APPLIED PSYCHOLOGY

This volume demonstrates how readers can become more effective parents, teachers, students, coaches, managers, or work supervisors, while also gaining practical skills to enhance their self-motivation, communication skills, and intervention acumen. The first eight chapters explain evidence-based principles from applied behavioral science (ABS) that can be used to improve the human dynamics of any situation involving behavior. Fundamentals from humanism are integrated strategically to show how an ABS intervention can be more acceptable, influential, and sustainable. The following twelve chapters detail the deployment of ABS interventions to optimize performance in a wide variety of fields, including occupational and transportation safety, quantity and quality of organizational work behavior, healthcare, athletic coaching, parenting, preschool and college education, environmental sustainability, and the control of obesity and alcohol abuse. *Applied Psychology* provides a thorough review of the latest research in relation to these domains and explores issues for future investigation.

E. Scott Geller is Alumni Distinguished Professor and Director of the Center for Applied Behavior Systems at Virginia Tech and Senior Partner of Safety Performance Solutions, Inc. He has written numerous books, research articles, and training manuals addressing the development, evaluation, and refinement of behavior-change interventions to improve quality of life on a large scale.

Applied Psychology

ACTIVELY CARING FOR PEOPLE

Edited by

E. Scott Geller
Virginia Tech

CAMBRIDGE
UNIVERSITY PRESS

32 Avenue of the Americas, New York, NY 10013-2473, USA

Cambridge University Press is part of the University of Cambridge.

It furthers the University's mission by disseminating knowledge in the pursuit of education, learning, and research at the highest international levels of excellence.

www.cambridge.org
Information on this title: www.cambridge.org/9781107417625

First published 2016

Printed in the United Kingdom by Clays, St Ives plc.

A catalog record for this publication is available from the British Library.

Library of Congress Cataloging in Publication Data
Geller, E. Scott, 1942–
Applied psychology : actively caring for people / E. Scott Geller.
pages cm
Includes bibliographical references and index.
ISBN 978-1-107-07166-7 (hardback) – ISBN 978-1-107-41762-5 (paperback)
1. Psychology, Applied. I. Title.
BF636.G4195 2016
158–dc23 2015024697

ISBN 978-1-107-07166-7 Hardback
ISBN 978-1-107-41762-5 Paperback

In loving memory and recognition, this book is dedicated to four individuals who walked a life of Actively Caring for People (AC4P) and throughout their journeys inspired many others to pursue an AC4P lifestyle.

JOHN HOWARD DEAN 1947–2014

John Dean was a faithful Christian, beloved husband, devoted son, and a loyal brother to four siblings. His life's work was that of an architect whose love for Jesus and artistic creations benefited countless numbers of people in Vero Beach, Florida. His perpetual spirit of truth, community service, and compassion for others led him and his wife – Carolyn – to meet Pope John in 1997.

ELIZABETH ALICE REICHLING 1989–2014

A graduate of Virginia Tech (cum laude), Alie was on the student-led team that initiated the Actively Caring for People (AC4P) Movement. She was passionate about the AC4P mission to cultivate a more compassionate and interdependent culture within schools, organizations, and entire communities. Alie exemplified an AC4P maxim: Making beneficial differences in other people's lives makes a life well lived.

RICHARD SANDERSON 1951–2014

Dick Sanderson exemplified AC4P in all his roles, from that of star athlete and coach to successful landscape architect and devoted husband and father. Dick gallantly battled ALS (Lou Gehrig's disease) for a decade, eventually becoming totally disabled and incapable of communicating in any way. Dick's extraordinary courage to remain positive and optimistic throughout his ordeal inspired everyone he met to avoid self-centered lamenting and to persevere with conviction in meeting life's challenges.

SUSAN ALICE GELLER WASHKO 1945–2013

Suzie epitomized the Actively Caring for People (AC4P) spirit as a loving wife and an attentive mother to Daniel Scott Washko and sixty-four blessed foster children. Throughout her spirited AC4P life, Suzie showed relentless courage and optimism during a forty-year struggle with severe and ever-increasing physical challenges caused by systemic lupus erythematosus.

CONTENTS

FOREWORD

I first crossed paths with Dr. E. Scott Geller at the annual meeting of the National Safety Council in 1987. A standing-room-only crowd of six or seven hundred safety professionals packed a session where Dr. Geller paced enthusiastically up and down aisles and across the speaker's platform. I couldn't even get into the room at first; his audience spilled out into the hallway.

As I listened I discovered something – I never heard anyone talk about workplace safety like the fellow I would come to know as "the Doc." His voice boomed off the ballroom walls. He joked, told personal stories, and ripped through a stack of overhead transparencies. This was 1987, remember. The man was passionate and positive. His vitality contagious. Laughs rolled through the ballroom and echoed out into the hall, where a group of us stood on our toes peeking through the door, trying to get a glimpse of this wiry, wired professor with the energy of a rock-and-roll drummer.

Scott was not another motivational safety speaker. What separated Scott was his message, his substance and depth. He had a knack for making ivory-tower research and principles somehow interesting and decipherable. Scott's scholarship is all about why we do the things we do, how to help people do better, and how to help people care for one another – to actively care.

I was intrigued when introduced to Scott's thinking. In those days, psychology wasn't talked about much in workplace safety circles. I took notes of that 1987 presentation. Two years later I spoke with Scott for the first time, by phone, for an October 1989 cover story on how to handle the "accident-prone" worker for my magazine, *Industrial Safety & Hygiene News*. "Accident-prone" is no longer part of the workplace safety lexicon; it's politically incorrect and perceived as a blame-the-victim concept. Even twenty-five years ago, Scott didn't like using the term, preferring "injury repeater." In our interview he said, "Where's the data, we don't know that certain people have more injuries." (Note that Scott has been screaming ever since I met him that we should avoid the popular term "accident" whenever knowledge is available to avoid the injury, because this term implies lack of control.)

That was, and is today, E. Scott Geller. Speak from empirical data. Accentuate the positive. Don't find faults, find fixes. In that first interview he also said, "I believe everyone's behavior is ultimately changeable. Some behaviors are tougher than others to improve. But I don't want to give up on anyone."

"Don't give up on anyone." "All behavior is ultimately changeable." These beliefs of Scott's are fundamental to his vision of an actively caring for people (AC4P) culture, the theme of this book you have in your hands.

In that same issue, October 1989, I listed Scott as one of the "people to watch" in the occupational-safety field over the coming decade. My summary: "E. Scott Geller is a psychologist at Virginia Tech, and a missionary for behavior modification programs. Safety pros are increasingly interested in this refreshing, positive approach to shaping work habits, and experts such as Geller will be traveling the country in the '90s explaining how it's done."

Well, "behavior modification" also fell victim to political correctness, with "modification" perceived as treating people like laboratory rats. I also learned that Scott would rather shape "mindful" behaviors than "mindless" habits. Habits are more superficial and less connected to thinking, attitudes, and values than mindful behaviors.

Travel far and wide Scott did in the 1990s and beyond – throughout the quarter century since 1989 leading up to today. Sometimes Scott was consulting; sometimes presenting daylong workshops; sometimes giving keynote addresses at professional conferences. Wherever he was, the Professor, "the Doc," was teaching, always teaching to help people make a difference, as he told his audiences.

Along the way I edited a monthly column Scott wrote for *Industrial Safety & Hygiene News* for nineteen years. And in those more than two hundred columns I observed as an editor how Scott was evolving. In the beginning his writing reflected the research and scholarship of B. F Skinner, the ABCs of applied behavioral science – activators, behaviors, and consequences. But the scope of his writing broadened noticeably over time. He wrote about Deming and the power of systems and Maslow's hierarchy of needs. He wrote about emotional intelligence, empathy, humanism, organizational cultures, servant leadership, behavioral coaching, commitment, mindfulness, selective perception, cognitive bias, savoring the moment, seeking success versus avoiding failure, systems thinking, and various internal dispositions such as optimism, self-esteem, personal control, self-efficacy, and a sense of belonging – all of which support a person's propensity to perform AC4P behavior on behalf of people's health, safety, or well-being. Scott called this scholarship *humanistic behaviorism*.

The ultimate humane behavior, Scott believes, is to go above and beyond what is asked of us in our daily lives on behalf of others. "Beyond the call of duty," he says, which infers that AC4P behavior should become routine, certainly not ignored. We are obliged to actively care because we have it within us to do so. Consider these real-world examples, taken from the December 2014 issue of *Mindfulness*:

- John McCormick, 65, suffered a fatal heart attack while mowing his lawn. Firefighters rushed him to the hospital – and then returned to finish his mowing.
- Lillian Weber, 99, every day sews a unique dress for a child in need. By her hundredth birthday, she will have sewn a thousand dresses.
- Thousands fled combat in the city of Donetsk, Ukraine, in 2014. A group of women, risking their lives, stayed to care for the many pets left behind.

This same issue of *Mindfulness* described the Native American tradition of "the Long Body." Through our senses the body extends beyond its immediate boundaries and is part of an interconnected whole. When the members of a tribe or a team are strongly connected to each other, they function as a single body. This level of connectivity and interdependence, "the Long Body," is embedded in the AC4P vision of worldwide humanistic behaviorism.

It's found in the chapters of this book, which range far and wide, covering organizational leadership; communication styles; social influence; proactive and reactive interventions of AC4P behavior; and actively caring for occupational safety, traffic safety, patient safety, and the environment and sustainable living; actively caring for preschoolers; actively caring for young athletes; actively caring for obesity; and AC4P behavior to prevent alcohol abuse; to prevent cruelty to animals; and for the purposes of higher education and effective parenting.

Scott is a distinguished authority on the foibles of human nature, and he'll tell you straight up that AC4P behavior is a tall order – for any number of reasons. We fear our good intentions will be misinterpreted or rejected. We don't believe ourselves capable. "I'm just not feelin' it, dude." "I just don't want to take the time or expend the energy." "Someone else will do it."

"Don't you see, I'm really an introvert, timid, and tend toward pessimism?"
"Actively caring is not in my DNA."

This book, *Applied Psychology: Actively Caring for People*, challenges these excuses and teaches you how to actively care effectively in everyday life, moment to moment, as a friend, a stranger, a parent, a teacher, a student, a coach, a caretaker, or a work supervisor. You'll learn how to motivate yourself and others to rise above your more independent, uncertain self. You'll learn how to solicit assistance from friends, family, teachers, peers, and strangers who can provide face-to-face encouragement, role modeling, and positive recognition. You'll acquire valuable observation, listening, and intervention skills and learn how to be empathic, action-oriented, self-motivated, and *other*-focused.

You will learn how to actively care effectively for others through the principles, practices, evidence-based research, and real-world lessons in this book, and through your related follow-up conversations and discussions. Armed with this profound knowledge, you can act competently on your caring and your compassion. You will learn how to bring the best out of yourself and others.

Dave Johnson
Editor, *Industrial Safety & Hygiene News*
March 2015

PREFACE: THE ACTIVELY CARING FOR PEOPLE (AC4P) MOVEMENT

I coined the term "actively caring" in 1990 while working with a team of safety leaders at Exxon Chemical in Baytown, Texas.[1] Our vision was to cultivate a brother/sister keeper's culture in which everyone looks out for each other's safety on a daily basis. This requires people to routinely go above and beyond the call of duty on behalf of the health, safety, and well-being of others. We agreed that "actively caring for people" was an ideal label for this company-wide paradigm shift. Most people do care about the well-being of others, but relatively few individuals "act" on behalf of this caring in the best ways. Our challenge was to get everyone to act effectively on their caring – to *actively care*.

We began systematic research in our Center for Applied Behavior Systems at Virginia Tech (VT) to develop, evaluate, and continuously improve intervention techniques to increase the frequency and improve the quality of interpersonal actively caring for people (AC4P) behavior throughout a work culture. We have continued this research to the present, broadening applications beyond the business world to educational settings and throughout communities, and targeting a variety of behaviors affecting human well-being. This book highlights evidence-based interventions developed by us and others to increase effective AC4P behavior in various environmental settings and under diverse circumstances.

Following the VT tragedy on April 16, 2007, when an armed student took the lives of thirty-two students and faculty and injured seventeen others,[2] the AC4P concept took on a new focus and prominence for my students and me. In a time of great uncertainty and reflection, those most affected by the tragedy were not thinking about themselves, but rather were acting to help classmates, friends, and even strangers heal. This collective effort was manifested in the AC4P Movement for culture change (see www.ac4p.org), making the belongingness spirit of the

Hokie community even stronger. My students and I envisioned applying the principle of positive reinforcement to spread this AC4P Movement beyond VT's Blacksburg campus.

We took the green wristbands, engraved with "Actively Caring for People," that I had been distributing at safety conferences for two decades and added a numbering system to enable computer tracking of the AC4P process: *see, act, pass,* and *share* (SAPS). The SAPS process asks individuals and groups to look for AC4P behavior (i.e., see) and reward such AC4P behavior with a green wristband (i.e., act). Wristband recipients are then requested to look for AC4P behavior from others and pass on the wristband (i.e., pass). They are asked to document this exchange (including the nature of their AC4P behavior) at the AC4P Website (www.ac4p.org), along with the wristband number. In this way, a positive recognition process is tracked worldwide (i.e., share) as positive AC4P communication.

In the fall of 2008, more than two thousand AC4P wristbands were given to university faculty, students, and staff to thank them for their AC4P behavior. But it didn't stop there. With a pay-it-forward mindset, wristband recipients passed on their wristbands to recognize the AC4P behavior of others. Thus, the AC4P Movement has spread far beyond VT, impacting individuals, organizations, universities, and communities worldwide.

What's the relevance of an applied-psychology textbook on the AC4P Movement for a college course or for an instructional workshop for parents, teachers, coaches, consultants, healthcare workers, work supervisors, or safety professionals? Simply put, the AC4P Movement is all about improving the human condition in the diverse circumstances we all experience throughout our daily lives. This book teaches you how practical applied psychology can be used to improve quality of life – your own and that of others. A fundamental premise: The solution to problems involving people requires beneficial behavior change.

The technology of applied behavioral science (ABS) is featured throughout this textbook, from the evidence-based principles of this extensive domain of psychology to real-world applications in multiple settings involving a variety of behavior-related challenges. However, after almost fifty years of developing and evaluating ABS interventions to manage and improve behavior in distinctly different environments (e.g., prisons, schools, corporations, and communities), I've learned that ABS-based technology is not sufficient for sustainable behavior change.

Yes, our applications of ABS resulted in dramatic improvement of the behavior of prisoners, students, teachers, supervisors, wage workers, drivers of motor vehicles, and residents of households. These short-term demonstrations of significant intervention impact (i.e., functional control of the target behavior) led to numerous publications of research articles in professional journals. But more often than not, the effective intervention process was removed from the setting after my research team left the scene. We had failed to convince the appropriate managers and indigenous personnel of the value of the intervention and the positive behavior change.

Plus, our exclusive reliance on extrinsic contingencies often inhibited the development of *self-persuasion* and *self-motivation* among both the agents and the recipients of the behavior-change intervention. Our introduction, implementation, and evaluation of successful ABS interventions were not accompanied by communication strategies to enhance *empowerment* and *buy-in* for initiation and institutionalization of the process. The notable exceptions to the typical short-term impact of successful interventions occurred when we applied methods beyond ABS.

The application chapters in this text detail exemplary occasions when effective applications of ABS, combined with select principles from psychological science, have resulted in maintenance of the behavior-change process and long-term continuous improvement of the targeted behavior. What principles beyond ABS, you ask? These are explained and illustrated throughout the first eight chapters of this text and are reflected in each of the chapters in Part II on applications.

For now, consider these four terms I used in a prior paragraph: *self-persuasion, self-motivation, empowerment,* and *buy-in*. These are concepts typically avoided by behavioral scientists because they are not directly observable. However, substantial research has demonstrated significant durable changes in behavior as the result of interventions targeting one or more of these constructs. This text will teach you how to incorporate intervention components that address these constructs, and thereby enhance the long-term impact of an ABS behavior-change process. For example, when giving someone supportive and corrective behavioral feedback (as detailed in Chapter 3), it's critical to consider the *humanistic* principles of empathy, empowerment, and compassion.

Yes, I refer to these nonbehavioral concepts as humanistic. In fact, the theme of this book – actively caring for people (AC4P) – integrates the best of humanism and behaviorism. The academic label is *humanistic behaviorism*. After all, *actively* means action (behavior) and *caring* reflects feeling (humanism). It's noteworthy the American Humanists Association, founded in 1941 to be a clear, democratic voice for humanism in the United States and to develop and advance humanistic thought and action, named B. F. Skinner (founder of behavioral science) "Humanist of the Year" in 1972.[3]

This book demonstrates the value of applying *humanistic behaviorism* when developing and implementing an intervention process to improve people's behavior. Plus, you will learn how to apply this approach to support an AC4P movement, and you'll realize why establishing an AC4P culture is fundamental to benefiting the human dynamics of so many situations worldwide.

CULTIVATING AN AC4P CULTURE

We are besieged by daunting societal problems. Thanks to the 24/7 news cycle and the Internet, social media, smartphones, tablet devices, and wearable sensor technology, we know more than perhaps we'd like about both ourselves, our day-to-day world, and broader, global problems of obesity, millions of medical errors, financial greed and scandal, online scams, cyberbullying, cyberhacking, violence and drugs in schools, bankrupt cities, terrorism, political gridlock, vehicle collisions, and climate warming. We live in a time of significant social problems. Since human behavior contributes to each of these societal ills, it must be part of every solution.

What if people were only more considerate of and empathic to the circumstances, opinions, and behaviors of others? Imagine the positive impact of a world with more compassion and AC4P behavior – more empathy and kindness. The practical research-based AC4P principles and interventions described in this book illustrate how such a culture change could be achieved. The AC4P Movement combines humanism and behaviorism (i.e., *humanistic behaviorism*) to improve behaviors related to the health, safety, and well-being of people worldwide.

In 1971, B. F. Skinner told us, "Our culture has provided the science and technology to save itself."[4] The AC4P Movement reflects his assertion. It empowers individuals to be self-motivated to actively care and to increase the occurrence of AC4P behaviors from others as well. Actively caring cultures empower people to improve their own school, work, and home environments, and as they do we will see AC4P cultures begin to flourish in organizations and communities worldwide.

Chapters 1 to 6 define evidence-based strategies for increasing AC4P behavior in various settings, while reviewing the supportive theory and research for each intervention approach. Chapter 7 introduces you to *positive* psychology, the science of understanding and advancing human happiness and well-being; Chapter 8 elucidates the industrial-organizational concepts of leadership and followership from an AC4P perspective. The lessons from Chapters 7 and 8 connect directly to cultivating an AC4P culture of interpersonal compassion.

Effective AC4P leadership to activate and support prosocial behavior and interpersonal welfare requires behavior-change (Chapter 1) and attitude-change (Chapter 2) technology, self-motivation (Chapter 3), moral courage (Chapter 4), communication skills (Chapter 5), and social-influence strategies (Chapter 6). We aren't talking about common-sense solutions here; we're sharing practical techniques verified through empirical research.

The chapters in Part II of this book were prepared in part by diverse subject-matter experts from various fields who have experienced firsthand the power of applying the AC4P principles to address critical large-scale problems, from injuries and fatalities in the workplace and ineffective teaching, coaching, and interpersonal conflict in educational settings to issues of obesity, alcohol abuse, athletic coaching, proper parenting, public health, patient safety, and environmental sustainability.

Most of the application chapters include details of the cost-effective procedures, as well as empirical results of the most functional implementations. We hope this information will inspire critical thinking and group discussions about practical ways to improve people's attitude and behavior on behalf of quality of life, happiness, and human well-being. Indeed, each chapter ends with a list of discussion questions that could be used to activate constructive verbal discourse about the contents of the chapter. I use these questions to develop discussion questions for exams, and my students are informed of this strategy.

THE QUALITY AND QUANTITY OF AC4P BEHAVIOR

Why isn't AC4P behavior more common? After all, the consequences of AC4P behavior are typically positive and rewarding for both the giver and the receiver. Boosts in self-esteem, self-efficacy, optimism, and belongingness that accompany an AC4P interaction can serve as both an activator and a reinforcer for participants. Plus, observers of AC4P behavior should experience vicarious reinforcement (see Chapter 6).

First, consider that AC4P behavior is more common than we realize. Daily occurrences of behavior that run counter to AC4P behavior make headlines, but there are many untold stories of people worldwide reaching out daily to help others deal with unfortunate situational and/or dispositional factors.

Thousands of these people are professionals – fire fighters, police officers, physicians, nurses, home health aides, social workers, ministers, teachers, and personnel in the safety and human relations departments of organizations. These AC4P professionals look out for the safety, health, and well-being of others – morning, noon, and night, every day and every shift. Consider too the vast number of ordinary people who volunteer their time daily on behalf of the health and well-being of others or who step out of themselves without forethought to actively care instantaneously for another person.

Quality of AC4P Behavior

I'm actually more concerned about the quality of AC4P behavior than the quantity. Our behaviors on the job, at school, on the road, and at home with our families often come across as top-down or self-serving and non-caring. Sure, most of our interpersonal behaviors might be well intentioned, but too often they are not well executed, or well received. We may want to do the right thing, but for a variety of reasons, including "unconscious incompetence," the behavior performed to help another person (e.g., offering feedback to improve someone's performance) is often not viewed as AC4P behavior.

Our society, thanks to our legal system, focuses too narrowly on using punitive consequences to stop individuals' undesirable behaviors, with limited attention to applying positive consequences to motivate desirable behavior. Our culture can be detrimental to AC4P behavior. Hundreds of self-help books and many TV and radio talk shows make behavior and attitudinal change seem easier than it is. Misinformed but popular authors proclaim that using incentives and rewards to increase the frequency of desirable behavior does more harm than good.[5] Indeed, the success of many positive AC4P interventions explicated in this book show the flaw in that assertion.

More important, the AC4P applications in Part II illustrate practical ways to improve any attempt to actively care by incorporating evidence-based principles of behavioral and psychological science. The quality of AC4P behavior can often be readily enhanced, and this book shows you how to do that.

Quantity of AC4P Behavior

Readers can increase the quantity of AC4P behavior by implementing the numerous successful applications of the AC4P principles and procedures illustrated throughout this book. Most influential, for me, are the personal stories of individuals who experienced the rewards of performing and receiving a simple AC4P act of kindness, as posted on the ac4p.org Website. Since January 2011, more than four thousand individuals have shared an AC4P story, illustrating the positive consequences of actively caring for both those performing and those receiving AC4P behavior. These stories simply inspire me. Sharing these AC4P experiences will contribute to eventually making AC4P behavior a social norm.

Any AC4P story you post on our Website connects immediately to your Facebook page and communicates to your friends the occasion of an AC4P behavior and its positive impact. As more and more people post their AC4P tales, people will begin to accept AC4P behavior as the norm – a "new normal." Successive approximations of a worldwide culture of compassion will follow. So we hope you will "think globally and act locally" with the research-based principles and applications explained in this text.

This book teaches you how psychology can improve the human condition and day-to-day communications and interactions on a large scale by applying principles of ABS and humanism to increase the quantity and improve the quality of AC4P behavior. Make your learning practical. Commit to being more intentional about actively caring for others and rewarding people for their AC4P behaviors. When you share your AC4P stories on our Website, others will see your kind acts and consider modeling your AC4P behavior.

HOW TO USE THIS BOOK

Book proposals define both the target audience and the presumed applications of the content. A proposed book could be intended as a textbook for a college or university curriculum. It could aim for introductory, advanced, or graduate students. Then again, a book might be suitable for professional workshops or seminars outside of academia. Applications of the text could vary from occupational safety, organizational management, interpersonal communication, parenting, environmental sustainability, job satisfaction, patient relations in healthcare, and so on. Also to be decided: What prior education or technical knowledge is required to learn and benefit from the content provided?

Every book I've authored or edited addressed these publishing prerequisites in order to shape the text's theme, scope, organization, editorial style, and language and to plan marketing strategies. Some were designed for use as a college textbook. Others were prepared for professional change agents, complete with instructional workbooks and a DVD series. Each book focused on aspects of psychology – behavioral and psychological science relevant to understanding and improving human dynamics in a particular application domain. The target areas varied widely – from behavior management in prisons and educational settings to environmental psychology, ecological sustainability, healthcare, behavioral community psychology, leadership and teamwork, and occupational health and safety.

How is all this relevant to the book you are about to read? Simply put, I cannot specify one intended audience, purpose, or application. Nor can I define a singular context for using this text. Why? The range of potential uses is so vast it's actually unlimited if the purpose – whatever it might be – connects to the application of psychology. The content of this textbook is germane any time and any place it's desirable to improve human behavior on behalf of learning; communicating; organizational, community, and/or family cultures; occupational and public safety and health; teamwork and leadership in any realm; and both individual and collective happiness and/or general well-being.

I intend to use this textbook as required reading for my graduate class in industrial/organizational (I/O) psychology, as well as for my annual occupational safety and health workshops for the National Safety Council and the American Society of Safety Engineers. It's worth noting the diverse range of prior knowledge of psychology among the various readers of this book. Graduate students in I/O psychology have an extensive background in psychological science, whereas many participants at my safety workshops have not had an introductory psychology course in high school or college.

This book on the science of applied psychology serves many purposes for audiences with quite different educational and professional experiences and interests. For anyone who aspires to improve human behavior, the first eight chapters on AC4P principles are directly relevant. The twelve application chapters pinpoint particular application domains for the AC4P principles introduced and illustrated in Chapters 1 to 8.

For my safety workshops I will focus on Chapters 1 to 8 and Chapters 9 to 11; for a seminar for healthcare professionals I will assign Chapters 12 to 14, after teaching the material in Chapters 1 to 8. Chapters 15 to 17 are suitable application chapters for a workshop on parenting and childcare. Educators will be particularly interested in Chapters 16 to 18 after learning the AC4P principles in Chapters 1 to 8.

As P. T. Barnum was famous for saying, "[H]ave a little something for everyone." If "everyone" includes any high school graduate interested in the human side of improving quality of life, this book follows P. T. Barnum's dictum. Read this book to understand and improve the behaviors of yourself and others in various contexts – and bring out the best in yourself and others.

Our world brims with untapped caring and compassion. A world filled with interpersonal compassion! This vision will become reality when more people reach out to help others more effectively and more often. Learn how you can make this happen while studying how psychology (i.e., humanistic behaviorism) makes positive differences in every realm of life, from improving education, parenting, family dynamics, athletic coaching, and interpersonal communication to protecting environmental resources, preventing bullying and alcohol abuse, appreciating our pets, and keeping people safe from harm at work, at school, at home, and when traveling in between.

REFERENCES

1. Geller, E. S. (1991). If only more would actively care. *Journal of Applied Behavior Analysis*, 24, 763–764.
2. Geller, E. S. (2008). The tragic shooting at Virginia Tech: Personal perspectives, prospects, and preventive potentials. *Traumatology*, 14(1), 8–20.
3. American Humanist Association (2008). Retrieved September 9, 2012, from http://www.americanhumanist.org/.
4. Skinner, B. F. (1971). *Beyond freedom and dignity*. New York: Knopf, p. 181.
5. Kohn, A. (1999). *Punished by rewards: The trouble with gold stars, incentive plans, A's, praise, and other bribes*. Boston: Houghton Mifflin; Pink, D. H. (2009). *Drive: The surprising truth about what motivates us*. New York: Penguin Group.

ABOUT THE AUTHORS

A beautiful tapestry has varied colors that blend, lines in harmony, textures, strands of different threads – all woven together with creativity to elicit admiration and appreciation. Our book is a tapestry woven by a diverse group of authors. These individuals are subject-matter experts in different fields, and all have used humanistic behaviorism to improve the quality of life in their corners of the world. With passion, thoughtful concentration, and care they have produced a book that will make a positive difference in your life and in the lives of those around you.

KATHLEEN B. BOYD, PH.D.
Director of Analysis
Acelero, Inc.
Early Childhood Education
LaGrange, GA

Katie completed her dissertation in industrial/organizational psychology at Virginia Tech in 2015. While a student, she focused a great deal of her research on the dynamic relationships between leaders and followers. Her dissertation looked at how follower behavior may alter the leadership style adopted by a leader. Katie now works as the Director of Analysis with Acelero Learning, a Head Start provider in many communities across the country with a unique outcome-focused approach to providing Head Start services. Katie oversees the data system used to track child and family outcome data, as well as the monitoring and compliance of centers in western Georgia.

> Exceptional leaders influence and transform. And those who experience such leaders are, as a result, more competent and capable.

CHRIS S. DULA, PH.D., LCP
Associate Professor, Department of Psychology
East Tennessee State University
Johnston City, TN

On arriving at ETSU in 2004, Chris established the Applied Psychology Laboratory, which is based on the model of Scott Geller's Center for Applied Behavior Systems, where students learn to do high-quality research in the service of improving our world. His work in traffic safety reflects his desire to see a Total Safety Traffic Culture, consistent with the AC4P Movement and consistent with his belief that AC4P is the way to go in life … the collective creation of a better world.

> If we all saw that we have flaws, and that we fail to consider the needs and safety of others, perhaps we would all work to make this a safer and more peaceful planet.

ROSEANNE J. FOTI, PH.D.
Associate Professor, Department of Psychology
Virginia Tech
Blacksburg, VA

Roseanne has received awards for excellence in both research and teaching. As a Fellow of the Society for Industrial and Organizational Psychology, she focuses her research on leadership perceptions, how leaders emerge in groups and teams, and leader-follower relationships. In addition to her teaching and research at Virginia Tech, she works with a variety of organizations on leadership training and development.

> Inspirational leaders instill a feeling that we are all accountable and that if one of us fails, we all fail. These leaders are on a mission to influence positive change for both the organization and the people they work with, and their energy and passion help fuel cohesion among peers and team members, allowing them greater outcomes than the sum of their parts.

ANGELA K. FOURNIER, PH.D., L.P.
Associate Professor, Department of Psychology
Bemidji State University
Bemidji, MN

As a parent, Angie uses the AC4P principles every day and sees the positive impact they have on her daughter's behavior and on their relationship. As a professional grounded in applied behavioral science (ABS), she has always felt uniquely prepared to manage parenting challenges and wished all parents had the benefit of training in basic ABS principles. So she is excited about having coauthored a book chapter on parenting, hoping a wide range of readers will benefit from practicing humanistic behaviorism with the children in their lives. Her research and scholarship focus on large-scale intervention to improve community health behavior and the psychological outcomes of animal-assisted intervention.

> All of my research is aimed at making a difference in others, and in the community, a passion that was ignited when working with Dr. Geller as a graduate student in the Center for Applied Behavior Systems.

CORY FURROW, M.S.
Graduate student, Department of Forest Resources and Environment Conservation
Virginia Tech
Blacksburg, VA

Cory recently completed the master's program in the Department of Forest Resources and Conservation at Virginia Tech, with his AC4P research focusing on the human dynamics of sustainability. He coauthored Chapter 6 on social influence for two primary reasons: (1) social influence is a personal interest and (2) to demonstrate how psychology can be used to promote AC4P behaviors. Consequently, readers will learn to identify moments when they are being targeted by social influence techniques.

> Sometimes people need a slight push to perform AC4P behavior. I believe the social influence principles can provide this push.

E. SCOTT GELLER, PH.D.
Alumni Distinguished Professor, Department of Psychology
Director of the Center for Applied Behavior Systems
Virginia Tech
Blacksburg, VA

Scott has authored or coauthored 33 books, 82 book chapters, 259 magazine articles, and more than 350 research articles addressing the development and evaluation of behavior-change interventions to improve quality of life. He is a Fellow of the American Psychological Association, the Association for Psychological Science, the Association for Behavior Analysis International, and the World Academy of Productivity and Quality Sciences. He has received Lifetime Achievement Awards from the American Psychological Foundation and the International Organizational Behavior Management

Network. In May 2011, the College of Wooster awarded Scott an honorary degree: Doctor of Humane Letters.

> The principles and applications presented in this book reflect the evolution of my forty-six-year career in applied psychology. I have contributed to no scholarship as important as this text.

KRISTA S. GELLER, PH.D.
Global People Based Safety & Human Performance Improvement Manager, Bechtel Corporation
Washington, DC

Pets have made a significant contribution to Krista's life; they have provided her with solidity, compassion, and understanding in her personal growth, exemplifying the love and caring humans should have for each other. She owes special recognition to her mom, Dr. Carol Hillis Geller, because of her love of animals. Krista cannot recall a time during her life when she didn't have a pet to love and care for. So, when it came time to choose a topic to research and develop for her master's thesis and Ph.D. dissertation, the "power of pets" was an obvious choice.

> I remain so grateful for all my furry friends, past, present, and future, who have participated so positively in my life and who will continue to actively care for me, and vice versa.

KATIE C. GOULET, ED.S.
School Psychologist
St. Croix River Education District
Finlayson, MN

Katie is a school psychologist at St. Croix River Education District in Northern Minnesota. She serves students prek-12th grade. Her passions include positive behavioral support, prevention, and teacher-student relationships.

> In my first year as an educator, I quickly learned that you cannot make change without first showing how much you care. I believe in building positive connections more than anything else, and making this my priority as a school psychologist.

KYRA HEIDELBERGER, M.S.E.D.
School Psychology Intern
St. Croix River Education District: Chisago Lakes Middle School
Lindstrom, MN

Kyra is a school psychology intern, completing her Education Specialists degree with the University of Wisconsin – La Crosse while serving the students, families, and staff at Chicago Lakes Middle School in Lindstrom Minnesota with the St. Croix River Education District. Her primary research interests include the effectiveness of behavior management strategies to support positive student outcomes in the classroom. She is especially passionate about intentionally promoting positive outcomes for all students within a school system through the use of prevention and early intervention techniques.

> I subscribe to the thought-process that all children benefit from positive and encouraging relationships; it is my hope that those relationships stem from the content shared in these pages.

THELMA S. HORN, PH.D.
Professor, Department of Kinesiology and Health
Miami University
Oxford, OH

Thelma's research examines how the behavior and psychosocial growth of children, adolescents, and young adults in sport and physical activity contexts are affected, or shaped, by factors in their social environment. In particular, she has conducted research projects that examine the role significant other individuals (primarily coaches but also parents and teammates) play in the lives of athletes and other physical-activity participants.

> Given that we, as a society, want children to develop a physically active lifestyle and to value their physical bodies by refraining from engagement in behaviors that can undermine their health, it would make sense that we try to hire (select) and train youth sport coaches to use an AC4P approach.

DAVE JOHNSON, B.A.
Chief Editor
Industrial Safety and Hygiene News

As a journalist, Dave researches a topic; learns its language, its history, its issues and trends; interviews subject-matter experts; observes and listens; studies and analyzes what he learns. He applied this process in coauthoring a chapter in this volume on patient-centered care. He deepened his understanding of this topic while coauthoring a book in 2007 with Scott Geller: *People-Based Patient Safety: Enriching Your Culture to Prevent Medical Error.*

> To make informed decisions about your healthcare, you can't be passive any longer. Realize the pressures your caregivers confront, and

prepare for office and hospital visits, do your homework, know the questions you want to ask, research treatments and medications. The healthcare you receive is largely up to the actions you take for your own well-being.

SALLIE BETH JOHNSON, MPH, MCHES
Ph.D. student, Department of Human Nutrition, Food, and Exercise
Virginia Tech
Blacksburg, VA
Adjunct Faculty Instructor, Jefferson College of Health Sciences
Roanoke, VA

Sallie Beth's research and scholarship focus on behavioral and community science. Her doctoral studies involve an integrated research-practice partnership with Carillion Clinic Department of Family and Community Medicine to prevent disease from obesity among healthcare workers and patients. Before Virginia Tech, she spent more than ten years working on the frontlines as a health educator with underserved populations in rural North Carolina and West Virginia. She implemented and evaluated evidence-based lifestyle interventions for improving nutrition, increasing physical activity, and promoting tobacco cessation in healthcare, school, worksite, and faith-based settings.

> As a Master-Certified Health Education Specialist, I am committed to making our world a healthier place to live, learn, work, and play.

KATE LETEXIER LARSON, PH.D.
Assistant Professor of Psychology
Bemidji State University
Bemidji, MN

Since childhood, Kate has had the opportunity to observe the principles of AC4P in action across several generations of care givers. Although her parents, grandparents, and great grandparents weren't formally trained in this discipline, they helped to establish a healthy, prosocial, compassionate worldview. The ability to provide an active, prosocial, caring environment for her three little ones is a direct result of those early role models.

Kate now believes it is her turn to actively care for and cultivate the spirit within the next generation. In addition to her parenting, she is an assistant professor of psychology at Bemidji State University in Bemidji, Minnesota. Kate is very passionate about working to reduce the stigma surrounding mental illness, finding ways to improve the general public's understanding of what it means for those who are living with a disorder, and helping to connect individual's with the appropriate resources. Additionally, her research interests include investigating the application of active learning techniques in large lecture and online courses.

> My hope in contributing this chapter to this great book is to demonstrate, through real-life application, how AC4P can easily be integrated into the lives of the reader. Meeting the reader where they are and then transforming their lives through this positive behavioral framework.

BENJAMIN A. MARTIN, M. A.
Behavior Support Specialist
New River Valley Community Services
Narrows, VA

On arriving at East Tennessee State University in 2005, Ben connected with Chris Dula and soon became a part of the newly created Applied Psychology Laboratory. After gaining experience on a myriad of research topics, he found his passion in traffic safety research. Increasing the safety of people on the roadways fueled his passion to help create a total traffic safety culture. His AC4P contribution is an attempt to recognize and promote positive driving behaviors to the same extent that we punish undesirable driving behaviors, if not more so.

> If we recognize what people do right just as much as what they do wrong, we can motivate them to care about their safety and the safety of others.

JOCELYN H. NEWTON, PH.D.
Associate Professor, Department of Psychology
University of Wisconsin
La Crosse, WI

Joci is a Nationally Certified School Psychologist and has worked with pre-k–12th grade populations in both rural and urban settings. Her primary clinical and research interests include examining and applying prevention and intervention techniques for effective early childhood development. She is interested in identifying environmental factors that positively enhance the academic, social, and emotional skills of young children, including positive parenting and teaching behaviors.

> I hope that people who read our chapter are inspired to initiate emotionally supportive adult-child relationships in professional careers.

DEREK D. REED, PH.D., BCBA-D
Associate Professor, Department of Applied Behavioral Science
University of Kansas
Lawrence, KS

Derek's laboratory views the education gap in the United States as a social injustice worthy of applied behavioral science. Toward this end, his team studies the efficacy of empirically based instructional techniques in their higher-education courses. Derek appreciates the significant support he received from his coauthors in preparing their chapter: Bryan T. Yanagita, Amel Becirevic, Jason M. Hirst, Brent A. Kaplan, Ellie Eastes, and Taylor Hanna.

> These ideas from humanistic behaviorism have transformed the way we approach our science.

FLORENCE D. DIGENNARO REED, PH.D., BCBA
Associate Professor, Department of Applied Behavioral Science
University of Kansas
Lawrence, KS

Florence's passion is to improve the lives of service recipients by addressing interventionist behavior. This is accomplished by the design of organizational systems that embody AC4P principles and simultaneously foster AC4P behavior among employees. She is excited about having coauthored her chapter in this volume with her colleagues: Amy J. Henley, Sarah R. Jenkins, Jessica L. Doucette, and Jason M. Hirst.

> As an organizational consultant, I believe the mission and content of this book have direct relevance to my day-to-day activities.

RYAN C. SMITH, PH.D.
Research Associate, Virginia Tech Transportation Institute
Virginia Tech
Blacksburg, VA

Ryan has dedicated much of his personal and professional life to eradicating the needless pain caused by alcohol-related tragedies. He hopes his chapter shows that punishment will not fix our current drinking culture. Rather, we need to create cultures that support interpersonal intervention to reduce alcohol abuse and ensure that drivers of vehicles are sober. He has authored more than one hundred peer-reviewed journal articles, book chapters, or conference papers on alcohol and drug use. He is the first person in Virginia

Tech history to have been named both the Undergraduate Man of the Year (2008) and Graduate Man of the Year (2013) – the university's highest honors.

Doing something does not mean you are doing the right thing.

KYLE A. SUHR, M.A.
Graduate Candidate, Department of Psychology
East Tennessee State University
Johnston City, TN

Kyle is a Clinical Psychology Graduate Candidate at East Tennessee State University. Working within Chris Dula's Applied Psychology Laboratory, Kyle conducted research on driving anger and aggressive driving to better understand how to reduce the risks associated with such dangerous behavior. His work on angry and aggressive driving reflects his desire to improve problematic driving behaviors.

Driving is part of our everyday lives, yet sometimes we forget how we impact other people on the road. The AC4P Movement reminds us to do the right thing on behalf of the safety and health of other vehicle occupants.

KEENAN TWOHIG, B.S.
Ph.D. student, Department of Industrial and Organizational Psychology
Virginia Tech
Blacksburg, VA

Keenan is a Ph.D. student in industrial/organizational psychology at Virginia Tech. With a desire to help others and a strong interest in positive psychology that he acquired during his undergraduate career, Keenan found it only natural to join the AC4P Movement and conduct related research in the Virginia Tech Center for Applied Behavior Systems.

It is my hope that the missions of AC4P and positive psychology will continue to spread and improve lives.

KELLI ENGLAND WILL, PH.D.
Associate Professor of Pediatrics
Eastern Virginia Medical School
Norfolk, VA

Since earning her Ph.D. from Virginia Tech in 2002, Kelli has continued the AC4P tradition in her professional career. She is now an Associate Professor in the Pediatrics' Division of Community Health and Research at Eastern Virginia Medical School. Kelli conducts research on the design and evaluation of large-scale behavior-change programs that benefit the health and safety of children, teens, and young adults. Her interest areas include injury control, motor vehicle safety, health behavior theory, and risk communication.

She is also a Licensed Clinical Psychologist, a Nationally Certified Child Passenger Safety Technician, and a Delegate of the American Academy of Health Behavior. She is involved in child injury prevention at the regional, state, and national levels, serving on a number of health and safety boards, coalitions, and committees.

> I apply behavioral principles in so many aspects of my life—as a teacher, a researcher, and a clinician. But perhaps one of the most surprising and useful applications of my training has been in raising my two children. I am delighted to be able to share some of these applications in our chapter on parenting.

JOSHUA H. WILLIAMS, PH.D.
Senior Project Manager
Safety Performance Solutions (SPS)
Blacksburg, VA

Josh is the author of *Keeping People Safe: The Human Dynamics of Injury Prevention* and co-editor of *Keys to Behavior-Based Safety* with Scott Geller. He has authored more than twenty publications in leading safety journals and received the Cambridge Center National First Prize for his research on behavioral-safety feedback. For the past eighteen years Josh has managed People-Based Safety and Safety Culture Assessment initiatives in both English and Spanish with leading organizations worldwide.

> Throughout my eighteen-year career as an organizational consultant and trainer, I've witnessed the substantial injury-prevention benefits of applying principles of behavioral science, and I've appreciated the evolution from behavior-based safety to people-based safety, and now AC4P.

ACKNOWLEDGMENTS

For more than thirty years I've taught AC4P principles and applications in workshops and keynotes at regional and national conferences, as well at various Fortune 500 companies. The evidence-based AC4P lessons have always been well received. But periodically my evaluations have included a critical comment such as "I appreciate the theory and principles presented by Dr. Geller, but I don't know how to apply his teachings. I like the ideas, but he didn't tell me what to do with them."

This book addresses this legitimate concern in the best way possible. How? By combining the principles with tried-and-true applications designed to resolve some of the relevant and consequential societal issues of our time. The diverse application chapters were written by authors who developed and/or implemented research-based AC4P interventions founded on humanistic behaviorism and who observed their beneficial effects. Plus, the four coauthors of chapters in Part I on AC4P principles conducted substantial research-based studies of their topics: social influence, positive psychology, and leadership versus followership.

It's fitting to acknowledge the thirty authors or coauthors of these chapters. The authors of chapters are listed in the preceding About the Authors section, along with their education and current positions. Thank you all for contributing original leading-edge scholarship to this unique text on real-world applied psychology. You have given readers specific direction for effectively teaching, implementing, and evaluating interventions designed to address the human dynamics of critical large-scale issues affecting the quality of human life.

The application chapters target distinct settings and circumstances. Yet many of these intervention methods can be adapted to different situations. Indeed, I hope readers will be inspired to customize and apply the cited interventions to problems beyond those addressed in a given chapter. I also hope students assigned this textbook in a college or university class will gain a special appreciation of the relevance and applicability of psychology in every aspect of everyday living and will practice the AC4P principles to benefit themselves and others.

The development, preparation, and refinement of the information shared in this book represent an interdependent team effort. The vision of a book about AC4P principles and applications could not have become a reality without the invaluable assistance of several individuals, beyond the authors and coauthors.

First, I am grateful for the inspiration and continual support of my wife, Joanne, who tolerated my endless and unfair substitution of book-work time for one-to-one relationship time. Not only did Joanne provide creative insight on various aspects of this book (e.g., the dedication page and the introduction to About the Authors), she sets an AC4P example in every aspect of her daily life.

As a professional health and fitness instructor for more than forty years, Joanne has guided and motivated the integration of health-enhancing exercise into the lives of countless individuals. Plus, Joanne continually goes beyond the call of duty to actively care for others – family, friends, and complete strangers. But she dislikes my use of the phrase "*beyond* the call of duty." Why? From her perspective AC4P behavior should not be an act that goes beyond a routine – it should be the routine. As they say in Australia, "It's our duty to care." For more than a decade, Joanne's AC4P spirit and actions have inspired numerous undergraduate and graduate students at Virginia Tech, and me too, of course.

I want to next acknowledge the consultancy of Safety Performance Solutions (SPS) – its team of partners, my collaborators, who have supported me and taught BBS, PBS, and now AC4P to organizations worldwide for more than two decades.

I am indebted to the long-term advice, alliance, and friendship of Dave Johnson, Chief Editor of *Industrial Safety & Hygiene News* (*ISHN*). Dave and I began collaborating in 1990 when I submitted my first five articles for publication in his magazine. Every time one of my articles was published, I learned something about communicating more effectively a principle or practice from humanistic behaviorism. This invaluable learning experience continued for the nineteen consecutive years of my monthly *ISHN* column: "The Psychology of Safety."

Dave was the editor of my first safety book – *The Psychology of Safety* (Chilton Publishers, 1996) – and two subsequent textbooks on people-based safety. Plus, we coauthored a book that teaches relevant humanistic behaviorism to healthcare workers – *People-Based Patient Safety: Enriching Your Culture to Prevent Medical Error* (Coastal Training Technologies Corp., 2009). In all four collaborations, including this book, Dave added his magic to the written expression and made it more concise, clear, and comprehensible.

Thank you, Dave Johnson, for continuing to help me make my scholarship in professional publications more accessible and appreciated by the general public. Indeed, if this book's content is not understood and embraced by people beyond the ivory towers of university and research institutions, it has no chance of making the beneficial cultural differences embodied by its founding vision.

Since 1990, my teaching, textbooks, and workbooks have benefited from the artistic talents of George Wills of Blacksburg, VA – the creator of the instructive and entertaining illustrations interspersed throughout this book. The chapter authors and I gave George a general verbal description of what we wanted to portray, and he did the rest. But without the craft of Zechariah (Zack) Robinson, the illustrations could not have been combined with the text for use by the publisher. In fact, Zack coordinated the processing of this entire book, combining tables and diagrams (which he refined) with George Wills's illustrations. He processed all the words from my original handwritten prose and from my substantial handwritten editing of authors' manuscripts. Plus, he handled the continual refinement of typed text by Dave Johnson and me.

I am also so very grateful for the dedication of my Virginia Tech students and associates in our University Center for Applied Behavior Systems (CABS) who collect and analyze endless streams of field data to test the effects of various AC4P interventions and inform the design of more effective procedures to increase the frequency and improve the quality of AC4P behavior.

The support system of CABS serves as a think tank for considering innovative approaches to understanding and influencing the human dynamics of interpersonal compassion and for developing research procedures to analyze variables that could affect the success of the AC4P Movement. In this regard, I am particularly beholden to my current or former graduate students: Michael Ekema-Agbaw, Devin Carter, Chris Downing, Micah Roediger, Ruth-Anne Poli, and Keenan Twohig; our CABS coordinators Alexandra Bazdar, Jeana Herring, Melissa Langerman, and Zack Robinson; and the CABS research scientist: Ryan C. Smith.

Last but certainly not least, I am so appreciative of the competent support of the staff of Cambridge University Press, beginning with the vision of David Repetto, who saw the potential of developing a textbook on applied psychology from the AC4P principles and applications we had disseminated in research documents, magazine articles, conference workbooks, and a self-published trade book. Then we were privileged to have the support of Vincent Rajan in formatting and refining our scholarship for publication, and text proofing by undergraduate research students in CABS.

Thank you all very much. The synergy of your past, present, and future sustenance enables a legacy – AC4P principles and practices readers can use to enrich their lives and contribute to cultivating cultures of interpersonal compassion at work, at school, at home, and in every environment where humanistic behaviorism can make a positive difference.

INTRODUCTION TO PART I: EVIDENCE-BASED PRINCIPLES OF AC4P

E. SCOTT GELLER

The first eight chapters of this textbook explain evidence-based principles that form the basis for the actively caring for people (AC4P) applications described in the twelve subsequent chapters. These applications range from employing the AC4P principles for most effective parenting, teaching, and coaching to optimizing safety, health, and well-being in educational, business, and hospital settings. Also included are applications of AC4P principles to address such issues as obesity, traffic safety, environmental sustainability, and alcohol abuse among college students. The authors of each application chapter have had firsthand experience implementing and evaluating the specific AC4P principles delineated and explained to improve the human dynamics of designated situations.

We start with the research-based AC4P principles derived from applied behavioral science (ABS) and humanistic psychology (i.e., *humanistic behaviorism*). What is a "principle" anyway? The first definition of *principle* in my *American Heritage Dictionary* is "a basic truth, law, or assumption."[1] How do truths, laws, or assumptions connect to the behavioral and psychological science referenced throughout this text?

Note we use the adjective *evidence-based* when referring to the AC4P principles. This means the principles are based on empirical research that demonstrates their validity. Does this mean an AC4P principle is a basic truth or fact? I think it's risky to consider these principles immutable or changeless, like the law of gravity. Still, the AC4P principles are as close to valid as any other principle in the domain of psychology – the science of human experience.

In contrast to evidence-based principles, let's consider a few select statements used frequently in society today to explain or influence human behavior; they are not evidence-based, but unfortunately are quite popular.

1

Some of these myths are in fact themes of self-help books and motivational seminars. I hope my comments make you skeptical of these so-called principles of human dynamics. Actually, many of the research-based principles presented in the first eight chapters directly contradict these trendy misconceptions of human nature.

1. We learn more from our mistakes. This first example of a common myth, along with the related slogan "trial-and-error learning," puts more emphasis on failure than success, and this can actually be detrimental to learning. Think about it. Animals, including humans, learn more when a consequence indicates their behavior was correct rather than incorrect. What do we learn from an error? What not to do? Throughout our lives we're informed time and again that there are a lot of "what not to do's" we need to be wary of. But when we're correct and know it, we learn what to keep doing or what to do next. That's efficient, effective, and positive learning.

2. After twenty-one times, behavior becomes a habit. There's no empirical evidence for this simplistic and silly statement. Many factors determine habit formation, especially the nature of the behavior. More important, many behaviors require mindful attention to be effective and should never become habitual. *Mindful fluency* is usually preferred over some mindless habit that is akin to acting without thinking, or being on "autopilot."

3. The secret to success is self-affirmation. Telling yourself you can do something is the surest way to personal accomplishment and happiness, right? Isn't "can do" thinking the secret to success? This made-in-America ideal may sound good, but it's wrong. Chapter 1 explains why the essential ingredient of achievement resides in the consequences of behavior, not the self-talk preceding your behavior. Self-talk can get you started, but if you see no benefits to your action, you will stop performing that behavior.

4. Live by the Golden Rule, meaning treat others the way you want to be treated. We've heard this maxim all our lives, yet in Chapter 2 you'll learn why this principle is not optimal. For now, consider the potential value in treating others the way *they* want to be treated. This requires the humanistic concepts of empathy, compassion, and nondirective advising or coaching.

5. Incentive and rewards are detrimental to self-motivation. This declaration is promulgated in self-help books, on TV, and over the Internet. Yet this assertion is rarely supported by research. In Chapter 2, you'll learn evidence-based ways to use rewarding consequences to improve behavior and increase self-motivation at the same time. For example, behavior-based rewards and supportive feedback (e.g., positive recognition) for competent effort are far more likely to increase than decrease an individual's self-motivation.

6. Reprimand privately and recognize publicly. Never recognize people publicly without their permission. Some people are embarrassed by public praise, especially if others on their team think they deserve recognition. Positive public exposure of individuals on a team can promote win/lose independency ("Aren't *I* great!") in place of win/win interdependency ("Aren't *we* great!"). Chapter 2 details evidence-based ways to recognize teams, and Chapter 3 delineates strategies for effectively rewarding individuals for their personal achievements.

7. Practice makes perfect. Practice without proper feedback can lead to permanence, but certainly not perfection. Evidence-based principles for improving behavior through feedback are detailed in Chapter 3.

I could list many more assumptions about human dynamics that are not supported by research. Some are incorrectly considered "principles" of human behavior. I hope these seven myths make my point. What's my point? Be skeptical about time-honored pop psychology "principles" that sound like common sense. Most important is the fact that the AC4P principles described in the next eight chapters and employed in the diverse application chapters are founded on empirical research.

The evidence-based principles explained in the following chapters were selected from literally hundreds of verifiable principles related to understanding, predicting, and influencing the psychology of human experience. Those discussed in Chapters 1 to 8 were selected because at this point in our understanding of AC4P behavior they are most relevant.

As we learn more about ways to increase the frequency of quality AC4P behavior in various situations, additional principles of behavioral and psychological science will become relevant. Plus, additional research and continuous learning could influence refinements or extensions of the AC4P principles defined and illustrated in Part I of this book. The next eight chapters elucidate state-of-the-art AC4P principles from behavioral and psychological science that we can use to cultivate cultures of compassion in multiple, everyday situations.

Chapter 1 defines the foundation of AC4P as applied behavioral science (ABS), but keep in mind that various AC4P principles have been derived from research attributed to the broader domain of psychology, which includes social, cognitive, and clinical science. As introduced in the Preface and emphasized throughout this book, the academic label for the AC4P principles most applicable to cultivating cultures of compassion and human well-being is *humanistic behaviorism*. Critical connections between ABS and humanism are drawn in Chapter 2, especially regarding how they relate to developing a culture in which AC4P behavior becomes commonplace – a social norm.

Assuming most AC4P behavior requires some self-direction and self-motivation, Chapter 3 defines self-motivation and reviews the research literature regarding ways to enhance this perception or person-state within ourselves and others. Too often, however, self-motivation alone is not sufficient to drive AC4P behavior, even when the potential benefactor (or the "actor") knows the specifics of how to actively care.

The missing factor is courage, as defined and discussed in Chapter 4. Here you are introduced to several easy-to-perform AC4P behaviors that can improve our human condition on a large scale – but only if individuals practice them on a scale that approximates a mass movement. Chapter 4 challenges you to consider what holds you back from performing simple and convenient AC4P behavior on behalf of the health, safety, happiness, and overall welfare of others.

Communication is another barrier to more frequent and more effective AC4P behavior. This is the theme of Chapter 5. Communication internal to ourselves (as self-talk) and external to others is usually necessary to activate behavior and determine whether behavior continues or stops. Indeed, much AC4P behavior relies on communication; and some AC4P behavior is inhibited by the communication context or interpersonal culture. So how can we communicate more effectively to ourselves and to others in order to promote rather than hinder the performance of AC4P behavior by ourselves and others? Practical answers to this critical question are multidimensional and rather complex. Some answers are revealed in Chapter 5 as you learn how to become a more effective AC4P communicator.

Chapter 6 connects the AC4P principles with research that demonstrated the impact of certain social-influence techniques on behavior and concomitant attitudes. The essence of this chapter is *applied social psychology*. Six key social-influence strategies (used by advertisers, entrepreneurs, and consultants, among many others, to market their wares) are shown to directly connect to the ABS foundation of AC4P. The overlap between particular evidence-based principles of humanistic behaviorism and applied social psychology are explained and made manifest with practical real-world examples.

Chapter 7 introduces you to *positive psychology*. This is the scientific examination of methods to advance human fulfillment by strengthening compassion, courage, self-control, optimism, socially responsible communities and cultures, and a deep sense of belonging and purpose. The connection between positive psychology and the AC4P theme of this text is obvious. This chapter illuminates similarities and distinctions between positive psychology and humanistic behaviorism, and shows how the principles and applications of each of these domains can benefit the other.

The final chapter in Part I discusses characteristics of effective leadership and followership, and draws parallels to promoting and supporting effective AC4P behavior. Any effort to effect change on a macro scale, including the AC4P Movement, implies critical roles for both leaders and followers. What are these roles and how can they be initiated and supported to promote beneficial behavior change? This chapter offers practical strategies that leaders of any group endeavor should consider in order to be more effective.

Read these chapters to learn the AC4P principles derived from ABS (i.e., behaviorism) and psychological science (i.e., humanism). You will appreciate the academic label for these principles of applied psychology – *humanistic behaviorism* – and recognize the relevance of these AC4P principles for improving people's behavior and attitude in various situations in your life. In some settings, you'll be able to practice certain principles as an appropriate change agent; in other contexts, you'll be the observer of a teacher, coach, parent, or supervisor who could be more effective if one or more AC4P principles were followed.

Your challenge: Learn these AC4P principles and potential applications so well that you'll be able to teach relevant AC4P principles to an individual you observe whose teaching, coaching, parenting, or supervising would be more effective and positive with your education and behavior-based feedback. My vision: You'll acquire the competence, commitment, and courage to teach relevant AC4P principles whenever you observe a need, and thus become a leader of the AC4P Movement.

REFERENCE

1. *The American Heritage Dictionary: Second College Edition* (1985), p. 985.

The Foundation: Applied Behavioral Science

E. SCOTT GELLER

> One can picture a good life by analyzing one's feelings, but one can achieve it only by arranging environmental contingencies.
> – B. F. Skinner

Countless societal problems are brought to our attention every day by the news media. Violence and drug abuse, highway crashes, epidemics such as obesity and bullying, untold numbers of medical errors, conflicts both geopolitical and intensely personal, and environmental degradation – particularly climate change – carry significant economic burdens. They all impose dehumanizing costs in terms of individual suffering and loss of life.

Human behavior contributes to each of these perplexing problems – but human behavior is also a critical part of the solution. For more than fifty years, applied behavioral scientists have helped people by developing, implementing, and evaluating interventions to increase the occurrence of positive acts of caring and decrease the frequency of damaging behaviors.

Effective applications of applied behavioral science (ABS) generally follow the seven key principles described in this chapter. Each principle is broad enough to include a wide range of practical operations, but narrow enough to define the ABS approach to managing behaviors useful for promoting an AC4P movement (e.g., to benefit safety, health, work productivity, parenting, coaching, and environmental conservation and to optimize teaching and learning).[1]

1. TARGET OBSERVABLE BEHAVIOR

B. F. Skinner conceptualized and researched the behavioral science upon which the ABS approach is founded.[2] Experimental behavior analysis and later applied behavior analysis[3] emerged from Skinner's research and teaching, and laid the groundwork for numerous therapies and interventions to improve the quality of life among individuals, groups, and entire communities.[4] Whether someone is working one-on-one in a clinical setting or with work teams throughout an organization, the intervention procedures always target specific behaviors relevant to promoting constructive change. Applied behavioral science focuses on what people do, analyzes *why* they do it, and then applies an evidence-based intervention to *improve* what they do.

Acting people into thinking differently is the focus. This contrasts with *thinking people into acting differently*, which targets internal awareness, intentions, or attitudes. Many clinical psychologists use the latter approach successfully in professional therapy sessions. But in group, organizational, or community-wide settings it's not cost-effective. To be effective, thinking-focused intervention requires extensive one-on-one interaction between a client and a trained intervention specialist.

Few intervention agents in the real world (e.g., teachers, parents, coaches, healthcare workers, and safety professionals) possess the educational background, training, and experience to implement an intervention focused on internal and unobservable person-states. A basic tenet of ABS is that interventions should occur at the natural site of the behavioral issue (e.g., corporation, school, home, or athletic field) and be administered by an indigenous change agent (e.g., work supervisor, teacher, parent, or coach).

2. FOCUS ON EXTERNAL FACTORS TO EXPLAIN AND IMPROVE BEHAVIOR

Skinner did not deny the existence of internal determinants of behavior (such as personality characteristics, perceptions, attitudes, and values). These unobservable inferred constructs were rejected by Skinner for *scientific study* as causes or consequences of behavior. Factors in both our external and internal worlds obviously influence what we do – how we act. But it's difficult to objectively define internal traits or states. It's simply more cost-effective to identify environmental conditions that influence behavior, and then change these factors when behavior change is called for.

Examining external factors to explain and improve behavior is a primary focus of organizational behavior management.[5] The ABS principles are used to develop interventions to improve work quality, productivity, and safety. *Behavior-based safety* (BBS) is the term for applying the ABS

approach to occupational safety. Behavior-based safety is currently used worldwide to increase the frequency of safety-related behaviors, decrease the occurrence of at-risk behaviors, and prevent workplace injuries and fatalities.[6] More recently, the ABS approach to organizational safety has been customized and applied in healthcare facilities to prevent medical error and improve patient safety.[7] These applications of ABS in industrial and healthcare settings are detailed in Part II – the applications section of this text.

The pertinent point here is that ABS focuses on the external environmental conditions and contingencies influencing a target behavior. A careful analysis of the situation is conducted before an intervention approach is chosen. The target behavior(s) and the individual(s) involved in any observed discrepancy between the behavior observed and the behavior desired (i.e., real vs. ideal behavior) are studied. A behavior-focused intervention is designed and implemented if the gap between the actual and the desired behavior warrants change. This is accomplished by adhering to the next three principles.

3. DIRECT WITH ACTIVATORS AND MOTIVATE
WITH CONSEQUENCES

This principle enables us to understand why behavior occurs and guides the design of interventions to improve behavior. It runs counter to common sense or "pop psychology." When people are asked why they did something, they say things like, "Because I wanted to do it," "Because I needed to do it," or "Because I was told to do it." Such explanations sound as if the cause of behavior precedes it. A multitude of pop psychology self-help books, audiotapes, and DVDs support the belief that we motivate our behavior with self-affirmations, positive thinking, optimistic expectations, or enthusiastic intentions.

The fact is, as Dale Carnegie put it, "Every act you have ever performed since the day you were born was performed because you wanted something."[8] We do what we do because of the consequences we expect to obtain or hope to escape or avoid by doing it. Carnegie cited Skinner's research and scholarship as the foundation for this basic principle of motivation.

Activators (or signals preceding behavior) are only as powerful as the consequences supporting them. Activators tell us what to do in order to experience a positive, pleasant consequence. Or they tell us what not to do to avoid a negative, unpleasant consequence. Take a ringing telephone. If we see from the "call waiting" phone number the call is from a friend we haven't spoken with in a long time, we pick up the receiver and begin a rewarding conversation. But if the "call waiting" number is unknown to us, we might not pick up the receiver. We might let the call go to voicemail.

How about the ringing of a doorbell? Years ago, people always answered the door. Now, due to fears of unknown strangers and a plethora of visitors who want something from us ("Would you sign this petition?" "Can I count on your vote?" "Do you need your driveway blacktopped?"), we're more likely to peer through a window to see who it is and decide whether the consequence of opening the door will be pleasant or unpleasant. We follow through with the particular behavior activated (from answering or ignoring a ringing telephone to opening or refusing to open a door) on the basis of whether we expect a pleasant consequence or can avoid an unpleasant consequence.

This principle is typically referred to as the ABC model or three-term contingency, with A for activator (or antecedent), B for behavior, and C for consequence. Behavioral scientists use this ABC principle to design interventions for improving behavior at individual, group, organizational, and community levels. More than fifty years of behavioral science research has demonstrated the efficacy of this general approach to directing and motivating behavior change. The ABC contingency is reflected in the illustration below.

The dog will move if he's hungry and expects to receive food after hearing the sound of the electric can opener. The direction provided by an activator is likely to be followed when it is backed by a soon, certain, and significant consequence. This operation is termed *operant* or *instrumental conditioning*. The consequence is a positive reinforcer when behavior is performed to obtain it. When behavior occurs to escape or avoid a consequence, the consequence is a *negative* reinforcer.

If the sound of the can opener elicits a salivation reflex in the dog, we have an example of *classical* or *respondent conditioning*. The can opener sound is a conditioned stimulus (CS) and the salivation is a conditioned response (CR). The food that follows the sound of the electric can opener is the unconditioned stimulus (UCS), which elicits the unconditioned response of salivating without any prior learning experience. This UCS–UCR reflex is natural or "wired in" the organism.

Perhaps you recall this terminology from a basic learning course in psychology. We review it here because ABS is founded on these learning principles, especially operant conditioning. People choose behavior to obtain a pleasant consequence or to escape or avoid an unpleasant consequence. But as shown in the illustration, operant (instrumental) conditioning and respondent (classical) conditioning often occur simultaneously. Although we operate on the environment to achieve a desired consequence or avoid an unwanted consequence, emotional reactions are often classically conditioned to specific stimulus events in the situation. We learn to like or dislike the environmental context and/or the people involved in administrating the ABC contingency. This is how the type of behavioral consequence influences attitude and why ABS interventions focus on positive consequences.

4. FOCUS ON POSITIVE CONSEQUENCES TO MOTIVATE BEHAVIOR

Skinner's concern for people's feelings and attitudes is reflected in his antipathy toward the use of punishment (or negative consequences) to motivate behavior. "The problem is to free men, not from control, but from certain kinds of control."[9] Skinner proceeds to explain that control by negative consequences must be reduced to increase perceptions of personal freedom.

The same situation can often be viewed both ways: control by punishment of unwanted behavior or control by positive reinforcement of desired behavior. Some students in my university classes, for example, are motivated to avoid failure (e.g., a poor grade). Other students are motivated to achieve success (e.g., a good grade or increased knowledge). Which of these groups of students feel more empowered and in control of their class grade? Which have a better attitude toward my classes? Of course, you know the answer. Reflect on your own feelings or attitude in similar situations where you perceived your behavior as influenced by positive or negative consequences.

Achieving Success versus Avoiding Failure

Years ago, John W. Atkinson and his associates[10] found dramatic differences when comparing the decision-making of individuals with a high need to avoid failure and those with a high need to achieve success. Those motivated to achieve positive consequences set challenging but attainable goals. Participants with a high need to avoid failure were apt to set goals that were either too easy or too difficult.

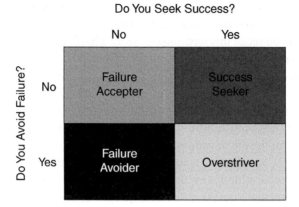

FIGURE 1.1. Four motivational typologies defined by achieving success vs. avoiding failure.

Setting easy goals ensures the avoidance of failure; setting unrealistic goals provides an excuse for failure – termed *self-handicapping* by more recent researchers.[11] Thus, a substantial amount of behavioral research and motivational theory justifies advocating the use of positive over negative consequences to motivate the occurrence of a designated behavior. This is the case whether an ABC contingency is contrived to improve someone else's behavior or imagined to motivate personal rule-following behavior.

Figure 1.1 depicts four distinct achievement typologies initially defined by Covington.[12] These four classifications have been researched to explain differences in how people approach success and/or avoid failure. It's most desirable to be a *success seeker*. These are the optimists, responding to setbacks (e.g., corrective feedback) in a positive and adaptive manner. They are self-confident and willing to take risks as opposed to avoiding challenges in order to avoid failure. They wake up each day to an *opportunity* clock rather than an *alarm* clock. It's a mindset or attitude toward life you can influence in yourselves and others. This book teaches you how to do that.

Overstrivers are diligent, successful, meticulous, and at times optimistic. But they have self-doubt about their abilities and experience substantial evaluation anxiety. This drives them to avoid failure by working hard to succeed. Covington and Roberts[13] found that overstrivers are preoccupied with perfection and often over-prepare for a challenge (e.g., a test of knowledge or ability).

Failure avoiders have a low expectancy of success and a high fear of failure. They do whatever it takes to protect themselves from appearing incompetent. They often use self-handicapping and defensive pessimism to shield themselves from potential failure.[14] These individuals are motivated but are not happy campers. They are the students who say, "I've *got* to go to class; it's a requirement," rather than "I *get* to go to class; it's an opportunity."

Finally, *failure accepters* score low in terms of both expecting success and fearing failure. Failure is merely accepted as indicative of low ability. Unlike failure avoiders, though, these individuals don't worry about failure or their inability to succeed. They have given up. Their attitude and behavior reflect learned helplessness.[15]

Interestingly, failure accepters are better adjusted psychologically than failure avoiders and overstrivers, according to Covington and Roberts.[13] They score relatively high on well-being, tolerance, self-control, and social presence. They report being relatively self-assured and self-disciplined. They have adopted a passive lifestyle relatively free of worry. Why? Perhaps because they've abandoned achievement, and in so doing they experience relatively few stressors throughout their days.

Personality Traits versus States

Much of the research literature addressing these four achievement typologies seems to imply that they reflect relatively stable and persistent qualities of individuals. They represent personality traits rather than states.[16] However, other researchers and practitioners, especially proponents of ABS, view these characteristics as fluctuating states. They exist under the influence of the environment and the three-term (ABC) contingency.

Environmental conditions and contingencies set the stage for success seeking, overstriving, failure avoiding, or failure accepting. The results or consequences of one's efforts can maintain or change one's perspective. Success seeking is cultivated through positive reinforcement. Overstriving and failure avoiding result from negative reinforcement and punishment. A failure accepter might simply surrender after a history of consistent failure. Passive failure accepters who have accepted their fate are apparently happier campers than failure avoiders and overstrivers. But in their surrendering they are not motivated to even try a challenging task. Wouldn't you rather have a failure avoider or overstriver on your team, and attempt to move their state toward success seeking?

The Contingency for Success Seeking

The ABS approach to promoting success seeking is to apply positive reinforcement contingencies strategically instead of negative reinforcement or punishment. Still, punishment contingencies are relatively easy to implement on a large scale. That's why our government selects this approach to behavior management. Simply pass a law and enforce it. And when monetary fines are paid for transgressions, the controlling agency obtains financial support for continuing its enforcement efforts. And punishment often seems to work, as the illustration below shows.

Control by negative consequences is seemingly the only feasible approach in many areas of large-scale behavior management, especially transportation safety. Consequently, the side effects of aggressive driving and road rage are relatively common and observed by anyone who drives. Most of us have experienced the anxious emotional reaction of seeing the flashing blue light of a police vehicle in our rearview mirror – another example of classical conditioning.

You've probably witnessed the temporary impact produced by this enforcement threat. Classic research in experimental behavior analysis teaches us to expect only temporary suppression of a punished behavior[17]

and to predict that some drivers in their "Skinner box on wheels" will speed up to compensate for the time they lost when slowing down in an enforcement zone.[18] As reviewed in Chapter 11, practical ways to apply positive reinforcement contingencies to driving are available,[19] but much more long-term research is needed in this domain. Various positive reinforcement contingencies need to be applied and evaluated to judge their ability to offset the negative side effects of the existing negative reinforcement contingencies.[20]

Regardless of the situation, managers, teachers, work supervisors, and parents can often intervene to increase people's perceptions that they are working to achieve success rather than avoid failure. Even our verbal behavior directed toward another person, perhaps as a statement of genuine approval of or appreciation for a task well done, can increase perceptions of personal freedom and self-motivation (see Chapter 3). Words of approval, though, are not as common as words of disapproval. So while ABS change agents focus their interventions on observable behavior, they are also concerned about attitude, as reflected in the next principle.

5. DESIGN INTERVENTIONS WITH CONSIDERATION OF INTERNAL FEELINGS AND ATTITUDES

Skinner was certainly concerned about unobservable attitudes or feeling states. This is evidenced by his criticism of using negative consequences to influence behavior. This perspective reflects a realization: Intervention procedures influence feeling states, and these can be pleasant or unpleasant, desirable or undesirable. Internal feelings or attitudes are influenced indirectly by the type of behavior-focused intervention procedure implemented, and this relationship must be carefully considered by the developers and managers of a behavior-change process.

The differential feeling state provoked by positive reinforcement versus punishment procedures is the rationale for using more positive than negative consequences to motivate behavior. Similarly, the way we implement an intervention process can increase or decrease feelings of empowerment, build or destroy trust, and cultivate or inhibit a sense of teamwork or belongingness.[21] Thus, it's important to assess feeling states or perceptions occurring concomitantly with an intervention process. This can be accomplished informally through one-on-one interviews and group discussions or formally with a perception survey.[22] However, surveys with few response alternatives have obvious limitations when it comes to assessing feelings or attitudes, as the illustration below shows.

Social Validity

Decisions regarding which ABS intervention to implement and how to refine existing intervention procedures should be based on both objective behavioral observations and subjective evaluations of feeling states. Often, it's possible to employ empathy to evaluate the indirect internal impact of an intervention. Imagine yourself going through a particular set of intervention procedures. Then ask the question, "How would I feel?"

Almost two decades ago when my daughter wanted to drive my car to her high school I installed a sign on the back, as shown in the illustration on the next page. I bolted the sign to my vehicle after she had achieved a percent-safe score of 100 on three consecutive coaching sessions with a critical behavior checklist (CBC), as described later in this chapter. We had this if–then contingency: "Achieve a perfect score on three consecutive trips with the CBC, and you may drive my car to school."

I was sure she'd accept the addition of the sign on my vehicle. Note how this activator is more than an awareness prompt; it implies a consequence. We talked about the value of positive or supportive consequences, so I thought Krista would view this sign as a fun and positive approach to promoting safe driving. "Let's be optimistic about this," I said to her, "and see how many positive phone calls I get about your safe and courteous driving behavior."

"Are you kidding me, Dad? There's no way I'd park that car and sign at my high school," Krista retorted. "I'd be the laughing stock of the whole school. I'll talk to Mom about this." My lesson: Don't assume you know how a well-intentioned intervention will be received by the participant(s); ask first.

Assessment of social validity is a comprehensive and systematic approach advocated by ABS researchers and practitioners.[23] Social validity assessment includes the use of rating scales, interviews, and focus-group discussions to assess (a) the societal significance of the intervention goals, (b) the social appropriateness of the procedures, and (c) the societal importance or clinical significance of the intervention effects.[24]

The Four Components of ABS Intervention

The four basic components of an ABS intervention process – selection, implementation, evaluation, and dissemination – are addressed in a comprehensive social validity evaluation.

Selection refers to the importance or priority of the behavioral problem and the people targeted for change. Addressing the large-scale problems of transportation safety, climate change, prison management, child abuse, interpersonal bullying, and medical errors is clearly important, but given limited resources, which issue should receive priority? The answer to this question depends partly on the availability of a cost-effective intervention.

Assessing the social validity of the *implementation* stage of an ABS intervention includes evaluating the behavior-change goals and procedures of the behavior-change process. How acceptable is the plan to potential participants and other parties, even those tangentially associated with the intervention?[25] In the case of a bullying-prevention program, answering this question entails obtaining acceptability ratings not only from teachers, students, and school administrators, but also from the students' family members and the community members whose tax dollars support the intervention. Are the intervention procedures consistent with the school's values and mission statement, and do they reach the most appropriate audience? And it's recommended that the recipients of an intervention be consulted regarding acceptability and methodology, as depicted in the illustration on the next page.

The social validity of the *evaluation* stage refers, of course, to the impact of the intervention process. This includes estimates of the costs and benefits of an intervention as well as measures of participant or consumer satisfaction. The numbers or scores obtained from various measurement devices (e.g., environmental audits, behavioral checklists, interview forms, output records, and attitude questionnaires) need to be reliable and valid. But they also need to be understood by the people who use them. If they are not, the evaluation scheme does not provide useful feedback and cannot lead to continuous improvement.

Meaningless or misunderstood evaluation numbers also limit the dissemination potential and large-scale applicability of an intervention. Now we're talking about the social validity of the *dissemination stage* of the ABS intervention process. This is the weakest aspect of ABS intervention, and perhaps

applied psychology in general. Intervention researchers and scholars justify their efforts and obtain financial support based on the scientific rigor of their methods and the statistical significance of their results. Rarely do these scholars address the real-world dissemination challenges of their findings.

Unfortunately, dissemination and marketability are left to corporations, consulting firms, and "pop psychologists." As a result, there are often disconnects between the science of ABS (and other psychological processes) and behavior-change intervention in the real world. One solution to this dilemma is to teach the real-world users of ABS how to conduct their own evaluations of intervention impact. This brings us to the next ABS principle.

6. APPLY THE SCIENTIFIC METHOD TO IMPROVE INTERVENTION

Some people believe dealing with the human dynamics of behavior change requires only "good common sense."[26] Surely you realize the absurdity of such a premise. Common sense is based on people's selective listening and

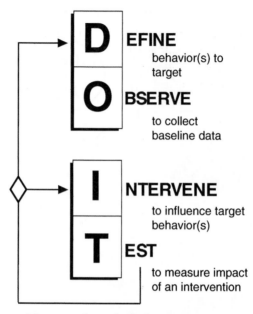

FIGURE 1.2. The scientific method of ABS as represented by DO IT.

interpretation and is usually founded on what sounds good to the individual listener, not necessarily on what works.[27] In contrast, systematic and scientific observation enables the kind of objective feedback needed to know what works and what doesn't work to improve behavior.

The occurrence of specific behaviors can be objectively observed and measured before and after the implementation of an intervention process. This application of the scientific method provides feedback for shaping behavioral improvement. I've frequently used the acronym DO IT depicted in Figure 1.2 to teach this principle of ABS to change agents (e.g., coaches, teachers, parents, work supervisors, and hourly workers) who are empowered to improve the behavior of others and who want to continuously improve their intervention skills. This process represents the scientific method that ABS practitioners have used for decades to demonstrate the impact of particular behavior-change techniques.

"D" for Define

We begin the process by defining specific behaviors to target, which are undesirable behaviors that need to decrease in frequency and/or desirable behaviors that need to occur more often. Avoiding certain unwanted behaviors often requires alternative behaviors, and so target behaviors might be behaviors that can substitute for particular undesirable behaviors. On the other hand, a desirable target behavior can be defined independently of undesired behavior.

An AC4P approach to preventing interpersonal bullying applied reward techniques to increase interpersonal caring and sharing behaviors, and resulted in a decrease in bullying behavior without ever mentioning bullying as a target.[28] A change agent can lower the frequency of an undesirable behavior(s) by targeting desirable behavior(s) incompatible with the unwanted behavior. Defining and evaluating ongoing behavior is often facilitated by the development of a behavioral checklist to use during observations. The development of behavioral definitions invokes an invaluable learning experience. When people get involved in deriving a behavioral checklist, they own a training process that can improve human dynamics on both the outside (behaviors) and the inside (feelings and attitudes) of people.

"O" for Observe

When people observe each other for certain desirable or undesirable behaviors, they realize everyone performs undesirable behavior, sometimes without even realizing it. Observation is not a fault-finding procedure. It's a fact-finding learning process to discover behaviors and conditions that need to be changed or continued in order for someone to be most competent at a task. No behavioral observation needs to be made without awareness and explicit permission from the person being observed. Observers should be open to learning as much (if not more) from the process as they expect to teach from completing the behavioral checklist.

The Critical Behavior Checklist. There isn't one generic observation procedure for every situation. Customization and refinement of a process for a particular setting never stops. You might begin the observation process with a limited number of behaviors and a relatively simple checklist. This reduces the possibility of people feeling overwhelmed at the beginning. Starting small also enables the broadest range of voluntary participation and provides numerous opportunities to improve the process successively by expanding coverage of both behaviors and environmental settings.

I used the critical behavioral checklist (CBC) depicted in Figure 1.3 to teach my daughter safe-driving practices. She actually thought the driver's ed. program she had in high school was sufficient. I knew better. We needed to develop and apply a CBC. Through one-on-one discussion, Krista and I derived a list of critical driving behaviors and then agreed on specific

Critical Behavior Checklist for Driving			
Driver:	Date:		Day:
Observer 1:	Origin:		Start Time:
Observer 2:	Destination:		End Time:
Weather:			
Road Conditions:			
Behavior	**Safe**	**At-Risk**	**Comments**
Safety Belt Use:			
Turn Signal Use:			
Left turn			
Right turn			
Lane change			
Intersection Stop:			
Stop sign			
Red light			
Yellow light			
No activator			
Speed Limits:			
25 mph and under			
25 mph–35 mph			
35 mph–45 mph			
45 mph–55 mph			
55 mph–65 mph			
Passing:			
Lane Use:			
Following Distance (2 sec):			
Totals:			
% **safe** = $\frac{\text{Total Safe Observations}}{\text{Total Safe + At-Risk Obs.}}$ = _____ %			

FIGURE 1.3. A critical behavior checklist for driver training.

definitions for each item. My university students practiced using this CBC a few times with various drivers, resulting in a refined list of behavioral definitions.

After discussing the revised list of behaviors and their definitions with Krista, I was ready to implement the second stage of DO IT – observation. I asked my daughter to drive me to the university – about nine miles from home – to pick up some papers. I overtly recorded behavioral observations on the CBC during both legs of this roundtrip. After returning home, I totaled the safe and at-risk checkmarks and calculated the percentage of safe behaviors. It turned out that 85 percent of her driving was safe. I considered this quite good for our first time. (Note the emphasis on achieving safe rather than avoiding at-risk driving.)

I told Krista her "percent-safe" score and proceeded to show her the list of safe checkmarks, while covering the few checks in the at-risk column. To my surprise, she was not impressed with her score. Rather she pushed me to tell her what she did wrong. "Get to the bottom line, Dad," she asserted. "Where did I screw up?"

This reaction was enlightening in two respects. First, it illustrated the unfortunate reality that the bottom line for many people is, "Where did I go wrong?" My daughter, at age 15, had already recognized that people evaluating her performance were more interested in mistakes than successes. This perspective activates an undesirable failure-avoiding mindset over a desirable success-seeking mindset, as introduced earlier.

The realization that people can be unaware of their at-risk behavior was a second important outcome of this CBC experience. Only through objective behavior-based feedback can we improve. Krista did not readily accept my corrective feedback regarding her four at-risk behaviors. She emphatically denied she did not always come to a complete stop at intersections with stop signs. However, she became convinced of her error when I showed her my data sheet and my comments regarding the particular intersection where there was no traffic and she made only a rolling stop before turning right.

Obviously, we are now in the intervention phase of DO IT, with interpersonal feedback being the ABS intervention tactic. I reminded Krista she used her turn signal at every intersection, and she should be proud of that behavior. To make this behavior-based coaching process a positive, success-seeking experience, I emphasized the behaviors I observed her perform correctly.

"I" for Intervene

During this stage, interventions are designed and implemented in an attempt to increase the occurrence of desired behavior and/or decrease the frequency of undesired behavior. As reflected in Principle 2, intervention means changing external conditions of the behavioral context or system in order to make desirable behavior more likely than undesirable behavior.

For the design of interventions, Principles 3 and 4 are critical: The most motivating consequences are soon, certain, and sizable (Principle 3), and positive consequences are preferable to negative consequences (Principle 4).

The process of observing and recording the frequency of desirable and undesirable behavior on a checklist is an opportunity to give individuals and groups valuable behavior-based feedback. When the results of a behavioral observation are shown to individuals or groups, they receive the kind of information that enables practice to improve performance. Considerable research has shown that providing people feedback regarding their ongoing behavior is a very cost-effective intervention approach.[29] Chapter 3 details techniques for giving AC4P feedback effectively.

The Hawthorne Effect. According to the classic Hawthorne effect, people change their behavior in desired directions when they know their behavior is being observed.[30] It turns out, however, people change their behavior not as a result of being observed but in response to receiving feedback. McIlvain Parsons[31] conducted a careful reexamination of the Hawthorne data (originally obtained at the Western Electric plant in the Hawthorne community near Chicago) and interviewed eyewitness observers, including one of the five female relay assemblers who were the primary targets of the Hawthorne studies. Here's what he found:

During the intervention phase, the five women observed systematically in the relay assembly test room received regular *feedback* about the number of relays each had assembled. Feedback was especially important to these workers because their salaries were influenced by an individual piecework plan. In ABS terminology this was a *fixed ratio reinforcement schedule.* The more relays each employee assembled, the more money each earned.

In addition to behavioral feedback, researchers have found a number of other intervention strategies to be effective at increasing desirable behaviors, including behavioral prompts, interpersonal coaching, behavior-change promise cards, individual and group goal setting, AC4P thank you cards, individual and group celebrations, as well as incentive/reward programs for individuals or groups. These intervention strategies, customized to target certain AC4P behaviors in particular situations, are described throughout this book.

"T" for Test

The test phase of DO IT provides work teams or change agents with intervention-based information they need to refine or replace the ABS intervention, and so improve the process. If observations indicate that significant improvement in the target behavior has not occurred, the change agents analyze and discuss the situation and refine the intervention or choose another intervention approach. On the other hand, if the target reaches the desired frequency level, the change agents can turn their attention to another set of behaviors. They might add new critical behaviors to their checklist, expanding the domain of their behavioral observations. Alternatively, they might design a new intervention procedure to focus only on the new behaviors.

Every time participants evaluate an intervention approach, they learn more about how to improve targeted behaviors. They have essentially become AC4P behavioral scientists, using the DO IT process to (a) diagnose a problem involving human behavior, (b) monitor the impact of a behavior-change intervention, and (c) refine interventions for continuous improvement. The results of such testing provide motivating consequences to sustain this learning process and keep the change agents and their participants involved.

7. USE THEORY TO INTEGRATE INFORMATION, NOT TO LIMIT POSSIBILITIES

B. F. Skinner was critical of designing research projects to test theory.[32] Nevertheless, much, if not most, research is theory-driven. Theory-driven research can narrow the perspective of the investigator and limit the extent of findings with the scientific method. Applying the DO IT process merely to test a theory can be like putting blinders on a horse. It can limit the amount of input gained from systematic observation.

Exploratory ABS investigation has resulted in many important findings. Systematic observations of behavior were made before and after an intervention or treatment procedure to answer the question, "I wonder what will happen if . . . ?" rather than "Is my theory correct?"

Applied behavioral scientists are not looking for a particular result, but are open to finding anything that can influence behavior. Then they modify their research design or observation process according to their behavioral observations, not a particular theory. Their innovative research has been data-driven rather than theory-driven, which is an important perspective for behavior-change agents, especially when applying the DO IT process.

It's often better to be open to many possibilities for improving performance than to be motivated to support a certain process. Numerous intervention procedures are consistent with the ABS approach, and an intervention process that works well in one situation will not necessarily be effective in another setting. Thus, it's usually advantageous to teach change agents to make an educated guess about what intervention procedure to use at the start of a behavior-change process, while being open to intervention refinement as a result of the DO IT process. Of course, Principles 1 to

4 should always be used as guidelines during the design of intervention procedures.

Distinct consistencies will be observed after many systematic applications of the DO IT process. Certain procedures will work better in some situations than others, with some individuals than others, or with some behaviors than others. Summarizing functional relationships between intervention impact and specific situational or interpersonal characteristics can lead to the development of a research-based theory of what works best under particular circumstances. In this case, theory is used to integrate information gained from systematic behavioral observation. Skinner approved of this use of theory, but cautioned that premature theory development can lead to premature theory testing and limited profound knowledge.[32]

EXAMPLES OF APPLIED BEHAVIORAL SCIENCE INTERVENTION

Most large-scale ABS interventions designed to improve behavior can be classified as either antecedent or consequence strategies. This section reviews four activator (or antecedent) strategies and three consequence strategies ABS change agents have used effectively to change socially important behaviors. The success of these ABS interventions was evaluated with a DO IT scheme.

Activators

Activators or antecedent interventions include (a) education, (b) verbal and written prompts, (c) modeling and demonstrations, and (d) commitment procedures.

Education. Before anyone attempts to improve a behavior, it's often important to provide a strong rationale for doing so. Sometimes this process involves making remote, uncertain, or unknown consequences more salient to the relevant audience. For example, an intervention designed to increase recycling could provide information about the negative consequences of throwing aluminum cans in the trash (e.g., wasted resources, unnecessary energy consumption, and overflowing landfills), as well as the positive consequences of recycling behavior (e.g., energy savings, decreased pollution, and reduced use of landfill space).

Educational antecedents can be disseminated through print or electronic media, or delivered personally in individual or group settings. Researchers have shown that education presented interpersonally is more effective when it's done in small rather than large groups and when it actively involves participants in relevant activities and demonstrations.[33]

Providing information and activating awareness of a problem are often important components of ABS intervention, but keep in mind that information alone is seldom sufficient to change behavior, especially when the desired behavior is inconvenient.[34] Education or awareness antecedents are often combined with other intervention components, as discussed later.

Prompts. Prompting strategies are verbal or written messages strategically delivered to promote the occurrence of a target behavior. These activators are reminders to perform target behaviors.

Geller, Winett, and Everett[35] identified several conditions for prompting antecedents. Prompts work best when (a) the target behavior is specifically defined by the prompt (e.g., "Buckle your safety belt" rather than "Drive safely"), (b) the target behavior is relatively easy to perform (e.g., using a designated trash receptacle vs. collecting and delivering recyclables), (c) the message is displayed where the target behavior can be performed (e.g., at a store where "green" commodities are sold vs. on the local news), (d) the message is stated politely (e.g., "Please buckle up" vs. "You must buckle up"), and (e) the activator implies a consequence, as already discussed.

Prompts are popular. They are simple to implement, cost relatively little, and can have considerable impact if used properly. Werner, Rhodes, and Partain increased dramatically the amount of polystyrene recycling in a university cafeteria by increasing the size of signs designed to prompt recycling and placing them next to recycling bins.[36] Geller, Kalsher, Rudd, and Lehman designed safety belt reminders to be hung from the rearview mirrors of personal vehicles.[37] In both of these successful applications, the prompts were displayed in close proximity to where the target behavior could be performed, and the behavior requested was relatively convenient to perform.

Modeling. Prompts can be effective for simple, convenient behaviors. Modeling is the more appropriate approach when the desired behavior is complex. Modeling involves demonstrating specific target behaviors to a relevant audience. This activator is more effective when the model or demonstrator receives a reward immediately after performing the target behavior.[38] Modeling can be accomplished via an interpersonal demonstration, but reaches a broader audience through electronic media. However, as the illustration on the next page shows, we sometimes model and teach undesirable behavior.

A large-scale modeling intervention to increase energy- conservation behaviors was evaluated by Winett and colleagues.[39] Participants who viewed a twenty-minute videotaped presentation of relevant conservation behaviors significantly decreased their residential energy use over a nine-week period. It's noteworthy the video specified the positive financial consequences of performing the conservation behaviors.

Behavioral Commitment. Behavioral commitment is straightforward and easy to implement, and it can be very effective. Although all ABS interventions request behavior change, a behavioral commitment takes this process a step further. Individuals are asked to agree formally to change their behavior. They make a behavioral commitment. Asking individuals to make a written or verbal commitment to perform a target behavior increases the likelihood the behavior will be performed.[40]

When individuals sign a pledge or promise card to increase a desirable behavior (e.g., buckling up, recycling, exercising) or cease an undesirable behavior (e.g., driving while impaired, smoking cigarettes, littering) they feel obligated to honor their commitment, and often do.[41] More examples of successful applications of this intervention strategy are discussed in Chapters 4 and 6.

Commitment-compliant behavior is explained by ABS professionals with the notion of *rule-governed behavior*. People learn rules for behavior, and through their experiences they learn that following the rule is linked to positive social and personal consequences (e.g., interpersonal approval), and breaking the rule can lead to the negative consequences of disapproval or legal penalties. This tendency to follow through on a behavioral commitment is attributed by social psychologists to the social norm of *consistency*. This norm creates pressure to be internally and externally consistent.[41] You'll read more about this in Chapter 6.

This behavioral commitment strategy can be conveniently added to many ABS interventions. At a time when vehicle safety belt use was not the norm, my students and I combined commitment and prompting strategies by asking university students, faculty, and staff to sign a card promising to use their vehicle safety belts. Participants also agreed to hang the "promise card" on the rearview mirror of their vehicles, which served as a proximal prompt to buckle up. As you may have guessed, individuals who signed the "buckle-up promise card" were already using their vehicle safety belt more often than those individuals who did not; but after signing the pledge, these individuals increased their belt use significantly.[42]

Consequence Strategies

Consequences are the primary determinant of voluntary behavior, according to ABS researchers and practitioners. The most effective activators make recipients aware of potential consequences, either explicitly or implicitly. Let's consider three basic consequence strategies: penalties, rewards, and feedback.

Penalties. These interventions identify undesirable behaviors and administer negative consequences to those who perform them. Although favored by governments, this approach is typically avoided by ABS practitioners in community interventions for a variety of reasons. One practical reason: It usually requires extensive enforcement to be effective, and enforcement requires backing by the proper authority. An ordinance that fines residents for throwing soda cans in the garbage would require some reliable way to observe this unwanted behavior, which obviously, would not be easy.

The negative impact of the penalty approach on the attitudes of the target audience is the main reason ABS practitioners have opposed the use of behavioral penalties. Most individuals react to a punitive event with negative emotions and attitudes.[43] Instead of performing a behavior because of its positive impact, they simply do it to avoid negative consequences. And when enforcement is not consistent, behaviors are likely to return to their previous state.

Astute readers will note the label *penalty approach* rather than *punishment*. And next, the term *reward* is used instead of *positive reinforcement*. This differentiates the technical and the application meanings of these consequence strategies. Reinforcement and punishment imply that the consequence changed the target behavior. If punishment does not decrease the occurrence of the target behavior, or reinforcement (positive or negative) does not increase the frequency of the target behavior, the relevant consequences were not punishers or reinforcers, respectively.

Punishment and reinforcement procedures are defined by the effects of the consequence on the target behavior. Because large-scale or community-based applications of consequence strategies rarely identify the behavioral impact per individual, the terms *penalty* and *reward* are more appropriate. Regardless of their behavioral impact, penalties are negative consequences and rewards are positive consequences.

Rewards. Because of the negative side effects associated with punishment, ABS practitioners favor following a desirable behavior with a positive consequence or reward. Rewards include money, merchandise, verbal praise, or special privileges, given as a consequence of the desired target behavior. Reward strategies have some problems of their own. Still, many community-based reward interventions have produced dramatic increases in targeted behaviors.

Because rewards follow behaviors, they are included in the consequence section of this chapter. However, as the illustration on the next page shows, rewards are often preceded by activators announcing the availability of the reward following a designated behavior. This activator is termed an *incentive*. An activator announcing punitive consequences for unwanted behavior is termed a *disincentive*. Sometimes rewards or penalties are used without incentives or disincentives. In these cases, the positive or negative consequence follows the behavior without an advanced announcement of the response-consequence contingency. These are "now-that" rewards (see Chapter 3).

A wide range of behaviors have been targeted with incentive/reward programs. Studies have shown that incentive/reward programs increase vehicle safety belt use,[44] medication compliance,[45] commitment to organ

donation,[46] and decrease the incidence of drug use,[46] environmental degradation,[47] alcohol abuse,[48] and interpersonal bullying.[28] In addition, incentives and rewards are used frequently and effectively by employers to increase worker productivity. A meta-analysis of thirty-nine studies using financial incentives to increase performance quantity found that, averaged across all studies, workers who were offered financial compensation for increased production increased their productivity by 34 percent over those who were not offered behavior-based rewards.[49]

Behavior-based incentive/reward strategies also increase the frequency of safety-related behaviors that prevent personal injury.[50] Given the consistent effectiveness of incentive/reward strategies, one might ask, "Why use anything else?" Unfortunately, incentive/reward interventions have a few disadvantages. An obvious practical disadvantage of using rewards is that they can be expensive to implement from both a financial and an administrative perspective.

A second limitation: Target behaviors tend to decrease when the rewards are removed, almost as dramatically as they increase when the rewards are introduced. In fact, this effect is so reliable ABS researchers often use it to evaluate intervention impact. They first measure the pre-intervention (baseline) rate of a target behavior, then assess the increase in the frequency of the behavior while rewards are in place, and finally document a decrease in behavioral frequency when the rewards are removed.

When a target behavior occurs more often while an intervention is in place and returns to near baseline levels when the intervention is withdrawn, ABS researchers demonstrate *functional control* of the target behavior. The intervention caused the behavior change. An obvious solution to this reversal problem is to keep a reward strategy in place indefinitely. Bottle bills, which provide a refund of 5–10 cents when bottles and cans are returned, illustrate an effective long-term incentive/reward strategy.

Finally, some researchers criticize reward interventions by contending rewards diminish *intrinsic motivation*.[51] Instead of focusing on the positive aspects of completing a task for its own sake, individuals become *extrinsically motivated* to perform the behavior. In essence, "If someone is paying me to perform a behavior, the activity must be unpleasant and not worth performing when the opportunity for a reward is removed."

The *over-justification effect*, as this perspective of extrinsic rewards is termed, is depicted in the illustration on the next page.[52] The prior extrinsic reward for solving a math problem takes the student's attention away from intrinsic or natural consequences of the behavior – solving an important problem. However, effective interpersonal recognition and feedback interventions call attention to the meaningfulness of the target behavior and can thus enhance intrinsic motivation. This issue, including how the use of certain positive consequences can actually increase self-motivation and behavioral sustainability, is entertained further in Chapter 3.

Feedback. Feedback strategies provide information to participants about their behavior. They can make the consequences of desirable behaviors more salient (e.g., money saved from carpooling, weight lost from an exercise program) and increase the frequency of behaviors consistent with desired outcomes.

Many early environmental-conservation interventions targeting home energy consumption used feedback strategies, and most of these interventions showed modest but consistent energy savings.[53] Feedback has been an effective strategy for addressing unsafe driving,[54] smoking cessation,[55] and depression.[56] Chapter 3 details communication techniques for giving supportive and corrective behavior-based feedback effectively in order to improve behavior.

Although these six nonpunitive ABS intervention techniques (education, prompts, modeling, commitment, rewards, and feedback) have been reviewed separately, in practice several are often combined in a single intervention process. Most interventions combine some sort of antecedent information component with a behavior-based consequence (e.g., reward and/or feedback). The reward or feedback can be based on participants' behavior

(i.e., process-based) or on the cumulative results of several behaviors performed by one individual or a team of individuals (i.e., outcome-based).

It's important to apply behavior-based and outcome-based consequences strategically. The behavior-consequence contingency defines an accountability system, which in turn influences the participant's behavior. Outcome-based feedback and reward programs to promote industrial safety are popular worldwide, because they are easy to implement and they decrease reports of injuries. Employees receive rewards (e.g., gift certificates, lottery tickets, or financial bonuses) when the company-wide injury rate is reduced to a certain level. The result: Rewards are received because the frequency of *reported* injuries decreases.

However, most of these outcome-based incentive/reward programs do more harm than good. Why? Because actual safety-related behaviors do not necessarily change – just the *reporting* of injuries. When the factual reporting of injuries is stifled by outcome-based incentives and rewards, the opportunity for critical conversations about injury prevention is lost. The illustration shows how rewards for outcomes can have a detrimental effect on behavior. Managers get what they reward.

THE CHALLENGE OF SUSTAINING
BEHAVIOR CHANGE

The intervention approaches reviewed in the preceding sections will change behavior, but will the target behavior continue when the intervention is removed? This is primarily a challenge of institutionalizing the ABC contingencies of the intervention process, contend some ABS professionals.[57] External or extrinsic activators and consequences need to be transferred from the intervention agent to the indigenous personnel of the organizational setting in which the target behavior occurs. The intervention is not removed; rather different individuals deliver the intervention contingencies.

Other behavioral scientists claim this maintenance challenge is about behavior continuing in the absence of the extrinsic intervention.[58] Some presume the objectives of the intervention need to be internalized. As indicated earlier, people act themselves into thought processes consistent with the new behavior.[59] As such, personal change is viewed as a continuous spiral of behavior causing thinking, thinking inducing more behavior, and then this additional behavior influencing more thinking consistent with the behavior, and so on. However, programmatic research indicates that some interventions do not facilitate an attendant change in thinking. This is reflected profoundly in Daryl Bem's classic theory of self-perception.

Behavioral Self-Perception

Bem prefaced his behavioral presentation of self-perception theory by saying, "Individuals come to 'know' their own attitudes, emotions, and other internal states by inferring them from observations of their own overt behavior and/or the circumstances in which this behavior occurs."[60] We write mental scripts or make internal attributions about ourselves from our observations and interpretations of the various three-term or ABC contingencies that enter our life space. "If external contingencies seem sufficient to account for the behavior, then the individual will not be led into using the behavior as a source of evidence for his self-attributions."[61]

Children who had the excuse of a severe threat for not playing with a forbidden toy did not internalize a rule and played with the forbidden toy when the threat contingency was removed.[62] Similarly, college students who were paid twenty dollars for telling other students a boring task was fun did not develop a personal view that the task was enjoyable.[63] The reinforcement contingency made their behavior incredible as a reflection of their personal belief or self-perception.

In contrast, participants who received a mild threat or low compensation (only one dollar) to motivate their behavior developed a self-perception consistent with their behavior. The children avoided playing with the forbidden toy in a subsequent situation with no threat, and the college students who lied for low compensation decided they must have liked the boring task. In theory, these participants viewed their behavior as a valid guide for inferring their private views, since their behavior was not under strong contingency control. This theory and its practical implications are explained further and illustrated in Chapter 6 as the *consistency principle* of social influence.

The More Outside Control, the Less Self-Persuasion

According to substantial research, self-persuasion is more likely when the extrinsic control of the three-term contingency is less obvious or perhaps indirect. When there are sufficient external consequences to justify the amount of effort required for a particular behavior, the performer does not develop an internal justification for the behavior. There is no self-persuasion, and performing the behavior does not alter self-perception.[64] Under these circumstances maintenance of the behavior is unlikely, unless it's possible to keep a sufficient accountability system (e.g., incentives or disincentives) in place over the long term, as was the case for a thirteen-year incentive/reward process that successfully reduced injuries in an open-pit mine.[65]

Intervening to improve behavior over the long term is more complex than applying the three-term contingency. Not only is it necessary to consider whether the performer needs instruction, motivation, or only support to improve or maintain behavior, it seems internal cognitive factors are important whenever external contingencies cannot remain in place to hold people accountable.[66] This implicates self-persuasion and self-directed behavior, topics not typically considered in ABS. These concepts imply that indirect influence is more likely to lead to sustained behavior change than is direct persuasion.

Direct Persuasion. Advertisers use direct persuasion. They show us actors enjoying positive consequences or avoiding negative consequences by using their products. They apply the three-term contingency or ABC paradigm to sell their goods and services. The activator announces the availability of a reinforcing consequence if the purchasing behavior is performed.

Advertisers also apply research-based principles from social psychology to make their messages more persuasive. Specifically, social scientists have shown advantages of using highly credible communicators and of arousing their audience's emotions.[67] Sales pitches are often delivered by authority figures (celebrities, chief executives) who attempt to get viewers emotionally involved with product-related issues. In today's social media world, one's friends can be influential if they indicate on Facebook they "like" a certain product. Advertisers are spending more and more money on this "peer persuasion" tactic.

These attempts at direct persuasion are not geared toward behavior that is inconvenient or difficult to execute. Normally, the purpose of an advertisement is to persuade a consumer to select a certain brand of merchandise s/he already uses. This boils down to merely choosing one commodity over another at the retail store. This is hardly a burdensome change in lifestyle.

AC4P behavior is usually more inconvenient and requires more effort than switching brands at a supermarket. Long-term participation in the AC4P Movement is far more cumbersome and lifestyle-changing than the consumer behavior targeted by advertisers.

In fact, direct attempts to persuade people to make inconvenient changes in their lifestyle have often yielded disappointing results. Communication strategies have generally been unsuccessful at persuading smokers to quit smoking,[68] drivers to stop speeding,[69] homeowners to conserve water[70] or insulate their water heaters,[71] bigoted individuals to cease prejudicial behavior, or sexually active people to use condoms.[64] Similarly, the "Just Say No to Drugs" campaigns have not brought about significant behavior change.

The direct approach can give the impression the target behavior is accomplished for someone else's benefit. This can cause a disconnect between the behavior and self-perception. Then there's no self-persuasion – and self-perception is the mindset needed for lasting change in the absence of incentives/rewards, disincentives/penalties, or another type of extrinsic/external accountability system.

The Indirect Approach. Self-persuasion is more likely to occur when the motivational strategy is less obvious. Compliments regarding a person's performance are often more powerful when they are more indirect than direct.[72] Imagine you overhear a person tell someone else about your superb achievement on a particular assignment. Or suppose a friend gives you secondhand recognition by sharing what another person said about your AC4P behavior. Both of these situations reflect indirect commendation and will likely have more influence on your self-perception than would a direct statement of praise. Why? Because the direct approach is tainted by the possibility that behind the flattery is an ulterior motive.

Indirect persuasion deviates significantly from the standard "command and control" method of promoting compliance. Both approaches might be equally effective at motivating immediate behavior change, but an indirect approach will be far more successful at enhancing the kind of internal dialogue needed to sustain behavior in the absence of an external motivator or accountability system.

Defining intervention conditions to make this happen is not easy. Start by asking, "Does the situation promote individual choice, ownership, and personal accountability?" "Does the context in which AC4P behavior is desired contribute to connecting or disconnecting the link between what people do and what they think of themselves?" "Are the AC4P activities only behaviors or do they stimulate supportive cognitive activity or self-persuasion?"

The role of psychological states or expectancies in facilitating AC4P behavior is reflected in these questions. If certain feelings or beliefs affect people's participation in the AC4P Movement, then enhancing these person-states can be a powerful indirect way to cultivate an AC4P culture of compassion. The next chapter explains this further by specifying both direct and indirect ways to increase the frequency and sustainability of AC4P behavior.

IN CONCLUSION

This initial chapter reviewed seven fundamental principles and related applications of ABS. These serve as the foundation of the AC4P Movement, from analyzing the behavioral components of social issues to implementing and disseminating practical, evidence-based strategies for large-scale behavior change. Some research-based examples of effective ABS interventions were presented, but the following chapters offer many more.

The need to consider self-talk and person-states in the design and implementation of AC4P interventions was explained. This domain of self-persuasion or self-motivation (see Chapter 3) justifies the label *humanistic behaviorism,* as introduced in the Preface. It takes us beyond traditional ABS. The principles and applications in this book illustrate ways to make ABS methods more effective and durable by incorporating concepts from humanistic theory and therapy. Still, when all is said and done, we have only scratched the surface regarding the potential of ABS and the AC4P Movement to mitigate numerous negative consequences resulting from the intimidating social and environmental problems we face every day.

DISCUSSION QUESTIONS

1. Explain with examples the difference between "acting people into thinking differently" and "thinking people into acting differently." Which approach do you think is more important, and why?
2. People often say that "a certain stimulus *triggered* a response." When is this statement correct and when is it incorrect?
3. Explain how classical and operant conditioning can occur simultaneously.
4. Distinguish between "success seeker" and "failure avoider" from both a dispositional and situational perspective.
5. Why is "punishment" or imposing negative consequences the intervention approach of choice in too many situations?

6. Distinguish between the deductive and inductive approaches to the development and application of theory. Which approach is more consistent with your current common sense? Why?

7. What is a "prompt," and what characteristics of a prompt determine its effectiveness in influencing behavior?

8. Distinguish between an incentive, disincentive, reward, and penalty with real-world examples.

9. When can extrinsic rewards be ineffective, and how might one overcome this liability?

10. Define "self-persuasion" and its relevance to sustaining behavior change.

REFERENCES

1. Geller, E. S. (1998). *Understanding behavior-based safety: Step-by-step methods to improve your workplace* (2nd ed.). Neenah, WI: J. J. Keller & Associates; Geller, E. S., & Williams, J. (Eds.). (2001). *Keys to behavior-based safety from Safety Performance Solutions.* Rockville, MD: Government Institutes; Geller, E. S. (2005). *People-based safety: The source.* Virginia Beach, VA: Coastal training and Technologies; Geller, E. S., & Johnson, D. J. (2007). *People-based patient safety: Enriching your culture to prevent medical error.* Virginia Beach, VA: Coastal Training and Technologies.

2. Skinner, B. F. (1938). *The behavior of organisms: An experimental analysis.* Acton, MA: Copley; Skinner, B. F. (1953). *Science and human behavior.* New York: Macmillan; Skinner, B. F. (1974). *About behaviorism.* New York: Alfred A. Knopf.

3. While the term *applied behavior analysis* is commonly used in the research literature, *applied behavioral science* is used here instead because it reflects a broader meaning with presumably more public appeal.

4. Goldstein, A. P., & Krasner, L. (1987). *Modern applied psychology.* New York: Pergamon Press; Greene, B. F., Winett, R. A., Van Houten, R., Geller, E. S., & Iwata, B. A. (Eds.) (1987). *Behavior analysis in the community: Readings from the "Journal of Applied Behavior Analysis."* Lawrence, KS: Society for the Experimental Analysis of Behavior.

5. Austin, J. (2000). Performance analysis and performance diagnostics. In J. Austin & J. E. Carr (Eds.). *Handbook of applied behavior analysis* (pp. 321–349). Reno, NV: Context Press; Austin, J., Carr, J. E., & Agnew, J. (1999). The need for assessing maintaining variables in OBM. *Journal of Organizational Behavior Management,* 19, 59–87; Bailey, J. S., &Austin, J. (1996). Evaluating and improving productivity in the workplace. In B. Thyer & M. Mattaini (Eds.). *Behavior analysis and social work* (pp. 179–200). Washington, DC: American Psychological Association.

6. Geller, E. S. (2001). *The psychology of safety handbook.* Boca Raton, FL: CRC Press; McSween, T. E. (2003). *The values-based safety process: Improving your safety culture with a behavioral approach* (2nd ed.). New York: Van Nostrand Reinhold; Sulzer-Azaroff, B., & Austin, J. (2000). Does BBS Work?

Behavior-based safety and injury reduction: A survey of the evidence. *Professional Safety*, 45, 19–24.

7. Geller, E. S., & Johnson, D. J. (2007). *People-based patient safety: Enriching your culture to prevent medical error*. Virginia Beach, VA: Coastal Training and Technologies.

8. Carnegie, D. (1936). *How to win friends and influence people*. New York: Simon & Schuster.

9. Skinner, B. F. (1971). *Beyond freedom and dignity*. New York: Alfred A. Knopf, p. 41.

10. Atkinson, J. W. (1957). Motivational determinants of risk-taking behavior. *Psychological Review*, 64, 359–372; Atkinson, J. W. (1964). *An introduction to motivation*. Princeton, NJ: Van Nostrand; Atkinson, J. W., & Litwin, G. F. (1960). Achievement motive and test anxiety conceived as motive to approach success and motive to avoid failure. *Journal of Abnormal and Social Psychology*, 60, 52–63.

11. Berglas, S., & Jones, E. E. (1978). Drug choice as a self-handicapping strategy in response to noncontingent success. *Journal of Personality and Social Psychology*, 36, 405–417; Rhodewalt, F. (1994). Conceptions of ability achievement goals, and individual differences in self-handicapping behavior: On the application of implicit theories. *Journal of Personality*, 62, 67–85; Rhodewalt, F., & Fairfield, M. (1991). Claimed self-handicaps and the self-handicapper: The relations of reduction in intended effort to performance. *Journal of Research in Personality*, 25, 402–417.

12. Covington, M. V. (1992). *Making the grade: A self-worth perspective on motivation and school reform*. Cambridge: Cambridge University Press; Martin, A. J., & Marsh, H. W. (2003). Fear of failure: Friend or foe? *Australian Psychologist*, 38, 31–38.

13. Covington, M. V., & Roberts, B. W. (1994). Self-worth and college achievement: Motivational and personality correlates. In P. R. Pintrich, D. R. Brown, & C. E. Weinstein (Eds.). *Student motivation, cognition, and learning: Essays in honor of Wilbert J. McKeachie* Hillsdale, NJ: Earlbaum.

14. Covington, M. V. (1992). *Making the grade: A self-worth perspective on motivation and school reform*. Cambridge: Cambridge University Press.

15. Maier, S. F., & Seligman, M. E. P. (1976). Learned helplessness: Theory and evidence. *Journal of Experimental Psychology: General*, 105, 3–46.

16. Wiegand, D. M., & Geller, E. S. (2005). Connecting positive psychology and organizational behavior management: Achievement motivation and the power of positive reinforcement. *Journal of Organizational Behavior Management*, 24, 3–25.

17. Azrin, N. H., & Holz, W. C. (1996). Punishment. In W. K. Honig (Ed.). *Operant behavior: Areas of research and application* (pp. 380–447). New York: Appleton-Century-Crofts.

18. Estes, W. K., & Skinner, B. F. (1941). Some quantitative properties of anxiety. *Journal of Experimental Psychology*, 29, 390–400.

19. Everett, P. B., Haywood, S. C., & Meyers, A. W. (1974). Effects of a token reinforcement procedure on bus ridership. *Journal of Applied Behavior Analysis*, 7, 1–9; Geller, E. S., Kalsher, M. J., Rudd, J. R., & Lehman, G. (1989). Promoting

safety belt use on a university campus: An integration of commitment and incentive strategies. *Journal of Applied Social Psychology*, 19, 3–19; Geller, E. S. (1992). Solving environmental problems: A behavior change perspective. In S. Staub & P. Green (Eds.). *Psychology and social responsibility: Facing global challenges* (pp. 248–270). New York: New York University Press; Hagenzieker, M. P. (1991). Enforcement or incentive? Promoting safety belt use among military personnel in the Netherlands. *Journal of Applied Behavior Analysis*, 24, 23–30; Rudd, J. R., & Geller, E. S. (1985). A university-based incentive program to increase safety-belt use: Toward cost-effective institutionalization. *Journal of Applied Behavior Analysis*, 18, 215–226.

20. Geller, E. S. (2001). Sustaining participation in a safety improvement process: Ten relevant principles from behavioral science. *Professional Safety*, 46, 24–29.

21. Geller, E. S. (2001). *The psychology of safety handbook*. Boca Raton, FL: CRC Press; Geller, E. S. (2002). *The participation factor: How to get more people involved in occupational safety*. Des Plaines, IL: American Society of Safety Engineers; Geller, E. S. (2005). *People-based safety: The source*. Virginia Beach, VA: Coastal Training and Technologies.

22. O'Brien, D. P. (2000) *Business measurements for safety performance*. New York: Lewis; Petersen, D. (2001). *Authentic involvement*. Itasca, IL: National Safety Council.

23. Geller, E. S. (1991). (Ed.). *Social validity: Multiple perspectives*. Monograph 5. Lawrence, KS: Society for the Experimental Analysis of Behavior.

24. Wolf, M. M. (1978). Social validity: The case of subjective measurement or how behavior analysis is finding its heart. *Journal of Applied Behavior Analysis*, 11, 203–213.

25. Schwartz, I. S., & Baer, D. M. (1991). Social validity assessments: Is current practice state of the art? *Journal of Applied Behavior Analysis*, 24, 189–197.

26. Eckenfelder, D. J. (1996). *Values-driven safety*. Rockville, MD: Government Institutes.

27. Daniels, A. C. (2000). *Bringing out the best in people: How to apply the astonishing power of positive reinforcement* (2nd ed.). New York: McGraw-Hill.

28. McCarty, S. M., & Geller, E. S. (2014). Actively caring to prevent bullying: Prompting and rewarding prosocial behavior in elementary schools. In E. S. Geller (Ed.). *Actively caring at your school: How to make it happen* (2nd ed.) (pp. 177–197). Newport, VA: Make-A-Difference; McCarty, S., Teie, S., McCutchen, J., & Geller, E. S. (in press). Actively caring to prevent bullying in an elementary school: Prompting and rewarding prosocial behavior. *Journal of Prevention Intervention in the Community*.

29. Alvero, A. M., Bucklin, B. R., & Austin, J. (2001). An objective review of the effectiveness and characteristics of performance feedback in organizational settings. *Journal of Organizational Behavior Management*, 21, 3–29; Balcazar, F., Hopkins, B. L., & Suarez, I. (1986). A critical, objective review of performance feedback. *Journal of Organizational Behavior Management*, 7, 65–89.

30. Mayo, E. (1933). *The human problems of an industrialized civilization*. Boston, MA: Harvard University Graduate School of Business Administration; Rothlisberger, R. J., & Dickson, W. J. (1939). *Management and the worker*.

Cambridge, MA: Harvard University Press; Whitehead, T. N. (1938). *The industrial worker*. Washington, DC: Howard University Press.

31. Parsons, H. M. (1974). What happened at Hawthorne? *Science*, 183, 922–932.
32. Skinner, B. F. (1974). *About behaviorism*. New York: Alfred A. Knopf.
33. Geller, E. S., & Hahn, H. A. (1984). Promoting safety-belt use at industrial sites: An effective program for blue-collar employees. *Professional Psychology: Research and Practice*, 15, 533–564; Lewin, K. (1958). Group decision and social change. In E. E. Maccoby, T. M. Newcomb, & E. L. Hartley (Eds.). *Readings in social psychology* (pp. 197–211). New York: Holt, Rinehart & Winston.
34. Geller, E. S. (1992). Solving environmental problems: A behavior change perspective. In S. Staub & P. Green (Eds.). *Psychology and social responsibility: Facing global challenges* (pp. 248–270). New York: New York University Press.
35. Geller, E. S., Winett, R. A., & Everett, P. B. (1982). *Environmental preservation: New strategies for behavior change*. New York: Pergamon Press.
36. Werner, C. M., Rhodes, M. U., & Partain, K. K. (1998). Designing effective instructional signs with schema theory: Case studies of polystyrene recycling. *Environment and Behavior*, 30, 709–735.
37. Geller, E. S., Kalsher, M. J., Rudd, J. R., & Lehman, G. (1989). Promoting safety belt use on a university campus: An integration of commitment and incentive strategies. *Journal of Applied Social Psychology*, 19, 3–19.
38. Bandura, A. (1977). *Social learning theory*. Englewood Cliffs, NJ: Prentice Hall.
39. Winett, R. A., Leckliter, I. N., Chinn, D. E., Stahl, B., & Love, S. Q. (1985). Effects of television modeling on residential energy conservation. *Journal of Applied Behavior Analysis*, 18, 33–44.
40. Geller, E. S., & Lehman, G. R. (1991). The buckle-up promise card: A versatile intervention for large-scale behavior change. *Journal of Applied Behavior Analysis*, 24, 91–94.
41. Cialdini, R. B., & Goldstein, N. J. (2004). Social influence: Compliance and conformity. *Annual Review of Psychology*, 55, 591–621.
42. Geller, E. S., Kalsher, M. J., Rudd, J. R., & Lehman, G. (1989). Promoting safety belt use on a university campus: An integration of commitment and incentive strategies. *Journal of Applied Social Psychology*, 19, 3–19.
43. Sidman, M. (1989). *Coercion and its fallout*. Boston, MA: Authors Cooperative.
44. Geller, E. S. (1983). Rewarding safety belt usage at an industrial setting: Tests of treatment generality and response maintenance. *Journal of Applied Behavior Analysis*, 16, 189–202.
45. Bamberger, J. D., Unick, J., Klein, P., Fraser, M., Chesney M., & Katz, M. H. (2000). Helping the urban poor stay with antiretroviral HIV drug therapy. *American Journal of Public Health*, 90, 699–701.
46. Silverman, K., Chutuape, M., Bigelow, G. E., & Stitzer, M. L. (1999). Voucher-based reinforcement of cocaine abstinence in treatment resistant methadone patients: Effects of reinforcement magnitude. *Outcomes Management*, 146, 128–138.
47. Lehman, P. K., & Geller, E. S. (2004). Behavior analysis and environmental protection: Accomplishments and potential for more. *Behavior and Social Issues*, 13, 13–32.

48. Fournier, A. K., Ehrhart, I. J., Glindemann, K. E., & Geller, E. S. (2004). Intervening to decrease alcohol abuse at university parties: Differential reinforcement of intoxication level. *Behavior Modification*, 28, 167–181; Glindeman, K. E., Ehrhart, I. J., Drake, E. A., & Geller, E. S. (2006). Reducing excessive alcohol consumption at university fraternity parties: A cost-effective incentive/reward intervention. *Addictive Behaviors*, 32(1), 39–48.

49. Jenkins, G. D., Mitra, A., Gupta, N., & Shaw, J. D. (1998). Are financial incentives related to performance? A meta-analytic review of empirical research. *Journal of Applied Psychology*, 83, 777–787.

50. Geller, E. S. (2001). *The psychology of safety handbook*. Boca Raton, FL: CRC Press; Geller, E. S. (2001). *Working safe: How to help people actively care for health and safety* (2nd ed.). New York: Lewis; McSween, T. E. (2003). *The values-based safety process: Improving your safety culture with a behavioral approach* (2nd ed.). New York: Van Nostrand Reinhold.

51. Deci, E. L., & Ryan, R. M. (1985). *Intrinsic motivation and self-determination in human behavior*. New York: Plenum; Kohn, A. (1993). *Punished by rewards: The trouble with gold stars, incentive plans, A's, praise, and other bribes*. Boston: Houghton Mifflin; Pink, D. H. (2009). *Drive: The surprising truth about what motivates us*. New York: Penguin Group.

52. Lepper, M., & Green, D. (1978). (Eds.). *The hidden cost of reward*. Hillsdale, NJ: Erlbaum.

53. Dwyer, W. O., Leeming, F. C., Cobern, M. K., Porter, B. E., & Jackson, J. M. (1993). Critical review of behavioral interventions to preserve the environment: Research since 1980. *Environment and Behavior*, 25, 485–505; Geller, E. S., Winett, R. A., & Everett, P. B. (1982). *Environmental preservation: New strategies for behavior change*. New York: Pergamon Press.

54. Ludwig, T. D., & Geller, E. S. (2000). Intervening to improve the safety of delivery drivers: A systematic, behavioral approach. *Journal of Organizational Behavior Management*, 19, 1–124.

55. Walters, S. T., Wright, J., & Shegog, R. (2006). A review of computer and internet-based interventions for smoking behavior. *Addictive Behaviors*, 31, 264–277.

56. Geisner, I. M., Neighbors, C., & Larimer, M. E. (2006). A randomized clinical trial of a brief, mailed intervention for symptoms of depression. *Journal of Consulting and Clinical Psychology*, 74, 393–399.

57. Malott, R. W. (2001). Occupational safety and response maintenance: An alternative view. *Journal of Organizational Behavior Management*, 21(1), 85–102; McSween, T., & Matthews, G. A. (2001). Maintenance in organizational safety management. *Journal of Organizational Behavior Management*, 21(1), 75–83.

58. Baer, D. M. (2001). Since safety maintains our lives, we need to maintain maintaining. *Journal of Organizational Behavior Management*, 21(1), 61–64; Boyce, T. E., & Geller, E. S. (2001). Applied behavior analysis and occupational safety: The challenge of response maintenance. *Journal of Organizational Behavior Management*, 21(1), 31–60; Geller, E. S. (2001). Dream–Operationalize–Intervene–Test: If you want to make a difference – Just DO IT. *Journal of Organizational Behavior Management*, 21(1), 109–121; Stokes, T. F., & Baer, D. M. (1977). An implicit technology of generalization. *Journal of Applied Behavior Analysis*, 10, 349–367.

59. Geller, E. S. (2001). Sustaining participation in a safety improvement process: Ten relevant principles from behavioral science. *Professional Safety*, 46(9), 24–29.

60. Bem, D. J. (1972). Self-perception theory. In L. Berkowitz (Ed.). *Advances in experimental social psychology*, Vol. 6 (pp. 1–60). New York: Academic Press, p.2.

61. Bem, D. J. (1972). Self-perception theory. In L. Berkowitz (Ed.). *Advances in experimental social psychology*, Vol. 6 (pp. 1–60). New York: Academic Press, p.3.

62. Lepper, M., & Green, D. (1978). *The hidden cost of reward*. Hillsdale, NJ: Erlbaum.

63. Festinger, L., & Carlsmith, J. M. (1959). Cognitive consequences of forced compliance. *Journal of Abnormal and Social Psychology*, 58, 203–210.

64. Aronson, E. (1999). The power of self-persuasion. *American Psychologist*, 54, 875–884.

65. Fox, D. K., Hopkins, B. L., & Anger, W. K. (1987). The long-term effects of a token economy on safety performance in open-pit mining. *Journal of Applied Behavior Analysis*, 20, 215–224.

66. Geller, E. S. (2001). Dream–Operationalize–Intervene–Test: If you want to make a difference – Just DO IT. *Journal of Organizational Behavior Management*, 21(1), 109–121.

67. Aronson, E. (1999). The power of self-persuasion. *American Psychologist*, 54, 875–884; Hovland, C., & Weiss, W. (1951). The influence of source credibility on communication effectiveness. *Public Opinion Quarterly*, 15, 635–650.

68. Elder, J. P., Geller, E. S., Hovell, M. F., & Mayer, J. A. (1994). *Motivating health behavior*. New York: Delmar.

69. Geller, E. S. (1998). *Applications of behavior analysis to prevent injury from vehicle crashes* (2nd ed.). Monograph published by the Cambridge Center for Behavioral Studies, Cambridge, MA.

70. Geller, E. S., Erickson, J. B., & Buttram, B. A. (1983). Attempts to promote residential water conservation with educational, behavioral, and engineering strategies. *Population and Environment*, 6, 96–112.

71. Geller, E. S. (1981). Evaluating energy conservation programs: Is verbal report enough? *Journal of Consumer Behavior*, 8, 331–334.

72. Allen, J. (1990). *I saw what you did and I know who you are: Bloopers, blunders and success stories in giving and receiving recognition*. Tucker, GA: Performance Management Publications; Geller, E. S. (1997). Key processes for continuous safety improvement: Behavior-based recognition and celebration. *Professional Safety*, 42(10), 40–44.

2

The Psychology of AC4P Behavior

E. SCOTT GELLER

We make a living by what we get, but we make a life by what we give.
– Winston Churchill

The large-scale, long-term health, safety, and welfare of people require us to routinely go beyond the call of duty on behalf of others. We call this "actively caring for people," or AC4P – the theme of this book. Usually AC4P behavior involves *self-motivation*, as explained in the next chapter. Often AC4P behavior requires a certain amount of *courage*, and this is clarified in Chapter 4. Research in social psychology,[1] applied behavioral science,[2] and person-based psychology[3] provides principles and practical strategies for increasing the occurrence and improving the quality of AC4P behaviors throughout a culture. These are reviewed in this chapter, as well as in Chapters 3 to 8.

WHAT IS AC4P BEHAVIOR?

Figure 2.1 presents a simple flow chart summarizing a basic approach to culture change. We start a culture-change mission with a vision or ultimate purpose – for example, to achieve an AC4P culture of compassion. With group consensus supporting the vision, we develop procedures or action plans to accomplish our mission. These are reflected in process-oriented goals that denote goal-related behaviors.

The popular writings of Covey,[4] Peale,[5] Kohn,[6] and Deming[7] suggest that behavior is activated and maintained by self-affirmations, internal motivation, and personal principles or values. Unfortunately, these authors, as well as many motivational consultants, miss a key component of human dynamics – the power of consequences.[8]

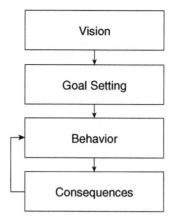

FIGURE 2.1. The flow of vision, goal setting, behavior, and consequences.

Consequences Are Critical

Appropriate goal setting, self-affirmations, and a positive attitude can indeed activate behaviors to achieve certain goals related to a vision. But we must not forget one of B. F. Skinner's most important legacies – *selection by consequences*.[9] As depicted in Figure 2.1, consequences follow behavior and are needed to support the right behaviors and correct wrong ones. Without support for the "right stuff," good intentions and initial efforts fade away. How long does a weight-loss plan last as a New Year's resolution (vision) if one cannot see initial weight loss (consequence) after the first few weeks of exercise (behavior) in an effort to lose 15 pounds (an outcome goal)?

In *How to Win Friends and Influence People*, Dale Carnegie affirms, "Every act you have ever performed since the day you were born was performed because you wanted something."[10] Sometimes natural consequences motivate desired behaviors, but often extrinsic consequences (or external accountabilities) need to be managed to motivate the behavior desired to achieve a goal. For example, I presume my students often have a vision of earning an A in my university classes, and they set relevant process goals to study regularly in order to achieve that ultimate A grade (an outcome goal). I hold them accountable for studying the material by giving exams periodically throughout the semester. When the days for exams are announced in the course syllabus, students typically adjust their study behavior according to this accountability scheme. They increase their frequency of studying successively as the day of the exam approaches, performing most of their studying behaviors the night before the exam.

However, when my assessment protocol is changed from announced to unannounced exams (pop quizzes), most students change their study behavior dramatically. Under this accountability system, students feel compelled to prepare for every class, anticipating a possible exam on any class day. Although students uniformly dislike this second approach, they are substantially more prepared for class when the occurrence of an exam cannot be predicted.

Some students study the course material consistently to reach their learning goals, regardless of the external accountability agenda set by their teacher. These individuals are self-motivated and implement their own self-management procedures to keep them on track. This special type of motivation is covered in the next chapter, as are ways to achieve this quality of personal responsibility.

Students' post-exam, course-related behaviors are usually affected by their test scores – the consequences of their test-taking behavior. But for a number of reasons, it's difficult to predict how a particular exam grade will influence an individual's goal-setting or study behavior. A high grade does not always motivate a higher rate of course-related studying, as expected from the principle of positive reinforcement; and a low grade does not necessarily lead to less studying, as would be predicted from punishment theory. A sense of competence or confidence from a high grade could lead to less study behavior; and fear of failure after receiving a low grade might lead to more study behavior, including some self-management goal-setting and feedback strategies.

As you can see, the driving motivators are consequences. This is a key lesson to learn and use. The pop psychology notion that people can overcome their challenges and achieve whatever they want through prior positive thinking, self-affirmations, and relevant goal setting is just not true. Without appropriate consequences to support the right behavior and correct the wrong behavior, goal-directed behavior will simply stop. People cannot reach their behavior-specific process goals unless they receive relevant feedback to keep them on track. We're talking about behavior-based feedback to support desirable behavior and correct undesirable behavior.

Empowerment Is Critical

In Figure 2.2, an empowerment box is added to the flow diagram in Figure 2.1. The point is simple but extremely important: A vision and a goal are not sufficient to activate a desirable behavior. People need to feel empowered to work for goal achievement, including the expectation of acquiring

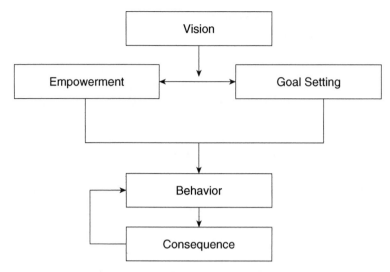

FIGURE 2.2. The connection between goal setting and empowerment.

desirable consequences and/or avoiding undesirable consequences. They need to believe in and own the vision. They need to feel encouragement from peers to attain process goals that support the vision. And peers need to give them supportive and corrective feedback to increase the quantity and improve the quality of behaviors consistent with vision-relevant goals.

Corrective feedback is critical for individuals to improve their future behavior. Supportive feedback is a powerful consequence for the maintenance of behavior, because it tells individuals what they are doing right. In most relationships, supportive feedback is rare, so special attention is needed to increase this important feedback process. Corrective feedback and supportive feedback are essential for continuous improvement and for achieving an AC4P culture of people contributing to one another's well-being. But for this to happen, empowerment is critical. So what is empowerment anyway?

Empowerment

In the management literature, empowerment typically refers to delegating authority or responsibility or sharing decision making.[11] When a manager says, "I empower you," s/he usually means, "Get 'er done." In contrast, the AC4P leader first assesses whether the "empowered" individual *feels* empowered. "Can you handle the additional assignment?" I'm convinced a

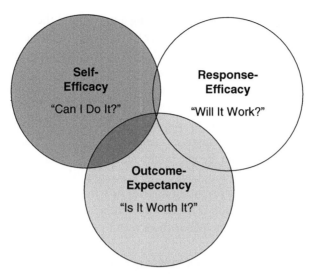

FIGURE 2.3. The three beliefs that determine empowerment (adapted from Bandura).[12]

proper assessment of *feeling empowered* involves asking three questions, as derived from social learning theory.[12]

As depicted in Figure 2.3, the first question –"Can I do it?" – asks whether the empowered individual or group has the resources, time, knowledge, and ability to handle the assignment. The knowledge and ability components refer to training, and the term *self-efficacy* places the focus on personal *belief*. An observer might think an individual has the competence to complete a task, but the person who needs to feel empowered might feel differently. Thus, a yes answer implies a belief in relevant personal effectiveness by those who received the assignment or who set a performance-improvement process goal.

The response-efficacy question asks whether those who should feel empowered believe pursuing and accomplishing the assignment or attaining the process goal (i.e., performing the requested behavior) will contribute to a valued mission of the organization, work team, or the individual. With regard to workplace safety, for example, this translates to believing a particular injury-prevention process (e.g., a peer-to-peer observation-and-feedback coaching process) will contribute to achieving the vision of an injury-free workplace. See Chapter 9 for details on this effective method to prevent occupational injuries.

Relatedly, a sports team would answer yes to this question if the team members believed their new workout routine or competition strategy would increase the probability of winning a game. And the student studying for an exam would give a yes answer to the response-efficacy question if s/he believed the study strategy would contribute to earning a higher exam grade. Of course, the behavioral outcome (or consequence) for these two examples could be more distal and substantive, like having a winning season or obtaining a college degree, respectively.

Whereas a yes answer to the *self-efficacy* question might require more training, education might be needed to obtain a yes answer to the *response-efficacy* question. People might believe they can accomplish a particular process or task, but not believe such accomplishment will contribute to the mission (e.g., of preventing injuries or winning an upcoming team competition). So education is needed, including an explanation of the relevant evidence-based principle or theory, and perhaps the presentation of convincing data.

The third empowerment assessment question – the *outcome-expectancy* question – targets motivation. Is the expected outcome worth the effort? Anticipating a positive consequence to achieve or a negative consequence to avoid motivates the occurrence of relevant behavior. And referring back to the critical distinction between working to achieve success and working to avoid failure, explained in Chapter 1, people feel more choice and are more likely to be self-motivated when they are working to achieve a positive consequence than when responding to avoid a negative consequence.

Empowering Goals. The benefits of behavior-focused goal setting as an activator of process activities are well documented.[13] A popular acronym used to define the characteristics of an effective goal is SMART. There are actually a few variations of the words denoted by these letters, with "M" representing "measurable" or "motivational," "R" reflecting "recordable" or "relevant," and "T" referring to "timely" or "trackable," for example.

I have proposed the following words: "S" for "specific," "M" for "motivational," "A" for "attainable," "R" for "relevant," and "T" for "trackable."[14] Later, I added "S" (i.e., SMARTS) for shared, because social support can increase commitment to work toward reaching a goal.[15] A rationale and procedural details for each component of effective goal setting are provided in Chapter 3. At this point I want only to show the connection between SMARTS goals and the empowerment model introduced here.

Specifically, SMARTS goals are empowering because they are *attainable* ("I can do it"), *motivational* ("It's worth it"), and *relevant* ("It will work"). This connection makes it clear that both empowerment and goal setting are interdependent behavioral antecedents, setting the stage (or activating) certain behavior(s). Each of these activators refers to motivation as the anticipation of a desirable consequence or outcome.

Empowerment versus Self-Motivation. A critical distinction exists between these two person-states. Empowerment is a behavioral antecedent (a dispositional factor or person-state); self-motivation reflects the impact of consequences, as implied by B. F. Skinner's legacy, "selection by consequences."[9] Feeling empowered means the individual is ready (or activated) to work toward achieving a given goal. A self-motivated person, in contrast, anticipates or has experienced a consequence that supports self-directed rather than other-directed behavior.[16]

THREE WAYS TO ACTIVELY CARE

When individuals perform an AC4P behavior, they can improve environmental factors, enhance person-states, or increase the frequency of others' AC4P behavior. When people alter environmental conditions or reorganize resources in an attempt to benefit others, they are actively caring from an environmental perspective. Examples of AC4P behavior in this category include attending to a housekeeping detail, posting a warning sign near an environmental hazard, shoveling snow from a neighbor's sidewalk, washing another person's vehicle, organizing a colleague's desk, helping a party-host collect recyclables, cleaning up a spill, or removing a trip hazard.

Person-based AC4P behavior occurs when people attempt to make others feel better. Often, it doesn't take much to improve an individual's emotion, attitude, or mood state. Examples of person-based AC4P behavior include listening to someone with empathy, expressing concern for another person's difficulties, complimenting an individual's academic or work performance, sending a get-well card, and posting birthday wishes on a person's Facebook page. These types of AC4P behavior will likely boost one's self-esteem, self-efficacy, personal control, optimism, and/or sense of belonging – potentially increasing one's propensity to perform AC4P behavior.

Reactive AC4P behaviors performed in crisis situations are also included here. For example, if you save someone from drowning, administer cardiopulmonary resuscitation (CPR), or give a drunk driver a ride home you're actively caring from a person-based perspective.

From a *proactive* perspective, behavior-focused AC4P is often the most challenging. This happens when people apply an instructive, supportive, or motivational intervention to improve another person's desirable behavior. When we teach others how to promote AC4P behavior or provide supportive comments or possible improvements regarding observed behavior, we are actively caring from a behavioral focus. Teachers and athletic coaches do this when they help a student or athlete achieve a desired performance goal. Plus, recognizing the desirable AC4P behavior of others in a one-to-one conversation is also actively caring with a behavior focus.

WHY CATEGORIZE AC4P BEHAVIORS?

Why go to the trouble of categorizing AC4P behaviors? Good question! Consider what these behaviors are trying to accomplish, and realize the relative difficulty of performing each of them. Environment-focused AC4P behavior might be the easiest approach for some people because it usually does not require interpersonal interaction. When people contribute financially to a charity, donate blood, or complete an organ-donor card, they do not interact personally with the recipient of the contribution. These AC4P behaviors are certainly commendable and may reflect significant commitment and effort, but the absence of personal encounters between giver and receiver is distinct from other types of AC4P behavior.

Certain situations and dispositions might facilitate or inhibit one type of AC4P behavior and not the other. For example, communication skills are needed for actively caring on the personal or behavioral level. And different aspects of those communication skills usually come into play.

Behavior-focused AC4P is more direct and usually more intrusive than person-focused AC4P. It's more risky and potentially confrontational to attempt to direct or motivate another person's behavior, in contrast to demonstrating concern, respect, or empathy for someone.

Helping someone in a crisis situation certainly takes effort and requires special skills, but there is rarely a possibility of rejection. On the other hand, attempting to step up to correct someone's behavior could lead to a negative, even hostile, reaction. Effective behavior-based caring, as in interpersonal coaching, usually requires interpersonal skills to gain the individual's trust, along with behavior-based skills to support desired behavior and correct undesired.

Behavior-focused AC4P is actually expected from parents, teachers, supervisors, and coaches who are in charge of improving the behavior of individuals in certain situations. Thus, some behavior-focused AC4P is part of one's job and is expected. But here the question is whether you apply the best AC4P methods (e.g., supportive and corrective behavioral feedback) that improve both behavior and attitude. Suppose you observe a stranger not using a vehicle safety belt or driving while talking on a cell phone. Would you say something to keep this person safe? Some people even hesitate to offer such proactive AC4P feedback for a friend, co-worker, or colleague.

Is it beyond the call of duty to look out for the well-being of a family member or friend? Most readers would say no. But when AC4P becomes a social norm or the expected behavior in a culture, actively caring for a stranger will also not stretch beyond one's normal routine. As legislated in Australia, it's your "duty to care." AC4P behavior occurs whenever you look out for the well-being of another, but the degree of self-motivation and courage needed to actively care varies dramatically as a function of situational and dispositional factors.

A HIERARCHY OF NEEDS

Probably the most popular theory of human motivation is the hierarchy of needs proposed by humanist Abraham Maslow.[17] Categories of needs are arranged hierarchically, and it's presumed people don't attempt to satisfy needs at one stage or level until the needs at the lower stages are satisfied.

First, we are motivated to fulfill physiological needs. These include basic survival requirements for food, water, shelter, and sleep. After these needs are under control, we are motivated by the desire to feel secure and safe from future dangers. When we prepare for future physiological needs, we are working proactively to satisfy our need for safety and security. Next we have our social-acceptance needs –to have friends and feel like we belong. When these needs are gratified, our concern focuses on self-esteem, the development of self-respect and feeling worthwhile.

When I ask audiences to tell me the highest level of Maslow's hierarchy of needs, several people usually shout "self-actualization." When I ask for the meaning of *self-actualization*, however, I receive limited or no reaction. The concept of being self-actualized is rather vague and ambiguous. In general terms, we reach a level of self-actualization when we believe we have become the best we can be, taking the fullest advantage of our potential as human beings. We labor to reach this level when striving to be as productive and creative as possible. Once we have accomplished this, we feel a sense of connection and affection for all human beings. We desire to help humanity as members of a single family – the human race.[18] Perhaps it's fair to say these individuals are most ready to perform AC4P behavior.

Maslow's hierarchy of needs is illustrated in Figure 2.4. Note that self-actualization is *not* at the top. Maslow revised his renowned hierarchy shortly before his death in 1970, placing self-transcendence above self-actualization.[19] Transcending the self means going beyond self-interest

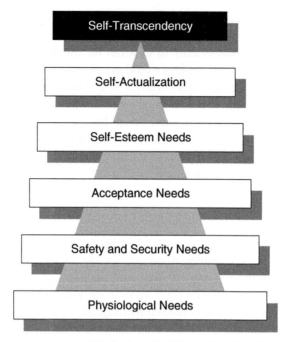

FIGURE 2.4. Maslow's revised hierarchy of needs.

and is quite analogous to the AC4P concept. According to Viktor Frankl, self-transcendence includes giving ourselves to a cause or to another person, and is the ultimate state of existence for the healthy individual.[20] After satisfying our physiological, safety, and security needs, and after reaching social acceptance, self-esteem, and self-actualization, we can attain self-transcendence by reaching out to help others – to perform AC4P behavior.

I'm sure you can think of individuals in your life, including yourself perhaps, who reached the top level of self-transcendence before satisfying needs in the lower stages. Note the connection between Maslow's need hierarchy and various potentially reinforcing consequences. An individual's position in the hierarchy certainly determines what types of consequences are likely to be most motivating at a particular time. Without food, shelter, or sleep, for example, most people will focus their efforts on satisfying these needs. But if this need level is satisfied, the motivation of human behavior requires consequences related to higher-level needs. In the next chapter, I explain the concept of self-motivation, and you'll see how reaching higher levels on Maslow's hierarchy suggests the relevance of certain consequences that can support and help sustain self-motivation.

BEHAVIORAL SCIENCE AND AC4P

Walking home on March 13, 1964, Catherine "Kitty" Genovese reached her apartment in Queens, New York at 3:30 A.M. Suddenly, a man approached her with a knife, stabbing her repeatedly, and then raped her. Kitty screamed, into the early morning stillness, "Oh my God, he stabbed me! Please help me!" Lights went on and windows opened in nearby buildings. Seeing the lights, the attacker fled. When he saw no one come to the victim's aid, he returned to stab her eight more times and rape her again.

The murder and rape of Kitty Genovese lasted more than thirty minutes and was witnessed by thirty-eight neighbors. One couple pulled up chairs to their window and turned off lights so they could get a better view. Only after the murderer and rapist departed for good did anyone phone the police. When the neighbors were questioned about their lack of intervention, they couldn't explain it.

The reporter who first publicized the Kitty Genovese story, and later made it the subject of a book,[21] assumed *bystander apathy* was caused by big-city life. People's indifference to their neighbors' troubles was a conditioned reflex in crowded cities like New York, he reasoned. Subsequently, this reporter's common-sense conclusion was discredited by hundreds of experiments conducted to determine causes of this so-called bystander apathy.[22] Several factors other than big-city alienation were shown to contribute to it.

Lessons from Research

Professors Bibb Latané, John Darley, and colleagues studied bystander apathy by staging emergency events observed by varying numbers of individuals. Then they systematically recorded the speed at which one or more persons came to the victim's rescue. As depicted in the illustration on the next page, the participants in these controlled studies of bystander apathy sat in separate cubicles and could not be influenced by the body language of other participants. In the first study of this type, the participants introduced themselves and discussed problems associated with living in an urban environment.

In each condition, the first individual introduced himself and then casually mentioned he had epilepsy and the pressures of city life made him prone to seizures. During the course of the discussion over the intercom, he became increasingly loud and incoherent, choking, gasping, and crying out before lapsing into silence. The experimenters measured how quickly the participants left their cubes to help him.

When participants believed they were the only witness, 85 percent left their cubicles within three minutes to intervene. But only 62 percent of the participants who believed one other witness was present left their cubicle to intervene, and only 31 percent of those who thought five other witnesses were available attempted to intervene. Within three to six minutes after the seizure began, 100 percent of the lone participants, 81 percent of the participants with one presumed witness, and 62 percent of the participants with five other bystanders left their cubes to intervene.

The hesitancy of observers of an emergency to intervene and help a victim when they believe other potential helpers are available has been termed the *bystander effect*. It has been replicated in several situations.[23] Keep in mind this research studied reactions in crisis situations only – behaviors we categorize as reactive, person-focused AC4P behavior. It seems intuitive, though, that the findings are relevant to both environment-focused and behavior-focused AC4P behavior in proactive situations. Research results suggest ways to prevent bystander apathy – a critical barrier to achieving an AC4P culture.

Diffusion of Responsibility. A key contributor to the bystander effect is the assumption that someone else should or could assume the responsibility. For example, many observers of the Kitty Genovese rape and murder assumed another witness would call the police or attempt to scare away the assailant. Perhaps some observers waited for a witness more capable than they to rescue Kitty. Does this factor contribute to lack of intervention when someone needs help? Do people ignore or deny opportunities to actively care for another person (i.e., a stranger) because they presume someone else will help? Perhaps some people assume, "If those who know the person seeking assistance don't care enough to help, why should I?"

Social psychologists have shown that teaching people about the bystander effect can make them less likely to fall prey to it themselves.[24] Often, people have a *we–they* attitude or a territorial perspective ("I'm responsible for the people in this area; you're responsible for those in that area"). Eliminating this *we–they* perspective increases people's willingness to actively care for others.[25]

An AC4P Norm. Many, if not most, U.S. citizens are raised to be independent rather than interdependent. However, a sincere commitment to interdependence is required to intervene for the benefit of others, whether reactively in a crisis situation or proactively to prevent potential crises. Social psychologists refer to a *social responsibility norm* as the belief that people should help those who need help. Subjects who scored high on a measure of this norm, as a result of childhood upbringing or special training sessions, were more likely to intervene in a bystander intervention situation, regardless of the number of other witnesses.[23]

Knowing What to Do. When people know what to do in a crisis, they do not fear appearing foolish and do not wait for another, more skilled person to intervene. The bystander effect was eliminated when observers had certain competencies, such as training in first-aid treatment, which enabled them to take charge of the situation.[26] Bystander apathy is decreased or eliminated when observers believe they possess the appropriate tools to help.

Recognizing others for performing AC4P behaviors is critical for the development of an AC4P norm and an AC4P culture. But our field studies have shown that this is easier said than done. Participants in these studies agreed with the mission to recognize others for their AC4P behavior. Still, the percentage who delivered such recognition in prescribed ways was always much lower than expected and desired. This percentage increased dramatically following role-playing to develop relevant interpersonal skills, accompanied by meetings of AC4P support groups.[27]

Most proactive AC4P action requires self-motivation (Chapter 3) and moral courage (Chapter 4) in addition to relevant interpersonal skills.

Much of our ongoing AC4P research, some of which is reviewed in this book, addresses ways to facilitate the occurrence and improve the effectiveness of AC4P behaviors and to remove barriers that hold us back from thanking others for their AC4P behavior.

The Value of Belonging. Bystander apathy is reduced, according to research, when observers know one another and have developed a sense of belonging or mutual respect from prior interactions.[28] Most, if not all, of the witnesses to Kitty Genovese's murder did not know her personally. It's likely the neighbors did not feel a sense of community with one another. Situations and interactions that reduce a *we–they* or territorial perspective and increase feelings of relatedness or community will increase the likelihood people will actively care for each other.

Mood States. People are more likely to offer help when they are in a good mood, according to several social psychology studies.[29] And the mood states that facilitated helping behavior were created very easily, for example, by arranging for potential helpers to find a dime in a phone booth, giving them a cookie, showing them a comedy film, or providing pleasant aromas. Are these findings useful for nurturing an AC4P culture?

Daily events can elevate or depress our moods. Some events are controllable, while others are not. Clearly, the nature of our interactions with others can have a dramatic impact on the mood of everyone involved. The research on mood and its effects on helping behavior might motivate those of us who want to facilitate an AC4P culture to interject more positivity and optimism into our interpersonal conversations with others.

Beliefs and Expectancies. Social psychologists have shown that certain dispositional characteristics or beliefs influence one's inclination to help a person in an emergency. Specifically, individuals who believe their world is fair and predictable, a place where good behavior is rewarded and bad behavior is punished, are more likely to help others in a crisis.[30] Also, people with a higher sense of social responsibility and a general expectancy that people control their own destinies showed a greater willingness to perform AC4P behavior.[31]

The beliefs and expectancies that influence the quantity and quality of AC4P behavior are not developed overnight and obviously cannot be changed overnight. But a particular culture, including its policies, appraisal and recognition procedures, educational opportunities, and approaches to discipline, can certainly increase or decrease perceptions or beliefs in a just world, social responsibility, and personal control, and in turn influence people's willingness to perform AC4P behavior.[32]

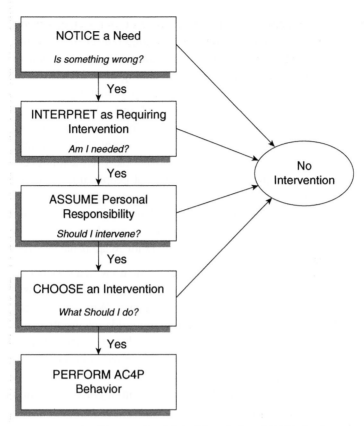

FIGURE 2.5. Four sequential decisions before AC4P behavior.

Deciding to Actively Care

An observer makes four sequential decisions before helping a victim, Latané and Darley proposed in their seminal research.[33] These four decisions (depicted in Figure 2.5) are influenced by the situation or environmental context in which an AC4P opportunity occurs, the nature of the crisis, the presence of other bystanders and their reactions, and relevant social norms and rules. Although the model was developed to evaluate intervention in emergency situations – where there's a need for direct, reactive, person-focused AC4P behavior – it's quite relevant to the other types of AC4P behavior as well.

Step 1: Is Something Wrong? The first step in deciding whether to intervene is simply perceiving something is wrong. Some situations or events naturally attract more attention than others. Most emergencies are novel and upset the normal flow of life. However, the onset of an emergency, such as a person slipping on ice or falling down a flight of stairs, will attract more attention and helping behavior than the aftermath of an *injury*, as when a victim is regaining consciousness or rubbing an ankle after a fall.[34] Of course, we should expect much less attention to *potential* problems in daily, non-emergency situations at work, in school, and at home.

In active and noisy work environments, people narrow their focus to what is personally relevant. We learn to tune out irrelevant stimuli. In these situations, environmental hazards are easy to overlook. Even less noticeable and attention-getting are the ongoing behaviors of people around us. Yet these behaviors need proactive AC4P support or correction. But even if the need for proactive participation is noticed, AC4P behavior will not necessarily occur. The observer must interpret the situation as requiring intervention. This leads us to the next question requiring a yes answer for AC4P behavior to occur.

Step 2: Am I Needed? Of course, we can come up with a variety of excuses for not helping. Distress cues, such as cries for help, and the actions of other observers can clarify an event as an emergency. When we are confused, we look to other people for information and guidance. In other words, by watching what others are doing, we figure out how to interpret an ambiguous event and how to react accordingly. The behavior of others is especially important when stimulus cues are not present.[35]

In situations where the need for intervention or corrective action is not obvious, we usually seek information from others to understand what's going on and to receive direction. This is the typical state of affairs when it comes to noticing a need for AC4P behavior or recognizing another person's AC4P behavior. In fact, the need for *proactive* AC4P behavior is rarely obvious. When I ask my students to look for AC4P behavior around them and then recognize the person with an AC4P thank you card (see Figure 2.6), I typically receive less than 10 percent compliance. The most frequent excuse for not recognizing AC4P behavior is, "I didn't see actively caring behavior worthy of a thank you card."

Step 3: Should I Intervene? "Is it my responsibility to intervene?" The answer is clear if you are the only witness to a situation you perceive as an emergency. But you might not answer yes to this question when you know other people are also observing the same emergency or cry for help. You have reason to believe someone else will intervene, perhaps a person more capable than you. This perception relieves you of personal responsibility. But what happens when everyone believes the other person will take care of it? This is likely what happened in the Kitty Genovese incident.

A breakdown at this stage of the decision model doesn't mean the observers don't care about the welfare of the victim. Actually, it's probably incorrect to call lack of intervention *bystander apathy*.[36] The bystanders might care very much about the victim, but defer responsibility to others because they believe other observers are more likely or better qualified to intervene. Similarly, employees might care a great deal about the safety and health of their co-workers, but feel relatively incapable of acting on their caring. People might resist taking personal responsibility to actively care because they don't believe they have the most effective tools to make a difference. They don't feel empowered because they lack self-efficacy.

In addition to having a *can do* attitude, people need to believe it's their personal responsibility to actively care for others. The challenge in achieving an AC4P culture is to convince everyone they have a responsibility to actively care for others. A social norm or expectancy has to be established: that all participants share equally in a daily assignment to keep everyone healthy and productive. Plus, AC4P leaders need to accept the special responsibility of teaching others any techniques they learn at conferences or group meetings that could increase a person's perceived competence (or self-efficacy) to actively care more effectively. If we don't meet this challenge, many people are apt to decide AC4P behavior is not for them.

Step 4: What Should I Do? The importance of education and training is reflected in the last step of the Latané and Darley decision model. Education gives people the rationale and principles behind a particular intervention approach. It gives people information they can use to design or refine intervention strategies, leading to a sense of ownership for the particular tools they help to develop. Through training, people learn how to translate principles and rules into specific behaviors or intervention strategies. Bottom line: People who learn how to intervene effectively through relevant education and training are more likely to feel empowered to be an AC4P intervention agent.

This decision logic suggests certain methods for increasing the likelihood people will perform AC4P behavior. Specifically, the model indicates a need to teach people how to recognize opportunities for AC4P behavior at the environment, person, and behavior levels; and then how to determine what intervention strategies are available and most effective in each case. Plus, people need to learn how to give supportive feedback and genuine recognition for those who exhibit AC4P behavior. It's also imperative to promote AC4P as a *core value* of your culture. This means everyone assumes responsibility for the health, safety, and well-being of others in the culture and never waits for someone else to act.

CULTIVATING AN AC4P CULTURE

Culture influences and sustains one's propensity to perform AC4P behavior. A work culture, for example, can incorporate an accountability system that encourages interpersonal helping. Plus, the daily interactions of people influence certain person-states that affect one's propensity to go beyond the call of duty for another person's well-being. The frequency of AC4P behavior varies *directly* with extrinsic-response contingencies and *indirectly* as a function of certain dispositional person-states.

The Direct Approach

For almost thirty years, I have promoted the use of a special actively caring thank you card at my university to recognize individuals for their AC4P behavior. Depicted in Figure 2.6, the front of this brightly-colored card includes the mascot of our university and two university sponsors. The

FIGURE 2.6. The front (on left) and back (on right) of the AC4P thank you card.

definition of AC4P behavior is given on the back of the card, along with some examples of AC4P behavior. Several organizations have customized this thank you card for their culture. I have seen this simple card cultivate a sense of interdependence and belonging throughout a work group, as well as help people feel good about their own AC4P behavior.

In their book, *Measure of a Leader*, Aubrey and James Daniels describe a creative device they have used successfully for years to motivate discretionary behaviors throughout an organization. Specifically, managers hang a chart in a conspicuous location that lists the names of all employees in a certain work area. Then they give each person a sticker identifying that individual. Whenever a worker is helped by a colleague, that person puts his or her identifying sticker on the chart, next to the name of the person who performed the AC4P behavior.

The Daniels brothers report dramatic culture change. "Not only does it give recognition for those who help, but it is an antecedent for others to take the initiative in finding ways they can help other team members."[37] In addition, for more than twenty years I've been promoting the use of a green wristband, engraved with the words "Actively Caring for People," to recognize people for their AC4P behavior. Throughout the years, I've distributed more than fifty thousand of these wristbands after my keynote addresses at conferences and organizations. More recently, my students have used this recognition approach to reduce bullying by promoting and rewarding AC4P behavior in various educational settings.[38]

For these latter applications, the AC4P wristbands were redesigned to include a different identification number per wristband as well as the name of the Website (www.ac4p.org), where people can (a) share their AC4P stories (with the number of the wristband they gave or received), (b) track worldwide where a particular AC4P wristband has been, and (c) order more AC4P wristbands to reward others for actively caring.

To date, more than three thousand AC4P stories have been shared on this Website, and more than a hundred thousand AC4P wristbands have been purchased, with proceeds going to the Actively Caring for People Foundation, Inc. We believe this particular accountability system for activating and rewarding AC4P behavior has great potential for spreading the AC4P Movement worldwide and inspiring the development of AC4P cultures.

Genuine appreciation and recognition can have dramatic positive effects on a person's attitude, mindset, and disposition. A recognition system that directly acknowledges AC4P behavior can result in a spiraling cycle of favorable culture change. Positive regard for people's AC4P behaviors increases the frequency of the target behavior directly, while simultaneously feeding five person-states or dispositions that can set the occasion for more AC4P behavior. These person-states, as well as ways to enhance them, are defined next.

The Indirect Approach

Psychological science considers both the observable (outside) and nonobservable (inside) aspects of individuals. The promise of a positive consequence or the threat of a negative one can sustain desired behavior while the response-consequence contingencies are in place. But what happens when they are withdrawn? What happens when people are in situations, at home, for example, when no one is holding them accountable for their behavior?

If people do not *believe* in the AC4P way of doing something and do not *accept* AC4P as a value or a personal mission, they will not choose AC4P behavior when no one's watching. If people are not self-motivated to actively care, the frequency of AC4P behavior will be much less than desired. The next chapter explains self-motivation further and reviews ways to enhance this person-state.

Figure 2.7 illustrates how person-factors interact with the basic activator-behavior-consequence (ABC) model of applied behavioral science (ABS) as introduced in Chapter 1.[39] Activators direct behavior, and

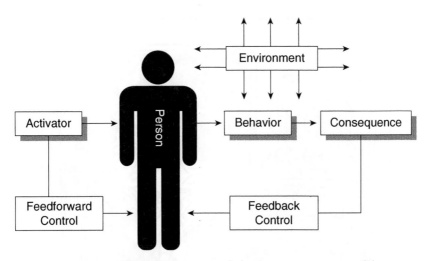

FIGURE 2.7. The activator, *person*, behavior, consequence model.

consequences motivate behavior. But as shown in Figure 2.7, these events are first filtered through the person. Numerous internal and situational factors influence how we mentally process activators and consequences. If we see activators and consequences as schemes to control us, our attitude about the situation will likely be negative.

On the other hand, when we believe the external contingencies are genuine attempts to help us do the right thing, our attitude will be more positive. Personal or internal dynamics determine how we receive activator and consequence information. This can influence whether environmental events enhance or diminish what we do. Let's consider five person-states that influence our propensity to perform AC4P behavior.

Self-Esteem ("I Am Valuable"). One's self-concept, or feeling of worth, is a central theme of most humanistic therapies.[40] According to Carl Rogers and his adherents, we possess both a real and an ideal self-concept. We have notions or aspirations of what we'd like to be (our *ideal* self) and what we think we are (our *real* self). Our self-esteem decreases as the gap between our real and ideal self-concepts increases. The mission of many humanistic therapies is to help a client reduce this gap.

A healthy level of personal self-esteem and acting to help others raise their self-esteem has obvious benefits. Research shows that people with high self-esteem report fewer negative emotions and less depression than people with low self-esteem.[41] Those with higher self-esteem also handle life's stresses better.[42] Individuals who score higher on measures of self-esteem

(a) are less susceptible to outside influences,[43] (b) are more confident of achieving personal goals,[44] and (c) make more favorable impressions on others in social situations.[45] Also, people with higher self-esteem help others more frequently than those scoring lower on a self-esteem scale.[46]

However, a comprehensive review of the extensive research on the effects of self-esteem on behavior suggests caution with a common assumption that "boosting self-esteem (by therapeutic interventions or school programs) causes benefits."[47] While success at a task can enhance one's self-esteem, the reverse is not necessarily the case, except that "high self-esteem facilitates persistence after failure."[47] Consider, for example, that noncontingent or "indiscriminate praise might just as easily promote narcissism with its less desirable consequences."[47] The authors of this comprehensive review do "recommend using praise to boost self-esteem as a reward for socially desirable behavior and self-improvement."[47] Of course, this suggestion is perfectly consistent with the ABS principles of AC4P, and the next chapter details methods for giving positive recognition to individuals and groups.

Self-Efficacy. As explained earlier and depicted in Figure 2.3, this person-state determines whether one feels empowered about pursuing a goal or accepting an assignment. I'm talking about your self-confidence. This is a key principle in social learning theory, determining whether a therapeutic intervention will succeed over the long term.[48] People who score relatively high on a measure of self-efficacy perform better at a wide range of tasks and work harder to achieve a specific goal, according to dozens of studies. These "can do" believers also demonstrate greater ability and motivation to solve complex problems at work, have better health and safety habits, and are more successful at handling stressors.[49]

Self-efficacy contributes to self-esteem, and vice versa; but these constructs are different. Self-esteem refers to a general sense of self-worth; self-efficacy refers to feeling successful or effective at a particular task. Self-efficacy is task-focused and can vary markedly from one task to another. One's level of self-esteem remains relatively constant across situations.

Personal Control. This is the sense that "I am in control" and connects to the person-state of autonomy or a perception of choice that determines self-motivation, as explained in the next chapter. J. B. Rotter[50] used the term *locus of control* to locate the forces controlling a person's life. People with an *internal* locus of control believe they usually have direct personal control over significant life events as a result of their knowledge, skill, and abilities. They believe they are captains of their life's ship. In contrast, persons with an *external* locus of control believe "outside" and random factors like chance, luck, or fate play important roles in their lives. Externals believe they are victims, or sometimes beneficiaries, of circumstances beyond their direct personal control.[51]

More than two thousand studies have investigated the relationship between perceptions of personal control and other variables.[52] Internals are more achievement-oriented and health-conscious than externals. They are less prone to distress and more likely to seek medical treatment when they need it.[53] Having an internal locus of control helps reduce chronic pain, facilitates psychological and physical adjustment to illness and surgery, and hastens recovery from some diseases.[54] Internals perform better at jobs that allow them to set their own pace, whereas externals work better when a machine controls the pace.[55]

Optimism. "I expect the best" sets the tone for optimism. It's the learned expectation that life events, including personal actions, will turn out well.[56] Optimism relates directly to achievement. Martin Seligman reported, for example, that world-class swimmers who scored high on a measure of optimism recovered from defeat and swam even faster than did swimmers scoring low. Following defeat, the pessimistic swimmers swam slower.[57]

In contrast to pessimists, optimists maintain a sense of humor, perceive problems or challenges in a positive light, and plan for success. They focus on what they can *do* rather than on how they *feel*.[58] Optimists handle stressors constructively and experience positive stress more often than negative distress.[59] They essentially expect to succeed at whatever they do, and so they work harder than pessimists to reach their goals. Optimists are beneficiaries of the self-fulfilling prophecy.[60]

Fulfilling an optimistic prophecy can enhance our perceptions of personal control, self-efficacy, and even self-esteem. Realizing this should motivate us to do whatever we can to make our interpersonal conversations positive and constructive. This will not only increase optimism in a certain culture, but also promote a sense of group cohesiveness or belonging – another person-state that facilitates AC4P behavior.

Belonging ("I Am a Team Member"). M. Scott Peck challenges us to experience a sense of true community with others in his best seller, *The Different Drum: Community Making and Peace.*[61] We need to develop feelings of belonging with one another regardless of our political preferences, cultural backgrounds, and religious beliefs. We need to transcend our differences, overcome our defenses and prejudices, and develop a deep respect for diversity. Peck claims we must develop a sense of community or interconnectedness with one another if we are to accomplish our best and ensure our sustainability as human beings.

It's intuitive that building a sense of community or belonging among our friends and colleagues will increase the frequency of AC4P behaviors. Improving behavior requires interpersonal observation, supportive and corrective feedback, and positive recognition. For this to happen, people need to adopt a collective win-win perspective instead of the individualistic win-lose orientation so common in many work and educational settings. A sense of belonging and interdependency leads to interpersonal trust and caring – essential features of an AC4P culture. In the next chapter, I explain how one's sense of community or perceived connection to others affects self-motivation – a person's drive to do something without an external incentive, disincentive, or accountability system.

At my group discussions with employees, someone inevitably raises the point that a sense of belonging or community at their plant has decreased in recent years. Belongingness is a fading concept; "We used to be more like family around here" is a common theme. For many companies, growth spurts, continuous turnover – particularly among managers – or "lean and mean" cutbacks have left many employees feeling less connected and trusting. People's need level on Maslow's hierarchy has regressed from satisfying social acceptance and belonging to concentrating on maintaining job security, in order to keep food on the table.

Figure 2.8 lists a number of special attributes prevalent in most families, where interpersonal trust and belonging are usually optimal. We are willing to actively care in special ways for the members of our immediate family. The result is optimal trust, belonging, and AC4P behavior for the health, safety, and welfare of our family members. Following the guidelines reflected in Figure 2.8 among members of our everyday peer group can lead to the achievement of an AC4P culture. Following the principles implied in Figure 2.8 develops trust and belonging among people, and leads to the

- We use more rewards than penalties with *family* members.

- We don't pick on the mistakes of *family* members.

- We don't rank one *family* member against another.

- We brag about the accomplishments of *family* members.

- We respect the property and personal space of *family* members.

- We pick up after other *family* members.

- We correct the undesirable behavior of *family* members.

- We accept the corrective feedback of *family* members.

- We are interdependent with *family* members.

- We actively care because they're *family*.

FIGURE 2.8. The connection between family and an AC4P culture.

quantity and quality of AC4P behavior expected among family members – at home, at work, at school, and everywhere in between.

A Self-Supporting AC4P Cycle

The five person-states presented here as influencing people's propensity or disposition to perform AC4P behavior are shown in Figure 2.9. Each of these person-states has a rich research history in psychology, and some of this research suggests ways to increase the quantity and/or improve the quality of AC4P behavior,[62] although much more research is needed in this domain. A particularly important question is whether the AC4P person-states are both antecedents and consequences of an AC4P act of kindness.

It seems intuitive that performing an act of kindness that is effective, accepted, and appreciated could increase the helper's self-esteem, self-efficacy, personal control, optimism, and sense of belonging. This,

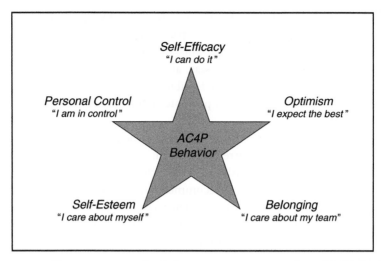

FIGURE 2.9. Five person-states that influence propensity to perform AC4P behavior.

in turn, should increase the probability of more AC4P behavior. In other words, one act of caring, properly appreciated, should lead to another and another. A self-supporting AC4P cycle is likely to occur.

ENHANCING THE AC4P PERSON-STATES

Sometimes participants in my workshops and seminars express concern that the AC4P person-states depicted in Figure 2.9 might not be practical. "The concepts are too soft or subjective" is a typical reaction. Teachers, parents, work supervisors, and individual employees accept the direct ABS approach for performance improvement because it's straightforward, objective, and clearly applicable to educational, work, and family settings. But person-based concepts like self-esteem, personal control, optimism, and belonging appear ambiguous, "touchy-feely," and difficult to deal with. "The concepts sound good and certainly seem important, but how can we wrap our arms around these 'warm fuzzies' and use them to promote an AC4P culture?"

To be sure, person-states are more difficult to define, measure, and manage than behaviors. But how people *feel* about a behavior-improvement process simply cannot be ignored. For people to accept a behavior-change process and sustain the target behaviors over the long term, we must confront internal person-states when designing and implementing an intervention.

After introducing the AC4P person-states at workshops on how to cultivate an AC4P culture, I often divide participants into discussion groups. I ask group members to define events, situations, or contingencies that decrease and increase the person-state assigned to their group. Then I ask the groups to derive simple and feasible action plans to increase their assigned dispositional state. This promotes personal and practical understanding of the concept.

The AC4P person-states may be soft and subjective, but feedback from these workshops shows they're not difficult to grasp. Action plans have been practical and quite consistent with techniques used by researchers. Substantial overlap of practical recommendations does exist – workshop groups dealing with different person-states have come up with similar contributory factors and action plans. Let's take a look at what my workshop participants have proposed regarding factors and strategies related to each of these person-states.

Self-Esteem

Participants suggest a number of ways to build self-esteem: (a) provide opportunities for personal learning and peer mentoring; (b) increase recognition for desirable behaviors and individual accomplishments; and (c) solicit and follow up on a person's suggestions.

It's essential to give more positive (or supportive) than negative (or corrective) feedback. When offering corrective feedback, focus on the act, not the actor. Pointing out an error only reflects behavior that can be corrected, not a deeper character flaw. Don't come off as a judge of character, implying that an observed mistake suggests some subjective personal attribute such as carelessness, apathy, bad attitude, or poor motivation.

Be a patient, empathic listener. Allow people to offer reasons for their error or poor judgment. Resist the temptation to argue. Giving a reason or excuse is just a way to protect one's self-esteem, and it's generally a healthy response. Remember, you already made your point by showing the error and suggesting ways to avoid the mistake in the future. Leave it at that.

If a person doesn't react constructively to corrective feedback, it might help to explore feelings. "How do you feel about this?" you might ask. Then listen empathically to assess whether self-esteem has taken a hit. You'll learn whether some additional communication is needed to place the focus squarely on what is external and objective rather than subjective and internal.

Self-Efficacy

As explained earlier, self-efficacy is more situation-specific than self-esteem, so it fluctuates more readily. Job-specific feedback should be directed only at what's needed to do a particular task successfully. It should not veer off in the nebulous direction of general self-worth. Keep in mind that repeated negative feedback can have a cumulative effect, chipping away at an individual's confidence or perception of competence. Then it takes only one remark, perhaps one you would think is innocuous and insignificant, to break the camel's back and activate what seems like an overreaction.

Our communication may not be received as intended. We might do our best to come across positively and constructively, but due to factors beyond our control, the communication might be misperceived. One's inner state can bias dramatically the impact of interpersonal feedback. Note that self-efficacy reflects a perception of competence, and in the next chapter you'll learn how feeling competent leads to self-motivation.

Achievable Tasks. What makes for a "can do" attitude? Personal perception is key. A supervisor, parent, or teacher might believe s/he has provided everything needed to complete a task successfully. However, the employee, child, or student might not think so. It's important to ask, "Do you have what you need?" We're checking for feelings of self-efficacy. This is easier said than done, because people often hesitate to admit their incompetence. Who wants to concede, "I can't do it"? Instead, we try to maintain the appearance of self-efficacy.

Ask open-ended questions when you give assignments to assess whether those on the receiving end feel prepared to get the job done. In large groups, though, this probing for feelings of self-efficacy is impossible. As a result, in large classes some students get left behind in the learning process, perhaps because they skipped classes or an important reading assignment. As they get farther and farther behind in a certain class, their low self-efficacy is supported by the self-fulfilling prophecy and diminished optimism. Sometimes this leads to feelings of helplessness.[63] All too often, these students withdraw from the class or resign themselves to receiving a low grade. In the workplace, employees who cannot keep pace with new procedures might withdraw into themselves or put up defensive resistance.

Personal Strategies. Watson and Tharp[16] suggest the following five steps to increase perceptions of self-efficacy. First, select a task at which you expect to succeed, not one at which you expect to fail. Then, as your feelings of self-efficacy increase, you can tackle more challenging projects.

A cigarette smoker who wants to stop smoking, for example, might focus on smoking 50 percent fewer cigarettes per week rather than attempting to quit cold turkey. With early success at reducing the number of cigarettes smoked, the individual could make the criterion more stringent (like smoking no cigarettes on alternate days). Continued success leads to more self-efficacy.

Second, it's important to distinguish between the past and the present. Don't dwell on past failures. Past failures are history. The present moment – right now – is the first moment of the rest of your life. Focus on a renewed sense of self-confidence and self-efficacy.

Third, it's important to keep behavioral records of progress toward reaching your goal. Our cigarette smoker should record the number of cigarettes smoked each day and note when the rate of smoking is 50 percent less for a week. This should be noted as an achievement, and then a new goal should be set. Focusing on your successes (rather than failures) represents the fourth step in building self-efficacy.

Fifth, develop a list of tasks or projects you'd like to accomplish; then rank them from easiest to most difficult to accomplish. Whenever possible, start with the easier tasks. The self-efficacy and self-confidence developed from accomplishing less demanding tasks will help you tackle the more challenging situations on your list.

Focus on the Positive. A basic principle – focus on the positive – is suggested by many of the strategies for improving this person-state. Whether attempting to build your own self-efficacy or that of others, emphasize success over failure. Whenever you have the opportunity to teach others or give them feedback, look for small-win accomplishments and give genuine approval before commenting on ways to improve. Again, this approach is easier said than done.

Failures are easier to spot than successes. They stick out and interrupt the flow. That's why most teachers are quick to give negative attention to students who disrupt the classroom, while giving only limited positive attention to students who remain on task and go with the flow. Plus, many of us have been conditioned (unknowingly) to believe negative consequences (penalties) work better than positive consequences (rewards) to influence behavior change.[64]

Personal Control

Employees at my seminars on cultivating an AC4P culture have listed a number of ways to increase perceptions of personal control: (a) set short-term

process goals and track progress toward long-term accomplishment; (b) offer frequent rewarding and correcting feedback for process activities rather than only for longer-term outcomes; (c) provide opportunities to set personal goals, teach others, and chart small wins;[65] (d) teach employees basic behavior-change intervention strategies (especially feedback and recognition procedures); (e) provide time and resources for people to develop, implement, and evaluate intervention programs; (f) show employees how to graph daily records of baseline, intervention, and follow-up data; and (g) post response-feedback graphs of group performance.

The perception of personal control is analogous to perceptions of personal choice and autonomy. When people believe they are in control of a situation or challenge, they generally feel a sense of personal choice: "I choose to take charge of the mission which is within my domain of influence." Appreciate the similarity between these person-states. The next chapter entertains the connection between perceptions of choice and self-motivation.

Optimism

Optimism flows from thinking positively, avoiding negative thoughts, and expecting the best to happen. Anything that increases self-efficacy should also increase optimism. When our personal control is strengthened, we perceive more influence over our consequences. This gives us more reason to expect the best. Again, we see how the person-states of self-efficacy, personal control, and optimism are intertwined. A change in one will likely influence the other two. Note also how these person-states relate to perceptions of choice and competence – determinants of self-motivation, as explained in the next chapter.

Belonging

Here are common proposals given by my seminar discussion groups for fostering and sustaining an atmosphere of belonging among employees: (a) decrease the frequency of top-down directives and "quick-fix," "flavor-of-the-month" programs; (b) increase team-building discussions, group goal setting and feedback, and group celebrations for both process and outcome achievements; and (c) use self-managed or self-directed work teams.

Feelings of empowerment and belonging can be enhanced when groups are given control over important matters such as developing a behavior-improvement observation-and-feedback process or a particular AC4P initiative. When resources, opportunities, and talents enable team members to assert, "We can make a difference," feelings of belonging occur naturally. This leads to synergy; the group achieves more than could be possible if participants were working independently.

A Critical Caveat

The intention (or goal) of the individual is positive, compassionate, and prosocial. This is a critical assumption about the five person-states discussed here as beneficial consequences of various environmental conditions and potential dispositional activators of AC4P. Consider that an individual intends to harm another person (e.g., from interpersonal bullying to ruthless decapitation). In these negative scenarios, high levels of these person-states would likely increase the propensity to cause harm. Plus, success at causing the intended negative consequences could certainly boost the perpetrator's sense of self-esteem, self-efficacy, personal control, and optimism, as well as belongingness with the particular antisocial group.

This caveat requires a return to Figure 2.2. The beneficial or harmful outcomes of boosting one or more of these five person-states depend on the participant's vision and goal. Is the mission to help or hinder human welfare? Are the intentions prosocial or antisocial, compassionate or heartless, humane or inhumane? Indeed, one can feel empowered to help or harm another person, and these five person-states can facilitate beliefs in self-efficacy, response efficacy, and outcome expectancy. Thus, a person-state can actually help or hinder the cultivation of an AC4P culture, depending on the individual's vision and goal.

IN CONCLUSION

Continuous positive improvement in any endeavor involving human behavior requires people to actively care for others as well as themselves. The research-based principles reviewed here are relevant to increasing the frequency and improving the quality of AC4P behavior throughout a particular culture. Some practical intervention procedures benefit AC4P behavior indirectly by enhancing dispositional person-states that can facilitate one's willingness to actively care. Other strategies target AC4P behaviors directly, but these often have an indirect positive effect on the person-states that increase one's propensity to perform AC4P behavior.

An intervention that increases a person's self-esteem, self-efficacy, personal control, optimism, or sense of belonging or interdependence in a system can indirectly benefit AC4P behavior if the behavioral goal is benevolent or prosocial. A number of communication techniques enhance more than one of these states simultaneously, particularly actively listening to others for feelings and giving genuine praise for another person's accomplishments.

Reflect on your own life to appreciate the power of personal choice, and how the perception of personal control makes you feel more self-motivated, involved, and committed to a particular mission. The perception of choice can help activate and sustain AC4P behavior.

Perceptions of belonging are important, too. They increase when groups are given control over important decisions and receive genuine recognition for their accomplishments. Synergy is the ultimate outcome of belongingness and win-win, interpersonal involvement. This occurs when group interdependence produces more than what's possible when individuals go it alone.

AC4P behaviors are the building blocks of an AC4P culture. The more often quality AC4P behaviors occur among people in a given work, school, or family setting, the more likely an AC4P culture will evolve. Self-motivation is usually necessary to initiate and sustain the kind of behavior needed for an AC4P culture, because people are rarely held accountable for performing AC4P behavior. The next chapter explains how you can increase perceptions of self-motivation in yourself and others, thereby setting the stage for effective AC4P behavior. You'll see several direct connections between the person-states that increase one's propensity to actively care and those that enhance one's self-motivation.

DISCUSSION QUESTIONS

1. What (if anything) is wrong with the pop psychology assertion "The secret to success is self-affirmation? What (if anything) is right with this "secret"?
2. Offer operational (or functional) definitions and distinctions between the following terms: vision, goal, empowerment, and consequence.
3. Distinguish between feeling empowered and feeling motivated.
4. Use examples to distinguish between person-based, environment-based, and behavior-based AC4P behavior.
5. Why or why not is it important or useful to distinguish between the three types of AC4P behavior?
6. Explain Maslow's hierarchy of needs with examples from your personal experience.
7. What holds people back from helping others in a crisis situation?
8. Contrast the *direct* and *indirect* approaches to cultivating an AC4P culture.
9. Offer specific suggestions for increasing a sense of belongingness among members of a work group. Why is this important?
10. Distinguish between an independent and an interdependent perspective with examples related to cultivating an AC4P culture of compassion.

REFERENCES

1. Cialdini, R. B. (2001). *Influence: Science and practice* (4th ed.). Needham Heights, MA: Allyn & Bacon; Schroeder, D. A., Penner, L. A., Dovidio, J. F., & Piliavin, J. A. (1995). *The psychology of helping and altruism.* New York: McGraw-Hill.
2. Geller, E. S. (1998). *Understanding behavior-based safety: Step-by-step methods to improve your workplace* (rev. ed.). Neenah, WI: J.J. Keller & Associates; Geller, E. S. (2001). *The psychology of safety handbook.* Boca Raton, FL: CRC Press; Geller, E. S. (2002). People-based safety: Seven social influence principles to fuel

participation in occupational safety. *Professional Safety, 47*(10), 25–31; Geller, E. S., & Williams, J. H. (Eds.) (2001). *Keys to behavior-based safety.* Rockville, MD: ABS Consulting; McSween, T. E. (1995). *The values-based safety process: Improving your safety culture with a behavioral approach.* New York: Van Nostrand Reinhold.

3. Geller, E. S. (1998). *Beyond safety accountability: How to increase personal responsibility.* Neenah, WI: J. J. Keller & Associates; Geller, E. S. (2001). Actively caring for occupational safety: Extending the performance management paradigm. In C. M. Johnson, W. K. Redmon, & T. C. Mawhinney (Eds.). *Organizational performance: Behavior analysis and management* (pp. 303–326). New York: Springer.

4. Covey, S. R. (1989). *The seven habits of highly effective people.* New York: Simon & Schuster; Covey, S. R. (1990). *Principle-centered leadership.* New York: Simon & Schuster.

5. Peale, N. V. (1952). *The power of positive thinking.* New York: Prentice Hall.

6. Kohn, A. (1993). *Punished by rewards: The trouble with gold stars, incentive plans, A's, praise, and other bribes.* Boston: Houghton Mifflin.

7. Deming, W. E. (1986). *Out of the crisis.* Cambridge, MA: Massachusetts Institute of Technology, Center for Advanced Engineering Study; Deming, W. E. (1993). *The new economics for industry, government, education.* Cambridge, MA: Massachusetts Institute of Technology, Center for Advanced Engineering Study.

8. Schneider, S. M. (2012). *The science of consequences: How they affect genes, change the brain, and impact our world.* Amherst, NY: Prometheus Books.

9. Skinner, B. F. (1981). Selection by consequences. *Science, 213,* 502–504.

10. Carnegie, D. (1936). *How to win friends and influence people.* New York: Simon & Schuster, p. 57.

11. Conger, J. A., & Kanungo, R. N. (1988). The empowerment process: Integrating theory and practice. *Academy of Management Review, 13,* 471–482.

12. Bandura, A. (1997). *Self-efficacy: The exercise of control.* New York: W.H. Freeman.

13. Locke, E. A., & Latham, G. P. (1990).*A theory of goal setting and task performance.* Englewood Cliffs, NJ: Prentice Hall.

14. Geller, E. S. (2005). *People-based safety: The source.* Virginia Beach, VA: Coastal Training and Technologies; Geller, E. S. (2008) *Leading people-based safety: Enriching your culture.* Virginia Beach, VA: Coastal Training and Technologies.

15. Geller, E. S. (2014). The psychology of self-motivation. In E. S. Geller (Ed.). *Actively caring for people: Cultivating a culture of compassion* (pp. 73–75). Newport, VA: Make-A-Difference.

16. Watson, D. C., & Tharp, R. G. (1987). *Self-directed behavior: Self-modification for personal adjustment* (7th ed.). Pacific Grove, CA: Brooks/Cole.

17. Maslow, A. H. (1943). A theory of human motivation. *Psychological Review, 50,* 370–396; Maslow, A. H. (1954). *Motivation and personality.* New York: Harper.

18. Schultz, D. (1977). *Growth psychology: Models of the healthy personality.* New York: D. Van Nostrand.

19. Maslow, A. H. (1971). *The farther reaches of human nature.* New York: Viking.

20. Frankl, V. (1962). *Man's search for meaning: An introduction to logotherapy.* Boston: Beacon Press.
21. Rosenthal, A. M. (1964). *Thirty-eight witnesses.* New York: McGraw-Hill.
22. Latané, B., & Darley, J. M. (1968). Group inhibition of bystander intervention. *Journal of Personality and Social Psychology,* 10, 215–221; Latané, B., & Darley, J. M. (1970). *The unresponsible bystander: Why doesn't he help?* New York : Appleton-Century-Crofts.
23. Latané, B., & Nida, S. (1981). Ten years of research on group size and helping. *Psychological Bulletin,* 89, 308–324.
24. Beaman, A. I., Barnes, P. J., Klentz, B., & McQuirk, B. (1978). Increasing help-ing rates through informational dissemination: Teaching pays. *Personality and Social Psychology,* 37, 1835–1846.
25. Hornstein, H. A. (1976). *Cruelty and kindness: A new look at aggression and altruism.* Englewood Cliffs, NJ: Prentice-Hall.
26. Shotland, R. L., & Heinold, W. D. (1985). Bystander response to arterial bleed-ing: Helping skills, the decision-making process, and differentiating the helping response. *Journal of Personality and Social Psychology,* 49, 347–356.
27. McCarty, S. M., Teie, S., & Furrow, C. B. (2012). *Training students to observe and reward actively-caring behavior.* Technical Research Report, Department of Psychology, Center for Applied Behavior Systems, Virginia Tech, Blacksburg.
28. Rutkowski, G. K., Gruder, C. L., & Romer, D. (1983). Group cohesiveness, social norms, and bystander intervention. *Journal of Personality and Social Psychology,* 44, 545–552.
29. Carlson, M., Charlin, V., & Miller, N. (1988). Positive mood and helping behav-ior: A test of six hypotheses. *Journal of Personality and Social Psychology,* 55, 211–229.
30. Bierhoff, H. W., Klein, R., & Kramp, P. (1991). Evidence for the altruistic person-ality from data on accident research. *Journal of Personality,* 59, 263–280.
31. Schwartz, S. H., & Clausen, G. T. (1970). Responsibility, norms, and helping in an emergency. *Journal of Personality and Social Psychology,* 16, 299–310; Staub, E. (1971). Helping a distressed person: The influence of implicit and explicit "rules" of conduct on children and adults. *Journal of Personality & Social Psychology,* 17, 137–145.
32. Geller, E. S. (1998). *Beyond safety accountability: How to increase personal responsibility.* Neenah, WI: J. J. Keller & Associates; Geller, E. S. (2001). Actively caring for occupational safety: Extending the performance manage-ment paradigm. In C. M. Johnson, W. K. Redmon, & T. C. Mawhinney (Eds.). *Organizational performance: Behavior analysis and management* (pp. 303–326). New York: Springer.
33. Latané, B., & Darley, J. M. (1970). *The unresponsible bystander: Why doesn't he help?* New York: Appleton-Century-Crofts.
34. Piliavin, J. A., Piliavin, I. M., & Broll, L. (1976). Time of arousal at an emergency and likelihood of helping. *Personality and Social Psychology Bulletin,* 2, 273–276.
35. Clark, R. D., III, & Word, L. E. (1972). Why don't bystanders help? Because of ambiguity? *Journal of Personality and Social Psychology,* 24, 392–400.
36. Schroeder, D. A., Penner, L. A., Dovidio, J. F., & Piliavin, J. A. (1995). *The psy-chology of helping and altruism.* New York: McGraw-Hill.

37. Daniels, A. C., & Daniels, J. E. (2005). *Measure of a leader.* Atlanta: Performance Management Publications, p. 158.

38. McCarty, S. M., & Geller, E. S. (2011, Summer). Want to get rid of bullying? Then reward behavior that is incompatible with it. *Behavior Analysis Digest International,* 23(2), 1–7; McCarty, S. M., & Geller, E. S. (2013). AC4P to prevent bullying: Prompting and rewarding prosocial behavior in elementary schools In E. S. Geller (Ed.). *Actively caring at your school: How to make it happen* (2nd ed.) (pp. 177–197). Newport, VA: Make-A-Difference; McCarty, S., Teie, S., McCutchen, J., & Geller, E. S. (in press). Actively caring to prevent bullying in an elementary school: Prompting and rewarding prosocial behavior. *Journal of Prevention Intervention in the Community.*

39. Kreitner, R. (1982). The feedforward and feedback control of job performance through organizational behavior management (OBM). *Journal of Organizational Behavior Management,* 4(2), 3.

40. Rogers, C. (1957). The necessary and sufficient conditions of therapeutic personality change. *Journal of Consulting Psychology,* 21, 95–103; Rogers, C. (1977). *Carl Rogers on personal power: Inner strength and its revolutionary impact.* New York: Delacorte.

41. Straumann, T. J., & Higgins, E. G. (1988). Self-discrepancies as predictors of vulnerability to distinct syndromes of chronic emotional distress. *Journal of Personality,* 56, 685–707.

42. Brown, J. D., & McGill, K. L. (1989). The cost of good fortune: When positive life events produce negative health consequences. *Journal of Personality and Social Psychology,* 57, 1103–1110.

43. Wylie, R. (1974). *The self-concept,* Vol. 1. Lincoln: University of Nebraska Press.

44. Wells, L. E., & Marwell, G. (1976). *Self-esteem.* Beverly Hills, CA: Sage.

45. Baron, R. A., & Byrne, D. (1994). *Social psychology: Understanding human interaction* (7th ed.). Boston: Allyn & Bacon.

46. Batson, C. D., Bolen, M. H., Cross, J. A., & Neuringer-Benefiel, H. E. (1986). Where is altruism in the altruistic personality? *Journal of Personality and Social Psychology,* 1, 212–220.

47. Baumeister, R. F., Campbell, J. D., Krueger, J. I., & Vohs, K. D. (2003). Does high self-esteem cause better performance, interpersonal success, happiness, or healthier lifestyles? *Psychological Science in the Public Interest,* 4(1), 1–44, p. 1.

48. Bandura, A. (1996). *Self-efficacy: The exercise of control.* New York: W.H. Freeman.

49. Bandura, A. (1982). Self-efficacy mechanism in human agency. *American Psychologist,* 37, 122–147; Betz, N. E., & Hackett, G. (1986). Applications of self-efficacy theory to understanding career choice behavior. *Journal of Social and Clinical Psychology,* 4, 279–289; Hackett, G., Betz, N. E., Casas, J. M., & Rocha-Singh, I. A. (1992). Gender, ethnicity, and social cognitive factors predicting the academic achievement of students in engineering. *Journal of Counseling Psychology,* 39, 527–538.

50. Rotter, J. B. (1966). Generalized expectancies for internal versus external control of reinforcement. *Psychological Monographs,* 80, No. 1.

51. Rotter, J. B. (1966). Generalized expectancies for internal versus external control of reinforcement. *Psychological Monographs,* 80, No. 1; Rushton, J. P.

(1984). The altruistic personality: Evidence from laboratory, naturalistic and self-report perspectives. In E. Staub, D. Bar-Tal, J. Karylowski, & J. Reykowski (Eds.). *Development and maintenance of prosocial behavior* (pp. 271–290). New York: Plenum.

52. Hunt, M. M. (1993). *The story of psychology.* New York: Doubleday.

53. Nowicki, S., & Strickland, B. R. (1973). A locus of control scale for children. *Journal of Consulting Psychology,* 40, 148–154; Stickland, B. R. (1989). Internal-external control expectancies: From contingency to creativity. *American Psychologist,* 44, 1–12.

54. Taylor, S. E. (1991). *Health psychology* (2nd ed.). New York: McGraw-Hill.

55. Eskew, R. T., & Riche, C. V. (1982). Pacing and locus of control in quality control inspection. *Human Factors,* 24, 411–415; Phares, E. J. (1991). *Introduction to personality* (3rd ed.). New York: HarperCollins.

56. Peterson, C. (2000). The future of optimism. *American Psychologist,* 55(1), 44–55; Scheier, M. F., & Carver, C. S. (1985). Optimism, coping and health: Assessment and implications of generalized outcome expectancies. *Health Psychology,* 4, 219–247; Seligman, M. E. P. (1991). *Learned optimism.* New York: Alfred A. Knopf.

57. Seligman, M. E.P. (1991). *Learned optimism.* New York: Alfred A. Knopf.

58. Carver, C. S., Scheier, M. F., & Weintraub, J. K. (1989). Assessing coping strategies: A theoretically-based approach. *Journal of Personality and Social Psychology,* 56, 267–283; Seligman, M. E. P. (2011). *Flourish: A visionary new understanding of happiness and well-being.* New York: Simon & Schuster; Peterson, C., & Barrett, L. C. (1987). Explanatory style and academic performance among university freshmen. *Journal of Personality and Social Psychology,* 53, 603–607.

59. Scheier, M. F., Weintraub, J. K., & Carver, C. S. (1986). Coping with stress: Divergent strategies of optimists and pessimists. *Journal of Personality and Social Psychology,* 51, 1257–1264.

60. Tavris, C., & Wade, C. (1995). *Psychology in perspective.* New York: HarperCollins.

61. Peck, M. S. (1979). *The different drum: Community making and peace.* New York: Simon & Schuster.

62. Geller, E. S. (2001). Actively caring for occupational safety: Extending the performance management paradigm. In C. M. Johnson, W. K. Redmon, & T. C. Mawhinney (Eds.). *Organizational performance: Behavior analysis and management* (pp. 303–326). New York: Springer; Geller, E. S. (2001). Sustaining participation in a safety improvement process: Ten relevant principles from behavioral science. *Professional Safety,* 46(9), 24–29.

63. Peterson, C., Maier, S. F., & Seligman, M. E.P. (1993). *Learned helplessness: A theory for the age of personal control.* New York: Oxford University Press; Seligman, M. E. P. (1975). *Helplessness: On depression, development, and death.* San Francisco: Freeman.

64. Notz, W. W., Boschman, I., & Tax, S. S. (1987). Reinforcing punishment and extinguishing reward: On the folly of OBM with SPC. *Journal of Organizational Behavior Management,* 9(1), 33–46.

65. Weick, K. E. (1984). Small wins: Redefining the scale of social problems. *American Psychologist,* 39, 40–44.

3

The Psychology of Self-Motivation

E. SCOTT GELLER

Whether you think you can or think you can't – you are right.
– Henry Ford

Exactly what is external accountability? In the work world, these are motivational tools such as time sheets, overtime compensation records, peer-to-peer behavioral observations, public posting of performance indicators, group and individual feedback meetings, and performance appraisals. In schools it's all about grades; teachers attempt to keep students motivated by emphasizing the relationship between the quality of their schoolwork and the all-important grade. Psychologists call these *extrinsic motivators*, and managers and teachers use them to keep employees and students on track, respectively.

Sometimes it's possible to establish conditions that facilitate self-direction, accountability, and self-motivation. When people go beyond the call of duty to actively care for the welfare of others, they are self-motivated to an extent. Achieving an AC4P culture requires more people to be self-motivated at more times and in more situations. This chapter presents evidence-based ways to make this happen, as gleaned from research in behavioral and psychological science.

SELF-MOTIVATION FOR AC4P BEHAVIOR

Without safety regulations, policies, and external accountability systems, many more employees would get hurt or killed on the job and on the road, and more students would be victimized in schools. Employers, police officers, safety professionals, and school teachers need extrinsic controls to hold people accountable for performing safe and AC4P behavior, while avoiding risky and confrontational behavior. Why do we need such extrinsic controls? The desired, safe AC4P behaviors are relatively inconvenient, uncomfortable, and inefficient. The soon, certain, positive consequences (or intrinsic reinforcers) of at-risk and other undesirable behavior often overpower our self-motivation to be as safe or caring as possible.

Every driver knows it's risky to talk on a cell phone or type a text message while driving, yet many drivers perform these behaviors regularly. Why? The immediate and naturally reinforcing consequences take priority over the low likelihood of a crash or traffic ticket. These risky drivers are not self-motivated to actively care for the safety of themselves and others on the road. (See Chapter 11 for AC4P approaches to traffic safety.)

Here's the key question: What can we do to overcome the human nature implied by these profound quotations from B. F. Skinner: "Immediate consequences outweigh delayed consequences," and "Consequences for the individual usually outweigh consequences for others"?[1] In other words, the performer of AC4P behavior is seemingly not rewarded by soon, certain, and positive consequences. Therefore, techniques are needed to overcome this natural tendency to avoid AC4P behavior. Some practical solutions are derived from psychological science, especially research conducted by Edward Deci and Richard Ryan.[2]

HUMAN NEEDS AND SELF-MOTIVATION

We have three basic psychological needs, and when these needs are satisfied, we are self-motivated, according to Deci and Ryan. Specifically, self-motivation is supported by situational factors (e.g., environmental contexts and other people) that facilitate the fulfillment of our needs for autonomy, relatedness, and competence. "Self-motivation, rather than external (or extrinsic) motivation, is at the heart of creativity, responsibility, healthy behavior, and lasting change."[3]

Autonomy

Autonomy is a matter of being self-governing or having personal control. In Chapter 2, this condition was introduced as a person-state related to one's propensity to actively care for the well-being of others.[4] Autonomous behavior is self-initiated, self-endorsed, and authentic. It reflects one's true values and intentions. Geller and Veazie[5] refer to this attribute as "choice," and plenty of research shows that people are more self-directed and self-motivated when they have opportunities to choose among action alternatives.[4]

Early Laboratory Research. More than forty years ago, when my students and I were conducting research in cognitive science, we designed a very simple experiment and obtained very simple results. The implications of the findings, however, are relevant to self-motivation in numerous situations. Half of the forty participants in this experiment were shown a list of five three-letter words (i.e., cat, hat, mat, rat, and bat) and asked to select one. Then, after a warning tone, the selected word was presented on a screen in front of the participant, and s/he pressed a micro-switch as fast as possible after seeing the word.

The latency in milliseconds between the presentation of the word and the participant's response was a measure of simple reaction time. This sequence of warning signal, word presentation, and participant reaction occurred for twenty-five trials. If a participant reacted before the stimulus word was presented, the reaction time was not counted, and the trial was repeated. The session took less than fifteen minutes per subject.

The word selected by a particular participant was used as the presentation stimulus for the next participant. Thus, this participant did not have the opportunity to choose the stimulus word. As a result, the word choices of twenty participants were assigned to twenty other participants. Consequently this simple experiment had two conditions – a Choice condition (in which participants chose a three-letter word for their stimulus) and an Assigned condition (in which participants were assigned the stimulus word selected by the previous participant). To our surprise, the mean reactions of participants in the Choice group were significantly faster than those of participants in the Assigned group.

Although these results were hypothesized and explained by presuming the opportunity to choose the stimulus word increased the motivation of the participants to perform in the reaction-time experiment, the large group differences were unexpected. How could the simple choice of a three-letter word influence faster responding in a simple reaction-time experiment? In fact, because I did not feel confident about a basic motivational explanation for these surprising results, I did not pursue the publication of these data in a professional research journal. Only years later did I appreciate the real-world ramifications of those findings.[4]

From Laboratory to Classroom. About a year after the simple reaction-time study just described, my students and I tested the theory of choice as a motivator in the college classroom. I was assigned to teach two sections of Social Psychology: one at 8:00 A.M. Monday, Wednesday, and Friday, and the other at 11:00 A.M. on these same days. There were about seventy-five students in each class.

On the first day of class, I did not hand out a syllabus with weekly assignments, but distributed only a general outline of the course that introduced the textbook, the course objectives, and the basic criteria for assigning grades (i.e., a quiz on each textbook chapter and a comprehensive final exam on classroom lectures, discussions, and demonstrations). In an open discussion and voting process, the eight o'clock class was given the opportunity to choose the order in which the ten textbook chapters would be read for homework and discussed in class. They could also submit multiple-choice questions for me to consider using for the ten chapter quizzes, and they could hand in short-answer and discussion questions for possible application on the final exam. The eleven o'clock class received the order of textbook chapters selected previously by the eight o'clock class, and this class was not given an opportunity to submit quiz or exam questions.

Thus, Choice and Assigned classroom conditions were derived, analogous to the two reaction-time groups we had studied one year earlier. Two of my undergraduate research assistants (RAs) attended each of these classes, posing as regular students, and systematically counted the frequency of behaviors reflecting class participation. These RAs did not know about my intentional Choice versus Assigned manipulations.

From the day the students in the eight o'clock class voted on the textbook assignments, these students seemed to be livelier than the students in the eleven o'clock class. My perception was verified by the participation records of the two classroom RAs. Furthermore, the ten quiz grades, the final exam scores, and my teaching evaluation scores from standard forms distributed during the last class period were significantly higher in the Choice class than the Assigned class. (Although several students from the eight o'clock class submitted potential quiz and final exam questions, none were actually used. Each class received the same chapter quizzes and final exam.)

It seems the Choice versus Assigned manipulation was a critical factor. The initial opportunity to choose reading assignments apparently increased students' motivation and class participation, and this extra motivation and involvement led to more involvement, perceived choice, self-motivation, and learning. Indeed, the students' attitudes toward the class improved as a result of their feeling more in control of the situation.

It's likely the "choice" opportunities in the eight o'clock class were especially powerful because they were so different from the traditional top-down classroom atmosphere at the time, as typified by the organization of my eleven o'clock class. In other words, the contrast of the Choice class with the students' other courses made the "choice" opportunities in the eight o'clock class especially salient, meaningful, and motivational.

A Corporate Safety Example. A decade after the laboratory and classroom research that showed the self-motivating impact of choice, I visited a chemical facility of 350 employees that exemplified the power of choice to impact occupational safety. The employees had initiated a behavior-focused AC4P observation, feedback, and coaching process in 1992 and had reaped amazing safety benefits for their efforts. In 1994, for example, 98 percent of the workforce had participated in sessions centered on behavioral observation and feedback, documenting a total of 3,350 coaching sessions for the year. A total of 51,408 behaviors were safe and 4,389 were at-risk.

Such comprehensive employee involvement in a behavioral observation-and-feedback process led to remarkable success. While numerous companies have improved their safety performance substantially with an AC4P behavioral coaching process (as detailed in Chapter 9),[6] this plant holds the record for sustaining optimal employee engagement in this injury-prevention process. I'm convinced a key factor in this organization's outstanding success was the employees' choice in the development, implementation, and maintenance of the process. The employees owned their AC4P observation-and-feedback process from the start because they applied the techniques *their way.*

There's no best way to implement an AC4P coaching process. Rather, the AC4P principles and procedures from applied behavioral science (ABS) need to be customized to fit the relevant work culture. The most efficient way to make this happen is to involve the target population in the customization process. At this facility, the entire workforce learned the AC4P principles by participating in ten one-hour small-group sessions spaced over a six-month period. These education/training sessions were facilitated by other employees who had received more intensive training in safety-focused AC4P principles and applications. At these group sessions, employees discussed specific strategies for implementing a plant-wide behavioral monitoring and coaching process, and they entertained ways to overcome barriers to total participation and sustain the process over the long term. They designed an AC4P process that included employee choice at its very core. Although some specifics of the process have changed since its inception in 1992, the choice aspect has remained a constant.

From the start, employees scheduled regular AC4P observation-and-feedback sessions with two other employees (i.e., observers). That is, they selected the task, and the day and time for the coaching session. Additionally, they selected two individuals to observe their performance and give them immediate and specific feedback regarding occurrences of safe and at-risk behaviors. Employees chose their observers (and coaches) from *anyone* in the plant. At the start of their process the number of *volunteer* safety coaches was limited (including only 30 percent of the workforce), but today everyone in the workforce is a potential safety coach. Personal choice facilitated involvement, ownership, and trust in the process.

At first, some employees did not have complete trust in the process and resisted active participation. Some tried to beat the system by scheduling their observation-and-feedback sessions at inactive times when the probability of an at-risk behavior was minimal (i.e., while they watched a monitor or completed paperwork). And most employees were certainly on their toes when the observers arrived at the scheduled times. At the same time, those observed were optimally receptive to constructive feedback and advice from the observers they had selected. Many people (whether observing or being observed) were surprised that numerous at-risk behaviors occurred in situations where employees knew the safe operating procedures and knew they were being observed for the occurrence of at-risk behaviors.

It wasn't long before most employees at this facility began scheduling their coaching sessions during active times when the probability of an at-risk behavior or injury was highest. Frequently, the observed individual pointed out an at-risk behavior necessitated by the particular work environment or procedure (e.g., a difficult-to-reach valve, a hose-checking procedure too cumbersome for one auditor, a walking surface made slippery by an equipment leak, a difficult-to-adjust machine guard). Many employees chose to use their observation-and-feedback process to demonstrate that some at-risk behaviors are facilitated or necessitated by equipment design or maintenance and/or by environmental conditions or operating procedures. This involvement often led to a beneficial change in environmental conditions or operation procedures.

We've All Been There. You need only reflect on your own life circumstances to realize how a *perception* of choice or personal control increases your self-motivation, involvement, and commitment. Please note we're talking about the *perception* of choice, as reflected in the illustration on the next page. We are not always in control of the critical events of ongoing circumstances, and thus we've experienced the frustration, discomfort, and distress of being at the mercy of environmental circumstances or other people's decisions. And we've certainly experienced the pleasure of having alternatives to choose from and feeling in control of those factors critical for successful performance. How sweet the taste of success when we can attribute the achievement to our own choices.

Bottom line: The message is clear. Whenever possible, give people opportunities to choose mission-relevant goals and the procedures to reach them. The result: increased self-motivation, engagement, and ownership. This may require relinquishing some top-down control, abandoning a desire for a quick fix, changing from focusing on outcomes to recognizing process achievements, and giving people opportunities to choose, evaluate, and refine their means to achieve the ends. The result: more people going beyond the call of duty on behalf of others when no one's watching.

Competence

Several researchers of human motivation have proposed that people naturally enjoy being able to solve problems and successfully complete worthwhile tasks.[7] In their view, people are self-motivated to learn, to explore possibilities, to understand what's going on, and to participate in achieving worthwhile goals. The label for this fundamental human motive is *competence*. "All of us are striving for mastery, for affirmations of our own competence."[8]

Motivation researchers assume the desire for competence is self-initiating and self-rewarding. Behavior followed by consequences that enhance feelings of competence becomes self-directed and often does not need extrinsic or extra rewards to keep it going. Feeling competent at doing worthwhile work motivates continued effort. When people feel more successful or competent, their self-motivation increases. As one behavioral scientist put it, "People are not successful because they are motivated; they are motivated because they have been successful."[9]

The Power of Feedback. How do we know we are competent at something? How do we know this competence makes a beneficial difference? You know the answer – feedback.

Feedback about our ongoing behavior tells us how we are doing and enables us to do better. That familiar slogan "Practice makes perfect" is actually incorrect. Practice makes permanence. Without appropriate feedback, well-practiced behavior can be wrong. We hone our skills through practice *and* behavior-focused feedback.

Some feedback comes naturally, as when we recognize that our behavior has produced a desired result. But often behavioral feedback requires careful and systematic observation by another individual – a trainer or coach – who later communicates his/her findings to the performer. In each case, feedback enables the development of perceived competence and self-motivation.

Feedback is essential to fulfill a basic human need – the need for competence. And helping people satisfy this need increases their self-motivation to perform the relevant behavior. But feedback regarding the *outcome* of a project or process does not reflect individual choices or competence, and thus can be ineffective. Only feedback that is behavior-focused and customized for the recipient can enhance an individual's perception of personal control and competence, and thus bolster self-motivation.

Is Feedback Reinforcing? Technically, a reinforcer is a behavioral consequence that maintains or increases the frequency of the behavior it follows. So, if behavior does not continue or improve after feedback, the feedback was not a reinforcer. Likewise, praise, bonus pay, and frequent flyer points are not reinforcers when they don't increase the frequency of behavior they target; and they often don't. However, interpersonal, behavior-based rewards can increase our perception of competence.

Can well-delivered supportive or corrective feedback increase our perception of competence and self-motivation? Absolutely, but it's not a payoff for doing the right thing. Rather, it's behavior-based information a person can use to feel more competent or to learn how to become more competent. There is perhaps no other consequence with greater potential to improve competence, self-motivation, and individual performance than behavior-focused feedback. Behavioral feedback, delivered with an AC4P mindset, is usually a reinforcer because it maintains or increases a certain desired behavior.

A Paradigm Shift. This discussion of feedback, competence, and self-motivation calls for a paradigm shift – a change in perspective about AC4P behavior. We should assume people are naturally self-motivated to help others, instead of calling on guilt or sacrifice to get people involved in improving the health, welfare, or safety of other people. Simply put, we hate feeling incompetent or helpless. We want to learn, to discover, to become more proficient at performing worthwhile tasks. We seek opportunities to ask questions, to study pertinent material, to work with people who know more than we do, and to receive feedback that can increase our competence and subsequent self-motivation.

Consequently, AC4P behavior is not a thankless job requiring self-sacrifice, obligation, or selfless altruism. Participation in an AC4P process provides opportunities to satisfy a basic human need – the need for personal competence.[7] Effective and frequent delivery of behavior-based feedback provides a mechanism for improving the quality of an AC4P process, as well as cultivating feelings of competence and self-motivation throughout a culture.[10]

Relatedness

The innate need for *relatedness* reflects "the need to love and be loved, to care and be cared for ... to feel included, to feel related."[11] This is analogous to the state of belonging – a person-state influencing one's propensity to actively care for the health, safety, and well-being of others. Geller and Veazie[5] use the term *community* to reflect this person-state because the concept of community is more encompassing than relatedness or belongingness.[12]

A community perspective reflects systems thinking and interdependence beyond the confines of family, social groups, and work teams, as explicated by Peter Block[13] and M. Scott Peck.[14] Community is an AC4P mindset for humankind in general – an interconnectedness with others that transcends political differences and prejudices, and profoundly respects and appreciates diversity.

Systems Thinking and Interdependence. Focus your efforts to optimize the system, W. Edwards Deming tells us in his best sellers on total quality management, *Out of The Crisis* and *The New Economics*.[15] Peter Senge stresses that systems thinking is *The Fifth Discipline*[16] and the key to continuous improvement. And Stephen Covey's discussion of interdependence, win-win contingencies, and synergy in his popular self-help book, *The Seven Habits of Highly Effective People*,[17] is founded on systems thinking and a community perspective. Plus, Geller and Veazie propose in *The Courage Factor*[18] that the amount of courage a person needs to intervene on behalf of another individual decreases as the degree of connectedness between the two people increases. (See Chapter 4 for more on courage and AC4P behavior.)

Developing a community or interdependent spirit in an organization, a classroom, or a family unit leads to two primary human performance payoffs: (a) Individuals become more self-motivated to do the right thing, and (b) people are more likely to actively care for the well-being of others. In their reality-based narrative, Geller and Veazie[5] illustrate the dos and don'ts of building an interdependent community perspective.

More Paradigm Shifts. A systems or community approach to improving people's welfare implicates a number of paradigm shifts from the traditional management of an organization, a classroom, and, yes, a family. We need to shift from trying to find one root cause of a problem (e.g., interpersonal bullying, sexual abuse, substance abuse, and occupational injuries) to considering a number of potential contributing factors from each of three domains – environment, behavior, and person. Interdependent systems thinking requires a shift from downstream outcome-based measures of individual or group performance (grades, injury rates, familial acceptance) to a more proactive and diagnostic evaluation of process variables within the environment, behavior, and person domains.

Systems thinking enables a useful perspective on basic principles of human motivation, attitude formation, and behavior change. The influence of activators and consequences on behavior is linear, or so we believe. But systems thinking implicates a circular or spiral perspective. While an event preceding a behavior might direct it, and a particular event following a behavior determines whether it will occur again, it's instructive to realize the consequence of one behavior can serve as the activator of the next behavior. With this perspective, behavior-based feedback can serve as a motivating consequence or a directing activator, depending on when and how it's presented.

Spiral causality and the consistency principle combine to explain how small changes in behavior can result in attitude change, followed by more behavior change and then more desired attitude change, leading eventually to personal commitment and total involvement in the process.[19] Similarly, the notion of spiral causality and the reciprocity principle explain why initial AC4P behavior by a few individuals can result in more and more AC4P behavior by many individuals. This *ripple effect* can eventually lead to families, work teams, and community groups performing AC4P behavior regularly on behalf of the health, safety, and well-being of each other with a win-win interdependent attitude and a proactive mindset. In the end we have AC4P synergy. It can all start with systems thinking and one intentional act of kindness from one person to another. (See Chapter 6 for more on this AC4P ripple effect.)

HOW TO INCREASE SELF-MOTIVATION

The C-words of choice, competence, and community are used by Geller and Veazie[5] as labels for the three evidence-based person-states that determine self-motivation. Dispositional, interpersonal, and environmental conditions that enhance these states, presumed to be innate needs by some psychologists,[8] increase personal perceptions of self-motivation. Researchers offer the following ten guidelines for increasing self-motivation by affecting one or more of the three person-states (or needs) defined earlier.

1. Explain Why

Rules and regulations should be accompanied by a meaningful explanation to provide a rationale for behavior that is not naturally reinforcing. Often, we tell people what to do (with rules and regulations) without including the rationale – the why. At work, managers often delegate quickly without connecting a specific task to the organization's larger mission or vision – the "big picture." In educational institutions, policies regarding student admissions, staff evaluation, and student grading, as well as changes in textbooks, are often announced without a reasonable rationale.

In the community, some people may choose to ignore residential speed laws (e.g., a 20 mph zone) because they don't understand how such a dramatic reduction in vehicle speed improves safety. In this case, it might help to know that pedestrians have an 85 percent chance of being killed when hit at 40 mph versus a 5 percent fatality rate when hit by a vehicle traveling 20 mph.[20] If individuals connected a speed restriction to saving a human life, as opposed to avoiding a speeding ticket, they might be less likely to speed. Or at least those complying with the 20 mph speed limit would more likely perceive personal choice and more self-motivation regarding their decision to obey mandates for reduced speed.

2. It's Not Easy

Acknowledge that "[p]eople might not want to do what they are being asked to do."[21] For example, admit that certain behaviors (e.g., safety-related behaviors) are relatively inconvenient and uncomfortable, but given the reasonable rationale provided, the personal response cost is worthwhile. And even though the value of AC4P coaching (i.e., giving a colleague interpersonal feedback to support right behavior and correct wrong behavior) is obvious, acknowledge that it's natural to feel awkward in this situation, whether feedback is being delivered or received. This justifies role-playing exercises to improve people's social skills at delivering and receiving behavior-based feedback. Guidelines 7 and 8 provide more on delivering and receiving feedback effectively.

3. Watch Your Language

Your language should suggest minimal external pressure. The common phrases "Safety is a condition of employment!" "All accidents are preventable!" "Bullying is a rite of passage!" and "Perform random acts of kindness!" reduce one's sense of autonomy. The slogan "AC4P is a core value of our organization, school, or community" implies personal authenticity, interpersonal relatedness, and human interaction.

In the workplace, injuries are typically referred to as "accidents," implying limited personal choice or control and making it reasonable to think, "When it's your time, it's your time." In schools, some teachers believe, "Students are just cruel at this age," or "Bullying just happens." As a result they exercise limited personal interaction to prevent bullying behavior. The problem is "beyond their control."

The common phrase "random acts of kindness"[22] has a disadvantage as a description of AC4P behavior. *Random* implies the behavior happened by chance, which suggests it's beyond individual choice or control. A kind act may appear random to the recipient, but it's intentionally performed and is usually self-motivated. Our preferred alternative: *intentional* acts of kindness. The language we use to prescribe or describe behavior influences our perceptions of its meaningfulness and its relevance to our lives. Language impacts culture, and vice versa.

4. Provide Opportunities for Choice

Participative management means employees have personal choice during the planning, execution, and evaluation of their jobs. People have a need for autonomy, regardless of dispositional and situational factors. In the workplace, managers often tell people what to do as opposed to involving them in the decision-making process. In schools, students are often viewed as passive learners, because teachers plan, execute, and evaluate most aspects of the teaching/learning process. Students' perceptions of choice are limited. Yet cooperative teaching/learning – where students contribute to the selection and presentation of lesson material – has been shown to be most beneficial over the long term.[23]

5. Involve the Followers

Rules established by soliciting input from those who will be affected by them support autonomy.[11] Employees are more likely to comply with safety regulations they helped to define. Shouldn't they have significant influence in the development of policy they will be asked to follow? Those on the front line know best what actions should be avoided versus performed in order to optimize the safety and quality of their production system.

Similarly, before a rule or regulation is implemented in an educational system, those affected (i.e., faculty and/or students) should certainly be given opportunities to offer suggestions. In a family, as the children mature, certain rules should be open to discussion before being mandated. This takes more time, but the marked increase in effectiveness justifies any loss in efficiency.

6. Set SMARTS Goals

Customize process and outcome goals with individuals and work teams. As introduced in Chapter 2, the most effective goals are SMARTS: specific, motivational, achievable, relevant, trackable, and shared.[19] Process goals reflect successive behavioral steps to achieve on route to accomplishing a significant outcome goal. A work team might set a process goal to complete a total of ten interpersonal observation-and-feedback sessions per week for one month, aiming to increase the percentage of safe behaviors recorded for their team. Of course, the long-term outcome goal is a reduction in personal injuries, but this can take substantial time to realize, especially if the group's injury rate is already low. It's important to note and celebrate the periodic accomplishment of measurable process goals related to more remote and nebulous visions such as "culture improvement" and "injury-free."

In educational settings, completing certain homework assignments and studying a certain number of hours per week serve as process goals, leading to the outcome of an improved exam grade and eventually a desirable grade in a particular course. Achieving such process goals and obtaining desirable grades leads to the more remote outcome goal of graduating with honors. In family settings, goal setting involving the participation of children may seem unreasonable, but at a certain point in the evolution of their maturity, full family involvement in defining required individual and group behaviors (e.g., daily chores, schoolwork, and budget management) to meet desired outcome goals (e.g., house and lawn maintenance, good school grades, and a family vacation) promotes mutual trust, perceived equity, and interdependent participation.

For optimal effectiveness, it's critical to apply SMARTS to the definition of a process goal. "S" for "specific" means the goal needs to be defined precisely with regard to the specific actions planned within a certain time period (e.g., perform ten coaching sessions per week for one month; complete a certain two-hour exercise routine three times a week for five consecutive months; recognize and reward five AC4P behaviors per week).

Is Your Goal Motivating? "M" for "motivational" refers to the realization of the extrinsic and/or natural consequences of goal attainment. For example, employees might look forward to a group pizza social (an extrinsic reward) after a month of averaging ten coaching sessions per week, and they might also anticipate improved communication skills and more AC4P relationships (an intrinsic reinforcer). Similarly, an individual could plan for a weekend at the beach after completing the weekly exercise routine for five months (extrinsic reward) and anticipate fitting well in a new bathing suit (intrinsic reinforcer). Moreover, it naturally feels good to reward the AC4P behavior of others with an AC4P wristband, and such action contributes to cultivating an AC4P culture.

"A" for "attainable" simply means the participants believe they can achieve the goal, although it will not be easy. Fitting in ten coaching sessions a week for a month, for example, might be considered challenging but feasible. And sticking to a specified exercise routine for five months will be difficult but doable. Recognizing and rewarding AC4P behavior is easier said than done, but it does get easier with practice.

"R" for "relevant" refers to a clear, rational connection between achieving the process goal and obtaining an eventual outcome. Participants need to believe working toward accomplishing the process goal is consistent with their mission to obtain an eventual outcome goal. Interpersonal coaching is relevant to the prevention of injuries; regular exercise will lead to improved fitness, health, and well-being; and recognizing people regularly for their AC4P behavior is consistent with cultivating an AC4P culture of compassion.

"T" for "trackable" reflects the need to track your progress toward attaining a process goal. This implies, of course, that goal-relevant behaviors can be counted successively as the participants get closer to realizing their process goal. For example, interpersonal coaching sessions are tallied and posted on a chart for team members to observe; every two-hour exercise routine completed is marked on the calendar; and occurrences of AC4P behavior are indicated on a spreadsheet that includes a space to specify the particular AC4P behavior rewarded.

Sharing Your Goal. Finally, "S" for "share" means it's useful to share your process goal with others. Public announcement of a group or individual goal increases commitment to work toward reaching that goal. And when others know your laudable goal and realize value in accomplishing that goal, they will likely help to support your progress.

For example, you might anticipate friends asking you about your goal-directed behavior, and such expected social accountability could enhance your self-motivation. In fact, just seeing those individuals who know about your goal can serve as a reminder to stay on course. You anticipate the question, "How's your goal progress these days," and you want to answer, "Very well, thank you."

So it's beneficial (a) for a work team to announce their coaching goals to other teams; (b) to tell others of a fitness-routine goal; and (c) for leaders of an AC4P movement to share their recognition goals with other advocates of an AC4P culture.

Observational learning is a positive side effect of such goal sharing. When others interested in the mission implied by your goal learn about your goal setting and view your progress, they might consider setting a similar goal for themselves or their team. Your shared goal setting and progress sets an impressive example for others to follow. This was a beneficial result of the following goal-setting story.

Joanne's AC4P Story. Five years ago, Joanne Dean made a New Year's resolution to perform an AC4P behavior every day until her sixtieth birthday on March 27. She announced her goal to family and friends, including leaders of our campus AC4P Movement. She also described each of her AC4P behaviors on the Website ac4p.org. I hope it's obvious this was a SMARTS process goal. Joanne knew she was setting a "stretch goal," but it was actually more challenging than she had expected. It took significant planning, preparation, and time to achieve daily AC4P behaviors, which varied widely from cooking meals and shoveling snow for neighbors to giving gift certificates to individuals she observed providing noteworthy community service.

Daily sharing of her AC4P actions sustained social support for her commitment and set an impressive example many AC4P advocates have attempted to emulate on a smaller scale.

For example, we periodically initiate the "AC4P Challenge" among the fifty to ninety research students in our Center for Applied Behavior Systems. We evaluate whether students can attain the goal of performing five intentional AC4P acts in one week. "If Joanne can do sixty in sixty," we say, "then surely you can accomplish five AC4P acts in seven days." Most students willingly sign an AC4P commitment card for the AC4P Challenge, but less than 50 percent report meeting this seemingly easy goal. Actively caring on a daily basis is easier said than done when AC4P behavior is defined as going beyond the norm to benefit the health, safety, or well-being of another person.

7. Use Behavior-Based Feedback and Rewards

Supervisors, teachers, and parents are more likely to notice and reprimand undesirable behavior than to discern and acknowledge desirable behavior. This is why the term *feedback* carries negative connotations. What is one to think if asked, "Can I give you some feedback about your behavior last night?"? Likewise, how do you feel after receiving an email from your supervisor saying he wants you to come to his office at the end of the day for some feedback? Has your day been ruined? For many of us, the illustration on the next page rings true.

Most people expect feedback to be more negative than positive. Of course, that perception can be changed if supervisors, teachers, and parents

verbalize more *supportive* than corrective feedback. Suppose a supervisor or teacher who asked to see you at the end of the day for a feedback session gives you only supportive feedback. She defines specific desirable behaviors she has observed you perform, and expresses genuine appreciation for the extra effort you consistently demonstrate to apply your notable skill sets on behalf of the organization's mission.

How would that make you feel? Would "feedback" take on a more positive meaning, at least with this supervisor? Would you share this positive experience with others and likely enhance others' perception of "feedback" and this supervisor's leadership skills? That's the power of interpersonal recognition and approval in cultivating a self-motivated AC4P culture.

If–Then Rewards. Use *if–then incentive/reward contingencies* when individuals are not already self-motivated to perform the desired behavior or intrinsic (i.e., natural) reinforcers are not available. This does not mean the if–then incentive/reward contingencies are bad or undesirable, as some uninformed authors have claimed.[24] Extrinsic rewards influence many behaviors and this is not detrimental to self-motivation; they just might not increase it. For example, I choose certain airlines and hotels in order to earn "points" that can translate to material rewards or improved service. My awareness of this "manipulation tactic" does not impact my disposition in any negative way. In fact, I'm pleased to be extrinsically rewarded for making certain choices. Indeed, knowing I can choose the airline or hotel that offers the if–then rewards has a beneficial impact on my overall self-motivation.

In the same view, it's not detrimental to reward students for performing certain behaviors relevant to their education, as authors uneducated in ABS have claimed.[24] The child who doesn't choose to read books, for example, cannot experience the inherent enjoyment (i.e., the intrinsic reinforcement) of reading. In this case, an if–then contingency can be invaluable. The child is extrinsically rewarded for performing a behavior previously emitted only infrequently. Subsequently, the child may enjoy reading, especially after s/he starts to feel competent at this worthwhile task. Then self-motivation takes control, and extrinsic incentives are no longer needed.

Now-That Rewards. At times, special rewards for excellence are given to individuals and groups for excelling at performance in a given domain, from accomplishments in teaching and learning to winning an athletic competition. These extrinsic consequences are well received, often to the applause of an approving audience. Such acknowledgment does wonders to an individual's sense of personal competence, leading to more self-motivation to sustain or even enhance the relevant skill set.

These examples of rewarding desirable behavior reflect a now-that contingency rather than if–then. These rewards do not include an incentive (i.e., the announcement of the availability of a reward if a designated behavior occurs). The behavior might be initiated for a variety of internal, intrinsic, or extrinsic reasons, but the unannounced *now-that* reward is given after the behavior occurs in order to support its occurrence. In some cases, this rewarding consequence increases the probability that the desirable behavior will recur. In most cases, a person's sense of competence increases following sincere *now-that rewards*, thereby fueling self-motivation to continue the rewarded behavior.

Behavior-Based Recognition. In the workplace, managers should intermittently communicate one-on-one with employees to express sincere appreciation for their specific behaviors that contribute to the organization. In school, teachers' one-on-one praise of their students' work is invaluable for boosting self-competence, confidence, and self-motivation. And every parent knows through personal experience the motivational benefits of demonstrating enthusiastic approval of a child's dedication to do well at a particular task.

Unfortunately, words of approval, appreciation, and praise are relatively rare, especially when compared with the use of verbal reprimands, as experience has taught us. Mistakes or disruptive behaviors stick out and invite corrective action; but desirable behavior does not naturally attract attention and seemingly does not require intervention.

8. Give Corrective Feedback Well

By now you certainly see the special advantages of supportive feedback in enhancing self-motivation, right? Still, there are times when it's necessary to correct undesirable behavior. How should this be done? Make use of empathy and compassion to correct undesirable behavior. Be nondirective, actively listen to excuses, and emphasize the positive over the negative. Still it can be uncomfortable to provide others with behavior-based corrective feedback, even when the recipient of your feedback is a family member or friend.

Remind yourself and the feedback recipient that only with specific behavioral feedback can performance be improved. Remember, practice does not make perfect unless the performer receives supportive feedback for right behavior and corrective feedback for wrong behavior. Incorrect or unsafe behavior is not an indictment of a person's attitude, values, or personality. Our unintentional mistakes do not reflect who we are. So it's critical to emphasize that your corrective feedback is only about behavior you have observed and is not a judgment of the person.

Continuous improvement occurs when observers have the courage to give relevant behavior-based feedback and when those observed have the humility to accept the feedback and make relevant behavioral adjustments. After all, we all want to improve behavior that's important to us, and this often requires behavioral feedback from others.

How should you approach someone to give corrective feedback? Your initial words are critical. If you come on too strong when directing a person to improve in a certain way, the "victim" may get defensive and offer excuses for a mistake. Or, if the observer has relevant authority over the victim, which is often the case, the victim might make the behavioral adjustments called for; but the change will not stick if the victim does not agree with and accept the behavioral advice.

How can you get buy-in for the behavioral feedback you have the courage to offer? Your opening words should be inquisitive rather than accusative. If the feedback targets a person's unsafe behavior, my good friend John Drebinger recommends beginning with a question like, "Could I look out for your safety?"[25] Who could say no to a request like this? Then, following a "Yes, of course," the observer mentions the behavior that needs adjustment for injury prevention. Often it's best if the observer can mention some desirable behavior first and then suggest where there's room for improvement.

My business partners at Safety Performance Solutions (www .safetyperformance.com) have been teaching behavioral coaching for occupational health and safety for two decades, and they've always emphasized the need to be empathic and nondirective when giving co-workers behavior-based feedback.[26] More specifically, an AC4P observer of a certain worker completes a critical behavior checklist (CBC) of safe versus at-risk behavior, previously designed through interactive group discussions among line workers representative of the relevant workforce.[27] Workers give permission to be observed, and they know what behaviors are being observed. Even with this set up, at-risk behaviors are often observed and observers are challenged to offer corrective feedback to a co-worker.

How do they do this? From the start it's emphasized that the observer (unlike a typical athletic coach) is not responsible for directing or motivating corrective action. The observer merely completes the CBC and then shows the results to the person observed. The two workers might discuss environmental or system factors that discourage safe behavior and encourage at-risk behavior. And they might consider ways to remove barriers to safe behavior. The observer, referred to as an AC4P coach, might offer positive words of approval to recognize certain safe behavior, but will make no disapproving statements or directives related to any observed at-risk behavior.

An AC4P coach is nondirective when communicating corrective feedback. The coach provides specific behavior-based feedback for the person observed to consider. There is no pressure to change. The only accountability is self-accountability. Any adjustment in behavior is self-motivated, activated by the results of a nonintrusive and anticipated application of a CBC. As explained earlier, the perception of personal choice increases the likelihood this kind of corrective feedback will be accepted and lead to a self-motivated behavioral adjustment. Workers choose to be observed by an AC4P coach and then choose to accept or reject the feedback provided by a CBC. (More details of this AC4P approach to the prevention of occupational injuries are given in Chapter 9.)

9. Celebrate to Increase a Sense of Community

Celebrations, when done correctly, can motivate teamwork and build a sense of belongingness and community among groups of individuals, boosting their self-motivation. Of course, the key words in the preceding sentence are "when done correctly." Let's consider seven guidelines for celebrating group accomplishments.

Reward the Right Behavior. In the domain of occupational safety, it's common for organizations to give groups of employees a celebration dinner after a particular number of weeks or months pass with no recordable injury. This kind of achievement is certainly worth celebrating, but let's be sure the record was reached fairly. If people cheat to win by not reporting their injuries, the celebration won't mean much.

If a celebration for a lower incidence of injuries is announced as an incentive, the motivation to cheat is increased. If employees are promised a reward when they work a certain number of days without an injury, it will be tempting to avoid reporting a personal injury if they can get away with it. This is, of course, peer pressure to cheat – a situation that reduces interpersonal trust and promotes a belief that improved levels of organizational safety cannot be reached fairly.

If the accomplishment of process activities is celebrated, then it's okay to establish an if–then behavior–consequence contingency, as discussed earlier. In this case, the behaviors the group needs to perform are specified in order to warrant a celebration. This is group goal setting. If the SMARTS principles discussed earlier are followed, teamwork for goal accomplishment will be motivated.

A group might decide to celebrate after everyone reports one observation of an AC4P behavior, or when every group member performs an AC4P behavior, or after the total number of AC4P behaviors observed and performed by the group members reaches a designated total. In these cases, a SMARTS group goal is set and progress is monitored. When the goal is reached, a celebration is warranted. It was earned for the completion of a successful journey, destined to eventually achieve an AC4P culture of compassion.

Focus on the Journey. Most of the corporate celebrations I've seen were for excellence in safety, and all of these gave far too little attention to the journey – the processes that contributed to reaching the milestone. Typically, the focus was on the end result, the outcome measure, like achieving zero injuries for a certain period of time. There was scant discussion about *how* the outcome was achieved. It's natural to toast the bottom line, but there's more to be gained from taking the opportunity to diagnose and recognize process success.

When you pinpoint processes instrumental to reaching a particular milestone, you give valuable direction and motivation. Participants learn what to continue doing for an effective journey. Those responsible for the behaviors leading to the celebrated outcome receive a special boost in competence, personal control, and optimism. Plus, information is added to these individuals' internal recognition scripts that in turn enhances their self-motivation.

Perhaps the most important reason to acknowledge journey activities leading to a noteworthy group outcome is that it gives credit where credit is due. Focusing on the process endorses the people and their competent actions that made the difference, fueling self-motivation. This leads to the next guideline.

Recipients Should Be Participants. Rarely do participants in a celebratory event discuss the processes they supported in order to reach the outcome.

And so a valuable teaching moment is missed. Instead, speeches from top management often kick off a corporate celebration. Sometimes charts are displayed to compare the past with the improved present. Often a sincere request for continuous improvement is made, and a manager points out the amount of money saved or profits earned by the group's accomplishment. Sometimes promises for a bigger celebration are made following continued success. Occasionally a motivational speaker or humorist gives everyone a lift and some laughs. Often special rewards are given to individuals or team captains, along with a handshake from a top management official. Certificates and trinkets might be handed out, along with a steak dinner.

In the typical corporate celebration, management gives and the employees receive – certainly an impressive show of top-down support. But the ceremony would be more memorable and beneficial as both a learning and a motivational opportunity if employees were more participants than recipients. Managers should listen more than speak, and employees should talk more about their experiences than listen to managers' satisfaction with the bottom line.

Relive the Journey. Managers should facilitate discussion of the activities that led to the celebrated accomplishment. The procedures that made the journey successful should be relived. This "reenactment" strengthens the participants' internal scripts that direct and motivate their ongoing support of the effective process. Managers who listen to these discussions with genuine interest and concern are rewarding the participation that enabled the success, and they're empowering employees to continue their journey toward higher-level achievement.

The best safety celebration I ever observed was planned by employees and featured a series of brief presentations by teams of hourly workers. Numerous safety ideas were shared. Some workers showed off new personal protective equipment, some displayed graphs of data obtained from environmental or behavioral audits, some discussed their procedures for encouraging reports of close calls and implementing corrective action, and one group presented its ergonomic analysis and redesign of a workstation.

Even the after-dinner entertainment was employee-driven. A skit illustrated safety issues. A talent show had entrants from all levels of the organization, including top managers. There was no need to hire a live band– a number of talented musicians were found in the workforce of six hundred. Luckily, they didn't find a drummer, allowing me to sit in and relive my rock 'n' roll gigging from the 1960s.

Discuss Successes and Failures. The work teams in this celebration discussed both successes and failures, displaying the positive results and recalling disappointments, dead ends, and frustrations. Pointing out the highs and lows made their presentations realistic and underscored the amount of dedication needed to complete their projects and contribute to the celebrated reduction in injuries.

Presentations that point out hardships along the journey to success justify the celebration. The celebrated bottom line was not a matter of luck. It took hard work by many people going beyond the call of duty. The payoff: small-win contributions, pronounced interdependence, win-win collaboration, and synergy.

Make It Memorable. Goal attainment is meaningful and memorable when people discuss the difficulties of reaching a goal. When managers listen to these presentations with sincere interest and appreciation, the event becomes even more significant and credible. And when a tangible reward is distributed appropriately at such an occasion, a mechanism is established to sustain the memory of this occasion and promote its value. Ideally, the memento should include words, perhaps a theme or slogan, that reflect the particular celebration. The tangible rewards should be something readily displayable or usable at work – from coffee mugs, placards, and pencil holders to caps, shirts, and umbrellas, for example.

When these keepsakes are delivered, it should be noted that they were selected "to help you remember this special occasion and what it has meant to all of us. This small token of our appreciation will remind us how we got here." One week after the safety celebration I described here, every participant received a framed group photograph of everyone who attended the event. That picture hangs in my office today, and every time I look at it, I'm reminded of the time several years ago when management did more listening than talking in a most memorable and educational group celebration.

Don't Neglect Your Leaders. In every group project, some individuals take charge and champion the effort, while others sit back and "go with the flow." Some people exert less effort when working with a group than when working alone. Psychologists call this phenomenon *social loafing*.[28]

So recognize the champions of a group effort one-on-one, and let them know you realize the importance of their leadership in a team accomplishment. You appreciate their extra-effort contributions. This positive consequence adds substantially to the self-motivation these individuals had already received from the earlier group celebration. As a result, you've increased the likelihood of their continued leadership for attaining further goals.

Solicit Ideas. When I mentioned to my graduate students I was writing a book chapter on how to celebrate, one of them quickly responded, "That's easy, a hundred-dollar bottle of cognac, a six-dollar cigar, and a special friend." I had to tell him, of course, my focus was on a different kind of celebrating. But it occurred to me that everyone has his/her own way of celebrating. And when it comes to group celebration, we often inadvertently impose our prejudices on others. We usually don't take the time to ask potential participants what kind of celebration party they would like.

When it comes to organizing a group celebration, many people don't know how to celebrate. Ask people what they want for their celebration, and the discussion likely focuses on tangible rewards. "What material commodity should we receive for our efforts?" This puts the celebration in a payoff-for-behavior mode and is not the real purpose of a group celebration. You want a meaningful and memorable event that increases a sense of belonging and community and can serve as a stepping-stone to even greater achievements.

10. Build Interpersonal Trust

To cultivate an AC4P culture, interpersonal trust is absolutely fundamental. Trust is the foundation for building a community of people who go beyond the call of duty to give each other behavior-based support and relevant corrective feedback. Seven C-words capture the essence of building interpersonal trust and interdependence: communication, caring, candor, consistency, commitment, consensus, and character. Let's consider how each of these C-words implicates interpersonal trust and community-building. The phrase associated with each C-word summarizes the key definitions given in my *American Heritage* and *New Merriam-Webster* dictionaries.[29]

Communication – *exchange of information or opinion by speech, writing, or signals.* What people say and how they say it influence our trust in both their capability and their intentions. As you've already heard many times, the way something is said, including intonation, pace, facial expressions, hand gestures, and overall posture, has a greater impact than what was actually said. And you've certainly experienced personal feelings of trust toward another person change as the result of how that individual communicated information.

Often we trust certain information because we respect the credentials of the communicator or we like the way the message is displayed. Personal

opinion or common sense is relied on if the message sounds good to us and is well presented– with clarity, confidence, and charisma. Those three C-words suggest how we get others to trust our knowledge, skill, or ability. But what about trusting one's intentions? Do you know people who have impressive credentials and communicate elegantly, but something makes you suspicious of their intentions? You believe they know what to do, but you're not convinced they will do what they say. They have the right talk but give the impression they don't walk it. This critical issue is reflected in each of the subsequent C-words for trust-building.

However, before moving on to the other C-words, let's consider the most powerful communication strategy for increasing trust in one's intentions – AC4P listening. There is probably no better way to earn someone's trust in your intentions than by listening attentively to that person's communication with an AC4P mindset. When you listen to others first before communicating your own perspective, you not only increase the chance they will reciprocate and listen to you, you also learn how to present your message for optimal understanding, appreciation, and buy-in.

Caring – *showing concern about or interest in what happens.* When people believe you sincerely care about them, they will care about what you tell them. They trust you will look out for them when applying your knowledge, skills, or abilities. They trust your intentions because they believe you care.

You communicate AC4P and build interpersonal trust when you ask questions about a particular task or set of circumstances. Questions targeting a specific aspect of a person's job send the signal that you care about him/ her. This communication is more credible than the general "How ya doing?" greeting. Take the time to learn what others are doing. Listen and observe. Here we're talking about "listening to the talk, and walking the talk." You want to "walk the talk" so people trust your intentions.

Candor – *straightforwardness and frankness of expression; freedom from prejudice.* We trust people who are frank and open with us. People who don't beat around the bush. When they don't know an answer to our questions, they tell us outright they don't know and they'll get back to us with an answer.

You have reason to mistrust individuals if their interactions with you reflect prejudice or the tendency to judge blindly. You question their ability to evaluate others and their intentions to treat people fairly. When people give an opinion about others because of their race, religion, gender, or birthplace, you should doubt these individuals' ability to make people-related decisions. And you should wonder whether their intentions to perform on behalf of another individual will be biased or tainted by a tendency to prejudge people on the basis of overly simple and usually inaccurate stereotypes.

Consistency – *agreement among successive acts, ideas, or events*. Consistency is a key determinant of interpersonal trust. Perhaps the *fastest* way to destroy interpersonal trust is to not follow through on an agreement. This is also the *easiest* way to stifle trust. How often do we make a promise we don't keep? Most promises are if–then contingencies. We specify that a certain consequence will follow a certain behavior. Whether the consequence is positive or negative, trust is diminished when the behavior is not rewarded or punished as promised.

When my daughters were young, I frequently caught myself impulsively making promises (or policy statements) I didn't keep. For example, when they misbehaved while their mom and I were packing the car for a trip, it was not uncommon for one of us to say, "Stop doing that right now or we're not going." Often our daughters stopped the undesirable behavior. The "policy maker" was then reinforced for making the promise.

But what happened when my daughters didn't stop their misbehavior or resumed the undesirable behavior after a brief hiatus? Sure, we still made the trip. The punishment contingency might be shouted a few more times, but regardless, we eventually piled into our car and took off. What did these empty threats teach our daughters?

We would have been far better off promising a less severe negative consequence we could implement consistently, such as delaying the trip until the behavior stopped. "We can't go until you stop fighting" would have been much better than a more severe if–then threat with inconsistent consequences. Chapter 15 on AC4P parenting provides more examples of effective versus ineffective contingency management by caregivers of children.

Commitment – *bound emotionally or intellectually to a course of action*. When you follow through on a promise or pledge to do something, you tell others they can count on you. You can be trusted to do what you say you will do.

The consistency principle reflects a spiral of causality and explains how behavior influences attitude, and vice versa. When we choose to do something, we experience internal pressure to maintain a personal belief system or attitude consistent with that behavior. And when we have a certain belief system or attitude toward something, we tend to behave in ways consistent with such beliefs or attitudes. This critical AC4P principle is discussed in greater detail in Chapter 6.

Commitment and total involvement result from a causal spiraling of action feeding attitude, then attitude feeding more action, which strengthens the attitude and leads to more behavior. Researchers have found three ways to make an initial commitment to do something lead to the most causal spiraling and total involvement.[30] First, people live up to what they write down, so ask for a signed statement of a commitment. Second, the more public the commitment, the greater the relevant attitude and behavior change, presumably because social pressures are added to the personal pressure to be consistent in word and deed.

Third, and perhaps most important, for a public and written commitment to initiate causal spiraling of behavior supporting attitude (and vice versa), the commitment must be viewed as a personal choice. When people believe their commitment was their idea, the consistency principle is activated. But when people believe their commitment was unduly influenced by outside factors, they do not feel a need to live up to what they were coerced to write down.

Consensus – *agreement in opinion, testimony, or belief.* Whenever the results of a group decision-making process come across as win-lose, some mistrust is going to develop. A majority of the group might be pleased, but others will be discontented and might actively or passively resist involvement. And even the "winners" could feel diminished interpersonal trust. "We won this decision, but what about next time?" And without solid backup support for the decision, the outcome will be less than desired. "Without everyone's buy-in, commitment and involvement, we can't trust the process to come off as expected."

How can group consensus be developed? How can the outcome of a heated debate be perceived as a win-win solution everyone supports? Consensus-building takes time and energy, and requires candid, consistent, and caring communication among all members of a discussion or decision-making group. When people demonstrate the C-words discussed earlier for building trust in interpersonal dialogue, they also develop consensus and more interpersonal trust regarding a particular decision or action plan.

There's no quick fix for this. It requires plenty of interpersonal communication, including straightforward opinion sharing, intense discussion, emotional debate, active listening, careful evaluation, methodical organization, and systematic prioritizing. But on important matters, the outcome is well worth the investment. When you develop a solution or process that every potential participant can get behind and champion, you have cultivated the degree of interpersonal trust needed for total involvement. Involvement in turn builds personal commitment, more interpersonal trust, and then more involvement.

Character – *the combined moral or ethical structure of a person or group; integrity; fortitude.* Generally, a person with "character" is considered honest, ethical, and principled. People with character are credible or worthy of another person's trust because they display confidence and competence. They know who they are; they know where they want to go; and they know how to get there.

All of the strategies discussed here for cultivating a trusting culture are practiced by a person with character. Individuals with character are willing to admit vulnerability. They are humble and realize they aren't perfect and need behavioral feedback from others. They know their strengths and weaknesses, and find exemplars to model.

By actively listening to others and observing their behaviors, individuals with character learn how to improve their own performance. And if they're building a high-performance team, they can readily find people with knowledge, skills, and abilities to complement their own competencies. They know how to make diversity work for them, their group, and the entire organization.

Having the courage to admit your weaknesses means you're willing to apologize when you've made a mistake and to ask for forgiveness. There is probably no better way to build trust between individuals than to own up to an error that might have affected another person. Of course, you should also indicate what you will do better next time or ask for specific advice on how to improve. This kind of vulnerability enables you to heed the powerful enrichment principle I learned from the late Frank Bird, "Good, better, best; never let us rest until our good is better; and our better best."[31]

While admitting personal vulnerability is a powerful way to build interpersonal trust, the surest way to reduce interpersonal trust is to tell one person about the weakness of another. In this situation it's natural to think, "If he talks that way about her, I wonder what he says about me behind my back." It's obvious how criticizing or demeaning others in their absence can lead to interpersonal suspiciousness and mistrust.

Backstabbing leads to more backstabbing, and eventually you have a work culture of independent people doing their own thing, fearful of making an error and unreceptive to any kind of behavior-based feedback. Key

aspects of continuous performance improvement – team-building, inter-personal observation, and coaching – are extremely difficult or impossible to implement in such a culture. Under these circumstances it's necessary to first break down barriers to interpersonal trust before implementing a behavior-based observation and feedback process.

Start to build interpersonal trust by implementing a policy of no back-stabbing. People with character, as defined here, always talk about other people as if they can hear you. In other words, to replace interpersonal mistrust with trust, never talk about other individuals behind their backs unless you're willing to say the same thing directly to them.

A Summary

The seven C-words offer distinct directives for AC4P trust-building behav-ior. *Communicating* these guidelines to others in a *candid* and *caring* way opens up the kind of dialogue that starts people on a journey of AC4P trust-building. Then people need to give each other *consistent* and *can-did* feedback regarding those behaviors that reflect these trust-building principles.

With *character* and *commitment,* they need to recognize others for doing it right and offer corrective feedback when there's room for improvement. And of course it's critical for the recipient of such *candid* behavior-based feedback to accept it with *caring* appreciation and a *commitment* to improve.

Then, the feedback recipient needs to have the *character* to thank the observer for the feedback, even when the *communication* is not all positive and is not delivered well. S/he might offer feedback on how to make the behavior-based feedback more useful. Dialogue like this is necessary to build *consensus* and sustain a journey of continuous AC4P trust and community-building.

IN CONCLUSION

An AC4P culture requires people to do the right thing on behalf of other people when no other person is holding them accountable. Such self-accountability and self-direction to perform AC4P behavior usually requires self-motivation. Although the initial proponents of self-motivation did not connect self-motivation with behavioral consequences,[32] this critical connection was indicated throughout this chapter. With this perspective, consequences that reflect personal choice, competence, and/or a sense of social support or community should enhance self-motivation and thereby increase the durability of a behavior-change intervention. Thus, an intervention that applies a positive consequence to increase the occurrence or improve the quality of AC4P behavior should have a longer-term impact if the intervention inspires self-motivation by linking the behavioral consequence with a perception of choice, competence, and/or community.

This research-based chapter introduced a number of practical ways to facilitate the self-motivation needed to achieve and sustain an AC4P culture. Throughout this book a number of real-world examples of the self-motivation principles and leadership lessons reviewed here are given, as are practical ways to use these principles and lessons for enhancing people's self-motivation to actively care for the health, safety, education, and well-being of others.

DISCUSSION QUESTIONS

1. Define self-motivation from a behavioral perspective. In other words, how can an observer determine objectively if another person is self-motivated?

2. Explain the three perceptions that influence self-motivation and provide examples from personal experience.
3. When is feedback a positive versus a negative reinforcer? Support your answer with real-world examples or personal experience.
4. Explain the meaning of this quotation from W. Edwards Deming: "Don't blame people for problems caused by the system."
5. What's wrong with the phrase "random acts of kindness"?
6. Explain the six components of SMARTS goals with a practical example.
7. The ABC model of behavioral science presumes behavior is *directed* by activators (or antecedent events) and *motivated* by consequences. Does this mean goal setting provides only direction and no motivation? Please explain.
8. Distinguish between "if–then" and "now-that" rewards with real-world examples.
9. List the components of a group celebration designed to promote a sense of group cohesion and to motivate employee inclusion and engagement.
10. Discuss the critical concept of interpersonal trust with reference to the following seven C-words: communication, caring, candor, consistency, commitment, consensus, and character.

REFERENCES

1. Chance, P. (2007). The ultimate challenge: Prove B. F. Skinner wrong. *Behavior Analyst, 30*, 153–160.
2. Deci, E. L. (1975). *Intrinsic motivation.* New York: Plenum; Deci, E. L., & Flaste, R. (1995). *Why we do what we do: Understanding self-motivation.* New York: Penguin Books; Deci, E. L., & Ryan, R. M. (1995). *Intrinsic motivation and self-determinism in human behavior.* New York: Plenum; Ryan, R. M., & Deci, E. L. (2000). Self-determinism theory and the foundation of intrinsic motivation, social development, and well-being. *American Psychologist, 55*, 68–75.
3. Deci, E. L., & Flaste, R. (1995). *Why we do what we do: Understanding self-motivation.* New York: Penguin Books, p. 9.
4. Geller, E. S. (2001). *The psychology of safety handbook.* Boca Raton, FL: CRC Press; Ludwig, T. D., & Geller, E. S. (2001). *Intervening to improve the safety of occupational driving: A behavior-change model and review of empirical evidence.* New York: Haworth Press; Monty, R. A., & Perlmuter, L. C. (1975). Persistence of the effect of choice on paired-associate learning. *Memory & Cognition, 3*, 183–187; Perlmuter, L. C., Monty, R. A., & Kimble, G. A. (1971). Effect of choice on paired-associate learning. *Journal of Experimental Psychology, 91*, 47–58; Steiner, I. D. (1970). Perceived freedom. In L. Berkowitz (Ed.). *Advances in experimental social psychology*, Vol. 5 (pp. 187–248). New York: Academic Press.
5. Geller, E. S., & Veazie, R. A. (2010). *When no one's watching: Living and leading self-motivation.* Newport, VA: Make-A-Difference.

6. Geller, E. S. (1994). Ten principles for achieving a Total Safety Culture. *Professional Safety*, 39(9), 18–25; Geller, E. S. (2001). *The psychology of safety handbook*. Boca Raton, FL: CRC Press; Geller, E. S. (2005). *People-based safety: The source*. Virginia Beach, VA: Coastal Training Technologies; Geller, E. S. (2008). *Leading people-based safety: Enriching your culture*. Virginia Beach, VA: Coastal Training Technologies.

7. White, R. W. (1959). Motivation reconsidered: The concept of competence. *Psychological Review*, 66, 297–321.

8. Deci, E. L., & Flaste, R. (1995). *Why we do what we do: Understanding self-motivation*. New York: Penguin Books, p. 66.

9. Chance, P. (2008). *The teacher's craft: The 10 essential skills of effective teaching*. Long Grove, IL: Waveland Press, p. 95.

10. Geller, E. S. (1996). *The psychology of safety: How to improve behaviors and attitudes on the job*. Radnor, PA: Chilton; Geller, E. S. (1998). *Understanding behavior-based safety: Step-by-step methods to improve your workplace* (2nd ed.). Neenah, WI: J. J. Keller & Associates; Geller, E. S. (2001). *The psychology of safety handbook*. Boca Raton, FL: CRC Press; Geller, E. S. (2005). *People-based safety: The source*. Virginia Beach, VA: Coastal Training and Technologies; Geller, E. S., Perdue, S. R., & French, A. (2004).Behavior-based safety coaching: Ten guidelines for successful application. *Professional Safety*, 49(7), 42–49; Krause, T. R., Hidley, J. H., & Hodson, S. J. (1996). *The behavior-based safety process: Managing improvement for an injury-free culture* (2nd ed.). New York: Van Nostrand Reinhold; McSween, T. E. (2003). *The values-based safety process: Improving your safety culture with a behavioral approach* (2nd ed.). New York: Van Nostrand Reinhold; Weigand, D. M. (2007). Exploring the role of emotional intelligence in behavior-based safety coaching. *Journal of Safety Research*, 38, 391–398.

11. Deci, E. L., & Flaste, R. (1995). *Why we do what we do: Understanding self-motivation*. New York: Penguin Books, p. 88.

12. Geller, E. S. (1994). Ten principles for achieving a Total Safety Culture. *Professional Safety*, 39(9), 18–25; Geller, E. S. (2001). *The psychology of safety handbook*. Boca Raton, FL: CRC Press; Geller, E. S. (2005). *People-based safety: The source*. Virginia Beach, VA: Coastal Training Technologies.

13. Block, P. (2008). *Community: The structure of belonging*. San Francisco: Berrett-Koehler.

14. Peck, M. S. (1979). *The different drum: Community making and peace*. New York: Simon & Schuster.

15. Deming, W. E. (1986). *Out of the crisis*. Cambridge, MA: Massachusetts Institute of Technology, Center for Advanced Engineering Study; Deming, W. E. (1993). *The new economics for industry, government, education*. Cambridge, MA: Massachusetts Institute of Technology, Center for Advanced Engineering Study.

16. Senge, P. M. (1990). *The fifth discipline: The art and practice of the learning organization*. New York: Doubleday.

17. Covey, S. R. (1989). *The seven habits of highly effective people*. New York: Simon & Schuster.

18. Geller, E. S., & Veazie, R. A. (2009). *The courage factor: Leading people-based culture change*. Virginia Beach, VA: Coastal Training and Technologies.

19. Geller, E. S. (2005). *People-based safety: The source* (pp. 95–98). Virginia Beach, VA: Coastal Training Technologies.

20. United Kingdom Department of Transport (1987). *Killing speed and saving lives.* London: Department of Transport.

21. Deci, E. L., & Flaste, R. (1995). *Why we do what we do: Understanding self-motivation.* New York: Penguin Books, p. 104.

22. Editors of Conari Press (1993). *Random acts of kindness.* Emeryville, CA.

23. Chance, P. (2008). *The teacher's craft: The 10 essential skills of effective teaching.* Long Grove, IL: Waveland Press.

24. Kohn, A. *Punished by rewards: The trouble with gold stars, incentive plans, A's, praise, and other bribes.* Boston: Houghton Mifflin; Pink, D. H. (2009). *Drive: The surprising truth about what motivates us.* New York: Penguin Group.

25. Drebinger, J. W. (2011). *Would you watch out for my safety? Helping others avoid personal injury.* Galt, CA: Wulamoc.

26. Geller, E. S. (2005). *People-based safety: The source.* Virginia Beach, VA: Coastal Training Technologies; Geller, E. S. (2008). *Leading people-based safety: Enriching your culture.* Virginia Beach, VA: Coastal Training Technologies; Geller, E. S., Perdue, S. R., & French, A. (2004). Behavior-based safety coaching: Ten guidelines for successful application. *Professional Safety, 49*(7), 42–49.

27. Geller, E. S. (1998). *Understanding behavior-based safety: Step-by-step methods to improve your workplace* (rev. ed.). Neenah, WI: J. J. Keller & Associates; Geller, E. S. (2001). *The psychology of safety handbook.* Boca Raton, FL: CRC Press; Geller, E. S. (2001). *Working safe: How to help people actively care for health and safety* (2nd ed.). Boca Raton, FL: CRC Press.

28. Latane, B., Williams, K., & Harkins, S. (1979). Many hands make light the work: The causes and consequences of social loafing. *Journal of Personality and Social Psychology, 37*, 822–832.

29. *The American Heritage Dictionary* (1991). Boston: Houghton Mifflin; *The New Merriam-Webster Dictionary* (1989). Springfield, MA: Merriam-Webster Publishers.

30. Cialdini, R. B. (2001). *Influence: Science and practice* (4th ed.). New York: HarperCollins College.

31. Bird, Jr., F. E., & Davies, R. J. (1987). *Commitment.* Loganville, GA: International Loss Control Institute, p. 111.

32. Deci, E. L. (1975). *Intrinsic motivation.* New York: Plenum; Deci, E. L., & Ryan, R. M. (1995). *Intrinsic motivation and self-determinism in human behavior.* New York: Plenum.

4

The Courage to Actively Care

E. SCOTT GELLER

Success is never final and failure is never fatal. It's the courage to continue that counts.

– Winston Churchill

It's often not enough to know what to do in order to actively care effectively (i.e., competence) and to be motivated to perform AC4P behavior (i.e., commitment). The missing ingredient is *courage*. The same five person-states introduced in Chapter 2 as determinants of AC4P behavior are discussed here as precursors to courage.

The simple AC4P intervention strategies presented in this chapter are practical for large-scale application and the achievement of evidence-based benefits. But none have been adopted on a broad scale. Why not? Is it lack of compassion, courage, commitment, competence, self-motivation, or something else? Exploring answers to this question will help us determine the next steps in nurturing an AC4P culture of compassion.

INTERPERSONAL INTERVENTION AND COURAGE

As with any program designed to improve behavior, people could claim they lack the resources and/or time to implement the intervention. They could doubt the effectiveness of the AC4P technique and wonder whether the time to implement the interpersonal intervention is worth the effort. However, these excuses are irrelevant for the techniques described here. Why? Because they are straightforward and easy to accomplish with minimal effort. More important, empirical research has demonstrated the beneficial impact of these simple interpersonal approaches to promoting human welfare and/or preventing harm to people.

Standard excuses for inaction cannot work here. So what is the barrier to large-scale implementation of simple-to-use interpersonal methods that clearly benefit everyone involved?

The key word is *interpersonal*. Each effective intervention method requires personal interaction with other people. It's likely many people lack the courage to intervene as an agent of change. This chapter discusses the level of courage needed and suggests ways to develop that courage in ourselves and others. Bottom line: What does it take for more people to become interpersonal change agents on behalf of the welfare of others? Effortless evidenced-based techniques to help people prevent harm to themselves and others are available, but at this time it seems too few people have the courage to use them.

WHAT IS COURAGE?

The American Heritage Dictionary defines courage as "the state or quality of mind or spirit that enables one to face danger with self-possession, confidence, and resolution."[1] This definition is consistent with the two-page description of courage in Wikipedia (http://en.wikipedia.org/wiki/courage), except that Wikipedia distinguishes between *physical courage* – when one is confronting physical pain, hardship, or threat of death – and *moral courage* – in the face of possible shame, embarrassment, or discouragement.[2]

Leaders certainly need competence and commitment to be effective change agents.[3] But interpersonal intervention to prevent possible harm to a person (i.e., proactive AC4P behavior) takes *moral courage*. A person could have both competence and commitment in a particular situation, but not be courageous. Consider the following two authentic incidents related to AC4P; the first was dramatic and reactive, while the other was temperate and proactive.

Responding to an Emergency

In the midst of a safety meeting, Joanne Dean, the safety director of a large construction firm in New Jersey, was notified of a horrendous "accident." The operator of an industrial equipment truck with an attached auger had been pulled into the auger by the weed mesh under the mulch on which he was standing. The worker chose not to stand on the safety platform provided for this task.

Joanne ran to help the bloody victim, whose body had been severed in half. She assisted the on-site nurse with the AED (automated external defibrillator), covered the body parts with a blanket, and stayed at the scene until the local EMS (emergency medical service) and coroner arrived.

It took commitment to step up and intervene in this horrible casualty. It's likely Joanne's competence as an emergency-response instructor contributed to her propensity to actively care, but her AC4P behavior took more than commitment and competence.

Indeed, three key safety professionals of the company that hired the construction firm chose not to intervene. They stood at a distance and watched Joanne and the other responders. We can assume these experienced, professional bystanders possessed both the competence and commitment required for their leadership positions. But on this day they appeared to lack moral courage.

Responding to a Risky Situation

While waiting in the lobby of a Fortune500 company, Bob Veazie, a safety consultant and former culture-change agent for a Fortune100 company, observed an at-risk behavior. A maintenance worker had climbed to the top of an eight-foot stepladder to change a light bulb. Because, the ladder was not tall enough for this job, the individual was standing with one foot on the top step of the ladder. A co-worker was looking up and talking to the man on the ladder, but he was not holding the ladder steady.

Imagining a serious injury from a fall to the hard marble floor of the lobby, Bob walked to the ladder and called up to the at-risk worker. Holding the bottom of the ladder, he requested that the man come down because "It doesn't seem safe to stand on the top of that ladder." Then he asked whether a longer ladder was available.

Bob Veazie showed moral courage by intervening with this at-risk stranger. Bob could have faced an unpleasant confrontation and been publicly embarrassed or humiliated. Bob's competence and commitment as a safety trainer and consultant certainly contributed to his inclination to speak up. But competence and commitment were not sufficient for the moral courage he showed. In fact, Bob's training partner, who has extensive competence and intense commitment for safety, saw the same at-risk behavior, but she chose not say or do anything about it.

HOW CAN COURAGE BE ENCOURAGED?

Courage is a human characteristic distinct from competence and commitment. But these three qualities of leadership are interdependent to a degree.

Individuals with greater competence and commitment in a given situation are more likely to demonstrate courage. One's propensity to demonstrate courage in certain circumstances is increased whenever relevant competence or commitment is augmented.

Developing Competence

As discussed in Chapter 3, behavior-focused training increases one's competence at a particular task. This involves (a) describing and demonstrating a desirable behavior or skill set, (b) giving specific behavior-based feedback during a participant's role-playing of designated target behaviors, (c) practicing the desired behaviors with both corrective and supportive feedback, and (d) implementing the new competency in real-world situations.[4] When learners teach this skill set to others, their perception of competence increases further, along with their personal commitment.[5]

Developing Commitment

Motivation or commitment to do something is determined by the intrinsic and extrinsic consequences of a task, as well as one's personal interpretation of those consequences.[6] While many tasks are performed for expected soon, certain, and significant consequences, we use self-talk to avoid impulsive reactive behavior and work for long-term goals.[7] Self-talk is also a potential means of overcoming anxiety and reinforcing a commitment to step up and be courageous when called upon.

Cultivating Courage

The moral courage of Joanne and Bob was due to many factors. This suggests that cultivating courage is more complex and less straightforward than developing competence and commitment. For example, both Joanne and Bob are extraverts. They gain energy from interacting with people. Both are naturally outgoing and inclined to communicate with others. They would be described as having excellent "people skills." Another of the "Big Five" personality traits that facilitated the courage of Joanne and Bob is conscientiousness.[8] I know each of them very well, and it's obvious they each carry an AC4P mindset with them at all times – both on and off the job.

Beyond personality *traits*, certain person-*states* increase one's propensity to show AC4P courage. These person-states – self-esteem, self-efficacy, personal control, optimism, and a sense of belongingness – were introduced in Chapter 2, along with ways to enhance these dispositions to increase the probability an individual will perform AC4P behavior.

CULTURE AND THE COURAGE TO ACTIVELY CARE

Many of the factors that influence one's propensity to demonstrate AC4P courage can be filed under the general label *culture*. Certain cultural factors related to the development and cultivation of courage are exhibited daily by people around us. Another real-life story not only illustrates physical courage, but also demonstrates some practical strategies for promoting the moral courage required for the kind of interpersonal intervention needed to achieve an AC4P culture.

Physical Courage to Actively Care

On January 16, 2007, Dr. Kevin Brothers, executive director of the Somerset Hills Learning Institute, was wheeled into St. Barnabas Renal Surgery Center. He was in top physical and mental health, and had never before experienced surgery. He underwent a three-hour surgical procedure – not for himself but for someone else. Dr. Brothers donated his kidney to his mentor and professional colleague, Dr. Patricia Krantz, executive director of the Princeton Child Development Institute. Seven months earlier Dr. Brothers had learned that Dr. Krantz was in severe kidney failure. Without a transplant, she would require dialysis within a few months.

Dr. Krantz was not aware that Dr. Brothers and several other colleagues had agreed to donate one of their kidneys to her. Among all of Dr. Krantz's family, friends, and colleagues who received extensive blood work and tissue sampling, there was only one viable match – Kevin Brothers.

The difference between physical and moral courage is evident in the three real-world incidents described here. When we risk social embarrassment or interpersonal confrontation on behalf of another person's welfare, we show *moral courage*. In contrast, when we risk physical harm to ourselves when looking out for another person's well-being, we demonstrate *physical courage*.[2] While Joanne Dean and Bob Veazie demonstrated moral courage, Kevin Brothers's elective surgery exemplified physical courage.

The AC4P courage of Dr. Brothers was extraordinary. Beyond a number of person-factors, including Dr. Brothers's self-esteem, self-efficacy, personal control, optimism, and sense of belongingness, several cultural factors facilitated this display of courage. Let's consider these cultural factors as potential guidelines for promoting AC4P courage in your culture.

A Group Commitment. Dr. Brothers's first courageous act was to pledge to give one of his kidneys to Dr. Krantz. When Kevin talked with me prior to his surgery, he admitted it was relatively easy to muster the courage to sign the donor pledge. The probability of him being the best antigen match was seemingly low. Surely one of Dr. Krantz's family members would be a better match. Although surprised he was the best match, Dr. Brothers affirmed strong motivation to honor his commitment to the group of potential donors. He acknowledged the value of this two-part approach to motivating his AC4P behavior – first the promise and then the action. This two-step approach is applicable to many situations.

Suppose each member of a work team signed a group declaration to give each other corrective feedback wherever they saw behavior that could jeopardize the quality or the safety of their job. This commitment could be called a "Declaration of Interdependence." In fact this was the label on a large poster at a leadership seminar for supervisors, safety leaders, and maintenance personnel of Delta Airlines.[9] The commitment poster was signed by more than a hundred Delta employees and is prominently displayed in the maintenance workers' break room at the Hartsfield-Jackson International Airport in Atlanta, Georgia. (This practical AC4P intervention is explained further in Chapter 6, along with the theoretical foundation.)

This group obligation, given voluntarily and publicly within a supportive social context, helps to sustain the moral courage required to give behavior-based feedback. Such courage increases the probability that workers will deliver AC4P coaching communications to their peers.

Group Support. Both before and after his surgery, Dr. Brothers received substantial social support for his physical courage. This is often crucial in deciding to move forward in a courageous way. His wife, Debbie, a registered nurse, and their four daughters totally supported Kevin's decision "to move ahead to give *our* kidney as soon as possible." Dr. Brothers said "*our* kidney, because this was a well-informed family decision made with the support of Debbie and our girls." Dr. Brothers's courage was also aided by the dedicated support of friends and colleagues who had pledged to donate a kidney.

Two weeks after successful surgery, Kevin Brothers returned to work. "What an outpouring of support our family received from our school's parents and staff," reported Debbie Brothers. The parents and staff of the Princeton Child Development Institute were also extremely supportive, sending thank you cards to Dr. Brothers for helping to prolong Dr. Krantz's life and enabling her to continue her important work worldwide.

Substantial research reports verify the beneficial impact of social sup-port on human performance, from enhancing motivation to engage in a challenging task to facilitating recovery from physical illness and injury.[10] This factor relates directly to the person-state of belongingness. If you feel you belong to a social network or circle of friends or peers, your inclination to actively care for another individual's health, safety, or general well-being is enhanced. If that AC4P behavior requires an act of courage, strong feel-ings of belonging create a sense of responsibility or obligation to not disap-point the group. Cultivating social support throughout a particular culture is extremely beneficial for increasing the courage factor and the frequency of AC4P behavior. Various interpersonal activities can enhance social support and courage, including team goal setting, interpersonal coaching, collab-orative work projects, and group celebrations (as described in Chapter 3).

A Trusting Culture. When Kevin Brothers honored his pledge to give Patricia Krantz one of his kidneys, his courage was bolstered by his belief that all of the others in his special donor group would follow through on their commitment if they had the best antigen match. He also trusted that the expert medical staff at St. Barnabas's Medical Center would give Dr. Krantz and him the very best healthcare. He expected a successful kid-ney transplant.

The topic of interpersonal trust, including the need to distinguish between trusting an individual's ability and his/her intentions, is addressed in Chapter 3, as well as in other publications.[11] In Chapter 3, specific ways to increase interpersonal trust were illustrated. In addition, you might consider asking colleagues or co-workers how specific events, policies, or communications impact their trust levels and their courage to speak up on behalf of the well-being of others.

Solicit ideas to eliminate barriers to interpersonal trust and nurture courage. Add policies and procedures that could enhance people's percep-tion that they can trust the intentions and abilities of their supervisors and co-workers. A number of practical action plans will likely result from this process, many similar to those suggested in Chapter 3. Still, just the pro-cess of soliciting ways to impact interpersonal trust will have a positive trust-building and courage-building effect.

A Common Worthwhile Purpose. Dr. Brothers and his colleagues in the kidney donor group admired and greatly appreciated the teaching and research of Dr. Patricia Krantz. Indeed, Dr. Krantz has pioneered the application of behavioral science to the treatment of autism, and she men-tored Dr. Brothers while he was a research intern and Ph.D. student. In

Dr. Brothers' words, "Dr. Krantz gave me the opportunity to learn science, and her teachings continue to be the underpinnings of my career ... [and] her guiding me into the field of autism treatment has given more children a chance for a better life."

The group that pledged to donate a kidney for Dr. Krantz had a common and commendable purpose. Likewise, advocates for an AC4P culture have a common and worthwhile mission. In fact, there is perhaps no more esteemed purpose than to actively care for another person's health, safety, and general welfare.

A Family Mindset

It certainly takes more courage to actively care for a stranger than a colleague. In fact, attending to the safety and/or welfare of a family member is usually not even considered courageous but rather an obligation. As proposed in Chapter 2 (see Figure 2.7), when members of a work team think of their co-workers as "family," actively caring for the well-being of these individuals becomes more an act of commitment than one of courage. In other words, the probability of AC4P behavior increases whenever interpersonal behavior supports a family mindset among friends, colleagues, or co-workers. Figure 4.1 illustrates this proposed relationship between the degree of courage needed for interpersonal AC4P behavior and the degree of relatedness or interpersonal connection between the person needing help and the observer.

It's unlikely many readers would undergo elective surgery to give a kidney to a stranger. Fortunately, AC4P does not require the *physical courage* shown by Dr. Brothers.

Indeed, proactive AC4P behavior doesn't require any physical courage – only the *moral courage* to face possible embarrassment, rejection, or conflict when giving feedback or advice to improve another person's behavior or giving personal approval to reward the AC4P behavior of another person. A supportive *family mindset* among people removes the fear of negative consequences from such proactive and behavior-focused AC4P efforts.

Actually, many AC4P behaviors do not require courage; they only present an inconvenience. If you saw a member of your immediate family get behind the steering wheel of a vehicle and neglect to buckle up, you would not hesitate to intervene. Courage would hardly enter the picture. But what would you do if you got into a hotel shuttle van at the airport and noticed that the driver and several passengers had not put on their safety belts?

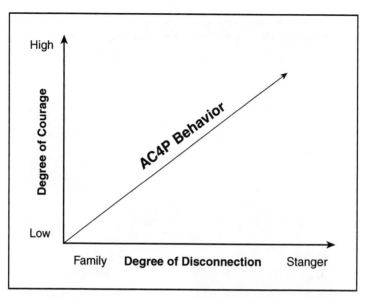

FIGURE 4.1. The amount of courage needed for AC4P behavior as a function of degree of disconnection between the observer and the person in need of assistance.

Would you offer some proactive AC4P corrective feedback? Would you have the moral courage to intervene on behalf of these at-risk strangers?

You have several excuses for not speaking up, right? It's only a short trip to the hotel and the probability of a crash is miniscule. These folks are adults, and if they want to travel at risk, that's their choice. Plus, if you say something about this, another occupant might be offended by your meddling and call you a "safety nerd." So why actively care in this situation? Here's a thought: Consider that your moral courage sets a memorable leadership example. Such behavior could start a constructive AC4P conversation and initiate a ripple effect of AC4P behavior.

Contemplating one's lack of moral courage can activate some disconcerting tension between what an individual thinks s/he *would* do in this and similar situations versus what the person knows s/he *should* do. The more one holds AC4P as a personal value, the greater the tension or cognitive dissonance.[12] Following through with moral courage relieves such tension and exemplifies AC4P leadership.

The following simple and convenient AC4P intervention strategies are straightforward and effortless, and they exemplify the kind of AC4P leadership needed to cultivate an AC4P culture. Question: Do you have the moral courage to apply any of these and encourage others to do the

FIGURE 4.2. Karly prompting an unbuckled driver (top) and thanking a driver for buckling up (bottom).

same? Implementing them on a large scale would move us one step closer to achieving our vision of an AC4P culture of compassion. And for the most part, they really do not require a great amount of courage.

THE FLASH FOR LIFE

Developed initially in 1984 and replicated in several other situations, this rather intrusive but effective intervention merely involves the change agent holding up a card to request a certain safety-related behavior (i.e., vehicle safety belt use); and if the target individual complies, the "flasher" flips the card over to reveal "Thank You." Figure 4.2 depicts a photo of my daughter Karly at age 3½ holding up the 11-by-14-inch sign to an unbuck-led driver at an intersection. When the driver buckled up, she turned over the bright yellow sign with bold black lettering to say thank you. Note the ABC (activator-behavior-consequence) contingency of this intervention.

TABLE 4.1. *Summary of "flash for life" results*[13]

Flasher	Number of observations	Number who looked	Number who buckled	Percentage who looked	Percentage who buckled
		Blacksburg, VA			
Karly, age 3½	179	154	37	86.0	24.0
David, age 5	31	21	5	67.7	23.8
Abby, age 7	68	47	16	69.1	34.0
Carrie, age 7	64	48	9	75.0	18.8
Dane, age 10	56	43	6	76.8	14.0
Hollie, age 22	206	177	43	85.9	24.3
Tim, age 23	183	148	41	80.3	27.6
Total	**787**	**634**	**157**	**80.9**	**24.6**
		Christiansburg, VA			
Tim, age 22	145	123	19	84.8	15.4
Hollie, age 23	155	133	16	85.8	12.0
Total	**300**	**256**	**35**	**85.3**	**13.7**

Here the courage factor is minimized by the physical distance between the actions taking place. In our first study, the "flasher" was positioned in the passenger seat of a vehicle stopped in the left lane at an intersection.[13] Table 4.1 depicts the impact of this simple intervention by specifying the percentage of vehicle drivers who fastened their safety belts after viewing the flashcard. As shown in Table 4.1, seven different vehicle passengers of various ages, ranging from 3.5 to 23, "flashed" a total of 787 unbuckled drivers in Blacksburg, Virginia, home of Virginia Tech, whereas only two of these passengers (i.e., Tim and Hollie) showed the "Flash for Life" card to 300 passengers in the adjacent rural town of Christiansburg, Virginia.

Some drivers did not turn their head to look at the sign, and therefore the compliance percentages are based on only those unbuckled drivers who looked directly at the sign. It's noteworthy that this prompting intervention was more successful in the university town than in Christiansburg (i.e., an average of 24.6 vs. 13.7 percent compliance, respectively). The age of the "flasher" did not have a reliable effect on the driver's compliance with the buckle-up prompt.

It's also noteworthy that this intervention did not result in any verbal or physical harassment, although the "flasher" did get a few hand signals that didn't mean right or left turn. When my daughter asked, "What do they mean, Daddy," I told her they were signaling, "You're number one, they're

TABLE 4.2. *Summary of results from positive versus negative buckle-up prompting*[14]

Intervention Sign	Percentage who buckled up	Percentage of positive hand gestures	Percentage of negative hand gestures	Percentage of positive expressions	Percentage of negative expressions
Flash for Life $n = 895$	33.6	13.2	0.9	25.0	3.9
Click It or Ticket $n = 927$	25.6	7.8	2.6	18.9	9.2

just using the wrong finger." Incidentally, none of these one-finger hand signals came from women.

The first applications of the "Flash for Life" occurred before laws mandating safety belt use were in effect, when only about 20 percent of U.S. drivers buckled up. Twenty years later, with about 80 percent of U.S. drivers using their vehicle safety belts, my students and I compared the impact of a positive reminder ("Please Buckle Up– I Care") with the more common disincentive prompt (i.e., "Click It or Ticket") on both behavioral compliance and body language.[14]

Table 4.2 reveals the percentage of unbuckled drivers who fastened their safety belts after viewing one of the two types of cards. This table also shows the percentage of drivers giving positive versus negative hand signals and facial expressions per type of prompt. It's noteworthy that not only was the positive "I Care" prompt more effective at activating buckle-up behavior than the threatening reminder, it also prompted more positive and less negative body language than did the disincentive message ($p<.05$ in each case).

THE AC4P-BEHAVIOR PROMISE CARD

This nonintrusive and straightforward strategy is suitable for numerous circumstances and target behaviors.[15] It requires little in the way of courage. It has been used effectively to increase the occurrence of specific safety-related behavior (e.g., the use of safety glasses, gloves, and vehicle safety belts),[16] as well as to promote an interdependent AC4P paradigm or mindset.[17]

Based on the powerful social-influence principle of consistency,[18] this behavior-change tactic merely asks participants to sign an individual "promise card" or a "group pledge" that declares an explicit commitment to regularly perform a particular AC4P behavior for a specified period of

AC4P Promise Card

I promise to ______________________________

____

From ______________ until ______________

____

Signature Date

FIGURE 4.3. A generic promise card to activate a behavioral commitment.

time. For maximum behavioral impact, the promise card signing should be public and voluntary. A generic promise card is depicted in Figure 4.3 that can be used to increase the occurrence of various AC4P behaviors.

THE AC4P POLITE LITE

Taking on the negative emotions of road-rage driving would seem to call for a greater degree of courage. But not so in this case. It involves the use of a vehicle light to signal a simple "courtesy code" under relevant conditions. Specifically, one flash means "Please," two flashes reflect "Thank you," and three flashes are used to signal "I am sorry." Vehicle emergency lights can be used to flash this "1-2-3 code," or a small green light as shown in Figure 4.4 can be affixed to the vehicle's rear window and operated with the convenient push of a button.

In a community-wide evaluation of this intervention strategy, the polite-driving code was promoted on radio stations and billboards throughout the town of Christiansburg, Virginia, and "polite lights" were distributed at various workshops. Results were encouraging, but the idea was not adopted. The success of this intervention relied not on courage but on marketing and outreach, and then for people to use the courtesy driving code. Marketing and the minor inconvenience of flashing the courtesy code were key barriers to the large-scale use of this AC4P behavior. More details of our evaluation of this potential "road-rage reducer" are given in Chapter 11.

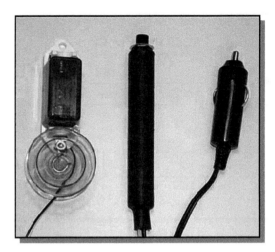

FIGURE 4.4. The three components of the polite lite (light, control button, and plug for cigarette lighter receptacle).

THE AIRLINE LIFESAVER

For this AC4P intervention, some courage is needed for one-on-one inter-action with a stranger. When boarding an airplane, a passenger can hand the 3 by 5 inch card depicted in Figure 4.5 to a flight attendant.

The lifesaver card shown in Figure 4.5 is the first one I used, beginning in 1985. In 1994, I began using an incentive card that offered the flight atten-dants a prize if they read the announcement. The back of this card, depicted in Figure 4.6, specifies an *if–then reward contingency*. Later, I alternated the distribution of these two types of reminders to determine the impact of an incentive intervention.

A seventeen-year study demonstrated substantial compliance with this airline lifesaver request,[19] but no current airline has adopted this simple safety-based intervention. And I know of no individual using this technique consistently when boarding an airplane. When the request was made with-out an incentive (i.e., prompt only), 35.5 percent of 798 recipients read the message. However, when the flight attendant was offered a prize for deliver-ing the buckle-up reminder, 53.3 percent of 245 recipients complied with the request.

Of course, showing that many flight attendants read the buckle-up reminder when asked to do so does not reveal behavior change directly related to people's welfare. Indeed, it is rare to see such direct benefits of proactive efforts to prevent personal injury. However, two behavior-change

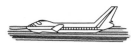

THE AIRLINE LIFESAVER

Airlines have been the most effective promoters of seat belt use. Please, would someone in your flight crew consider announcing a statement like the following neat the end of the flight?

"Now that you have worn a seat belt for the safest part of your trip – the flight crew would like to remind you to buckle-up during your ground transportation."

This announcement will show that your airline cares about transportation safety. And who knows – you might start the buckle-up habit for someone and help save a life! Thank you.

FIGURE 4.5. The first lifesaver card distributed, 1985–1994.

benefits of the airline lifesaver have been documented.[20] In one case, a passenger who heard the buckle-up reminder asked the driver of the airport commuter van to buckle up, claiming, "If a flight attendant can request safety belt use, so can I."

As a second testimony, I received a letter from a passenger who said he used the back-seat safety belt in a taxi cab because he had just heard the buckle-up reminder at the end of his flight. Traveling more than 70 mph, the taxi hydroplaned on a wet road and struck the guardrail. Serious injuries were prevented because this person had buckled up. The letter from this individual is printed in my first book on the behavioral science of safety.[21]

After you read the "buckle-up reminder," a passenger will give you a coupon redeemable for various prizes.

1 coupon $5.00*

2 coupons $15.00

3 coupons.... $30.00

(* Prize equivalent)

For more information call (540)-231-8145
Center for Applied Behavior Systems

FIGURE 4.6. The back of the incentive lifesaver card.

THE DRIVER-TRAINING SCORE CARD

As mentioned earlier, it often requires less moral or physical courage to actively care for family members than for strangers, as in a class of workplace safety trainees. But here is an intervention that has proved successful in both applications. More than fifteen years ago, I documented an effective behavior-change intervention for driver training, which led to numerous adaptations in work settings.[21] Specifically, I worked with my fifteen-year-old daughter to develop a critical behavior checklist (CBC) for driving. As detailed in Chapter 1, this CBC lists a number of driving-related behaviors, along with columns to record whether each behavior is safe or at-risk and a column to write comments relevant to a follow-up feedback session.

While much research and even common sense indicates that this process works to improve safety-related behaviors, I am unaware of a single adoption of this technique for driver education/training. However, this behavior-change technique is the foundation of behavior-based safety (BBS), and there is much empirical support for the BBS approach to increasing safety-related behaviors and preventing injuries.[22] As introduced in Chapter 1, BBS has evolved to people-based safety (PBS) and now to AC4P. More details regarding this approach to cultivating an AC4P culture are given in Chapter 9.

THE TAXI-CAB FEEDBACK CARD

At keynote addresses to large audiences, I have proposed that safety leaders record the safety-related driving behaviors of cab, bus, and limo drivers on a simple observation feedback card and, after the trip, show the results to the driver for valuable behavior-based feedback.[23] A sample feedback card, applicable to numerous driving situations, is shown in Figure 4.7. The top half of the card is given to the driver, while the bottom half has a return address and stamp on the back. This enables tracking of the driver behaviors observed by the passengers of public transport vehicles.

This observation-and-feedback technique reflects another adaption of a basic process of BBS, applied in industries worldwide with remarkable improvements in injury statistics. However, I know of no large-scale application of this evidence-based process for public transportation. It does take substantial moral courage to use this proactive AC4P strategy in taxi cabs, limos, and buses.

THE AC4P THANK YOU CARD

For many years, I have promoted the use of a simple thank you card for delivery to people following their performance of AC4P behavior.[24] In fact, thank you cards have been customized for particular industrial sites and educational settings. For example, I have distributed the Virginia Tech thank you card depicted in Chapter 2 for more than twenty years.

Every semester I make these cards available for my students in introductory psychology classes to use to acknowledge the AC4P behavior of others, but relatively few students take them. Student leaders in our Center for Applied Behavior Systems (CABS) have regularly used this recognition technique for more than two decades, because this recognition process has been institutionalized in our CABS culture. However, beyond applications in CABS, university use of a thank you card is rare.

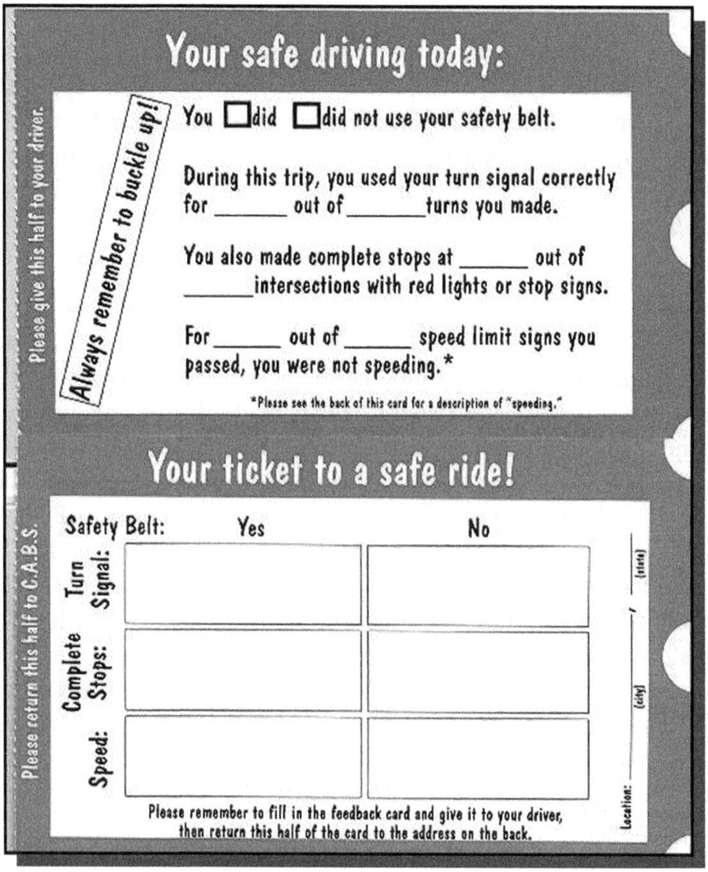

FIGURE 4.7. The feedback card used for taxi-cab drivers.

Given the power, generic applicability, and relative convenience of one-to-one recognition, it's appropriate to end this chapter with evidence-based details about how to give and receive interpersonal recognition. Both prior chapters on the theoretical and research foundation of AC4P refer to one-to-one recognition. In Chapter 2, actively caring thank you cards" were introduced as a way of nurturing a sense of connectedness and an AC4P mindset throughout an organization. In Chapter 3, interpersonal recognition was discussed within the context of supportive feedback to sustain and potentially increase the occurrence of AC4P behavior. Here specific behavioral strategies are offered for delivering and receiving recognition. First, it's critical to understand and believe in the importance of giving quality AC4P recognition.

In terms of the courage factor, it's worth noting that many people are uncomfortable communicating rather intimately on a one-to-one, face-to-face basis regarding their behavioral observations. But the value of this sort of interaction makes it important to use whatever means you have at your disposal to overcome fears of interpersonal interaction. Ask for coaching on this critical skill set. Observe other behavior-focused coaches who are competent at up-close and personal interaction and model techniques that fit your style.

WE LEARN MORE FROM SUCCESS

"We can't learn unless we make mistakes." How many times have you heard this? This might make us feel better about the errors of our ways and provide an excuse for focusing more on people's failures than on their successes, but in reality nothing could be further from the truth.

Behavioral scientists have shown convincingly that success – not failure – produces the most effective learning.[25] Edward Lee Thorndike, for example, studied intelligence at the start of the last century by putting chickens, cats, dogs, fish, monkeys, and humans in situations that called for problem-solving behavior. Then he systematically observed how these organisms learned. He coined the "law of effect" to refer to the fact that learning depends upon behavioral consequences.

When a behavior is followed by a "satisfying state of affairs" the probability of that behavior occurring again increases. But if an "*annoying* state of affairs" follows a behavior, that behavior (considered an error) is less likely to recur.[26] Which kind of consequence – positive or negative – leads to the most learning? Does an error have to occur in order for a problem to be solved? We can reflect on our own experiences to answer these questions. A pleasant consequence gives us direction and motivation to continue the behavior. We know what we did to receive the reward, and are thus motivated to earn another. In contrast, a negative consequence following a mistake only tells us what not to do. It provides no specific direction for problem solving. An overemphasis on a mistake can be frustrating and discouraging, and de-motivate us to continue the learning process.

Errors are not necessary for learning to occur. In fact, when training results in no errors, made possible with certain presentation techniques, learning occurs most smoothly and is most enjoyable. Errors disrupt the teaching/learning process and can lead to a negative attitude, especially if negative social consequences accentuate the mistake. Even subtle reactions to an error – a disappointed face or verbal tone – can increase feelings of helplessness or despair and turn a person off to the entire learning process.

From the courage perspective, the less focus and talk of errors, the less courage is called for. Offering positive consequences (e.g., supportive feedback) requires substantially less courage, right? The antidote to depressed learning from the negative consequences of incorrect behavior is to provide positive consequences for correct behavior. And the most powerful positive consequence to support a learning process is interpersonal recognition – the theme of this discussion. But some attempts to be positive are ineffective, as the illustration below shows.

Before leaving this topic of learning from success versus failure, it's worth noting that Thorndike referred to the type of learning discovered in his problem-solving situations as "trial and accidental success."[27] Many textbook authors have used the term "trial-and-error learning" when describing Thorndike's research, even though Thorndike himself disliked the term because of its inaccurate implications. But let's not focus on this error; rather consider the need to support AC4P behavior with quality recognition. In what follows, seven guidelines are specified for giving such recognition.

1. Be Timely

In order for recognition to provide optimal direction and support, it needs to be associated directly with the desired behavior, as *not* demonstrated in the illustration. This is not necessarily an act of courage, but recognition should be delivered promptly. People need to know what they did to earn the appreciation. Then they might be motivated to continue performing that behavior.

If it's necessary to delay the recognition, the conversation should relive the activity deserving recognition. Talk specifically about the behavior warranting special acknowledgment. Don't hesitate to ask the recipient to recall aspects of the situation and the commendable behavior. This provides the direction and motivation needed to continue the desired behavior.

2. Make It Personal

Recognition is most meaningful when it's perceived as personal. Recognition should not be generic, fit for any situation, as in "Nice job." Rather, it has to be customized to fit a particular individual and circumstance. This happens naturally when the recognition is linked to designated behavior. When you recognize someone, you're expressing personal thanks. Sometimes it's tempting to say "*we* appreciate" rather than "*I* appreciate" and to refer to company gratitude rather than *personal appreciation*. Speaking for the company can come across as impersonal and insincere.

Of course, it's appropriate to reflect value to the organization when giving recognition, but the focus should be personal: "I saw what you did to support our AC4P process and I really appreciate it. Your example illustrates the kind of leadership we need around here to achieve an AC4P culture." This second statement illustrates the next guideline for quality recognition. Again, being positive and proactive shouldn't require that much courage, but some people are not at ease delivering interpersonal praise.

3. Take It to a Higher Level

Recognition is most memorable and inspirational when it reflects a higher-order quality. Adding a universal attitude like leadership, integrity, trustworthiness, or AC4P to your recognition statement makes the recognition more meaningful and thus rewarding. It's important to state the specific behavior first and then make an obvious linkage between the behavior and the positive attribute it reflects.

Our attempts to get college students to recognize others for their AC4P behavior have been less successful than desired. Many claim they didn't observe AC4P behavior worthy of special recognition, whereas others admit they lack the courage to present a thank you card or a Hershey Payday candy bar (relabeled "Pay-It-Forward") as a reward for AC4P behavior.

Some say, "It's unnatural or silly," while others resist because it could come across as manipulative. A sincere verbal thank you is okay, they declare, "But giving someone a material reward could be seen as a ploy to control them."

One of my graduate students claimed he's more comfortable rewarding a stranger with a candy bar or a thank you card than a friend because "[t]he embarrassment of using a behavior modification technique would be more personal and aversive among close friends than strangers." My comeback: "It's all in the delivery." My students hear this and review the seven steps given here for giving quality AC4P recognition, but the use of thank you cards and candy bars to recognize AC4P behavior has not markedly increased. However, we have found less resistance to passing on an AC4P wristband when the wristband is viewed as more than a reward for behavior.

More specifically, when the wristband is presented as a symbol of AC4P leadership and worn to show membership in an elite group of individuals dedicated to cultivating an AC4P culture of compassion, my students show more interest and willingness to participate in such a recognition process. In other words, the AC4P wristband is given to not only reward AC4P behavior, but to signify membership in a movement to cultivate AC4P cultures of compassion. This connection brings the interpersonal recognition to a higher level, enabling positive impact on this recipient's self-esteem, competence, and sense of interdependence and belongingness. As mentioned earlier, courage should not be a significant issue here, but the benefactor's depth of commitment and passion for the AC4P Movement can make "taking it to a higher level" more or less genuine.

4. Deliver It Privately

Because quality recognition is personal and indicative of higher-order attributes, it needs to be delivered in private and one-on-one. This requires a certain degree of courage for those not comfortable in private, one-on-one conversations, especially with people they don't know well. But consider this: The recognition is special and relevant to only one person. So it will mean more and seem more genuine if it's given from one individual to another.

It seems conventional to recognize individuals in front of a group. This approach is typified in athletic contests and reflected in the pop psychology slogan, "Praise publicly and reprimand privately." Many managers take the lead from this common-sense statement and give individuals recognition in group settings. Indeed, isn't it maximally rewarding to be held up as an exemplar in front of one's peers? Not necessarily, because many people feel embarrassed when singled out in front of a group. Part of this embarrassment could be due to fear of subsequent harassment by peers. Some peers might call the recognized individual an "apple-polisher" or "brown-noser," or accuse him or her of "sucking up to management."

When I was in third grade, my teacher recognized me in front of the class for doing "an excellent job" on my homework. As depicted in the illustration on the next page, I was so embarrassed. Then after school, a gang of boys beat me up on the playground. Unfortunately, that teacher never found out that her public recognition had a negative side effect.

In athletic events the participants' performance is measured fairly and the winners are objectively determined. However, in educational and work settings it's usually impossible to assess everyone's relevant behaviors objectively and obtain a fair ranking for individual recognition. Therefore, praising one individual in public may lead to perceptions of favoritism on the part of individuals who feel they did equally well but did not get praised. Plus, such ranking sets up a win-lose atmosphere – perhaps appropriate for some sporting events but not in settings where interdependent teamwork is needed to achieve group goals.

It's beneficial, of course, to recognize teams of participants for their accomplishments, and this can be done in a group setting, as discussed in Chapter 3. Since individual responsibility is diffused or dispersed across the group, there is minimal risk of individual embarrassment or later peer harassment. However, as indicated in that chapter, it's important to realize that group achievement is rarely the result of equal input from all team members. Some take the lead and work harder, while others loaf and count

on the group effort to make them look good. Thus, it's important to deliver personal and private recognition to those individuals who went beyond the call of duty for the sake of their team.

5. Let It Sink In

In this fast-paced age of trying to do more with less, we try to communicate as much as possible when we finally get in touch with a busy person. After recognizing an individual's special AC4P effort, we are tempted to tag on a bunch of unrelated statements, even a request for more such behavior. This comes across as, "I appreciate what you've done, but I need more."

It does take a certain amount of courage or guts to tell someone, "I need more out of you." All the more reason to drop the request and let the praise sink in. Resist the temptation to do more than praise the AC4P behavior you saw. If you have additional points to discuss, it's best to reconnect later, after the rewarding recognition has had a chance to sink in and become part of the individual's self-talk for self-recognition and self-motivation.

By giving quality AC4P recognition, we give people a script they can use to reward their own behavior. In other words, our quality recognition strengthens the other person's self-reward system. And positive self-talk (or self-recognition) is critical for long-term maintenance of AC4P behavior. Thus, by allowing our recognition communication to stand alone and sink in, we enable the internalization of rewarding words that can be used later for self-motivation of additional AC4P behavior.

6. Use Tangibles for Symbolic Value

Tangible rewards can detract from the self-motivation aspect of quality recognition. If the focus of an AC4P recognition process is placed on a material reward, the words of appreciation can seem less significant. In turn, the beneficial impact on one's self-motivation is lessened.

On the other hand, tangible rewards can add to the quality of interpersonal recognition if they are delivered as tokens of appreciation. Rewards that include a relevant AC4P slogan, as on the AC4P wristband, can help to promote the desired behavior. But how you deliver a tangible reward will determine whether it adds to or subtracts from the long-term benefit of your praise.

The benefit of interpersonal recognition is weakened if the tangible is viewed as a payoff for the AC4P behavior. However, if the reward is seen as symbolic of going beyond the call of duty for another person's well-being, it strengthens the praise. Have the courage to tell it like it is: The AC4P wristband or another tangible reward is a token of appreciation or a symbol of going beyond the call.

7. Consider Secondhand Recognition

Up to this point, we've been considering one-on-one verbal communication in which one person recognizes another for a particular AC4P behavior. It's also possible to recognize a person's outstanding efforts indirectly, and such an approach can have special advantages. Suppose, for example, you overhear me talk to another person about your outstanding presentation about the AC4P Movement. How will this secondhand recognition affect you? Will you believe my words of praise were genuine?

Sometimes people are suspicious of the genuineness of praise when it's delivered face-to-face. Is there an ulterior motive? Perhaps a favor is expected in return. Or maybe the recognition is seen merely as an extension of a communication exercise and thus devalued as sincere appreciation. Secondhand recognition, however, is not as easily tainted with these potential biases. Therefore, its genuineness is less suspect.

Suppose I tell you that someone else in your workgroup told me about the superb job you did leading a certain group meeting. What will be the impact of this type of secondhand recognition? Chances are you'll consider the recognition authentic because I was only reporting what someone else said. Because that person reported your success to me rather than you, there was no ulterior motive for the indirect praise. Such secondhand praise can build a sense of belongingness or group cohesion among individuals. When you learn someone was bragging about your behavior, your sense of friendship with that person will likely increase.

As emphasized in Chapter 3 in the section on trust-building, gossip can be beneficial – *if it's positive*. When we talk about the achievement of others in behavior-specific terms, we begin a cycle of positive communication that can support desired behavior, as well as activate self-talk for self-recognition and self-motivation. So have the courage to initiate this cycle of positivism. This is the kind of interpersonal communication that enhances self-esteem, self-efficacy, personal control, optimism, and group cohesion. As explained in Chapter 2, these are the very person-states that increase the potential for AC4P behavior and the achievement of an interdependent culture of compassion.

A Summary

Referring to classic learning research, the case was made that success is more important than failure in developing and maintaining desired behaviors. This emphasis on success rather than corrective feedback should lessen the need for courage. It's usually more important to recognize people for their correct behaviors than to correct them for their mistakes. But how we recognize people dramatically influences the impact of our interpersonal interactions.

Seven basic guidelines were offered for giving people quality recognition for their AC4P behavior. This list of guidelines is not exhaustive, but it does cover the basics. Following these guidelines will increase the positive impact of interpersonal recognition. The most important point is that more recognition for AC4P behavior is needed, whether given firsthand or indirectly through positive gossip. It takes only a few seconds to deliver quality AC4P recognition.

Start giving AC4P recognition today – even for behaviors that occurred yesterday. Delayed recognition is better than no recognition. And quality recognition does not need to occur face-to-face. Leaving a behavior-based and personal recognition message on voicemail or in an email or a written memo (formal or informal) can make a person's day. It shows you appreciate what you saw and helps to build that person's self-recognition script for later self-motivation. This behavior takes minimal courage and can reap benefits far greater than the little inconvenience required. Perhaps realizing the positive impact we can have on people's behaviors and attitudes with relatively little effort will be self-motivating enough for us to muster the courage, if that is what is needed, to do more recognizing.

Consider the social consequences of giving quality recognition. Specifically, the reaction of the people who are recognized can have a dramatic impact on whether AC4P recognition increases or decreases throughout a culture. We need to know how to respond to recognition in order to ensure such AC4P recognition continues. This is the next and final topic of this chapter.

ACCEPT RECOGNITION WELL

Most of us get so little recognition from others we are caught completely off guard when acknowledged for our commendable actions. We don't know how to accept recognition when it finally comes. Don't shy away when it does come; have the courage to embrace it. Remember the basic behavioral science principle: Consequences influence preceding behaviors. Thus, quality recognition increases the probability that the behavior recognized will continue, and one's reaction to the recognition influences whether the behavior of recognizing someone will be attempted again. It's crucial to react appropriately when we receive recognition from others. Let's consider seven basic guidelines for receiving recognition.

1. Don't Deny or Disclaim

Often when I attempt to give quality AC4P recognition, I get a reaction that implies I'm wasting my time. I get disclaimer statements such as, "It really was nothing special" or "Just doing my job." The most common reply is, "No problem." This implies that the commendable behavior is not special and should not have been recognized.

We need to accept recognition without making denial or disclaimer statements, and without deflecting the credit to others. It's okay to show pride in our small-win accomplishments, even if others contributed to the successful outcome. After all, the vision of a compassionate AC4P culture includes everyone going beyond the call of duty for the well-being of others. In this context, numerous people deserve recognition daily.

Accept the fact that recognition will be intermittent at best for everyone. So when your turn comes, accept the recognition for your most recent AC4P behavior and for the many prior AC4P behaviors you performed that went unnoticed. Keep in mind that your genuine appreciation of the recognition will increase the chance that more recognition will be given by others.

2. Listen Actively

Listen actively to the person giving you recognition. You want to learn what you did, right? Plus, you can evaluate whether the recognition is given well. If the recognition does not pinpoint a particular behavior, you might ask the person, "What did I do to deserve this?" This will help to improve that person's method of giving recognition. Of course, it's important to not seem critical but rather to show genuine appreciation for the special attention.

Consider how difficult – yes, how courageous – it is for many people to go out of their way to recognize others. So revel in the fact you're receiving some recognition, even if its quality could be improved.

3. Use It Later for Self-Motivation

Most of your AC4P behaviors will go unnoticed. You perform many of these behaviors when no one else is around to observe you. Even when other people are present, they will likely be so preoccupied with their own routines they won't notice your extra effort. So when you finally do receive recognition for AC4P behavior, take it in as well deserved.

Don't hesitate to relive this moment later by talking to yourself. Such self-recognition can motivate you to continue going beyond the call of duty on behalf of other people's well-being. As mentioned earlier, self-talk can help you muster the courage to perform more AC4P behavior.

4. Show Sincere Appreciation

You need to show sincere gratitude with a smile, a thank you, and perhaps special words like, "You've made my day." Your reaction to being recognized can determine whether similar recognition is apt to occur again. So be prepared to offer a sincere thank you and words that reflect your pleasure in the memorable interaction. And consider the courage the other person might have needed in order to give you the recognition.

I find it natural to add, "You've made my day," because it's the truth. When people go out of their way to offer me quality recognition, they *have* made my day. I often relive such situations to improve a later day.

5. Reward the Recognizer

When you accept recognition well, you reward the person for their appreciation. This can motivate that individual to do more recognizing, especially if the person is an introvert and requires courage to step out and speak up to give recognition. Sometimes, you can even do more to ensure the occurrence of more quality recognition. Specifically, you can recognize the person for recognizing you. You might say, for example, "I really appreciate you noticing my AC4P behavior and calling me a leader of the AC4P Movement." Such rewarding feedback provides direction and motivation for those aspects of the AC4P recognition process that are especially worthwhile and need to become routine.

6. Embrace the Reciprocity Norm

Some people resist receiving recognition because they don't want to feel obligated to give recognition to others. This is the reciprocity norm at work. If we want to achieve an AC4P culture, we need to embrace this norm. When you are nice to others, as when providing them with special praise, you increase the likelihood they will reciprocate by showing similar behavior. You might not receive the returned favor, but someone will.[28] (See Chapter 6 for more on the cascading effects of reciprocity.)

It's important to realize that your genuine acceptance of quality recognition will activate the reciprocity norm; and the more this norm is activated by positive interpersonal communication, the greater the frequency of interpersonal recognition and AC4P behavior. So accept recognition well, and embrace the reciprocity norm. The result will be more interpersonal involvement consistent with the vision of an AC4P culture of compassion. Again, interpersonal involvement does not come easy to all of us. The quality of AC4P interactions can go a long way to easing one's resistance to involvement.

7. Ask for Recognition

If you feel you deserve recognition, why not ask for it? In terms of courage, yes, asking for praise is easier if you are an extrovert rather than an introvert. Your request might result in recognition viewed as less genuine than if it were spontaneous, but the outcome of such a request can be quite beneficial. You might receive some words worth reliving later for self-motivation. Most important, you will remind the other individual in a nice way that s/he missed a prime opportunity to offer quality recognition. This could be a valuable learning experience for that person.

Consider the possible beneficial impact of your statement to another person that you are pleased with a certain outcome of your extra effort, including your performance of particular AC4P behavior. With the right tone and affect, such verbal behavior will not seem like bragging but rather a declaration of personal pride in a small-win accomplishment – something more people should feel and relive for self-motivation. The other person will surely support your personal praise with supportive testimony, and this will bolster your self-motivation. Plus, you will teach the other person how to support the AC4P behavior of others.

Many years ago, I instituted a self-recognition process among my research students that increased our awareness of the value of receiving praise, even when it's self-initiated. I told my students during class or group meetings they could request an ovation at any time. All they had to do was specify the behavior they felt deserved recognition and then ask for an ovation. Obviously, such recognition is not private, personal, and one-to-one, and therefore it's not optimal. Plus, the public aspect of this process inhibited many personal requests for a standing ovation.

However, over the years a number of my students have requested public recognition, and the experience has always been positive for everyone. Each request has included a solid rationale. Some students express pride in an exemplary grade on a project; others acknowledge an acceptance letter from a graduate school, internship, or journal editor. Such public recognition is fun and feels good, both on the giving and receiving ends. Plus, we all learn the motivating process of behavior-based recognition, even when it doesn't follow all of the quality principles.

The Craving

William James, the first renowned American psychologist, wrote, "The deepest principle in human nature is the craving to be appreciated."[29] A little later John Dewey, the famous American educator who developed the field of school psychology, claimed, "The deepest urge in human nature is the desire to be important."[28] Then in 1936, Dale Carnegie proposed that the key to winning friends and influencing people is to "always make the other person feel important."[28] How can we readily fulfill the human need to feel appreciated and important? The answer, of course: Give and receive recognition well.

IN CONCLUSION

Many excuses and barriers can be offered for the lack of large-scale application of effective AC4P interventions analogous to those described in this chapter. Three C-words reflecting the leadership qualities needed to achieve an AC4P culture of compassion were explained: competence, commitment, and courage. Many people are competent at and committed to achieving an AC4P culture. In other words, they know what to do and are motivated to do whatever it takes to increase the quantity and quality of AC4P behaviors in educational, work, and community settings. However, the missing link is often *moral courage*, or the audacity to step up, take an *interpersonal risk*, and go beyond one's predictable routine on behalf of the well-being of other people, especially complete strangers.

Beyond competence (or self-efficacy), four person-states that influence courage in this context were discussed in Chapter 2 (i.e., self-esteem, belonging, personal control, and optimism), and guidelines for cultivating an AC4P culture have been entertained in the first three chapters of this book. The chapters in Part II of this text specify cost-effective techniques for increasing the frequency and effectiveness of AC4P behaviors in particular settings and for a designated meaningful purpose. Many of the AC4P applications describe the profound personal and interpersonal advantages of a particular AC4P intervention. These are the special reinforcing consequences that keep all of us in pursuit of an AC4P culture of compassion.

DISCUSSION QUESTIONS

1. Explain how competence and commitment contribute to an individual's courage to perform AC4P behavior.
2. Discuss distinctions between person-*traits* and person-*states* with realistic examples.
3. Explain the connection (or correlation) between the courage required to perform a proactive AC4P behavior and the state of belongingness.
4. How does the "Flash-for-Life" intervention exemplify the ABC model of applied behavioral science?
5. What situational factors increase the influence of an "AC4P Promise Card"?
6. How could the Critical Behavior Checklist for Driving be used to improve a driver education course? Is this education or training? Please explain.
7. Why or why not would you use the "Taxi-Cab Feedback Card" on your next trip in a taxi cab?
8. What's wrong (if anything) with the common suggestion, "Reprimand privately and recognize publicly"?
9. Discuss strategies for receiving recognition. Why is it important to follow these suggestions?
10. What does "Embrace the Reciprocity Norm" mean to someone receiving interpersonal recognition?

REFERENCES

1. *The American Heritage Dictionary* (1991) (2nd College Edition), p.333. New York: Houghton Mifflin.
2. McCain, J., & Salter, M. (2004). *Why courage matters: The way to a braver life.* New York: Random House.

3. Blanchard, K. P., Zigarmi, P., & Zigarmi, D. (1985). *Leadership and the one minute manager.* New York: William Morrow.
4. Geller, E. S. (1996). *The psychology of safety: How to improve behaviors and attitudes on the job.* Radnor, PA: Chilton; Geller, E. S. (1998). *Practical behavior-based safety: Step-by-step methods to improve your workplace.* Neenah, WI: J. J. Keller & Associates; Geller, E. S. (2001). *The psychology of safety handbook.* Boca Raton, FL: CRC Press.
5. Kouzes, J. M., & Posner, B. Z. (2006). *A leader's legacy.* An Francisco: John Wiley.
6. Geller, E. S. (1996). *The psychology of safety: How to improve behaviors and attitudes on the job.* Radnor, PA: Chilton; Geller, E. S. (2001). *The psychology of safety handbook.* Boca Raton, FL: CRC Press; Geller, E. S. (2005). *People-based safety: The source.* Virginia Beach, VA: Coastal Training Technologies; Geller, E. S. (2006). Reinforcement, reward, & recognition: Critical distinctions and a reality check. *Industrial Safety & Hygiene News,* 40(3), 12, 14; Geller, E. S. (2007). Why do people act that way? *Industrial Safety & Hygiene News,* 41(10), 21–22.
7. Mischel, W. (2004). Toward an integrative model for CBT: Encompassing behavior, cognition, affect, and process. *Behavior Therapy,* 35, 185–203.
8. Geller, E. S. (2008). *Leading people-based safety: Enriching your culture.* Virginia Beach, VA: Coastal Training Technologies; Geller, E. S., & Weigand, D. M. (2005). People-based safety: Exploring the role of personality in injury prevention. *Professional Safety,* 50(12), 28–36.
9. Geller, E. S. (2001). *The psychology of safety handbook.* Raton, FL: CRC Press, p. 378.
10. Reif, C. D, & Singer, B. (2000). Interpersonal flourishing: A positive health agenda for the new millennium. *Personality & Social Psychology Review,* 4, 30–44; Sarasson, B. R., Sarasson, I. G., & Gurung, R. A. R. (1997). Close personal relationships and health outcome: A key to the role of social support. In S. Duck (Ed.). *Handbook of personal relationships* (2nd ed.) (pp. 547–573). New York: Wiley; Sarasson, B. B., Sarasson, I. G., & Pierce, G. R. (1990). *Social support: An interactional view.* New York: Wiley.
11. Geller, E. S. (1999). Interpersonal trust: Key to getting the best from behavior-based safety coaching. *Professional Safety,* 44(4), 16–19; Geller, E. S. (2002). *The participation factor: How to increase involvement in occupational safety.* Des Plaines, IL: American Society of Safety Engineers.
12. Festinger, L. (1957). *A theory of cognitive dissonance.* Stanford, CA: Stanford University Press.
13. Geller, E. S., Bruff, C. D., & Nimmer, J. G. (1985). The "Flash for Life": A community prompting strategy for safety-belt promotion. *Journal of Applied Behavior Analysis,* 18, 145–159.
14. Cox, M. G., & Geller, E. S. (2011). Community prompting of safety-belt use: Impact of positive versus negative reminders. *Journal of Applied Behavior Analysis,* 43(2), 321–325; Farrell, L. V., Cox, M. G., & Geller, E. S. (2007). Prompting safety-belt use in the context of a belt-use law: The "Flash-for Life" revisited. *Journal of Safety Research,* 38, 407–411.
15. Geller, E. S., & Lehman, G. R. (1991). The buckle-up promise card: A versatile intervention for large-scale behavior change. *Journal of Applied Behavior Analysis,* 24, 91–94.

16. Streff, F. M., Kalsher, M. S., & Geller, E. S. (1993). Developing efficient work-place safety programs: Observations of response covariation. *Journal of Organizational Behavior Management*, 13(2), 3–15.
17. Geller, E. S. (2001). *The psychology of safety handbook*. Boca Raton, FL: CRC Press.
18. Cialdini, R. B. (2001). *Influence: Science and practice* (4th ed.). New York: HarperCollins College.
19. Geller, E. S., Hickman, J. S., & Pettinger, C. B. (2004). The Airline Lifesaver: A 17-year analysis of a technique to prompt safety-belt use. *Journal of Safety Research*, 35, 357–366.
20. Geller, E. S. (2005). *People-based safety: The source*. Virginia Beach, VA: Coastal Training Technologies.
21. Geller, E. S. (1996). *The psychology of safety: How to improve behaviors and attitudes on the job*. Radnor, PA: Chilton, p. 148.
22. Sulzer-Azaroff, B., & Austin, J. (2000). Does BBS work? Behavior-based safety and injury reduction: A survey of the evidence. *Professional Safety*, 45(7), 19–24.
23. Geller, E. S. (1998). *Practical behavior-based safety: Step-by-step methods to improve your workplace*. Neenah, WI: J. J. Keller & Associates.
24. Geller, E. S. (1998). *Practical behavior-based safety: Step-by-step methods to improve your workplace*. Neenah, WI: J. J. Keller & Associates; Geller, E. S. (2005). *People-based safety: The source*. Virginia Beach, VA: Coastal Training Technologies.
25. Chance, P. (1999). *Learning and behavior* (4th ed.). Belmont, CA: Wadsworth.
26. Thorndike, E. L. (1911). *Animal intelligence: Experimental studies*. New York: Hafner, p. 174.
27. Thorndike, E. L. (1931). *Human learning*. Cambridge, MA: MIT Press.
28. Cialdini, R. B. (2001). *Influence: Science and practice* (4th ed.). New York: HarperCollins College; Gouldner, A. W. (1960). The norm of reciprocity: A preliminary statement. *American Sociology Review*, 25, 161–167.
29. Carnegie, D. (1936). *How to win friends and influence people* (1981 ed.), New York: Simon & Schuster, p. 19.

5

Effective AC4P Communication

E. SCOTT GELLER

> You don't manage people, you have conversations that get them to do things.
> – Kim Krisco

You've heard the expression "Talk is cheap." Now consider the remarkable influence of "talking" on our feelings, attitudes, perceptions, knowledge, skills, and behavior. You cannot deny the fact that talking is the most cost-effective intervention we have to improve the human dynamics of any situation. Simply put, both the quantity and the quality of AC4P behavior can be influenced by *interpersonal* and *intrapersonal* conversation. Our *interpersonal* communication, or how we talk to others, can influence their AC4P behavior directly or indirectly by affecting *their* current attitude and person-states, which in turn can increase their propensity to perform AC4P behavior, as covered in Chapter 2.

Our *intrapersonal* communication, or how we talk to ourselves, directs our own behavior and influences our attitude and person-states. We can commend ourselves for our AC4P behavior, and thereby increase the probability of performing another kind act. Plus, we use self-talk to direct our ongoing activity, which could include AC4P behavior. Furthermore our self-talk can increase our sense of self-efficacy and personal control regarding the successful performance of an act of kindness, as well as optimism that our kind act will result in beneficial consequences, including an increased sense of self-esteem and belonging for our self and the beneficiary. Thus, the intervention power of conversation to ourselves and others is compelling and prevailing.

Prior chapters in this book have already covered aspects of effective conversation. For example, guidelines for communicating supportive and corrective feedback and for celebrating group achievements were provided in Chapter 3, and techniques for giving and receiving positive words of recognition for AC4P behavior were covered in Chapter 4. Plus, each of the six social-influence principles explained in the next chapter (Chapter 6) involves interpersonal communication to some extent. This chapter brings us to some basics in communicating more effectively to others and to ourselves, with the overall mission of increasing the quantity and improving the quality of AC4P behavior. Yes, talk is cheap, but it can make or break our efforts to cultivate an AC4P culture of compassion.

THE POWER OF CONVERSATION

Let's start with a common-sense bottom line: Participation in AC4P conversations is key to preventing interpersonal conflict and cultivating cultures of compassion and caring. We're not talking about the high-tech communication referenced in the illustration below, but about one-to-one interpersonal conversation related to AC4P behavior. Such improvement, in turn, benefits our own self-talk or intrapersonal communication and relevant person-states, leading to more AC4P behavior. Yes, we're talking about conversations having the power to activate and maintain an AC4P ripple effect.

This chapter offers guidelines and techniques for getting more beneficial impact from our communications with others, and with ourselves. Then four types of behavior management are presented, each defined by the nature of interpersonal conversation. First, however, let's consider the beneficial consequences of effective conversation. Realizing these consequences can motivate us to dedicate personal time and effort to improving our interpersonal conversations per the guidelines offered here.

Building Interpersonal Barriers

Surely you've seen how lack of communication can cause a minor incident to escalate into major conflict. Here's an example: You see a colleagues and say, "Hello," yet she passes by without reacting. What do you say to yourself? Maybe she didn't see you or had other thoughts on her mind. Still, it's easy for you to assume the person is unfriendly or doesn't like you. So the next time you see this person you avoid a friendly "Hello." You might even talk to others about that person's "unfriendliness." Can you see how an interpersonal barrier might start to develop?

This is only one of many situations that can stifle further interpersonal communication with an individual and lead to negative feelings and judgments. The result: the possible perception of interpersonal conflict, an unpleasant relationship, diminished cooperation, and reduced willingness to perform AC4P behavior for that person.

Resolving Interpersonal Conflict

If the lack of conversation can initiate or energize conflict, it's not surprising that the occurrence of conversation can prevent or eliminate conflict. "Let's talk it out," as the saying goes. Of course, the quality of that conversation will determine whether any perceived conflict is heightened or lessened. This issue of conversation quality is covered later in this chapter. Here I only want you to consider the potency of interpersonal talk. It can make or break interpersonal conflict, which in turn enables constructive or destructive relationships. And the nature of relationships determines whether individuals are willing to actively care for another person's safety and health.[1]

Bringing Reality to Intangibles

What are love, friendship, courage, loyalty, happiness, and forgiveness? Of course, you can describe behaviors that reflect these constructs, but where is the true meaning? Don't we derive the meaning of these common words from our conversations? Consider how we "fall in or out of love" depending on how we talk to ourselves and to others. Similarly, we convince ourselves we're happy through our self-talk, and this inner conversation is obviously influenced by what we hear others say about us.

We define another person's friendship, courage, or loyalty by talking about that individual in certain ways, both to ourselves and to others. Our internal mental scripts and external verbal behaviors rule. They give practical meaning to concepts that define the very essence of human existence. Then when groups, organizations, or communities communicate to explain these concepts, we have a "culture." In fact, our culture is defined by conversations – both spoken and unspoken – and the behaviors influenced by such communication.

Defining Culture

What about "unspoken conversation"? I'm referring to customs or unwritten rules we heed without mention. We might realize, for example, the teacher's pet sits in the front row; or the coach doesn't want to hear about a star athlete missing a class; or Mom is more lenient than Dad regarding certain rule-breaking behavior. We might also know characteristics that bias a particular supervisor's performance appraisals, from gender and seniority to one's ability on the golf course.

It might be understood, for example, that someone with high seniority and a low golf handicap is more likely to get the special training assignment, but such prejudice is certainly not expressed. If it were, a productive conversation would be possible – one that could reduce the barriers to optimal interpersonal trust and the achievement of an AC4P culture. Bottom line: Spoken and unspoken words define a culture, and the culture can change, for better or worse, through interpersonal and intrapersonal conversation.

Influencing Self-Esteem

How we talk to ourselves both influences and reflects our self-esteem. In fact, it's probably fair to say our mental scripts about ourselves reflect our self-esteem. We can focus our self-talk on the good things people say about us or on other people's critical statements about us. The result is a certain kind of self-talk we call *interpretation*. Such intrapersonal communication can influence how we feel about ourselves. In other words, our self-esteem can go up or down according to how we talk to ourselves about the way others talk about us. As the illustration below shows, negative self-talk can detract from the consequences of positive experiences that should increase one's self-esteem.

Enabling Breakthroughs

In his provocative book *Leadership and the Art of Conversation*, Kim Krisco[2] defines a breakthrough as going beyond business as usual and getting more than expected. This requires people to realize new possibilities, commit to going for more, and then make a concerted effort to overcome barriers. In most situations, achieving an AC4P culture requires a breakthrough. So how can we visualize possibilities, show commitment to go for a breakthrough, and identify barriers to overcome? You guessed it – through conversation.

Krisco warns us to expect barriers and resistance to change. And the greater the change, the greater the resistance. But remember, most barriers to change are perceptions or interpretations derived through people's self-talk about their perceived reality. Conversation, both interpersonal and intrapersonal, enables us to overcome the barriers that hold back the accomplishment of breakthroughs.

THE ART OF IMPROVING CONVERSATION

Given the power of conversation to resolve interpersonal conflict, define culture, and affect the person-states that influence one's propensity to perform AC4P behavior, we need to apply this powerful tool to support and advance the AC4P Movement. But how do we maximize the impact of our interpersonal and intrapersonal conversations? What kinds of conversations are more likely to provoke and maintain beneficial participation in the AC4P Movement? That's the theme for the remainder of this chapter. Let's start with the most basic aspect of communication – the words we use.

Watch Your Language

Words shape our feelings, expectancies, attitudes, and behavior.[3] How you talk about something influences how others feel about it, especially yourself. In other words, our verbal behavior affects our attitudes and beliefs, and these in turn determine more behavior. Question: How might your language increase or decrease involvement in a movement to cultivate an AC4P culture? Consider, for example, how some words used in the safety and health fields are counterproductive. They are negative and uninspiring, and probably have a detrimental effect on people's voluntary involvement in organized efforts to actively care for the safety, health, and well-being of others.

Accident Implies Chance. The word *accident* implies "a chance occurrence" outside one's immediate control. When a young child has an "accident" in his pants, we presume he was not in control. He couldn't help it. Occupational and vehicle "accidents" are usually unintentional, of course, but are they truly chance occurrences? There are usually specific controllable factors, such as changes in the environment, behaviors, and/or attitudes that can prevent "accidents."

Years ago President Bill Clinton at the time stumbled on the steps at the home of golf pro Greg Norman in West Palm Beach, Florida. It happened on the morning of March 14, 1997. When asked about the incident, Clinton was quoted in our local newspaper (the *Roanoke Times*) as saying what's depicted in the illustration on the next page. The logical follow-up comment is "When

it's my time, it's my time." How many times have you heard someone say
something like that?

Clinton's remarks reflect the implied meaning of *accident*. "Accidents are
bound to happen somewhere to someone. It's just a matter of time before
it happens here. I just hope my luck doesn't run out and it happens to me."
These statements are not far-fetched. They follow logically from the implied
meaning of *accident*.

Incidentally, do you recall any reports from an "accident investigation"
of Clinton's injury? We heard much about the extent of his injury – a tear
of his quadriceps tendon, which connects the upper thigh to the kneecap.
And we were told about the surgery to his knee at Bethesda Naval Hospital.
We even got a play-by-play of his recovery, progressing from a big brace and
crutches to a cane over several weeks. But nothing was mentioned about the
factors contributing to the injury.

Were the steps slippery? Did someone distract the president? Did the president fail to use the handrail, or was a handrail unavailable? Did someone "accidentally" push Mr. Clinton? Where were the bodyguards? Could a bodyguard have warned the president about an environmental hazard or offered feedback about his at-risk behavior? This is just a sample of AC4P questions that could have been asked to enable the kind of "injury analysis" needed to prevent similar future mishaps from happening to the president and to others in similar circumstances.

Imagine the nationwide impact if a careful AC4P analysis of the potential contributing factors to Clinton's injury had been conducted and reported. Consider the benefits of broad media coverage of the potential environmental, behavioral, and person-based factors that led to the president's injury and the techniques that could be implemented to prevent future mishaps like this one. Bodyguards might even add observations of safe versus at-risk behaviors of the president and his companions to the regular protective audits they perform. However, none of this AC4P participation for injury prevention is likely to occur with the attitude, "It was just an accident, and accidents happen to people."

We want to develop the belief and expectation in our culture that injuries can be prevented by controlling certain factors. Therefore, *accident* is the wrong word to use when referring to unintentional injuries. It can reduce the number of people who believe with true conviction that their AC4P involvement in safety efforts can prevent personal injuries. Besides, the word *injury* has more emotional impact than *accident*. For the same reason, it's not a vehicle "accident"; it's a vehicle "crash."

Restraints Don't Invite Use. For more than three decades I've been urging transportation and safety professionals to stop using the terms *occupant restraint* and *child restraint* for vehicle safety belts and child safety seats. These terms imply discomfort and lack of personal control, as shown in the illustration on the next page. Furthermore, these labels fail to convey the true function of these devices. *Seat belt* is better than *occupant restraint*, but this popular term is not really adequate because it doesn't describe the function or appearance of today's lap-and-shoulder belts. We need to get into the habit of saying "safety belt" and "child safety device." But actually *life belt* and *lifesaving seat* are more appropriate terms.

Priority or Value. Priority implies importance and a sense of urgency. Safety and healthcare professionals are often quick to urge us to make safety and a healthy lifestyle priorities. Similarly, most flight attendants begin their safety announcements with, "Your safety is our priority." This seems

appropriate, since my dictionary defines *priority* as "taking precedence logically or in importance."[4]

But everyday experience teaches us that priorities come and go. Depending upon the demands of the moment, one priority often gets shifted for another. Do we really want to put AC4P on such shifting ground? An AC4P culture requires actively caring to be accepted as a value. The relevant definition of *value* in my dictionary is, "something (as a principle or ideal) intrinsically valuable or desirable."[5] Shouldn't safety and AC4P be a "value" that people bring with them every day, regardless of the ongoing priorities or task requirements?

Don't Say "Behavior Modification." Over the years I've seen "behavior modification" used many times for titles of research presentations and keynote addresses at regional and national conferences. I've heard teachers, consultants, coaches, parents, and students use this term to describe behavior-focused approaches to improving individual and group functioning in educational, athletic, and industrial settings, as well as the residence facilities for individuals with developmental, physical, and/or psychological challenges. Indeed, a flagship research journal of ABS since 1977 is entitled *Behavior Modification*. And I've often been introduced at conferences as a specialist in "behavior modification." This is the wrong choice of words if we want acceptance and involvement from the folks who are to be "modified." Who wants to be "modified"?

This lesson was learned the hard way more than thirty years ago by the behavioral scientists and therapists who developed the principles and techniques of "behavior modification." Whether it was applied to teachers, students, employees, or prisoners, the term *behavior modification* was a real turnoff. It conveyed images of manipulation, top-down control, loss of personal control, and "Big Brother."

Unfortunately, the term *behavior* alone carries negative associations for many – as in "Let's talk about your behavior last night." However, I can't see any way around using this term. Behavior refers to a process, or the ongoing actions that result in certain output or outcomes. We need to teach and demonstrate the benefits of focusing on behaviors and on defining behaviors correctly. And, if we focused more on desirable than undesirable behaviors, as should be the case, the term *behavior* would have more positive than negative connotations.

As detailed elsewhere,[6] the words used to describe behavior should be chosen for *clarity* to avoid being misinterpreted, *precision* to fit a specific activity, *brevity* to keep it simple, and *objectivity* to refer to actions explicitly observed. Without a clear and precise definition of *behavior*, most action words can have more than one interpretation, as depicted in the illustration below – a reaction to another of President Clinton's "accidents."

If you want to encourage participation in an AC4P process, don't link the term *modification* with behavior. *Behavior analysis* and *behavioral science* are the terms used by researchers and scholars in this area of applied psychology, as explained in Chapter 1. This implies that behavior is analyzed first, and *if* change is called for, an evidence-based intervention process is developed with input from the client(s). Given that "analysis" can sound cold or bring to mind Sigmund Freud and psychoanalysis, we use *science*, as in "applied behavioral science" (ABS) throughout this text. Besides, *science* implies both analysis and intervention based on empirical research.

I hope the basic message is clear. We need to realize how our language can activate feelings and even behaviors we don't want. It can hinder voluntary participation. If we want to communicate in order to "sell" an AC4P process, we must consider how our language will be perceived by those whose participation is needed to make the process work. That's why the principles and applications of ABS are referred to as humanistic behaviorism, combining the science of behaviorism with the interpersonal-caring philosophy of humanism.[7]

Ponder the following words and phrases related to the human dynamics of safety, health, or well-being. Do some of the words or phrases on the left suggest negative associations that can stifle involvement in an AC4P movement? I suggest alternatives on the right, but you might have a better idea.

"air bag" or "safety cushion"?
"requirement" or "opportunity"?
"peer pressure" or "peer support"?
"program" or "process"?
"training" or "coaching"?
"loss-control manager" or "injury prevention facilitator"?
"mandate" or "expectation"?
"compliance" or "accomplishment"?
"I've *got* to do this" or "I *get* to do this"?
"I must meet this deadline" or "I choose to achieve another milestone"?
"I wake up to my *alarm* clock" or "I awaken to my *opportunity* clock"?

It's a good personal or group exercise to consider the ramifications of using these terms and phrases. Adding alternatives to this list is even more beneficial. But understanding the critical relationship between words, attitudes, and voluntary participation is only half the battle. We need to change our verbal habits, and this is easier said than done. Also, the effectiveness of our communication to facilitate participation depends on more than the words we use. Let's turn to other aspects of our interpersonal conversations that affect their behavioral and attitudinal impact.

Get Beyond the Past

Has this ever happened to you? You ask for more AC4P involvement from a particular individual and you get a reaction like, "I've tried that AC4P behavior more than once and got no appreciation, so count me out." Or have you attended a group meeting where people spend more time going over past accomplishments or failures than discussing future possibilities and deriving new action plans?

These are examples of conversations stuck in the past. The dialogue might be enjoyable or a nice diversion, but little or no progress is made. Conversations about past events help us connect with others and recognize similar experiences, opinions, and motives. But such communication does not permit progress toward problem solving or continuous improvement. For this to happen, the conversation must leave the past and move on.

Kim Krisco[2] maintains leaders need to help people move their conversations from the past to the future and then back to the present. If you want conversation to fuel engagement in an AC4P movement, possibilities have to be entertained (future talk) after the past is acknowledged, followed by the development of practical action plans (present talk). This is the case for group conversation at a team meeting, as well as for one-on-one advising, counseling, or coaching.

To direct the flow of a conversation from past to future and then to the present, it's first necessary to recognize and appreciate the other person's perspectives. Practice AC4P listening, as discussed later in this chapter. Then shift the focus to the future. "Yes, I understand we've had difficulties with this issue in the past, but what is your vision for an ideal resolution. What specific improvements would you like to see?" After the ideal AC4P possibilities are explored, shift back to the present. "What can we do today to move us forward toward those ideals?"

Seek Commitment

You know your interpersonal conversation is especially constructive when someone makes a commitment to participate. This reflects success in moving conversation from the past to the future and then to a specific action plan for the present. As addressed in Chapter 6, a verbal commitment also tells you something is happening on an intrapersonal level. The person is becoming self-motivated (Chapter 3), increasing the probability participation will continue in the absence of an external accountability system.[8]

Now you can proceed to talk about ways to support the commitment, or methods to hold participants mutually accountable. For example, one person might offer to help a colleague meet an obligation through verbal reminders. Or an individual might agree to honor a commitment by showing a coach behavioral records that verify AC4P involvement. This is the kind of follow-up conversation that facilitates continued involvement.

Stop and Listen

Sometimes, in their eagerness to make things happen, managers, coaches, teachers, or parents give corrective feedback in a top-down, seemingly controlling manner. In other words, their passion to make a difference can lead to an overly directive approach to getting others to change their behavior. An indirect or nondirective approach to giving advice is usually more effective, especially over the long term,[9] and this is a basic tenet of humanistic therapy.[10]

Think about it: How do you respond when someone tells you exactly what to do? Now it certainly depends on who is giving the directive, but I bet your reaction is not entirely positive. You might follow the instructions, especially if they come from someone with the power to control consequences. But how will you feel? Will you be self-motivated to make a lasting change? You might if you asked for the direction. But if you didn't request feedback, you could feel insulted or embarrassed. Try to be more nondirective when using interpersonal conversation to effect behavior change. This requires empathic listening, or as we say, "AC4P listening."

Dale Carnegie wrote about the value of empathic listening more than fifty years ago in his classic book: *How to Win Friends and Influence People.*[11] His wisdom is reflected in the writing of many authors of popular self-help books, including Stephen Covey, whose fifth habit of highly effective people is "Seek First to Understand … Then to be Understood."[12] Carnegie, Covey, and others offer the same basic strategies for AC4P listening; and if you've had any training in effective communication, you've heard the same advice. Let's review these guidelines with four easy-to-remember words, each beginning with the letter "R."

For readers who have received communication training, this review will at least provide a mnemonic for remembering how to listen with an AC4P mindset and teach others to do the same. To be sure, the increasing "lean and mean" and "win/lose" paradigms of contemporary organizations, as well as the focus on impersonal emails and text messages, suggest a dire need to teach and use these humanistic guidelines for AC4P listening.

Repeat. This is the easiest technique to use. Simply mimic (or repeat) what you hear, using the same words. This clarifies that you heard correctly and, most important, prompts the person to say more. Remember, the purpose of AC4P listening is to motivate the other person to say more so you can truly understand the problem.

So if a friend tells you he's dropping out of school, you might repeat this statement by asking, "You're dropping out?" This shows you're attentive and interested, and waiting for more information. Hearing how drastic the statement sounds, the person might reply, "Well, at least I feel like dropping out." Then what would you say? Following this "repeat" technique, you would say, "You mean you feel like dropping out?" Or you might use different words to echo the same meaning. This is the next AC4P listening technique.

Rephrase. Instead of mimicking the content, you might rephrase the statement. In other words, say the same thing but in different words. In our example, you might say, "You mean you don't like the life of a college student anymore?" By putting the statement in your own words, you're showing genuine interest while also asking for more information. You're also checking for understanding. If you can rephrase the statement correctly, you have received and interpreted the communication accurately.

It's possible your friend miscommunicated or you misperceived something. Your rephrasing gives the other person a chance to explain. And this is what you want – more disclosure of the problem. Suppose your friend clarifies, "Well, it's not that I don't like being a student here, it's just that some of my teachers get me so frustrated at times, I feel like quitting." Now your friend has revealed a more specific aspect of the problem. What do you say?

You could use the *repeat* strategy and return with, "Your teachers get you frustrated." Alternatively, you could attempt to *rephrase* with something like, "You mean some of your teachers get you so angry that your motivation to continue attending classes is sapped." Or perhaps this statement calls for the next "R" of AC4P listening – *ratification*.

Ratify. With this AC4P listening strategy you demonstrate affirmations or support for the individual's statement by confirming your understanding. In other words, you offer words that show approval of what is being said, and this in turn encourages more explanation. In our example, you might ratify your appreciation of the statement by saying, "I know the feeling, I've been frustrated with some of my teachers at times and wonder whether this college life is for me."

At this point, you might be tempted to jump in with probing questions to find out more about the frustration, the teachers, or the situation. What teachers got you so upset? What did they do? Why are you so frustrated that you want to quit? You should resist this temptation to be directive. You probably have not heard enough about the problem to begin a structured (and biased) analysis. More AC4P listening could reveal problems beyond the teachers. Perhaps it's not a teacher per se, but a particular homework assignment or exam grade. Or the problem might stem from interactions with another student, or a family member, or from feelings of personal inadequacy, including a perceived loss of confidence, self-efficacy, or personal control.

Bottom line: A person's distress signals can have many sources, and these will probably not come to the surface quickly in one-to-one communication. And, if the relevant causes of a problem were disclosed early, it's unlikely you could give optimal advice at this point – directive action that is both useful and accepted. Usually, the best we can do is listen actively with repeat, rephrase, and ratify strategies in order to get the problem out in the open. Ultimately, we want the person to express true feelings, as indicated by the fourth "R" word.

Reflect. When people reflect their inner feelings about a situation, they are at the personal root of the problem. Such self-disclosure of person-states can lead to insight into the true cause of the problem (for both the speaker and the listener) and suggest strategies for intervention. However, even at this stage (with outer layers of the onion peeled away), it's usually better to let the speaker entertain a variety of possible intervention approaches.

If you've been an AC4P listener, you might eventually get the ultimate reward for your sensitivity, patience, and emotional intelligence. The speaker will ask you for specific advice. When you hear words like, "What do you think I should do," you have mastered AC4P listening. You have shown you actively care, and now your thoughtful direction will likely be most relevant, understood, and accepted.

Ask Questions First

Suppose the conversation is not about a serious issue like personal distress, frustration, or apathy, but only about a less-than-desired behavior. You see an opportunity for a person to show more or better AC4P behavior in a particular situation. What should you say? Instead of telling the person what to do, try this. Get the individual to tell you, in her/his own words, what s/he should have done to reflect the AC4P principles. You can do this by asking questions with a sincere and AC4P demeanor. Avoid at all costs a sarcastic or demeaning tone.

First, point out certain AC4P behaviors you noticed – it's important to start with positives. Then move on to the undesirable behavior by asking, "Could you have been more actively caring in that situation?" Of course, you hope for more than a yes or no response to a question like this. But if that's all you get, you need to be more precise in follow-up questioning. You might, for example, point out a particular situation where AC4P behavior was called for and ask what that behavior should be. Now we're talking about giving corrective feedback. This was addressed in Chapter 3 with regard to communicating the results of observations with a critical behavior checklist (CBC). But even without a CBC and a systematic feedback process, start corrective feedback with questions.

By asking questions, you're always going to learn something. If nothing else, you'll hear the rationale for not performing in an optimal AC4P manner. You might uncover a barrier to AC4P behavior you can help the person overcome. A conversation that entertains ways to remove obstacles that hinder AC4P behavior is especially valuable if it translates possibilities into feasible and relevant action plans.

Beware of Bias

Every conversation you have with someone is biased by prejudice or pre-judgment filters – in yourself and within the other person. You can't get around it. From personal experience, people develop opinions and attitudes, and these in turn influence subsequent experience. With regard to interpersonal conversation, we have subjective prejudgment filters that influence what words we hear, how we interpret those words, and what we say in response to those words.[13] Every conversation influences how we process and interpret the next conversation.

The illustration on the next page makes my point. The female driver is merely trying to inform the other driver of an obstacle in the road. But that's not what the driver of the pickup truck hears. This driver's prior driving experience leads to a biased interpretation of the warning. You could call such selective listening an "autobiographical bias."[12] Of course, factors besides prior experience can bias interpersonal communication, including personality, mood state, physiological needs, and future expectations.

It's probably impossible to escape completely the impact of this premature bias in our conversations. But we can exert some control. Actually, each of the conversation strategies discussed here are helpful. For example, in the nondirective approach, an individual attempts to overcome this bias by listening actively and asking questions before giving instruction. With this approach a person's biasing filters can be identified and considered in the customization of a plan for corrective action.

Certain words or phrases in a conversation can be helpful in diminishing the impact of a prejudice filter. For example, when you say "as you know" before giving advice, you're limiting the perception of a personal insult and the possibility of a "tune-out" filter. By asking people for their input up front, you reduce the likelihood they will later tune you out. It's the principle of reciprocity (Chapter 6). By listening first, you increase the odds the other person will listen to you without a tune-out filter.

If you think a person might tune you out because s/he heard your message before, you could use opening words to limit the power of tune-out filters. Specifically, you might start the conversation with something like, "Now, I realize you might have heard something like this before, but . . ." In this way you are anticipating the kind of intrapersonal conversation (or mental script) that activates a tune-out reaction, and thereby you reduce such filtering.

In the same vein, don't let your prejudices about a speaker limit what you hear. Do you ever listen less closely to certain individuals because they seldom had anything useful to say in the past or because you think you can predict what they will say? If so, you've let your past conversations with these people bias future conversation. Becoming aware of this "stuck-in-the-past" prejudice can enable more AC4P listening.

Don't let a speaker limit what you hear. Tell yourself you're not listening *to someone*; rather you're listening *for something.*[2] You're not listening reactively to confirm a prejudice – you're listening proactively for possibilities. Pay close attention to the body language and tone in conversations. I'm sure you've heard many times that a person's delivery can hold as much or more information as the words themselves. Listen for passion, commitment, or caring. If nothing else, you could learn whether the messenger understands and believes the message. Perhaps you'll learn a new way to deliver a message yourself. Bottom line: Our intrapersonal conversations can either facilitate or hinder what we learn from an interpersonal conversation.

Plant Words to Improve Self-Image

How we talk about others influences interpersonal perceptions. How we hear others talk about us shapes our own self-image. And how we talk to ourselves about these viewpoints can make them a permanent feature of our self-concept or self-esteem. Want to change how others perceive you? Change the conversations people are having about you. Through proactive AC4P listening, you can become aware of negative interpersonal conversations about you. Then you can interject new statements about yourself into conversations, especially with people who have numerous contacts with others.

If you suspect, for example, colleagues consider you to be forgetful and disorganized, you could mention certain self-management strategies you've been using lately to improve memory and organization. Of course, you need to actually practice these techniques so you'll also change your self-talk. If you focus on new positive qualities rather than past inadequacies in your conversations with others and with yourself, you'll surely improve your

self-image and self-esteem. Plant key messages about your commitment to become a more effective AC4P person, and you'll eventually see yourself that way and behave accordingly.

In Summary

The strategies covered here for getting the most from interpersonal conversation are reviewed in Figure 5.1. Each technique is relevant for getting more AC4P involvement from others. Plus, applying these strategies effectively can improve a person's self-talk or intrapersonal conversation. This leads to increased self-esteem, self-efficacy, and personal control – person-states that enhance an individual's willingness to perform AC4P behavior.

First, consider the tendency to focus interpersonal and intrapersonal conversation on the past. This helps us connect with others, but it also feeds our prejudice filters and limits the potential for a conversation to facilitate

---

Conversation Checklist

✓ Listen attentively and proactively.

✓ Focus on the positive actions observed.

✓ Draw out responses from the other person.

✓ Influence others to tell you how they could support the AC4P Movement.

✓ Ask questions with a sincere and AC4P demeanor.

✓ Act as if you don't know the answer, even though you think you do.

✓ Shift a past focus to future possibilities for improvement.

✓ Bring the conversation back to the present and develop an action plan.

✓ Seek a verbal commitment to follow the action plan.

✓ Plant words to improve public and self-image.

FIGURE 5.1. Guidelines for improving interpersonal conversation.

beneficial change. We enable progress when we move conversations with ourselves and others from past to future possibilities and then to goal setting for present-day behavior.

Expect people to protect their self-esteem with excuses for their past mistakes. Listen proactively for barriers to AC4P behavior reflected in these excuses. Then help the conversation shift to a discussion of possibilities for improvement and personal commitment to applying a practical action plan. This is more likely to occur with a nondirective than directive approach in which more questions are asked than directives given, and when opening words are used to protect self-esteem and limit the impact of reactive bias.

Remember that planting certain words in self-talk and conversations with others can improve your self-image and confidence as a facilitator of beneficial change. Tell others of your increased commitment to facilitate more effective AC4P conversations. Then tell yourself the strategies you will use to improve interpersonal conversation, and be sure to commend yourself when you see improvement. In this way, intra- and interpersonal conversations work together to help achieve an AC4P culture of compassion.

CONVERSATION FOR BEHAVIOR MANAGEMENT

Behavior is managed through conversation, and the success of behavior management is determined in large part by the effectiveness of interpersonal

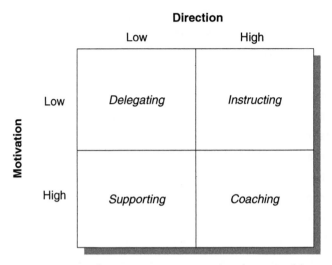

FIGURE 5.2. Four types of management conversation determined by amount of direction and motivation communicated.

communication. This starts with listening proactively to understand the other person's situation before giving direction, advice, or support. Then one of four types of interpersonal conversation should occur, depending on what kind of management is called for. As depicted in Figure 5.2, a management conversation can reflect coaching, supporting, instructing, or delegating,[14] depending on the amount of direction and motivation given by the manager (the benefactor) and received by the beneficiary.

Coaching Conversation

Coaches give direction and provide feedback. They present a plan, perhaps specific behaviors needed for a certain task, and then follow up with support and AC4P feedback to pinpoint what worked and what did not. Periodic reminders keep people on the right track, while intermittent recognition provides support to keep people going.

Delegating Conversation

Sometime it's best to give an assignment in general terms (without specific direction) and to limit interpersonal behavioral feedback. This is when team members are already motivated to do their best and will give each other direction, support, and feedback when needed. These individuals should be self-accountable or self-motivated, and expected to use self-management techniques (activators and consequences) to keep themselves motivated and on the right track.[15]

Instructing Conversation

Some people are already highly motivated to perform well, but don't know exactly what to do. This is often the case with new hires, beginning students, interns, and trainees. They want to make a good first impression, and the newness of the situation is naturally motivating. They are nervous, however, because of response uncertainty. They aren't sure what to do in the relatively novel situation. In this case, managers, teachers, or coaches need to focus on giving behavior-focused instruction.

This type of conversation should also be the coaches' approach at most athletic events. Individuals and teams in a sports contest do not typically need motivation. The situation itself, from fan support to peer pressure, usually provides plenty of extrinsic motivation. Such competitors need directional focus for their motivation. They need to know what specific behaviors are desired to win in various situations. This said, my personal experience with athletic coaches is not consistent with this analysis. For example, are the half-time speeches of team coaches more likely to be directional or motivational?

Supporting Conversation

What about the experienced person who does the same tasks day after day? This individual doesn't need direction but could benefit from periodic expressions of sincere thanks for a job well done. There are times when experienced workers know what to do but don't consistently perform up to par. This is not a training problem, but rather one of execution.[16] Through proactive listening a manager can recognize this and provide the kind of support that increases motivation. This could involve broadening a job assignment, varying the task components, or assigning leadership responsibilities. But at least it includes the delivery of one-to-one recognition in ways that increase a person's sense of importance and self-efficacy. See Chapter 3 for ways to give quality AC4P recognition.

A celebration with top-down support and bottom-up involvement encourages teamwork and builds a sense of belonging among participants. Therefore, the most effective celebrations are planned by representatives from the group whose efforts warrant the celebration. At these celebrations, managers do more listening than talking. They show genuine approval and appreciation of the challenges addressed and the difficulties handled in achieving the bottom line. Discussions of the journey help participants write internal scripts for continued self-talk and self-motivation to achieve more to justify the next celebration. See Chapter 3 for more details about planning the most effective celebration for group support.

CHOOSING THE BEST MANAGEMENT CONVERSATION

So how can we know what type of behavior-management conversation to use? This is where empathy is critical. Your assessment of situations and people – through observing, listening, and questioning – will determine which approach to use. And given the dynamic characteristics of most work and educational settings and the changing nature of people, you need to make this assessment periodically per situation and participant.

Consider, for example, the new employee who needs specific direction at first. Then, as this person becomes familiar with the routine, more support than instruction is called for. Later, you decide to expand this individual's work assignment with no increase in financial compensation. This situation will likely benefit most from a coaching conversation whereby both direction and support are given, at least at first. Eventually, a delegating approach might be most appropriate, whereby varying assignments are given with only a specification of your outcome expectations. These workers are able to manage themselves with self-direction and self-motivation. But as discussed earlier, these individuals still benefit from genuine words of appreciation and gratitude when expectations are met.

The AC4P leaders of work teams change their interpersonal conversations quite dramatically as groups get more familiar with team members and their mission. In the beginning, during the forming and storming stages of team progress, work groups need structure, including specific direction and support. This implies a coaching or directing format. Later, when the group members become familiar with each other's interests and talents, and progress to the norming and performing stages of team development, supporting and delegating conversations are needed.[17]

The Role of Competence and Commitment

Figure 5.3 illustrates how two critical characteristics – competence and commitment – should influence a manager's conversation approach.[14] When competence is high, people know what to do and therefore do not need

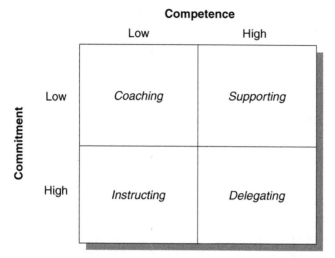

FIGURE 5.3. Four management conversations determined by the beneficiary's level of competence and commitment.

a directing conversation. However, they need supporting conversations when their motivation or commitment is low. This is particularly evident when students, employees, or athletes perform irregularly or inconsistently. Their good days indicate they know what to do, while bad days suggest a motivation issue.

Causes of low commitment vary dramatically, from interpersonal conflict on the job or athletic field to emotional upheaval at home. Such causes can be discovered only through AC4P listening. At times, the diagnosis and subsequent treatment of a motivational problem require special assistance. In this case, the best a manager can do is recognize a need for professional help and offer AC4P advice and support.

In Summary

Coaching conversations are needed when a person's competence and commitment regarding a particular task or assignment are relatively low. You can improve competence through behavior-focused direction and feedback, and increase commitment by giving authentic appreciation and AC4P support. Anything that increases a person's perception of importance or competence can enhance commitment. What makes that happen? The answer is not always obvious, but if you listen, observe, and ask questions you'll find out.

Delegating is relevant when people know what to do (competence) and are motivated to do it. You can often know when an individual or team advances to this level by observing successive progress. But it's often useful to ask people whether they are ready for this level of conversation. If they say no, then ask them what they need to reach this stage. Do they need more competence through direction or more commitment through some kind of support the institution or organization could make available?

FIVE TYPES OF INTERPERSONAL CONVERSATION

We end our discussion of the power of interpersonal and intrapersonal conversation by defining five types of one-to-one communication. Each plays an essential role in cultivating an AC4P culture of compassion. The strategies illustrated in this chapter for improving the beneficial impact of interpersonal communication connect to each of these types of conversation in unique and important ways. In other words, each of these types of conversation reflects particular communication techniques aimed at benefiting the human dynamics of a school, work, or home environment. In particular, each type of conversation can play a critical role in increasing the quantity and/or improving the quality of AC4P behavior.[18]

Relationship Conversation

Relationship conversations are relatively easy, yet critical to developing a trusting and AC4P culture. Simply put, these conversations occur whenever you show sincere interest in another person, from his/her home life to challenges at school or work. This happens, of course, when you talk about particular aspects of a person's family, health, hobbies, work processes, or AC4P-related perceptions. Indeed, showing genuine interest and appreciation in what a person is doing is probably the best way to give supportive recognition. As Dale Carnegie said years ago, and Ken Blanchard and Spencer Johnson later reiterated, "Help people feel important at doing worthwhile work."[19] This is relationship-building – the foundation of an AC4P connection between people.

Specific behaviors you find desirable might surface during a relationship-building conversation. If so, you should certainly acknowledge their occurrence and show appreciation. But your intention is more about developing support and interpersonal trust than influencing behavior. This approach to interpersonal recognition and support removes the perception of manipulation or "behavior modification" and is therefore more acceptable to both the initiator and receiver of this type of communication. The key is to show genuine interest in the other person's situation, performance, and/or perspective.

Possibility Conversation

Relationship conversations often refer to an individual's past. Indeed, we build interpersonal relationships by comparing our prior experiences and looking for commonalities. In contrast, *possibility* conversations focus on the future. These conversations occur when you share visions with another person. Leaders of the AC4P Movement are motivated by the vision of an AC4P culture of compassion with interpersonal support predominant over conflict and bullying. Possibility conversations target any future situation that reflects desired improvement in environment/engineering conditions, behavioral competence, or person-states.

As discussed earlier, Kim Krisco recommends we begin coaching conversations with a discussion of a person's past, analogous to the relationship conversation just discussed, then progress to a discussion of future possibilities, as defined here.[2] Subsequently, Krisco proposes the coaching conversation transition back to the present, whereby people define process goals or behavioral strategies relevant to achieving certain possibilities. The next three types of conversation reviewed here help make this happen through improvement-focused interpersonal coaching.

Action Conversation

Action conversation is behavior-based communication. Given a vision or possibility for improvement, this conversation focuses on what an individual or project team could do to move in a desirable direction. The conversation might be between individuals, as in coaching, or between members of a group.

The action conversation could define a number of behaviors, some to continue and others to decrease or eliminate. When these conversations occur in group meetings, individual assignments are often needed. Also, action goals are set according to the SMARTS acronym (for specific, motivational, achievable, relevant, trackable, and shared) explained in Chapter 3.

This goal-setting exercise should include an accountability system for tracking progress toward goal attainment. With work groups or teams, it's usually best to monitor both individual achievements with regard to specific assignments and the group's progress as a team. Next, people look for opportunities to perform their newly defined and desirable behavior(s).

Opportunity Conversation

So you've learned how to do behavior-based coaching and set a goal for completing a certain number of coaching sessions in one month. Now it's time to look for opportunities to conduct such a one-on-one session. In some cultures this can be any situation that involves human behavior. However, in other settings the potential participants must agree to be observed before the process can be implemented.

Suppose an individual or a project team chooses to adopt an achievement or success-seeking perspective on AC4P behavior by tracking all AC4P behaviors performed beyond a person's daily routine. This requires an action conversation about the types of behavior that indicate going beyond the call of duty, and an *opportunity* conversation about the situations that call for various AC4P behavior.

Bottom line: A practical action plan for achieving particular possibilities includes a definition of behaviors and situations – behaviors needed to fulfill the plan (an *action* conversation) and the times and places for these behaviors to occur (an *opportunity* conversation). After an action plan is completed, it's beneficial to celebrate small-win achievements (see Chapter 3) and set the stage for additional action and opportunity discussions. This is the fifth type of interpersonal conversation.

Follow-up Conversation

It's important to acknowledge the achievement of a SMARTS goal. These follow-up conversations are rewarding and promote a success-seeking mindset – a valuable person-state introduced in Chapter 1. After noting the acquisition of an action/opportunity outcome, a *follow-up* conversation turns to discussion of a subsequent challenge. This could include an identification of new possibilities, relevant and acceptable action plans, and opportunities calling for certain action.

Follow-up conversations target the end result or outcome of an action plan, but they often focus on the process first. In other words, it's useful to have periodic follow-up conversations to check on progress toward a designated outcome. Suppose, for example, you communicate with a teacher or supervisor regarding a need to have more one-on-one interaction with students or workers. After exploring possibilities, you discuss specific actions

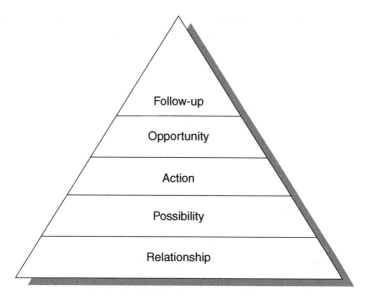

FIGURE 5.4. Five levels of interpersonal conversation.

and opportunities for meaningful teacher/student or supervisor/employee contacts. You might set a SMARTS goal and even a follow-up reward for goal attainment. But process-focused monitoring could also be quite helpful. In other words, it would probably be useful to contact this teacher or supervisor periodically for follow-up conversations regarding his/her progress toward goal attainment.

Figure 5.4 illustrates this five-way classification system, which provides an intuitive sequence for constructive interpersonal talk. For example, action plans will be all the more accepted and accomplishment will be all the more likely if they are preceded by appropriate relationship conversations. Please note, however, that one type of conversation does not stop with the implementation of the next in the sequence. Relationship conversations, for example, continue throughout action planning, accomplishment, and follow-up. And while it makes sense to define the behaviors in an action plan before considering opportunities, in actual practice people look for opportunities for their action-plan behavior before performing.

Actually, interpersonal communication varies unsystematically between all five conversation types. Perhaps understanding these different conversations and their differential objectives will contribute to increasing the quantity and improving the quality of communications aimed at nurturing an AC4P culture of compassion. When it comes to advancing the AC4P Movement, we can't have too many quality interpersonal conversations.

IN CONCLUSION

I hope you're convinced the level of AC4P in your culture is greatly determined by interpersonal and intrapersonal conversation. We often focus our interpersonal and intrapersonal conversations on the past. This helps us connect with others, but it also feeds our prejudice filters and limits the potential for conversation to facilitate beneficial behavior change. We enable progress when we move conversations with ourselves and others from past to future possibilities and then to the development of an action plan.

Expect people to protect their self-esteem with excuses for their past mistakes. Then help the conversation shift to a discussion of possibilities for improvement and personal commitment to applying a feasible action plan. This is often more likely to happen with a nondirective than directive approach in which more questions are asked than directives given. It's also useful to use opening words to protect the listener's self-esteem and limit the impact of reactive bias.

AC4P listening enables one to determine whether a coaching, instructing, supporting, or delegating conversation is most appropriate. Coaching involves both direction and support, and is needed when a person's competence and commitment in a particular setting are relatively low. In contrast, delegating is relevant when people know what to do and are motivated to do it. In this case, they are both competent and committed, and can direct and motivate themselves. Then, delegating conversations provide clear expectations and show sincere appreciation for worthwhile behavior.

When people are self-motivated to perform well but don't know how to maximize their efforts for optimal performance, an instructive conversation is called for. In other situations, people know what is needed for optimal performance but don't always work at optimal levels. This reflects an execution problem that can't be solved with directive conversation. Rather, supportive conversation is needed. Actually, everyone can benefit from supportive recognition.

Bottom line: Interpersonal conversation defines our culture at home, at school, at work, and everywhere in between. It can create conflict and build barriers to performing AC4P behavior. Or it can cultivate the kind of culture needed to make a major breakthrough in cultivating a culture of compassion. Interpersonal conversation also affects our intrapersonal conversations or self-talk, which in turn influences our willingness to look out for the health, safety, and well-being of ourselves and others.

DISCUSSION QUESTIONS

1. How has high-tech communication (i.e., the Internet) influenced interpersonal relationships? Please consider both benefits and liabilities.
2. Explain with specific examples how language (e.g., the words we use) can affect attitudes, behavior, and even a culture.
3. Define the past–future–present sequence of interpersonal conversation with an example, and explain the value of this sequence for constructive conversation (e.g., communication aimed at identifying and improving a relationship issue).
4. Explain each of the following R-words with regard to empathetic listening: Repeat, Rephrase, Ratify, and Reflect.
5. How can personal bias or "prejudgment filters" limit the impact of interpersonal conversation?
6. Define the following four types of management conversation in terms of the amount of direction and motivation offered: Coaching, Delegating, Instructing, and Supporting.
7. How does the level of competence and commitment of the receiver of management conversation influence whether the manager should use a Coaching, Delegating, Instructing, or Supporting approach?
8. Distinguish between the following five types of interpersonal conversation with personal or realistic examples: relationship, possibility, action, opportunity, and follow-up.
9. Offer a rationale for the particular sequence of the five types of conversation, from relationship to follow-up conversations.
10. What types of intrapersonal and interpersonal conversations contribute to nurturing an AC4P culture?

REFERENCES

1. Geller, E. S. (1994). Ten principles for achieving a Total Safety Culture. *Professional Safety*, 39(9), 18–24; Geller, E. S. (2001). Actively caring for occupational safety: Extending the performance management paradigm. In C. M. Johnson, W. K. Redmon, & T. C. Mawhinney (Eds.). *Handbook of organizational performance: Behavior analysis and management* (pp. 303–326). New York: Haworth Press.
2. Krisco, K. H. (1997). *Leadership and the art of conversation*. Rocklin, CA: Prima.
3. Hayakawa, S. I. (1978). *Language in thought and action* (4th ed.). New York: Harcourt Brace Jovanovich.

4. *New Merriam-Webster Dictionary* (1989). Springfield, MA: Merriam-Webster, p. 577.
5. *New Merriam-Webster Dictionary* (1989). Springfield, MA: Merriam-Webster, p. 800.
6. Geller, E. S. (2001). *Building successful safety teams*. Rockville, MD: Government Institutes.
7. Dinwiddie, F. W. (1975). Humanistic behaviorism: A model for rapprochement in residential treatment milieus. *Child Psychiatry and Human Development*, 5(4), 254–259; Krasner, L. (1978). The future and the past in the behaviorism-humanism dialogue. *American Psychologist*, 33(9), 799–804.
8. Cialdini, R. B. (2001). *Influence: Science and practice* (4th ed.). New York: HarperCollins College; Geller, E. S., & Veazie, R. A. (2010). *When no one's watching: Living and leading self-motivation*. Newport, VA: Make-A-Difference.
9. Bandura, A. (1997). *Self-efficacy: The exercise of control*. New York: W. H. Freeman; Geller, E. S. (2002). *The participation factor: How to increase involvement in occupational safety*. Des Plaines, IL: American Society of Safety Engineers; Ryan, R. M., & Deci, E. L. (2000). Self-determinism theory and the foundation of intrinsic motivation, social development, and well-being. *American Psychologist*, 55, 68–75.
10. Rogers, C. R. (1957). The necessary and sufficient conditions of therapeutic personality change. *Journal of Consulting Psychology*, 21, 95.
11. Carnegie, D. (1936). *How to win friends and influence people* (1981 ed.). New York: Galahad Books.
12. Covey, S. R. (1989). *The seven habits of highly effective people: Restoring the character ethic*. New York: Simon & Schuster.
13. Langer, E. J. (1989). *Mindfulness*. Reading, MA: Addison-Wesley.
14. Blanchard, K. (1999, November). *Building gung ho teams: How to turn people power into profits*. Daylong workshop presented at the Hotel Roanoke, Roanoke, VA; Blanchard, K., & Bowles, S. (1998). *Gung ho! Turn on the people in any organization*. New York: William Morrow; Blanchard, K., Zigarmi, P., & Zigarmi, D. (1985). *Leadership and the one minute manager*. New York: William Morrow.
15. Geller, E. S. (1998). *Understanding behavior-based safety: Step-by-step methods to improve your workplace* (2nd ed.). Neenah, WI: J. J. Keller & Associates; Geller, E. S. (2001). *Beyond safety accountability*. Rockville, MD: Government Institutes.
16. Geller, E. S. (2000). Ten leadership qualities for a Total Safety Culture: Safety management is not enough. *Professional Safety*, 45(5), 38–41.
17. Geller, E. S. (2001). *Building successful safety teams*. Rockville, MD: Government Institutes; Tuckman, B. W. (1965). Developmental sequence in small groups. *Psychological Bulletin*, 63, 384–399.
18. I was introduced to these five conversation labels during a Progressive Business audio conference in 2003, featuring Bob Aquadro and Bob Allbright.
19. Carnegie, D. (1936). *How to win friends and influence people* (1981 ed.). New York: Galahad Books; Blanchard, K., & Johnson, S. (1981). *The one-minute manager*. New York: William Morrow.

6

Social Influence and AC4P Behavior

CORY FURROW AND E. SCOTT GELLER

Don't criticize them; they are just what we would be under similar circumstances.

– Abraham Lincoln

For an AC4P culture to thrive over the long term, self-motivation is essential (see Chapter 3). However, people sometimes need a slight extrinsic nudge to perform AC4P behavior. Six social-influence principles, founded on more than fifty years of research by social psychologists, offer practical techniques to help make this happen – strategies to activate and/or support occurrences of AC4P behavior.

Social influence is defined as perceived pressure or support from others that results in notable change in an individual's behavior. Do not confuse this with *persuasion*. This is more than changing one's opinion or attitude, although such change might follow a change in behavior, as we discuss later in this chapter. Persuasion does not necessarily change observable behavior.[1]

In this chapter we explain practical behavior-change techniques derived from six basic social-influence principles – consistency, liking, reciprocity, social proof, authority, and scarcity. We illustrate how these principles and related techniques have been (or could be) used to nudge others to perform AC4P behaviors or to increase the probability certain AC4P behavior will continue.[2] Appropriate interventions based on these principles can help cultivate an AC4P culture of compassion and propel expansion of the AC4P Movement worldwide.

Before defining the social-influence principles and their applications, let's review the concepts related to the applicability of these principles – three types of behavior change and their connection to the activator-behavior-consequence (ABC) model of applied behavioral science (ABS), as explained in Chapter 1.

THREE TYPES OF BEHAVIOR CHANGE

Conformity, compliance, and obedience are three types of behavior change that result from social influence. Note that conformity occurs when explicit social pressure is relatively low, whereas obedience follows the perception of high social pressure.[1]

Conformity

Conformity is an attempt to fit-in. We conform when we alter our behavior to match the behavior of others.[1] A student will likely drink more beer at a college party if peers consume lots of beer. And one's attire at the party will be formal or informal to match the attire of other partygoers.

Compliance

Compliance comes about when we are directly or indirectly requested to change a behavior.[1] A *direct request* emanates from an interpersonal interaction, usually verbal communication. An *indirect request* uses a message or sign to solicit compliance. Ask a passenger to buckle up in a vehicle and you're taking a direct route to gaining compliance. A billboard message, like "Click It or Ticket," is an indirect request.

Obedience

When a perceived authority figure requests (or orders or commands) a change in behavior, people obey in order to appease the authority.[1] Obedience reduces one's sense of personal control or choice. This in turn reduces self-motivation, as explained in Chapter 3. The de-motivating effect of obedience occurs whether the authority's request is direct (i.e., interpersonal) or indirect.

THE ABC MODEL

How activators and consequences influence behavior is exemplified by the ABC model of ABS. Simply put, behavior is directed by activators and motivated by consequences.[3] As illustrated in Chapter 1, activators can be education/training programs, written/verbal prompts, online webinars, and modeling/demonstrations.[4] A stop sign at an intersection is a written prompt, directing a driver to halt at the intersection.

An announcement that a certain behavior will result in a certain consequence is the most influential type of activator. Incentives activate behavior by indicating a certain reward will follow a designated behavior. In contrast, a disincentive warns people of the negative consequence of a penalty if a designated undesired behavior occurs (e.g., a hundred-dollar fine for littering) or if a certain desirable behavior does not occur (e.g., "Click It or Ticket").

Consequences vary from rewards to penalties, social approval to disapproval, and from insignificant to significant outcomes.[4] Failing to brake and stop at an intersection stop sign can produce irritating but temporary social disapproval (e.g., other drivers angrily honking their car horn), the more permanent financial cost of a penalty if the behavior is observed by a police officer, or a dramatic, even fatal incident – colliding with a pedestrian or another vehicle.

According to Robert Cialdini and Noah Goldstein,[5] social or interpersonal consequences are desirable to the extent they (a) offer an accurate perception of reality, (b) contribute to the development or maintenance of meaningful social relationships, or (c) contribute to a desirable self-concept. An accurate, reality-based decision can have the consequence of helping the decision maker attain a goal. Developing meaningful relationships with classmates can make a course more enjoyable and also cultivate support for cooperative learning. A favorable self-concept increases self-esteem and enhances one's propensity to perform AC4P behavior.[6]

Accuracy, social affiliation, and a favorable self-concept – motivating characteristics of consequences from social interaction – connect to three of the five person-states proposed in Chapter 2 to increase one's propensity to perform AC4P behavior – self-efficacy/competence (accuracy), belonging (social affiliation), and self-esteem (a positive self-concept).

One behavior can produce these three desirable consequences. You observe your peers make a financial donation to a charity after hearing a persuasive presentation, and you follow up by making a similar donation. This environment-based AC4P behavior (see Chapter 2) is supported by each of three motivating consequences. Your behavior is an "accurate" consequence of a persuasive speech and reflects relevant compliance from peers. You gain social approval and avoid social disapproval from your peers by making a donation. And upon making the AC4P donation, you view yourself more favorably.

Social-influence principles and related techniques can be understood and executed within the framework of the ABC model of ABS. The six principles and techniques covered in the remainder of this chapter are essentially activators. But each infers desirable or undesirable consequences following relevant behavior. Most of these consequences relate to conformity, compliance, and obedience either in combination or alone – the three consequence categories defined by Cialdini and Goldstein.[5]

THE CONSISTENCY PRINCIPLE

The first of the six social-influence principles is consistency. Here is how it can work: To pay his way through college, Cory worked as a cook at a local restaurant in Blacksburg, Virginia. Of the kitchen staff, he was the only one who didn't smoke cigarettes. During one of the cigarette breaks, a co-worker said he would like to quit smoking for his health. Cory perceived that his co-worker felt guilty about smoking, but this smoker verbalized a convincing rationalization: "Cigarettes relieve my stress." Before the smoker headed back into the kitchen, any guilt about smoking seemed nearly dissipated. Self-talk had this man believing reducing stress overshadowed any future and uncertain costs to his health.

According to Leon Festinger's *Theory of Cognitive Dissonance*, people are uncomfortable when they realize their behaviors are inconsistent with their beliefs, attitudes, or values.[7] The smoker experienced dissonance when he said cigarettes were bad while continuing to smoke. To ease this disturbing dissonance, he identified what he perceived as an immediate and certain psychological benefits from smoking (i.e., stress relief).

Self-perception theory, an extension of cognitive dissonance theory, was proposed ten years later by Daryl Bem.[8] According to self-perception theory, we validate our values, attitudes, or beliefs (internal attributes) by observing our own behaviors. For example, Tim is passionate about sports (e.g., football, baseball, and basketball) and fitness. He believes these passions emanate from his dedicated participation in sports ever since elementary school. As an athlete in high school, he trained in a gym and won multiple awards. Tim includes fitness as a personal value after reflecting on his past fitness behaviors and he *chooses* to continue performing behaviors consistent with that value.

Note the critical word *chooses*. Self-perception is influenced only by behavior perceived to be personally chosen. Behavior perceived to be influenced completely by external contingencies (e.g., incentives/rewards or disincentives/penalties) generally does not come to define personal values, attitudes, or beliefs. Likewise, cognitive dissonance is absent when attitude-discrepant behavior is perceived to be controlled by extrinsic consequences (e.g., financial compensation).

The techniques explained in the following sections – foot-in-the-door, social labeling, and commitment – make use of the *consistency principle* to influence the behavior of others. Remember the critical role of *choice*. When we believe our inconsistent behavior or attitude was controlled by outside factors, we are not disrupted by cognitive dissonance and do not feel compelled to adjust our behavior, attitude, or perception of self.[9]

Foot-in-the-Door

The *foot-in-the-door* (FITD) technique gains compliance to a relatively large request by first obtaining compliance to a smaller, related request.[10] If you want your roommate to help wash the dishes, ask him/her first to take out the trash– a less time-consuming task. After your roommate takes out the trash, follow with the dish-washing request.

Jonathan Freedman and Scott Fraser demonstrated the FITD technique empirically with a seminal field study.[10] Research assistants (RAs) went door-to-door and asked homeowners to post a large sign on their front lawn. For the Large-Request-First condition, homeowners were shown a picture of a large obtrusive sign stating "Drive Carefully," and asked if they would allow the RAs to place the same sign in their yard. Of these twenty-four homeowners, only 16.7 percent complied.

In contrast, another group of homeowners were asked if they'd be willing to place a small 3 by 3inch sign in their window that stated, "Be a Safe Driver," as a Small-Request-First (or FITD) condition. Two weeks later, those homeowners who complied with the small-sign request were asked if they would place the same large sign used in the Large-Request-First condition in their front yard. Of the twenty-five homeowners who agreed with the small request first, 76 percent permitted the large sign in their yard.

Social Labeling

When an individual is assigned an attribute, attitude, or belief and is then asked to comply with a behavior related to that label, *social labeling* has occurred.[11] If the social label is desirable, the individual wants to behave consistently with it. For example, labeling a driver as a careful and safe driver can increase his/her safe-driving behaviors. Of course, a reckless-driver label may prompt the driver to drive recklessly.

Supportive Research. To increase charitable donations, Robert Kraut applied a similar social-labeling technique.[12] An RA acting as a door-to-door volunteer asked homeowners to make a charitable donation to the American Heart Association. The participants were split into two conditions, depending on whether they agreed to make a donation (i.e., the Charitable or Uncharitable condition). In both conditions, participants received the same leaflet supporting the charity.

Participants in the Charitable condition were randomly assigned to one of two groups. One group received the leaflet with a card stating, "Charitable people give generously to help a good cause and those less fortunate than themselves. Are you one?"[13] Participants in the other group received the same leaflet and card, but the RA added the personal statement, "You are a generous person. I wish more of the people I met were as charitable as you."[13] Similarly, those who didn't make a donation were randomly assigned to one of two groups. One group received the same leaflet given to those in the Charitable condition, but the attached card stated, "Uncharitable people give excuses and refuse to help others. Are you one?"[14] The second group in the Uncharitable condition received the same leaflet and card, but a personal label was added: "Let me give you one of our health leaflets anyway. We've been giving them to everyone, even people like you who are uncharitable and don't normally give to these causes."[14]

One to two weeks after the leaflets, cards, and personal labels had been first distributed, the same homeowners were asked by a different RA, posing as a door-to-door volunteer, whether they would like to donate to help raise money for multiple sclerosis. Individuals in the Charitable condition ($n=37$) who had received the personal label donated an average of $0.70 (equivalent to approximately $3.76 in 2013),[15] whereas those in the Charitable condition who had not received the personal label ($n=62$) donated an average of $0.41 (equivalent to approximately $2.20 in 2013[15]). This group difference was significant ($p<.05$).

Interestingly, individuals in the Uncharitable condition who received the uncharitable label ($n=27$) donated significantly less money ($p<.05$) than those who had not previously received the uncharitable label ($n=27$). More specifically, those who got the uncharitable label donated an average of $0.23 (equivalent to approximately $1.20 in 2013),[15] whereas those in the group without the personal statement that implied an uncharitable label donated an average of $0.33 (equivalent to approximately $1.73 in 2013).[15]

These results suggest people behave consistently with reasonable labels given to them. Participants given a charitable label through a personal statement donated more than participants who were not given the label. Similarly, participants who received a label reflecting uncharitability donated less than uncharitable participants who did not receive a personal statement implying uncharitability.

Consider the disadvantage of giving someone a negative label. A person might behave undesirably to be consistent with a negative label such as being lazy, a poor reader, or an underachiever. A negative label like "underachiever" can be an excuse to put less effort into achieving a personal or group goal. A positive label might activate and/or support desirable behaviors such as being energetic, conscientious, or a diligent worker. However, the type of positive label is critical, according to programmatic research by Carol Dweck.[16]

Ability vs. Effort Labels. Dr. Dweck and her colleagues gave hundreds of early adolescents a set of ten fairly difficult problems from the nonverbal portion of an IQ test. Afterward, all participants were praised individually for their performance on the test, but the nature of the praise was varied systematically. For half of the students, the praise was based on their *ability*. They were each told, "Wow, you got eight right. That's a really good score. You must be smart at this."[17] The other students were each praised with a positive social label for their *effort* with these words: "Wow, you got eight right. That's a really good score. You must have worked really hard."[18]

Both groups scored equivalently on the IQ test. But researchers noted significant differences in students' behavior following their *ability* vs. *effort* label. All students had the choice to work on a challenging new task from which they could learn. Most of those with the ability label rejected this opportunity. Apparently "they didn't want to do anything that could expose their flaws and call into question their talent."[18] In contrast, 90 percent of the students praised for their effort welcomed the opportunity of a challenging new task from which they could learn.

Later, when all of these students performed less effectively on some additional, more difficult problems, their reaction to failure feedback was influenced by the prior label given them. The ability kids felt like failures. They believed they did not live up to their ability, and they rated the task as "not fun anymore." The effort group saw in their failure a need to try harder. They did not perceive any indictment of their intellect and did not indicate they didn't enjoy the problem-solving task. "Many of them said that the hard problems were the most fun."[18]

After experiencing these difficult problems, the adolescents were given some easier problems to solve. The performance of the ability-labeled students plummeted. The effort-labeled students performed increasingly more effectively. In the profound words of Dr. Dweck, "Since this was a kind of IQ test, you might say that praising ability lowered the students' IQs. And that praising their effort raised them."[19]

A final difference showed up when the adolescents were asked to write out their opinions of the problem-solving tasks for the benefit of students at other schools. A space was provided on this form for the students to report the personal scores they had received. To the researchers' surprise and disappointment, 40 percent of the ability-labeled students reported higher grades than they actually earned. In the author's words, "We took ordinary children and made them into liars by telling them they were smart."[19]

Bottom line: Focus on the process (or effort) rather than the outcome (or results) when praising another person's performance.

Commitment

Marriage is probably the most meaningful commitment a couple can make. While dating, they often choose to increase their commitment through engagement. For some, the ordeal of meticulous wedding planning then begins. Selecting a venue, caterer, baker, wedding colors, groomsmen, and the bridal party is an involved process. After a wedding date is set and a location chosen, wedding invitations and announcements are mailed. Engagement, bachelor, and bridal parties soon follow. Then on the wedding day, in front of invited guests, the couple exchange wedding rings and publicly state their vows – often customized for each other. Then comes the big moment. Each person chooses to say publicly, "I do," and this is followed by the "public commitment" kiss.

Perceived Choice. Imagine helping a young boy dress in nice clothes you have selected for him to wear on his first day of school. This might feel like top-down control to the boy, and he might resist in order to assert his individuality or personal freedom. Consider an alternative approach: Select two school outfits you would like the boy to wear, and let him choose between the two. More than likely, the young boy will be less resistant because he feels he has some choice in the clothes he wears to school. Little does he know you're happy with either outfit.

When a decision maker perceives a sense of choice, his or her decision is considered authentic and self-endorsed.[20] People who make a commitment without perceiving some choice are less likely to honor it.[7] In the wedding example, choice is abundant: The couple choose to get married. They choose all of the wedding arrangements (e.g., venue, caterer, guests). Each person chooses personal wedding vows. Finally, the bride and groom choose to say, "I do."

Active. The second component of increasing one's propensity to honor a commitment is to make it active.[21] Signing a document, shaking hands, and succumbing to fraternity hazing are active commitments involving behavior. It can take months to plan the perfect wedding. All of the steps prior to the wedding day reflect an active investment in a lifelong commitment. At the altar, the behaviors of two individuals exemplify an active commitment. First, wedding rings are exchanged. Then the words, "I do" and a kiss. Without such action, a commitment is passive and less binding.

Public. Making a commitment in front of others also increases the propensity to honor that commitment. Behaviors consistent or inconsistent with a

FIGURE 6.1. Scott making the first public commitment.

FIGURE 6.2. Workshop participants making a public commitment.

public commitment have relevant social consequences. A public commitment implies possible social approval or disapproval following behavior consistent or inconsistent with the commitment, respectively.[22] Wedding guests exemplify this point. Invitations are sent to people most relevant in the couple's life. It's expected that deviations from their commitment will be met with social disapproval.

Figures 6.1 and 6.2 depict a public-commitment intervention applied at an AC4P safety seminar for safety leaders, supervisors, and maintenance personnel at Delta Airlines. After giving a half-day workshop on the AC4P principles and applications for the safety and well-being of others, Scott Geller walked to the back of the auditorium and signed his name to a "Declaration of Interdependence" as a public commitment to look out for the safety and well-being of others (Figure 6.1). Then Scott requested the audience to follow suit.

The social context was probably critical in influencing most of the workshop participants to sign this declaration (Figure 6.2), which is displayed in the breakroom for the maintenance employees of Delta Airlines at the Hartsfield-Jackson Atlanta International Airport. Scott's request was both public and voluntary in nature. This contributed to the effectiveness of an active exercise to inspire awareness of the AC4P concepts and the development of relevant action plans.

Consider the discussion of SMARTS goal setting in Chapter 3. The final "S" in the SMARTS acronym represents *shared* – making a goal public. Sharing goals with others creates internal and external accountability. Not only are people motivated to make their behavior consistent with their commitment to achieve a particular goal (i.e., internal accountability), they also want others to see them living up to their commitment (i.e., external accountability).

THE LIKING/INGRATIATION PRINCIPLE

We like to be liked, asserts the *liking principle*.[23] Naturally, people are more likely to comply with a request from others they like. *Ingratiation* refers to attempts to get others to like you.[1] Relatively convenient strategies for getting others on board with the AC4P Movement are provided by this social-influence principle of liking.

Similarity

We tend to like people who are similar to us, and we are more likely to comply with requests from these individuals. Similarities can vary from comparable opinions and attitudes to backgrounds and past experiences, attire, and notable behaviors.[23] It's more likely "birds of a feather flock together" than "opposites attract."

Gaining compliance through similar attire was tested in a field study conducted at Purdue University in 1971. Research assistants (dressed in either collegiate or hippy attire) randomly asked for a dime to make a long-distance phone call from either collegiate or hippy-dressed students

(n=384) they encountered in a hallway near a dining facility. Participants were more likely to give the RA a dime when their attire matched that of the RA (i.e., collegiate or hippy attire).[24]

In a related study, the experimenter told an RA and the participant they shared a similar fingerprint type. In the Common-Fingerprint condition, the participant and RA were told they shared a common fingerprint type; while in the Rare-Fingerprint condition, the shared fingerprint type was considered rare. In a Control condition, the experimenter did not comment on the relative uniqueness of their shared fingerprint type. After the experimenter dismissed the two individuals, the RA asked the participant to review a document for a class and provide feedback.[25] Of twenty-nine participants in the Control-Fingerprint condition, 48.3 percent complied with the RA's request. In the Common-Fingerprint condition, compliance increased to 54.8 percent of thirty-one participants. In the Rare-Fingerprint condition, 82.1 percent of twenty-eight participants complied with the RA's request.

Interestingly, a person can gain favor or compliance by faking or claiming a false similarity. In the fingerprint study, for example, the RA and participant didn't really share the same fingerprint type, but this false similarity was enough to gain compliance. Consider this true story: At a calling agency, Stephanie's task was to convince others to make a donation to an organization helping with the cleanup process after Hurricane Katrina. Stephanie was the best at convincing others to make large donations. Her secret: "Appear to be like them." When Stephanie heard a southern accent over the phone, she faked a southern accent. If the person stated a personal opinion or interest, Stephanie faked similarity: "I feel the same" or "I do that too." Stephanie's ability to create a fake similarity enabled her to gain more compliance than her co-workers. Of course, it's critical the apparent similarity is believable, which is not the case in the illustration below.

Compliments

Who doesn't like to receive a compliment? Complimenting people is a quick and easy way to gain their favor.[26] You increase the target's self-esteem and perhaps a sense of competence or self-efficacy. You also set the stage for reciprocity (as discussed later in this chapter). Interestingly, even if the target is aware of an ulterior motive behind the flattery, the target still views the person giving the compliment as favorable.[23]

Professors are suckers for flattery. Many undergraduates seeking a letter of recommendation or acceptance into a graduate program flood professors with compliments and flattery. A student approaches Scott and says, "Dr. Geller, your inspirational teaching of the introductory psychology course convinced me to change my major to psychology!" A few weeks later the same student comes to Scott with a request: "Dr. Geller, would you write me a letter of recommendation for a summer internship program?"

Even if Scott suspected an ulterior motive behind the prior compliment, the undergraduate still increased the probability of receiving a letter of recommendation. Since students seldom give these kinds of "life-changing" compliments to their professors, the compliment in this case was impacted by the *principle of scarcity*, as explained later in this chapter. Similarly, compliments from a child to a parent might be viewed as uncommon and perhaps insincere. Still, parents who receive compliments from their children are extremely pleased and more likely to comply with a child's request. Bottom line: When people say, "Flattery will get you everywhere," they are probably more right than wrong.

Mere-Exposure Effect

When a new song is first played on the radio, it may not get a positive review from listeners. However, as the song continues to be played, it may grow on the listeners. From mere exposure, listeners can develop a positive attitude toward a song. The impact of repeated exposure was demonstrated in a series of studies conducted by Robert Zajonc.[27] In one of his experiments, each participant was shown a series of photos. The relative frequency of showing each photo varied among participants. After viewing the photos, the participants rated how much they liked each photo. Higher favorability ratings went to those photos viewed more frequently.[27]

Advertisers use the mere-exposure effect constantly to sell their products. We see Coca-Cola products on billboards, vending machines, in TV commercials, in restaurants, and on the sides of trucks. Does such excessive exposure increase sales of Coke products? Apparently the Coca-Cola Company believes so, given the amount of money spent to promulgate these exposures.

The mere-exposure effect can apply to interpersonal relationships. Initially, one's attitude toward a teacher, co-worker, or neighbor may be neutral. However, through frequent interaction, one's impression of another person can become positive. This exposure can then influence one-on-one communication and relationship-building. Now we have the possibility of true friendship and increased potential for interpersonal AC4P behavior.

THE RECIPROCITY PRINCIPLE

On occasion, when a customer enters a supermarket, someone offers free samples. This gives the customer an opportunity to try a new product without having to purchase it. However, this free sample is not so free. There's a good chance the customer will purchase this product or spend more money at the supermarket. Our advice, avoid the "not so free" sample.

Norm of Reciprocity

The norm of reciprocity was identified by Alvin Gouldner in 1960 as an obligation to help individuals who have provided you with help and to retaliate against those who have caused you harm.[28] Many laws and governing societies originate from the norm of reciprocity (e.g., Babylon's Code of Hammurabi).[29] Plus, many human interactions, exchanges, and traditions existing on a smaller scale involve this social norm. In Western culture, gift exchanges occur on special occasions such as birthdays, weddings, baby showers, and holidays. Other reciprocal behaviors develop as families take turns preparing holiday dinners or alternating as host. After being a dinner guest at a friend's home, a couple typically reciprocates with a dinner at their home.

Exchanging holiday cards in December is an enduring tradition in the American culture. Many families go to great lengths to ensure they send holiday cards (e.g., Christmas, Hanukkah, and Kwanzaa) to important individuals/families in their lives. Plus, when a family receives a holiday card from people to whom they originally failed to send a card, they typically send one in return or at least put the sender on their holiday card list for the following year.

This norm of reciprocity was tested by two social psychologists, Philip Kunz and Michael Woolcott. They sent 578 Christmas cards to a random group of Chicago residents they didn't know. To their surprise, 20 percent of the recipients responded by either calling the researchers to reestablish a lost connection or sending them a Christmas card. Some recipients continued to send these researchers Christmas cards for a number of consecutive years after the experiment was conducted.[30]

The norm of reciprocity occurs in two forms: (1) direct reciprocity and (2) indirect reciprocity. Direct reciprocity is the exchange of helpful or harmful behavior between two individuals.[31] It's helpful when one AC4P act begets another; it's harmful when an individual seeks revenge or payback for an unkind act directed toward him/her.

As shown in the illustration on the next page, a time delay may exist between these behavioral exchanges. Still, the initial exchange can lead to repeated interactions and/or exchanges in the future. Indeed, it's common to experience these repeated interactions between friends, families, and acquaintances. If exchanges are consistently harmful, the two individuals can easily become long-term enemies. Even though the negative side of reciprocity is noteworthy, for the remainder of this section we focus on the positive side of reciprocity and its connection to AC4P behavior.

Direct Reciprocity

As depicted in Figure 6.3 and explained previously with reference to the Christmas card study, the first AC4P behavior is initiated by Person A. Person B's reciprocation is based upon the initial behavior of Person A. For example, direct reciprocity occurred for Cory when he hosted a spaghetti dinner at his apartment. After dinner, one of the dinner guests cleaned all of the dirty dishes. This mirrors what many couples do; one cooks, the other cleans.

Make the First Move. Reciprocity is a powerful activator of compliance. For this to occur, though, it's important to make the first move (e.g., to be the first to give a gift, provide help, or make a donation); then follow with a request for AC4P behavior by the recipient.

One study found that students who *received* gifts (e.g., T-shirt and travel mug) *before* they were asked to reward people's pro-environmental

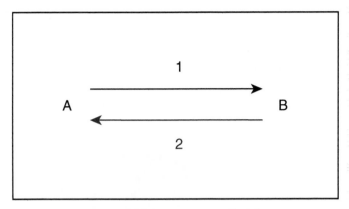

FIGURE 6.3. A representation of direct reciprocity. Each letter represents an individual, and "1" represents the initial AC4P behavior, whereas "2" is the reciprocal AC4P behavior.

behaviors with thank you cards were more likely to pass out the thank you cards than were students who were *promised* the same gifts *after* passing out five thank you cards.[32] Helping or gift-giving prior to a request is one way to increase probable compliance from others. Making a concession is another way to obtain agreement with a request. *Door-in-the-face* is the term for this influence technique, discussed later.

In another study, the norm of reciprocity was used to increase the reuse of hotel towels to save energy, cut down on costs, and help protect the environment.[33] Researchers gained 30 percent participation in the reuse of hotel towels with the following if–then contingency: "Partner with us to help save the environment. In exchange for your participation in this program, *we at the hotel will donate* a percentage of the energy savings to a nonprofit environmental-protection organization. The environment deserves our combined efforts. You can join us by reusing your towels during your stay."[34]

Participation grew to 42.5 percent with the following reciprocity message: "We're doing our part for the environment. Can we count on you? Because we are committed to preserving the environment, *we have made a financial contribution* to a nonprofit environmental-protection organization on behalf of the hotel and its guests. If you would like to help us in recovering the expense, while conserving natural resources, please reuse your towels during your stay."[35] This study suggests the norm of reciprocity is more effective at getting people to participate in a hotel towel-reusing program than an if–then contingency. Again, by being the first to perform an AC4P behavior it is possible to activate the norm of reciprocity and gain compliance with a follow-up request.

Door-in-the-Face. A person asks you, "Can I have ten dollars?" More than likely you will turn the person down, unless the plea comes from a friend who gave you money in the past. After you reject this first request, the person asks, "Could I have one dollar instead?" If you have the dollar, you might honor this request. Here's the critical question: Would you be more inclined to give up one dollar after your refusal to give up ten dollars than if you had never received the first request?

The answer is yes, according to empirical research. People are more likely to comply after rejecting a request that is more costly, in terms of time, effort, or money. This is called *door-in-the-face* (DITF).[36] Someone using the DITF technique increases compliance to a small request by first making a larger related request that is expected to get rejected.

In a seminal study, Cialdini et al. used the DITF technique to get college students to volunteer two hours of their time as chaperons for juveniles.[36] As expected, a low proportion of college students (four of twenty-four) agreed to volunteer. But when the same request followed a larger request to chaperon a group of juveniles for two hours a week for a minimum of two years, significantly more students (12 of twenty-four) volunteered.

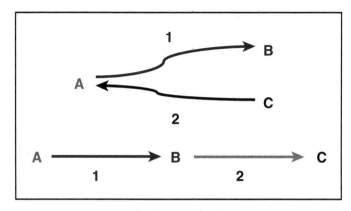

FIGURE 6.4. A representation of two types of reciprocity.
Top: Vicarious reciprocity: Person A helps Person B and then Person C helps Person A. Bottom: Pay-it-forward reciprocity: Person A helps Person B, then Person B helps Person C.

Now, what if someone asks you for a thousand dollars and then follows up with a request for one dollar. Would you give up the dollar? Research evidence suggests a small request is likely to be declined if the initial request is too large. The request may seem manipulative and illegitimate, and the credibility of the requester is impaired.[37] Additionally, counter-control or psychological reactance may decrease compliance, as discussed later in this chapter.

Indirect Reciprocity

Indirect reciprocity occurs when the behavior of a third individual is activated following awareness of a previous AC4P interaction between two other individuals.[38] Figure 6.4 illustrates two types of indirect reciprocity: (1) *vicarious reciprocity* and (2) *pay-it-forward reciprocity*.[39]

Vicarious Reciprocity. Vicarious reciprocity occurs when Person C observes Person A helping Person B, and then Person C chooses to help Person A as a result. Recall the research by Goldstein et al. which found that the incidence of reuse of hotel towels depended on the message left for the hotel guests. In their Reciprocity condition, the researchers induced vicarious reciprocity. That is, the hotel (A) made a financial contribution to an environmental-protection organization (B), and the hotel guest (C) is asked to help the hotel recover financially from its donation by reusing towels.

> # Last semester, the Actively Caring for People Movement paid for meals to increase intentional acts of kindness.
>
> ## You can actively care as well by paying for the next person's meal.
>
>
>
> ac4p.org

FIGURE 6.5. The sign at the cash register during all four phases of the study.

Pay-It-Forward Reciprocity. The behavior of Person C differentiates *pay-it-forward reciprocity* from vicarious reciprocity. Unlike vicarious reciprocity, where Person C rewards Person A, in pay-it-forward reciprocity, Person C is a recipient of the helpful act.[38] Suppose at a coffee shop, Person A purchases the next customer's coffee (Person B); then Person B performs a similar AC4P behavior for Person C by purchasing his/her muffin. Additionally, Person C might continue this linear chain of reciprocity by paying-it-forward to another individual.

Analogously, the Center for Applied Behavior Systems conducted an observational field study of pay-it-forward reciprocity at a university cafeteria.[39] To enter the buffet-style cafeteria, students pay a six-dollar admission fee. Due to the high volume and a rather slow financial transaction process, a long entrance/payment line was common. Periodically, an RA entered this line, and unobtrusive observers recorded whether specified behaviors occurred.

For all conditions, an 8½ by 11 inch sign (illustrated in Figure 6.5) was posted at the cash register, suggesting diners pay for the next person's meal. In the No-Reciprocity condition, the RA entered the line, paid for his/her meal, and did not interact with any of the diners standing in line. In the No-Interaction Reciprocity condition, the RA did not interact with the next diner but paid for his/her meal. In the Interaction-Reciprocity condition, the RA turned to the person behind him/her, pointed to the sign, and said, "I just read this sign and I want to support the Actively Caring for People Movement, so I am going to buy your meal." The RA then paid for the meal of this next diner.[39]

In the No-Reciprocity condition, only 6.8 percent of 148 diners paid for the next person's meal. In the No-Interaction Reciprocity condition, 15.6 percent of 122 diners paid for the next person's meal; and in the Interaction-Reciprocity condition, 24.6 percent of 183 diners paid for the next person's meal. Thus, in this setting, pay-it-forward reciprocity was most likely to occur when the norm of reciprocity was activated with both a supportive verbal exchange (a direct request) and a prompt (indirect request) that suggested how to reciprocate.

THE SOCIAL PROOF PRINCIPLE

At a local restaurant, Jocelyn joins a group of friends for dinner. For some time the group exchanges opinions on which entrée seems the most appetizing. From their discussions, Jocelyn assumes a wide variety of entrees will be ordered. Brittany is the first to order and selects the grilled chicken salad. Next is Jocelyn, who also orders the grilled chicken salad. Then Joanne does the same. Each of the girls at the table orders the grilled chicken salad.

According to the *social proof principle*, we look to others for guidance about which behaviors are appropriate or inappropriate in a particular situation, especially in an unfamiliar setting.[23] For instance, the individuals in this example discussed which entrée seemed the best to order and then each ordered the same entrée.

The social-proof principle is reflected by conformity. *Conformity* occurs when people imitate or copy the behavior of one or more persons.[40] Brittany's ordering the grilled chicken salad influenced Jocelyn's decision to order the same entrée. Of course, after Brittany and Jocelyn ordered the grilled chicken salad, the remaining girl at the table conformed by ordering the same entrée.

Conforming behaviors are more likely to occur in uncertain or unfamiliar situations.[41] In an unfamiliar situation, it's best to observe and imitate the behaviors of the most credible individual. However, because expectations vary across cultures, indigenous people often set the best example to follow. In China, for instance, it's customary to belch and leave a mess of food on your plate. This behavior is unacceptable in other countries. However, in China belching is a compliment to the cook. And leaving food on your plate indicates the cook provided ample food.

Laser-Dot Experiments

Social norms are rules or guidelines for appropriate/inappropriate behaviors.[42] Social approval results from behaviors consistent with a social norm. Behaviors inconsistent with a social norm risk social disapproval. When someone is riding in an elevator, the social norm (in the United States) is to face the elevator door for the duration of the ride. Don't believe us? Break this social norm by turning and facing the back wall of the elevator. We guarantee some passengers' reactions will be priceless.

Muzafer Sherif conducted a series of classic conformity experiments when studying the development of social norms.[43] Many variations of Sherif's paradigm exist, but the basic procedure is as follows. Each participant sits in a dark room. A laser dot is displayed on the wall across from the participant, who is instructed to tell the researcher how far the laser dot has moved on each trial. Unbeknownst to the participant, the laser dot is stationary. With a dark room eliminating a visual frame of reference and occasional rapid eye movements, a stationary laser dot appears to move. Perceived movement of the laser dot is an illusion called the *autokinetic effect.*

In the first experiment, each participant evaluated the distance the laser dot appeared to move.[44] The participants' responses ranged from 0.4

to 9.6 inches. The wide range of responses allowed Sherif to conduct two more studies to measure conformity. The second experiment consisted of four trials per participant.[42] The first trial followed the same procedure as in the first experiment. Then the participants were placed in groups of two or three, and three additional trials followed. On the second trial, the group members announced their responses publicly, and their responses varied quite a bit from each other. But on Trials 3 and 4, the variation in the group members' responses decreased significantly. Each group member's response was within 1 inch of the others' responses.

Interestingly, the groups' responses varied across groups. Toward the end of each group's trial, a norm had been developed regarding the observed distance the dot had moved. For one group, the laser dot moved 1 inch; for another group, the norm was established at 5 inches. This showed how group behavior can determine different social norms and how these norms can affect perception.

When a participant was removed from the group, Sherif found the group's social norm still existed.[45] In this study, a participant and an RA reported the distance a laser dot moved for fifty trials and a social norm was established (i.e., the distance the laser dot moved). After the first fifty trials, the RA left and the participant continued to evaluate the distance the laser dot moved for another fifty trials. Sherif found that the participants' responses given in the second set of fifty trials were similar to the responses in the first fifty trials. This suggests the social norm established in the first fifty trials remained after the RA left.

Because there wasn't a correct response in Sherif's experiments, participants could question their perception after hearing a conflicting view. As a result, perceptions were apparently altered to conform to those of others. Question: Will people conform to a group's incorrect response when the correct answer is obvious? The answer is yes, according to research conducted by Solomon Asch.

Matching Line Length Experiments

In a series of studies analogous to those by Sherif, the participants in Solomon Asch's studies selected one of three lines to match the length of a specified line – the standard.[46] The correct answer was always obvious. On successive trials, a participant publicly selected the line that matched the standard after a number of RAs publicly announced their judgments one by one. The RAs made correct selections for the first few trials. Then, the RAs gave uniformly incorrect judgments for the remaining trials. Even though the correct answer was obvious, in all twelve trials the judgments for only 23 percent of 123 participants remained completely independent of the group's response. Most participants (77 percent) denied reality in order to conform to the unanimously incorrect judgment of the RAs.

Normative and Informational Influence

Other people's judgments can have a dramatic impact on an individual's decisions, as demonstrated by the Sherif and Asch studies. In Sherif's experiments, participants' reports of the movement of a stable dot were influenced by the reported observations of others. In Asch's studies, participants denied their comparative judgments of line lengths in order to conform to the inaccurate judgments of a group. Why did these participants choose to conform?

People conform in anticipation of two possible consequences (i.e., social approval or disapproval). People conform to gain approval from others and/or avoid disapproval of others. They also gain information by observing the behavior of others. This is considered normative influence.[41] In Sherif's laser-dot studies, conforming participants modified their perceptions after becoming aware of another participant's reported perception. In Asch's line-judgment studies, incorrect information from others influenced most participants to deny their own perceptions. As in Sherif's experiments, the judgments of others were considered by individuals in order to be correct in their decisions and/or to gain a sense of social affiliation. These benefits reflect two of the three motivating consequences proposed by Cialdini and Goldstein: accuracy/competence and affiliation/community.[5]

Changing behavior to gain social approval (or peer support) or to avoid social disapproval (typically viewed as peer pressure) results from *normative influence*. In contrast, changing behavior for accuracy or competency is referred to as *informational influence*. Informational and normative influence can occur simultaneously. At the dinner setting, diners sought information from each other about their opinion on which was the best entrée. When Jocelyn and Megan selected grilled chicken salads, the other girls might have selected the same entrée because of both normative and informational influence.

Strength in Numbers

The more people who perform a certain behavior, the more likely others will imitate the same behavior. Makes sense, doesn't it? But this is not always the case. To test the impact of group size on conformity, Stanley Milgram, Leonard Bickman, and Lawrence Berkowitz conducted a simple field study.[47] A particular number of RAs (i.e., one, two, three, five, ten, or fifteen) simultaneously looked toward the sky on a busy sidewalk in New York City. Observers noted that 42 percent of 1,424 pedestrians looked up when one RA looked up. When three RAs looked up, about 60 percent of pedestrians looked up. When five RAs looked skyward nearly 86 percent of the pedestrians followed suit. But as the number of RAs increased beyond five, the proportion of pedestrians who looked up remained at approximately 80 percent.

In the line-judgment studies, Solomon Asch found a participant's conformity to a group's decision increased as the group size increased to three people.[46] But the percentage of conforming people remained the same as the group size increased beyond three people. What does this mean? Results from these studies suggest the increase in people performing the same specific behavior can prompt others to conform. However, as the number of people observed performing the same behavior increases beyond a certain point, one's propensity to conform is only slightly increased, if at all.[48]

Similarity

A person is more likely to conform to someone when the individual is similar to that person with regard to gender, age, career/education, and/or cultural background.[23] Being of similar age and gender could explain why all of the girls at the restaurant chose the grilled chicken salad.

Injunctive and Descriptive Norms as Activators

As explained earlier, a social norm is a rule or guideline for performing or avoiding a certain behavior. Social norms are injunctive or descriptive. An *injunctive norm* defines desirable and/or undesirable behavior. An injunctive norm is what one "ought to do," as Robert Cialdini put it.[49] In the United States, walking on the right side of the stairs is an injunctive norm. Strong disapproval is expressed via shouting, horn honking, and/or hand gestures when a driver is observed driving on the left side of the road.

A *descriptive norm* is the common and observed behavior of other people. Are people hiking, running, or biking on a trail? In this case, whichever activity most people are undertaking would be considered a descriptive norm.

An individual can activate behavior change in someone by changing that person's perception of the injunctive and/or descriptive norm.[49] A credible person performing a certain behavior can alter one's perception of the descriptive norm. One person littering can prompt onlookers to litter. Of course, the same is true if a person picks up litter. In this example, picking up litter is obviously an injunctive norm, while littering is a descriptive norm.

A sign is a low-cost way to inform people of the injunctive norm. Messages stating "no food or drink" are commonly found in office areas and classrooms. The message describes the desirable social norm for that setting. If most people comply, then a descriptive norm is implied. As depicted in the illustration below, a descriptive norm can put social pressure on a person to conform even when the norm is not injunctive.

THE AUTHORITY PRINCIPLE

The *authority principle* relates to compliance with a request coming from an authority figure.[23] The term *authority* has negative connotations because many historical examples and studies have illustrated the top-down coercive influence of people abusing their authority.[50] Still, many people with authority (e.g., physicians, ministers, teachers, and parents) set the stage for desirable behavior.

Obedience to authority can lead to undesirable behavior. This was shown by Stanley Milgram in a series of seminal experiments in the 1970s.[51] Ordinary people administered an electrical shock to another person at the request of a perceived authority figure. Note the participant's body language in the illustration of Milgram's experiment below. She's visibly distressed, as was the case for many participants, while following the anti-AC4P instructions from an authority figure.

In the first study, all forty participants administered at least 300 volts before refusing to continue administering an electrical shock.[52] Surprisingly, 65 percent of the forty participants administered the maximum voltage of 450 volts, even after the shock recipient (a stranger to the shock administrator) pounded on the wall and shouted "Ouch, this hurts!" Fortunately, the shock recipient in these studies was an RA and never actually received a shock.

There's a flip side to Milgram's horrific and surprising findings. According to a 1988 study, ordinary people will also *help* others at the request of a perceived authority figure.[53] A female RA (the requester) dressed as a perceived authority figure requested that a passerby give a nickel to a second RA (the recipient). The recipient posed as if he needed a nickel to pay for a parking meter. The three conditions in this study were defined by the requester's attire. In the Common-Attire condition, the requestor was dressed as a panhandler, wearing an old T-shirt, tattered pants and shoes. The RA in the Business-Attire condition wore well-tailored business clothes. And the RA in the Uniform condition wore an official uniform with a patch and badge. Of the 150 participants in the Uniform condition, 72 percent complied with the request. In contrast, compliance in the Business and Common-Attire conditions was 48 and 52 percent, respectively.

In addition to recording the number of participants who gave a nickel per each condition, the researchers recorded the participants' verbal behaviors accompanying the gift and classified them into four categories: (a) altruism, (b) unquestioned obedience, (c) compliance, and (d) ambiguous. Altruistic responses reflected a desire to help (e.g., "I saw you were in need of a nickel and I wanted to help"). The unquestioned obedience responses reflected a lack of desire to help (e.g., "That person told me to give you a nickel"). A mixture of unquestioned-obedience and altruistic responses were categorized as compliance (e.g., "I was told to help you, and I figured, why not?"). Finally, vague responses for helping were categorized in the ambiguous category.

The results: 27 percent of twenty-six participants viewed their gift of a nickel as more altruistic when the requester wore common clothes compared with tailored business attire (12.5 percent of 24 twenty-four participants) and a uniform (14 percent of thirty-six participants). On the other hand, 62.5 percent of twenty-four participants in the Business-Attire condition and 72 percent of 36 participants in the Uniform condition gave unquestioned-obedience responses while giving a nickel to the "beggar." In contrast, only 27 percent of twenty-six participants in the Common-Attire condition gave unquestioned-obedience responses.

So why do people obey an authority figure? In childhood, obeying a parent's decision is supported by positive and negative consequences, Stanley Milgram proposed.[52] Even in adulthood, consequences are often controlled by an authority figure (e.g., a manager or judge). In fact, authority is often defined by the person who controls the most consequences for others in a given situation. Complying with a request from a manager can increase job security and determine a raise. Disobeying a supervisor can lead to job termination.

Bottom line: Human behavior is motivated by consequences, and people are likely to comply with requests from those in control of those consequences –authority figures.

Harsh versus Soft Factors

Authority figures can gain compliance through situational or dispositional factors. These factors are categorized as harsh versus soft factors.[54] An authority figure who gains obedience from others based on a hierarchical position within a particular social structure represents the *harsh factor* approach. Managers, event staff, and administrators employ harsh factors to gain obedience. A staff member at a football game can instruct a fan to empty a cooler full of alcoholic beverages before entering the stadium.

In contrast, the *soft factor* approach applies dispositional factors, or one's attributions (e.g., experience, education, and credibility) to gain obedience. Physicians, professors, and ministers typically can use their dispositional factors or attributions to gain obedience within the relevant environmental context. Because of their education and experience, we usually don't question the medicine and dosages prescribed by a physician.

Authority Heuristics

Matt was recently duped by a car salesman. Before Matt purchased the car, the salesman agreed to have it inspected. The salesman took the car to the onsite mechanic. After the car passed the inspection, Matt purchased the car. Within a week, the motor seized up and the car stopped running. Matt immediately went back to the car salesman to return the car and get a refund. When Matt investigated the issue, he discovered the mechanic was a relative of the car salesman, who shared the profits made on each sale. Their ploy caused Matt to lose several thousand dollars, and he still was without a functional vehicle.

In this real-life example, Matt became a victim of heuristics. *Heuristics* are mental shortcuts used to make a decision.[55] These shortcuts can save lots of time and effort in making a decision. For instance, we often don't question a prescription from a medical doctor. After all, the physician is the expert and is looking out for our best interests, right? In the car salesman example, Matt made two heuristic mistakes. First he allowed the salesman to find a mechanic. This saved Matt the trouble of finding a mechanic and an inspection station. The second mistake: assuming the mechanic was a nonbiased third party, as is usually the case.

Bottom line: Individuals can gain obedience from others by creating the perception they are an authority figure. Bearing titles and wearing certain clothes are two methods people can use to influence the perception that they warrant authority impact.[23]

Attire. As a bystander, Jenna witnessed a person stealing a road sign. Another onlooker approached the thief and strongly suggested he return the sign. The thief ignored the onlooker's request. Shortly after the onlooker's intervention, two police officers approached the thief and requested the sign be returned. Without questioning the officers, the thief immediately obeyed and returned the sign. A uniform gains more obedience to a request than regular clothes, especially when potential consequences are implied.[56]

To empirically test the impact of attire on onlookers' behavior, an RA dressed differently in two conditions.[57] In the Low-Status condition, the RA wore common clothes. In the High-Status condition, the same RA wore a pressed suit. In both conditions, the RA was the first of a number of pedestrians to disobey a pedestrian traffic signal by crossing the street when it indicated "Wait." Observers recorded the number of people who illegally crossed the street with the RA and the number of individuals who waited to cross the street legally. Significantly more people (14 percent of 290) crossed the street illegally when the confederate's clothes suggested high status than when the attire of the illegal pedestrian reflected low status (4 percent of 288).

Titles. Titles define a level of authority because they offer insight into the background of the individual (e.g., education, experience, and leadership). The military uses titles/ranks to signify the chain of command. A doctor's title (e.g., cardiologist, surgeon, and dentist) provides insight into his/her educational background and expertise. Even when a title is not authentic, it can influence someone's decision.[58] Recall Matt getting duped by a car salesman and mechanic. The mechanic may not have been a mechanic at all. Because the individual held the title of mechanic, Matt trusted his decision regarding the condition of the vehicle. This trusting of the mechanic's credentials as a result of his title relates to an instructive study.

Over the phone a researcher claimed he was a medical doctor and instructed different nurses to give a patient a specific drug s/he did not need.[59] The results were terrifying. Almost all (95 percent) of the twenty-two nurses who answered the phone complied with the researcher's request. Fortunately, an RA stopped each nurse before the medicine was administered and informed him/her of the study. This research was conducted in

1966. We doubt the same results would be found today, given the current context of frequent Internet scamming and phone call solicitation.

THE SCARCITY PRINCIPLE

In the mid-1800s, Napoleon III invited the royal family to a banquet. To show off, he permitted the royal family to use special aluminum utensils; silver and gold utensils were used by ordinary folk. Today, allowing the royal family to use aluminum utensils over silver and gold would seem preposterous. But in Napoleon's era, aluminum was held in higher esteem than silver and gold because it was more difficult to process. Near the end of the nineteenth century, the value of aluminum dropped substantially as more effective processing systems were discovered.

According to the *scarcity principle*, we value things that are rare or becoming rare.[23] People valued aluminum more than silver or gold in the 1850s because it was more difficult to obtain. The value of aluminum dropped when it became abundant. Our attraction to limited numbers and our attempts to preserve personal control reflect the scarcity principle.

Limited Numbers

Having a limited quantity of a certain product, and increasing one's awareness of the limited availability, increases one's propensity to purchase the product.[23] When advertising, companies often implement the limited-number technique to sell their products. They claim the item has a "limited release," is a "limited edition," or is "one of a few left in stock." In this latter example, the scarcity principle works in conjunction with the social proof principle. That is, the message "one of a few left in stock" implies the product is in high demand and becoming scarcer.

Psychological Reactance

We act to regain our personal control when we perceive a restriction or limitation on our freedom or individuality, according to *psychological reactance* theory.[60] For this reason, top-down control tactics can backfire. A young boy might fight back when his parents insist he wear certain clothes to school. The fighting-back behavior presumes an attempt to regain some personal control or demonstrate counter-control.[61]

Recall from the section on the authority principle that a harsh tactic is one way to gain obedience from others. Due to psychological reactance, though, a top-down approach can be counterproductive.[4] For example, university students who got the most intoxicated on Thursday and Friday nights were those whose parents used the most punitive strategies to stop them from consuming alcohol, according to field research conducted by the Virginia Tech Center for Applied Behavior Systems (see Chapter 12). It's called the *forbidden fruit phenomenon*. Restricting the use of an item makes it scarce, and so the item seems more valuable, and the restrictions are often disregarded when one can avoid the implied punitive consequences.

Leaders of the AC4P Movement have applied social-influence principles to activate and motivate occurrences of AC4P behavior. This section connects specific social-influence principles with real-world strategies for fueling the AC4P Movement. Plus, we suggest techniques you can use to increase the frequency of AC4P behavior and help create a more compassionate and AC4P culture.

AC4P APPLICATIONS

Consistency

The consistency principle is the basis for a plethora of AC4P applications. The foot-in-the-door technique can increase the occurrence of AC4P behavior among friends, colleagues, and even strangers. First, start with a small request like, "Please wear the AC4P wristband to signify your intention to join the AC4P Movement." Then follow with a larger request like, "Please give another person supportive and/or corrective feedback regarding behavior related to AC4P."

Social labeling is a subtle way to promote the occurrence of AC4P behavior. Simply give a person a particular desirable and suitable social label like, "You seem to be someone who really cares about the well-being of others," and then follow with a request, "Would you join our AC4P coaching team, which provides behavior-based feedback to individuals regarding the safety of their job-related behavior?" The AC4P label will increase the probability the targeted individual will comply with your request.

Leaders of the AC4P Movement have used the social-labeling tactic to cultivate an AC4P culture in elementary schools. Teachers in elementary schools rewarded two students daily with an AC4P wristband to wear the day after they performed or wrote an AC4P story. These two students were publicly labeled the "Actively Caring Heroes of the Day," and they proudly wore the AC4P wristband. Systematic evaluations indicated these students performed more AC4P behavior on the days when they wore the AC4P wristband, presumably to live up to the positive social label they had received and displayed for one day.

A commitment strategy to promote AC4P behavior for environmental conservation was used recently by research students in the Center for Applied Behavior Systems. Customers leaving a large grocery store were asked by researchers if they'd like to increase their use of reusable grocery bags for purchased groceries. When a customer gave a positive response, the RA offered a hangtag to hook on a vehicle's rearview mirror as a reminder to bring reusable bags into the grocery store. Then the customer was asked to sign the back of the hangtag as a part of his/her commitment to use reusable grocery bags.

Notice how this social-influence strategy applied three consistency techniques to enhance people's propensity to honor their commitment. First, customers *chose* to use reusable grocery bags. Subsequently, they signed the hangtag in front of the RA, making the commitment *active* and *public*. Subsequently, they were presumably reminded of their pro-environment commitment whenever they looked at the card hanging from their vehicle's rearview mirror.

Liking

The AC4P interventions accomplished by Virginia Tech students at Chardon High School (CHS) exemplify the influential power of claiming similar backgrounds.[62] Both educational settings were sites of tragic school shootings. After the shootings at CHS in 2012, student leaders contacted AC4P leaders at Virginia Tech to help recover and move forward. When the AC4P leaders talked with leaders and students at CHS, they discussed their "common background" to make critical connections. Also, when giving workshops and coaching CHS staff and students, AC4P leaders wore blue jeans and an AC4P t-shirt customized for CHS (see Figure 6.6), approximating the common attire of most high school students.

The AC4P Movement gains favorable exposure it needs to expand and grow through the mere-exposure effect, like companies advertising their products. Leaders of the AC4P Movement are already using various strategies to acquire favorable exposure, including T-shirts, Facebook, the ac4p. org Website, scholarship,[63] media exposure (e.g., radio interviews and local/ national television stations), keynote addresses at professional conferences, webinars, as well as the AC4P wristband.

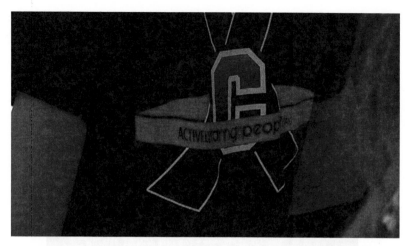

FIGURE 6.6. The AC4P T-shirt customized for Chardon High School.

Reciprocity

Reciprocity is a fundamental influence tactic in the *see, act, pass, share* (SAPS) process of the AC4P Movement.[64] To clarify: A person rewards another person with an AC4P wristband for performing an AC4P behavior. Once the wristband has been accepted, the recipient might feel a sense of indebtedness. The rewarding individual asks the wristband recipient to use the wristband to reward someone else for his/her AC4P behavior. Such pay-it-forward behavior will alleviate any sense of indebtedness. Thus, compliance with the request to pass on the wristband for AC4P behavior is increased through reciprocity.

The door-in-the-face technique can be used to activate others to perform AC4P behavior. You could challenge people to perform an AC4P act every day for a month. For most people, this would be a difficult task. When this request is rejected, follow it with an easier request like, "Try performing an AC4P act two times a week for a month." Of course, this same technique can be used to ask others to reward AC4P behavior they observe or to provide behavior-based feedback to benefit another person's health, safety, or welfare.

Let's say you actively cared for an individual and this individual wants to reciprocate. Reciprocity may take place in the form of money, a free meal, or a promise to help you in the future. Regardless, as a result of your AC4P behavior, this individual may feel a sense of obligation to return the favor. We recommend specifying how this sense of indebtedness can be

FIGURE 6.7. The logo on the first AC4P T-shirts.

relieved: "Simply pay it forward by actively caring for another person." Your suggestion may nudge pay-it-forward reciprocity, enabling your one AC4P behavior to initiate a ripple effect that spreads AC4P behavior.

Social Proof

Large-scale behavior change is influenced daily through the social proof principle. Many people conform to fashion trends or fads because others are doing so. Seeing others wearing the AC4P wristband encourages others to do the same. This demonstrates social approval of the AC4P Movement, and perhaps awareness of how this wristband gets passed on among individuals. Such social proof could activate interpersonal conversation about the AC4P Movement and a discussion of ways to get involved. For example, a common reaction following our passing of the AC4P wristband is, "Oh thank you, I've seen these around campus and have always wanted one of my own."

The AC4P T-shirt. The social proof principle is one of many social-influence techniques used by the leaders of the AC4P Movement. During the early stages of the AC4P Movement, the original AC4P T-shirt included the line "Join the Movement" (see Figure 6.7). The phrase, "Join the Movement" implies that other people are already a part of the AC4P Movement – a descriptive norm. This message should be more influential in getting others to join the AC4P Movement than a message like "Actively Care for People."

The AC4P Website. The AC4P Website applies the social proof principle in different ways. It offers a way for others to see the number of wristbands that have been registered and how the wristbands are traveling around the world. During AC4P presentations, AC4P leaders show a map of the world and tell AC4P stories connected to particular AC4P wristbands that have traveled across several countries.[65]

A second way the social proof principle promotes the AC4P Movement on the Website is linking the AC4P Website to Facebook. On Facebook pages, individuals share their AC4P stories with friends and others. Here we have the influence of both interpersonal liking and a descriptive norm. In this case, the descriptive norm matches the injunctive norm.

Injunctive and Descriptive Norms. Some schools and communities have organized an AC4P Day to align the injunctive and descriptive norms. For example, leaders in Newton, Connecticut (site of a tragic school shooting), implemented an "Acts of Kindness Day" on September 14, 2013. Community leaders gave speeches and distributed materials to initiate and maintain an AC4P buzz. Similarly, thousands of students at Virginia Tech participate annually in "the Big Event" – a day when students volunteer their AC4P service for homeowners throughout the university community. They assist residents with a variety of projects, from planting trees and grooming gardens to cleaning home garages and basements.

Authority

AC4P leaders have used various strategies from the authority principle to spread the AC4P Movement. Soft-Factor approaches are commonly used by AC4P leaders. Examples of experience, education, and credibility can be found in resources like the AC4P brochure and on the AC4P Website (ac4p.org):

> Actively Caring, coined by Dr. E. Scott Geller, refers to any behavior going above and beyond the call of duty for others. For decades, Dr. Geller, Alumni-Distinguished Professor at Virginia Tech, has applied behavioral science to keep people safe at work and on the road.

To gain credibility via a title, the leaders of the AC4P Movement are introduced as college students and campus leaders to an assembly of elementary, middle, or high school students. The same leaders wear AC4P T-shirts to display their involvement in the AC4P Movement. To enhance the leaders' credibility, they could add the social label "AC4P Leader" to their shirts.

Scarcity

The scarcity principle can be used to increase the perceived value of the AC4P wristband. For example, at professional conferences and workshops, AC4P leaders inform audience members they brought a limited number of wristbands to the event. And the AC4P wristbands can be purchased *only* at the ac4p.org Website. Of course, a social-proof message can be added as an explanation for the limited number of AC4P wristbands. For instance, one can account for the scarcity of wristbands by explaining that a large number of people had requested the wristband prior to the presentation – a descriptive norm.

IN CONCLUSION

The six social influence principles and strategies described and illustrated here can help initiate and sustain the AC4P Movement at your school, community, and workplace. Throughout this chapter we suggested ways to use the social-influence principles and techniques to increase another person's propensity to perform AC4P behavior.

The method of delivering an influence technique can be more important than the technique itself. This is worth remembering. A top-down application can actually do more harm than good by activating psychological reactance or counter-control. That's why we call the AC4P approach to cultivating compassion on a large-scale *humanistic behaviorism*.

We incorporate evidence-based principles of ABS to activate and sustain beneficial behavior change. We also use person-centered principles of humanism to ensure personal ownership and perceived empowerment. In other words, behavior-change methods are taught, coached, and implemented so both the benefactors and the beneficiaries believe in their effectiveness and want to support the AC4P Movement.

DISCUSSION QUESTIONS

1. Explain the Consistency Principle and its connection to Leon Festinger's Theory of Cognitive Dissonance (1957).
2. Use self-perception theory to explain why intrapersonal conversation should accompany prosocial behavior. In other words, why is planned

and mindful AC4P behavior preferable to random and mindless acts of kindness?

3. How does the ability versus effort research by Carol Dweck define ways to give and not to give performance feedback to others?

4. Explain the role of perceived choice in self-perception (i.e., transferring behavior to attitude) and commitment (i.e., following through with a behavioral promise).

5. Why is the "Door-in-the-Face" technique classified as a Reciprocity Principle? What other social influence principle(s), if any, connect(s) to this interpersonal phenomenon? Please explain.

6. Distinguish operationally between injunctive and descriptive norms with regard to their influence on behavior.

7. Distinguish with realistic examples between harsh versus soft determinants of compliance from authority figures.

8. How does psychological reactance connect to the Scarcity Principle?

9. Discuss ways each of the six social-influence principles can be (or are) applied to increase the frequency or improve the quality of prosocial or AC4P behavior

10. Discuss the validity and relevance of the opening quotation of this chapter from Abraham Lincoln, "Don't criticize them; they are just what we would be under similar circumstances."

REFERENCES

1. Kenrick, D. T., Neuberg, S. L., & Cialdini, R. B. (2002). *Social psychology: Unraveling the mystery* (2nd ed.). Boston: Pearson.

2. Thaler, R. H., & Sunstein, C. R. (2009).*Nudge: Improving decisions about health, wealth, and happiness.* New York: Penguin Group.

3. Geller, E. S. (1996). *The psychology of safety: How to improve behaviors and attitudes on the job.* Radnor, PA: Chilton; Geller, E. S. (2001). *The psychology of safety handbook.* Boca Raton, FL: CRC Press; Geller, E. S., & Veazie, B. (2014). Behavior-based safety versus actively caring: From other-directed compliance to self-directed commitment. *Professional Safety, 59*(10), 44–50.

4. Lehman, P. K., & Geller, E. S. (2008). Applications of social psychology to increase the impact of behavior-focused intervention. In Steg, L., Buunk, A. P., & Rothengatter, T. (Eds.). *Applied social psychology: Understanding and managing social problems* (pp. 117–136). New York: Cambridge University Press.

5. Cialdini, R. B., & Goldstein, N. J. (2004). Social influence: Compliance and conformity. *Annual Review of Psychology, 55,* 591–621.

6. Geller, E. S. (2001). *The psychology of safety handbook.* Boca Raton, FL: CRC Press; Geller, E. S., Roberts, D. S., & Gilmore, M. R. (1996). Predicting propensity to actively care for occupational safety. *Journal of Safety Research, 27,* 1–8.

7. Festinger, L. (1957). *A theory of cognitive dissonance*. Stanford, CA: Stanford University Press.

8. Bem, D. J. (1967). Self-perception: An alternative interpretation of cognitive dissonance phenomena. *Psychological Review, 74*, 183–200.

9. Bem, D. J. (1972). Self-perception theory. In L. Berkowitz (Ed.). *Advances in experimental psychology*, Vol. 6 (pp. 1–62). New York: Academic Press.

10. Freedman, J. L., & Fraser, S. C. (1966). Compliance without pressure: The foot-in-the-door technique. *Journal of Personality and Social Psychology, 4*, 195–202.

11. Cialdini, R. B., Eisenberg, N., Green, B. L., Rhoads, K., & Bator, R. (1998). Undermining the undermining effect of reward in sustained interest: When unnecessary conditions are sufficient. *Journal of Applied Social Psychology, 28*, 249–63; Tybout, A. M., & Yalch, R. F. (1980). The effect of experience: A matter of salience? *Journal of Consumer Research, 6*, 406–413.

12. Kraut, R. E. (1973). Effects of social labeling on giving to charity. *Journal of Experimental Social Psychology, 9*, 551–562.

13. Kraut, R. E. (1973). Effects of social labeling on giving to charity. *Journal of Experimental Social Psychology, 9*, 551–562, p. 554.

14. Kraut, R. E. (1973). Effects of social labeling on giving to charity. *Journal of Experimental Social Psychology, 9*, 551–562., p. 555.

15. Retrieved from www.bls.gov/cgi-bin/cpicalc.pl, July 23, 2015.

16. Dweck, C. S. (2006). *Mindset: The new psychology of success*. New York: Ballotine Books.

17. Dweck, C. S. (2006). *Mindset: The new psychology of success*. New York: Ballotine Books, p. 71.

18. Dweck, C. S. (2006). *Mindset: The new psychology of success*. New York: Ballotine Books, p. 72.

19. Dweck, C. S. (2006). *Mindset: The new psychology of success*. New York: Ballotine Books, p. 73.

20. Geller, E. S. (2001).*The psychology of safety handbook*. Boca Raton, FL: CRC Press; Geller, E. S, & Veazie, B. (2010). *When no one's watching: Living and leading self-motivation*. Newport, VA: Make-A-Difference; Ludwig, T. D., & Geller, E. S. (2001). *Intervening to improve the safety of occupational driving: A behavior-change model and review of empirical evidence*. New York: Haworth Press; Monty, R. A., & Perlmuter, L. C. (1975). Persistence of the effect of choice on paired-associate learning, *Memory & Cognition, 3*, 183–187; Perlmuter, L. C., Monty, R. A., & Kimble, G. A. (1971). Effect of choice on paired-associate learning. *Journal of Experimental Psychology, 91*, 47–58; Steiner, I. D. (1970). Perceived freedom. In L. Berkowitz (Ed.). *Advancements in experimental social psychology*, Vol. 5 (pp. 187–248). New York: Academic Press.

21. Fazio, R. H., Sherman, S. J., & Herr, P. M. (1982). The feature-positive effect in the self-perception process. Does not doing matter as much as doing? *Journal of Personality and Social Psychology, 42*, 404–411.

22. Schlenker, B. R., Dlugolecki, D. W., & Doherty, K. (1994). The impact of self-presentations on self-appraisals and behavior. The power of public commitment. *Personality and Social Psychology Bulletin, 20*, 20–33; Tedeshi, J. T.,

Schlenker, B. R., & Bonoma, T. V. (1971). Cognitive dissonance: Private ratiocination or public spectacle? *American Psychologist*, 26, 685–695.

23. Cialdini, R. B. (2001). *Influence: Science and practice* (6th ed.). Boston: Pearson.

24. Emswiller, T., Deaux, K., & Willits, J. E. (1971). Similarity, sex, and requests for small favors. *Journal of Applied Psychology*, 1, 284–291.

25. Burger, J. M., Messian, N., Patel, S., Prado, A., & Anderson, C. (2004). What a coincidence! The effects of incidental similarity on compliance. *Personality and Social Psychology Bulletin*, 30, 35–43.

26. Berscheid, E., & Walster, E. (1978). *Interpersonal attraction*. Reading, MA; Addison-Wesley; Howard, D. J., Gengler, C., & Jain, A. (1995). What's in a name? A complimentary means of persuasion. *Journal of Consumer Research*, 22, 200–211; Howard, D. J., Gengler, C., & Jain, A. (1997). The name remembrance effect. *Journal of Social Behavior and Personality*, 12, 801–810.

27. Zajonc, R. B. (1968). Attitudinal effects of mere exposure. *Journal of Personality and Social Psychology*, 9, 1–27.

28. Gouldner, A. (1960). The norm or reciprocity: A preliminary statement. *American Sociological Review*, 25(2), 161–178.

29. Babylon's Code of Hammurabi is one of the earliest known set of laws. It is based upon *lextalionis* (eye for an eye), which means for every crime committed an equitable punishment should be issued.

30. Kunz, P. R., & Woolcott, M. (1976). Season's greetings: From my status to yours. *Social Science Research*, 5(3), 269–278.

31. Trivers, R. L. (1971). The evolution of reciprocal altruism. *Quarterly Reviews of Biology*, 46(1), 35–57.

32. Boyce, T. E., & Geller, E. S. (2001). Encouraging college students to support pro-environmental behavior: Effects of direct versus indirect rewards. *Environment and Behavior*, 33, 107–125.

33. Goldstein, N. J., Griskevicius, V., & Cialdini, R. B. (2007). Invoking social norms: A social psychology perspective on improving hotel's linen-reuse programs. *Cornell Hotel and Restaurant Administration Quarterly*, 48(2), 145–150.

34. Goldstein, N. J., Griskevicius, V., & Cialdini, R. B. (2007). Invoking social norms: A social psychology perspective on improving hotel's linen-reuse programs. *Cornell Hotel and Restaurant Administration Quarterly*, 48(2), 146.

35. Goldstein, N. J., Griskevicius, V., & Cialdini, R. B. (2007). Invoking social norms: A social psychology perspective on improving hotel's linen-reuse programs. *Cornell Hotel and Restaurant Administration Quarterly*, 48(2), 147–148.

36. Cialdini, R. B., Vincent, J. E., Lewis, S. K., Catalan, J., Wheeler, D., & Darby, B. L. (1975). Reciprocal concessions procedure for inducing compliance: The door-in-the-face technique. *Journal of Personality and Social Psychology*, 31, 206–215.

37. Schwartzwald, D., Raz, M., & Zwibel, M. (1979). The applicability of the door-in-the-face technique when established behavior customs exit. *Journal of Applied Social Psychology*, 9, 576–586.

38. Nowak, M. A., & Sigmund, K. (2005). Evolution of indirect reciprocity. *Nature*, 437, 1291–1298; Stanca, L. (2009). Measuring indirect reciprocity: Whose back do we scratch? *Journal of Economic Psychology*, 30(2), 190–202.

39. Furrow, C., McCarty, S., & Geller, E. S. (in press). Intervening to promote pay-it-forward behavior: Impact of prompting an act of kindness. *Journal of Prevention Intervention in the Community.*

40. Brecker, S. J., Olson, J. M., & Wiggins, E. C. (2006). *Social psychology alive.* Belmont, CA: Thomson Wadsworth.

41. Deutsch, M., & Gerard, H. B. (1955). A study of normative and informational social influences upon individual judgment. *Journal of Abnormal and Social Psychology, 51,* 629–636.

42. Sherif, M. (1936). *The psychology of social norms.* Oxford: Harper.

43. Sherif, M. (1935). A study of some social factors in perception. *Archives of Psychology, 27*(187), 1–60; Sherif, M. (1936). *The psychology of social norms.* Oxford: Harper; Sherif, M. (1937). An experimental approach to the study of attitudes. *Sociometry,* 1, 90–89.

44. Sherif, M. (1935). A study of some social factors in perception. *Archives of Psychology, 27*(187), 1–60.

45. Sherif, M. (1937). An experimental approach to the study of attitudes. *Sociometry,* 1, 90–89.

46. Asch, S. E. (1951). Effects of group pressure upon the modification and distortion of judgments. In H. Guetzkow (Ed.). *Groups leadership and men* (pp. 177–190). Pittsburgh: Carnegie Press; Asch, S. E. (1952). *Social psychology.* New York: Prentice Hall; Asch, S. E. (1956), Studies of independence and conformity: A minority of one against a unanimous majority. *Psychological Monographs: General and Applied,* 70(9), 1–70.

47. Milgram, S., Bickman, L., & Berkowitz, L. (1969). Note on the drawing power of crowds of different size. *Journal of Personality and Social Psychology,* 13, 79–82.

48. Latane, B. (1981). The psychology of social impact. *American Psychologist,* 35(4), 343–356.

49. Cialdini, R. B., Kallgren, C. A., & Reno, R. R. (1991). A focus theory of normative conduct: A theoretical refinement and reevaluation of the role of norms in human behavior. *Advances in Experimental Social Psychology,* 24, 201–234.

50. Examples are the Stanford Prison Experiment, Milgram studies, rape of Rwanda, and the Holocaust.

51. Milgram, S. (1974). *Obedience to authority: An experimental view.* New York: Harper & Row.

52. Milgram, S. (1963). Behavioral study of obedience. *Journal of Abnormal and Social Psychology,* 67, 371–378.

53. Bushman, B. J. (1988). The effects of apparel on compliance: A field experiment with a female authority figure. *Personal and Social Psychology Bulletin,* 14, 459–467.

54. Koslowsky, M., Schwarzwald, J., & Ashuri, S. (2001). On the relationship between subordinates' compliance to power sources and organizational attitudes. *Applied Psychology: International Review,* 50, 455–476; Raven, B. H., Schwarzwald, J., & Koslowsky, M. (1998). Conceptualizing and measuring a power/interaction model of interpersonal influence. *Journal of Applied Social Psychology,* 6, 161–168.

55. Kahneman, D., Slovic, P., & Tversky, A. (1982) (Eds.). *Judgments under uncertainty: Heuristics and biases.* New York: Cambridge University Press.

56. Bickman, L. (1974). The social power of a uniform. *Journal of Applied Social Psychology*, 4, 47–61.
57. Lefkowitz, M., Blake, R. R., & Mouton, J. S. (1955). Status factors in pedestrian violation of traffic signals. *Journal of Abnormal and Social Psychology*, 51, 704–706.
58. Cialdini, R. B. (2001). *Influence: Science and practice* (6th ed.). Boston: Pearson; Hofling, C. K., Brotzman, E., Dalrymple, S., Graves, N., & Pierce, C. M. (1966). An experimental study of nurse–physician relationships. *Journal of Nervous and Mental Disease*, 143, 171–180.
59. Hofling, C. K., Brotzman, E., Dalrymple, S., Graves, N., & Pierce, C. M. (1966). An experimental study of nurse–physician relationships. *Journal of Nervous and Mental Disease*, 143, 171–180.
60. Brehm, J. W. (1966). *A theory of psychological reactance.* New York: Academic Press.
61. Skinner, B. F. (1971). *Beyond freedom and dignity.* New York: Alfred A. Knopf.
62. Teie, S. Y., McCarty, S. M., & McCutchen, J. (2014). Sustaining compassion after tragic school shootings: Applying the AC4P Principles at Virginia Tech and Chardon High School. In E. S. Geller (Ed.). *Actively caring at your school: How to make it happen* (pp. 225–236). Newport, VA: Make-A-Difference, LLC.
63. Geller, E. S. (Ed.). (2014). *Actively caring at your school: How to make it happen* (2nd ed.). Newport, VA: Make-A-Difference; Geller, E. S. (Ed.). (2014). *Actively caring for people: Cultivating a culture of compassion* (4th ed.). Newport, VA: Make-A-Difference.
64. McCarty, S., Teie, S., McCutchen, J., & Geller, E. S. (in press). Actively caring to prevent bullying in an elementary school: Prompting and rewarding prosocial behavior. *Journal of Prevention Intervention in the Community*; McCarty, S. M., & Geller, E. S. (2014). Actively caring to prevent bullying: Activating and rewarding prosocial behavior in elementary schools. In E. S. Geller (Ed.). *Actively caring for people: Cultivating a culture of compassion* (4th ed.) (pp. 177–197). Newport, VA: Make-A-Difference.
65. Case studies are available on the ac4p.org Website.

7

The Intersection of Positive Psychology and AC4P

KEENAN TWOHIG, MATT FORNITO AND E. SCOTT GELLER

[I]n the last ten years, we've seen the beginnings of a science of positive psychology, a science of what makes life worth living.
– Martin Seligman

When you think about psychology, what comes to mind? Perhaps a therapist or marriage counselor helping patients work through emotional and relationship issues or a licensed psychiatrist prescribing an antidepressant to a clinically diagnosed patient. Maybe you imagine a cognitive behavioral therapist treating someone's crippling social phobia or post-traumatic stress disorder. Common to all these impressions is this: The focus is predominantly on correcting a negative psychological state and alleviating mental and emotional suffering. Psychology, it would seem, is all about identifying and eliminating mental afflictions, negative emotions, and disruptive, destructive behaviors – attempting through various techniques and medications to bring abnormality back to normality.

But why this preoccupation with negativity? Negative disorders. Negative behaviors. Depression. Anxiety. Phobias and traumas. After all, humans possess many, many strengths – positives. We are curious, creative, brave, kind, and loving – we can actively care. We appreciate integrity, wisdom, gratitude, mindfulness, and fair play. We seek out and celebrate warm, nurturing social relationships; we inspire others and are inspired in return. Plus, we are resilient; we can sustain hope through many trials and tribulations. We genuinely care for the well-being and the safety and health of people who are close to us – even strangers we know nothing about. And within us and for others we have the capacity to activate and nurture these strengths just as a gardener waters seeds and watches them bloom.

The truth is psychology is about both sides of the human condition and fulfilling lives as well as curing people of mental and emotional suffering.[1]

As the twenty-first century began, a few researchers sought to revive a genuine, scientific interest in promoting the positive dimensions of psychology. They began foundational work in the domain known today as *positive psychology*.[1] This is not to say positive psychology suddenly became a new field, bursting out of nowhere. Applied behavioral science (ABS) focused on the application of positive over negative consequences to improve behavior for many years before the evolution of this "new" positive psychology. As a subfield of psychology, positive psychology attempts to identify interventions to support positive psychological growth – emotional fulfillment and happiness.

Christopher Peterson and Martin Seligman's *VIA Character Strengths* was a primary initial catalyst for the blossoming of positive psychology.[2] They defined particular character strengths as reflecting humans' capacity for thinking, feeling, and behaving. We view their analysis as integrating the humanistic person-focus of positive psychology and the positive behavior-change focus of ABS. We conceptualize this as humanistic behaviorism, also known as actively caring for people (AC4P).

DEFINING POSITIVE PSYCHOLOGY

Positive psychology is the scientific study of people's strengths and virtues.[3] It's considered the "science of positive subjective experience, positive individual traits, and positive institutions [that promise] to improve quality of life and prevent the pathologies that arise when life is barren and meaningless."[4] The primary mission: Build positive qualities in people by adopting an open, nonjudgmental perspective toward human potential, motives, and capacities.[1]

The advent and public acceptance of positive psychology are credited in large part to clinical psychologist Martin Seligman. His epiphany and subsequent paradigm shift occurred when he realized his job as a parent was not to focus on correcting his daughter's shortcomings, but rather to nurture her strengths and virtues in order for her to live an enriching life full of potential and positive outcomes.[5] His parental role was not to simply punish his daughter in order to correct her behavior; he needed to be the driver – an AC4P agent – who promoted a positive vision of healthy possibilities and opportunities and relevant goal setting. Both positive psychology and the AC4P Movement aim to enhance human welfare and well-being. Positive psychology asks, "What are people doing right?" ABS and AC4P take it a step further to formulate and implement interventions in order to increase the frequency of "right" behavior.

Helping Others

Much of Seligman's early research was crucial for the subsequent popularity of the positive psychology movement, which continues to this day. This is especially germane since negative-focused publications in psychology far exceed positive-focused publications at a ratio of 14:1.[6]

In one classroom study, Seligman posed an assignment to his students: Engage in one pleasurable activity and one philanthropic activity, then write about each.[5] Pleasurable activities included watching a movie, spending time with friends, or eating a favorite meal; philanthropic activities required the physical expression of gratification or kindness. Philanthropic activities were further divided into structured versus spontaneous choices.

A *structured* philanthropic exercise might include volunteering at a soup kitchen every Friday night. In contrast, a *spontaneous* philanthropic activity was defined as an emergent moment in which the decision to provide (or not provide) support and kindness occurs without any apparent external cause. You listen empathically to a colleague who is distraught over a nasty divorce. You help an elderly woman carry her groceries to her car. Perhaps you simply hold the door open for a stranger at a convenience store. Your choice occurs in the present moment, to help or not to help, and it reflects a certain courage to transcend one's selfish interests.

Seligman described the results of this study as *life-changing*. Spontaneous philanthropic acts made the day for these students. Pleasurable self-centered activities were in no way as effective – in duration or intensity – as a means of boosting a person's positive mood for the day. Subsequent research supports this notion that philanthropic acts of kindness and caring (i.e., AC4P behaviors) increase personal happiness significantly more than experiencing personal pleasurable activities.[7]

Well-Being

Well-being is defined as "optimal psychological functioning and experience" and is classified as *hedonic* and *eudemonic*.[8] Hedonic well-being, often known as subjective well-being (SWB), has been thoroughly researched. Aristotle claimed that hedonism referred simply to obtaining gratification from pleasurable behaviors and consciously choosing to do things that are enjoyable or intrinsically reinforcing (as explained in Chapter 1). As such, SWB serves and benefits only our self-interests. What hasn't been emphasized enough is the fact that SWB reflects the entire spectrum of an individual's life satisfactions[9] as well as positive and negative experiences.[10]

Eudaimonic well-being is more neglected in research and is not a well-known concept. The word *eudaimonia* comes from the Greek word *daimon*, meaning one's true self or spirit.[8] Eudaimonia is sometimes considered pure happiness, but it's actually more akin to the satisfaction that comes with developing and realizing our maximum potential. It goes beyond the easily accessible pleasures of a hedonistic lifestyle and emphasizes that pleasure must be accompanied by realizing one's potential in order to give life more purpose.[11] Eudaimonic well-being focuses on more global measures such as mastery of one's environment or circumstances, autonomy, choice (Chapter 3), positive relationships with others, purpose in life, personal growth, and self-acceptance.[12]

Aristotle refers to the combination of hedonic and eudemonic well-being as *the good life*.[7] Central to this theme is the notion that one's character is constructed from ethics and virtues, and helping others promotes the pursuit of ethical behavior. *Happiness* is the composite of high eudemonic well-being and hedonic well-being. From the ABS perspective, positive consequences of meaningful behavior promote happiness; negative consequences of undesirable behavior promote negative affect.

Finding Happiness

It's natural to seek and want to sustain "the good life."[13] In 1967, psychologist Warner Wilson concluded that a happy person is a "young, healthy, well-educated, well-paid, extraverted, optimistic, worry-free, religious, married person with high self-esteem, job morale, modest aspirations of either sex and of a wide range of intelligence."[14] But this definition has been refuted because research indicates all people can be happy regardless of their dispositions (their personality) and situations (e.g., their age, job, wealth, marital status, and education). Plus, much of people's happiness is within their control.[15] What is astounding is that no negative factors (e.g., being homeless, poor, sick, disabled, obese, lonely, aging, or having dysfunctional social relationships – inside and outside one's family) – *prevent* an individual from attaining happiness.

Happiness levels indeed might be systematically lower for certain income groups (e.g., a $70,000 income vs. being 200 percent below the poverty level) due to the desire to obtain societal and material necessities (e.g., home, food, and education). However, people's levels of happiness are dispersed across the spectrum of dispositional and situational factors. True happiness is culturally, economically, and socially resilient. It's important to mention here that social extraverts tend to be happier than introverts.

Extraverts, on average, are more motivated than introverts to maintain and strengthen positive emotions and a cheerful mood. Extraverts, more than introverts, also have an inherent desire to repair a negative mood.[16]

The positive psychology literature indicates that happiness is observable. For instance, observers studied women's photos in college yearbooks. Those expressing a Duchenne smile (increased emotional expression, use of the muscles around the eyes and cheek) were rated more favorably on several personality dimensions.[17] More important, the women with expressive, smiling faces were contacted as they reached their 20s, 40s, and 50s. Researchers found that those with the Duchenne smile experienced better marriage outcomes and well-being thirty years later.

Positive affect is also a strong predictor of longevity and health. A group of 2,822 Mexican Americans participated in a longitudinal study of in-home interviews in 1993–1994 and in follow-up interviews in 1995–1996. Demographic variables, daily activities, health conditions, performance-based mobility, and a rating of positive and negative affect were collected at both interview times. Researchers found happy people were half as likely to die or become disabled as unhappy people.[18] These odds may be partially due to happier individuals enjoying better habits, stronger immune systems, and lower blood pressure than less happy individuals.

Implications of happiness and longevity can be gleaned from various sources. Researchers scored the emotional content of autobiographies written by elderly nuns (75–102 years old) when they were younger. They found that positive emotional content was inversely correlated with risk of mortality late in life.[19] In other words, those nuns with more positive emotional content in their autobiographies written when they were in their 20s lived longer.

Self-perceptions also play a role in aging. Self-perceptions on aging reflect an individual's stereotypes of older people and perhaps have psychological effects. Participants completed an "Attitudes Towards Own Aging" scale. Researchers discovered that individuals with more positive self-perceptions of aging (e.g., have a positive attitude toward getting older, dismiss age-related stereotypes) live 7.5 years longer than individuals with less positive self-perceptions of aging.[20]

The strongest indicators of happiness involve AC4P interactions with others. Happy people spend the least time alone, the most time socializing, and maintain higher-quality relationships with others compared with moderately happy or unhappy individuals (i.e., they tend to be extraverts).[21] Performing five acts of kindness (i.e., AC4P behaviors) weekly over the course of a mere six weeks increased perceptions of well-being. These acts of kindness can include calling a relative you haven't spoken to in a long time, donating blood to the Red Cross or clothing to Goodwill, or helping a younger sibling with her homework.[15] Individuals who spend money on other people experience more happiness than those who spend money on themselves.[22]

Positive Psychology at Work

Psychological scientists have applied positive psychology to various domains. Principles of positive psychology have been integrated into the field of organizational behavior to shift the focus away from what is *wrong* with organizations toward what is *right* with organizations and the individual workers (e.g., employees, supervisors, corporate executives) who work within those organizations.[23] As you know, focusing on what is *right* as opposed to what is *wrong* is a theme of ABS (see Principle 4 in Chapter 1). Applying positive psychology to increase desirable behaviors such as courtesy and interpersonal AC4P behavior within an organizational is called *positive organizational behavior,* or POB.

Within the field of empirical POB, Fred Luthans' work has been seminal. Luthans coined and published leading-edge research on a construct called psychological capital (PsyCap), which had a significant impact on the field of POB. This construct appeals to both positive psychology researchers and organizational consultants due to its potential to cultivate happier and more engaged employees, generating a greater return on investment.[24] PsyCap is considered to be a higher-order construct that includes self-efficacy, hope, optimism, and resilience. These constructs share some similarities but have distinct differences that contribute uniquely to the construct of PsyCap.

Later in this chapter, we elaborate on the differences between two of these in particular: hope and optimism. The organizational interventions that have been used to increase the strength of PsyCap within workers have been very self-focused. These interventions attempt to increase PsyCap mainly through the use of personal cognitions or self-talk,[25] to "think people into acting differently." "Acting people into thinking differently" is not considered. We are convinced, however, that the AC4P principles reviewed in Chapters 1 to 6 as humanistic behaviorism contribute substantially to the PsyCap of workers, indeed to the well-being of everyone in almost any setting.

Organizations constantly strive to recruit and cultivate talent – high-quality leaders. A leader's positive emotions can augment organizational learning and transformation.[26] As detailed in Chapter 8, authentic leaders possess high self-awareness and "lead with purpose, values, and integrity ... build enduring organizations, motivate their employees to provide superior customer service, and create long-term value for shareholders."[27]

THE MISSING LINK

Since its resurgence in the early 2000s, positive psychology has succeeded in analyzing and promoting concepts such as love, courage, forgiveness, talent, interpersonal skills, spirituality, and perseverance in an empirical context.[1] Despite this burgeoning body of promising research, something has been missing from all this analysis and consumer-type marketing. Positive psychology has ignored the *behavior-based* approach to increasing happiness – assessing and studying the *behaviors* linked to character strengths and virtues.[28] Positive psychology to date ignores the principles and applications of behavioral science, including the impact of positive consequences on behavior and concomitant attitudes, person-states, and self-motivation (Chapter 3).[29]

Most research in positive psychology uses surveys to assess individuals' levels of perceived happiness as an affect or person-state. This measurement methodology is limiting and at times useless. It's very unlikely that scores on a questionnaire alone can change feelings of happiness, sadness, anxiety, or anger. They cannot actively make a difference. What if an individual could *practice behaviors* when s/he was feeling sad, perhaps self-satisfied, or even happy that would *improve her*/his perception of well-being? What if one could act oneself into feeling happier?

One of the most cited positive psychology articles asked this very question. Researchers recruited almost six hundred people online to participate in the study. To motivate participation, subjects were informed they would be entered into a lottery for cash awards after completing a certain exercise. The participants were administered the Steen Happiness Index, the Center for Epidemiological Studies Depression Scale, and the Character Strengths and Virtues (CSV) Survey. After completing these surveys, the subjects were randomly assigned one of six exercises to complete. At a later date, the participants completed the same questionnaires. It was hypothesized that the happiness of the participants would increase and their depressive symptoms decrease as a result of their assigned exercise.[30]

The exercises included(1) *a gratitude visit* – write a letter expressing gratitude to a person who has been kind or influential and deliver the letter to him/her; (2) *three good things in life* – each day for a week, write down three things that went well and their causes; (3) *you at your best* – write about a time when you were at your best and reflect on the personal strengths you displayed; (4) *identifying signature strengths* – take the CSV survey (discussed in the next section) and practice one of your top strengths every day for a week; (5) *using signature strengths in a new way* – take the character strengths inventory and practice one of your top strengths every day for a week in a novel way. The sixth exercise was a *control*; the placebo exercise involved writing early childhood memories in a journal.

The results: Two exercises – using signature strengths in new ways and the three good things in life – increased happiness levels for six months. The gratitude visit revealed the greatest positive change from initial message delivery to five weeks after the delivery. Unfortunately, this is one of very few studies to use behaviors to increase happiness.[15]

It's important to note a common concern in psychological research: experimenter bias. Researchers want results that support their hypothesis, and they can inadvertently present aspects of the experiment (e.g., the happiness exercises, the administration of questionnaires, and their body language and verbal behavior) in ways that support their hypothesis. And participants might complete surveys in ways that please the researchers – to support their hypothesis.

Still, this study provided convincing evidence that a behavioral approach could be advantageous for increasing subjective well-being. What can we do to facilitate expanded practice of these positive behavioral exercises? How will the consequences of these behaviors affect an individual's level of happiness? In the next section, we explore answers to these questions by integrating ABS and the AC4P principles with positive psychology.

CHARACTER STRENGTHS

Character Strengths and Virtues: A Handbook and Classification[31] may be the most ambitious project completed in positive psychology. This handbook presents a comprehensive classification of psychological well-being characteristics, much as the *Diagnostic and Statistical Manual of Mental Disorders*[32] provides an inventory of psychological afflictions. It includes strengths of character – positive characteristics that amplify good feelings and gratification.

In determining what characteristics to include in their list of character strengths, Seligman, Peterson, and many others developed specific criteria for defining a human strength. Each strength had to be ubiquitous, global, fulfilling, morally valued, not diminishing to others, something with negative antonyms, trait-like, measurable, distinct, a paragon, prodigious, selectively absent in some individuals, and promoted by society.[30]

Every strength is encompassed by one of six virtue categories: wisdom and knowledge, courage, humanity, justice, temperance, and transcendence. For example, the virtue of justice contains the character strengths of citizenship, fairness, and leadership.[31] For the interested reader, the VIA Inventory of Strengths Survey developed by the late Christopher Peterson is available to take free of charge online.[33]

The twenty-four universal character strengths Peterson and Seligman ultimately retained are listed in Table 7.1. As we mentioned at the beginning of this chapter, character strengths are capacities humans have for thinking, feeling, and behaving. All of these strengths are taken into account to fully explicate the six stated human virtues.[31] People can possess any of the twenty-four character strengths in varying degrees.

Some strengths, though, are more pronounced or more easily expressed in a particular individual than in others. These are classified as *signature strengths* – those at the core of your attitudes and behaviors. Though Peterson and Seligman view character strengths as mostly stable during

TABLE 7.1. *The twenty-four universal character strengths*

Creativity	Vitality	Humility
Curiosity	Love	Prudence
Open-mindedness	**Kindness**	Self-regulation
Love of Learning	**Social Intelligence**	Appreciation of Beauty and Excellence
Wisdom	**Citizenship**	**Gratitude**
Courage	Fairness	**Hope**
Persistence	**Leadership**	Humor
Integrity	Forgiveness	Spirituality

Note: The ten bolded words are the character strengths explained in this chapter.

one's lifespan, they do suggest that character strengths can change in a person over time. These strengths interact with one another, influence one another, and are expressed as a function of the situation.

Cultivating the Character Strengths

As we have stated, scant research in positive psychology has assessed or targeted behavior. Yet behavior influences character strengths and, in turn, character strengths influence behavior. Also, certain behaviors can be changed to enhance a character strength. Behaviors can lead to positive consequences that can augment one or more character strengths. For example, setting SMARTS goals (Chapter 3) and obtaining behavior-based feedback can help develop certain character strengths.

Ten of the twenty-four character strengths listed in Table 7.1 seem to be the most relationship-based and reflect behaviors that can be readily observed and influenced. Others are unobservable (e.g., one can't count the number of times someone demonstrates vitality) or are not relationship-based (e.g., creativity, humor, love of learning). We focus on relationship-based character strengths because the related behaviors (a) are observable and can be tracked; (b) allow opportunities for providing interpersonal feedback; (c) can change in frequency and intensity; and (d) align with the AC4P mission of connecting positively with others in a community.

We now proceed to define these ten character strengths and show the relationship between each character strength and other variables. We demonstrate how each character strength relates to AC4P behavior or to the AC4P Movement. Then we provide a scenario in which the character strength is reflected in behavior. Finally, we list some behaviors that enhance each character strength.

We recommend choosing a character strength and attempting to complete at least one relevant behavior per day. Take time to reflect on the positive consequences of performing that behavior. The result: You will realize a greater sense of happiness and well-being.

Curiosity

The innate pursuit, recognition, and regulation of experiences in challenging circumstances epitomize curiosity. We all experience curiosity, but the depth of and willingness to engage in this pursuit vary from individual to individual. Curious individuals tend to seek novel experiences. By their nature, these experiences have a propensity for risk – curious individuals are willing to endure higher levels of risk. They typically have the courage and sociability to communicate with strangers and have a greater propensity to help others. Practicing behaviors that reflect curiosity can be rewarding; curiosity-driven behavior is often intrinsically or naturally reinforced.[31]

Curiosity correlates significantly with positive affect, creativity, a desire for challenging work, and self-control.[34] As a motivational state, curiosity promotes goal perseverance,[35] complex decision-making,[36] and excitement/enjoyment.[38] By compiling and analyzing data and evidence from multiple studies on curiosity, research suggests that curiosity accounts for 10 percent of the differences in individuals' behavior during and after learning a task.[38]

In the workplace, curiosity-related behaviors exhibited by workers (e.g., seeking out new tasks, asking questions) relate to contextual learning as well as overall self-rated quality of interpersonal and technical work performance.[39] In interpersonal friendships and romantic partnerships in which both members are highly curious, there is a tendency to have more positive experiences, better conversations, a higher degree of intimacy, and more fun.[31]

It's important to keep in mind that high levels of curiosity can be undesirable because individuals with high novelty-seeking behaviors are likely to act impulsively, use drugs, steal, or engage in promiscuous sexual activities.[40] This, in turn, can be detrimental to curiosity; internal and external pressures such as guilt or the threat of punitive consequences can diminish one's curiosity toward novel tasks.[31]

The positive impact of curiosity makes it a perfect character strength to be nourished in meaningful contexts such as educational settings and the workplace. Not much is known about the malleability of curiosity; still, it's worth considering methods to increase the occurrence of curiosity-related behavior. Seligman and Peterson suggest curiosity can be enhanced over the short and long-term by increasing mindfulness (using all your senses to be aware of your body, feelings, perceptions and the environment in the present moment), facilitating autonomy, and setting up mentor relationships in specific domains.[31]

The AC4P Movement was fueled, in part, by curiosity. We asked, "How can we create a culture of compassion and AC4P behavior?" We began taking steps to answer that question for organizations and schools, as reviewed in this book. Leaders of the AC4P Movement are naturally curious. As applied behavioral scientists, we look for ways to improve behaviors as situations present themselves; and as humanistic behaviorists, we want to develop and deliver practical behavior-change interventions that enable and support perceptions of empowerment to perform AC4P behavior.

Example. James walks into his boss's office to deliver the day's reports. His boss, Steve, is staring at his computer screen looking flustered; he's not technologically savvy. Being naturally *curious*, James asks his boss what is wrong and if he can help. With an exasperated sigh, Steve says all of his documents have disappeared and he can't finish the reports for his client.

Though James lacks formal software training, in his free time at home he is often on his computer learning how the operating system and software operate because it *interests* him. James discovers the company's new anti-virus software has labeled the document folder as spam and sent all of its contents into "quarantine." After another quick scan, James is able to restore the documents and make his boss very happy and appreciative.

Cultivating Curiosity:
- Schedule an hour each day to spend time on something that interests you. Learn and engage in something you are curious about that does not relate directly to your job.
- Partake in cognitively difficult tasks – such as crossword puzzles or Sudoku.
- Have your work team participate in a weekly trivia night.
- Converse with a stranger and learn about his/her life.
- Find a colleague who works on a different project or in a different department. Spend time asking about and learning about his/her current work.
- Take a training course to build a new skill.
- Take an online education course to explore new topics.
- In an occupational setting, work with someone in a different department.
- Explore new ways to accomplish a routine task.

- Share "fun facts" or information about positive behaviors with friends and family through email in order to stimulate their curiosity.
- Rearrange your study or work space. Shuffle your routines. Be open to change.
- Encourage innovation by asking your peers questions about their education or work projects and relevant skills.
- Explore ways to improve interpersonal relatedness at school or at work.
- Study how ABS can be used to enable teachers, managers, and coaches to be more effective.
- Attend a professional convention and network with others in your field.
- Create or join a listserv with discussions/news from leaders, teachers, and relevant content experts.
- Give presentations or host discussion sessions on topics related to your unique knowledge, experience, and/or skill sets.
- Organize an AC4P club to promote AC4P behavior in your organization.

Wisdom

Picture a wise person. You might envision a venerable philosophical figure, similar to the likes of Confucius, Socrates, or the Buddha. Perhaps an older relative or authority figure comes to mind. What characteristics do these people possess? According to Seligman and Peterson, the character strength most associated with such people is perspective, also referred to as wisdom. It's the character strength characterized by optimal knowledge acquisition, the highest capacity to give counsel to others, and an outlook on life most congruent with that of others. Wise individuals are honored, respected, and consulted for their perspective.[5]

One of the most accepted definitions of wisdom is known as the Berlin wisdom paradigm. This paradigm characterizes wisdom as general expertise in understanding what makes for a meaningful life and understanding how to conduct oneself in order to have a meaningful life.[41] Wisdom is often assessed by measuring individuals' levels of intelligence and personality traits or presenting them with social dilemmas and evaluating their solutions.

The AC4P Movement aims to achieve significant positive impact – to make a beneficial difference in people's lives and in society. By reflecting on and working through social dilemmas, you can increase your own capacity to exhibit appropriate AC4P behavior. People with wisdom see multiple perspectives, and this requires empathy – a key factor in humanism.

Here's an example of a dilemma that requires wisdom: You are talking to a close friend who has recently lost a loved one and is seriously depressed and stricken with grief. How do you respond? What do you say? What factors do you consider in your reaction? Do you possess sufficient wisdom to save your friend from diving deeper into despair?

According to the Berlin wisdom paradigm, wisdom is assessed through five criteria. The first two criteria are basic: comprehensive factual knowledge (e.g., social norms) and comprehensive procedural knowledge (e.g., how to offer advice). The third criterion is lifespan contextualism. This is essentially knowledge that accepts, considers, and integrates all domains of life, including work, school, family, leisure, and society. Lifespan contextualism, as the term implies, also considers these domains temporally, with separate emphasis on the past, present, and future.

The fourth criterion is relativism of values. Wisdom requires the ability to see and appreciate the greater good from the moral perspectives of many and varied individuals (i.e., humanism). The fifth criterion is recognition and management of uncertainty. Wise people can honestly admit they know nothing about a particular subject; they accept the limitations of human knowledge and foresight.[31]

Understanding when and how wisdom develops has been an important catalyst for future research in positive psychology. Seligman and Peterson have proposed that interventions to nurture wisdom can occur successfully in the adolescent stage of development. This assumption is largely based on findings that wisdom is not dependent upon age; the wisdom ratings for individuals as young as 20 have been similar to that of seniors in their 90's.[31]

An important aspect of wisdom development connects directly to AC4P principles. Paul Baltes and Ursula Staudinger emphasized the role of mentoring in fostering wisdom development.[42] Longitudinal results identified factors that enable or inhibit wisdom: life tasks, adjustment, coming to terms with life choices, life changes, and stressful life experiences.[31] This suggests that an individual gains wisdom through active participation in life, adjusting to unexpected and unfamiliar life experiences, handling critical events related to interpersonal relationships, and managing life stressors. The connection to AC4P behavior is obvious – wisdom is accompanied by an increased capacity for kindness.

The consequences of our actions shape our behavior – and most likely our character strengths, including wisdom. This does not mean overloading yourself with stressful situations with the expectation that subsequent "trial-by-fire" experiences will deliver wisdom. Rather, be aware of situations that potentially might be challenging, and appreciate the role of your prior experience as you attempt to manage these situations. We recommend that you take a humanistic behaviorism approach when assessing and responding to the human dynamics inherent in challenging interpersonal circumstances.

Example: Frank, a colleague on your work team, is middle-aged, is a good worker, and for all intents and purposes has no qualities that make him stand out above his co-workers. He is, in essence, the epitome of normal – at a glance. But it turns out Frank is the go-to guy for everyone on the team. Johnny asks Frank for marriage advice. Kim has him review her reports. Stephen discusses the meaning of life with him for hours after work. Frank has a certain quality that none of his co-workers can describe in behavioral terms. All we can observe is that Frank consistently treats everyone with respect, actively listens, is never demeaning, and is always thoughtful. He has a perspective that seems to give him life expertise, and his expert knowledge in many areas is magnetic, causing others to gravitate toward him.

Cultivating Wisdom:
- Assess your relative expertise in specific domains.
- Before giving advice, assess the situation with empathy and offer a rationale for your perspective.
- Coach others with behavior-focused supportive and corrective feedback (see Chapter 3).
- Become a mentor for others in situations where you have gained useful experience.
- Ask elders for their advice regarding basic life decisions.
- Ask colleagues to define their special talents/abilities to others in order to promote relevant interpersonal mastery and achieve synergy from collaboration.
- Seek opportunities or relationship-based conversation (Chapter 5) in one-to-one and group sessions.
- Before expressing your point of view, put yourself in the other person's shoes (i.e., actively listen with empathy).
- Seek out new individuals who offer their unique perspectives for learning opportunities.
- Contemplate ways to perform AC4P behavior for the sake of others and the larger community.
- Be available, be accessible and present, to offer advice.

Courage

Courage is a disposition that gives you the propensity to act voluntarily while weighing the risks and consequences of that action. Courage does not necessarily assume the absence of fear. Acts of courage aim to preserve or attain a perceived favorable result for yourself or for others, even when it's understood success is uncertain.[43]

Seligman and Peterson propose this definition of courage, but split it into three character strengths: bravery, persistence, and integrity. Bravery seems to align more strongly with their virtue of courage than the other two character strengths.[31] Peterson and Seligman recognize in courage the necessity of interpersonal interaction, but they don't express the crucial interdependence between courage, commitment, and competence (as explained in Chapter 4).

Courage can be motivated by extrinsic factors, but can also be self-motivated (Chapter 3). When observing someone being bullied, you might decide to intervene without an incentive. But if someone requests that you intervene, doing so is not truly courageous, according to Seligman and Peterson. Stopping a bully involves risks; you could become the victim of an attack. But with the proper competence and commitment, you might be courageous and act as an AC4P change agent – but not necessarily (Chapter 4).

Choosing to be courageous is often not easy, even if you know it's the right thing to do. Imagine this scenario: A group of high school students are notoriously renowned for being boorish, selfish, and contemptuous of those who are different from them. A popular student hanging with this clique notices a student with a physical challenge struggling to open his locker. The popular student risks his popularity when he helps the other student with his locker. This is an example of *moral courage* in the face of others' negative opinions.

Moral courage exemplifies AC4P behavior, as explained in Chapter 4. Physical courage is exhibited by soldiers during combat. The Time Magazine "Persons of the Year" in 2014 who took care of people with the Ebola virus showed physical courage. However, the opportunity to demonstrate physical courage is less evident in tranquil, everyday situations; moral and psychological courage (Chapter 4) are much more likely to occur in daily routines.

Ironically, the anxiety that often stops an individual from being courageous due to potentially negative opinions from others all but disappears when the act is completed. Friends will more likely see you as courageous for initiating the risky act, rather than judge you for doing something outside the social norm.

Research indicates a number of correlates with courage, including prosocial orientation,[44] self-efficacy,[45] valuing socially important achievements,[46] delayed gratification,[47] risk taking,[48] and experiencing relationships with others or with humanity.[49] Individuals who feel they have a great deal of control over their environments and the events that unfold around them have relatively high self-efficacy and are able to delay gratification.

Courageous individuals usually have more self-efficacy because they believe "they can do it." They know what to do to benefit a situation. It's within their personal control. In addition, having experiential or learned knowledge allows an individual to interpret or "read" a situation properly and react accordingly. But individual personal values are clearly relevant. Without a concern for or commitment to uphold the welfare of others, an individual will not be self-motivated to perform AC4P behavior and will not choose to act courageously if another person is in need of help.

Example: New York City firefighters, police, and emergency workers displayed immense *physical courage* on the morning of September 11, 2001, when two airliners piloted by suicidal terrorists tore into the North and South Towers of what was known as the Twin Towers in Manhattan.

At 8:46 A.M., five hijackers crashed American Airlines Flight 11 into the northern facade of the World Trade Center's North Tower,[50] and at 9:03 A.M., five hijackers crashed United Airlines Flight 175 into the southern facade of the South Tower.[51] Five hijackers also flew American Airlines Flight 77 into the Pentagon at 9:37 A.M.[52] A fourth flight, United Airlines Flight 93, under the control of four hijackers, crashed near Shanksville, Pennsylvania, southeast of Pittsburgh, at 10:03 A.M. after the passengers fought the hijackers.[53]

A total of 2,606 people died at Ground Zero, the World Trade Center in New York, due to the initial explosions and fires, and subsequent implosions of both towers within hours.[54] At least 200 people jumped or fell to their deaths from offices high up in the towers.[55] No plan existed for helicopter rescues, and the combination of roof equipment and thick smoke and intense heat prevented helicopters from approaching.

Fully aware of the trapped and panicked occupants high up in the towers and completely uncertain as to the structural damage, whether one or both towers might collapse, and how much time they had to rescue those trapped, firefighters (weighed down by heavy equipment and hauling hoses), police, and emergency medical technicians climbed stairwells choked with smoke and cluttered with debris, and with fires raging all about, to try to rescue as many people as possible and extinguish the fires. It was a futile firefighting plan, but the only plan.

The rescuers, many of whom showed up to help while off-duty, showed courageous, professional indifference to their own safety and took tremendous risks. A total of 411 emergency workers died as they tried to rescue people and fight fires. The New York City Fire Department lost 340 firefighters, a chaplain, and two paramedics.[56] The New York City Police Department lost 23 officers.[57] The Port Authority Police Department lost 37 officers.[58] Eight emergency medical technicians and paramedics from private emergency medical services units were killed.[59]

Cultivating Courage:
- Report observations of interpersonal bullying.
- Recognize and report counterproductive or antisocial behavior.
- Report a safety hazard or clean up your local park to promote health or safety (i.e., environment-based AC4P behavior, Chapter 2).
- Share honest opinions contrary to the majority viewpoint in group meetings.
- Speak up when an instructor or coach is saying something you know is incorrect; or in a healthcare setting, when you see potential for a medical error.
- Offer corrective feedback (i.e., behavior-based AC4P action) after observing an undesirable behavior of a friend or colleague.
- Do what you think is right even when everyone else is doing what you think is wrong.
- Suggest a participant at a party stop consuming alcoholic beverages.
- Lead a meeting on a controversial topic.
- Volunteer to do a household chore that nobody else wants to do.
- Take an education or training course that teaches you how to intervene effectively with others on behalf of their safety, health, or well-being.
- Give someone positive recognition after you observe that person performing AC4P behavior.
- Teach behavior-based feedback strategies and role-play techniques for giving supportive feedback to someone observed performing AC4P behavior.
- Apply one of the behavior-change techniques detailed in Chapter 4 (e.g., the airline lifesaver, the flash-for-life for unsafe driving, or the taxi cab feedback card).

Integrity

It's more important to be myself than to be popular. To thy own self be true. The character strength of integrity includes honesty, authenticity, trustworthiness, and self-worth. Integrity is based on regular patterns of behavior that reflect one's values. Integrity requires moral conviction and compassion toward others – even when the relevant behavior counters popular opinion.

Many constructs correlate directly with measures of integrity, including positive mood, empathy, self-actualization, and life satisfaction.[60] There is also evidence of direct correlations between integrity and three of the Big Five personality traits: conscientiousness, agreeableness, and emotional stability.[61] For some public figures it's difficult to be honest and authentic when success is defined by public appeal, as depicted in the illustration below.

Integrity is important to all individuals, as it begets interpersonal trust. Trust is essential for AC4P behavior to be frequent, authentic, and effective.

This interpersonal trust requires individuals to maintain integrity by putting others' needs ahead of their own and by helping for the pure sake of helping rather than for personal gain. The members of a peer group or an organization should have high integrity, reflecting positive, prosocial values; or at the very least, they should accept corrective feedback for behaviors inconsistent with organizational values and adjust them accordingly. Helping others sets an AC4P example, reflects the character strength of integrity, and can initiate a pattern of prosocial behavior for both the benefactor and the beneficiary.

Example: Erin is working late at the office of her financial firm on a Friday night. As she leans back in her chair, she notices her colleague John sneaking into their boss's office. The open window of the boss's office provides Erin a clear view of John's next move. He pulls out a key to the boss's filing cabinet and opens a drawer. After a quick search, he selects three files and closes the cabinet.

Erin wonders why John has a key to the filing cabinet, but before she can even consider the possibilities, she hears the mechanical sounds of a copier. John snatches the copies and silently replaces the folders. He turns off the light, closes the door, and leaves the office. Erin knows the filing cabinet holds key financial data from other companies. It appears John illegally took proprietary information. What should she do?

Maybe he's stealing it to sell for personal gain, or he secretly works for a competitor. If Erin has integrity, she considers the impropriety of John's behavior and feels compelled to act. She can choose to confront John directly about the copies. Or Erin could set up a private meeting with the boss and make him aware of John's transgression. Or she could do nothing. Will her morals supersede her concern that a report of her observations could get John fired?

Cultivating Integrity:
- Identify the behaviors of a friend, colleague, or co-worker with high integrity and model those behaviors.
- Act in ways that represent your values as opposed to public opinion.
- Give open and honest behavior-based feedback (Chapter 3).
- Speak up and tell others when a person deserves positive recognition for AC4P or discretionary behavior.
- Own up to your mistakes and apologize if your error had an impact on another person.
- Tell the truth, even when it could result in a negative consequence for you and/or for colleagues.

- Extend an offer to mediate interpersonal conflict between others.
- Consider the ethics of every decision that has an impact on others.
- Make an attempt to return a lost item, even when it's cash.
- Report cheating.
- Adjust your behavior to be consistent with your values.
- Follow through on personal commitments.
- Offer and request behavior-based feedback.
- Speak up at group meetings when verbal behavior or decisions are inconsistent with your values.
- Conduct group 360-degree feedback sessions – participants write down and then openly discuss answers to three questions: (1) What are my strengths? (2) What are my weaknesses? (3) How can I improve?

Kindness

Compassion and AC4P behavior toward others reflect kindness. Kindness or generosity often appears visible when it helps an individual achieve personal goals. Some people might behave nicely to a customer service representative in order to get a discount. These same people might become annoyed and hostile when the customer service representative can't provide a discount. This is not authentic kindness.

Behavior reflects kindness when it's not performed for an extrinsic gain. Still, such AC4P behavior will likely result in positive verbal behavior from the beneficiary and a boost in a positive person-state of the benefactor. Those possessing the kindness character strength treat all people as worthy and important, bring joy to others, and focus on giving above receiving.

Three person-factors activate kindness: empathy, moral reasoning, and social responsibility.[62] Empathy allows an individual to understand and internalize the emotions experienced by another individual. Altruistic or AC4P behavior increases with higher levels of empathy.[63] In other words, thinking beyond self and visualizing walking in another person's shoes leads to more acts of kindness.

Moral reasoning also increases the propensity for AC4P behavior. Those who focus on the needs of others and connect those observations with the AC4P Movement tend to perform more prosocial behaviors.[64] Socially responsible individuals feel concern and personal responsibility for others. Behaviorally, this reflects a higher propensity to intervene when they witness an incident or conflict that puts another person at risk or in harm's way. Prosocial AC4P behaviors are significantly more likely to occur when the benefactor is in a relatively positive mood.[65]

The AC4P Movement exemplifies kindness and operates through a multi-step process. Those who consistently practice AC4P behavior sincerely believe that doing good on behalf of others is a healthy, rewarding, fulfilling way to live. For them, interpersonal kindness is a value. AC4P behavior is important for everyone, not only for those we know and love. Your own interpersonal helping can influence the development of this AC4P-related character strength. Yes, you can act yourself into an AC4P mindset and eventually a personal value.

The next time you're sitting in a coffee shop or restaurant and you see someone struggling to open the door, go help. If you see someone fall, help them up. If you see a stray dog wandering while you're driving home, try to place it somewhere safe from moving vehicles. You may think these opportunities are far and few between, but you might be surprised to see how many opportunities there are to perform AC4P behaviors when you have an AC4P mindset, aiming to cultivate kindness. Such AC4P behavior will be rewarded with good feelings, a boost in your self-esteem, belongingness, and optimism.

Example: Take a few moments to reflect about kindness. Describe a recent or memorable moment when you performed AC4P behavior or were the subject of a kind act. How did you feel after the AC4P intervention? What behaviors occurred in this situation? This could be a written or verbal exercise in a group setting, followed by a discussion of observations and implications. Entertain the consequences of the AC4P act that could influence the occurrence or nonoccurrence of subsequent AC4P behavior.

Cultivating Kindness:
- Smile frequently to put yourself in a good mood and enhance your inclination to show kindness.
- Step in to interrupt interpersonal conflict.
- Look for opportunities to perform AC4P behaviors in places you frequently visit.
- Share office supplies or snacks.
- Help others with their work assignments.
- Simply ask people if they need any help.
- Create an email listserv where people can describe their expertise and offer their AC4P service.
- Volunteer to help others on projects or provide advice.
- Pair people with different skills and weaknesses on a project where their complementary skills could facilitate a productive process.

- Write a thank you card to express gratitude to someone who has helped you recently (Chapter 2).
- Give someone an AC4P wristband or an AC4P thank you card (Figure 2.6) for AC4P behavior you observe.
- Send out a group email to recognize people for performing kind acts.
- Ask for reports of interpersonal helping behaviors at group meetings.
- Observe helping behaviors at social gatherings and try to incorporate them into your own life.

Social Intelligence

Intelligence is recognized as intellectual or cognitive ability. Social intelligence refers to the ability to understand others. Subsumed under social intelligence are the terms *emotional intelligence* and *personal intelligence*.[31] This domain of literature is quite expansive and here we provide only a brief overview.

Emotional intelligence (EI) is the ability to identify, understand, and process the emotions of others and apply that knowledge to our own reasoning. *Personal intelligence* is self-appraisal and self-assessment to understand internal motivations, emotions, and other similar dynamic processes. *Social intelligence* focuses more broadly on relationships, including how relationships are created and sustained through a combination of interpersonal trust, persuasion, membership (belongingness), and power.

The study of social intelligence began more than ninety years ago with Edward Thorndike,[66] and research in this area has made great strides. According to Harold Gardner, a more recent researcher in this field, personal intelligence includes two domains: *intrapersonal* intelligence and *interpersonal* intelligence.[67] The intrapersonal aspect is the awareness of one's self and an understanding of one's own emotions, moods, and mental processes. The interpersonal aspect overlaps considerably with social intelligence and focuses on being aware of other people's behaviors, attitudes, and emotions.

Peter Salovey and John Mayer created a four-branch model of EI: (1) perceiving emotions; (2) using emotions to facilitate thought; (3) understanding emotions; and (4) managing emotions.[68] The advent of the Mayer-Salovey-Caruso Emotional Intelligence Test popularized EI among researchers and organizations.[69] Subsequently, Daniel Goleman popularized EI for the public.[70]

Though much research has been produced in the EI literature, and more broadly in the social intelligence literature, the work has been largely assessment-based.[31] These studies maximize the use of knowledge structure, processes, and individual differences, but little research has been conducted from an AC4P standpoint. More research is needed on the correlates of emotional, personal, and social intelligences – especially understanding how AC4P behaviors and consequences influence these intelligences. Despite some relational shortcomings, we see social intelligence as crucial to the AC4P Movement. In order to recognize others in need of help, you must possess qualities of both social and emotional intelligence.

Example: Karen notices Mike's somber mood after leaving his boss's office to go to lunch. His normal upbeat gait is replaced by his feet dragging heavily, as if he were walking in mud. She knows how caustic their boss can be and follows Mike. As she approaches him, she focuses on trying to *read his emotions* and behaviors and to empathize with his plight. As it turns out, their boss had just trashed Mike's project – one he had been working on for the better part of five months – because it "didn't reflect the mission of the company."

Observing Mike's body language and social cues, Karen realizes he's distraught. She proceeds to validate the worth of his project and his self-worth. She affirms the discretionary effort he dedicated to the project and confirms justification for his disappointment. She asserts the boss' decision does not reflect poorly on his skills or on his ability to rebound successfully. Mike gives Karen a hug and walks away. She can't help but notice he has a trace of a smile on his face and a slight bounce in his step. Mike will recover; he's been "talked off the ledge."

Cultivating Social Intelligence:
- Convince a nervous friend s/he is perceived well by others.
- Practice empathic listening daily by listening actively to the spoken words of others and putting yourself in the other person's shoes throughout the conversation.
- Ask people for their perspective before attempting to sell your own.
- Listen actively to the words of others before planning your next comment.
- Promote open dialogue among colleagues.
- Re-read that email carefully from the perspective of the recipient before pressing the "send" button.
- Throughout a conversation, maintain awareness of your social and emotional cues (e.g., tone of voice, body language).
- Interpret others' behavior within the context of the situation, and don't fall victim to the fundamental attribution error (Chapter 9).

- After giving someone behavior-based feedback, ask about personal feelings or emotions.
- Explain the concept of high versus low self-monitoring and give participants the available assessment tool to measure their level of self-monitoring.[71]

Citizenship

Individuals reflecting this character strength go beyond self-interest and feel obliged to support the common good. Supporting another as a friend (or even as a stranger) becomes a moral necessity and reflects AC4P behavior. According to Peterson and Seligman, people high in citizenship perceive a personal responsibility to help others and improve the world, and they believe other people should feel the same, and contribute time for the good of their community.[31]

Citizenship implicates a social responsibility mindset and AC4P behavior.[72] People with this character strength want to hold group membership and to feel included by others on the team.[31] This belief in belongingness is reciprocal. When the group/community fosters a sense of caring, the individual is more likely to care and act in the best interests of the community members.[73]

Research in this domain is quite intensive: Citizenship correlates with high regard for social and moral issues, social responsibility, behaving in conventional ways, acting less rebelliously, and holding trust and confidence in one's community. People with high citizenship are less cynical, less anxious, less hostile, more tolerant, more sociable, and more secure in social interactions than are people with low citizenship.[74] Still, as depicted in the illustration, citizenship behavior might be punished rather than rewarded.

Starrett's Global Social Responsibility Scale (GSR) identifies two distinct clusters of social responsibility that reflect the mission of the AC4P Movement.[75] One subscale of the GSR assesses a person's attitudes about individual responsibility for global issues such as deforestation of rainforests, climate change, and sustainability of agriculture. The other subscale, Responsibility for People, reflects the importance of community and interdependency, as do the AC4P wristbands.

Measures of citizenship have strong reliability and validity, but rely on attitudes and perceptions toward community. This measurement approach misses a critical aspect of citizenship. People may perceive themselves in a certain way on a paper assessment form, but when AC4P behavior is called for, will they stand and deliver? Reporting a willingness to help someone in

need and actually performing relevant AC4P behavior are entirely different matters.

Research designed to observe whether AC4P behavior actually occurs in certain situations is clearly needed. One way to go beyond the self-report assessments of citizenship is through service interventions. Participation in service learning (i.e., projects that help others) could certainly be observed and correlated with specific dispositions presumed to reflect citizenship or social responsibility.

Example: It had been three years since Rachel's son was killed in a drunk-driving crash. She initially retreated into a shell, struggling to cope and constantly asking herself, "Why him?" Her sadness and anger gave way to a new motivation: determination to make a difference. Rachel researched and learned that drunk driving is, tragically, all too common among youth. Her mission: to prevent as many fatalities from alcohol-impaired drivers as possible.

She started groups in her community, joined Mothers Against Drunk Driving (MADD), and gave speeches at local high schools and universities. Talking with teenagers about making proactive decisions was AC4P behavior. Rachel attempted to create a better, more caring community by promoting interpersonal support to prevent alcohol-impaired driving.

Cultivating Citizenship:
- Arrange group socials to foster citizenship among all participants.
- Promote interdependent collaboration on a project requiring diverse skill sets.
- Build and maintain camaraderie within the workplace by offering support to co-workers who seem to be struggling.
- Complete your part of *team* projects before the deadline.
- Promote the special skills and abilities of *team* members.
- Provide information or advice for the individual or team projects of others.
- Arrive early and/or stay late for meetings in order to help set up and/or clean up, respectively.
- Help others in emergencies (e.g., take lecture notes for a student who has to miss class; trade work shifts with someone who cannot make it to his shift; collect donated cans of food for the local homeless shelter).
- Promote and coordinate cooperative-learning groups for the workplace and for schools.
- Create tasks or objectives within educational or work settings that require teamwork.
- Discuss synergy – how various individual contributions can merge and multiply into a meaningful outcome greater than the sum of individual results, and one that is unattainable without the collaborative contributions of individuals with diverse skills and abilities.
- Maintain an AC4P accountability chart on which employees place a sticker with their name next to the person they helped (Chapter 2).

Leadership

Leadership has a long and varied history, not just in the psychological literature, but throughout recorded history. From the Bible, to Beowulf, Hercules, Odysseus, and to more modern models, leadership has constantly been exemplified, promoted, mythologized, and idealized as a character strength. The foundations of "great man theory," trait theory,[76] behavior-based leadership,[77] and revolutionary work in transformational leadership have led to a diverse literature – all of which attempt to define and understand leadership.

Leadership effectiveness correlates with many individual, team, and organizational outcomes. Creating better leaders requires communication and adherence to organizational goals. In addition, leadership correlates strongly with socialized power, charisma, authority, self-control, risk-taking, and dominance.[31] Leaders account for 44–47 percent of the variance in organizational performance, and newly promoted leaders account for 5.6–24.2 percent of that variance.[78]

The quality of a leader's relationship with others significantly affects job satisfaction, organizational commitment, job performance, and turnover rates.[79] The next chapter (Chapter 8) reviews the recent research literature on leadership and followership, and highlights the characteristics of AC4P leaders.

Example: Margaret accepts a job running a team of chemical engineers. She is nervous because engineering is a largely male-dominated field. On her first day, Margaret pulls her employees into a meeting to discuss the team's current strengths and limitations. She also sets deadlines for each project. Some individuals struggle to meet the deadlines. She later meets individually with each team member, asking those who are struggling, "What do you need in order to succeed?" One worker didn't know the programming language and was learning it from scratch. Margaret pairs him up with a colleague who's an expert on the language to expedite the coding process.

Another individual appears apathetic toward his job, and his teammates have labeled him "lazy." She calls him into her office and tells him they need a strong team that is cohesive and mutually supportive. Margaret tells him to take the rest of the day off (with pay) to decide if he wants to continue as a supportive member of the team or find opportunities elsewhere. If he decides to return, he needs to prepare a behavior-focused action plan that specifies what he will do to demonstrate more interdependent support of the team.

Margaret has grabbed hold of responsibility, held employees accountable, set goals, and fostered communication between team members. Margaret's future in this organization looks bright.

Cultivating Leadership:
- Promote high expectations of leadership among subordinates via the self-fulfilling prophecy.
- Take a leadership role when you have expertise in a particular area.
- Act as a mediator to foster and maintain positive relationships.

- Spread the notion that everyone can be a leader in the domain of his/ her expertise or talent.
- Take charge in emergencies.
- Ask people if they have what they need to do their job, including knowledge, resources, and time.
- Anticipate and plan for mistakes in a project.
- Set incremental goals and ask others to hold fellow group members accountable.
- Set periodic SMARTS goals with each individual and with teams (Chapter 3).
- Give supportive and corrective feedback effectively (Chapter 3).
- Resolve interpersonal conflicts to keep groups working constructively on an interdependent team.
- Provide opportunities for others to take leadership roles.
- Rotate team members to lead group meetings.
- Support others as they work toward completing challenging or novel tasks.
- Define competence, choice, and community for particular people and circumstances, and implement strategies to enhance these person-states among individuals (Chapter 3).

Gratitude

Gratitude is a sense of thankfulness and joy that comes in response to receiving a gift. Derived from the Latin *gratia*, this character strength relates to "kindness, generousness, the beauty of giving and receiving, or getting something for nothing."[80] Gratitude is highly valued across all cultures and times. It can be environment-focused, "I appreciate the beauty of the world today" (a gift from the earth), or person-focused (Chapter 2), "I am grateful to my mother for supporting me in this difficult time" (a gift from a person).

Peterson and Seligman state that the grateful disposition of individuals is a function of the intensity, frequency, density, and generality of gratitude they feel on a regular basis. These four qualities of gratitude vary dramatically among individuals who receive the same act of kindness.[31]

Gratitude has both diverse measures and significant correlations with other characteristics. Measures of gratitude are diverse because some scholars believe gratitude is a potentially transitory state; others believe it's an embedded trait. Higher levels of gratitude appreciation correlate directly with self-control, spirituality, and life satisfaction.[31] Keeping weekly gratitude journals led to participants' experiencing fewer negative physical symptoms, feeling better about their lives, and becoming more optimistic about the future.[81] Grateful people experience greater levels of positive emotion, life satisfaction, vitality, and optimism.[82]

As a person-state, gratitude appears to directly benefit cardiovascular and immune functioning.[83] From an AC4P perspective, gratitude is a form of positive self-talk and becoming mindful of the positive consequences of helping others. Indeed, the AC4P Movement is based on gratitude. First, giving an AC4P wristband to someone represents an exercise in showing gratitude for that person's helping behavior. Second, not only does a pay-it-forward exercise exemplify personal gratitude; but as a reinforcer, the wristband increases the likelihood the recipient will perform more AC4P behavior, and perhaps pass on the wristband to another person as a display of gratitude for his/her AC4P behavior (Chapter 6).

Example: Richard feels alone and isolated. He sits on his couch, in the dark, playing the phone conversation with his doctor over and over again in his head. "Cancer? But I'm not even forty!" He is scared. Nervously, he dials his old friend James. James answers on the first ring with his normal, upbeat attitude, "Richard, my man! How's it going?" Richard begins to cry. Somehow, he stutters out the news that his life could be cut short. James replies, "Give me an hour," and hangs up.

An hour later, James shows up with pizza, beer, and a handful of their closest friends. Each gives Richard a hug, assures him he's not alone, and promises they will be with him through everything. Being with his friends manages to take Richard's mind off of the unfortunate, unnerving news and helps him cope. After his friends leave, Richard is overwhelmed with gratitude and begins to recall the other things in life for which he is extremely grateful. Richard doesn't realize it at the time, but this represents a major step in his road to emotional healing.

Cultivating Gratitude:

- Begin keeping a gratitude journal of the positive things you appreciate each day.
- Write a letter of gratitude to someone who has helped or influenced you.
- Reflect on how others facilitated your path to where you are today.
- Thank janitors, maintenance crew, cafeteria workers, or other people who may often be underappreciated in your school or workplace.
- Give a "thumbs-up thank you" hand signal to drivers of vehicles who stop and give you the right-of-way at a pedestrian crosswalk.

- Recognize the AC4P behavior of others.
- Apply a reciprocity or pay-it-forward mindset when you're the recipient of kindness.
- Thank your classmates when they help you with anything, even if it seems insignificant at first.
- Schedule appreciation lunches.
- Take one minute out of your day to recognize and show appreciation in a one-on-one conversation with a friend or colleague.
- Express gratitude for others through things like an AC4P thank you card and AC4P wristband (Chapter 2).
- Acknowledge AC4P behavior via letters, emails, text messages, phone calls, and commendation.
- Show your appreciation to friends, family, and co-workers by sincerely communicating to them your gratitude.
- Ask team members to express one-to-one gratitude privately, but publicly recognize group accomplishments at the beginning of each shift.

Hope

Hope, in a colloquial sense, is sometimes viewed as a desperate stab by someone on the verge of plummeting into the depths of despair. It might be characterized by not wanting to lose hope, or needing to hope for the best. Students may hope they have studied well enough for a test, or hope they are doing well with sticking to their diet.

One can also have high hopes of winning the lottery and becoming a millionaire or catching a foul ball at a baseball game. In this latter context, some people like to be hopeful in situations in which they have little to no control (e.g., a fan cannot control where a foul ball goes during a baseball game). We characterize this as *false hope* and do not acknowledge it as *true hope*. True hope is a resource that can be applied to situations in which one *does* have some personal control.

One of the popular theories of hope in the positive psychology literature was conceived by Charles Snyder, who characterized hope in terms of goal setting. Hope, according to this theory, is a quality of striving in which people envision multiple *pathways* toward a desired goal, as well as feel they contain the *agency* – the personal control – to achieve the intended goal.[84]

The pathways component of hope is crucial; it prevents individuals who envision multiple means of achieving their goal from faltering if one pathway becomes blocked. For example, if an individual who hopes to lose weight by exercising daily fractures a leg and is unable to exercise for months, s/he would not be instantly discouraged because s/he can still achieve a weight-loss goal by practicing healthy eating habits. This conceptualization does not include hope for the attainment of unrealistic consequences. As mentioned, this would be false hope.

Let's differentiate this construct from the similar construct of *optimism*. Optimism is the general belief that good things will happen. Optimism does not take into account whether one has agency, or personal control. One can, for example, be generally optimistic about the future of the economy. Hope is similar to optimism in that it can be characterized by wishful thinking (e.g., I believe I will lose weight), but it's not *true* hope unless it's also characterized by some personal control.

Charles Snyder puts the distinction succinctly: "Hope is similar to optimism in that it is conceptualized as a stable cognitive set reflecting general rather than specific outcome expectancies. Hope and optimism differ, however, in the hypothesized relationship between outcome and efficacy expectancies and the role this relationship plays in the prediction of goal-directed behavior."[85] Note that the man asking for help in the illustration below is both optimistic and hopeful because he has prepared for his wishful expectancy.

The pathways component of hope also distinguishes it from optimism; hope involves striving toward making a particular wish come true by envisioning multiple pathways toward an intended goal. An optimistic individual can feel the same way about an anticipated goal, but optimism also involves a reaction to the consequences of an event. Specifically, when faced with negative consequences, an optimist might make external, unstable, and specific attributions to that outcome. This is known as the *optimistic explanatory style*.[86] By Snyder's theory, hope allows one to react to a perceived consequence by perhaps shifting to a different pathway.

Correlates of hope and optimism are numerous: high achievement, reduced anxiety and depression, positive social skills, self-efficacy, and well-being.[87] People who are hopeful and optimistic in the face of undesired consequences are more likely to achieve their goals, and do so without wavering. Hopeful and optimistic individuals also feel more confident in their abilities to obtain their desired outcome.

As the measures of hope and optimism and associated studies are relatively new, more similarities and differences might eventually emerge. It should be easy to see, then, how similar hope and optimism are to the AC4P model (Figure 2.9).[88] The model presumes that optimism, self-efficacy, and personal control enhance one's propensity to perform AC4P behavior. The combination of personal control and optimism reflects hope.

Example: Matt is having a rough year. Cartilage in his knee joint wore away, which required surgery. His heart began to beat irregularly, preventing normal breathing and requiring many visits to the doctor. Plus, his compact car stalled and was totaled by a truck going 50 mph. For all intents and purposes, Matt has rights to a negative outlook on life.

But Matt doesn't raise the white flag and surrender. He vows to keep his chin up, focus on the positive accomplishments and relationships in his life, and realize that bad situations occur for everyone. By telling himself these unfortunate circumstances are merely onetime occurrences that do not reflect on himself as a person, he is being *optimistic*. By striving and making an active effort to recover his health and get a new car, Matt takes personal control and is *hopeful*.

Cultivating Hope:

- Sustain a success-seeking attitude, so you are always trying to expect the best, based on effort exerted.
- Make a list of accomplishments and share it with friends. Refer to this list when you experience a setback.
- Discuss goals and visions for the future with family, friends, and colleagues.

- Share the best moments of your workday with family, friends, or colleagues.
- Celebrate the accomplishments of process goals with others and connect these successes with the actual or expected attainment of outcome goals.
- Set SMARTS goals in keeping with an ultimate vision (Chapter 2).
- Help others set SMARTS goals, and help them monitor their accomplishment of each component of a SMARTS goal (Chapter 3).
- Discuss the mission and vision of your organization and connect these to your daily tasks. Help others do the same and see the big picture. "You're not laying bricks, you're building a community center!"

IN CONCLUSION

Positive Psychology and AC4P

Character strengths are the foundation of positive psychology and relate closely to the person-state principles of AC4P. But it's important to note that the ABS focus on positive consequences has apparently been unnoticed by the founders and proponents of the "new" positive psychology. Indeed, most of the proposed and researched strategies for enhancing critical character strengths and in turn increasing happiness reflect activators or antecedents of behavior, rather than consequences. The focus seems to be on "thinking people into feeling better" rather than "acting people into feeling better." The latter behavior-based approach connects obviously to the use of ABS principles (Chapter 1) to increase the frequency of behaviors that augment happiness.

Considering Maslow's revised hierarchy of needs (Chapter 2), after satisfying basic physiological and safety needs, we perform behaviors that increase perceptions of self-worth, confidence, and a sense of social support or community to promote happiness and well-being. How can we increase the frequency of such behaviors? With consequences, of course – both extrinsic and intrinsic. Also, recall that AC4P behavior is at the top of Maslow's revised hierarchy, and the consequences of such behaviors fuel the very person-states that enhance one's propensity to perform AC4P behavior.

Successful enhancement of a particular character strength requires a vision and relevant goal setting to develop an AC4P mindset and lifestyle. Consider, for example, an aspiration to be more socially aware and to notice individuals in need of AC4P behavior. Relevant SMARTS goals (Chapter 3) are implicated, such as (a) speak to one stranger per week for a month; (b) perform two AC4P behaviors per week for one month; (c) record two AC4P behaviors per week at the ac4p.org Website.

Behaviors and intentions are not always synonymous. Personal accountability and contingencies can help keep you motivated. Don't simply record your AC4P interactions; have a daily phone conversation with a friend or relative about your AC4P behavior. Not only will your friend or relative acknowledge your act of kindness with positive recognition, s/he might even give you an idea for your next AC4P act.

Some of the character strengths and their characteristics from positive psychology are analogous to the AC4P person-states defined in Chapter 2: self-esteem, self-efficacy, personal control, optimism, and belongingness. Since behavior can influence both person-states and character strengths, by performing AC4P behaviors we do more than merely assist another person. Our actions enhance our own character strengths and lead to an increase in the happiness of the other person. Plus, happiness interventions succeed most often when individuals acknowledge, endorse, and commit to implementing happiness interventions.[89] This could also apply to the happiness exercises described in the seminal research reviewed previously in this chapter.[30]

Future Directions

Research is needed to identify and expand on the behaviors that reflect each dimension of the character strengths we have discussed. As indicated earlier in the chapter, positive activities such as keeping gratitude journals and sending thank you letters do increase perceptions of well-being. To date, though, a paucity of research has targeted the identification of specific behaviors that secure and increase happiness. Since Seligman and Peterson's character strengths are integral to the mission of positive psychology – to increase well-being – identifying and practicing behaviors related to each character strength should increase well-being.

Some questions related to the challenge of identifying the AC4P behaviors that might increase well-being are revealed in the following scenario. An individual decides to hand out AC4P wristbands to fulfill a desire to help others and increase a sense of community and interpersonal appreciation – person-states that contribute to this person's sense of well-being. Research indicates that distributing these wristbands increases interpersonal sharing and reduces bullying.[90]

Consider dosage. What quantity, frequency, and dispersion of an activity maximize one's perceived well-being? Should an AC4P wristband be distributed to one person per day or per week, or perhaps three times per week or three times daily? Another important question: Whose happiness is being augmented? To what extent does recognizing another person's AC4P behavior increase happiness for both the benefactor (the giver of the AC4P wristband) and the beneficiary (the recipient of the AC4P wristband)?

Of course, practicing certain behaviors other than distributing wristbands might increase perceived happiness as well. For instance, counting your blessings each night is a self-oriented positive activity; in contrast, writing and delivering a thank you letter is other-oriented. To date, no research has compared the impact of different activities as determinants of happiness.

The same can be said for social versus personal behaviors. Which behavior contributes more to well-being: counting one's blessings or helping an elderly woman cross a heavily trafficked pedestrian crosswalk? We hypothesize that the latter, other-oriented behavior will have a greater impact on one's perception of well-being.

Dispositional versus Situational Impact

The impact on happiness of dispositional attributes such as self-motivation, self-efficacy, and various affective states requires systematic investigation. Take the hypothetical case of two people, John and Aaron. John is a mid-30s successful businessman and former Eagle Scout with a captivating smile. He travels regularly across the country and speaks to thousands of people on how to better their lives. No matter where he's speaking, he always manages to find local places with people in need and donates twenty hours each week to help them.

In contrast, Aaron is an 18-year-old college freshman. He hasn't made any friends yet on campus, not that he's made much of an effort. When he's not in classes, he's glued to his computer in his dorm playing online fantasy games. For hours and hours each day, he plays until it's time for bed. Every day, he continues this cycle: classes, computer games, sleep.

Now let's suppose an AC4P leader approaches John and Aaron, explains the mission of the AC4P Movement, and hands each of them fifty wristbands, with a request for each to recognize and reward the observed AC4P behaviors of others. How do you think each will react to this request, and what will be the behavioral and person-state impact?

The task is probably right in John's wheelhouse, as they say in baseball. It connects directly with the message he preaches. It likely won't require an excessive amount of energy because John is usually surrounded by others. He also has a high level of self-efficacy, in that he believes he can deliver fifty or more wristbands since he will have audiences of more than fifty thousand people in the next two months.

Aaron has a contrary reaction. He doesn't think he can pass out two wristbands, let alone fifty. Low self-efficacy limits his hope and optimism. Not having a history of effective interpersonal communication, he has little motivation to gain any traction to begin now. For him, it will be very inconvenient and uncomfortable to personally acknowledge fifty AC4P behaviors and offer an AC4P wristband each time. He's quite satisfied, even happy, to endlessly play video games in the seclusion of his dorm room.

Both dispositional and situational factors influence the relative ease or difficulty of complying with this request, as well as the immediate and long-term consequences of delivering an AC4P wristband. John could readily deliver fifty wristbands with his perceived well-being remaining rather steady and unchanged; Aaron could deliver a single wristband and experience a huge increase in his perceived well-being. Suppose Aaron subsequently befriends an individual whom he recognized for AC4P behavior. That individual happens to be a research student in the Center for Applied Behavior Systems (CABS), where the AC4P Movement originated on the Virginia Tech campus.

Aaron joins CABS and eventually takes a lead on a research project studying ways to increase the frequency of AC4P behavior. He later presents his findings at a professional conference. So enthralled with explaining his AC4P research to others, Aaron advances through college, then graduate school, and is now a professor at a large university. He is currently speaking at conferences to thousands of people on how practicing AC4P behavior can better their lives.

A Mutual Mission

Obviously, the complementary domains of positive psychology and the AC4P Movement are ripe for intervention research, and more important, they are critical for enhancing the well-being of society as a whole. Unfortunately, the seemingly widening gulf between ABS and positive psychology researchers can slow progress toward what seems to be a mutual mission. What is the point of identifying scales that test levels of happiness perceptions if we don't develop interventions to increase the quantity and quality of AC4P behaviors that can fuel happiness?

Behavioral intervention seems to be a logical next step for progress in positive psychology. For example, large-scale increases in the frequency of AC4P behavior should enhance perceived happiness for both the giver and the receiver. Research is needed to empirically demonstrate this impact and to develop interventions to increase occurrences of such behavior. In any case, we hope the harmony and synergy between positive psychology and the AC4P Movement provide effective interventions for promoting AC4P behavior, happiness, and well-being at the same time. Reflect on what this chapter has outlined.

Take time to build up your character strengths. Consider it a form of exercise. Work toward becoming happier, and apply these positive psychology principles to increase the frequency of AC4P behavior throughout your day. Finally, consider that the happiness studied by positive psychologists is a personal perception. This person-state can benefit a person's viewpoint and interpretation, as reflected in the illustration on the next page.

However, behavior change can reap more long-term and widespread advantages. We issue a call for more synergistic collaboration between the teachers, researchers, and scholars of positive psychology and humanistic

behaviorism. In fact, positive psychology and the AC4P Movement should be one and the same reciprocal movement.

DISCUSSION QUESTIONS

1. Offer a brief definition of "positive psychology" as opposed to traditional psychology.
2. Differentiate between hedonic and eudemonic well-being.
3. What factors or behaviors predict happiness?
4. Explain the construct of psychological capital (Psy Cap) as conceptualized and researched by Fred Luthens.
5. What do the authors mean by their proposal of a "missing link" between ABS and positive psychology?
6. Of the following character strengths: Curiosity, Wisdom, Courage, Integrity, Kindness, Social Intelligence, Citizenship, Leadership, Gratitude, and Hope, which three do you most admire? Why?

7. Propose one practical way to enhance each of the three character strengths you selected in the prior question.
8. How can ABS inform the burgeoning domain of positive psychology and vice versa?
9. In what ways are the Positive-Psychology Movement and the AC4P Movement similar and different?
10. The authors propose the Positive-Psychology and AC4P movements should be one and the same. Why or why don't you agree with their proposal?

REFERENCES

1. Seligman, M. E. P., & Csikszentmihalyi, M. (2000). Positive psychology: An introduction. *American Psychologist*, 55(1), 5–14.
2. *VIA Character Strengths*, http://www.viacharacter.org/.
3. Sheldon, K. M., & King, L. (2001). Why positive psychology is necessary. *American Psychologist*, 56(3), 216–217.
4. Seligman, M. E. P., & Csikszentmihalyi, M. (2000). Positive psychology: An introduction. *American Psychologist*, 55(1), 5.
5. Seligman, M. E. (2002). *Authentic happiness: Using the new positive psychology to realize your potential for lasting fulfillment*: New York: Simon &Schuster.
6. Seligman, M. E., & Gillham, J. (2000). Hope and happiness. In *The science of optimism and hope: Research essays in honor of Martin E. P. Seligman* (pp. 323–336). Philadelphia: Templeton Foundation Press.
7. Ryan, R. M., & Deci, E. L. (2001). On happiness and human potential: A review of research on hedonic and eudaimonic well-being. *Annual Review of Psychology*, 52(1), 141–166.
8. Ryan, R. M., & Deci, E. L. (2001). On happiness and human potential: A review of research on hedonic and eudaimonic well-being. *Annual Review of Psychology*, 52(1), 142.
9. Deci, E. L., & Ryan, R. M. (2008). Hedonia, eudaimonia, and well-being: An introduction. *Journal of Happiness Studies*, 9 (1), 1–11.
10. Watson, D., Clark, L. A., & Tellegen, A. (1988). Development and validation of brief measures of positive and negative affect: The PANAS scales. *Journal of Personality and Social Psychology*, 54(6), 1063–1070.
11. Keyes, C. L. M., Shmotkin, D., & Ryff, C. F. (2002). Optimizing well-being: The empirical encounter of two traditions. *Journal of Personality and Social Psychology*, 82(6), 1007.
12. Ryff, C. D. (1989). Happiness is everything, or is it? Explorations on the meaning of psychological well-being. *Journal of Personality and Social Psychology*, 57(6), 1069–1081.
13. Diener, E. (2000). Subjective well-being: The science of happiness and a proposal for a national index. *American Psychologist*, 55(1), 34–43.
14. Wilson, W. R. (1967). Correlates of avowed happiness. *Psychological Bulletin*, 67(4), 294.

15. Lyubomirsky, S., Sheldon, K. M., & Schkade, D. (2005). Pursuing happiness: The architecture of sustainable change. *Review of General Psychology, 9*(2), 111–131.

16. Lischetzke, T., & Eid, M. (2006). Why extraverts are happier than introverts: The role of mood regulation. *Journal of Personality, 74*(4), 1127–1161.

17. Harker, L., & Keltner, D. (2001). Expressions of positive emotion in women's college yearbook pictures and their relationship to personality and life outcomes across adulthood. *Journal of Personality and Social Psychology, 80*(1), 112–124.

18. Ostir, G., Markides, K., & Black, S. (2000). Emotional well-being predicts subsequent functional independence and survival. *Journal of the American Geriatrics Society, 48*(5), 473–478.

19. Danner, D. D., Snowdon, D. A., & Friesen, W. V. (2001). Positive emotions in early life and longevity: Findings from the nun study. *Journal of Personality and Social Psychology, 80*(5), 804–813.

20. Levy, B. R., Slade, M. D., Kunkel, S. R., & Kasl, S. V. (2002). Longevity increased by positive self-perceptions of aging. *Journal of Personality and Social Psychology, 83*(2), 261–270.

21. Diener, E., & Seligman, M. E. (2002). Very happy people. *Psychological Science, 13*(1), 81–84.

22. Dunn, E. W., Aknin, L. B., & Norton, M. I. (2008). Spending money on others promotes happiness. *Science, 319*(5870), 1687–1688.

23. Luthans, F. (2002). The need for and meaning of positive organization behavior. *Journal of Organizational Behavior, 23*(6), 695–706.

24. Luthans, F., Luthans, K. W., & Luthans, B. C. (2004). Positive psychological capital: Beyond human and social capital. *Business Horizons, 47*(1), 45–50.

25. Luthans, F., Avey, J. B., & Patera, J. L. (2008). Experimental analysis of a web-based training intervention to develop positive psychological capital. *Academy of Management Learning & Education, 7*(2), 209–221.

26. Fredrickson, B. L. (2003). The value of positive emotions: The emerging science of positive psychology is coming to understand why it's good to feel good. *American Scientist, 91*(4), 330–335.

27. Avolio, B. J., & Gardner, W. L. (2005). Authentic leadership development: Getting to the root of positive forms of leadership. *Leadership Quarterly, 16*(3), 316.

28. Gable, S. L., & Haidt, J. (2005). What (and why) is positive psychology? *Review of General Psychology, 9*(2), 103–110.

29. Wiegand, D. M., & Geller, E. S. (2005). Connecting positive psychology and organizational behavior management. *Journal of Organizational Behavior Management, 24*(1–2), 3–25.

30. Seligman, M. E., Steen, T. A., & Peterson, C. (2005). Positive psychology progress: Empirical validation of interventions. *American Psychologist, 60*(5), 410–421.

31. Peterson, C., & Seligman, M. E. (2004). *Character strengths and virtues: A handbook and classification.* Washington, DC: American Psychological Association.

32. American Psychiatric Association. (2013). *Diagnostic and statistical manual of mental disorders* (5th ed.).Washington, DC: American Psychiatric Association.

33. Assess your relative character strength at no cost at www.viame.org.

34. Cacioppo, J. T., Petty, R. E., Feinstein, J. A., & Jarvis, W. B. (1996).Dispositional differences in cognitive motivation: The life and times of individuals varying in need for cognition. *Psychological Bulletin*, 119(2), 197–253.

35. Sansone, C., & Smith, J. L. (2000). The "how" of goal pursuit: Interest and self-regulation. *Psychological Inquiry*, 11(4), 306–309.

36. Kreitler, S., Kreitler, H., & Zigler, E. (1974). Cognitive orientation and curiosity. *British Journal of Psychology*, 65(1), 43–52.

37. Kashdan, T. B., & Roberts, J. E. (2004). Social anxiety's impact on affect, curiosity, and social self-efficacy during a high self-focus social threat situation. *Cognitive Therapy and Research*, 28(1), 119–141.

38. Schiefele, U., Krapp, A., & Winteler, A. (1992). Interest as a predictor of academic achievement: A meta-analysis of research. In A. Renninger, S. Hidi, & A. Krapp (Eds.).*The role of interest in learning and development* (pp. 183–212).Hillsdale, NJ: Lawrence Erlbaum.

39. Reio, T. G., & Wiswell, A. (2000). Field investigation of the relationship among adult curiosity, workplace learning, and job performance. *Human Resource Development Quarterly*, 11(1), 5–30.

40. Aluja-Fabregat, A. (2000). Personality and curiosity about TV and film violence in adolescents. *Personality and Individual Differences*, 29(2), 379–392.

41. Baltes, P. B., & Staudinger, U. M. (2000). Wisdom: A meta-heuristic (pragmatic) to orchestrate mind and virtue toward excellence. *American Psychologist*, 55(1), 122–136.

42. Baltes, P. B., & Staudinger, U. M. (1993). The search for a psychology of wisdom. *Current Directions in Psychological Science*, 2(3), 75–80.

43. Shelp, E. E. (1984). Courage: A neglected virtue in the patient–physician relationship. *Social Science and Medicine*, 18, 351–360.

44. Shepela, S. T., Cook, J., Horlitz, E., Leal, R., Luciano, S., Lutfy, E., et al. (1999). Courageous resistance: A special case of altruism. *Theory & Psychology*, 9(6), 787–805.

45. Finfgeld, D. L. (1999). Courage as a process of pushing beyond the struggle. *Qualitative Health Research*, 9(6), 803–814.

46. Larsen, K. S., & Giles, H. (1976). Survival or courage as human motivation: Development of an attitude scale. *Psychological Reports*, 39(1), 299–302.

47. Goldberg, C., & Simon, J. (1982). Toward a psychology of courage: Implications for the change (healing) process. *Journal of Contemporary Psychotherapy*, 13(2), 107–128.

48. Spreitzer, G. M., McCall, M. W., & Mahoney, J. D. (1997). Early identification of international executive potential. *Journal of Applied Psychology*, 82(1), 6–29.

49. Golden, L. (1996). The economics of work time length, adjustment, and flexibility. *Review of Social Economy*, 54(1), 1–45.

50. National Transportation Safety Board (2002). *Flight Path Study: American Airlines Flight 11*. http://www.ntsb.gov/about/Documents/Flight_Path_Study_AA11.pdf, retrieved February 19, 2002.

51. National Transportation Safety Board (2002). *Flight Path Study: United Airlines Flight 175*. http://www.ntsb.gov/about/Documents/Flight_Path_Study_UA175.pdf, retrieved February 19, 2002.

52. National Transportation Safety Board (2002). *Flight Path Study: American Airlines Flight 77.* http://www.ntsb.gov/about/Documents/Flight_Path_Study_ AA77.pdf, retrieved February 19, 2002.

53. Snyder, D. (2002). Families hear flight 93's final moments. *Washington Post,* April 19. http://www.washingtonpost.com/archive/politics/2002/04/19/families -hear-flight-93s-final-moments/de9e0830-f706-4cad-84d2-f1a8a4e2e690/; http://www.foxnews.com/story/2006/04/12/text-flight-3-recording.html, retrieved November 12, 2013.

54. CBC News (2011). *Winnipegger heads to NY for 9/11 memorial.* http://www.cbc.ca/ news/canada/manitoba/winnipegger-heads-to-ny-for-9-11-memorial-1.991431, retrieved November 13, 2013. A total of 2,996 people died: 19 hijackers and 2,977 victims.

55. Cauchon, D., & Moore, M. (2002). Desperation forced a horrific decision. *USA Today,* September 2. http://usatoday30.usatoday.com/news/sept11/2002-09 -02-jumper_x.htm, retrieved September 2, 2011.

56. Grady, D., & Revkin, A. C. (2002). Threats and responses: Rescuer's health; Lung ailments may force 500 firefighters off job. *New York Times,* September 10. http://www.nytimes.com/2002/09/10/us/threats-responses-rescuer-s-health -lung-ailments-may-force-500-firefighters-off.html, retrieved September 2, 2011.

57. Associated Press (2002). Post-9/11 report recommends police, fire response changes. *USA Today,* August 19. http://usatoday30.usatoday.com/news/nation/ 2002-08-19-nypd-nyfd-report_x.htm, retrieved September 2, 2011.

58. CNN (2002). Police back on day-to-day beat after 9/11 nightmare. July 21. http://edition.cnn.com/2002/US/07/20/wtc.police/index.html?related, retrieved November 12, 2013.

59. Joshi, P. (2005). Port Authority workers to be honored. *Newsday,* September 8. http://www.newsday.com/news/port-authority-workers-to-be-honored-1.695524, retrieved September 2, 2011.

60. Ryan, R. M., & Deci, E. L. (2000). Self-determination theory and the facilitation of intrinsic motivation, social development, and well-being. *American Psychologist,* 55(1), 68–78.

61. Ones, D. S., Viswesvaran, C., & Schmidt, F. L. (1995). Integrity tests: Overlooked facts, resolved issues, and remaining questions. *American Psychologist,* 50(6), 456–457.

62. Eisenberg, N., Miller, P. A., Schaller, M., Fabes, R. A., Fultz, J., Shell, R., et al. (1989). The role of sympathy and altruistic personality traits in helping: A reexamination. *Journal of Personality,* 57(1), 41–67.

63. Unger, L. S., & Thumuluri, L. K. (1997). Trait empathy and continuous helping: The case of voluntarism. *Journal of Social Behavior & Personality.* 12(3), 785–800.

64. Carlo, G., Koller, S. H., Eisenberg, N., Silva, M. S., & Frohlich, C. B. (1996). A cross-national study on the relations among prosocial moral reasoning, gender role orientations, and prosocial behaviors. *Developmental Psychology,* 32(2), 231–240.

65. Carlson, M., Charlin, V., & Miller, N. (1988). Positive mood and helping behavior: A test of six hypotheses. *Journal of Personality and Social Psychology,* 55(2), 211–229.

66. Thorndike, E. L. (1920). Intelligence and its uses. *Harper's Magazine*, 140, 227–235.
67. Gardner, H. (2004) *Frames of mind: The theory of multiple intelligences.* New York: Basic Books.
68. Salovey, P., & Mayer, J. D. (1989). Emotional intelligence. *Imagination, Cognition and Personality*, 9(3), 185–211.
69. Mayer, J. D. (2003). *Mayer-Salovey-Caruso Emotional Intelligence Test: MSCEIT.* North Tonawanda, NY: MHS, Multi-Health Systems.
70. Goleman, D. (1995). *Emotional intelligence.* New York: Bantam Books.
71. Snyder, M. (1974). Self-monitoring of expressive behavior. *Journal of Personality and Social Psychology*, 30, 4, 526–537.
72. Berkowitz, L., & Lutterman, K. G. (1968). The traditional socially responsible personality. *Public Opinion Quarterly*, 32(2), 169–185.
73. Ball, T., Farr, J., & Hanson, R. L. (1989). *Political innovation and conceptual change.* New York: Cambridge University Press.
74. Gough, H. G., McClosky, H., & Meehl, P. E. (1952). A personality scale for social responsibility. *Journal of Abnormal and Social Psychology*, 47(1), 73–80.
75. Starrett, R. H. (1996). Assessment of global social responsibility. *Psychological Reports*, 78, 535–554.
76. Mann, R. D. (1959). A review of the relationships between personality and performance in small groups. *Psychological Bulletin*, 56(4), 241.
77. Fleishman, E. A. (1953). The description of supervisory behavior. *Journal of Applied Psychology*, 37(1), 1–6.
78. Day, D. V., & Lord, R. G. (1988). Executive leadership and organizational performance: Suggestions for a new theory and methodology. *Journal of Management*, 14(3), 453–464.
79. Gerstner, C. R., & Day, D. V. (1997). Meta-analytic review of leader–member exchange theory: Correlates and construct issues. *Journal of Applied Psychology*, 82(6), 827–844.
80. Pruyser, P. W. (1976). *The minister as diagnostician: Personal problems in pastoral perspective.* Philadelphia: Westminster Press, p. 69.
81. Emmons, R. A., & Crumpler, C. A. (2000). Gratitude as a human strength: Appraising the evidence. *Journal of Social and Clinical Psychology*, 19(1), 56–69.
82. McCullough, M. E., Emmons, R. A., & Tsang, J. (2002). The grateful disposition: A conceptual and empirical topography. *Journal of Personality and Social Psychology*, 82(1), 112–127.
83. McCarty, R., Atkinson, M., Tiller, W. A., Rein, G., & Watkins, A. D. (1995). The effects of emotions on short-term power spectrum analysis of heart rate variability. *American Journal of Cardiology*, 76(14), 1089–1093.
84. Snyder, C. R., Harris, C., Anderson, J. R., & Holleran, S. A. (1991). The will and the ways: Development and validation of an individual-differences measure of hope. *Journal of Personality and Social Psychology*, 60(4), 570–585.
85. Snyder, C. R., Harris, C., Anderson, J. R., & Holleran, S. A. (1991). The will and the ways: Development and validation of an individual-differences measure of hope. *Journal of Personality and Social Psychology*, 60(4), p. 571.

86. Scheier, M. F., & Carver, C. S. (1992). Effects of optimism on psychological and physical well-being: Theoretical overview and empirical update. *Cognitive Therapy and Research*, 16(2), 201–228.

87. Buchanan, G. M., & Seligman, M. E. (1995). *Explanatory style*. Hillsdale, NJ: Lawrence Erlbaum.

88. Geller, E. S. (2001). *The psychology of safety handbook*. Boca Raton, FL: CRC Press.

89. Lyubomirsky, S., Dickerhoof, R., Boehm, J. K., & Sheldon, K. M. (2011). Becoming happier takes both a will and a proper way: An experimental longitudinal intervention to boost well-being. *Emotion*, 11(2), 391.

90. McCarty, S. M., & Geller, E. S. (2014). Actively caring to prevent bullying: Prompting and rewarding prosocial behavior in elementary schools. In E. S. Geller (Ed.). *Actively caring at your school: How to make it happen* (2nd ed.) (pp. 177–197). Newport, VA: Make-A-Difference; McCarty, S., Teie, S., McCutchen, J., & Geller, E. S. (in press). Actively caring to prevent bullying in an elementary school: Prompting and rewarding prosocial behavior. *Journal of Prevention Intervention in the Community*.

8

Leadership, Followership, and AC4P

ROSEANNE J. FOTI AND KATHLEEN B. BOYD

A good leader inspires people to have confidence in the leader; a great leader inspires people to have confidence in themselves.
                                    – Eleanor Roosevelt

Have you ever been in a group in which someone took control by conveying a clear group vision with actively caring for people (AC4P) passion, and made the rest of the group feel recharged and energized? These are characteristics of an AC4P leader. AC4P leadership inspires positive change in followers. These leaders are energetic, enthusiastic, and passionate.

AC4P leaders are concerned and involved in reaching SMARTS goals (Chapter 3). They focus on helping every member of the group succeed in the process. These leaders create beneficial behavior change within a group or an organization, and they facilitate self-motivation among their followers. The measure of a leader, you see, can be defined by the amount of discretionary or self-directed behavior performed by followers.[1]

Now, have you ever been in a group in which someone takes over by telling everyone what to do, and precisely how to do it? These are behaviors of a *manager*. Managers expect followers to be compliant, and they ensure compliance with an accountability system – positive and negative behavioral consequences. Managers do not seek any type of transformation or change; their aim is simply to keep people on track to reach existing group or organizational goals. Followers are carefully monitored to ensure expectations are met. The power of managers comes from their formal authority and designated responsibility in the group; the power of an AC4P leader comes from inspiration.

Finally, have you ever belonged to a group in which you were sometimes a leader and at other times a follower, depending on the task or the challenge at hand? People often switch between leader and follower roles many times in a single day, and task success depends as much on effective followership as it does on effective leadership.

So what is *leadership*? Leadership is the process of influencing others toward the accomplishment of goals (recall the discussion of SMARTS goals in Chapter 3). Leadership is not inherently good or bad. It becomes good or bad depending on the intentions, goals, and behavior of both leaders and followers. Goals can be constructive or destructive, helpful or harmful, legal or illegal, self-serving or prosocial. They can reflect actively caring for self or for others. The beneficial or harmful outcomes of boosting one or more of the five person-states (Chapter 2) depend on the leader's intentions, vision, and goal. Consequently, we have good AC4P leaders and destructive leaders.

WHAT IS AC4P LEADERSHIP?

In the leadership literature, AC4P leaders are acknowledged as transformational leaders.[2] You find transformational leaders everywhere in daily life, not just at the helm of major corporations, social movements, religious organizations, or entire countries. To gain a better understanding of what constitutes a transformational leader, you need look no further than the family in which you were raised. In the family environment, parents can be considered transformational leaders, because they guide the development – or transformation – of children into adults. Coaches and religious leaders can also be considered transformational leaders when they use their intentions, vision, and charismatic attitudes and behaviors to transform the attitudes and behaviors of the players or followers.

Transformational leadership creates positive cultural and environmental change (e.g., in communities, organizations, societies, and governments) and achieves goals both large and small, and it can also create positive change in the individuals who follow. In essence, transformational leaders focus on their followers, motivating them to achieve optimal levels of performance. In the process, they help followers develop their own leadership potential.

To accomplish their goals, transformational leaders are attentive to the needs and person-states of their followers, and they try to help followers reach their full potential. Transformational leaders adopt a developmental orientation toward followers and encourage them to focus not only on their own needs, but also on the needs of a collective group, society, or nation. In so doing, transformational leaders model the espoused values of the culture and use charismatic methods to attract people to these values and vision.[3] To be sure, transformational leaders are humanistic behaviorists. They care deeply. And they are action-oriented. They actively care.

Transformational leaders can choose to use their charisma to lead followers toward a more positive vision of the future (e.g., Martin Luther King, Mahatma Gandhi). These are AC4P leaders. However, visionary leaders can also be narcissistic and dangerous; their charisma gives them power to pursue their self-serving goals (e.g., Adolf Hitler, Attila the Hun). This phenomenon is referred to in the leadership literature as the dark side of transformational leadership or destructive leadership.[4] First, we describe the behaviors and characteristics of an AC4P or transformational leader, before describing destructive leadership and how it occurs.

Transformational Leadership Behavior

Transformational leaders motivate followers beyond immediate self-interests by applying a set of four leadership behaviors. In practical terms, transformational leaders come to their tasks willing to listen empathically and consider the needs of others. They take the time to get to know the people with whom they work, to remove roadblocks so people can perform at their best, and to understand how far their followers can be challenged.[5]

Idealized Influence. Transformational leaders are AC4P role models for their followers. They set exemplary examples, often by willingly sacrificing personal gain for the sake of others. These leaders are consistent, rather than arbitrary, in their actions and display determination and confidence. Modeling, as described in Chapter 1, is an effective intervention strategy; a transformational leader who combines the character strengths defined in Chapter 7 with a notable work ethic lays the foundation for an AC4P culture.

Inspirational Motivation. Transformational leaders promote cooperation among followers and encourage them to work interdependently to achieve a common goal. Transformational leaders create a vision of a desirable future and articulate possible ways to achieve it. They understand and apply the motivational influence of soon, certain, and positive consequences (Chapter 1) while implementing principles of self-motivation (Chapter 3), and help followers set SMARTS goals (Chapter 3) en route toward achieving a meaningful, consensual vision.

While it's important to help people appreciate the intrinsic (or natural) consequences of their work, transformational leaders realize at times it's advantageous to provide extrinsic consequences for desirable behavior. As depicted in the illustration on the next page, some tasks are not inherently reinforcing and extrinsic rewards are needed for optimum performance. Transformational leaders demonstrate unwavering commitment to their vision, and in doing so empower their followers to achieve relevant process goals.

Intellectual Stimulation. Transformational leaders set expectations rather than specify exactly what behaviors are required. They stimulate their followers to be innovative and creative by questioning assumptions, reframing problems, and approaching old situations in new ways. They realize followers must confront problems, and if they contribute to finding solutions, they will be more self-motivated to do their part.

Followers' ideas are not ignored simply because they might differ from those of the leader. Transformational leaders recognize and embrace the value of diverse viewpoints and encourage suggestions from followers with different experiences and knowledge. Intellectual stimulation can be achieved when transformational leaders perform person-based AC4P behaviors such as listening empathically to their followers' ideas and showing genuine appreciation for a follower's suggestions. By actively caring, the transformational leader activates and supports self-motivated initiatives of followers.

Individualized Consideration. Transformational leaders pay close attention to each follower's particular needs for achievement and growth by acting as an AC4P coach or mentor. Through empathic listening, transformational leaders accept individual differences. Each follower is unique, and transformational leaders recognize not all followers are created equal. By creating a culture of interpersonal trust and providing opportunities for personal growth in self-efficacy, transformational leaders increase the frequency and improve the quality of AC4P behavior among their followers.

How to Become a Transformational Leader

Everyone has opportunities to be a transformational leader. Transformational leadership starts with awareness – awareness of your own thoughts, perceptions, and feelings. As your awareness grows, you begin to see what drives you – your passions and values – and how these affect your actions and the attitudes and behavior of those around you. It's about leading with an integrity and authenticity that resonates with others and inspires them to follow.[6] But it doesn't stop there. Followers become leaders themselves.

This approach to leadership requires an evolution from a model of competition between individuals, teams, or nations that constricts growth, to an interdependent connection with the big picture – the all-encompassing context of goals, vision, and aspirations. Leadership genuinely serves for the good of all. This is an AC4P transformational leader. How can you become such a leader?

- Be inspired in your heart and mind, and show it.
- Be connected to yourself, the world, and the people around you.
- Have a vision and communicate it with passion and purpose.
- Pay personal attention to others; engage them and generate interpersonal trust and commitment.
- Genuinely care about others, what they want, and how you can serve them.
- Be curious, open to new ideas, and learn constantly.[7]

It's Not All about Leaders

Leadership necessarily requires followership. Without followers and the behaviors of following there is no leadership. Leadership does not exist in a vacuum. This means the behavior of followers is crucial to the leadership process. Followership requires behaviors that reflect a willingness to defer to another person in some way. You allow yourself – you grant permission – to be influenced by another person.

The most frequently cited early work on followership is that of Robert Kelley.[8] He distinguishes followers by their behavior and personality characteristics, and defines five types of followers: alienated, effective, passive, conformist, and pragmatist. These five archetypes are based on two important behavioral dimensions. One dimension measures the degree to which followers think independently and critically; the other assesses the level of a person's engagement as active or passive in a group or organization.

Do You Think? Independent, critical thinkers go beyond manuals and procedures. They reflect on the impact of their own actions and the actions of others, and they are willing to be creative and innovative and to offer corrective feedback when it's appropriate.

In contrast, dependent uncritical thinkers do not consider any possibilities beyond what they are told, do not contribute to the creative nurturing of the organization or group, and accept their leader's ideas without a second thought. They strictly adhere to procedures or instructions – even when circumstances demand responsible discretion.

Do You Act? The second dimension of the follower style is active versus passive behavior. Active followers demonstrate a sense of ownership. They participate fully in the group, take the initiative in problem-solving and decision-making, interact with other group members, and go beyond the basic necessities required by the task.

In contrast, passive followers require constant supervision and encouragement. Their level of involvement or interaction is limited to following instructions. They pointedly avoid responsibilities beyond what the task specifically requires.

The interaction of these two dimensions is shown in Figure 8.1 and determines the type of follower: conformist, passive, alienated, pragmatist, or exemplary. *Conformists* are the "yes people" who are active but dependent. They allow their leader to do most of the thinking and acting for them; they are generally positive and always loyal to their leader. *Passive* followers are the stereotypical "sheep." They are extrinsically motivated by their leader rather than by themselves.

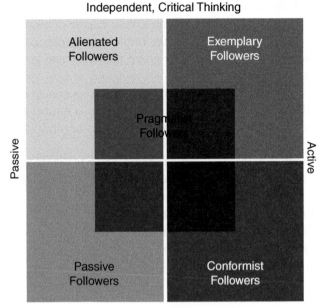

FIGURE 8.1. Kelley's five types of followers.

In contrast, *alienated* followers are independent, critical thinkers but are often perceived as cynical and disengaged. They think for themselves, but do not contribute to the positive direction of the group. In the center of Figure 8.1 are the *pragmatists*, who avoid taking a strong position and desire to keep conflict to a minimum; they are motivated to maintain the status quo. Finally, *exemplary* followers think for themselves, have positive energy, and are actively engaged. They agree with their leader's vision, but are willing to challenge the methods used to achieve the vision.

Kelley advocates turning all followers into exemplary followers, arguing the best followers are anything but passive sheep or cautious defenders of the status quo – they are actively engaged and exhibit courageous principles. Exemplary followers are committed to the group and to a purpose, belief, or mission that transcends self-interest. Transformational leaders aim to positively motivate and transform all followers into exemplary ones.[9]

In essence, transformational leaders want to help followers reach the top of Maslow's hierarchy of needs – self-transcendence and AC4P (Chapter 2). Kelley argues the same qualities that make effective leaders are those that make effective followers, and he emphasizes the importance and purpose of followers. Followers and leaders can be viewed as partners who move with ease from one role to another within the same group as a function of contextual factors such as task, interest, and expertise; and they switch roles with each other to perform the role that best meets the group's or organization's needs at the time.[10] They match a person's talent with function.

TRANSFORMATIONAL VERSUS
DESTRUCTIVE LEADERSHIP

What happens when a leader's vision for a group or organization is driven by narrow self-interests? These leaders behave in a way geared to obtain benefits for themselves at the expense of followers.[11] When leaders are pre-occupied by self-interests, they fail to consider the broader goals, interests, and needs of their followers. The result: an undesirable leadership process and unfortunate outcomes.

Jean Lipmann-Blumen refers to destructive leadership as a process in which leaders, by virtue of their harmful behavior and/or dysfunctional personal characteristics, inflict serious and enduring harm on their follow-ers, their organizations, and society as a whole.[12] Obviously, a destructive leader weakens the possibilities of cultivating an AC4P culture of compassion. This is anything but positive transformation. Many destructive leaders nurture and promote behaviors incompatible with the AC4P spirit.

Two Examples

Leaders can create a vision that inspires their followers to put the interests of others above their own needs; or their vision can create excessive dependency on the leader. Depending on the vision and the goals, leaders can inspire followers to perform behaviors that are constructive or destructive for human welfare or societal well-being.[13] Here are two examples of historical figures who have employed inspirational leadership tactics. One possessed positive intentions; the other, negative.

John F. Kennedy. "The New Frontier" was President Kennedy's vision for America in the early 1960s. The New Frontier consisted of a list of challenges facing the American people, challenges in the areas of science, space, foreign affairs, race and economic equality. He appealed to a younger generation through his conscious display of vigor and energy. During his speeches, John F. Kennedy challenged the nation's new generation, with famous quotes such as, "And so, my fellow Americans, ask not what your country can do for you; ask what you can do for your country."

In essence, JFK promoted selflessness; the New Frontier could be reached only if everyone actively contributed. Post–World War II America was already the greatest global force for freedom and prosperity; yet his idea of American greatness was not measured in power or material wealth, but by the very nature and intentions of Americans and how much they would actively care for the value of their country.

JFK backed up his vision of America with a public initiative, the founding of the Peace Corps in February 1961. President Kennedy appealed to the self-sacrifice of American youth, urging them to use their skills in the service of peace away from home. Seventy-one percent of the American public approved of the initiative. After almost five decades of service, the Peace Corps is more vital than ever and still growing. From JFK's inspiration came an agency devoted to world peace and friendship, and volunteers who continue to help individuals far from the shores of the United States build a better life for themselves, their children, their community, and their country.

Adolf Hitler. Adolf Hitler is one of the most infamous characters in world history, known for his leadership of the Nazi Party and his role as chancellor of Germany in the early 1930s. Once chancellor, Hitler consolidated his power by persuading the German parliament to pass the Enabling Act, which made the German chancellor the dictator of Germany and gave him absolute power. Two months later, Hitler began "cleaning house"; he abolished trade unions and ordered mass arrests of members of rival political groups. By the end of 1933, the Nazi Party was the only political entity allowed in Germany.

Throughout his rule, Hitler espoused the vision that the "Aryan race" was superior to all. Hitler and the Nazi Party started the "new order" on the basis of the Nazi concept of racial hygiene. New laws banned marriage between non-Jewish and Jewish Germans and deprived "non-Aryans" of the benefits of German citizenship. Hitler's early eugenic policies targeted children with physical and developmental disabilities, and later authorized a euthanasia program for disabled adults.

The Holocaust was conducted under the auspices of racial cleansing. Between 1939 and 1945, the Nazis and their collaborators were responsible for the deaths of 11 to 14 million people, including about 6 million Jews, representing two-thirds of the Jewish population in Europe. Deaths took place in concentration and extermination camps and through mass executions.

Other persecuted groups included Poles, Communists, homosexuals, Jehovah's Witnesses, and trade unionists.

Recently, leadership researchers have focused on understanding the factors underlying destructive leadership. These factors are at least as important as, and may be even more important, than the positive effects of transformational leadership on followers' attitudes and behaviors, due to their potential for horrific crimes against humanity. Obviously, a destructive leader is willfully blind to the possibilities of cultivating an AC4P culture of compassion. Many destructive leaders directly and systematically nurture and promote behaviors diametrically opposed to an AC4P movement.

How does destructive leadership develop? Like all leadership, it evolves from the interplay of the leader's motivations and behaviors, the followers' need for direction and authority, plus various situational factors.

Destructive Leadership: The Toxic Triangle

Destructive leadership is seldom absolutely or entirely adverse. Why? Because most leadership of any sort results in both favorable and unfavorable outcomes. Leaders, in conjunction with followers and the environmental context, contribute to outcomes distributed across a destructive–constructive continuum. Unfavorable outcomes can be a function of the leader, susceptible followers, or a context conducive to destructive leadership. Art Padilla calls this the "toxic triangle."[14] His model of the toxic triangle is depicted in Figure 8.2. These factors interact in complex ways to make destructive leadership possible; here we discuss them one at a time.

Destructive Leaders. Destructive leaders are not incompetent; they deliberately misuse positions of power and influence for their own interests. They know what they're doing; they consciously and actively abuse their power and position. Destructive leaders can be charming and energetic and will oversell their own achievements (often through propaganda). They may contaminate others with their own twisted confidence, but they are ultimately solely interested in bettering themselves.

Destructive leaders often enable and encourage failure because they are interested only in their own agenda, despite costs to the group or individuals in the group. Unlike positive-minded transformational leaders, destructive leaders hinder and impede AC4P behaviors among their followers. They propagandize their own beliefs and self-serving plans, leading to cultures deficient in AC4P behavior. They might ask for feedback, but from a disingenuous or self-serving perspective, as shown in the illustration on the next page.

Susceptible Followers. Destructive leaders will not get far without strong and active supporters. But why are certain followers unable or unwilling to resist domineering and abusive leaders? Most research suggests these followers yearn for safety, security, group membership, and predictability in a perceived uncertain world.[15] Ambitious people may support toxic, narcissistic leaders to secure their own positions; they might truly believe in the leader's agenda; or they may have negative feelings about themselves and/or their country, which they believe can be improved by the destructive leader.

There are two groups of susceptible followers: *conformers* and *colluders*. Conformers comply with destructive leaders out of fear; colluders actively participate in a destructive leader's agenda. Both are motivated by self-interest, but their concerns are different. Conformers try to minimize the consequences of *not* going along. Colluders seek personal gain through association with a destructive leader. Conformers are *failure avoiders*, while colluders are perverse *success seekers* (Chapter 1).

The vulnerability of conformers is based on unmet basic needs, negative self-evaluations, and psychological immaturity. Conformers lack the

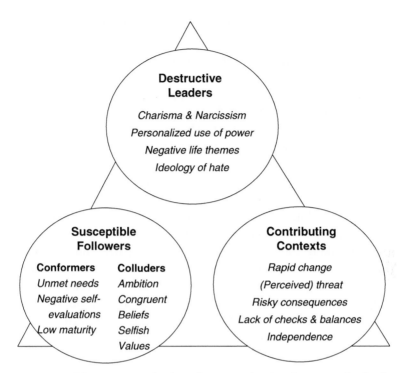

FIGURE 8.2. The toxic triangle: three domains related to destructive leadership.

strength and courage to transcend destructive leadership and actively care for their peers, team, organization, and/or country. In contrast, colluders are ambitious, self-serving and share the destructive leader's world views. Colluders seek security and acceptance from destructive leaders, even when their supportive behavior makes an AC4P culture improbable.

Contributing Contexts. The third element in the toxic triangle is the environmental context surrounding leaders, followers, and their interactions. The context is, in essence, everything external to the leader and followers, including the resources available to help accomplish goals. To detect and prevent destructive leadership, it's important to understand the situational factors that facilitate versus inhibit destructive leadership.

Certain situations, organizations, and cultural issues make it relatively easy for destructive leaders to thrive. One key contextual factor is the degree of discretion or personal choice the leader is granted.[16] When discretion is high, leaders are relatively free to do as they wish and wield their power as they desire. Rapid change in an organization or country may also enable leaders to centralize power and control more easily, thus increasing their own personal discretion.

Alternatively, certain contextual factors can inhibit leader discretion and serve as a check-and-balance system for destructive leadership. These factors include a free news media, external experts, and independent government agencies and advisory boards. Likewise, groups, organizations, and countries can prevent destructive behavior by promoting integrity and humility, interdependence over independence, and AC4P behavior over self-serving behavior.

Creating an environmental context to inhibit destructive leadership is critical, because once destructive leaders achieve power they consolidate control by abolishing existing policies and procedures.[17] Creating an AC4P culture of compassion is key to preventing destructive leadership behaviors from taking root, growing, and producing undesirable outcomes. When leaders and followers perform AC4P behaviors, they improve the culture and enhance positive person-states, which in turn can increase the frequency of others' AC4P behaviors. Clearly, AC4P behavior is the foundation of an AC4P culture. The more often quality AC4P behavior occurs among people in a given work, school, family, or societal setting, the more likely an AC4P culture will evolve.

USING AC4P PRINCIPLES TO BE AN EFFECTIVE LEADER AND FOLLOWER

As indicated earlier, without followership there is no leadership. Specifically, three types of followership behavior are critical for AC4P leadership: (a) Followers exhibit discretionary behavior directed toward the leader's goals or vision – they freely *donate* some of their time and energy to the leader's cause; (b) Followers make sacrifices for the leader's cause; this implies a commitment to the leader and his/her cause and is another example of a voluntary choice rather than forced or mandated behavior; (c) Followers offer supportive and corrective feedback relevant to achieving the leader's goals.[1]

Follower behavior is critical to AC4P leadership. Just as important, AC4P leaders inspire followers to hold themselves accountable to doing the right thing. These transformational leaders facilitate self-motivation by promoting perceptions of competence, choice, and community among their followers (Chapter 3), while also enhancing the five person-states that influence one's propensity to perform AC4P behavior (Chapter 2). Leaders' position of influence in a group or organization gives them substantial opportunity to influence followers' five person-states and consequently the propensity for AC4P behavior.

A large body of research literature has addressed the question: "Are leaders born or made?" Within this research there is evidence of genetic factors influencing leadership development. There is also strong support for environmental or extrinsic determinants of leadership, corroborating the premise that transformational leadership can be achieved through training and education.

In his provocative book, *The Science of Leadership*, Julian Barling discusses transformational leadership behaviors that have the potential to (a) make followers feel more appreciated; (b) increase followers' self-esteem and self-efficacy; (c) empower followers to feel ownership over their accomplishments; and (d) increase the overall effectiveness of both leaders and followers.[18] In addition to being constructive, these behaviors inherently increase the person-states that fuel one's propensity to perform AC4P behavior. Let's review these leadership behaviors that can contribute to establishing an AC4P culture.

Walk the Talk!

An AC4P leader builds respect and mutual trust among followers by consistently choosing to do the right thing instead of doing what is merely expedient. This simple component of transformational leadership might not always be easy and can leave the leader in a difficult position.

One example of doing the right thing is accepting responsibility for failure and apologizing sincerely. A leader must face the brutal facts of less-than-desirable outcomes and hold him/herself accountable without blaming other people or just "bad luck." Deciding to always do the right thing means you are a leader, a teacher, an AC4P person who understands that transformational leadership is not about benefiting self-interests, but elevating the individuals around you.[19]

AC4P Coaching is Infectious!

By providing followers with the inspiration to go the extra mile, AC4P leaders help them attain more than they believed possible. Chapter 3 provides ten guidelines for increasing self-motivation by enhancing one or more of three perceptions: competence, choice, and community. The most effective athletic coaches communicate behavioral feedback so team members learn from an interpersonal exchange and increase their self-motivation to continuously improve.

C are
- *show that you care*
- *set caring examples*

O bserve
- *define target behaviors*
- *record behavioral occurrences*

A nalyze
- *identify existing contingencies*
- *identify potential contingencies*

C ommunicate
- *listen actively*
- *speak persuasively*

H elp
- *recognize continuous improvement*
- *teach and encourage the process*

FIGURE 8.3. The five basic components of AC4P coaching.[21]

The five letters in the word *coach* represent the critical sequential steps of AC4P coaching: care, observe, analyze, communicate, and help. Scott Geller has applied this instructional acronym for the improvement of occupational safety, but this AC4P coaching process (summarized in Figure 8.3) is clearly useful for improving follower behaviors and enhancing self-esteem, self-efficacy, and personal control in various situations, including home, school, athletics, and the workplace.[20]

"C" for "Care." Caring is the basic underlying motivation for coaching. AC4P leaders need to demonstrate a caring attitude throughout their personal interactions with others and act on this caring. When people realize – by a leader's words and body language – that s/he cares, they are more apt to listen to and accept the leader's counsel. When people know you care, they care what you know.

"O" for "Observe." Effective coaches observe the behavior of others objectively and systematically, with an eye to supporting goal-directed behavior and correcting off-task behavior. Behavior that transcends the call of duty for the group should be especially supported. Observing behavior for supportive and constructive feedback is easy if the coach (a) knows exactly what behaviors are desired and undesired; and (b) takes the time to observe whether these behaviors take place in the work or task setting. Involving followers in the creation of the critical behaviors increases their ownership of and commitment to the process. Behavior that contributes significantly to goal accomplishment can be increased through supportive feedback and positive recognition.

"A" for "Analyze." When interpreting observations, coaches draw on their understanding of the ABC contingency (for activator-behavior-consequence) introduced in Chapter 1. They realize that observable reasons usually exist to explain why behavior occurs. They know certain destructive behaviors are prompted by activators such as work demands, peer pressure, and inconsistent and/or contradictory messages from those in power. This understanding is critical if effective coaching is to be a fact-finding rather than fault-finding process. It also leads to an objective and constructive analysis of the situations observed.

"C" for "Communicate." An AC4P coach is an effective communicator. This means being an active listener and persuasive speaker. Anyone giving behavioral feedback must actively listen to reactions. This is how an effective coach shows sincere concern for the feelings and self-esteem of the person on the receiving end of feedback. As detailed in Chapter 5, the best listeners give empathic attention with facial cues and posture, paraphrase to check understanding, prompt for more details, and accept stated feelings without subjective interpretation.

"H" for "Help." It's critical, of course, that a coach's help be accepted. Words corresponding to the four letters of *help– humor, esteem, listen, praise* – outline strategies for increasing the probability a coach's advice, directions, or feedback will be integrated into performance. Once followers experience the benefits of AC4P coaching, such behavior-focused coaching becomes a shared responsibility and part of the culture of the group or work organization.

Inspiring Self-Direction

Transformational leadership involves intellectual stimulation. These leaders encourage followers to think about work- or school-related challenges in new ways. This provides followers with opportunities to develop and grow. By reminding followers of their existing knowledge, skills, and abilities and allowing them to take ownership of a problem, a leader inspires self-motivation and provides followers a greater sense of accomplishment when the issue is resolved.

By developing an interdependent perspective, a transformational leader helps followers become holistic systems thinkers and see widespread benefits of AC4P behavior. This may require relinquishing some top-down control; abandoning a desire for a quick fix; changing from focusing on outcomes to recognizing process achievements; and giving followers opportunities to choose, evaluate, and refine their means to achieve the ends. The result: more followers going beyond the call of duty on behalf of others when no one's watching.[22]

Often followers will come to a leader and ask for assistance when they already know the answer. They are simply asking for the leader's support. Consider the opposite: The leader knows the answer but does not tell the followers. Instead s/he sets up the situation for them to find the answer themselves. This epitomizes humanistic behaviorism and achieves optimal learning and buy-in.

Promoting Respect and Appreciation

A final vital component of AC4P transformational leadership involves compassion, appreciation, and positive recognition to establish a symbiotic relationship between leader and follower. One easy behavioral strategy is to learn and use followers' names in conversations and emails. Followers should be assured you have confidence in them, but they should also be reminded when they are doing well. The fulfillment of certain psychological needs is critical for healthy psychological development and well-being. Though psychological need fulfillment is not necessary for the occurrence of AC4P behavior, as discussed in Chapter 2, it certainly makes AC4P behavior more likely.

Recall that exemplary followers are actively engaged with their leader and with the group or organization, whether the leader is a professor in the classroom, a student leader of a project group, or the CEO at a Fortune 500 company. Supportive behavioral feedback is a vital AC4P behavior for the maintenance of the desirable behavior.

Recall a time when you were on the receiving end of positive recognition of your behavior. How did it make you feel? Did it increase your sense of competence and self-motivation? Did it increase your sense of empowerment and self-efficacy, as in "I can do it"? Did you feel more optimistic? Providing relevant supportive feedback takes time, but it's the glue that binds you in a lasting constructive relationship with existing followers and helps to attract additional followers.

THE DIRECT APPROACH TO CULTIVATING AN AC4P CULTURE

Chapter 2 discussed direct and indirect approaches to increasing the frequency and improving the quality of AC4P behavior. The preceding section gave examples of ways transformational leaders can increase the frequency of AC4P behavior indirectly by impacting certain dispositional person-states. A transformational leader can also increase the frequency of AC4P behavior directly with extrinsic now-that rewards (Chapter 3). Recognizing someone for exceeding expectations (e.g., via a thank you card or an AC4P wristband) creates interdependence and belongingness among followers. Here are additional ways to nurture an AC4P culture with ABS activators and consequences:

- Leaders can ask followers to make a verbal and/or written commitment to increasing their interdependence mindset and become active members of the organizational community.
- Leaders can openly support (e.g., though wristbands, thank you cards, employee-of-the-moment recognition) individuals who stand tall as leaders and oppose damaging decisions and plans.
- Leaders can create a system by which behavioral feedback can be conveyed and appreciated across all levels of an organization (peer-to-peer, follower-to-leader, and leader-to-follower).

IN CONCLUSION

Creating an AC4P culture is a continuous journey for leaders and followers. Organizations, schools, and businesses are always seeking ways to be more successful. We believe desirable outcomes often begin with AC4P leadership. A key mistake people make is thinking that leadership means focusing on large-scale changes, the big picture, such as developing and implementing a new strategic plan or policy initiative (recall the Peace Corps). Yet when researchers talk to followers and leaders about what inspires them, it's usually the little things, interpersonal communication between the leader and the follower, that have the most frequent and meaningful impact on individuals and their motivation to do amazing work.

We get back to the basics of human interaction and relationship-building. The guiding question: Rather than acting in a way that typically belittles or demeans people, what can I do as a leader to help them feel better about themselves? Everyone wants to improve, but many people resist giving and receiving the kind of communication that is critical for beneficial change. Some people perceive feedback that implies personal change as an indictment of their current work style, job skills, or diligence. This reaction most likely happens when someone is asked to change dramatically and when the current routine has been followed for years.

To overcome this natural resistance, AC4P leaders steer clear of disruptive and dramatic communication and emphasize incremental "fine-tuning" or successive approximations. They also facilitate beneficial change in both behavior and attitude by accentuating the positives – occurrences of desirable behavior. This enables the transformational development of authentic interpersonal relationships and the community spirit needed for behavioral feedback to be given and received frequently, constructively, and in a non-adversarial manner. When these "transformed" relationships develop in the workplace or educational setting, the ability to inspire and influence achievement of goals and objectives is optimized.

Focus on the one or two things you can do as a leader to help people feel they are the most important person to you in the moment of the interaction. It's not "employee of the *month*" but "employee, student, or athlete of the *moment*." Transformational leadership does not require the impossible from leaders, but rather daily AC4P communication that shows sincere appreciation of the *effort* of others who contribute to the group or organizational mission.

AC4P leaders inspire us to hold ourselves accountable to doing the right thing. AC4P leaders facilitate self-motivation by influencing person-states (e.g., perceptions, attitudes, and/or emotions) that facilitate self-motivation. Self-motivation often leads to discretionary behavior – behavior beyond that which is required. Vision, goals, and consequences are not sufficient for culture change. Followers need to *actively care* about the goals, action plans, and consequences. They need to believe in and own the vision. They need to feel empowered and encouraged to attain process goals that support the vision (Chapter 2).

When performing these transformational leadership behaviors, AC4P leaders model the espoused values of an AC4P culture. They attract people, peers, and followers to similar values and a noble, mutually beneficial vision. Our vision: a culture of interdependence, compassion, and AC4P behavior by all.

DISCUSSION QUESTIONS

1. What are some differences between a transactional leader (a manager) and a transformational leader?
2. How can one become a transformational leader?
3. Define the role(s) of followership and point out advantages of this behavioral pattern.
4. List characteristics of "exemplary" followers as opposed to other types of followers.
5. Discuss motives and behaviors of destructive leaders.
6. Can a destructive leader be inspirational and therefore transformational? Please explain your answer.
7. Explain the role of the environmental context in determining constructive versus destructive leadership.
8. Explain how the COACH acronym reflects the kind of AC4P coaching that can improve follower behavior and attitudes.
9. Discuss the "interdependent" perspective with regard to facilitating effective leadership and followership.
10. How do the direct and indirect approaches to nurturing an AC4P culture connect to constructive transformational leadership?

REFERENCES

1. Daniels, A. C., & Daniels, J. E. (2005). *Measure of a leader.* New York: McGraw-Hill: Performance Management Publications.
2. Burns, J. M. (1978) *Leadership.* New York: Harper & Row.
3. Bass, B. M. (1985). *Leadership and performance beyond expectation.* New York: Free Press; Bass, B. M. (1998). *Transformational leadership.* New York: Lawrence Erlbaum.
4. Schyns, B., & Hansbrough, T. (2010). *When leadership goes wrong.* Charlotte, NC: IAP.
5. Avolio, B. J. (2011). *Full range leadership development* (2nd ed.). Thousand Oaks, CA: Sage; Bass, B. M., & Riggio, R. E. (2006). *Transformational leadership* (2nd ed.). Mahwah, NJ: Lawrence Erlbaum.
6. Bass, B. M., & Riggio, R. E. (2006). *Transformational leadership* (2nd ed.). Mahwah, NJ: Lawrence Erlbaum.
7. Lussier, R. N., & Achua, C. F. (2004). *Leadership: Theory, application, skill development* (2nd ed.); Eagan, MN: Thomson-West; Tichy, N. M., & Devanna, M. A. (1986). *The transformational leader.* New York: John Wiley.
8. Kelley, R. E. (1988). *In praise of followers. Harvard Business Review, 66,* 141–148.
9. Kelley, R. E. (1992). *The power of followership.* New York: Doubleday Business.
10. Kelley, R. E. (2008). Rethinking followership. In R. Riggio, I. Chaleff, & J. Lipman-Blumen (Eds.). *The art of followership: How great followers create great leaders and organizations* (pp. 5–16). San Francisco: Jossey-Bass.

11. Craig, B. S., & Kaiser, R. B. (2013). Destructive leadership. In M. G. Rumsey (Ed.). *The Oxford handbook of leadership* (pp. 439–454). New York: Oxford University Press.
12. Lipman-Blumen, J. (2005). *The allure of toxic leaders: Why we follow destructive bosses and corrupt politicians – and how we can survive them.* New York: Oxford University Press.
13. Howell, J. M., & Avolio, B. J. (1992). The ethics of charismatic leadership: Submission or liberation? *Academy of Management Executive*, 6, 43–54; Kark, R., Shamir, B., & Chen, G. (2003). The two faces of transformational leadership: Empowerment and dependency. *Journal of Applied Psychology*, 88, 246–255. http://www.biography.com/people/john-f-kennedy-9362930; http://www.bbc.co.uk/history/people/adolf_hitler; http://www.biography.com/people/adolf-hitler-9340144.
14. Padilla, A., Hogan, R., & Kaiser, R. B. (2007). The toxic triangle: Destructive leaders, susceptible followers, and conducive environments. *Leadership Quarterly*, 18, 176–193.
15. Kellermann, B. (2004). *Bad leadership: What it is, how it happens, why it matters.* Cambridge, MA: Harvard University Press.
16. Kaiser, R. B., & Hogan, R. (2007). The dark side of discretion: Leader personality and organizational decline. In R. Hooijberg, J. Hunt, J. Antonakis, & K. Boal (Eds.). *Being there even when you are not: Leading through strategy, systems and structures, Monographs in leadership and management*, Vol. 4 (pp. 177–197). London: Elsevier Science.
17. Furnham, A. (2010). *The elephant in the boardroom.* London: Palgrave Macmillan; Padilla, A. (2012). *Leadership: The leaders, the followers and the environment.* New York: John Wiley.
18. Barling, J. (2014). *The science of leadership: Lessons from research for organizational leaders.* New York: Oxford University Press.
19. Geller, E. S. (2005). *People-based safety: The source.* Virginia Beach, VA: Coastal Training Technologies, pp. 130–135.
20. Adopted from Geller, E. S. (2001). *The psychology of safety handbook.* Boca Raton, FL: CRC Press, p. 241.
21. Geller, E. S (2001). *The psychology of safety handbook.* Boca Raton, FL: CRC Press, pp. 233–263.
22. Geller, E. S., & Veazie, B. (2010) *When no one's watching: Living and leading self-motivation.* Virginia Beach, VA: Coastal Training and Technologies.

INTRODUCTION TO PART II: APPLICATIONS
OF AC4P PRINCIPLES

E. SCOTT GELLER

I started my professional career in 1969 as assistant professor of psychology at Virginia Polytechnic Institute and State University (Virginia Tech). Assisted by undergraduate and graduate students, I developed a productive laboratory and research program in cognitive psychology. My tenure and promotion to associate professor were based entirely upon my professional scholarship in this domain. However, in the mid-1970s I became concerned the laboratory work had limited potential for helping people. This conflicted with my personal mission to make beneficial large-scale differences in people's quality of life. Consequently, I turned to another line of research.

I was convinced behavior-based psychology or applied behavioral science (ABS) had the greatest potential for solving organizational and community problems. Accordingly, I focused my research on finding ways to make this happen. Inspired by the first Earth Day in April 1970, my students and I developed, evaluated, and refined a number of community-based techniques to increase the frequency of environmentally responsible behavior (ERB) and decrease the occurrence of environmentally harmful behavior (EHB). This prolific research program culminated with the 1982 book, *Preserving the Environment: New Strategies for Behavior Change*, which I coauthored with Dr. Richard A. Winett and Dr. Peter B. Everett.[1]

My students and I applied behavioral science to a number of issues beyond environmental protection. These included prison administration, school discipline, community theft, transportation management, and alcohol-impaired driving. In the mid-1970s we began researching strategies for increasing the use of vehicle safety belts. This led to a focus on the application of behavioral science to the prevention of unintentional injuries in organizational and community settings.

FROM BASIC TO APPLIED RESEARCH

My early scholarship was divided between basic (i.e., reaction time) and applied (i.e., behavioral science) research. Once awarded tenure in 1976, I started giving more attention to behavioral community psychology, which was clearly not mainstream in those days. My students and I continued to demonstrate the efficacy of applying behavior-focused psychology in community and organizational settings to benefit the environment and people's health, safety, and well-being. By 1979, the year I was promoted to the rank of professor, my research and scholarship had transitioned completely from basic to applied psychology, particularly the practice of ABS to improve people's quality of life on a macro scale.

Applied Behavioral Science

Every semester since 1979, thirty to seventy undergraduate students have conducted ABS research with me that reflects our university motto: "That I may serve." Students learn the methodology of applying rigorous behavioral science in the field by doing, and their doing contributes in turn to people's health, safety, and welfare or to environmental sustainability. Beyond learning the principles and procedures of ABS through personal involvement, these students learn the value of actively caring for people (AC4P).

A University Research Center

By 1987 our applied-psychology research had been awarded enough extramural grant support to fund a research center in the Department of Psychology at Virginia Tech. That year marked the beginning of the Center for Applied Behavior Systems (CABS). We wanted to be more than a center for contracts and grant-funded research; we wanted a significant focus on teaching through active involvement.

Following the advice of the wise Confucian principle, "Tell them and they'll forget, demonstrate and they'll remember, involve them and they'll understand," our ABS research has always involved students in some type of community service. By "putting knowledge to work" (our university slogan at the time), students experienced the value of helping others. As we grew into an official university research center, we were empowered to declare our research, teaching, and service-learning objectives in an official mission statement.

The Center for Applied Behavior Systems was developed to:

1. Help students, undergraduate and graduate, learn how to conduct research that combines the technology of applied behavioral science with theories from experimentatl, social, and applied psychology.
2. Give students real-world, hands-on research experience, from designing methodology and data-analysis strategies to documenting findings in professional publications.
3. Teach, develop, and evaluate community-based interventions.
4. Give students opportunities to participate in leading-edge professional activities.
5. Improve quality of life in the VT and Blacksburg community, and beyond.
6. Teach and demonstrate the value of actively caring for people (AC4P).

FIGURE II.1. The mission statement for the Virginia Tech Center for Applied Behavior Systems.

Our Mission Statement

Our mission statement, shown in Figure II.1, defines our purpose and our values as a teaching/learning research center. The mission outlines standards for directing our daily process activities and the types of consequences that are worth celebrating as a group.

Every semester the Virginia Tech students who learn and conduct research in CABS receive a comprehensive handbook that provides an overview of the research planned for the semester and explains procedures and research projects for the semester. The handbook changes each semester to reflect administrative variations and different research topics and methods. What has never changed since its inception in 1987 is the mission statement.

EXAMPLES OF CABS RESEARCH

All of the research discussed in this book is founded on the same ABS and humanism principles (i.e., humanistic behaviorism) as the research conducted by the undergraduate and graduate students in CABS. Ten of the chapter authors (including coauthors) received research education/training in CABS, and five completed their Ph.D. dissertation research in CABS. The other chapter authors have a solid foundation in ABS; seven currently teach ABS courses at a college or university. While most of these professionals may not have considered *humanistic behaviorism* to be a label for their domain of expertise, I'm convinced the preparation of their chapters activated a relevant, personal paradigm shift. All chapter authors have expressed sincere appreciation of the AC4P Movement and the direct connection of the AC4P principles to their scholarship.

The first two chapters in this section target the well-being of employees in the workplace. The senior author of Chapter 9 led substantial ABS research in CABS and earned a Ph.D. in industrial/organizational psychology; since 1999 he has worked as senior project manager for Safety Performance Solutions, Inc. – a leading-edge training and consulting firm specializing in behavior-based and people-based safety since 1985 (safetyperformance.com).

Chapter 9 is the longest chapter in Part II. Why? Behavior-based safety (BBS), the use of ABS to keep workers and workplaces injury-free, has been a worldwide phenomenon since the early 1990s, and there is much to report about this make-a-difference domain of applied psychology. As explained in this chapter, we now refer to BBS as people-based safety (PBS) because the most successful applications have incorporated AC4P principles that involve evidence-based concepts from psychological science, especially humanism – a more broad-based domain of human dynamics than ABS.

In Chapter 10, an organizational behavior management team at the University of Kansas takes a perspective that goes beyond occupational safety and explains how humanistic behaviorism can be applied in an organization to nurture an AC4P culture of win-win interdependency and interpersonal compassion. The result: greater productivity and job satisfaction, and lower rates of job turnover.

The lead authors of the next two chapters conducted their PhD dissertation research in CABS. These chapters target behaviors in the community at large to address two tragic social ills: injuries and fatalities from vehicle crashes and alcohol abuse among university students. Each chapter documents successful applications of behavior-focused interventions based on AC4P principles. Some of the practical behavior-change strategies relevant to cultivating an AC4P traffic safety culture have already been applied extensively; others have evidence-based potential but have not been tried on a macro scale; additional interventions described in this chapter are in the conceptual or prototype stage, calling for research testing and dissemination.

Chapter 12 explores a variety of AC4P attempts to decrease intoxication and its obvious negative side effects. Alcohol consumption among university students at fraternity parties and community bars is targeted, and empirical evidence discredits many common-sense and popular intervention approaches. A few AC4P-based strategies show promise for alleviating critical aspects of this at-risk behavior if practiced on a large scale.

The next two chapters address healthcare, one from a problem-specific focus (i.e., obesity) and the other concerning the general care of patients in healthcare facilities. Chapter 13 is proactive, discussing AC4P approaches for the prevention of disease from obesity; Chapter 14 is reactive, showing how adopting the fundamental humanistic principle of patient-centered care can improve healthcare dramatically. This is easier said than done. An AC4P healthcare culture is needed to instruct and encourage patients to provide healthcare workers with specific behavior-focused feedback and to motivate healthcare workers to consider the corrective feedback from their patients and adjust their behavior accordingly.

The next three chapters address the AC4P care of children by parents and teachers, and the coaching of young athletes. The first two authors of Chapter 15 conducted their dissertation research in CABS; after establishing their professional careers, they became moms. Each has applied AC4P principles (i.e., ABS and humanism) throughout the childhood years of their children. Their successful behavior-change approaches are documented in their chapter, accompanied by substantial research evidence for the efficacy of their techniques.

Speaking of mothers and children, the senior author of Chapter 16 is the daughter of the author of Chapter 17. Both have solid graduate school education and training in ABS, teach applied psychology at different universities, and conduct leading-edge research on the topics of their respective chapters. Chapter 16 explains convincingly that parents should send their children to preschool and delineates the AC4P tactics of the most effective preschool teachers. Perhaps most important, this chapter explains how preschool teachers can be trained to be more effective AC4P teachers.

In Chapter 17 we learn how the behaviors of coaches of young athletes can be systematically observed, evaluated, and then improved with an AC4P training program. The behavioral observation and training techniques are applicable for coaches of any sport and athletes of any age. If coaches used more positive than negative consequences to shape the behavior of their athletes, more athletes would practice and compete to succeed rather than to avoid failure – and therefore be more self-motivated to perform well and be the best they can be at their sport.

The next chapter continues a focus on training and education; here the target is higher education. Many readers are in the midst of their college or university education right now. What aspects of this expensive experience, with consequences that last a lifetime, are working well for you? Which ones do you not find effective or efficient? The authors of this chapter have studied the relevant literature and have tested various ABS-based attempts to make university education more effective. Read this chapter to learn how the application of AC4P principles could improve the quality and efficiency of higher education at colleges and universities.

Chapter 19 addresses an enduring and ultimately life-threatening issue many people deny or simply choose to ignore – the continuous degradation of our planet. This chapter explains the relevance of human behavior to solving the paramount issue of ecological sustainability. It's ironic that the earliest applications of ABS technology in community settings targeted behavior associated with environmental conservation (i.e., littering, recycling, residential energy consumption), yet relatively little ABS research addresses this issue today. The reason? I believe the paucity of research stems from minimal large-scale improvements resulting from the prior ABS interventions in this domain. They were merely short-term demonstrations.

This chapter explores why effective techniques for increasing the frequency of ERB and reducing the occurrence of EHB have not been adopted and suggests how applications of AC4P principles can have a more profound, durable, and positive impact on ecological sustainability.

Finally, the last application chapter offers a unique perspective on the AC4P concept. Here the author proposes that pets be considered AC4P agents. Why? Because pets exemplify the unconditional and loyal positive regard that increases perceptions of happiness and well-being among pet owners, as well as enhance those person-states of pet owners that intensify their propensity to perform AC4P behavior.

Read these chapters to learn the potential of an AC4P approach to improve people's lives in diverse environments and cultural settings (organizations, communities, families, athletic teams, and healthcare facilities) and among all age groups. The need to directly confront many societal problems through AC4P-based interventions at home, in the workplace, in classrooms, during travel on the road, at play in recreational settings, and in the communities where we live is clearly evident.

Still, these chapters reflect only a tip of the iceberg. Sure, we want these chapters to inspire more people to perform AC4P behaviors in the contexts discussed here. But more than that, we hope these application chapters stimulate broad-based exploration of how AC4P principles can bring understanding, compassion, and improvement to the various trials and tribulations that affect human lives and require a sustainable change in behavior to improve quality of life.

REFERENCE

1. Geller, E .S., Winett, R. A., & Everett, P. B. (1982) *Preserving the environment: New strategies for behavior change.* New York: Pergamon Press.

9

Actively Caring for Occupational Safety

JOSHUA H. WILLIAMS AND E. SCOTT GELLER

Vision without execution is hallucination.
– Thomas Edison

For decades we've been fortunate to work with leading organizations around the world to help them achieve an actively caring for people (AC4P) safety culture. Many of these organizations use behavior-based safety (BBS) to address the human dynamics of workplace injuries. This application of behavioral science was created by the second author in 1979 and has been widely effective in reducing injuries at thousands of organizations worldwide. However, many applications of BBS are too narrow, inflexible, and limiting. This chapter addresses people-based safety (PBS), which is an evolution of BBS for organizations working to achieve an AC4P safety culture.[1]

Like BBS, PBS targets human behavior and uses behavioral observation and feedback to correct risky behaviors and reward safe behaviors. Unlike traditional BBS, PBS involves other key factors required to achieve an AC4P safety culture. As depicted in Figure 9.1, key factors of PBS for achieving an AC4P safety culture include *behavior, person-states, leadership*, and *systems/conditions*. We examine the principles and execution of each of these key organizational cultural factors in this chapter.

BEHAVIOR

Most workplace injuries and fatalities have a behavioral component. Employees may strain their back because of improper lifting techniques, injure an eye because they chose not to wear safety glasses, or even die on the job because they didn't use a safety harness at extreme heights. In order to prevent injuries and fatalities, it's important to understand why employees perform risky behaviors.

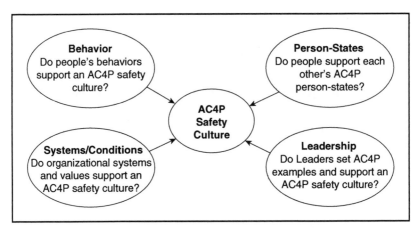

FIGURE 9.1. The key organizational factors addressed by PBS to achieve an AC4P safety culture.

The ABC Model

Behavioral psychologists frequently use the ABC model to explain occurrences of safe and at-risk behaviors.[2] As detailed in Chapter 1, activators (A) get our attention to behave (B) in a certain way. Our motivation to perform the behavior depends on consequences (C), those we want, to obtain, avoid, or escape. Activators include safety signs, meetings, posted rules, verbal reminders, and the presence of a supervisor. Behaviors (safe or at-risk) are observable actions and include using a safety harness, locking out the power of moving equipment, and driving a forklift at a safe speed. Positive consequences include a "thank you" hand signal, as well as personal pride for following safe work practices and setting the right example. Negative consequences include injuries and verbal reprimands for at-risk work practices.

Consequences are considered strong or weak. *Strong consequences* are probable, soon, and significant, and *weak consequences* are improbable, delayed, and insignificant. These distinctions are critical for understanding the occurrence of at-risk versus safe behaviors on the job.

Let's use the ABC model to explain the occurrence of a certain at-risk behavior: grinding without a face shield. Activators that encourage the use of face shields include posted safety signs, prior training, and the presence of a supervisor. Activators that discourage face shield use include time pressure, scratched face shields, and lack of availability of this personal protective equipment (PPE).

Primary consequences encouraging face-shield use include avoiding an eye injury or a supervisory reprimand. These consequences are soon and significant, but they are improbable. On the other hand, consequences that discourage face-shield use include saving time, better vision, convenience, and more comfort. All of these consequences are powerful because they are probable, positive, soon, and significant. As a result, employees often avoid wearing a face shield–not because they're uninformed, but because the natural consequences of not wearing this PPE are stronger than the consequences of wearing it. It's simply a matter of the ABCs. This is especially true when system factors (e.g., excessive production pressure, uncomfortable PPE) support the at-risk behavior.

Smoking cigarettes is another example. The positive consequences of smoking are probable, soon, and significant. However, thousands of smokers die every year from lung cancer associated with smoking. Why do so many people continue smoking in spite of this fatal consequence? This natural consequence is not viewed as soon or even probable. For this reason countless people delay or abandon their efforts to quit smoking every day.

Bottom line: Human beings are often rewarded naturally for taking risky shortcuts. Such behavior is often easier, faster, more comfortable, and more convenient than the safer alternative. The individual without PPE in the illustration is at-risk for an injury, but an injury is improbable and he is clearly having a better time because of soon, certain, significant, and positive consequences.

Critical Behavior Checklist

Area: _____   Immediate follow-up Needed: YES NO

Date: _____   Observer: _____

	Safe	At-Risk	Comments
1. PPE:			
A. Eye/Face			
B. Hearing			
C. Head			
D. Hearing			
E. Breathing			
F. Body			
2. Body Positioning:			
A. Cramped			
B. Ergonomics			
C. Extended			
D. Lifting			
E. Line of fire			
F. PinchPoints			
3. Tools and Equipment:			
A. Use			
B. Condition			

FIGURE 9.2. A portion of a critical behavior checklist (CBC).

Behavioral Observation and Feedback

The primary tool of BBS is behavioral observation and feedback (BOF). Workers create a critical behavior checklist (CBC) of relevant safe versus at-risk behaviors for their job (see Figure 9.2). Then they use this CBC while systematically observing each other on the job and then offering behavioral feedback. Showing a co-worker the completed CBC brings recognition for safe work practices and awareness when risky behaviors are observed. Subsequently, the CBC data are compiled, enabling work teams to identify behavior(s) needing special attention. This could include altering the work environment to make a safe behavior more comfortable or convenient. These days BOF data are often tracked with smartphones and tablets, making it more convenient for recording and reviewing behavioral observations.

It's hoped this formal use of a CBC sets the stage for workers to speak up at any time to acknowledge co-workers for their safety-related behaviors and warn them of at-risk behaviors. Execution of this formal BOF process provides practice for the ultimate vision – an AC4P safety culture in which all employees provide informal supportive and/or corrective feedback (Chapter 4) whenever it's warranted.[3]

Although BOF should be a bottom-up employee-driven process to maximize cultivation of an AC4P safety culture, managers, union leaders, and supervisors play a key role in the success of a BOF process. Employees are more likely to sustain their involvement in BOF when they understand leadership is fully supportive.

Regarding execution, company managers and union leaders should (a) ensure the BOF steering team has the necessary resources (e.g., time, training, money) to be effective; (b) discuss observation process metrics at group meetings; (c) communicate one-on-one with employees about the BOF process; (d) recognize the BOF accomplishments of individuals and teams; (e) collaborate regularly with supervisors to support the BOF process; and (f) give legitimate power to the BOF steering team for managing the process.

In addition, company supervisors should(a) attend BOF training to understand the process; (b) discuss BOF regularly at safety meetings; (c) allow time for peer-to-peer observations, even with high production demands from management; (d) offer to be observed by employees; (e) help use BOF data to remove barriers to safe behavior; (f) keep up-to-date on process information/data and celebrate process successes (see Chapter 4); and (g) praise employees for their BOF participation (see Chapter 3).

Unfortunately, BBS has often been rolled out improperly. Many organizations fail to train and educate their workers properly. They use workbooks instead of interactive education/training, failing to get the participants involved and customizing the examples per their particular work culture. Also, contractors are often not briefed on BOF efforts or included in the process. Furthermore, employees are often held responsible for the number of CBCs completed but not the quality of the BOF report (e.g., the comments). This "quota effect" leads to incomplete observations and "pencil whipping" (i.e., checking behavioral categories without careful observation).[3]

Many employees report filling out a card but not talking to the person after completing the CBC. Providing BBS feedback can be anxiety-provoking (especially in the beginning of a process), but it's critically important. As discussed in Chapter 5, it's best to be nondirective and ask questions (at least at first) rather than give directions. But, in a culture with limited interpersonal trust and belongingness, this post-observation feedback discussion takes substantial moral courage (Chapter 4).

The improvement and encouragement of behavior-focused communication between employees are the primary benefits of BOF. "It's not an *observation* without a *conversation*," we remind participants. Keep in mind that these discussions are informal conversations designed to solve problems and encourage AC4P behavior. It's not about telling people what to do, catching their risky actions, or getting people in trouble. It's also important to note these peer-to-peer conversations need to occur between *all* employees, including contractors and employees outside an observer's work area. The purpose: to cultivate an AC4P brother/sister keeper's culture.

Consider the employee at a soft-drink facility who developed the habit of scraping off excess glue on sharp label-cutting blades by jabbing at the clumps of glue with a rag. This normally worked to remove the glue and kept the line moving. Otherwise, he'd have to spend several minutes shutting down the line and locking out the equipment in order to clean the blade properly and safely.

This method worked for years until one day the rag dragged his hand into the equipment and the blade cut off two of his fingers. This would not have happened if one of his co-workers had spoken up and warned him about his risky behavior. In another example, a construction worker in Mexico walked across a beam 150 feet in the air without putting on a safety harness. None of his co-workers said anything to him. The outcome: He slipped off the beam and fell to his death.

The BOF process of PBS encourages peers to provide corrective feedback to one another respectfully without being critical. Note that the observer in the illustration on the next page starts positive but then gets too critical. What will the worker remember from this feedback? How will he feel? In addition to one-on-one feedback, group behavioral data are displayed in the form of graphs and charts to help reduce risky behavioral trends and support safe ones.[4]

Implementing and sustaining a successful BOF process is not easy. Employees may be initially skeptical that the process is truly anonymous or that management will support their BOF efforts over the long term. Also, it may be difficult to keep the process "evergreen" (i.e., fresh and interesting) once the process is underway. Finally, managers and supervisors may allow production demands (or new initiatives) to supersede BOF efforts.

Despite these challenges, organizations have been using BOF to prevent workplace injuries for decades. The benefits of BOF in numerous settings are well documented.[5] In summary, a proper BOF process helps to cultivate an AC4P safety culture because it:

- Focuses employees' attention on safe and at-risk behaviors
- Gives employees an excuse to provide safety-related feedback to their co-workers

- Increases the amount of praise for safe work practices
- Increases the amount of corrective feedback for at-risk behaviors
- Fosters open communication among employees about safety
- Improves the quality and quantity of safety communication through-out the organization
- Raises safety awareness
- Increases employee involvement for safety
- Provides a mechanism for employees to learn from each other
- Allows safety professionals to track proactive, behavioral data

Improving AC4P Communication with BOF

When done correctly, BOF improves the quality and increases the quantity of informal safety-related feedback, even when a CBC card is not used. Such BOF communication fosters a positive and healthy AC4P culture and reduces the chances employees will get hurt on the job. Specific items on the SPS Safety Culture Survey address employees' beliefs and expectations regarding safety communication.[6] For instance, these three

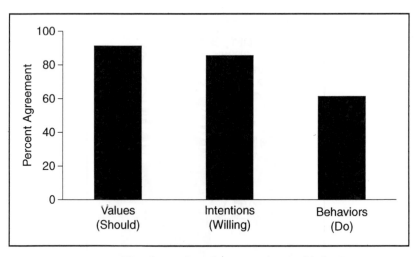

FIGURE 9.3. The observed gap between values and behaviors.

items on the survey focus on the issue of cautioning co-workers when they're working at-risk:

- Employees should caution co-workers when observing them perform at-risk behaviors.
- I am willing to caution co-workers when observing them perform at-risk behaviors.
- I do caution co-workers when observing them perform at-risk behaviors.

The first item assesses participants' values, while the second addresses their intentions. The third item targets employees' behavior. Approximately 90 percent of 300,000 employees surveyed by SPS for many years indicate you "should" give employees feedback when they're performing an at-risk behavior. Nearly 85 percent of these same respondents reported they're "willing" to give corrective feedback when a co-worker is performing an at-risk behavior. But, only about 60 percent of these participants said they actually "do" provide corrective feedback when a co-worker is performing an at-risk behavior (see Figure 9.3).

It's alarming that people are reluctant to warn others of their risky behavior, especially since at-risk behavior contributes to most injuries. In addition, 74 percent of respondents to the SPS survey confirmed they welcome peer observations for the purpose of receiving safety-related feedback. Yet only 28 percent believed *other* employees feel the same. Lesson: We underestimate how much others are willing to receive AC4P feedback about their safety-related behavior.

When addressing this gap between values and behaviors, employees often say they fail to give corrective behavioral feedback because:

- It will create conflict with co-workers.
- It's the job of the supervisor or safety director to give safety-related feedback.
- I've never given peer feedback before and I question my ability to give safety feedback effectively.
- I don't know enough about that job to give quality feedback.
- I don't want to disrespect a more experienced employee.

Through repeated administrations of the SPS culture survey, organizations often find the gap between "employees should caution co-workers" and "I do caution co-workers" diminishes following effective PBS training and implementation. Indeed, with PBS, the BOF process is designed to institutionalize peer-to-peer BBS feedback as a normal, established way of doing business, with or without a CBC card.[3]

PERSON-STATES

When an employee gets hurt on the job, managers are often quick to blame the employee. But they rarely gauge or even understand the person-states that influence the risky behaviors contributing to injuries. A key aspect of the AC4P approach is getting leaders to better understand how to influence employees' person-states so employees become *self-motivated* to improve occupational safety (Chapter 3).

We've asked several groups of employees to tell us which of the following attributes of co-workers is most important in cultivating an AC4P safety culture: experience, intelligence, or attitude. We expected most employees, especially those with more tenure, to tell us "experience." However, people have overwhelmingly said "attitude," regardless of their age, position, location, or industry. This next section addresses employees' attitudes and other person-states that impact workplace safety.

Employee Attitudes

As introduced in Chapter 6, people experience cognitive dissonance when their attitudes/beliefs and behaviors are incongruent. This unpleasant state motivates them to either change their behavior or their attitude so they're consistent.[7] For instance, a manager who considers himself a nice person will feel guilty if he finds himself yelling regularly at employees. This realization will motivate him to either stop yelling or change the way he views himself.

With this principle in mind, employees with a positive safety attitude are more likely to exhibit AC4P behaviors that support safety, such as following safety procedures, reporting safety hazards, participating in safety initiatives, and cautioning co-workers about safety hazards. However, when employees have a bad attitude about safety, they are apt to hide injuries, take shortcuts, resist safety-improvement efforts, and avoid providing safety feedback to others.[8]

Employees can be classified as complainers, spectators, or champions.[9] These attitudinal person-states are not set in stone and can be improved with AC4P leadership. Indeed, effective leaders help people become champions.[10] In our efforts to help organizations improve their safety, we've observed each of the attitude types described below. Have you experienced these types of people?

Complainers. These employees usually voice safety concerns to express displeasure, not to make improvements. Also, they often verbalize these complaints to other employees instead of to safety personnel or supervisors who have the authority to make changes. In general, complainers seek out ways to find fault with the organization and other employees. They also believe(a) other people cause their problems, (b) change is inherently bad, and (c) people don't have much personal control over their own lives, leading to feelings of anger, resentment, doubt, frustration, and fear with regard to occupational safety.

Spectators. These employees rarely discuss safety concerns. They believe their actions will have little effect on the company. As a result, they seldom get involved in safety-related efforts. Spectators typically believe (a) other people will solve important problems, (b) change is unnecessary, (c) most improvement initiatives are no big deal, and (d) people have minimal control over their lives. As a result, spectators often feel uninspired, detached, unemotional, and indifferent regarding AC4P safety efforts.

Champions. These employees normally express safety concerns constructively and work effectively with others to make improvements. They also have a positive outlook on most employees and the organization as a whole. Champions generally believe (a) problems create opportunities for improvement, (b) change is a sign of growth, and (c) people control their own lives. They also deal with negative aspects of the company in a reasonable, mature fashion. This leads to feelings of confidence, happiness, contentment, personal control, and optimism in working to achieve the vision of an AC4P safety culture.

Facilitating Attitude Change

Again, the three person-states defined here are not permanent traits. Effective safety leaders deploy the following AC4P techniques to move their employees (and themselves) from being complainers or spectators to champions:

Own up to past organizational mistakes. And, look to the future to make improvements. All organizations make mistakes and employees often remember them for years. During one training session, the first author found the entire group to be nonresponsive and angry. Group discussions revealed that seven years earlier a new plant manager had fired a number of employees in a single day, and they were given only a few hours to take all of their belongings out of the facility. The new management team had not addressed or apologized for the incident, and hostility lingered within the workforce.

Treat mistakes as learning opportunities. Do not consider them as occasions to punish. It's common to feel one will be severely reprimanded and/or fired after an injury that was due in part to one's at-risk behavior. Beyond the pain and discomfort of getting hurt on the job, employees are often embarrassed and worried about losing their job. To the contrary, elite AC4P organizations use most workplace injuries as teachable moments to understand why the injury occurred and define ways to prevent its occurrence in the future. This may include key system changes such as improving equipment, education/training, and work procedures.

Solicit input from employees. Ask them about safety concerns and respond to these concerns in a timely manner. Responding quickly to employee concerns is critical. When employees' safety issues or suggestions are delayed or ignored, an attitudinal problem is created, contributing to lower morale. The common feeling is, "They don't care." Companies are well served by responding quickly to employee concerns, even if they're unable to fix the problem immediately and/or completely. In these cases, short-term solutions should be used and plans for more permanent fixes should be spelled out clearly to the concerned employee(s). The worst possible news for employees who raise a safety-related concern is no news at all.

Create opportunities for employees to get involved in safety initiatives. Actively engaged employees experience self-motivation (Chapter 3) and go beyond the call of duty for the safety of others. Organizations should help institutionalize employee engagement by (a) supporting safety-improvement teams among hourly employees, (b) soliciting employee input regarding new equipment and procedures, (c) promoting group celebrations for safety achievement (Chapter 3), (d) connecting safety programs with a family perspective (Chapter 2), and (e) involving employees in behavioral and facility audits. Non-engaged employees lack the sense of competence, personal control, and belongingness needed to fuel AC4P behavior.

Improve and increase one-on-one conversations. "Management by walking around" (MBWA) is not enough. It's critical to build relationships through empathic conversations (Chapter 5). When organizational leaders spend time on the floor interacting effectively with employees, they demonstrate AC4P by considering important safety issues and concerns. When employees regularly see managers on the floor, they sense leaders genuinely care about their safety.

Not only does the application of AC4P principles encourage more safety engagement from champions, it puts social pressure on complainers who find themselves in the minority. Such complainers may feel compelled to conform with the majority (i.e., champions) by either minimizing their distracting negative communication with others or improving their own attitudes. (Recall the discussion of consistency and social-proof principles in Chapter 6.)

As discussed in Chapter 2, five key person-states impact people's attitudes and willingness to perform AC4P behavior: self-esteem, self-efficacy, personal control, optimism, and belongingness.[11] Improving these person-states also improves employee engagement. Employees who feel in control of safety issues and initiatives are more likely to participate in an organization's safety efforts.[12] In fact, we found that employees at a Virginia company who were directly involved in developing their own CBCs were six times more likely to use them than co-workers in different areas who were handed a CBC to use.

Consider this real-world example of diminished employee engagement and personal control. An offshore oil rigger was coping poorly with a difficult divorce. His company's work schedule put employees on the rig (i.e., an island in the ocean) for a month at a time and then sent them home for a month. This distressed employee returned to the rig and learned of a new mandate requiring employees to wear hard hats and steel-toed boots *at all times*. This new rule was accompanied by a myriad of signs on the rig telling employees to always wear their boots and hard hats. The embittered employee reacted by showing up on the rig wearing his hard hat and steel-toed boots but *nothing else*. This emotional, volatile, and now completely naked employee strolled around the rig doing his job. Clearly, his sense of engagement and personal control on the job was less than desirable.

As discussed in Chapter 5, empathy reflects our ability to put ourselves in someone else's shoes. Realize people see the same situations from a personal perspective, as depicted in the illustration below. Empathizing with others is critical for healthy interpersonal relationships at home and on the job, and is at the core of an AC4P safety culture. Empathy often occurs nonverbally, as we tune into the voice tones, gestures, mannerisms, and facial expressions of others. People who have strong empathy toward others are more sensitive, outgoing, and popular than people who are less empathic.[13]

Reminders to be more empathic are helpful at all levels of an organization. This can be executed by one-on-one discussions, safety meetings, and sensitivity or diversity education, and especially through testimonials whereby workers share personal experiences (e.g., injuries) that have impacted their lives. Increasing empathy also helps minimize the "us versus them" mindset (e.g., salary versus hourly workers) that can divide a workforce and decrease the occurrence of AC4P behavior.

Self-Monitoring. Self-monitoring is another key person-state affecting the human dynamics of occupational safety. It's defined as one's motivation and ability to interpret social cues from the environment and respond to those cues in a socially desirable way. Low self-monitors act similarly regardless of the occasion; high self-monitors alter their behavior effectively to fit the particular situation.[14] This has also been referred to as the *if–then behavioral signature.*[15]

In research tests, high self-monitors better understand subtle undercurrents in human interactions[16] and perform better on novel tasks.[17] They also become emergent leaders in ambiguous situations,[18] receive higher job performance evaluations,[19] and usually ascend to leadership positions within organizations more rapidly and more frequently than low self-monitors.[20]

To use a boxing analogy, Muhammad Ali famously beat George Foreman in the "Rumble in the Jungle" by eschewing his typical movement, "float like a butterfly, sting like a bee," and employing the "rope a dope." After losing the first round, Ali laid against the ropes for the next seven rounds as Foreman pummeled him. Throughout the entire fight Ali whispered to Foreman, "Is that all you got, George?" Afterward, Foreman admitted he was thinking near the end of the fight, "Yeah, that's about it." After Foreman wore himself out, Ali used a five-punch combination to floor Foreman and earn an eighth-round TKO to help cement his legacy as the greatest heavyweight boxer of all time.

What separated Ali from other greats in the golden age of heavyweights? Among other things, *flexibility.* Unlike Foreman, Frazier, Holmes, and others, Ali was able to fight a number of different ways depending on the situation. He was a high self-monitor.

This same flexibility is key for effective communication. Certain types of education (e.g., sensitivity education) and interpersonal mentoring with open and candid behavior-based feedback can facilitate higher self-monitoring. Individuals who become high self-monitors will manage conflict better, empathize with others' perspectives, and be more successful on the job.[20] They're also more likely to perform AC4P behavior on behalf of their co-workers' safety.

LEADERSHIP

An AC4P safety culture cannot happen without genuine leadership support from management – the third crucial factor we are examining here. When managers and supervisors demonstrate AC4P behavior on behalf of the safety of employees, the safety culture is improved and injuries are less likely to occur. Some examples of such AC4P behavior include spending time interacting with employees, fixing equipment issues immediately, providing effective and interesting training/education, establishing employee-focused safety programs, encouraging near-hit (or close-call) reporting, and using more positive than negative consequences to motivate behavior.

It's critical that company presidents, vice presidents, plant managers, and other top leaders exhibit desired behaviors to support safety. In many cases these leaders support safety but may not fully understand the *behaviors* needed to demonstrate this support. Safety Performance Solutions uses a 360-degree feedback tool to assess leaders' safety-supportive behaviors, along with ratings from their bosses, peers, and hourly employees. These ratings give leaders a better understanding of their strengths and weaknesses along the following dimensions.

Vision for Safety. Do leaders establish broad health, safety, and environment (HSE) expectations for their organization? Do they support proactive safety performance efforts? Do they maintain a focus on safety even when other aspects of the business (e.g., production, quality, reliability, share price) are doing poorly?

Engagement in Safety. Do leaders actively participate in safety activities within the organization(s) they oversee? Do they seek opportunities to speak one-on-one with frontline employees about safety? Do they review relevant results of corporate HSE audits/assessments and take appropriate action?

Rewards and Recognition for Safety. Do leaders include safety as a key component of operation reviews – praising exemplary site/workgroup performance and challenging managers whose performance is poor? Do they seek opportunities to provide positive recognition for specific safety-related behavior by individuals at all levels of the organization? Do they informally recognize sites for their safety efforts and achievements?

Trust in Ability and Intent for Safety. Do leaders' decisions demonstrate concern for safety? Do they confer with relevant experts regarding the safety impact of their decisions? Are they willing to invest the necessary resources to help keep employees injury-free?

Communication for Safety. Do leaders consistently and openly communicate specific proactive HSE goals and objectives? Do their safety-related communications focus on efforts and activities – not just safety outcome statistics? Do they encourage open and honest safety communication throughout the organization?

Teamwork for Safety. Do leaders sponsor or support safety networking across the organization? Do they ensure that unhealthy competition does not develop between sites or teams related to safety performance (e.g., discouraging injury reporting, encouraging risk taking to get a job done)? Do they praise the efforts of others in their absence?

Empowerment for Safety. Do leaders include input from the appropriate organizational levels when making decisions? Do they use an appropriate management style for the situation when working with others to address safety concerns (e.g., delegating, coaching, directing, or supporting, as explained in Chapter 5)? Do they set expectations but allow autonomy and flexibility on goal setting and attainment?

Management Behaviors that Inhibit AC4P Behavior

Managers and supervisors may inadvertently encourage at-risk behavior by failing to praise safety-related behaviors, ignoring at-risk behaviors, overemphasizing production at the expense of safety, and modeling risky behaviors. These behaviors put employees at risk for an injury and hinder the cultivation of an AC4P safety culture.

Failure to Praise Safety-Related Behaviors. Managers and supervisors may fail to praise safety-related behaviors because they don't notice them, don't want to take time to address them, or think it's unwarranted ("That's what they get paid to do"). However, praise increases the likelihood employees will continue to perform these behaviors, even though offering praise takes time or is inconvenient. It also helps workers feel better about the entire organization. (See Chapter 3 for advice on how to give behavior-based recognition.)

Failure to Give Corrective Feedback. Managers and supervisors may fail to give corrective feedback for at-risk behavior because they don't want to interfere with production goals and/or confront employees. They might also consider the particular risk inconsequential, especially when employees frequently take this risk without getting hurt. Unfortunately, failure to give corrective feedback for risky behavior implies acceptance and increases the likelihood employees will continue taking shortcuts. Eventually, someone will get hurt.

Rewarding Production over Safety. Managers and supervisors typically reward production more than safety. After all, production is readily measured as achievement and makes money for the organization. Safety is perceived as controlling losses (i.e., loss control) and avoiding failure; and as discussed in Chapter 1, it's easier to get self-motivated to achieve success than to avoid failure. Most important, overemphasizing a production-focused mindset minimizes the importance of safety and increases the likelihood of safety-related shortcuts and injuries. The best safety leaders stress safe production.

Modeling At-Risk Behavior. Managers and supervisors may model risky behaviors themselves because they're unaware of the risk, they've developed risky habits, or they don't think others will notice or care. But, as shown in the illustration below, workers *do* notice the at-risk behavior of their supervisors. Such behavior sends the message that safety isn't really that important, increasing the probability employees will take similar risks.

In one Brooklyn company, the safety department fought for months to get employees to accept stricter requirements for using PPE such as safety glasses, safety shoes, and hearing protection devices. Unfortunately, their efforts were undermined by a television interview in which the company CEO answered a reporter's questions about company profits from the shop floor during operations and was not wearing any of the required PPE. Many employees saw the interview on the news and decided they no longer needed to use their PPE.

Demonstrating Management Support for Safety

Most managers say they support safety and don't want to see employees get hurt. However, this concern about safety does not necessarily filter down to employees. Managers need to discuss safety consistently at group meetings and in one-on-one conversations with employees. These conversations should include contactors and part-time employees, who are often left out of these important safety discussions. Managers also need to work effectively with union leaders (when applicable) to advance safety efforts.

Several years ago, we were conducting interviews with groups of four to five people as part of a safety-culture assessment. We noted that the plant manager and head of the union responded quite differently to questionnaire items about the site's safety culture. More specifically, the plant manager's responses were much more favorable than those of the union leader. So we asked these leaders to attend the same survey review session.

It was eye-opening for the plant manager to hear about the union leader's concerns and for the union leader to learn about recent management efforts and money spent to improve safety. They left the session more empathic to each other's viewpoints. Ultimately, both parties discussed ways to resolve existing safety concerns as well as to publicize their safety successes.

It has been our experience that managers underestimate how much employees appreciate their presence on the production floor, walking around and talking with employees. As mentioned earlier, this MBWA (management by walking around) provides a great opportunity for managers to interact with employees, listen to their concerns, demonstrate an AC4P mindset, and generally improve the overall safety culture. The value of such relationship-building conversations (Chapter 5) cannot be overestimated. Consider the following guidelines for managers to demonstrate their AC4P support for employee safety:

Safety versus Production. Emphasize safety as much as production and quality, both formally (e.g., at meetings) and informally. Production and moneymaking are obviously critical for an organization's survival. However, being productive and being safe are *not* mutually exclusive. In fact, safety (e.g., proper proactive planning, hazard removal, good housekeeping) benefits production. Plus, safe companies don't have to endure the financial cost of employee injuries, increased insurance premiums, rehiring replacement employees, and losing business with clients who select vendors on the basis of their injury record.

Organizational Decision Making. Leaders with an AC4P mindset always consider safety when making organizational decisions, from those related to the purchase of new equipment to those concerning a change in work schedules and procedures. Overly aggressive schedules (especially with excessive overtime) lead to fatigued employees. This increases the probability of at-risk safety shortcuts, unsafe behaviors, and injuries.

Also, engineering departments may introduce new equipment without consulting with safety professionals and employees who'll be using the equipment. This may lead to hidden safety hazards and other problems (e.g., egress and body positioning around the equipment). Plus, complicated procedures may be enacted without input from relevant employees who can recommend simpler and safer operation methods.

Exhibiting Safety Success. Most organizations miss crucial opportunities to show off their safety excellence and create an organizational identity that could motivate safety-related behavior through the social-influence principle of consistency (Chapter 6). Leaders often spend substantial time, energy, and money to improve organizational safety, but they might not keep employees informed of all these efforts. An employee may perseverate on his/her own safety concerns without realizing the many safety improvements the company has already made. Appreciating these safety efforts improves perceptions of management and their AC4P actions, while also putting responsibility on employees to behave consistently with management's value for their personal safety.

Accountability. Hold supervisors accountable for balancing safety and production demands. This is challenging because supervisors often feel pressure from management to meet aggressive production schedules. Management may support safety, but messages to supervisors that stress production over safety will filter down to employees and negatively affect their behavior.

Improving Organizational Culture

Organizational culture represents the collective feelings, thoughts, behaviors, attitudes, and values of its employees. The manner in which organizational powerholders execute their leadership skills impacts directly the culture of the organization.[21] Unfortunately, culture-improvement efforts are often resisted because change is seen as a loss of stability, clarity, and predictability and may take years to accomplish.

The first step in organizational culture change is to acknowledge that change is a constant. Because change is inevitable, leaders should create a vision that the organization will be further strengthened as a result of cooperative change efforts.[22] Also, everyone from management to wage workers needs to realize culture change does not happen overnight, contrary to the message in the illustration.

Of course, bombarding people with change initiatives reflects the flip side of this quick-fix perspective. This occurs when organizational leaders implement too many new programs at the same time (i.e., flavors of the month), especially when the new "programs" aren't integrated but are presented independently (i.e., the silo approach). This results in employees tuning out new initiatives because they presume they won't really work that well and will be soon forgotten.

Culture change is especially important in terms of safety. Traditional safety approaches have been top-down and compliance-driven. More positive, employee-driven philosophies are used by leading organizations to manage safety.[23] Figure 9.4 highlights the progression from outdated top-down *dependent* cultures to more progressive AC4P collaborative *interdependent* cultures. In these more empowered and interdependent organizations, hourly employees are more likely to appreciate safety training, participate in safety-related efforts, discuss safety concerns, and fix safety hazards themselves when possible.[24] Also, improving the safety culture

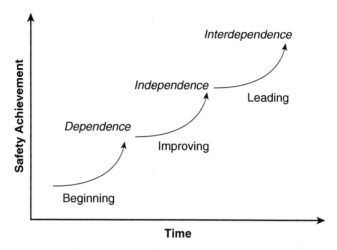

FIGURE 9.4. The progression from dependence to interdependence.

positively impacts *all* aspects of organizational performance, including production and quality.[25]

Tracking Safety-Culture Change

Injury numbers are often the sole indicator of safety-improvement efforts. This is unfortunate because injury statistics can be misleading in a number of ways. Companies may exhibit poor safety practices but have the temporary good fortune of employees not getting hurt. This is especially common for smaller companies. Conversely, companies may be taking numerous proactive, positive steps to ensure safety and still find that employees occasionally get injured. This is particularly common at larger companies.

Plus, injuries are typically infrequent and offer no useful information regarding the success of ongoing safety-improvement endeavors. A focus on injury rate as a safety index can also lead to employees and/or organizations under-reporting injuries. For example, some companies have been known to put injured employees on light duty so the company can avoid reporting a lost-time injury.

Still, some changes in a safety culture are relatively easy to evaluate. Employees' beliefs and attitudes about safety (which influence behavior) can be assessed with safety-culture assessment tools. Safety professionals use these perception surveys to demonstrate progress toward achieving an AC4P safety culture, in the context of injury data that are inconclusive and usually uninformative regarding proactive injury prevention.

Also, company leaders can better understand the organization's safety culture by engaging in quality conversations with employees, both formally (through structured interviews) and informally (through one-on-one conversations). Safety culture surveys should supplement these conversations.

Validated safety-culture surveys accurately assess employees' perceptions of management support for safety, peer support for safety, personal responsibility for safety, and awareness of the various safety-management systems. Employees from all organizational levels (e.g., supervisors, contractors), work areas (e.g., warehouse, lab), and job types (e.g., maintenance, operations) should complete these surveys.

These surveys can be developed in-house or purchased from outside consulting firms. With validated surveys, normative responses from similar industries should be provided for benchmarking purposes. Also, results from the survey should be made available to *all* employees in the organization.

The comprehensive safety-culture assessment provided by Safety Performance Solutions[6] includes a safety-culture survey, structured interviews, 360-degree feedback for leaders (i.e., self-assessment, peer assessment, and employees' assessment of safety performance), and a comprehensive analysis of the organization's safety-management systems. Organizational leaders are well served by using such safety-culture assessments to gauge their current safety culture, recognize specific domains needing improvement, and assess what it will take to achieve an AC4P safety culture.

SYSTEMS/CONDITIONS

The fourth important aspect of working to achieve the vision of an AC4P safety culture is providing effective safety-management systems and a safe work environment. Employees are more likely to be injured if the organization has management-system failures such as inadequate manpower, unreasonable production pressure, excessive overtime, faulty equipment, insufficient safety training, unclear safety policies, nonexistent safety meetings, poor safety-related communication, and blame-oriented discipline procedures.[8] Managers improve their safety culture by optimizing these key safety-management systems: close-call reporting, injury reporting, injury analysis, rules and policies, safety education/training, hazard recognition, facility audits, communication, engagement, and an AC4P BOF process.

Close-Call Reporting

Organizations should have a formal process for employees to report close calls (i.e., an unplanned event that did not result in injury but had the potential to do so). For example, an employee at a local soft-drink bottling company reported that a large stack of empty pallets nearly fell on him as he walked through the warehouse. The safety director assessed the situation and determined that all empty pallets needed to be stored in a covered outdoor area with limits set on how high pallets could be stacked. By filling out a close-call form, this employee helped ensure he and other employees won't be injured by falling pallets in the future.

It's extremely important that close-call reporting be nonpunitive. If employees believe reporting a close call will have a negative consequence, they won't do it. In fact, it's a good idea for managers and supervisors to reward employees and work groups (through praise or other small tokens of appreciation) for filling out a quality close-call form.

Seminal work by Herbert William Heinrich suggests an inverse relationship between the severity and the frequency of injuries.[26] As depicted in Figure 9.5, Heinrich's law, developed almost a century ago, holds true today. Fatalities are very rare. While somewhat rare, serious injuries are more common. Minor injuries happen more often than serious ones, and close calls occur more frequently than minor injuries. Finally, at-risk behaviors are more common than close calls, injuries, and fatalities. Heinrich

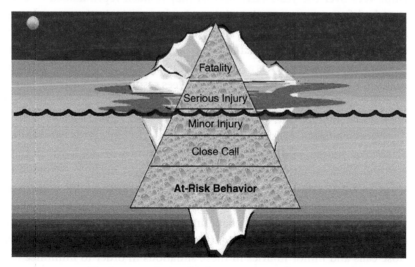

FIGURE 9.5. The inverse relationship between injury frequency and severity.

demonstrated that decreasing at-risk behaviors and close calls reduces injuries and fatalities. Unfortunately, only 42 percent of 300,000 employees who took the SPS Safety Culture Survey believed close calls are consistently reported and analyzed at their work site.

Reporting Minor Injuries

Employees should report all minor injuries. Referring back to Heinrich's law, correcting factors that contribute to minor injuries decreases the chance of an employee having a more serious injury in the future. Reports of minor injuries allow the organization to take steps to minimize the chance of that kind of injury happening again, and that kind of injury could be more serious next time.

For instance, an employee in a packaging department cut her hand when she reached into a trash can to retrieve a piece of paper she had thrown away. She cut her hand on a discarded retractable blade (from a box cutter) someone had tossed in the trashcan. Employees routinely discarded these blades (which would sometimes snap off) in nearby trashcans. After she reported her minor injury, the company set up durable lockboxes to collect the discarded blades. If it had not done so, another employee might have experienced the same injury or a more serious laceration/amputation.

As with close calls, employees should be encouraged to report minor injuries without fear of negative consequences. Unfortunately, numerous employees over the years have told us they've been reprimanded or even punished for reporting a minor injury. In these organizations, employees soon learn to hide their minor injuries in order to avoid punitive consequences. This is referred to as the *bloody pocket syndrome*. Having to complete excessive paperwork is an additional negative consequence of a minor injury. Only 57 percent of 300,000 employees responding to the SPS Safety Culture Survey agreed with the statement, "If I received a minor injury on the job I would report it."

Reporting close calls and minor injuries decreases the probability of *serious injuries and fatalities* (SIFs), especially with high-risk behaviors and tasks. From our experience, SIFs are most likely to occur when the prescribed safe behaviors are not performed in the following situations: (a) work requiring a lock-out of the power, (b) working at heights requiring a safety harness, (c) handling chemicals, (d) operating mobile equipment, and (e) entering a confined-space area. It's critical to report close calls and minor injuries in these situations in order to minimize the occurrence of SIFs.

Injury Analysis and Discipline

When an employee is injured on the job, a company will typically conduct an injury analysis to determine what happened and why. This process should be done to correct system factors and environmental hazards contributing to the particular injury. Unfortunately, employees often view this process as blame-oriented, especially when it's done inconsistently and called an *accident investigation* (see Chapter 5). In fact, one of the surest ways to damage employees' safety-related performance, empathy, and attitudes is to use negative consequences inconsistently.[27] It's noteworthy that approximately two-thirds of 300,000 employees from the SPS survey reported their company's discipline (or corrective-action) process was used inconsistently.

With an injury analysis and corrective-action process, it's imperative managers (a) establish a consistent use of negative consequences, (b) effectively explain this corrective-action process to all employees, (c) assess system factors contributing to injuries, (d) use punitive consequences consistently but sparingly, and (e) correct identified system problems as soon as possible.

Behavior should be viewed as an outcome of the system rather than the cause of an injury. In our experience, far too many companies define the "root cause" of an injury (actually there are many) as operator error and propose retraining as the corrective action. Too many of these "investigations" ignore the variety of system factors contributing to the injury.

Two system factors contribute to numerous injuries: unreasonable production pressure and excessive overtime. More than half of all those who completed the SPS survey indicated that production pressures sometimes trump safety concerns for both managers and supervisors. When leaders apply unreasonable production pressure, employees are motivated to take risky shortcuts to save time and please their supervisor.

Excessive overtime, often the result of insufficient manpower, is another major contributor to at-risk behavior and workplace injuries. We once talked with a utility technician who said he'd worked forty-one straight days during an outage because he had to finish the job. He told us he was "absolutely fried" and no longer had the mental capacity to "work completely safe." Excessive overtime and production pressure are hidden precursors to many workplace injuries worldwide.

Figure 9.6 provides a heuristic for assessing an injury (following an at-risk behavior) and determining whether a punitive consequence (unfortunately termed "discipline" in most organizations) is warranted. The first question to ask is whether the employee knew s/he was performing an

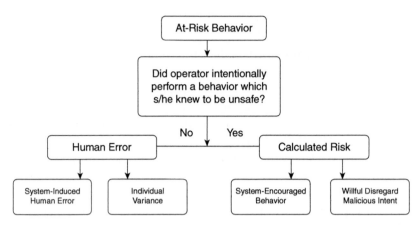

FIGURE 9.6. Flow chart of issues to consider after a critical at-risk behavior has been identified.

at-risk behavior. If the answer is no, this constitutes human error that was either system-induced (e.g., faulty equipment) or an individual variance (e.g., a brain cramp). In these cases, negative consequence should not be used as a corrective technique.

If the answer is yes, the individual took a calculated risk. This is either system-encouraged (e.g., the supervisor ignored the occurrence of an at-risk behavior) or is willful negligence or sabotage (e.g., an employee failed to lock out power despite numerous reminders and warning). Negative consequences are warranted only for this latter situation.

Unfortunately, organizational leaders often underestimate system factors that contribute to injuries. For example, a national pizza chain once had a policy whereby customers would receive their pizza within thirty minutes or it would be free. Whenever the delivery was late, the cost of the "free" pizza was deducted from the driver's paycheck. In many cases, delivery drivers who had to deliver numerous pizzas at a given time received speeding tickets or were involved in a traffic crash. This is an example of system-encouraged risky behaviors. In this case, a company-induced penalty for risky driving would not be warranted.

A punitive consequence is justified only in those rare cases when an employee intentionally violates a cardinal rule (e.g., not using a safety harness at 50 feet) or *continues* to defy a safety rule while other employees follow the rule. In these cases, not only is a negative consequence warranted, it's necessary. Employees get frustrated when the company fails to penalize a co-worker who breaks a cardinal rule that everyone else follows. In fact,

71 percent of 300,000 employees surveyed believed a punitive consequence is warranted for serious safety violations, and only 34 percent of these individuals believed penalties are used enough in these situations.

Safety Rules

Safety rules and procedures keep employees from getting hurt or killed on the job. They should be consistently enforced to avoid perceptions of favoritism or incompetence. In creating safety rules and standard operating procedures, safety professionals are well served by consulting with engineers, managers, supervisors, and hourly employees to ensure the safety rules are clear, practical, and written in user-friendly language. Too often safety protocols are overly complicated and confusing. Safety rules must also align with regulations established by the Occupational Safety and Health Administration (OSHA) in 1871 to protect workers. Leading organizations often set standards that go well beyond these OSHA compliance minimums.

As an example, managers and supervisors at one Pennsylvania steel mill were concerned about compliance problems with lock-out/tag-out (LOTO) procedures. Rather than immediately threatening those employees who did not comply, managers spoke with the hourly employees running the equipment. They found out the LOTO procedures were overly complicated and the standard operating procedures (SOPs) for LOTO were written for engineers, not hourly employees. To solve this problem, they brought in engineers, safety professionals, supervisors, and hourly employees to collectively – and interdependently – streamline the LOTO process and revise the SOPs with user-friendly language. Overnight, the LOTO issue became a non-issue.

Conversely, leaders at an automanufacturing facility overreacted to an employee's eye injury by mandating safety glasses be worn in all areas of the plant (even where glasses weren't needed). This is referred to as the *shotgun approach*. Although most employees begrudgingly wore their safety glasses, several employees got creative by popping out the lenses and simply wearing the frames over their noses in areas where safety glasses weren't really needed. As explained in Chapter 6, such behavior reflects psychological reactance.[28]

Safety Education and Training

Effective safety education/training engages employees in safety endeavors and improves workplace safety. Unfortunately, employees often complain that safety education/training is boring and repetitive. Effective managers improve safety education/training by (a) providing hands-on experience with behavior-based feedback (e.g., using actual fire extinguishers during fire safety training), (b) bringing in dynamic guest speakers, (c) hiring training consultants for special programs, and (d) ensuring new employees receive all necessary education/training before working, and more experienced employees get periodic refresher education/training.

In addition, "online training" and webinars are increasingly cost-effective and convenient ways to provide education. The astute reader will note that the term *online training* is an oxymoron – an impossibility. Only education can occur online. Training requires hands-on role-playing with corrective and supportive behavioral feedback (Chapter 3). In our experience, many employees complain their "online training" was either ineffective or improperly used (e.g., people skipped to the end, passed along cheat sheets to co-workers so they could complete the process more quickly). Finally, education/training sessions led by hourly employees are effective because fellow employees can readily relate to (and trust) the speaker.

Facility Audits

Facility audits should be conducted regularly by employees (including wage workers, safety personnel, managers, and supervisors) to identify safety-related hazards. This is particularly important because employees often become complacent about the hazards around them. Most employees we've talked to who had been seriously injured on the job told us they got hurt doing routine tasks in the same manner they had always done them. By their own admission, they got complacent or mindless (i.e., worked habitually without relevant self-talk).

Workers usually believe serious injuries won't happen to them. We often ask employees, "If you had to bet your mortgage on it, how many of you would venture to say that someone at the facility will have a serious injury in the next five years?" Almost everyone raises a hand. Next, we ask, "If you had to bet your mortgage on it, how many of you would venture to say that *you* will have a serious injury in the next five years?" No one raises a hand (unless they weren't paying attention). But now ask workers, "Where do you think the next injury will occur?" You'll get some specific answers, and you might be surprised by the consistency among these answers. This can be very valuable information. You might learn about certain work areas that require more regular auditing.

Hazard Recognition Traps

Various cognitive biases beyond complacency impair people's thinking or self-talk. These include the fundamental attribution error, confirmation bias, conservation bias, risk homeostasis and the anchoring effect.[29] Regarding the *fundamental attribution error*, people blame environmental factors (e.g., production pressure) for their own failures but attribute similar failures in others to person-states (e.g., laziness). This attribution error is depicted in the illustration below by the golfer blaming his poor performance on external or situational factors, while the caddie identifies a personal ability or dispositional factor. As a result of this common error, employees are apt to blame the situation for their injuries and overlook their own person-states. As determinants of an injury to another person, this attribution error results in overemphasis of person-states or dispositional factors.

Also, employees may get hurt because they're resistant to change. They may believe new safety rules, procedures, and equipment are unnecessary. These beliefs are reinforced by the *anchoring effect* (i.e., overreliance on past information) in which employees believe what they were taught decades ago doesn't need updating. Also, the *confirmation bias* (i.e., new information is automatically aligned with preconceived beliefs) and the *conservation bias* (i.e., being unmoved by new evidence) can cause employees to resist new safety efforts.

In an extreme example, an older employee told us he would never wear a safety belt because he was afraid he might get run off the road, flip over into the ocean, and drown. He lived in Kansas with no water within a hundred miles and was unmoved (conservation bias) when we told him tens of thousands of drivers are killed each year and more than half of them could have survived if they had buckled up.[30] He went on to tell us a woman died in San Diego ten years ago because she was run off the road and drowned (confirmation bias).

Employees may increase their risky behaviors when situational factors make them feel safe. For instance, employees wearing a back brace may overestimate the protection it provides and lift objects that are too heavy for them. Or people may drive too fast in snow and ice because they believe their four-wheel-drive vehicle will automatically protect them and prevent them from sliding off the road. This error is termed *risk homeostasis* or risk compensation, as depicted in the illustration on the next page.[31]

People also tend to underestimate everyday hazards because they aren't as memorable as dramatic ones. A simple example: an individual's fear of flying. Many people are more nervous flying in a plane than driving to and from the airport, despite the fact more than 45,000 people were killed while driving in the United States in 2007 compared with 2 on U.S. airlines during the same time period.[32] In fact, the odds of dying in a plane crash on a major U.S. airline are 1 in 13.6 million.[33]

Fix Environmental Concerns Immediately

Safety audits help raise employees' awareness of safety hazards in their environment. They also help leaders identify and correct safety hazards that can injure or kill people. Fixing identified hazards in a timely fashion improves morale as well as the safety of the work environment. It's important to let employees know when safety hazards will be addressed if they can't be fixed right away. Also, alternative fixes should be provided when employee concerns can't be addressed. For instance, one employee suggested building a dome over the site to deal with excessive heat. Instead, the safety director

brought in big fans and water containers and instituted two-minute breaks every hour to combat heat exhaustion.

Sometimes a simple environmental fix can have a dramatic impact on employees' attitudes. In one Pennsylvania company, the safety director bought brighter lightbulbs, and more of them, when an employee in one area repeatedly complained about the lack of lighting. Making this simple change immediately improved the employee's attitude and the work environment. As mentioned earlier, the worst possible response to employees' concerns about safety-related hazards is a non-response, which is interpreted as, "The company doesn't care about us."

Communication

Management should effectively convey information about safety improvement efforts to all employees. This includes sharing information about recent injuries and close calls. Because managers are held accountable for injury statistics, they sometimes inadvertently overemphasize injury numbers at the expense of demonstrating genuine empathy for employees' safety. In fact, most of the 300,000 employees who completed the SPS survey indicated a belief that managers care more about the injury numbers than employees' actual safety.

In one very powerful safety presentation, a manager showed a slide of a young man with his wife and two kids. The manager gave details about the man, including job position, education, hobbies, and so on. He then told the audience the young man had been killed the week before in an explosion. No graphs or statistics were needed to emphasize the importance of safety at this meeting. Managers are well served by remembering that testimonials and genuine discussions about actively caring for employees' safety are more influential than safety-related statistics. Emotions, not statistics, make people more empathic, caring, and motivated.

Mentoring

Effective mentoring of inexperienced employees by highly experienced employees is important for increasing employee engagement in safety and supporting the vision of an AC4P safety culture. This is especially true when a large number of employees with special skill sets are retiring. Indeed, many companies don't backfill these positions, thereby requiring the remaining employees to do more work with fewer people and less craft knowledge.

To formalize mentoring, an energy company in Tennessee implemented a "buddy for a week" system. Experienced employees (with high job knowledge and positive attitudes about safety) spent one week with newer employees working together, eating together, and socializing. This process improved rapport between newer and older employees and provided an AC4P method for experienced employees to pass on specific craft knowledge in a direct, hands-on way.

Extrinsic Rewards

Managers sometimes misuse outcome-based rewards to demonstrate their support for safety. This may lead to decreased morale and less-than-desired employee involvement for safety. With typical outcome-based safety rewards, employees who go a certain amount of time without a recordable injury are rewarded monetarily. An unintended effect of this approach is that employees hide injuries and may pressure others to do the same in order to get the reward. (See Chapter 1 on critical distinctions between behavior-based and outcome-based rewards.) Two examples demonstrate the problem with traditional outcome-based safety rewards.

In one Canadian company, a woman slipped on the ice outside of her building in front of a group of co-workers and was injured. Despite her embarrassment and injury, some of her co-workers were angry with her for "screwing up" their reward (a $75 gift card), which they normally received each month if no one got hurt.

In another organization, management brought in a huge television and placed it in the middle of the plant. Next to it they placed a raffle wheel with the names of all employees typed on index cards. During the next twelve months, management removed the names of employees from the raffle wheel who received an injury that required serious medical attention. At the end of the year, one index card was randomly pulled from the raffle wheel and a lucky employee received the television. Until the actual drawing, the employees loved the idea.

So what happened? First, employees quit reporting any injuries they could hide (i.e., the bloody pocket syndrome). Second, employees who had a serious injury they couldn't hide were angry because they were no longer eligible to win the television. In one case, a man was seriously injured when a co-worker accidentally burned him while welding. Management removed the victim's name from the raffle wheel in order to maintain consistency with their original agreement.

After twelve months, a manager pulled the winning index card at a big safety celebration that included everyone at the facility as well as corporate executives. Ironically, the worker who burned his co-worker ended up winning the television. His co-workers were upset and management was embarrassed. This is a classic example of good intentions for safety gone awry. This kind of experience decreases the subsequent involvement of workers in safety-improvement efforts. The illustration on the next page depicts humorously this problem with outcome-based safety incentive/reward programs.

Safety incentive/reward programs should be behavior-based and process-oriented, and luck or chance should not be a factor. Everyone who performs the desired behavior or reaches the process goal should receive the prize. And the rewards should be presented as small tokens of appreciation, not as a payoff. Monetary rewards are ill-advised. Rather, items with a safety theme should be used, such as smoke detectors, fire extinguishers,

and first-aid kits. If articles of clothing are used as safety rewards (e.g., hats, shirts, or jackets) they should display a safety logo or message (e.g., "Actively Caring for People").

When a reward includes a safety logo or message, it becomes an activator for the relevant safety-related behavior displayed. Also, if the safety message or logo was designed by representatives from the target population, the reward takes on special meaning. Special items like those shown in the illustration on the next page cannot be purchased anywhere, and from the perspective of self-motivation (Chapter 3), they are more valuable than money.

Most important, sincere and behavior-focused praise should be the default reward managers give employees on a regular basis to improve their involvement in injury-prevention ventures. "Employee of the Month," is wrong, rather "Employee of the Moment" is the appropriate mindset. People need words of approval on the spot to enhance their perception of competence and self-motivation (Chapter 3).

IN CONCLUSION

This chapter on real-world applications of ABS reviewed what leading-edge organizations are doing to deliver on their vision for an AC4P safety culture. The progression from traditional behavior-based safety (BBS) programs to

more advanced people-based safety (PBS) efforts was explained. Safety is managed more effectively with PBS than BBS because PBS addresses four key components of an AC4P safety culture: behavior, person-states, leadership, and systems/conditions. This chapter reviewed connections between AC4P principles and each of these components as we have experienced in our own safety training and consulting. Progressive organizations are continuously working to improve each of these domains, en route to creating and sustaining an AC4P injury-free work culture.

DISCUSSION QUESTIONS

1. Use the ABC (activator-behavior-consequence) model to explain why unsafe or risky behavior is usually more common than safe behavior.
2. Illustrate an application of the primary tools of behavior-based safety (BBS), i.e., behavioral observation and feedback (BOF) with a critical behavior checklist (CBC).

3. How does SPS (Safety Performance Solutions, Inc.) distinguish between values, intentions, and behaviors with an employee survey?

4. Distinguish between high and low self-monitors with a personal or realistic example. Which type do you trust more? Why?

5. Explain the progression of a culture from dependent to independent and interdependent as it relates to occupational safety.

6. Why is it critical to promote employees' reporting of close calls and minor injuries? What should they report about a close call?

7. When is it appropriate to administer a negative consequence (unfortunately referred to as "discipline") following a workplace injury?

8. How does the fundamental attribution error bias "investigations" of occupational injuries?

9. How might *risk homeostasis* contribute to at-risk behavior and an injury?

10. Discuss the Do's and Don'ts of using incentives/rewards to reduce the frequency of workplace injuries.

REFERENCES

1. Geller, E. S. (2003). People-based safety: The psychology of actively caring. *Professional Safety*, 48(12), 33–43; Geller, E. S. (2006). People-based safety: An evolution of behavior-based safety for greater effectiveness. *Proceedings of the 2006Professional Development Conference for the American Society of Safety Engineers*; Geller, E. S. (2011). Psychological science and safety: Large-scale success at preventing occupational injuries and fatalities. *Current Directions in Psychological Science*, 20(2), 109–114; Geller, E. S. (2005). *People-based safety: The source*. Virginia Beach: Coastal Training and Technologies; Geller, E. S. (2008). *Leading people-based safety: Enriching your culture*. Virginia Beach: Coastal Training and Technologies; Geller, E. S., & Johnson, D. (2008). *People-based patient safety: Enriching your culture to prevent medical error* (2nd ed.). Virginia Beach, VA: Coastal Training and Technologies.

2. Geller, E. S. (1996). *Working safe: How to help people actively care for health and safety*. Radnor, PA: Chilton; Geller, E. S. (1996). *The psychology of safety: How to improve behaviors and attitudes on the job*. Boca Raton, FL: CRC Press; Geller, E. S. (Ed.). (2014).*Actively caring for people: Cultivating a culture of compassion* (4th ed.). Newport, VA: Make-A-Difference, LLC.

3. Geller, E. S., & Veazie, B. (2014). Behavior-based safety versus actively caring: From other-directed compliance to self-directed commitment. *Professional Safety*, 59(10), 44–50; Veazie, B. (2014). Commitment-based safety. In E. S. Geller (Ed.). *Actively caring for people: Cultivating a culture of compassion* (4th ed.) (pp. 227–233). Newport, VA: Make-A-Difference, LLC.

4. Geller, E. S., & Williams, J. H. (2001). *Keys to behavior-based safety from Safety Performance Solutions*. Rockville, MD: Government Institutes; Krause, T. R., Hidley, J. H., & Hodson, S. J. (1996). *The behavior-based safety process: Managing*

involvement for an injury-free culture (2nd ed.). New York: Van Nostrand Reinhold; McSween, T. E. (1995). *The value-based safety process: Improving your safety culture with a behavioral approach.* New York: Van Nostrand Reinhold.

5. Cooper, M. D. (2003). Behavior based safety: Still a viable strategy. *Safety & Health*, 4, 46–48; Daniels, A. C. (1989) *Performance management.* Tucker, GA: Performance Management Publications; Fellner, D. J., & Sulzer-Azaroff, B. (1984). Increasing industrial safety practices and conditions through posted feedback. *Journal of Safety Research*, 15, 7–21; Geller, E. S., & Williams, J. H. (2001).*Keys to behavior-based safety from Safety Performance Solutions.* Rockville, MD: Government Institutes; Geller, E. S. (1998). *Understanding behavior-based safety: Step-by-step methods to improve your workplace* (2nd ed.). Neenah, WI: J. J. Keller & Associates; Geller, E. S. (1999).Behavior-based safety: Confusion, controversy, and clarification. *Occupational Health and Safety*, 68, 1, 40–49; Krause, T. R., Hidley, J. H., & Hodson, S. J. (1996). *The behavior-based safety process: Managing involvement for an injury-free culture* (2nd ed.). New York: Van Nostrand Reinhold; McSween, T. E. (1995). *The value-based safety process: Improving your safety culture with a behavioral approach.* New York: Van Nostrand Reinhold; Sulzer-Azaroff, B., & de Santamaria, M. C. (1980). Industrial safety hazard reduction through performance feedback. *Journal of Applied Behavior Analysis*, 13, 287–297; Williams, J. H., & Geller, E. S. (2000). Behavior-based interventions for occupational safety: Critical impact of social comparison feedback. *Journal of Safety Research*, 31, 135–142; Zohar, D., Cohen, A., & Azar, N. (1980) Promoting increased use of ear protectors in noise through information feedback. *Human Factors*, 22(1), 69–79.

6. Safety Performance Solutions (SPS) is a leading BBS/PBS training and consulting firm that for two decades has assessed the safety culture of organizations with the SPS Safety Culture Survey (www.safetyperformance.com).

7. Festinger, L. (1957). *A theory of cognitive dissonance.* Evanston, IL: Row, Peterson.

8. Geller, E. S., & Williams, J. H. (2001). *Keys to behavior-based safety from Safety Performance Solutions.* Rockville, MD: Government Institutes; Williams, J. H. (2010). *Keeping people safe: The human dynamics of injury prevention.* Lanham, MD: Government Institutes/Scarecrow Press.

9. Yanna, M. M. (1996) *Attitude: The choice is yours.* Des Moines, IA: American Media.

10. Williams, J. H. (2002). Personality styles which influence organizational safety. *Proceedings on compact disk for the American Society of Safety Engineers Conference*, Nashville, TN; Williams, J. H. (2003) People-based safety: Ten key factors to improve employees' attitudes. *Professional Safety*, 2, 32–36.

11. Geller, E. S. (2005) *People-based safety: The source.* Virginia Beach, VA: Coastal Training Technologies; Geller, E. S. (2008). *Leading people-based safety: Enriching your culture.* Virginia Beach, VA: Coastal Training Technologies; Geller, E. S. (Ed.). (2014). *Actively caring for people: Cultivating a culture of compassion* (4th ed.). Newport, VA: Make-A-Difference, LLC; Geller, E. S., & Veazie, B. (2014). Behavior-based safety versus actively caring: From other-directed compliance to self-directed commitment. *Professional Safety*, 59(10), 44–50.

12. Geller, E. S. (2002). *The participation factor: How to increase involvement in occupational safety.* Des Plaines, IL: American Association of Safety Engineers.

13. Goleman, D. (1995). *Emotional intelligence.* London: Bantam Books.
14. Snyder, M. (1974). Self-monitoring of expressive behavior. *Journal of Personality and Social Psychology,* 30, 526–537.
15. Geller, E. S. (2008). How to remain cool when facing risks: Forget OSHA regulation, we're talking self-regulation. *Industrial Safety and Hygiene News,* 42, 12, 20–21.
16. Mill, J. (1984). High and low self-monitoring individuals: Their decoding skills and empathic expression. *Journal of Personality,* 52, 372–388.
17. Haverkamp, B. E. (1999). Using assessment in counseling supervision: Individual differences in self-monitoring. *Measurement and Evaluation in Counseling and Development,* 27, 316–324.
18. Cronshaw, S. F., & Ellis, R. J. (1991). A process investigation of self-monitoring and leader emergence. *Small Group Research,* 22, 403–420; Kent, R. L., & Moss, S. E. (1990). Self-monitoring as a predictor of leader emergence. *Psychological Reports,* 66, 875–881.
19. Zaccaro, S. J., Foti, R. J., & Kenny, D. A. (1991). Self-monitoring and trait-based variance in leadership: An investigation of leader flexibility across multiple group situations. *Journal of Applied Psychology,* 76, 308–315.
20. Snyder, M. (1986). *Public appearances/private reality.* New York: W. H. Freeman.
21. Yukl, G. A. (1997). *Leadership in organizations.* Englewood Cliffs, NJ: Prentice Hall.
22. Lawson, R. B., & Shen. Z. (1998). *Organizational psychology.* New York: Oxford University Press.
23. Saal, F. E., & Knight, P. A. (1995). *Industrial/organizational psychology* (2nd ed.). Pacific Grove, CA: Brooks/Cole.
24. Geller, E. S., & Williams, J. H. (2001). *Keys to behavior-based safety from Safety Performance Solutions.* Rockville, MD: Government Institutes.
25. Krause, T. R. (2005). *Leading with safety.* Hoboken, NJ: John Wiley.
26. Heinrich, H. W. (1931). *Industrial accident prevention: A scientific approach.* New York: McGraw-Hill.
27. Daniels, A. C. (1989). *Performance management.* Tucker, GA: Performance Management Publications. Geller, E. S. (2008). *Leading people-based safety: Enriching your culture.* Virginia Beach, VA: Coastal Training and Technologies.
28. Brehm, J. W. (1966). *A theory of psychological reactance.* New York: Academic Press; Brehm, J. W. (1972). *Response to loss of freedom: A theory of psychological reactance.* New York: General Learning Press.
29. Baron, J. (2000). *Thinking and deciding* (3rd ed.). New York: Cambridge University Press.
30. Geller, E. S. (1996). *Working safe: How to help people actively care for health and safety.* Radnor, PA: Chilton.
31. Wilde, G. J. S. (1994). *Target risk.* Toronto: PDE.
32. National Highway Traffic Safety Administration (NHTSA). Traffic safety facts. www.nhtsa.dot.gov (retrieved March 17, 2009).
33. Kebabjian, R. (2009) *Accident statistics.* www.planecrashinfo.com/cause (2009).

10

Cultivating an AC4P Culture
in Organizations

FLORENCE D. DIGENNARO REED, AMY J. HENLEY,
SARAH R. JENKINS, JESSICA L. DOUCETTE,
AND JASON M. HIRST

> Culture does not change because we desire to change it. Culture changes when the organization is transformed; the culture reflects the realities of people working together every day.
> – Frances Hesselbein

Have you ever had a job you loved and felt empowered to fulfill your responsibilities? If so, what was it about your co-workers, your manager/supervisor, and your work environment that made your experience so positive? Perhaps you've never felt that way about a job and, instead, you've dreaded heading to work every morning. Your boss might have rarely recognized your efforts. It's possible you weren't sure how to perform your job, but felt uncomfortable asking for help. Your co-workers might have seemed like characters from the movie *Mean Girls*. In this perfect storm of the forces of disengagement, we suspect you didn't last too long at that job. Or you felt overwhelmed with too much to do, with too little support, as depicted in the illustration on the next page.

According to a 2013 survey,[1] more than half of workers in the United States were dissatisfied with their jobs. This statistic is alarming; after all, we spend approximately one-third of our waking hours and energy at work, plus dissatisfied employees tend to find new employers. Because we spend so much of our time and energy at work, the organizational culture can have a profound impact on our lives and the lives of those around us. If work cultures support interdependent, prosocial behavior instead of individualism and competition, we believe the business world, indeed our everyday lives, will be more positive and productive for almost everyone.

Any organization's mission will benefit from employees who care about their work and their colleagues. It's a win-win scenario. What

factors influence employee job satisfaction? Aside from the obvious – job security, pay, and benefits (e.g., health insurance) – employees report that feeling safe at work, having a positive relationship with their immediate supervisor, and communicating openly and cooperatively with other employees and senior management contribute significantly to their work satisfaction.[2] The bad news: In many organizational cultures, managers/supervisors struggle with these very issues, resulting in unacceptably high rates of employee dissatisfaction and turnover and a climate of distrust.

Imagine these disgruntled employees as supervisors who are responsible for mentoring newly recruited employees. Clearly, these interpersonal problems and a toxic work culture will only worsen if this cycle of apathy and disengagement continues. The good news: The actively caring for people (AC4P) principles – applied behavioral science (ABS) and humanism – can be used in an organization to improve the human dynamics of its culture and the work satisfaction of its employees. In fact, decades of research in a sub-discipline of ABS, known as *organizational behavior management* (OBM), supports the application of AC4P principles at all levels of an organization.

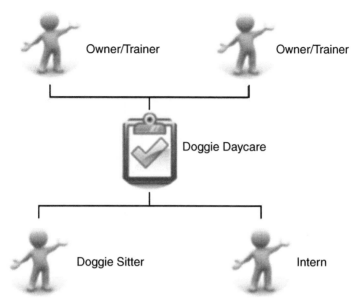

FIGURE 10.1. The full organizational chart for a doggie daycare firm.

CREATING AN AC4P CULTURE

An organization is a *system* – a group of interrelated elements that form a discrete entity.[3] Organizational systems can range from fairly simple to quite complex. Complexity increases as the organizational chart grows – the number of people, departments, services, products, and management levels multiply.[4] Figure 10.1 shows the organizational chart for a local doggie daycare and dog-training firm several of us frequent. The company is a relatively simple system with few layers and departments. In contrast, Figure 10.2 depicts a small segment of the organizational chart for a company that serves children and adults with disabilities with which we consult. Departments not represented in the figure include human resources, information technology, and others. Even without these details, the organizational chart shows much greater complexity than that of the doggie daycare company.

Cultivating an AC4P culture can be challenging in more complex systems, but it certainly is not impossible. We believe an AC4P culture involves integrating AC4P principles into expectations communicated by executives and managers/supervisors and reflected in the policies, standard operating

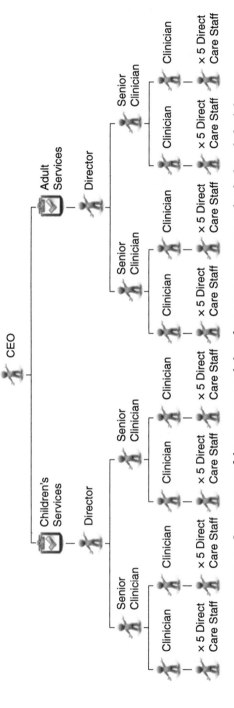

FIGURE 10.2. One segment of the organizational chart for a company serving individuals with disabilities.

procedures, and practices at all levels of an organization no matter the complexity. Ideally, executives and managers/supervisors model AC4P behavior in their own daily work practices, demonstrating alignment between what they say they value and how they behave (i.e., *say–do* correspondence). The purpose of this chapter is to describe potential applications of AC4P principles within organizational systems and practices in order to foster AC4P behavior. The chapter concludes with recommendations for addressing common workplace issues by removing barriers to AC4P behavior.

Mission and Values Statements

Developing an AC4P culture begins with a vision and relevant goal setting (Chapter 3). The *vision* for a particular organizational culture is embodied in its mission statement. It reflects the purpose of the organization and presumably drives the activities of all employees.[3] *Values statements* have a slightly different purpose – to communicate an organization's core values and guiding beliefs. Mission and values statements contribute to cultivating an AC4P culture in at least two ways. First, one or both of these statements can articulate and emphasize the relevant AC4P behaviors valued by the organization. If the stated mission and values drive action effectively, they foster the evolution of an AC4P culture. The values statement of Starbucks' exemplifies an AC4P purpose. It reads:

> With our partners, our coffee, and our customers at the core, we live these values: Creating a culture of warmth and belonging, where everyone is welcome. Acting with courage, challenging the status quo and finding new ways to grow our company and each other.
> Being present, connecting with transparency, dignity, and respect.
> Delivering our very best in all we do, holding ourselves accountable for results.
> We are performance driven, through the lens of humanity.

This statement clearly reflects AC4P. Even more impressive is that the Starbucks Website hosts a thirty-two-page manual outlining expectations for employee behavior with respect to AC4P business ethics and compliance.[5] The first section of this guide communicates standards regarding the treatment of co-workers and customers, workplace safety, and the support of diversity. Note that these sections align almost perfectly with the variables linked to employee satisfaction described earlier in this chapter and speak directly to enhancing person-states that facilitate AC4P behavior (personal control, self-esteem, and belonging).

Mission and values statements influence behavior if executives, managers, and supervisors ensure all employees understand them and specify how their individual roles and responsibilities contribute to the organization's mission and values. Accomplishing this is the very essence of achieving an AC4P workplace.[6] Why? Clearly relaying why and how each employee's job has relevance and importance and aligns with the values of the organization communicates to employees that all stakeholders matter to the organization. Doing so informs employees (a) what to do; (b) that their actions can lead to beneficial outcomes; and (c) that *all* employees are valuable. Although mission and values statements may establish a commitment to AC4P, they will not translate into day-to-day AC4P behavior without the sustained support of leaders and frontline supervisors.

Executives as AC4P Leaders

History provides us with numerous examples of uncaring and unethical leaders. A quick Internet search for unethical leaders yields more than 3 million results and produces names from our not-too-distant past. In 2001, a scandal that revealed faulty accounting practices or "cooked books" ultimately resulted in prison sentences for leaders of Enron Corporation, an energy company, and devastating financial losses for its employees and stockholders.

In a very public and humiliating scandal, Eliot Spitzer resigned from his post as governor of New York in 2008 after his constituents learned he had spent tens of thousands of dollars on prostitutes. We are all aware of the atrocities of the Holocaust (1941–1945) resulting from the actions and dictates of Adolph Hitler, one of the most immoral leaders of the twentieth century. Unfortunately, there is no shortage of leaders whose behaviors are antithetical to AC4P principles.

What qualities and behaviors produce an effective leader? How can we build on these behaviors to shape an effective *and* AC4P leader? The answers to these questions depend in part on time, place, and context. Some leadership behaviors are well suited for specific environments and times, but not others. For readers interested in learning more about effective leadership, we recommend the book *Measure of a Leader* by Aubrey and James Daniels.[7]

Leaders can and do emerge at any level of an organization, irrespective of title and rank. But effective leadership is especially important at the top levels of an organization, where individuals are charged with communicating the mission and values of the business, identifying strategies for achieving the mission, articulating how values can be exemplified at work (e.g., how employees should treat one another), providing resources, designing and communicating organizational contingencies, and motivating employees.[8]

An AC4P perspective can be embedded in all of these activities. When executives provide guidance in lieu of coercion, they represent AC4P values. When they express clear and attainable expectations rather than mandates, and model and support collaboration rather than competition, they exemplify AC4P behavior. AC4P behavior is also evident when executives solicit input from others and listen with empathy instead of judging and blaming. These are exemplary AC4P leadership behaviors.

Effective AC4P leaders foster perceptions of interdependence and personal control while also building a sense of interpersonal relatedness (belongingness) and community.[9] AC4P leaders also ensure the design and implementation of systems, including relevant education, training, and support to empower all employees to perform their jobs in ways that align with the mission and vision of an AC4P organization.

AC4P Managers and Supervisors

Managers and supervisors implement the strategies and contingencies designed by the organization's executives.[7] These individuals commonly have more frequent interactions with employees than do corporate leaders in executive suites, and as a result, they have the most direct influence on employee success and work satisfaction. Recall that employees' relationship with their immediate supervisor is a critical determinant of their on-the-job satisfaction.[2]

When we consult with companies or teach employees OBM skills, the most common complaint is the lack of effective supervision skills among those charged with managing the day-to-day work of others. Another complaint is the absence of a constructive AC4P manager/supervisor–employee relationship. All too often, hardworking employees are promoted to a supervisory position and then fail miserably because they lack the necessary skills to be an effective manager of people. In other words, they are promoted to a level of incompetency. To make matters worse, most organizations do not provide effective training and education, as well as other resources, for their frontline supervisors.[10] In these circumstances, we should not be surprised when managers fail to effectively supervise their staff or behave in ways inconsistent with AC4P principles.

For example, two common approaches – management by perception and management by exception[8] – stand in direct contrast to the principles of AC4P and often alienate employees. Management by perception occurs when a manager bases performance evaluations or recommendations for promotion on his/her subjective impressions of the employee rather than objective behavioral observations or performance (i.e., outcome) data.

Management by exception occurs when managers attend to employees only when they make mistakes or fail to perform as expected. This approach relies heavily on negative consequences to motivate employees. We strongly encourage managers to avoid these approaches and instead, use research-supported AC4P techniques, as discussed in Chapters 1, 2, and 3.

How does an AC4P workplace prepare its supervisors to properly support frontline workers? In Chapter 2, you read how goal setting activates designated behaviors for achieving goals related to a vision. In Chapter 3, you learned the advantage of pursuing SMARTS goals (specific, motivational, achievable, relevant, trackable, and shared). Using Figure 2.2 as a guide, an AC4P workplace employs leaders and managers/supervisors who generate SMARTS goals and then give each other supportive and corrective feedback regarding their supervisory skills. To be successful, managers/supervisors must first feel empowered and believe they can supervise effectively (self-efficacy), that doing so contributes to the mission and values of the organization (response efficacy), and that it's worth the effort (outcome expectancy) (see Figure 2.3).

Empowerment can be accomplished through management training and education, delivering supportive and corrective feedback on a manager's supervisory behaviors, and documenting the benefits of effective supervision. For readers interested in learning more about effective supervision, we recommend the book *Bringing out the Best in People* by Aubrey Daniels.[11]

How do AC4P managers behave? The same goal-setting and empowerment model applies here. Managers help employees achieve the organization's vision by empowering employees, setting SMARTS goals, and providing positive consequences for desirable behavior. Of course, employees need to be adequately prepared to perform their job effectively by receiving relevant education and training, having their progress measured objectively, and receiving supportive and corrective feedback. AC4P managers/supervisors behave as AC4P leaders. They foster interdependence, collaboration, and the AC4P behavior of employees. These are not easy tasks. They require the time and resources to ensure employees know how to perform their job well while also actively caring for their co-workers.

Managers/supervisors with an AC4P mindset also strive to facilitate open, respectful, and bidirectional communication with their employees. This means AC4P managers/supervisors take steps to build a personal relationship with their employees by arranging time to meet regularly with them to entertain concerns, help set professional goals, and solicit feedback. When employees express legitimate concerns or offer advice about how to improve the workplace, the AC4P manager/supervisor listens empathically and responds with humility and appreciation.

Employees of various companies recently shared with us that their supervisors felt uncomfortable delivering one-on-one corrective feedback, and did so only in the context of email correspondence or in a group meeting. Group feedback came across as rude and angry, not constructive, and employees often felt publicly humiliated. This form of feedback is the antithesis of effective AC4P communication. Some managers/supervisors incorrectly assume they need to be tough and feared by employees to earn respect. This is ineffective leadership. Rather, managers/supervisors who adopt AC4P principles in their interactions with employees and provide the relevant training and support we describe next are effective, trusted, *and* respected.

Training

Suppose you are about to board a plane to head to your favorite vacation destination. You and your family have spent months planning the itinerary and you desperately need some rest and relaxation away from classes and work. Imagine learning that your pilot has logged tens of thousands of hours flying an Airbus A319 with another airline, but has never received training to fly the Boeing aircraft you are about to board. Knowing that airplanes vary widely, how comfortable would you be trusting your life with this pilot?

Now imagine you are a healthcare worker in a busy hospital and receive news that a patient on your floor has tested positive for the Ebola virus, a serious disease that can be fatal if left untreated. The virus is transmitted through direct contact with bodily fluids of an infected person or by contact with contaminated surfaces. As a result, the patient must be cared for in an isolation room and you are required to wear personal protective equipment (PPE) from head to toe, including a half- or full-face piece respirator, goggles, rubber boots, two pairs of sterilized gloves, and a waterproof apron. You also learn that removing this PPE is a common way to contract the disease. This is scary because you have never cared for a patient with this serious illness. What type of training would you want to ensure your safety? Would you insist on a rigorous training program to prevent the spread of infection, or would you accept whatever training was offered regardless of its quality?

When you started your most recent job you probably participated in training before beginning work on your own. What were the activities? We bet most of you read an employee manual and perhaps watched an orientation lecture that reviewed safety rules and regulations. Then you might have watched someone perform the tasks detailed in your job description. Many of you had to pass a written test before working on your own. We suspect fewer of you practiced important job-relevant tasks with a trainer who coached you with behavior-based supportive and corrective feedback. We also bet that once you started working, your supervisor did not regularly observe you and provide relevant behavioral feedback.

Did you feel lost? Did you wish you had received better training? Many employees and managers/supervisors express dissatisfaction with the quality of their training, but do not really know what activities characterize a good training program. Because training is an important component of an AC4P organization, we next elaborate on the research-supported components of an effective employee training process.

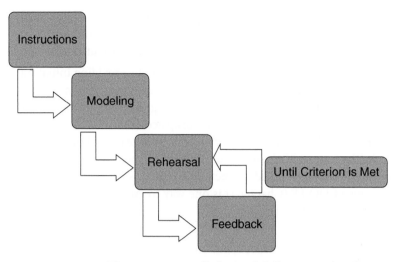

FIGURE 10.3. The components of behavioral skills training (BST).

Initial Training or Orientation. The examples we provided about the pilot and healthcare worker are extreme and ones you are not likely to encounter. We shared these to emphasize the importance of training, particularly when employees are new or the task is novel and challenging. Although it may seem like common sense to provide training under these circumstances, organizations often fail to do so, or provide low-quality and ineffective training. An AC4P approach adopts an effective, research-supported training program known as *behavioral skills training* (or BST).[12] This is the framework we recommend to organizations for structuring new-hire orientations and job-specific training programs.

Figure 10.3 depicts the four components of BST: instructions, modeling, rehearsal, and feedback. The first component of BST involves providing behavior-focused *instructions* to employees. These instructions specify the particular behaviors required for a task and can be given verbally or in written format, as in a manual. When used as the only training procedure, the process is not very effective;[13] yet this is often the only training experienced by newly hired employees.

The next component of BST is *modeling*, which happens when the trainer demonstrates how to perform a task correctly. It can be accomplished live (face-to-face) or through the use of videos, known as video modeling.[14] The third component of BST is *rehearsal*, which involves practicing the target skill. The final component consists of supportive and corrective behavioral *feedback*, which includes detailed information about correctly and incorrectly performed behaviors. Rehearsal and feedback are repeated until the employee meets a predetermined performance criterion, such as completing the task perfectly three consecutive times without assistance.

Ongoing Behavior Management. In addition to providing initial training using BST, an AC4P approach includes ongoing behavior-management support.[15] Minimally, this includes the following tasks for on-the-job coaches or supervisors: (a) be present in the workplace; (b) formally and informally observe the job-relevant behavior of target employees; (c) provide immediate, in-the-moment behavioral coaching (assistance, praise); and (d) deliver consistent supportive and corrective feedback (see Chapter 3). Following the steps of DO IT (Chapter 1) is one way to ensure effective adoption of behavior management.

Define. The first step is to define the behaviors that are correct and those that have room for improvement. This might include how to implement a procedure correctly, the number of times a certain behavior should occur, or what verbal behaviors are desirable. One way to ensure managers/supervisors and employees are in agreement about what behaviors are appropriate is to develop a behavioral checklist (recall the critical behavior checklist introduced in Chapter 1 and applied to occupational safety in Chapter 9).

Figure 10.4 shows a behavioral checklist we used when consulting with an early childhood education program that aimed to improve the quality of interactions the teachers had with parents when they dropped off or picked up their children from school.[16] We specified each behavior of a

Teacher Behavior	Was Behavior observed?
Greets the parent and child within five seconds ot their arrival to the classroom (e.g, Good morning!).	Yes
Moves within double arms reach of the parent and stays there for at least ten seconds.	Yes
States the parent's name.	No
States the child's name.	Yes
Makes a socially appropriate inquiry (e.g., How are you?).	Yes
Makes eye contact with the parent at least once during the greeing.	Yes
Smiles at least once during the interaction.	Yes
Facilitates an exchange of information about the child.	No
Scans the room for safety.	Yes
Makes a closing statement (e.g., Have a nice day!).	Yes
TOTAL (percentage of behaviors observed)	**80%**

FIGURE 10.4. Our teacher–parent interaction checklist.

quality teacher–parent interaction. This is called operationalizing desired behaviors, defining what interaction behaviors are expected of the teachers.

Observe. The next step in the process is to observe each target behavior regularly and note the contexts in which the behavior does and does not occur. Some questions to consider during observation: Which behaviors does the employee perform correctly? Do employees have the resources to complete the task? Do employees enjoy or even want to complete the task? Do employees have the skills to complete the task?

Using the checklist provided in Figure 10.4 as an example, the results of the completed observation indicate the teacher correctly completed eight of the ten behaviors and scored 80 percent. Behaviors requiring improvement include stating the parent's name and exchanging information about the child's day. The teacher performed all of the other behaviors on the checklist correctly.

In addition, the observation includes determining why the teacher made the errors (e.g., Does s/he know the parent's name?) or what the barriers were to completing all behaviors (e.g., Was s/he assisting other children at the time?). Collecting this information allows the manager or supervisor to intervene appropriately. For example, employees may make errors due to a skill deficit, which means they lack the behavioral knowledge for task performance. In these instances, additional training or task clarification may be all that's needed to score 100 percent on the behavioral checklist.

Employees may also make errors due to an effort deficit, which means they lack the motivation to perform the task even though they have the execution skills. In these instances, additional training will not improve performance because the employees know what to do; they just don't execute the desired skills consistently. Quite possibly, the consequences of completing the task well are not salient, immediate, or significant enough to motivate the employees to contribute their best efforts. When effort deficits are identified, managers/supervisors should consider positive and negative consequences that might enhance motivation. It's also possible the factors that facilitate self-motivation are lacking (see Chapter 3) and one or more of these could be added as an intervention.

Intervene. The next step in the DO IT process involves addressing the behaviors identified during the observation by implementing an intervention. AC4P leaders take the time to recognize the quality efforts of employees. Sincere approval can be a powerful motivator for many employees; hearing supportive feedback from the boss helps to maintain desired behavior over time.

When behavior is not meeting expectations, corrective feedback delivered in a respectful manner can help the employee address a particular error. Behavior-focused training that clarifies the appropriate behaviors helps to remedy skill deficits. To address effort deficits, managers/supervisors must examine the current motivating consequences and make adjustments. The observations could reveal that an employee is operating with few or inadequate resources or other environmental constraints. Ameliorating these issues can help the employee to better meet expectations.

Regarding our consultation referred to earlier, we determined that low-quality teacher–parent interactions were due to teachers' skill deficits and a lack of high-quality initial training. To help the teachers interact better with parents, we provided a video-based training program hosted on a secure Website. Teachers logged into the Website and viewed a video containing written and verbal instructions, video models, and a quiz. While watching the video, teachers completed a training guide that included a behavioral checklist. We implemented this intervention for approximately one semester and tested its effectiveness, which we discuss next.

Test. Test is the last step in the DO IT process. During this stage, managers test the effectiveness of an intervention and make adjustments as needed. Observations continue during the intervention process to determine if the intervention improved employee behavior. This step enables organizations to avoid wasting valuable resources on ineffective interventions and ensures effective interventions.

When we tested our teacher intervention, we provided the video-based training only to teachers who worked the afternoon shift. When we saw performance improvements in the afternoon, we then introduced the training for the morning-shift teachers. Eventually we made adjustments to maximize improvements by sharing the classroom's checklist scores, discussing correct and incorrect behaviors, and brainstorming ways to intervene more effectively.

Peer Training. Organizations might also adopt a peer-training approach in which co-workers train each other. As summarized in Figure 10.5, this model is appealing because it can be a cost-effective way to prepare and support employees. First, a manager or human resources (HR) professional receives training from a professional – generally an outside consultant – on effective ways to train others in the organization.[17] This training typically addresses the use of evidence-based training techniques (such as BST), perhaps relevant to creating and maintaining an AC4P culture within the organization.

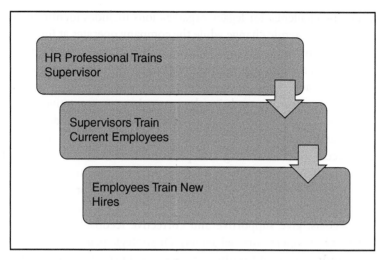

FIGURE 10.5. The peer-training approach.

Next, the manager or HR professional trains supervisors, and they in turn train employees in their respective departments. Each employee then trains newly hired employees in his/her department. Rather than a single trainer or training department assuming responsibility for training new employees, existing employees serve as peer trainers. One benefit of this peer-training approach is that it solicits employee involvement, not only ensuring team members have the skills necessary to complete their job responsibilities but also maintaining an AC4P culture of interpersonal helping.

Getting Started

An organizational system that incorporates an AC4P mission and values statement, effective leadership and management/supervisory practices, ongoing training and support of leaders, and ongoing training and support of frontline employees using the AC4P approach just described will go a long way toward cultivating an AC4P culture. These practices serve to establish expectations; reward desired AC4P behavior; correct anti-AC4P behavior; and create ownership, accountability, and a satisfying and fulfilling work environment.

Readers with "start-up" aspirations – to form their own company – have an advantage. You can design your company's systems so they incorporate AC4P principles from the ground up and hire employees with an AC4P mindset. The challenge for legacy organizations includes identifying ways to bring about systemic change while the company operates at full capacity and is staffed with employees who may or may not have an AC4P mindset.

How does one pursue organizational change in this latter context? Recognize that achieving an AC4P culture will be a journey, a process, and not a quick fix. One approach involves engaging representatives from all levels of the organization in strategic planning, which includes identifying a strategy for achieving an AC4P workplace and allocating resources to ensure success. Because managers/supervisors have the most direct influence over employee success and work satisfaction, the strategic planning process might institute change at the manager/supervisor level first (e.g., empower managers by supervisors providing education and training, set SMARTS goals, give supportive and corrective feedback about effective management or supervisory behaviors). Or strategic planning might identify the training needs of frontline employee as a priority necessitating the need for change at this level first (e.g., develop a BST program).

One benefit of strategic planning is customizing the culture-change process to the unique needs and strengths of the organization. If it also involves executives, managers/supervisors, and frontline employees, strategic planning will ensure the proper perspective and priorities of all stakeholders, thereby increasing the likelihood of engagement, ownership, and success.

The strategic planning process may adapt the DO IT method described previously in this chapter and in Chapter 1. An AC4P behavior relevant to an employee's job description and responsibilities could be *defined* clearly (operationalized) and *observed*. The systemic change identified by the strategic planning process and informed by the behavioral observations would serve as the *intervention*. Finally, a *test* of the effects of the intervention could be accomplished by post-intervention observations.

Changes will take time to identify, implement, and test. Accept the challenge of continually refining processes designed to maximize beneficial effects on AC4P behavior and grow an AC4P culture. In the meantime, organizational leaders will likely encounter myriad social problems and other obstacles to AC4P that must be addressed.

COMMON SOCIAL PROBLEMS IN THE WORKPLACE

Even though a system may incorporate ABS and AC4P principles, employees can still behave in ways inconsistent with the values of the organization and an AC4P mission. Several social or interpersonal issues arise in the workplace, including negative gossip, bullying, competition and sabotage, poor communication, and low morale. Many of you have likely experienced at least one, or potentially a number, of these detrimental circumstances. In this section, we focus on three of these issues, which we hope will serve as examples of other interpersonal workplace challenges. We also discuss potential ways AC4P can combat these.

Negative Gossip

Most people are aware of the adverse effects of negative gossip on one's personal and social well-being, but negative gossip in the workplace can also harm a person's career. Employees might discuss hearsay regarding personal or privileged information that is potentially false or misleading, and this may result in the spread of rumors. Negative gossip is often focused on the attributes or behaviors of other employees, managers, or supervisors within an organization (e.g., "Akeem is the boss's favorite; I wonder if they're having an affair"). Such backstabbing can interfere with teamwork and collaboration among co-workers and also unjustly influence a manager's perception of an employee.

For example, employees might not want to work with a particular co-worker who is the target of negative gossip. A manager might provide a biased performance evaluation if s/he believes the false rumors spread about an employee s/he supervises. Such destructive communication stifles interpersonal trust ("I wonder what he says about me behind *my* back") and subverts an AC4P work culture.

Solving the issue of negative workplace gossip can take several directions, depending on its root cause. Negative gossip is a part and parcel of modern culture – reality TV shows, radio talk shows, texting, instant messaging, and social media. Negative gossip is antithetical to AC4P behavior. Employees should support one another rather than tear each other down. Indeed, they should spread *positive* gossip by talking about the positive attributes of co-workers.

As B. F. Skinner said, "The organism is always right."[18] There is a reason gossip occurs – it's organic to modern culture as we described – and to put an end to malicious gossip its origins must be identified and changed. Unflattering, disrespectful gossip occurs for any number of reasons, so the solution is not a one-size-fits-all approach. It could spread simply as a function of the organizational culture. Leaders might need to make adjustments to the organization on a systems level, building AC4P at the cultural level. Incorporating prosocial values and humanism into the organization's values can help to extinguish negative gossip and promote positive culture change.

As discussed in Chapter 1, behavior occurs in response to activators and is maintained by consequences. Starting with activators, ask what is happening when employees begin to gossip. Is the problem an issue of perception, such as, "Johnny is lazy" or "Susan gets all the perks because the manager is playing favorites"? False perceptions occur in the absence of fact. We can prevent employees from making their own misguided judgments by being open and honest in the workplace. "Johnny isn't lazy; he reached his sales goal early this month so he can afford to take some time off." "Susan has consistently met her goals and is rightfully being rewarded." The opposite is also true. If an employee isn't productive, the availability of objective measures of performance, such as completed behavioral checklists, raises accountability issues and flags areas needing corrective action.

Destructive gossip is likely sustained in an organization because it's reinforced. Humans are social beings and gossip can enliven a conversation. A simple solution for reducing negative gossip: Refuse to listen to it. You could say, "I'm not interested in negative judgments, but if you have some positive gossip, I'm all ears!"

If social reinforcement is no longer available, employees will stop engaging in negative gossip, particularly if the behavior is maintained by this type of reinforcement. As a manager/supervisor, you might not be able to stop the contingency for negative gossip, but you can implement a contingency of your own for a competing behavior. Recall the DO IT strategy. *Define* what you would like to see employees doing instead. For example, employees should provide support for one another, motivate employees who could be doing better, and celebrate each other's achievements. They could also actively care and spread positive gossip.

Observe the occurrence of both your desired behavior and the behavior you are replacing. The *intervention* phase is when you introduce a competing consequence. The success of the AC4P wristband campaign, the thank you cards, and other means of promoting AC4P behaviors might suggest directions. Create a way for employees to be social in a positive way and to be rewarded for it. Did Joe coach a fellow employee through a tough task, or did Omar show courage and stand up for an unpopular employee? Provide a way to recognize Joe, Omar, and other employees who engage in similar AC4P behavior. Finally, you can *test* the effectiveness of the intervention.

Competition/Sabotage

Competition can have a positive impact on performance in the workplace,[19] but it can increase the risk for unintended and counterproductive side effects – sabotage and bullying.[20] Workplace sabotage consists of any subversive activity that worsens the appearance of another employee's work or impedes the ability of another employee to complete his/her work. It's usually covert and can be subtle, making it difficult to prove any wrongdoing.

For example, sabotage occurs when an employee intentionally fails to communicate information to a co-worker, such as the date and time of an important meeting (this is the "Shoot … Sorry, I forgot" excuse). Sabotage may occur because winning – as in "My department performed better than yours" or "I performed better than my co-workers" – is based not only on the merit of one's own performance or group performance, but also on the performance of the competition.[21]

Competition can also disrupt teamwork and cooperation. Employees might become more concerned with winning or beating another department or co-worker than with helping their peers. Imagine receiving the brush-off after innocently asking a co-worker for information about where work materials, such as a mop and pail, are located. This sort of behavior and lack of support obviously interferes with developing an AC4P culture.

If competition is used to motivate employees, managers/supervisors must consider the counterproductive effects of win-lose contingencies. In game theory, interactions between individuals can be described in terms of how the outcome of that interaction is perceived by each person involved. A win-win outcome is one in which all those involved feel they contributed and benefited. In win-lose outcomes, one person or work group reaps some benefit, while others feel they have lost in some way or missed out on an opportunity. The illustration on the next page depicts our point.

If competition becomes problematic, the solution is to reverse course and support cooperation. An ABS analysis of sabotage and competition suggests they are caused by the "zero-sum game" in some workplace situations. In other words, your colleague's loss is your gain (win-lose). It might be easier to prevent others from succeeding than to honestly do better yourself. To stop counterproductive competition, managers/supervisors need to abolish these harmful win-lose contingencies. Instead, they should bring employee goals into alignment with the win-win mission of the organization and an AC4P culture.

For example, employees might be given positive recognition and/or tangible rewards for helping their co-workers rather than sabotaging them (see the direct approach introduced in Chapter 2). An intervention in a data entry center highlights the importance of aligning incentives with AC4P goals.[8] When pay was linked only to individual data entry, operators refused to help each other because it meant taking a pay cut for

lost processing time. But an intervention that rewarded the group (i.e., the sum of the individual entries) would likely lead to more cooperation. Because behavior is supported by consequences, take a close look at what behaviors are being supported formally by policy and informally by peers and leaders.

Interpersonal Bullying

Interpersonal bullying in the workplace is often subtle, but still harmful to the individual being bullied (hereafter referred to as the target). Workplace bullying can be defined as repeated mental and physical health-harming mistreatment of an individual that (a) can be threatening, humiliating, or intimidating; (b) interferes with ongoing work (e.g., sabotage); and (c) could be considered verbal abuse.[22] Bullying can range from insidious actions, such as exclusion (e.g., omission from a meeting invitation or an important email correspondence) to more blatant actions, such as a manager or supervisor yelling critical or belittling comments in a public or private forum.

In 2014, the Workplace Bullying Institute (WBI) surveyed 1,000 adults in the United States regarding the prevalence of workplace bullying. According to the WBI report, 27 percent of Americans have been subject to abusive conduct at work, another 21 percent have witnessed it, and 72 percent are aware that workplace bullying happens.[22] This translates to roughly 37 million U.S. workers being on the receiving end of abusive conduct and another 28.7 million witnessing such acts. Alarm bells should be going off – bullying in the workplace is far too common. Unfortunately, many of you have or will likely experience this in some form during your lifetime.

The high prevalence of interpersonal bullying translates to real consequences. Bullying negatively affects the victim's professional development and results in financial costs for the organization and decreases in organizational productivity. For targets of bullying, negative work outcomes may include job loss and poor performance. According to the WBI report, victims lose their jobs at a much higher rate than perpetrators (82 vs. 18 percent).

Job loss may occur because the target quits, the employer terminates the target, or the employer forces the target to resign. Victims may also experience sabotage (a form of bullying); absenteeism due to negative health and emotional side effects associated with being a target of bullying; presenteeism – physically being at work but mentally distracted by bullying acts; and difficulty completing work tasks or meeting deadlines due to low morale or retreating into a shell. Plus, bullying results in fewer opportunities for professional growth and development for victims. Relatedly, organizations pay the price of accommodating bullies through employee turnover, absenteeism, presenteeism, and decreased productivity.

Two aspects of the WBI survey shed light on potential reasons bullying is alive and well in the workplace. First, the survey indicated that 56 percent of bullies are bosses. This power differential between a boss and subordinate – wherein the job and livelihood of the target/subordinate are under the control of the perpetrator/boss – makes it difficult and risky for the targeted individual to report the abuse. The survey also revealed that despite being made aware of the abuse, 72 percent of employers either condone or explicitly sustain bullying (e.g., denying, discounting, or rationalizing the bullying behavior) and less than 20 percent of American employers take action to stop it. Why? Because the common perception is that beneficial consequences will not follow the reporting of bullying behavior and a change in the bullying behavior is unlikely.

Of course, bullying is the antithesis of actively caring. The antidote to bullying might lie partially in the establishment of an AC4P culture in the organization. Actually, suggestions for practical solutions can be gleaned from success stories in another setting where bullying is common – schools. The AC4P principles have been applied to bullying prevention in elementary, middle, and high schools and consist of three components: rewards, expectations, and social competence.[23] Although the intervention was directed toward school-aged children, the same basic AC4P principles apply in a vast range of other settings, including the workplace.

First, we can assume those who bully do so to obtain some sort of social reward: praise and encouragement from peers, for example. We have already discussed the basic strategy for changing a behavior. Define a behavior you'd like to see replace bullying, and then arrange for that behavior to have positive consequences. Expectations are set largely by rules and values statements from leaders of the organization and by the actions of these respected individuals. Similarly, social competence can be built through modeling and practice with behavioral feedback.

Organizations looking to prevent or eliminate bullying should begin with ensuring AC4P expectations are set for interpersonal communication. These expectations should be consistently modeled by organizational leaders, managers, and supervisors. And words of appreciation should follow observations of AC4P interactions between employees. In the school setting, AC4P wristbands were used to reward prosocial behaviors.[23] We have seen success with these wristbands among college adults, and a similar reward for acts of kindness could be successfully adapted for work settings as well.

A survey or assessment could be conducted to determine (a) the relative occurrence of interpersonal bullying; (b) the barriers to reporting observations of bullying; and (c) suggestions for promoting prosocial AC4P behavior in lieu of bullying behavior. As with confronting other social issues, consistency is key. It's not sufficient to make an example out of one bully. Bullying cannot be permitted to be a part of the organizational culture at any level. We agree with Kid President, a character played by Robby Novak, who said, "Don't be a bully. Don't even be a bully to the bullies … it just makes more bullies!"[24]

Compound Effects of Social Issues

An organization experiencing one of these three social issues is likely to be experiencing others. They may be intertwined or co-occur due to a type of chain reaction. For example, an employee may gossip negatively about a co-worker, stating, "Kelly gets all of the attention from our boss but her work really isn't that good." This statement might create competition between employees involved in such gossiping, which could lead to personal sabotage or bullying. For example, Kelly may not be sent important group emails and miss meetings as a result. As a result, Kelly's co-workers might not involve her in important projects and exclude her from other group socials. The impact on Kelly's attitude toward work and her performance on the job could be devastating.

These sorts of behaviors and their compound effects must be stopped immediately. Interpersonal conflict is extremely detrimental to productivity. Negative gossip and sabotage not only take time away from work; resolving the issues also drains resources and talented personnel may be lost. Such problematic social issues cause personal distress and obviously decrease the likelihood employees will engage in AC4P behaviors. As such, it's important to identify and address all of the negative social issues that exist in an organization.

BARRIERS TO CREATING AN AC4P CULTURE

A number of barriers can interfere with the successful adoption of a movement designed to promote AC4P behavior. Because AC4P behavior needs to occur at all levels of the organization, barriers might exist at each of these levels (e.g., the behavior of leaders, managers, and supervisors as well as wage workers). Barriers might also exist within the systems and processes of the organization. Prior to implementing an AC4P movement, it's important to identify any potential barriers. This section reviews some common barriers to creating an AC4P culture.

Individual Level

Lack of Buy-in. Employees often witness numerous organizational-change programs during their time with a company. These programs come and go typically without producing meaningful benefits, while at the same time disrupting employees' work routines. As a result, employees often view programs as a cynical, short-term quick fix or gimmick that introduces challenges to the success of an AC4P movement. In fact, some employees may not support a presumed "flavor of the month" program, and take action to impede its progress.

This ultimately results in the unsuccessful adoption of the program and further confirms the employees' suspect thinking that the program was no good or never going to work. It's critical that employees "buy in" to the AC4P Movement, which means they believe it's necessary, worthwhile, and will likely make a positive difference in the workplace. Employees need to feel empowered to participate and support the Movement.

Recall the empowerment model presented in Chapter 2. It includes three beliefs that contribute to empowerment: self-efficacy, response efficacy, and outcome expectancy (see Figure 2.3). Employees who answer yes to the question "Can you do it?" communicate they have the resources, time, knowledge, and ability to participate in the AC4P Movement (self-efficacy). Employees who are unable to respond positively to this question could benefit from additional training to help improve their skills and ability. An analysis of the allocation of resources might also reveal that employees require additional materials, time, or other resources to successfully participate in the Movement.

The response-efficacy question of the empowerment model asks, "Will it work?" Employees who respond in the affirmative believe the Movement contributes to the organizational mission and AC4P values statements. Alternatively, employees who believe the Movement will be ineffective do not see how it will contribute to the mission or help establish an AC4P culture. These employees will benefit from education that highlights the rationale for and principles of the AC4P Movement as well as data showing it produced meaningful and beneficial change in other settings.

The outcome-expectancy question of the empowerment model ("Is it worth it?") assesses whether employees believe the outcomes of participating in the AC4P Movement are worth the effort. Motivation to participate results from anticipation of short- and long-term consequences. If the long-term consequences of participation are too delayed, managers need to ensure AC4P behaviors result in immediate, positive consequences so employees are motivated to participate every single day. Plus, maximizing positive consequences in lieu of using negative consequences will foster self-motivation.

If a sense of belonging or community has been established, employees will also believe they can work with their peers interdependently to effect positive change. Involving employees in cultivating the Movement can contribute to self-motivation and empowerment. An employee will be more likely to support the Movement if s/he believes the organization has made use of his/her experience/expertise, and relevant concerns have been addressed.

Developing appropriate systems to sustain the Movement fosters employee support. Finally, a strong message of commitment from leadership might lead to employee commitment, ownership and accountability. Leadership might accomplish this by allocating appropriate resources for the AC4P Movement and telling employees what they will do to support AC4P behavior and sustain a successful process.

Person-States. Various person-states can also serve as a barrier to the success of an AC4P movement. Certain person-states facilitate or inhibit AC4P behavior. For example, an employee working within a peer-training model who is uncomfortable providing behavioral feedback to a trainee inhibits AC4P behavior in two ways: (a) the AC4P behavior of the peer trainer is inhibited when s/he avoids supportive and corrective feedback (i.e., providing behavioral feedback *is* actively caring); and (b) if the trainee's AC4P behavior does not have positive consequences, the likelihood of that AC4P behavior occurring in the future will diminish.

To address this barrier, organizations need to ensure that expectations about AC4P behavior are communicated in mission and values statements, policies and procedures, and that employees are educated about the AC4P principles and the four sequential decisions that lead to AC4P behavior: Is something wrong? Am I needed? Should I intervene? What should I do? (see Figure 2.5).

Training and education can improve person-states that facilitate AC4P behavior, such as effective communication skills (Chapter 5). Education will also help to increase self-efficacy, courage, cohesion, and belongingness, and consequently increase the frequency and quality of AC4P behaviors.

Systems Level

Allocation of Resources. Programs are often unsuccessful due to a lack of support. Imagine working for a company that instituted a new workplace initiative mandating employees to work as teams, but you were not permitted to meet with your team during work hours. Instead, you and your co-workers were required to come to work early or stay late and you were not paid for your extra time. Would you be excited about this new initiative? Would you feel as though you owned it or were accountable to it? Organizational leaders and managers/supervisors can inadvertently design an initiative to fail in part because they do not allocate appropriate resources for its success.

Demonstrating that sufficient resources will be allocated to support the AC4P Movement will improve the likelihood of success and help to dispel the negative preconceptions employees might have about empty "flavor-of-the-month" changes in workplace practices. Resources include but are not limited to money, personnel time and staffing, and materials for the provision of training and education, adaptation of policies and procedures, or implementation of systems and processes directed toward the Movement. Making available these or other appropriate resources not only aids in creating a sustainable movement, but also helps to increase buy-in from employees and sends a strong message of commitment to the long-term success of the AC4P Movement from leadership.

Real or Perceived Pressures. Adopting a movement designed to promote AC4P behavior will likely result in a transition period as new practices and cultural expectations are developed. These new practices can create additional responsibilities for employees, take extra time to complete, and detract from the completion of current job tasks. For example, human resource professionals may be asked to update an employee manual so the policies and procedures incorporate AC4P principles. This task requires time and effort.

Relatedly, an organization that adopts peer training with BST as part of an AC4P movement must prepare its employees to take on the responsibilities associated with peer training. Employees may become frustrated and view peer training as one more thing "they pile on us." This frustration can lead to a lack of employee support and participation. If the system is not adjusted to alleviate some of these pressures (e.g., by teaching employees to juggle all responsibilities, reassigning tasks), employees may be in a situation where they perceive a need to choose between peer training and fulfilling other job responsibilities.

Additionally, it takes time for individuals to learn new behaviors, including AC4P behaviors, and to become proficient at performing them. This is especially true if certain person-states inhibit AC4P behavior. For example, taking the time to actively care for a colleague may require extra effort at first until AC4P behavior becomes the norm or at least until the employee becomes skilled at performing AC4P behavior. During this acquisition or learning period, employees may struggle with keeping up with their job responsibilities while meeting new expectations. If managers/supervisor do not anticipate and plan for this real or perceived pressure, employees may opt out of the Movement, sabotage the Movement, or simply leave the company.

To address this barrier, leaders and managers/supervisors should expect that employees will benefit from guidance on how to incorporate new expectations within existing job responsibilities. Employees might also require training and/or education to address person-states that inhibit AC4P behavior. Employers might need to adjust job tasks if substantial changes are made to employee responsibilities as part of adopting the AC4P Movement. Using the example just described, ensuring employees have sufficient time in their schedule for peer training may require shifting responsibilities or adjusting deadlines. Minimally, AC4P principles and behaviors must be integrated with job responsibilities and expectations of employees so these "extras" are not viewed as piling on extra work or competing with one's job.

IN CONCLUSION

Organizations can initiate and sustain an AC4P work culture. The AC4P Movement is a feasible solution for addressing common detrimental issues in the workplace no matter how widespread they are or hopeless they may seem. We believe it's possible to employ individuals who will answer yes to the first question we posed at the beginning of this chapter: Have you ever had a job you loved and felt empowered to fulfill your responsibilities?

An AC4P work culture requires an infrastructure that supports AC4P behavior on a daily basis and adopts a values-based AC4P mission statement with (a) organizational leaders who model AC4P behavior; (b) training programs that prepare managers/supervisors to effectively lead employees in an AC4P manner; (c) training programs that prepare employees to perform their jobs well and in ways consistent with the AC4P Movement; (d) ongoing support and relevant behavior management; and (e) creative ways to address problems with an AC4P mindset.

Developing and implementing these systems require commitment, coordinated planning, and resources. The return on investment: the development of competent employees who are satisfied, self-motivated, and fulfilled by a work environment that exemplifies qualities all of us should emulate. Organizations might also expect to see an increase in cost savings and/or earnings that more than make up for the investment in AC4P through (a) reduced employee turnover and training/hiring expenses; (b) improved productivity driven by dedicated employees taking the initiative and actively caring for their colleagues; and (c) a reputation in the eyes of the public and shareholders as a trustworthy and caring "brand" that attracts investors, customers, positive media coverage, and business partners.

DISCUSSION QUESTIONS

1. Write a mission statement and list the values of a company for which you'd love to work.
2. Define with examples the four components of behavioral skills training (BST): Instructions, Modeling, Rehearsal, and Feedback.
3. Consider a job situation you were once involved in and explain how a DO IT process could have improved performance on that job.
4. Explore the advantages and disadvantages of "peer training."
5. Discuss an incident when you heard negative or destructive gossip. What was your response? What could you do to decrease the frequency of such gossip?
6. To optimize an organizational system, W. Edwards Deming advised, "Ranking people, teams, or divisions induces conflict, destroys moral, and prevents optimization." How does this recommendation conflict with a typical U.S. organization in which individualism and competition are the norm?
7. Describe a situation in which you observed or were subjected to interpersonal bullying. What do you think motivated the bullying behavior? How might such bullying be decreased?
8. Describe individual and system barriers to initiating a nurturing mindset and sustaining an AC4P culture in a particular organization.
9. What specific person-states could facilitate or inhibit the success of an AC4P movement in an organization?
10. What employee experiences and expectations interfere with the initiative of a new AC4P process?

REFERENCES

1. Ray, R. L., Rizzacasa, T., & Levanon, G. (2013). *Job satisfaction: 2013 edition* (Report No. TCB_R-1524-33-RR). Retrieved September 4, 2014 from http://www .conference-board.org/publications/publicationdetail.cfm?publicationid=2522.
2. Society for Human Resource Management (2009). *2009 employee job satisfaction: Understanding the factors that make work gratifying.* Alexandria, VA: Author.
3. Malott, M. E. (2003). *Paradox of organizational change: Engineering organizations with behavioral systems analysis.* Reno, NV: Context Press.
4. Glenn S., & Malott, M. E. (2004). Complexity and selection: Implications for organizational change. *Behavior and Social Issues*, 13, 89–106.
5. Starbucks Coffee Company (2011). *Business ethics and compliance. Standards of business conduct.* Retrieved September 4, 2014 from http://globalassets .starbucks.com/assets/eecd184d6d2141d58966319744393d1f.pdf.

6. Geller, E. S., & Veazie, R. A. (2010). *When no one's watching: Living & leading self-motivation.* Newport, VA: Make-A-Difference.

7. Daniels, A. C., & Daniels, J. E. (2007). *Measure of a leader: The legendary leadership formula for producing exceptional performers and outstanding results.* New York: McGraw-Hill.

8. Abernathy, W. B. (1996). *The sin of wages: Where the conventional pay system has led us, and how to find a way out.* Tucker, GA: Performance Management Publications.

9. Geller, E. S. (2003). Leadership to overcome resistance to change. *Journal of Organizational Behavior Management, 22,* 29–49.

10. DiGennaro Reed, F. D., & Henley, A. J. (2015). A survey of staff training and performance management practices: The good, the bad, and the ugly. *Behavior Analysis in Practice, 8,* 16–16. doi: 10.1007/s40617-015-0044-5.

11. Daniels, A. C. (2000). *Bringing out the best in people: How to apply the astonishing power of positive reinforcement.* New York: McGraw-Hill.

12. Miltenberger, R. G. (2007). Behavioral skills training procedures. In R. G. Miltenberger. (Ed.) *Behavior modification: Principles and procedures* (5th ed.) (pp. 251–266). Belmont, CA: Wadsworth, Cengage Learning.

13. Reid, D. H., Parsons, M. B., & Green, C. W. (2011). *Evidence-based ways to promote work quality and enjoyment among support staff: Trainee Guide.* Washington, DC: American Association on Intellectual and Developmental Disabilities.

14. Reid, D. H., & Parsons, M. B. (1995). *Motivating human service staff: Supervisory strategies for maximizing work effort and work enjoyment.* Morganton, NC: Habilitative Management Consultants.

15. Sugai, G., Bullis, M., & Cumblad, C. (1997). Provide ongoing skill development and support. *Journal of Emotional and Behavioral Disorders, 5,* 55–64.

16. Berc, H., Doucette, J., DiGennaro Reed, F. D., Neidert, P. L., & Henley, A. J. (2014). Evaluating the effects of brief training on parent-teacher interactions in an early childhood classroom. *Behavior Analysis in Practice, 7,* 41–50.

17. Pence, S., St. Peter, C., & Giles, A. (2014). Teacher acquisition of functional analysis methods using pyramidal training. *Journal of Behavioral Education, 23,* 132–149.

18. Skinner, B. F. (1938). *The behavior of organisms: An experimental analysis.* New York: D. Appleton-Century.

19. Kortick, S. A., & O'Brian, R. M. (1996). The world series of quality control: A case study in the package delivery industry. *Journal of Organizational Behavior Management, 16* (2), 77–93.

20. Samnani, A., & Singh, P. (2014). Performance-enhancing compensation practices and employee productivity: The role of workplace bullying. *Human Resource Management Review, 24,* 5–16.

21. Johnson, D. A., & Dickinson, A. M. (2010). Employee-of-the-month programs: Do they really work? *Journal of Organizational Behavior Management, 30* (4), 308–324.

22. Workplace Bullying Institute (2014). *2014 WBI U.S. workplace bullying survey.* Retrieved from http://workplacebullying.org/multi/pdf/WBI-2014-US-Survey.pdf.

23. McCarty, S. M., & Geller, E. S. (2011).Want to get rid of bullying? Then reward behavior that is incompatible with it. *Behavior Analysis Digest International,* 23(2), 1–7; McCarty, S. M., & Geller, E. S. (2014). AC4P to prevent bullying: Activating and rewarding prosocial behavior in elementary schools. In E. S. Geller (Ed.). *Actively caring at your school: How to make it happen* (2nd ed.) (pp. 177–197). Newport, VA: Make-A-Difference, LLC.

24. Kid President (2013, September 12). Kid president's pep talk to teachers and students [Video file]. Retrieved from https://www.youtube.com/watch?

11

Actively Caring for Traffic Safety

CHRIS S. DULA, BENJAMIN A. MARTIN, AND KYLE A. SUHR

We hear about lives lost on our Nation's roadways every day in the news, but none of us should ever forget that these are not nameless, faceless people. They are mothers, fathers, sisters, brothers, children, and friends.
– David L. Strickland

Traffic safety is a serious public-health issue worldwide. In the United States alone, motor vehicle crashes (MVCs) are the leading cause of death for people ages 5–34.[1] In 2012, more than 2.3 million MVCs were reported in this country, representing more than 30,000 deaths and 2 million injuries. Based on 2010 data, annual crash-related costs were estimated at $277 billion, while the total societal harm was estimated at $871 billion.[2] Worldwide, the annual costs of MVCs are truly inestimable.

Efforts to improve traffic safety are long-standing. Many grassroots programs combat this terrible toll on the highways. When available, local and state police are on the alert for dangerous drivers. Corporations sponsor ads aimed at promoting responsible drinking and reducing texting people do while driving. The National Highway Traffic Safety Administration is devoted to improving transportation safety.

Prevention of injury to vehicle occupants is our AC4P mission. To reduce the tragic losses from vehicle crashes, traffic safety must become a *core value of* our country, not just a priority to be shifted up and down a list of many other societal issues. Discussions about traffic safety should be a regular topic of communication among families, friends and co-workers, students in classrooms, employees in training workshops, and other groups. Why aren't conversations about keeping people safe from an MVC common?

Many psychological principles contribute to this lack of dialogue, including (a) a lack of cognitive dissonance (e.g., not perceiving an inconsistency between one's driving behavior and an attitude of safety); (b) the fundamental attribution error (e.g., assuming there is something fundamentally wrong with someone who caused an MVC); (c) the self-serving bias (e.g., failing to appreciate our own mistakes and seeing ourselves as more skilled and less risky than other drivers); (d) inherent difficulties in changing long-held beliefs or attitudes (e.g., the confirmation bias, Chapter 9); (e) conformity (e.g., texting while driving because "everyone does it"), and other factors. Ironically, these same principles could be used to benefit traffic safety if people understood and applied them for systematic positive change.

It's likely you feel overwhelmed by the magnitude of traffic and driving problems. You may not see how you can personally make a difference. We all know someone who has been adversely affected by an MVC, and you'll likely experience an MVC sometime during your life, if you haven't already. At any given moment in a vehicle your personal risk of an MVC seems small, but motor vehicle occupants are continually at risk.

As pointed out throughout this textbook, many people feel it's not their responsibility to suggest to others, especially strangers, that they change their behavior. Many lack the courage to challenge another person's at-risk behavior (Chapter 4). Recall the unique challenges of behavior-based AC4P introduced in Chapter 2. In this chapter, we discuss how AC4P principles can be used to improve traffic safety, both personally and collectively. We use relevant ABS research to support our suggestions. First, it's helpful to define the types of dangerous driving.

DANGEROUS DRIVING

While some MVCs are caused by factors beyond one's control (e.g., an accelerator sticks due to a manufacturing defect), most MVCs are preventable. That's why we call them crashes or collisions, not accidents. As discussed in Chapter 5, "accident" implies that the consequences of a situation were beyond our control. It's important to consider how we can personally prevent an MVC or lessen the chances of injury or death from an MVC.

Dangerous driving includes aggressive driving, driver distraction, drowsiness, and intoxication. Driver behavior is the critical factor in most MVCs. Attitudes, emotions, cognitive processes, and the behavior of other drivers all affect our behavior behind the wheel. Drivers must constantly interpret information from the highway environment and make choices about how to respond to dangers as they arise. Some environmental situations are more dangerous than others.

Types of Dangerous Driving

Aggressive driving, negative cognitive-emotional driving, and risky driving[3] have been identified by research as three types of dangerous driving. This list deviates from early views on *aggressive driving* and *road rage*, which lumped together most dangerous driving behaviors, such as speeding, weaving in and out of traffic lanes, and running red lights, along with physical and verbal assaults. Today, *aggressive driving* must include intent *to harm*, consistent with decades of research on aggression in other contexts.

Someone can be aggressive without having any negative emotions; psychopathic individuals take pleasure in tormenting others or putting them at risk. This is rare, though. Researchers now think of road rage as a blend of negative thoughts and feelings accompanied by aggressive and risky driving behaviors. Negative reactions to others' driving may lead to aggression, but more often will lead only to intensely negative emotions and ruminative thinking.

Yet negative affect and cognitions alone can be very distracting to drivers. Drivers who experience cognitive-emotional distractions are at heightened risk for an MVC, and it's very common for people to get upset while driving, as much research has shown (some is detailed later in this chapter). But people scoring relatively high on the AC4P person-states discussed in Chapter 2 are less likely to experience negative emotions while driving, according to empirical research.[4] Even intense emotions arising from other situations (e.g., anger at a significant other, intense grief over the recent loss of a loved one) can distract a driver.

Most drivers who speed, run red lights, or weave in and out of traffic do not *intend* to harm anyone. These behaviors are indeed risky, but they're not considered aggressive. These drivers cannot know how those around them will maneuver at any given time, and other drivers may have negative reactions to their risky behavior. Any behavior with the potential to imperil others is dangerous driving. Understanding the affective, behavioral, and cognitive experiences of drivers is critical for reducing the frequency of dangerous driving and improving traffic safety.

Safe Driving Practices

Some safe-driving practices seem simple enough: stop for red lights and stop signs; follow speed limits; signal lane changes; stay in the rightmost lane, except to pass; maintain alertness/attention at all times; reduce speed in bad weather; and maintain vehicle equipment (e.g., headlights, signal lights, tire pressure, brakes). These all serve to reduce risk for an MVC or lessen the severity of injury from an MVC. However, many drivers fail to consistently engage in these safe behaviors.

Even if you follow all of these practices, other drivers may not, and their failures may result in a collision with your vehicle. You can mitigate potential harm by using vehicle safety equipment, even when you cannot prevent an MVC. Unfortunately, many drivers fail to consistently buckle their safety belt; install and use child safety seats properly; or wear helmets and other safety gear when riding a motorcycle or bicycle.

What if all vehicle drivers consistently abided by all safe-driving practices and reminded other drivers to do the same? Crash-related deaths and injuries would be dramatically reduced. Can such a lofty vision be achieved? We contend it's possible through a nationwide (and eventually worldwide) application of the humanistic behaviorism principles of the AC4P Movement.

In fact, a national movement has already been launched to improve our driving culture. The AAA Foundation for Traffic Safety assembled a compendium of articles in the handbook, *Improving Traffic Safety Culture in the United States: The Journey Forward*. One of those articles, "Creating a Total Safety Traffic Culture,"[5] written by Dula and Geller, makes the case that large-scale applications of ABS principles within an AC4P framework can dramatically improve traffic safety. We revisit those ideas here.

AN AC4P SAFETY CULTURE

As discussed in Chapters 2 and 9, an occupational AC4P safety culture involves open and honest input about safety issues and possible solutions; commitment from management to enable changes to systems; behavior-based observation and coaching; monitoring of leading (proactive) and lagging (reactive) indicators of safety; use of relevant data to adjust intervention strategies whenever necessary; and proactive multilevel communication regarding all aspects of an organization's safety.

The AC4P safety principles and ABS methods aim to develop an interdependent culture of compassion. The relevant AC4P education/training process teaches people how to put their caring in motion by giving and receiving behavioral feedback in a respectful, supportive, and constructive manner. Continually thinking and talking about ways to make workplace safety the norm is the mission.

People in our individualistic culture take a fairly negative stance toward giving and receiving behavioral feedback. This is one barrier to achieving an AC4P social norm. Many drivers (perhaps more males) resist asking for feedback on something as simple as directions, even when help is clearly needed, as depicted in the illustration below. They worry about being viewed as incompetent.

Think how you would feel if your supervisor said, "I would like to talk with you for a minute." We bet you would worry about what you did wrong. Why? Because people rarely take the time to talk about what others have done well. But we can learn to ask for feedback; and as described in Chapter 3, we can learn how to give behavioral feedback constructively rather than destructively. This encourages continual performance of desirable behavior.

In an AC4P work culture, people proactively promote and support safety on a daily basis. This translates into continuous behavioral improvement and helps ensure mindfulness regarding workplace safety.[5] This is certainly feasible for cohesive groups like factory or office workers, as has been demonstrated time and time again across many organizations (see Chapter 9).

But how can such behavioral improvement occur throughout an increasingly diverse and fragmented society, much less the entire world? Bringing about such a movement is indeed the theme of this book. So how do these occupational applications apply to traffic safety?

CREATING AN AC4P TRAFFIC SAFETY CULTURE

Persistent attention to safety issues is central to many traffic safety behaviors. Driving is also an inherently social activity. We may not see it that way, especially if we do our daily driving alone, but other people in vehicles flow all around us. Most do not want strangers giving them feedback about their driving. People we know may be in our vehicles, though, and can certainly provide us with behavioral feedback – if we're open to receiving it.

We all belong to various and relatively large cohesive groups, family, friends, and co-workers, at home, at school, in places of worship, as well as on the job. We care about certain people in all these settings, and others in these situations care about us. What if it were the norm to continually and mindfully think and talk about ways to protect these folks when they're occupants in a motor vehicle? The successful applications of AC4P practices that keep people safe in the business world can be adopted by people in various groups and organizations and applied directly to traffic safety.

Top-down is the current traffic safety culture in the United States. Someone in an authority role (e.g., legislator, administrator, police officer) decides which driving-related behaviors are acceptable and unacceptable. The "system" typically uses threats and penalties to promote desired behaviors and reduce undesirable behaviors. Legislators are comparable to managers within a company. And law enforcement officers can be thought of as supervisors. Individual drivers are the equivalent of line workers seeking a safer workplace.

Traffic safety laws and their enforcement have improved our collective safety. They are vital for preventing MVCs, because few citizens feel personally accountable for improving our traffic safety system. Yet personal accountability, starting with the driver, is the direction in which we need to move. In the business world this is considered a *bottom-up* approach to safe behaviors and safety improvement.

An AC4P mindset implies a shift in responsibility toward individuals and small groups. We need to empower people to promote safe-driving practices and openly discuss risky versus safe driving. These conversations will reveal contributing factors and reinforcers of at-risk driving. As with occupational safety (Chapter 9), any analysis of factors influencing risky driving, near crashes, and collisions should consider three critical domains: environment (e.g., road conditions, equipment, and climate), person (e.g., attitudes and person-states), and behavior (e.g., driving routines and interpersonal dialogue).[6]

The bottom-up AC4P approach to driving safety requires individual drivers and their passengers to define at-risk and/or safe behaviors and intervene appropriately. To begin, we should encourage those who already drive very safely to become community AC4P leaders for traffic safety. With training in behavior-based coaching, safe drivers can provide guidance and support to others in community-based programs to improve traffic safety. Let's consider a few relevant areas in which the AC4P approach can be quickly and immediately applied. Keep in mind these are only a few examples, but with collective dedication, effort, creativity, and persistence, the sky's the limit.

Secure Your Sister and Buckle Your Brother

There is no disputing the value of safety belts for saving lives and reducing injuries after an MVC. Instead of *seat* belt, we say *safety* belt; it's an important distinction (see Chapter 6). Interestingly, *safety belt* was the original label when the device was first patented by Edward Claghorn in 1885.[7] Safety belts were introduced on a large scale as options by some manufacturers in the 1950s, but did not become standard equipment in most vehicles until the early 1960s. Still, very few drivers used them regularly.

Interventions developed in the 1980s were designed to increase the use of safety belts, and ranged from engineering devices (e.g., dashboard reminders and ignition interlock systems that would not allow the vehicle to start until the driver-side safety belt was buckled) to top-down legal policies (e.g., safety belt mandates enforced by local police officers), and community-based efforts (e.g., media campaigns and educational programs). Fast forward a few decades and various interventions increased usage to about 87 percent in 2013.[8] As safety belt use increased, the percentage of fatalities due to occupants being unrestrained correspondingly fell substantially.[8]

Negative reinforcement systems (e.g., interlock systems or buzzer/light warnings installed in vehicles) were relatively effective in increasing safety belt usage between 1972 and 1980.[9] But many drivers had these controlling devices disconnected, perhaps to regain a sense of personal control or freedom.[10] Similarly, the "Click It or Ticket" program initiated in 1994 also helped increase safety belt use, but these increases eventually leveled off.[11]

Positive ABS techniques, such as "flash-for-life," whereby a vehicle occupant flashes a card with the message, "Please Buckle Up– I Care," were also effective in increasing safety-belt use.[12] In a later study, the impact of the "flash-for-life" card was compared with a "Click It or Ticket" prompt. Both of these techniques increased safety belt use, but the positive prompt was significantly more effective (i.e., 34 percent of unbuckled drivers followed the positive prompt and 26 percent complied with the negative prompt).[13] See Chapter 4 for more details about these AC4P techniques founded on ABS.

Today we are more consistent than ever in our use of safety belts; still, universal usage has yet to be achieved. The persistent few who choose not to buckle up report a variety of excuses for their risky behavior: discomfort, forgetting, inconvenience, and laziness. Plus, many actually believe they are not at risk for injury and don't need to buckle up.[14] More has to be accomplished in this domain, and this should be a critical behavioral target of an intervention to cultivate an AC4P traffic safety culture.

When seeing an unbuckled vehicle occupant, a believer in safety belts and the AC4P Movement should feel the need to ask this person to buckle up. Consider the opening, "May I actively care for your safety?"[15] It could be hard to refuse this request. With a yes response and a foot in the door (Chapter 6), you will likely have the courage you need to ask the person to please buckle up, and the probability of compliance with the request will be increased.

Some large-scale interventions consistent with ABS and the AC4P Movement have already been used to increase safety belt use. In the 1980s, Geller and others showed the positive advantages of incentive/ reward approaches to increasing safety belt use in community, university, and occupational settings.[16] Indeed, personal feedback and positive consequences have been shown to effectively promote the use of both safety-belts[17] and child safety seats.[18] And researchers have increased safety belt use with promise cards, flash cards, and various safety belt reminders.[19] See Chapter 4 for examples of these AC4P techniques for increasing the use of vehicle safety belts.

CALMING COGNITIVE-EMOTIONAL COMMOTION

Most of us occasionally get angry in relatively common traffic situations, such as getting cut off by another driver or being stuck in gridlock. One study found drivers felt anger toward another driver on about 10 percent of their trips and felt frustrated by another driver on about 30 percent of their trips.[20] Approximately 34 percent of drivers elicit aggressive driving behaviors annually, though the prevalence of such behaviors is difficult to determine.[21] Drivers may stew in negative thoughts/emotions, even if they don't express them openly. Suhr and colleagues found that simmering rumination actually increases anger and risk of aggressive driving.[22]

Driving while you are angry or frustrated is dangerous; it diverts your attention and reduces your concentration. Any powerful negative emotion that is at work while you drive, such as severe sadness or jealousy, is likely to pose risks not only to you but to vehicle occupants and others on the road. One scholar found that grieving for the recent loss of a loved one while driving poses a danger because grieving is "an intensely demanding process."[23] Theoretically, even a powerful positive emotion can take one's focus off of driving.

Generally, a positive attitude helps alleviate negative emotions, creates a more charitable interpretation of others' driving behavior, and promotes forgiveness and compassion – not anger. Adopting an AC4P mindset facilitates a positive attitude and mindfulness while driving. As a driver, how often do you make negative judgments about other drivers? Do these judgments usually lead to negative emotions? Actually, it's common to label drivers who are seemingly unconcerned about our safety as "jerks," or perhaps worse. Many drivers fall prey to committing the fundamental attribution error.

The Fundamental Attribution Error

As explained in Chapter 9, when we attempt to explain someone's behavior we usually assume the cause is due to some dispositional characteristic (or person-state) of the other person. This is called the fundamental attribution error (FAE) or correspondence bias.[24] We overemphasize others' internal attributes to explain their behavior and ignore the fact that situations play a significant role in determining their behavior. In contrast, we explain our own behavior by pointing to situational or environmental factors.

Think about being cut off by another driver. Do you reflexively say, "You stupid jerk"? (Or perhaps your negative label for this driver is more colorful.) You assumed the driver was callous or uncaring. Now, think about when *you* cut off another driver. You most likely didn't say, "I'm a stupid jerk!" You know your cutting-off behavior was unintended. You may even want to apologize. Some aspect of the situation likely explains your mistake, not some dispositional self-judgment that you are a stupid unconcerned jerk. As you can see, we attribute our own driving errors to situational factors, and we cut ourselves slack we don't typically extend to other drivers.

Maybe you just didn't check your blind spot. Perhaps you were engrossed in thinking about school, home, a relationship, or work. Possibly you got distracted by another person in your vehicle. Maybe you were doing something you shouldn't have been doing, like texting or talking on a cell phone. At any rate, you probably forgave yourself for your mistake and you would want the other driver to know you didn't intend any harm. If you didn't intend any harm, you shouldn't get scolded, right? Think about it. If you usually aren't a careless or thoughtless driver, why should you automatically attribute such negative qualities to other drivers?

What if we drove with an AC4P mindset? What if we gave other drivers the benefit of the doubt and assumed their errors were as unintentional as our own? What if we were willing to forgive instead of condemn? Such compassion would promote a more positive perception of other drivers and diminish the anger or frustration we might otherwise feel. As shown in the illustration below, this can be quite a challenge.

Becoming more mindful of the FAE can improve our attitude and our behavior when we are confronted with drivers who slow our progress or put us at momentary risk for a crash. What if drivers had a courteous way to unambiguously request help from another driver, thank him/her for a courtesy, or communicate an apology?

The "Polite Lite"

Say *you* cut someone off in traffic. Maybe you raise your hand to wave a sign of guilt or humility, hoping it's seen as an apology. Or you may avoid such gesturing for fear it could be misinterpreted as insulting or hostile. We can't communicate unambiguously to another driver when we're separated by steel and glass at high speed. The need to communicate clearly and efficiently on the road inspired the development of "the Polite Lite."

Scott Geller and Jerry Beasley designed and tested the Polite Lite to provide intervehicular communication. As described in Chapter 4, this was a small but very bright green light affixed to the rear windscreen of a vehicle (see Figure 4.4 for a photo of the device). Vehicles displayed a static-cling window decal defining a "courtesy code" as follows: 1 flash = "Please" (e.g., allow me to merge into traffic); 2 flashes = "Thank you" (e.g., for letting me in); and 3 flashes = "I am sorry" (e.g., for cutting you off).

A major advertising campaign made the courtesy code widely known in the target community. Radio and newspaper ads urged drivers to use hazards lights to flash the code if they didn't have a Polite Lite. As depicted Figure 11.1, the code was displayed on large billboards along main roads in the town. The marketing campaign succeeded; after ten weeks, 75 percent of 599 randomly polled local drivers were aware of the code.

Drivers who participated in a community-based evaluation of this AC4P intervention were randomly assigned to three groups: (1) Polite Lite group, told to use the Polite Lite to flash the code when appropriate; (2) Hazard Light group, told to use their hazard lights to signal the code when suitable; and (3) No Code group (control). (This last group was not told anything about the code, but would see it on billboards and community advertisements.) Participants filled out driving diaries, reporting behaviors and emotions they experienced while driving on a regular basis. All participants took pre- and post-intervention surveys as well.

FIGURE 11.1. A community billboard displaying the courtesy code.

Some interesting findings emerged. Drivers instructed to use the code reported sending an average of twelve positive messages during the eight-week intervention. Compared with drivers in the No-Code group, participations in both the Polite Lite and Hazard Light groups reported less speeding on the part of other drivers, less tailgating, less failure to use a turn signal, less drifting from a lane, and fewer refusals to let other drivers into their lane. Drivers who used the code also reported making fewer negative remarks about other drivers and scored lower on a post-intervention measure of aggressive driving.

These differences suggest some social validity for a courtesy code. However, it should be noted the group sizes decreased markedly by the end of the study; some group differences approached only statistical significance; and some differences in verbal reports could have been due to other factors.[20] Thus, replication of this field study is warranted.

Still, trends clearly showed that people instructed to engage in positive intervehicular communication reported more AC4P driving behaviors. Further, in a random phone interview of 423 drivers who said they were aware of the courtesy code after the intervention, 64 percent stated it would be "somewhat" or "very helpful" if it were widely used. From these data we might assume most people want to be more courteous and engage in AC4P behavior while driving.

On the other hand, 22 percent felt it would be unhelpful. Among the minority who thought the code would be unhelpful, many presumed some drivers would make some negative use of the code (e.g., using two flashes to mean something radically different than "Thank you"). Plus, some thought being "flashed" without awareness of the code might be seen as a threat or insult.

Widely deployed positive intervehicular communication is not currently feasible, though in the future "smart" vehicles may create opportunities for such communication. In the meantime, you can at least communicate positively to yourself. Mindful self-talk helps you remain calm and civil when driving (e.g., deep breathing, avoiding the FAE, choosing to forgive others' risky behavior). Plus, AC4P-focused passengers can use relevant AC4P principles to help their drivers reduce frustration, anger, or distress. By avoiding reactionary judgments about others, we are far less likely to be distracted by our own anger or frustration, and we are more likely to have a peaceful, mindful driving experience. Quelling negative thoughts and emotions can help us focus on safe driving. Yet other forms of distraction are also powerful risk factors.

DITCH THE DISTRACTIONS

Driver inattention is without a doubt a major contributor to MVCs. The Department of Transportation reported in 2012 that 16 percent of reported

MVCs, 10 percent of fatal crashes, and 18 percent of injury crashes were caused by distraction.[25] Distracted driving in 2013 contributed to at least 3,300 fatalities and about 421,000 injuries in MVCs. Distraction occurs when your attention is diverted from safe driving behavior, such as closely watching the road or regularly checking mirrors. No doubt a wide variety of stimuli compete for your attention when you drive. But you can also lose focus simply by being lost in thought.

The use of a cell phone (i.e., texting, using apps or the Internet, and talking with both handheld and hands-free devices) is one of the most common forms of distraction while one is driving. The risks of using these devices when one is behind the wheel are well documented and have been known for some time; yet these behaviors are still widespread.[26] In 2012, at least 7 percent of MVCs resulting in injury and 12 percent of those resulting in fatalities involved cellphone use.[25] It seems difficult for most of us to completely comprehend all of the dangers of driving while distracted (DWD). Let's draw a parallel to another issue once thought not to be that dangerous – driving while intoxicated (DWI).

DWI in the United States was not considered a serious problem until the late twentieth century. It took a steady stream of research beginning in the mid-1960s[27] to show the dangers of DWI. Crash risk increases precipitously with relatively small increases in blood alcohol concentration (BAC). Researchers, law enforcement officials, and traffic safety advocates tried desperately to get DWI on the nation's agenda, but many legislators resisted the creation of anti-DWI laws.[27]

As reported by Chuck Hurley, a former executive director of Mothers Against Drunk Driving (MADD), "Before the 1980s, drinking and driving was how people got home. It was normal behavior."[28] It took the grassroots effort of MADD to initiate an anti-DWI social norm. Candy Lightner and Sue LeBrun-Green started MADD after Candy's 13-year-old daughter, Cori, was killed by a drunk driver. These AC4P-oriented leaders vowed to do whatever it took to eliminate this mindless, tragic behavior.

They teamed up with Cindy Lamb, whose five-month-old daughter, Laura, was the nation's youngest paraplegic victim of a DWI-related crash. On October 1, 1980, they held a press conference in Washington, DC. "On that day, public tolerance of alcohol-impaired driving changed forever."[28] Anti-DWI laws were soon put in place across the country, and the public began to change its attitude toward DWI. While it is still a significant problem, today many more people view DWI as unacceptable as they did thirty years ago. Psychology made the difference. It took an understanding of people to change their attitudes and behavior regarding DWI.

DWI versus DWD: Which Is Worse?

A similar grassroots movement will likely be needed to change the public's view of DWD. Though DWD is clearly unsafe, the public is much less negative and more accepting of DWD than DWI, though it's at least as dangerous. For example, driving-simulator researchers found talking on the phone while driving was *more* dangerous than DWI at a BAC of 0.08 percent, the upper legal limit in every U.S. state.[29]

Yet in 2011, a survey showed drivers agreed in the abstract that DWD *could be* dangerous, but many saw the risk as tolerable.[30] Today progress is being made. In 2014, an Iowa study suggested people believed cell-phone usage was a serious or somewhat serious threat to traffic safety.[31] But the researchers found a strong relationship between behaviors and attitudes: Drivers who reported engaging in more distracted driving were less likely to view distracted driving as a safety concern.

The actual risk an intoxicated driver will crash in any particular DWI-related incident is statistically low.[32] But the public has collectively decided such risks are unacceptable. Laws with serious penalties have been enacted to prevent DWI. Laws and public campaigns have helped substantially, and alcohol-related crashes have declined significantly.[33] Though DWD laws have begun to emerge, they do not impose the severe penalties seen with anti-DWI laws. Plus, they do not seem to be making a difference, at least not yet.

One law to curtail cellphone use by drivers seems to have had no effect.[34] Another national study of the impact of DWD laws on MVCs found a strong effect of texting bans on single-vehicle, single-occupant crashes, one month following ban imposition.[35] However, MVCs returned to normal levels in about three months. Clearly, more studies are needed. If laws against DWD are in place, and many people believe such behavior is risky, why does DWD continue? The answer lies within the ABS principles explained in Chapter 1.

We know behavior that has soon, certain, and positive consequences is likely to continue. The immediate positive-reinforcing aspects of using a phone or texting while driving clearly outweigh the seemingly remote risk of a negative outcome. We know convenience, task accomplishment, social connectedness, curiosity satiation, and fun are powerful intrinsic (i.e., natural) reinforcers. As depicted in the illustration below, a device that enables us to communicate with anyone we want and anytime we want is extremely valuable.

Using a cell phone is extremely reinforcing. And again, personal experience informs most drivers, incorrectly, that there is no risk. Every time a driver engages in a distracting task and arrives safely at a destination, the belief of no risk is supported. Thus, DWD continues. How might punishment, or its absence, contribute to alleviating this problem?

Those who have experienced the punishing trauma of a DWD-related MVC, or who are close to someone who has had such an experience, may be more likely to desist in this behavior. But that's an outcome we want to prevent, and this consequence is also statistically unlikely to happen on any single DWD-related trip. Extrinsic punishment contingencies are added to the system, and to be effective the negative consequence or penalty should be swift, certain, and sufficiently severe.

But legal penalties for DWD are not nearly as severe as those for DWI. For example, a 2009 legislative act doubled the penalties for texting while driving in New Jersey.[36] First-offense fines increased to $200, $400 for the second, and $600 for the third. Only on a fourth offense was a three-point license penalty applied. Compare those consequences with those of a first-time DWI, which in all states results in automatic arrest, points on one's license, loss of some driving privileges, stiff fines, and legal costs. Often a third DWI offense results in automatic and substantial jail time and, in some states, permanent revocation of one's license to drive.

In all legal proceedings, the penalty comes in two forms: the initial citation/arrest and the conviction. The first consequence is swift; it happens on the scene upon contact with a law enforcement officer. But the impact of a ticket is substantially less severe than an arrest, and a conviction is neither swift nor certain. Due process takes time (unless one immediately pleads guilty), and the intricacies of prosecutorial/defense maneuvering often lead to reduced or dismissed charges and mitigated sentences. The ultimate negative consequence may not be nearly as severe as intended by the spirit of the law. Plus, there is virtually no certainty a person will be caught when engaging in DWD, even if a crash results.

As with DWI, unless it's blatantly obvious, DWD can be difficult for officers to detect.[37] Plus, many states do not have laws against using cell phones for GPS functions. How is a police officer to know whether a driver is texting or using the GPS function? And cell-phone use of all types is relatively easy for drivers to conceal if they are conscious of a patrol car. New and effective approaches to this problem are needed if we are to intervene effectively, and AC4P may well provide us with some guidance.

Connections to the AC4P Movement

People on this very day will be hurt and some will be killed as a result of DWD (search YouTube for "texting while driving" to see horrific consequences of this DWD behavior). Do you care? Of course you care! Nobody wants anyone to be seriously hurt or killed because of DWD. But do you send the message that you want it to stop? Do you engage in such behavior yourself, if only on rare occasions? If so, reflect on the fact that DWD behavior viewed by passengers in your vehicle and in adjacent vehicles on the road sets a risky example.

No DWD behavior is acceptable. If you agree, please use your knowledge of ABS to eliminate DWD from your driving. By doing so, you will set an AC4P example for others. You will help create an anti-DWD norm. And when you live safety-driving ideals yourself, you will intervene more effectively to increase the frequency of AC4P driving behavior among others.

The AC4P Movement applies supportive and corrective feedback effectively (see Chapter 3) to promote this safety-based standard with friends, family, colleagues, and even strangers. Do you have the moral courage (Chapter 4) to be an effective change agent? To help you develop the necessary courage, let's review some of the fundamentals again.

Be compassionate but not self-righteous when reminding others you care about their safety and would like to talk about their DWD behavior. Remember, most people engage in DWD behavior because it's convenient to multitask while driving, and they *believe* they are safe. As it happens, they probably don't know about the research that refutes this notion, or they feel they are among the minimal 2.5 percent who can multitask effectively.[38] Most people don't take risks because they are irrational, uncaring daredevils; they just don't understand the seriousness of the risks.

Let's move beyond safety belts, FAE, DWI, and DWD and talk about broader applications of the AC4P Movement to traffic safety issues. An AC4P perspective reminds us of the positive potential we have to be supportive of the many desirable behaviors of people. Initiating a movement for the purpose of individual change is relatively easy; but changing a culture and sustaining that change is another story.

Will you be part of the AC4P Movement for Traffic Safety? Will you tell others why you changed your driving behavior and why you wish they'd do the same? We hope so! AC4P behavior for traffic safety can make driving without a cell phone the norm and help cultivate an AC4P culture of compassion. How might we proceed to champion the creation of a traffic safety culture?

INTERVENING FOR TRAFFIC SAFETY
AND CULTURE CHANGE

We can use a host of AC4P approaches to transform organizations, as well as families, places of worship, and schools. The AC4P principles illustrated in Chapters 1 to 8 can transform even children from passive observers to effective change agents. With simple ABS education and training (see Chapters 1 and 9), people learn how to design safety interventions, conduct systematic behavioral observations, and effectively give and receive feedback. Those students then teach the process. To see how we might bring about a traffic safety culture, let's consider the seven procedural guidelines of ABS introduced in Chapter 1, termed people-based safety (PBS) by some organizations.[39]

1. Start with Observable Behavior

Select an observable behavior to change – a safe-driving behavior to increase in frequency or an unsafe-driving behavior to decrease in frequency. The behavior can be safe or unsafe, and range from using a safety belt or turn signal, to keeping one's eye on the road, or performing various at-risk behaviors such as DWD, speeding, passing in the right lane, and so on. The focus is on *what* people do. *Why* they do what they do becomes a later focus in the development of evidence-based and behavior-based interventions. Attitudes are not targeted directly, but will change to support the target behavior if the behavior-based intervention facilitates perceptions of empowerment and self-motivation (Chapter 3).

2. Look for External and Internal Factors to Improve Behaviors

Many external factors affect our driving behavior. Someone texts or calls us or pressures us to reach our destination at a certain time. Internal factors also influence our driving behavior. We want to see who is trying to reach us on the phone, or we feel the pressure to get somewhere by a certain time. We want to make a positive difference on both sides of this equation. We want to reduce external incentives to engage in risky driving and simultaneously increase incentives to engage in safe driving. Self-talk, for example, can support safe driving rather than risky driving and enhance one's courage to speak up about another person's at-risk driving. (See Chapter 4 on ways to increase courage in yourself and others.)

3. Direct with Activators and Motivate with Consequences

As detailed in Chapter 1, we want to use activators (e.g., signs, posters, stickers, and/or verbal reminders) to promote mindfulness of specific safe and risky driving behaviors. The most effective activators remind us of positive versus negative consequences of target behaviors. Most government-sponsored strategies focus on disincentives/penalty-based interventions (e.g., speed enforcement zones and "Click It or Ticket" programs). But as noted, psychologists have developed and evaluated a number of large-scale incentive/reward programs to increase occurrences safe-driving behavior (e.g., using a safety belt, using the turn signal, stopping completely at intersections, and driving the speed limit).

4. Focus on Positive Consequences

By now you realize the AC4P Movement puts a positive spin on talking about behavior and focuses on rewards rather than penalties. We want people to become success seekers, working to achieve desirable consequences, rather than failure avoiders (Chapter 1). Success seekers are more optimistic and more likely to go beyond what's required. As discussed in Chapter 3, the self-motivation needed for AC4P behavior is fueled by positive consequences (e.g., supportive feedback and genuine appreciation). Next, we add the scientific method to the mix.

5. Apply the Scientific Method to the Design and Improvement of Interventions

The DO IT (define, observe, intervene, and test) process detailed in Chapter 1 is essentially the scientific method in a concise step-by-step format. First, *define* target behavior(s) you wish to change. Safe behaviors to increase might include using a safety belt and a turn signal, coming to full stops at intersections, turning off a cell phone before driving, and pulling over to a safe location before making a call or sending a text message. Risky behaviors to decrease in frequency might include turning without signaling, speeding, rolling through stop signs, or talking on the phone or texting while driving.

Second, *observe* the frequency of the target behavior(s) to obtain a baseline. During these observations, look for natural consequences in the environment that might support risky driving or prevent safe driving. Baseline rates determine whether the target behavior(s) change as a function of an intervention.

Third, create a behavior-change process to *intervene* by using positive consequences to increase the frequency of safe behaviors. Positive consequences might be withheld and/or additional activators provided (e.g., reminding someone to buckle up) to decrease the frequency of risky driving behaviors. Of course, negative consequences can be used, but much research evidence shows positive consequences to be more effective at activating and supporting behavior change, and the side effects of negative consequences can be avoided (as discussed in Chapter 1).

Finally, *test* the impact of the intervention. Through continual observing and recording, determine whether the frequency of a targeted safe behavior is higher or lower than baseline.

6. Use Theory to Integrate Information

Once you go through the DO IT system several times, patterns emerge. Some approaches work better for some people, for some situations, or in some organizations. As you discover and analyze consistencies, you may develop a data-driven theory to explain your findings. If you are adventurous and academically minded, you could integrate them with other findings from the research literature. This type of inductive theory development often facilitates the design of more effective interventions. Plus, summarizing your findings in an integrative theory facilitates the dissemination of helpful information to others.

7. Consider the Feelings and Attitudes of Others

Feelings and attitudes of course differ profoundly from person to person and influence the impact of an intervention. The AC4P Movement fosters a concern for the well-being of others, and this includes emotional well-being. The development and maintenance of valued relationships, as well as the fostering of genuine interpersonal trust, promote the kind of interdependent teamwork needed to attain an AC4P-based traffic safety culture. The AC4P perspective directly targets behavior, but it also indirectly influences feelings and attitudes. Thus, Scott Geller has appropriately termed this approach *humanistic behaviorism*[40] – the academic theme of this textbook.

IN CONCLUSION

We could go on and on about dangerous driving and the application of AC4P principles to the prevention of vehicle collisions. For example, driving while drowsy (i.e., sleep-deprived) is yet another prevalent dangerous-driving behavior[41] that could be prevented through increased awareness, knowledge, and application of AC4P principles. Other dangerous driving issues have not been addressed directly here, including a wide range of risk-taking behaviors (e.g., running red lights and stop signs, speeding, weaving, and tailgating), and a host of critical issues (e.g., proper use of infant/child safety seats, teenage driver training, and senior drivers).

We have not discussed how policy changes might incorporate an AC4P perspective. The idea of stopping drivers to give them a reward for safe-driving behavior has not been well received; still it's possible to use intersection cameras to detect safe driving and not just speeding through red lights. And the ongoing advancement of intelligent transportation systems will enable the monitoring of individual drivers, including in-car vocal and written feedback for safe and risky driving behaviors. Those who have excellent driving records could thus be rewarded through some if–then contingency. Imagine insurance companies adjusting your monthly premium contingent on the frequency of your safe versus at-risk driving behaviors. Indeed, at least one insurance company advertises an incentive/reward plan that approximates this ABS approach.

AC4P principles can be applied in any number of ways to mitigate many of our collective societal problems. Bottom line: Traffic safety affects us all, and we all care about the safety of the occupants in our own and others' motor vehicles. We need to apply ABS principles with an AC4P mindset to increase the frequency of safe-driving practices. We need to do this in a systematic, consistent, persistent fashion. This is how we will cultivate a culture that values compassion, safety, health, security, and well-being for everyone, in every situation.

DISCUSSION QUESTIONS

1. In your opinion, why is traffic safety such a serious problem in our country and worldwide?
2. Why don't we take traffic safety issues as seriously as terrorist threats or war casualties?
3. What's the distinction (if any) between risky driving and aggressive driving?
4. How could AC4P principles be used to increase the frequency of safe driving?
5. Do you believe the authors' proposal to cultivate an AC4P safety culture is realistic? Why or why not?

6. Explain connections between cognitive psychology and driving behavior.
7. How does the fundamental attribution error contribute to aggressive driving or road rage?
8. Offer an opinion of "the Polite Lite" and suggest how research could be used to support or invalidate your opinion.
9. Explain similarities and distinctions between DWI (driving while intoxicated) and DWD (driving while distracted).
10. Imagine you're a well-paid consultant who is asked to give a talk at a town council meeting on "practical applications of behavior-based safety to the improvement of traffic safety on a large scale." What would you say, given that you want to plant seeds for the development of cost-effective community-wide intervention?

REFERENCES

1. Centers for Disease Control and Prevention (2011). *10 Leading Causes of Death, United States.* Retrieved March 10, 2014: http://www.cdc.gov/injury/wisqars/; *Injury prevention and control: Motor vehicle safety.* Retrieved May 15, 2012: www.cdc.gov/motorvehiclesafety/index.html; National Highway Traffic Safety Administration (2013). *Traffic safety facts: 2012 data.* Retrieved July 27, 2014: http://www-nrd.nhtsa.dot.gov/Pubs/811856.pdf.
2. Blincoe, L. J., Miller, T. R., Zaloshnja, E., & Lawrence, B. A. (2014). *The economic and societal impact of motor vehicle crashes, 2010.* Washington, DC: National Traffic Safety Administration.
3. Dula, C. S., & Ballard, M. E. (2003). Development and evaluation of a measure of dangerous, aggressive, negative emotional, and risky driving. *Journal of Applied Psychology*, 33(2), 263–282; Dula, C. S., & Geller, E. S. (2004). Risky, aggressive, or emotional driving: Addressing the need for consistent communication in research. *Journal of Safety Research*, 34(5), 559–566; Dula, C. S., Geller, C. S., & Chumney, F. L. (2011). A social-cognitive model of driver aggression: Taking situations and individual differences into account. *Current Psychology*, 30(4), 324–334.
4. Martin, B. A., Taylor, D. A., Dula, C. S., & Geller, E. S. (2012). *Who cares about dangerous driving: Applying the actively caring model to automobile crash prevention.* Technical Report. Blacksburg: Virginia Tech, Center for Applied Behavior Systems.
5. Dula, C. S., & Geller, E. S. (2007). *Creating a total safety traffic culture. In Traffic safety culture in the United States: The journey forward.* Washington DC: American Automobile Association Foundation for Traffic Safety. Retrieved May 28, 2012: www.aaafoundation.org/pdf/DulaGeller.pdf.
6. Geller, E. S. (2001). *The psychology of safety handbook. Boca* Raton, FL: Lewis; Geller, E. S., Bolduc, J. E., Foy, M. J., & Dean, J. (2013). In pursuit of an actively-caring safety culture: Practical methods, empirical results, and provocative implications. *Professional Safety*, 57 (1), 44–50.

7. U.S. Patent and Trademark Office (2012). *Safety-Belt. U.S. Patent Number: 312085.* Retrieved July 26, 2012: http://patft.uspto.gov/netahtml/PTO/srchnum.htm.

8. National Highway Traffic Safety Administration (2013). *Traffic safety facts: Seat belt use in 2013– Overall results.* Retrieved May 20, 2014: http://www-nrd.nhtsa .dot.gov/Pubs/811875.pdf.

9. Geller, E. S., Casali, J., & Johnson, R. (1980). Seat-belt usage: A potential target for applied behavior analysis. *Journal of Applied Behavior Analysis,* 13, 669–675; Robertson, L. (1975). Safety-belt use in automobiles with starter-interlock and buzzer-light reminder systems. *American Journal of Public Health,* 65, 1319–1325; Westefeld, A., & Phillips, B. (1976). *Safety-belt usage survey.* Technical Report DOT H5-801. Princeton, NJ: Opinion Research.

10. Brehm, J. W. (1966). *A theory of psychological reactance.* New York: Academic Press; Skinner, B. F. (1971). *Beyond freedom and dignity.* New York: Alfred A. Knopf.

11. Williams, A., Reinfurt, D., & Wells, J. (1996). Increasing seat-belt use in North Carolina. *Journal of Safety Research,* 27, 33–41; Williams, A., & Wells, J. (2004). The role of enforcement programs increasing seat-belt use. *Journal of Safety Research,* 35(2), 175–180.

12. Geller, E. S., Bruff, C., & Nimmer, J. (1985). The "flash-for-life": Community-based prompting for safety-belt promotion. *Journal of Applied Behavior Analysis,* 18, 309–314; Farrell, L., Cox, M., & Geller, E. S. (2007). Prompting safety-belt use in the context of a belt-use law: The flash-for-life revisited. *Journal of Safety Research,* 38, 407–411; Thyer, B., Geller, E. S., Williams, M., & Purcell, E. (1987). Community-based "flashing" to increase safety-belt use. *Journal of Experimental Education,* 55, 155–159.

13. Cox, M., & Geller, E. S. (2010). Prompting safety-belt use: Comparative impact on the target behavior and relevant body language. *Journal of Applied Behavior Analysis,* 43, 321–325.

14. Begg, D. J., & Langley, J. D. (2000). Seat-belt use and related behaviors among young adults. *Journal of Safety Research,* 31(4), 211–220; Kim, K., & Yamashita, E. Y. (2007). Attitudes of commercial motor vehicle drivers towards safety belts. *Accident Analysis and Prevention,* 39(6), 1097–1106.

15. Drebinger, J. W. (2011). *Would you watch out for my safety? Helping others avoid personal injury.* Galt, CA: Wulamoc.

16. Geller, E. S. (1983). Rewarding safety-belt usage at an industrial setting: Tests of treatment generality and response maintenance. *Journal of Applied Behavior Analysis,* 16(2), 189–202; Geller, E. S., Johnson, R. P., & Pelton, S. L. (1982). Community-based interventions encouraging safety-belt use. *American Journal of Community Psychology,* 10, 183–195; Geller, E. S., Paterson, L., & Talbot, E. (1982). A behavioral analysis of incentive prompts for motivating seat-belt usage. *Journal of Applied Behavior Analysis,* 15, 403–413.

17. Boyce, T. E., & Geller, E. S. (1999). Attempts to increase vehicle safety-belt use among industry workers: What can we learn from our failures? *Journal of Organizational Behavior Management,* 19, 27–44; Campbell, R. J., Hunter, W. W., & Stutts, J. C. (1984). The use of economic incentives and education to modify safety-belt use behavior of high school students. *Health Education,* 15, 30–33;

Geller, E. S., Davis, L., & Spicer, K. (1983). Industry-based incentives for promoting seat-belt use: Differential impact on white-collar versus blue-collar employees. *Journal of Organizational Behavior Management*, 5, 17–29; Geller, E. S., Kalsher, M. J., Rudd, J. R., & Lehman, G. (1989). Promoting safety-belt use on a university campus: An integration of commitment and incentive strategies. *Journal of Applied Social Psychology*, 19, 3–19; Geller, E. S., Rudd, J. R., Kalsher, M. J., Streff, F. M., & Lehman, G. R. (1987). Employer-based programs to motivate safety-belt use: A review of short and long-term effects. *Journal of Safety Research*, 18, 1–17; Grant, B. A. (1990). Effectiveness of feedback and education in an employment-based seat-belt program. *Health Education Research*, 5, 2–10; Kello, J. E., Geller, E. S., Rice, J. C., & Bryant, S. L. (1988). Motivating auto safety-belt wearing in industrial settings: From awareness to behavior change. *Journal of Organizational Behavior Management*, 9, 7–21; Pastò, L., & Baker, A. G. (2001). Evaluation of a brief intervention for increasing seat-belt use on a college campus. *Behavior Modification*, 25, 471–486; Roberts, D. S., & Geller, E. S. (1994). A statewide intervention to increase safety-belt use: Adding to the impact of a belt-use law. *American Journal of Health Promotion*, 8, 172–174.

18. England, K. J., Olson, T. M., & Geller, E. S. (2000). Behavioral observations find unsafe use of child safety seats. *Behavior Analysis Digest*, 12, 11–12; Greenberg-Seth, J., Hemenway, D., Gallagher, S. S., Ross, J. B., & Lissy, K. S. (2004). Evaluation of a community-based intervention to promote rear seating for children. *American Journal of Public Health*, 94, 1009–1013; Roberts, M. C., Fanurik, D., & Wilson, D. (1988). A community program to reward children's use of seat belts. *American Journal of Community Psychology*, 16, 395–407; Roberts, M. C., & Layfield, D. A. (1987). Promoting child passenger safety: A comparison of two positive methods. *Journal of Pediatric Psychology*, 12, 257–271; Task Force on Community Preventive Services (2001). Recommendations to reduce injuries to motor vehicle occupants: Increasing child safety-seat use, increasing safety-belt use, and reducing alcohol-impaired driving. *American Journal of Preventive Medicine*, 21, 16–22; Will, K. E., & Geller, E. S. (2004). Increasing the safety of children's vehicle travel: From effective risk communication to behavior change. *Journal of Safety Research*, 35, 263–274; Zaza, S., Sleet, D. A., Thompson, R. S., Sosin, D. M., Bolen, J. C., & Task Force on Community Preventive Services (2001). Reviews of evidence regarding interventions to increase use of child safety seats. *American Journal of Preventive Medicine*, 21, 31–47.

19. Geller, E. S., & Lehman, G. R. (1991). The buckle-up promise card: A versatile intervention for large-scale behavior change. *Journal of Applied Behavior Analysis*, 24, 91–94; Geller, E. S., Bruff, C. D., & Nimmer, J. G. (1985). The "Flash for Life": A community prompting strategy for safety-belt promotion. *Journal of Applied Behavior Analysis*, 18, 145–159; Geller, E. S. (1989). The Airline Lifesaver: In pursuit of small wins. *Journal of Applied Behavior Analysis*, 22, 333–335; Geller, E. S., Hickman, J. S., & Pettinger, C. B. (2004). The Airline Lifesaver: A 17-year analysis of a technique to prompt the delivery of a safety message. *Journal of Safety Research*, 35, 357–366.

20. Positive Driving Systems (2003). *Final report for the National Institutes of Health Project: Innovative approaches to anger management*. Grant 1 R43 MH62263-01A2. Washington, DC: National Institutes of Health.

21. Galovoski, T., Malta, L., & Blanchard, E. (2006). *Road rage: Assessment and treatment of the angry, aggressive driver*. Washington, DC: American Psychological Association.

22. Suhr, K., & Nesbit, S. (2013). Dwelling on 'road rage': The effects of a trait rumination on aggressive driving. *Transportation Research Part F*, 21, 207–218.

23. Rosenblatt, P. C. (2004). Grieving while driving. *Death Studies*, 28(7), 684.

24. Ross, L. (1977). The intuitive psychologist and his shortcomings: Distortions in the attribution process. In L. Berkowitz(Ed.). *Advances in experimental social psychology* (pp. 173–220). New York: Academic Press.

25. U.S. Department of Transportation, National Highway Traffic Safety Administration. (2014). *Traffic safety facts research note. Distracted driving 2012*. Retrieved August 5, 2014: http://www-nrd.nhtsa.dot.gov/Pubs/812012.pdf.

26. Briem, V., & Hedman, L. R. (1995). Behavioural effects of mobile telephone use during simulated driving. *Ergonomics*, 38, 2536–2562; Bener, A., Crundall, D., Özkan, T., & Lajunen, T. (2010). Mobile phone use while driving: A major public health problem in an Arabian society, State of Qatar – Mobile phone use and the risk of motor vehicle crashes. *Journal of Public Health*, 18(2), 123–129. doi:10.1007/s10389-009-0286-1; Cook, J., & Jones, R. (2011). Texting and accessing the web while driving: Traffic citations and crashes among young adult drivers. *Traffic Injury Prevention*, 12(6), 545–549; Haque, M., & Washington, S. (2014). A parametric duration model of the reaction times of drivers distracted by mobile phone conversations. *Accident Analysis & Prevention*, 62, 42–53; Ishigami, Y. & Klein, R. (2009). Is a hands-free phone safer than a handheld phone? *Journal of Safety Research*, 40(2), 157–164; McEvoy, S. P., Stevenson, M. R., & Woodward, M. (2006). Phone use and crashes while driving: A representative survey of drivers in two Australian states. *Medical Journal of Australia*, 185, 630–634; Nemme, H. E., & White, K. M. (2010). Texting while driving: Psychosocial influences on young people's texting intentions and behaviour. *Accident Analysis and Prevention*, 42(4), 1257–1265; Stavrinos, D., Jones, J., Garner, A., Griffin, R., Franklin, C., Ball, D., et al. (2013). Impact of distracted driving on safety and traffic flow. *Accident Analysis & Prevention*, 61, 63–70.

27. Borkenstein, R . F., Crowther, R. F., Shumate, R. P., Ziel, W. B., & Zylman, R. (1974). The role of the drinking driver in traffic accidents: The Grand Rapids Study. *Blutalkohol*, 11(1), 1–131.

28. Mothers Against Drunk Driving (2005). 25 years of saving lives: 1980–2005. *Driven*. Retrieved July 31, 2012: www.madd.org/about-us/history/madd25thhistory .pdf, p. 10.

29. Strayer, D. L., Drews, F. A., & Crouch, D. J. (2006). A comparison of the cell-phone driver and the drunk driver. *Human Factors*, 48(2), 381–391.

30. Hallett, C., Lambert, A., & Regan, M. A. (2011). Cell-phone conversing while driving in New Zealand: Prevalence, risk perception and legislation. *Accident Analysis and Prevention*, 43(3), 862–869; Harrison, M. A. (2011). College students' prevalence and perceptions of text messaging while driving. *Accident Analysis and Prevention*, 43(4), 1516–1520.

31. Li, W., Gkritza, K., & Albrecht, C. (2014). The culture of distracted driving: Evidence from a public opinion survey in Iowa. *Transportation Research*

Part F: *Traffic Psychology and Behaviour26*, Part B, 337-347 doi:10.1016/j. trf.2014.01.002.

32. Dula, C. S., Dwyer, W. O., & LeVerne, G. (2007). Policing the drunk driver: Measuring law-enforcement involvement in reducing alcohol-impaired driving. *Journal of Safety Research*, 38(3), 267–272; Peck, R., Gebers, M., Voas, R., & Romano, E. (2008). The relationship between blood alcohol concentration (BAC), age, and crash risk. *Journal of Safety Research*, 39(3), 311–319.

33. U.S. National Highway Traffic Safety Administration (2012). *Fatality Analysis Reporting System (FARS) Encyclopedia*. Retrieved July 26, 2012: www-fars.nhtsa .dot.gov/Main/index.aspx.

34. Foss, R. D., Goodwin, A. H., McCartt, A. T., & Hellinga, L. A. (2009). Short-term effects of a teenage driver cell phone restriction. *Accident Analysis and Prevention*, 41(3), 419–424; Goodwin, A. H., O'Brien, N. P., & Foss, R. D. (2012). Effect of North Carolina's restriction on teenage driver cell phone use two years after implementation. *Accident Analysis and Prevention*, 48, 363–367. doi:10.1016/j.aap.2012.02.006.

35. Aboulk, R., & Adams, S. (2013). Texting bans and fatal accidents on roadways: Do they work? Or do drivers just react to announcements of bans? *American Economic Journal*, 5(2), 179–199.

36. Friedman, M. (2012). *N.J. Senate passes bill doubling penalty for texting while driving*. Retrieved August 28, 2012: www.nj.com/news/index.ssf/2012/06/nj_ senate_passes_bill_doubling.html.

37. Logana, D. (2012). *How do police enforce laws against texting while driving?* On Live 5 WCSC. Retrieved August 21, 2012: www.live5news.com/story/12937810/ how-do-police-enforce-laws-against-texting-while-driving; Associated Press (2012). *Oregon cops to face problems enforcing cell phone ban*. Retrieved August 21, 2012: www.policeone.com/communications/articles/1985732-Ore-cops-to-face -problems-enforcing-cell-phone-ban/.

38. Watson, J. M., & Strayer, D. L. (2010). Supertaskers: Profiles in extraordinary multitasking ability. *Psychonomic Bulletin & Review*, 17(4), 479–485.

39. Geller, E. S. (2005). *People-based safety: The source*. Virginia Beach, VA: Coastal Training and Consulting; Geller, E. S. (2005). Seven basics of people-based safety: Embracing empowerment, ownership, & trust. *Industrial Safety and Hygiene News*, 39 (6), 14, 16.

40. Geller, E. S. (2015). Seven life lessons from humanistic behaviorism: How to bring the best out of yourself and others. *Journal of Organizational Behavior Management*, 35, 151–170.

41. Scott, L., Hwang, W. T., Rogers, A., Nysse, T., Dean, G., & Dinges, D. (2007). The relationship between nurse work schedules, sleep duration, and drowsy driving. *Sleep*, 30(12), 1801–1807; Stutts, J., Wilkins, J., & Vaughn, B. (1999). *Why do people have drowsy driving crashes? Input from drivers who just did*. Washington, DC: AAA Foundation for Traffic Safety; Vanlaar, W., Simpson, H., Mayhem, D., & Robertson, R. (2008). Fatigued and drowsy driving: A survey of attitudes, opinions and behaviors. *Journal of Safety Research*, 39, 303–309.

12

Actively Caring to Prevent
Alcohol Abuse

RYAN C. SMITH AND E. SCOTT GELLER

Alcohol gives you infinite patience for stupidity.
– Sammy Davis, Jr.

Makayla Greathouse, a Virginia Tech student in Professor Scott Geller's senior seminar on self-motivation in 2012, told this story:

> Danny Gilliam lived right above my apartment. We spent a lot of time hanging out. One Saturday night, Danny and his roommates were about to leave for a party. We shared several minutes of conversation and laughs, and they went on their way.
>
> Around 2:30 A.M. I saw a good friend crying outside of my apartment and immediately approached her to see what was wrong. The news knocked me off my feet. Danny Gilliam was dead.
>
> It took me days to process what happened. I watched his family move out his belongings with tear-streaked faces. I watched his roommates go through denial, anger and depression. Losing a roommate – a best friend – is heartbreaking. The mood of our building was solemn. It would take months for life to return to a new reality.

Makayla's good friend Michael had been at Whipple Drive, where the incident happened. Michael reported:

> I was at a friend's house and the party above us was huge, probably two hundred people. Suddenly everyone rushed out and we decided to see what had happened. We didn't see cop cars anywhere and when we asked the fleeing partiers what's going on, they just said, "Someone fell." I went around the building, and saw a body on the ground. Someone had fallen from a balcony while trying to climb the roof. Three friends were there, all in hysterics. I told someone to call 911 and as a first responder, I began CPR and checked his vitals. The police soon arrived

and performed CPR, as well. The guy didn't make it; we tried everything but it was too late.

Why did everyone flee the scene?

Makayla responded:

Many students who consume alcohol in college are underage; they are scared of getting caught. So many people were present; I'm sure many thought someone else would take care of Danny. Perhaps bystander apathy took place.

Proactive bystander intervention could have saved Danny's life that night. If someone had stopped him from climbing the balcony, he wouldn't have fallen. There are so many ways Danny could have been convinced to get down. Someone could have told him how dumb it was or said, "Hey, come get another drink with me," or "Come meet my friend."

A RECURRING TRAGEDY ON COLLEGE CAMPUSES

This tragic story at Virginia Tech represents only one of approximately 1,800 alcohol-related college student deaths in the United States each year. It seems unimaginable this could be a frequently recurring story. It seems impossible that in 2011 nearly four times more college students died as a result of alcohol consumption than Americans died in both the Iraq and Afghanistan wars combined during the same year.[1]

Not only do college students drink significantly more alcohol than their peers who don't attend a college or university, they are also more likely to drive under the influence of alcohol.[1] College alcohol consumption is such a major public-health concern that one of Healthy People 2010's major ten-year initiatives was to reduce the percentage of college students who binge-drink from 39 percent in 2000 to 20 percent by 2010.[2] Binge drinking is typically defined as consuming four standard alcoholic beverages in one sitting for a female and five standard alcoholic beverages for a male. This corresponds directly to the number of drinks linked to a host of negative outcomes.

Healthy People is sponsored by the U.S. Department of Health and Human Services as a ten-year blueprint to monitor and improve areas of extreme health risk. Unfortunately, during the decade spanning the Healthy People 2010 initiative, the percentage of binge drinkers actually increased to 44.7 percent.[1] Healthy People 2020 again set a reduction in college binge drinking as a major initiative, but this time the ten-year goal was 36.0 percent by 2020.[3] This target would still only barely reduce the percentage of binge drinkers 3 percent below the level of 39.0 percent in 2000.

Our nation's approach to decreasing alcohol use and abuse among college students calls for drastic behavior change. Innovative AC4P interventions are urgently needed. New ways of addressing this public-health risk with data-driven solutions must be embraced in order to make a beneficial difference. Traditional top-down directives and punitive enforcement tactics are not working. The Center for Applied Behavior Systems (CABS) at Virginia Tech has been at the forefront of research on this public-health crisis, pioneering creative ways to understand and address alcohol abuse from an AC4P perspective.

THE CENTER FOR APPLIED BEHAVIOR SYSTEMS

For more than twenty-five years CABS has studied alcohol use and abuse among university students. The Center has worked closely with various university organizations, including fraternities and sororities, to provide critical insight into this national problem. To date, CABS has received more than 3 million dollars in grant funding in this domain, published dozens of scientific publications, given hundreds of professional conference presentations, and received multiple community service awards for researching and preventing excessive alcohol consumption among college students.

These efforts and their promising outcomes stem from the unique perspective and approach of CABS. Specifically, the field research is demarcated by data collection in the very locations where people are drinking, and the intervention approaches are founded on applied behavioral science (ABS) and humanism – humanistic behaviorism. Some of this research and solution-relevant interventions are reviewed in this chapter.

Actively Caring for Alcohol Abuse

The research of CABS has uncovered promising areas for AC4P intervention. It's evident from the previously cited data that traditional top-down directives and policies that address college drinking are not sufficient. Paradigm shifts are required to reduce the significant harm from alcohol abuse among college students. But before we discuss these shifts, let's consider the research methodology of CABS, which has revealed many intervention challenges and at-risk consequences created by the college drinking culture. Perhaps most important, we assess actual levels of intoxication rather than rely on self-report, which has been used often in this research domain. Across all fields of psychological research, self-report is notorious for its inaccuracies.[4] For a variety of reasons, this is particularly true for alcohol research.

To ensure the accuracy of self-reported alcohol consumption and survey data, students must understand the alcohol concentration of their drinks and accurately recall each and every drink they consume. It's troubling that most alcohol research relies on students' understanding the precise definition of a standard drink in order to report the number of drinks consumed. Both research and common sense show that students clearly do not have this level of understanding.[5]

For instance, Virginia Tech students frequently consume a drink called a "Rail." Despite containing the amount of alcohol contained in more than five standard drinks, a Rail is often considered to be one alcoholic beverage. This impacts more than research accuracy when students think they are safe to drive because they only had one or two "drinks."

Self-reported alcohol consumption is also problematic due to the effects of fatigue, blacking out, and social desirability – all of which impede a drinker's ability and motivation to accurately recall and report the number of drinks s/he consumed.[6]

The CABS research is not limited by self-report. Armed with breathalyzers (the same used by police) and clipboards, dozens of undergraduate researchers give up their Thursday, Friday, and Saturday nights to visit fraternity parties, private parties, and downtown bars between the hours of 10:00 P.M. and 2:00 A.M. Yes, these students get academic research credit for collecting data at frat parties and downtown bars.

Three teams of four undergraduates set up assessment tables outside high-risk drinking locations. Two team members serve as data collectors who read survey questions to downtown passersby or partygoers and mark their responses. As shown in Figure 12.1, one researcher administers the breathalyzer to the participant after s/he completes the survey. The final researcher serves as a team leader to ensure all research assistants follow protocol.

Some results of these field efforts have been startling and revealing. Perhaps the most astonishing result is the average level of intoxication among students across all types of drinking settings. Specifically, during the past ten years of data collection, the average blood alcohol concentration (BAC) of drinkers was 0.082g/dL at private parties, 0.093g/dL at fraternity parties, and 0.087g/dL near bar establishments in downtown Blacksburg, home of Virginia Tech. This translates into the average drinker at all locations being above the per se legal limit (0.08 g/dL) to drive in all fifty states.

The increasing trend in average BACs among college students is also troubling. In 2007, the average downtown BAC was 0.087g/dL. Yet the five-year average downtown BAC from Fall 2009 to Fall 2014 was 0.102g/dL.

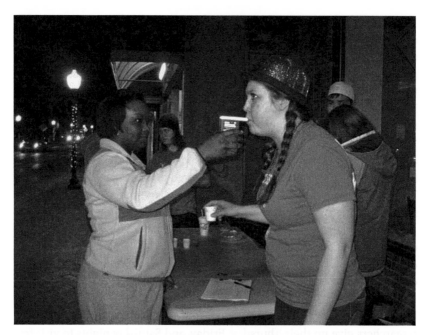

FIGURE 12.1. The process of assessing blood alcohol concentration.

Of more than 12,000 drinkers who were breathalyzed over those three years, nearly 15 percent were in fact twice the legal limit to drive or higher.

Another disappointing, yet consistent, finding is the lack of students' awareness regarding their level of intoxication. Results have consistently shown a weak relationship ($r < .15$) between a student's intended BAC and actual BAC as measured by the breathalyzer.[7] Students are wildly inaccurate in guessing their current level of intoxication. On average, students' estimates of their BAC are incorrect by 0.034g/dL. Ironically, students at lower BAC levels tend to *over*estimate their BAC, while students at higher BAC levels generally *under*estimate it.

These findings shed light on a dangerous drinking culture in which many college student drinkers are neither in control nor aware of their level of intoxication. But the work performed by CABS leads us to five research-inspired paradigm shifts we believe are critical to finding practical AC4P solutions to the nationwide quandary of alcohol abuse on college campuses.

Paradigm Shift 1: From Reactive Responding to Proactive Intervening

Makayla's story about Danny serves as a devastating demonstration of the negative consequences of acting *after* tragedy has struck. The reactive measures of performing CPR and calling 911 after Danny's fall showed competence and courage – AC4P behaviors indeed – but they came too late. If someone had merely talked to Danny about his excessive alcohol consumption, offered to take him home when he became obviously intoxicated, pulled him down from the balcony he was climbing, and encouraged his friends to look after him, he would be here today. If only someone had actively cared from a proactive stance.

Alcohol-abuse problems are almost always handled reactively. Parents, friends, and society in general adhere to the apparent misconception that alcohol-abuse problems need to be addressed only when someone gets caught or when a serious at-risk line is crossed. Problem drinkers go to counseling *after* they become dependent on alcohol or when excessive alcohol consumption interferes with interpersonal relationships. Parents speak to their children about drinking alcoholic beverages *after* they come stumbling home intoxicated, slurring words, or falling down, or after a call from police. Friends encourage friends to slow down their alcohol consumption only *after* they are obviously not in control of their own behavior. This delayed AC4P behavior is particularly dangerous when it comes to alcohol-impaired driving.

Alcohol-Impaired Driving. As detailed in Chapter 11, the consequences of drunk driving are self-evident and appalling. In 2013, alcohol-impaired driving resulted in 10,076 deaths.[8] In fact, more than 30 percent of all traffic fatalities are the result of alcohol-impaired driving.[9] Penalties for drunk driving vary by state, but a similar reactive approach is applied nationwide. Until a drunk driver is caught by police or is involved in a vehicle crash, very little of consequence happens to a drunk driver. This reactive approach has consistently failed to reduce the number of alcohol-impaired drivers on our nation's roadways.

The effectiveness of these reactive measures is further called into question due to their rare enforcement. The Centers for Disease Control and Prevention (CDC) estimates the average first offender drives drunk at least eighty times prior to his/her first conviction.[10] Regardless of the type of reactive punitive measures imposed, drunk-driving recidivism is extremely high.[11] It has been estimated that between 50 and 75 percent of those whose licenses are suspended because of alcohol-impaired driving continue to drive, sometimes while intoxicated.[12]

Our CABS research sheds a similar dispiriting light on just how deep-rooted the problem of drunk driving really is. In the past five years CABS researchers have surveyed and breathalyzed more than 500 designated drivers (DDs) in downtown Blacksburg. During this time, we found

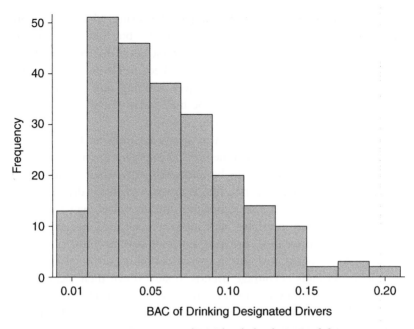

FIGURE 12.2. Frequency of BAC levels for designated drivers.

that more than 60 percent of DDs consumed alcohol. The average BAC of these alcohol-consuming DDs was 0.061g/dL. Considering impairment begins at 0.05g/dL or less, this means the average DD was at increased risk for a vehicle crash.

Figure 12.2 shows the BAC distribution of over 500 DDs who had consumed some alcohol on the night their BAC was assessed. Nearly 70 percent of these DDs had BACs over 0.05g/dL. Greater than 25 percent of these DDs had BACs over 0.08g/dL. There was even a DD with a BAC of 0.201g/dL. Many of these individuals said they were chosen as the DDs because they "were the least intoxicated." Thus, the selection of a DD is too often reactive rather than proactive, as well as flawed by poor judgment.

These high BACs are particularly troubling because university students are generally unaware of their BAC. Indeed, CABS research has found that 39.8 percent of self-reporting drivers with a measured BAC over 0.08g/dL believed they were actually under the legal limit to drive of 0.08g/dL.[13] This is strongly indicative of the need for a proactive intervention for DDs. These DDs should be assigned at the beginning of the night, before drinking begins. It must be emphasized that a true DD does not consume any alcohol. Reactively selecting as a DD the person who seems "least drunk" is inappropriate and risky.

A proactive approach to preventing alcohol-impaired driving is obviously needed. Society cannot simply rely on reactive legal consequences to sober up drivers. AC4P agents are needed to intervene proactively with AC4P behavior. This could involve taking someone's keys, calling a taxi, or arranging some alternative form of transportation. Also, a shift toward being proactive in selecting our DDs is needed. People simply cannot wait until everyone is intoxicated before making such a critical and too often misguided decision.

Sure, it can be uncomfortable to take keys from a friend or stranger, or to bring up the topic of a DD before the drinking begins; but remember AC4P is all about looking out for other people's health, safety, and well-being. It's about not letting friends, people we just met, or even total strangers put themselves and others in harm's way. It's about having the courage and self-motivation to take a proactive AC4P step toward preventing a tragedy.

Paradigm Shift 2: From Penalizing to Rewarding

Traditional approaches to reducing alcohol use and abuse focus almost entirely on penalizing the drinker. This makes sense; after all it's convenient and efficient to resort to punishment. When people who are driving while intoxicated (DWI) get pulled over by police, there is a law to penalize them. When people consume too many alcoholic beverages in public, police can penalize them by throwing them into the "drunk tank." If adolescents come home intoxicated, parents have a variety of penalties they can levy.

Punishment is logical, convenient, and at times necessary. It's foolish to argue for removing all punitive consequences. However, punishment often backfires and produces unintended attitudinal and behavioral consequences, as discussed in Chapter 1. Critical to this discussion is the distinction between *punishers* and *penalties*.

Punishers versus Penalties. Penalties are negative consequences intended to decrease or discourage a designated undesirable behavior. Punishers are consequences that actually decrease the probability the behavior they follow will recur. Penalties do not necessarily decrease the occurrence of the target behavior. Punishers by definition decrease the frequency of the behavior they follow.

This distinction might seem unimportant, but several implications are worth noting. It's often assumed penalties are punishers. But consider that a seemingly undesirable consequence does not necessarily have the desired effect. Some penalties actually create resentment, which can *reinforce* or increase the very behavior they were intended to stop.[14] A top-down threat issued by an authority figure, for example, can activate behavior contrary to the intention of the rule, as illustrated below.

Another key distinction: Punishers target a specific behavior; penalties target an individual. We say a certain person was *penalized* for a certain action. Actually that action was *punished* if the consequence decreased the frequency of the behavior it followed. Effective punishers typically follow an undesirable behavior immediately and are clearly linked to that behavior. On the other hand, penalties are often delayed and target the individual for misbehaving. This personalization is often internalized and can activate reactance or motivation to perform the undesired behavior more often.[14]

Parenting and Alcohol Consumption. Consider penalties used by parents to "punish" their children for consuming alcohol. CABS research tracked the current alcohol consumption of more than 300 college students and asked them about their parents' strategies for confronting the students'

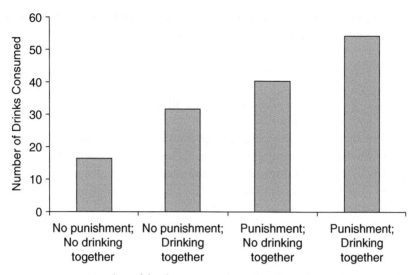

FIGURE 12.3. Number of drinks consumed as a function of parenting method.

alcohol consumption when they were in high school. The parents used a variety of penalties, including a curfew, no access to television/phone, no time with friends, chores, and even physical consequences. Yet across all types of punitive strategies one consistent finding emerged. Students who were penalized for drinking alcohol in high school consumed significantly more alcohol in college than students who were not penalized.

It could be that students who were penalized in high school for drinking consumed more alcohol in college because they drank more alcoholic beverages in the first place. However, when our statistical tests controlled for the amount of alcohol consumed in high school, this observed relationship between high school penalties and college drinking still held. The penalties backfired. Parental "punishment" for alcohol consumption was not punishment at all.

As shown in Figure 12.3, this effect was even greater if parents let their children drink, but only with them. College students were asked if they were punished for drinking in high school and if they were allowed to consume alcohol only with their parents. Students fell into the four categories along the x-axis of Figure 12.3. The y-axis shows the average frequency of drinks consumed in the previous two weeks. As can be seen, not only did those students penalized for drinking in high school consume more alcohol in college, but this effect was even greater if parents allowed their children to drink with them.

We call this phenomenon an *interpersonal hypocrisy effect*, distinct from the *intra*personal hypocrisy researched earlier by social psychologists and explained later in Chapter 19.[15] *Inter*personal hypocrisy means the person penalized perceives an inconsistency in the behavior of the individual administrating the penalty. In this case, the parents were hypocritical because they penalized selectively (i.e., allowed alcohol consumption at home but not elsewhere).

Note that the *behavior* of underage drinking is not punished by parents who allow alcohol consumption under their own supervision. When these students are penalized for drinking elsewhere, the penalty is internalized. It's no longer about the *behavior*, and this can create resentment and confusion, and actually lead to increased drinking in college. Interestingly, this same hypocrisy effect was observed if parents kept alcohol in the house and penalized their children for alcohol consumption.

This research does not inform parents to refrain from using punitive consequences, especially when it comes to underage drinking. It says, instead, mothers and fathers should not wait until after their child starts drinking alcoholic beverages before starting AC4P parenting on this life-and-death issue. The AC4P Movement advocates rewarding your child for smart, healthy behaviors, rather than just punishing undesirable behavior. As explained in Chapter 1, sometimes the best way to eliminate undesirable behavior is to reward desirable behavior that is incompatible with alcohol consumption.

Parents should not just punish their children for drinking, but encourage them to develop positive friendships with those who do not consume alcohol. Adolescents should be encouraged to attend events and gatherings where alcoholic beverages are not served. The AC4P Movement is about developing positive AC4P relationships and finding opportunities to proactively facilitate desirable behaviors with positive attention and support.

Alcohol Abuse at Fraternity Parties. Fraternity parties are among the most notorious college environments for excessive alcohol consumption. CABS researchers have observed a wide variety of outlandish behaviors and outrageous themes in fraternity houses that set the stage for abusing alcohol. A few of the observed party themes included Mardi Gras, Cowboys and Indians, Bosses and Secretaries, Teachers and School Girls, and Around the World, in which each fraternity room contains alcohol specific to a certain country. Several themes were too inappropriate to put in print.

As expected, our field research showed the average BAC to be markedly higher at fraternity parties than at any other typical drinking location.

In our sample of 1,525 university students at nineteen separate parties, we found BACs were significantly higher at fraternity parties (BAC = 0.093g/dL) than non-fraternity, private parties (BAC = 0.082g/dL).[16] Along the same lines, fraternity brothers at fraternity parties had a significantly higher BAC than fraternity brothers at private parties. More than just the drinking tendencies of fraternity brothers themselves, it could be the environment of fraternity parties that drives at-risk drinking. We also found BACs tend to be higher at fraternity parties than in downtown Blacksburg bars, even during "alcoholidays" such as Halloween and St. Patrick's Day.[17]

Colleges and universities annually make significant investments in time and money to tackle at-risk drinking at fraternity parties. Similarly, CABS has spent years conducting intervention research aimed at preventing alcohol abuse at Virginia Tech fraternity parties. We have tried every positive approach imaginable, from education to one-on-one demonstrations with behavioral feedback.

For one intervention, we tried a simple educational approach. Research assistants (RAs) passed out educational cards to drinkers. These cards contained tips for keeping a "buzzed" but safe level of intoxication. The cards also had a BAC chart on the back to help individuals figure out how many drinks it would take to reach a desired BAC. Unfortunately, this approach proved wholly ineffective at reducing BACs.

We also tried setting up sobriety stations at fraternity parties. These stations provided traditional sobriety tests and a few dexterity-based games. For one of these simple tests, participants placed their thumb and index finger an inch apart while an RA dropped a ruler between their two fingers. Participants could see how many inches the ruler fell before they were able to catch it with their fingers. This exercise clearly demonstrated the severe effect of alcohol on reaction time, but it had no effect on reducing BACs, as measured when partygoers exited the fraternity parties at the end of the night.

We even served pizzas and provided nonalcoholic beverages at some fraternity parties. Food slows the absorption of alcohol, and nonalcoholic drinks help individuals pace their level of alcohol consumption. Yet again, even this approach was ineffective at reducing the intoxication of partygoers.

In all the years we attempted to reduce at-risk drinking at fraternity parties by various means, only one tactic was effective at reducing the mean BAC of party participants as they exited the fraternity house. Instead of focusing on the negative consequences of alcohol consumption, CABS

WIN $100 TONIGHT!	WIN $100 TONIGHT!
	Virginia Tech researchers wil be giving free BAC (blood alcohol concentration) assessments tonight.
Virginia Tech researchers wil be giving free BAC (blood alcohol concentration) assessments tonight.	If your BAC is **below .05**, you will be registered in a drawing for $100 to be given away tonight.
If you choose to participate, you will be registered in a drawing for $100 to be given away **tonight**.	Here are some tips to help you keep a safe buzz: * Drink a glass of water between each alcoholic beverage * Snack on food before and while drinking * Partake in physical activity, life dancing * Use the attached chart to estimate a safe number of drinks.

FIGURE 12.4. The flyers handed to partygoers entering the Control parties (left) and the Incentive parties (right).

researchers rewarded partygoers for their low-risk alcohol consumption. This created a fun and effective technique for reducing the rates of at-risk drinking.

The success of this intervention was assessed with two field studies. In each study, fraternity parties were divided into Control parties and Incentive parties. At the Control parties, partygoers were informed they would be entered into a raffle for $100 at the end of the night simply by having their BAC taken. At Intervention parties, partygoers were informed they could be entered into a raffle for $100 if their BAC was below 0.05g/dL at the end of the night. These two conditions were defined on flyers handed out to each partygoer as s/he entered the party location (see Figure 12.4).

In our first study of this incentive/reward intervention, BACs were assessed at the end of the night at four consecutive parties at the same fraternity. The first two parties served as Baseline or Control parties, and the final two parties served as Incentive parties. As shown in Figure 12.5, partygoers at the Incentive parties had significantly lower BACs. Also, significantly greater numbers of drinkers were below the critical BAC benchmarks of 0.050g/dL and 0.080g/dL at the Incentive versus Control parties.[18]

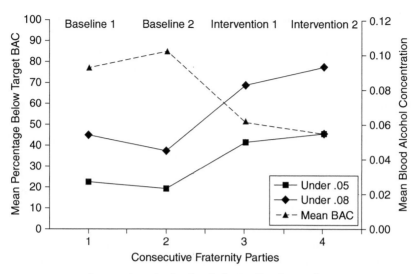

FIGURE 12.5. Average intoxication levels during Baseline and Incentive parties.

The results of this study were replicated in a larger follow-up study of 207 participants at six different parties at six different fraternities. The significant beneficial impact of the incentive/reward intervention was demonstrated. While individuals at three Control parties had a mean BAC of 0.098g/dL, individuals at the three Incentive parties had a significantly lower BAC average of 0.079g/dL. Furthermore, while 40.1 percent of participants at the three Control parties were over the legal limit to drive at 0.08g/dL, 30.6 percent of participants in the Incentive condition were over the legal limit to drive.[19]

Again, all interventions based on education and negative consequences from alcohol abuse were ineffective at reducing alcohol consumption among college students. However, a focus on positive consequences for desirable behavior reduced at-risk drinking at one of the most challenging and high-risk environments – fraternity parties. Several partygoers (especially women) who did not expect to win the cash prize reported an appreciation for the lottery because it gave them an excuse to turn down an alcoholic beverage.

Are you thinking this successful intervention for reducing alcohol abuse at the next party you host is impractical? Well, consider that the cash price for this incentive/reward intervention could be obtained from party participants as a request for donations. A slotted "prize money" box at the party entrance with the sign "Please donate cash for the end-of-the-party lottery" would not only prompt partygoers to read the flyer with contest specifics and then donate some cash; it might also lower the rate of alcohol consumption for some individuals. The only expense would be a BAC breathalyzer (which could be borrowed from the local police department at no cost) and the response cost of measuring the BAC of partygoers interested in participating in the lottery. We have found that most partygoers greatly appreciate receiving BAC feedback from a breathalyzer.

The awareness activated by such an intervention regarding an AC4P mission to reduce excessive alcohol consumption and the likely reduction in the rate of drinking by some partygoers are consequences well worth the small monetary cost and the inconvenience of implementing this incentive/reward contingency at a large party where alcoholic beverages are served. Plus, imagine if the reduced alcohol abuse motivated by your AC4P intervention prevented a serious injury or fatality caused by excessive alcohol consumption at your party. This positive approach to preventing harm from intoxication would set the kind of effective AC4P example people need to see and talk about.

Paradigm Shift 3: From Good Intentions to Data-Driven Solutions

Alcohol interventions often involve the misconception that good intentions produce good results. Just because an intervention makes sense or sounds good doesn't mean it works in practice. As we are fond of saying, "Without data you're just a jerk with an opinion." Yet too many attempts to prevent alcohol abuse are based on someone's common sense rather than empirical evidence.

AC4P is not just about feeling good or blindly trying to help people. Effective AC4P behavior requires that AC4P change agents be knowledgeable about the problem, the relevant intervention research, and the people they are trying to influence or help. Hope and caring cannot substitute for data-driven interventions.

Multiple empirical studies demonstrate this very point. The parental punishment study detailed above provides a relevant example. Well-intentioned parents without proper knowledge mistakenly increase their children's alcohol consumption, thus putting them at risk, through misguided penalty strategies. Unfortunately, this result is quite common for interventions designed to reduce harm from excessive alcohol consumption. Consider, for example, the variety of interventions designed by well-intentioned high school faculty and staff to reduce alcohol consumption among students on prom night. These have included awareness assemblies, pledge cards, and school-sponsored after-prom parties.

One of the most noteworthy of these interventions makes use of Fatal Vision® goggles. When worn, these popular and expensive goggles ($150) simulate alcohol impairment of a certain level. In the intervention we investigated, students wore these goggles while driving a golf cart around a course marked by traffic cones. A sheriff's deputy sat in the passenger seat of the golf cart to answer students' questions.

This is an innovative and common intervention at high schools and universities. Students at the event we studied had a great time, laughing hysterically while their peers veered around the course. By all "feel-good" indicators this was a huge success. School administrators felt strongly about repeating this event annually. Unfortunately, our data pointed to a very different reality than their perceptions. Students who attended the goggles event were nearly twice as likely to report consuming alcohol on prom night than were their peers who had not attended the event. This significant difference held even when we controlled for students' previous alcohol consumption.

Of course, one field study is insufficient and inconclusive. Follow-up studies are needed before we can draw strong conclusions that "drunk goggles" increase students' consumption of alcoholic beverages. However, our underlying point is that despite well-intentioned efforts, many programs, interventions, treatments, and therapies lack practical effectiveness. Even worse, many of these efforts could actually promote the very behavior they are designed to decrease.

Bottom line: Compassion, caring, and empowerment are fundamental to making a difference through AC4P principles and applications, but these motivating person-states must be supplemented with empirical results from relevant research.

Paradigm Shift 4: From Blame to Empathy

We offer this paradigm shift with a point of caution. It's not intended to remove all responsibility from the drinker, but to encourage greater thoughtfulness regarding the effect alcohol has on the body. For example, many alcoholics have a strong desire to remove alcohol from their lives. Most are deeply troubled by the hurt they cause those around them through their drinking. In this case, simply blaming a drinker without considering the addictive properties of alcohol lacks compassion and does not suggest feasible intervention strategies.

Throughout this book, the importance of dispositional variables (e.g., person-states), situational variables (e.g., environmental context and behavioral consequences), and their interaction are revealed. AC4P is about taking the time and effort to understand each of these determinants of human behavior. It's easy to blame a person for his/her behavior, but this is rarely an effective platform for offering effective help. Well-intentioned AC4P behavior requires sufficient empathy to see the complete picture and the compassion to act accordingly.

This is certainly true for alcohol-affected behavior. Alcohol consumption provides a context and a physiological change that makes many good people do bad things. This is the case not only for individuals addicted to alcohol, but for all persons with alcohol in their system. Most people have experienced or observed the negative effects of intoxication. Physical impairment is a consequence. Drunks may stumble, fall, or slur their words. Mental impairment is a consequence. Those intoxicated may have trouble remembering the occasion; they may say inappropriate things, and their cognitive ability may temporarily decline.

However, few people consider just how significant and fundamental these changes can be for an individual. Few people realize how profoundly someone's perceptions can be altered after only a few drinks. CABS research on sexual assault and victimization provides some relevant evidence.

Sexual Assault and Alcohol Consumption. It's estimated an astonishing one in four women experience some form of sexual assault or victimization in college.[20] In approximately 85–90 percent of these sexual assaults the victim knew her attacker.[21] What's not surprising is that almost all of these incidents involved alcohol.[22] It's easy to blame the perpetrator of these horrendous acts, and this is understandable. But a more comprehensive analysis is required to address this problem with any hope of reducing the number of sexual assaults and victimizations.

If we examine only the people who commit such acts we ignore reality and context. Most of these individuals are at least slightly intoxicated at the time of the assault. This is hardly coincidental, but rather a result, in part, of the effects of alcohol. CABS research provides evidence for this phenomenon across two studies.

In one study, 1,240 drinkers were read a brief vignette by a trained researcher. This story described a fictional, alcohol-related sexual assault between two characters – Steve and Julie. In the most extreme vignette, Steve has sex with Julie while she is completely incapacitated by alcohol. After hearing the vignette, researchers then asked participants several questions about the story.

Even those participants at very low levels of intoxication (BACs ≈ 0.020g/dL) were significantly more likely than completely sober individuals to say the sexual assault and victimization was not a rape, that Steve was not responsible, and that this was a consensual encounter. Individuals with higher BACs were not more immoral; rather alcohol drastically changed their perception of the situation.

Recognizing Facial Emotions. Another CABS study examined the impact of alcohol consumption on the recognition of facial emotions. One's ability to quickly recognize emotions is viewed as a fundamental social skill, but is often taken for granted. In this study, researchers showed 695 participants pictures of several faces from a validated facial emotion database and asked them to guess the emotion depicted.

On various trials the photo exposure was manipulated between one second versus three seconds and included one face versus two faces. In the Two-Faces condition, one face served as a distracter and researchers asked for the perceived emotion of the second face. Participants who had consumed alcohol performed significantly worse than those who consumed no alcohol at identifying the negative emotions of *disgust* and *surprise*.

This inability to detect certain facial emotions was present even at low BACs, and offers an explanation for the initiation and continuance of inappropriate sexual advances in a drinking setting. The antagonist may quite literally not be able to detect the negative reaction of the victim. This suggests negative facial expressions are not sufficient to ward off unwanted harassment from an intoxicated individual. The courage to verbalize direct disapproval is likely necessary.

Again, the purpose of this paradigm shift is not to justify inexcusable behavior, but rather to encourage AC4P intervention agents to consider the entire context of the alcohol consumption. Alcohol can have many pleasing effects, but it can also be the source of addiction and undesirable behavior change. AC4P means going beyond the simple solution of blaming the drinker. It's about being empathic and showing compassion for the victims of alcohol. And this includes the drinker.

Paradigm Shift 5: From Overreliance on Technology to AC4P Behavior

Technology is rapidly overwhelming our world. Instead of finding time to meet people at a coffee shop, we often send them a quick text or impersonal message on Facebook. After all, who needs to spend an in-person moment with a single friend when we can quickly connect with 1,000 Facebook friends? We often think about tweetable moments and Snapchat pictures rather than the value of connecting in person with those presently near us.

It's disheartening to imagine the number of times someone in the office next door sends a question over instant message or email rather than walk a few feet to engage in a one-to-one conversation. Social media and technology have become what connects us, how we think, and how we spend our time. Unfortunately, technology has also become a crutch for solving social problems, including excessive alcohol consumption.

Consider how often we defer to the supposed power of technology rather than implement AC4P principles. Reflect on the number of opportunities to help others that were snatched away because either we were too busy with our electronic world or we thought technology would do the work for us. Technology not only creates a distraction and safety risk (e.g., texting while driving), but also gives us an easy out to believe it's not our responsibility to intervene or help others. Common sense and research evidence both paint a grim picture regarding the new ways people interact with both technology and each other. This problem extends well beyond the issue of alcohol abuse.

The horrible reality of sexual assaults on college and university campuses has already been described. Let's consider how technology has addressed this critical human problem. In 2014, the state of California enacted the "yes means yes" law. This law requires both parties in a sexual situation to verbally consent to having sex. Nonverbal cues no longer suffice. This chapter has already detailed the shortcomings of merely writing laws to address societal issues. A law helps formalize societal standards or social norms, but does anyone really believe legislation can completely stop sexual assaults, particularly when alcohol is involved?

Once again, technology has "come to the rescue" to support this legislative top-down directive to control human behavior. Numerous phone applications now tackle college and university sexual assault. One app is "Good2Go." Both interested sexual parties whip out their smartphones and respond to whether they are "Good2Go?" Responding Good2Go means your consent to the sexual activity is recorded and logged by the phone application. The app also asks potential partners if they are intoxicated. If the user self-selects s/he is wasted, the phone application tells the person s/he cannot provide consent for sexual activity. The app also reminds participants sexual consent can be withdrawn at any time.

While well-intended, can a phone application contribute to stopping the horror stories of sexual assault on our college campuses? Will this help young females at university parties protect themselves while they are at near black-out levels of intoxication? We are convinced interpersonal AC4P communication is key to successful prevention, but not with impersonal technology. People need to protect themselves, be alert when they know alcohol is involved, have honest and candid AC4P conversations with a potential sexual partner prior to alcohol consumption, and have the courage to intervene when they observe a friend or stranger in a precarious situation – be they a potential victim or potential antagonist.

Phone applications have also been developed to inform people when they are too intoxicated to drive. In fact, CABS systematically evaluated eight of the most popular BAC-estimation phone applications (four Android; four iPhone). These apps usually require users to enter how long they've been drinking, the number of drinks they've consumed, their gender, and their weight. Then the app provides an estimated BAC to the user. These phone applications have reported hundreds of thousands of downloads by users throughout the United States.

We tested their accuracy among 583 participants. Our RAs helped the participants enter their drinking information. The estimate provided was then compared with the BAC obtained via a breathalyzer. To our surprise and disappointment, the average phone application was incorrect by 0.043g/dL. Furthermore, if the user had a BAC over the legal limit to drive, on 14.2 percent of these occasions the phone application told the individual s/he was actually *under* the legal limit. Sadly, it's often considered easier to trust an app to say you are safe to drive than to call a taxi or trust a friend.

When technology advances faster than people's ability to cope with advancement, technology can have negative consequences. Overreliance on various technologies has dramatically diminished human-to-human connections. We need to move beyond our many behavior-controlling screens (e.g., television, phone, computer, car display) and reach out to people with an AC4P mindset. It's people who give our lives purpose and meaning, and it's people who have the power to help other people in need.

IN CONCLUSION

To seriously address the extreme rates of alcohol consumption at colleges and universities, drastic changes are called for. The paradigm shifts detailed in this chapter reflect a general blueprint for making AC4P behavior a significant part of the solution.

Reactive, punitive, and rarely research-based laws and the legal system will not curb the prevalence of excessive alcohol consumption among college students. The optimum solution is the cultivation of AC4P cultures. The AC4P Movement calls on all of us to take personal responsibility and ownership of this serious societal problem.

Danny's life was lost because no bystander had the compassion and courage to step to the plate and actively care. Don't ask why there is a college binge-drinking culture; ask why more people are not willing to actively care for those around them. Every alcohol-related death is preventable. We have the power to drive alcohol-related college deaths to zero. Traditional top-down and punitive interventions are not working well. But the more effective humanistic behaviorism approach requires AC4P behavior from people – people with the competence, commitment, and courage to intervene when they perceive others at risk for injury to themselves or others due to alcohol abuse.

Are you ready and willing to help? Are you committed to go beyond the call of duty and intervene proactively before words are slurred, coordination is lost, judgment is fogged, and the legal limit of alcohol consumption is surpassed?

DISCUSSION QUESTIONS

1. Describe the typical protocol used by CABS (Center for Applied Behavior Systems) to study alcohol abuse in the community. What

are the advantages (if any) of this approach over the more standard research in this domain?

2. What evidence suggests the designated-driver approach to the DWI problem is not as successful as expected and desired?

3. What's the difference (if any) between a penalty and a punisher?

4. Explain the relationship between parenting and alcohol abuse among university students, as discovered by the CABS researchers.

5. List the various intervention strategies implemented and evaluated by the CABS researchers to reduce intoxication at fraternity parties.

6. Which intervention approach was markedly successful at reducing intoxication at fraternity parties?

7. Provide a critical evaluation (positive and negative) of the successful intervention used to reduce alcohol abuse and intoxication at fraternity parties. Why or why not is this approach practical?

8. Discuss the role of empathy in understanding and preventing alcohol abuse and its negative side effects.

9. To what extent do you believe alcoholism is a disease?

10. How does the AC4P Movement relate to the prevention of alcohol abuse and its negative side effects?

REFERENCES

1. Hingson, R. W., Zha, W., & Weitzman, E. R. (2009). Magnitude of and trends in alcohol-related mortality and morbidity among U.S. college students ages 18–24: 1998–2005. *Journal of Studies on Alcohol and Drugs*, Suppl. 16, 12–20; Slutske, W. S. (2005).Alcohol use disorders among U.S. college students and their non-college-attending peers. *Archives of General Psychiatry*, 62, 321–327; Slutske, W. S., Hunter-Carter, E. E., Nabors-Oberg, R. E., Sher, K. J., Bucholz, K. K., Madden, A. A., et al. (2004). Do college students drink more than their non-college-attending peers? Evidence from a population-based longitudinal female twin study. *Journal of Abnormal Psychology*, 113(4), 530–540.

2. U. S. Department of Health and Human Services. (2000). *Healthy People 2010*. Washington, DC: USD-HHS, pp. 26–29.

3. U.S. Department of Health and Human Services. *Healthy People 2020*. Washington, DC. Retrieved from http://www.healthypeople.gov/2020/topicsobjectives2020/pdfs/HP2020objectives.pdf.

4. Schwarz, N. (2007). *Retrospective and concurrent self-reports: The rationale for real-time data capture*. In A. A. Stone, S. S. Shiffman, A. Atienza, & L. Nebeling (Eds.). *The science of real-time data capture: Self-reports in health research* (pp. 11–26). New York: Oxford University Press; Schwarz, N. (1999). Self-reports: How the questions shape the answers. *American Psychologist*, 54, 93–105.

5. Kerr, W. C., & Stockwell, T. (2012). Understanding standard drinks and drinking guidelines. *Drug and Alcohol Review*, 2, 200–205; Lemmens, P. H. (1994). The alcohol content of self-report and "standard" drinks. *Addiction*, 89, 593–601.

6. Shillington, A. M., Clapp, J. D., Reed, M. B., & Woodruff, S. I. (2011). Adolescent alcohol use self-report stability: A decade of panel study data. *Journal of Child & Adolescent Substance Abuse*, 20, 63–81; Waterton, J. J., & Duffy, J. C. (1984). A comparison of computer interviewing techniques and traditional methods in the collection of self-report alcohol consumption data in a field study. *International Statistical Review*, 52(2), 173–182; Whitford, J. L., Widner, S. C., Mellick, D., & Elkins, R. L. (2009). Self-report of drinking compared to objective markers of alcohol consumption. *American Journal of Drug and Alcohol Abuse*, 35, 55–58.

7. Smith, R. C., Bowdring, M. A., & Geller, E. S. (2015). Predictors of at-risk intoxication in a university field setting: Social anxiety, demographics, and intentions. *Journal of American College Health*, 63(2), 134–142.

8. National Highway Traffic Safety Administration (2014). *Alcohol-impaired driving*. DOT HS 812 102. Department of Transportation. Retrieved from www-nrd.nhtsa.dot.gov/Pubs/811606.pdf.

9. National Highway Traffic Safety Administration (2004). *Traffic safety facts: Young drivers*. DOT HS 809 774. Department of Transportation. Retrieved from http://www-nrd.nhtsa.dot.gov/pdf/nrd-30/NCSA/TSF2003/809774.pdf.

10. Centers for Disease Control and Prevention (2011). *Vital Signs: Alcohol-impaired driving among adults – United States, 2010*. Retrieved from www.cdc.gov/mmwr/preview/mmwrhtml/mm6039a4.htm.

11. Rauch, W. J., Zador, P. L., Ahlin, E. M., Howard, J. M., Frissell, K. C., & Duncan, G. D. (2010). Risk of alcohol-impaired driving recidivism among first offenders and multiple offenders. *American Journal of Public Health*, 100(5), 919–924; Rauch, W. J., Zador, P. L., Ahlin, E. M., et al. (2002). Any first alcohol-impaired driving event is a significant and substantial predictor of future recidivism. In R. Daniel, Mayhew and C. Dussault (Eds.). *Proceedings of the 16th International Conference on Alcohol, Drugs and Traffic Safety*. Montreal: Council on Alcohol, Drugs and Traffic Safety, pp. 161–167.

12. Nichols, J. L., & Ross, H. L. (1990). The effectiveness of legal sanctions in dealing with drinking drivers. *Alcohol, Drugs and Driving*, 6(2), 33–55.

13. Smith, R. C., & Geller, E. S. (2014). Field investigation of college student alcohol intoxication and return transportation from at-risk drinking locations. *Transportation Research Record*, 2425(1), 67–73.

14. Brehm, S. S., & Brehm, J. W. (1981). *Psychological reactance: A theory of freedom and control*. New York: Academic Press

15. Aronson, E., Wilson, T. D., & Akert, R. M. (2013). *Social psychology* (8th ed.). Upper Saddle River, NJ: Pearson Education.

16. Glindemann, K. E., & Geller, E. S. (2003). A systematic assessment of intoxication at university parties: Effects of the environmental context. *Environment and Behavior*, 35(5), 655–664.

17. Glindemann, K. E., Wiegand, D. M., & Geller, E. S. (2007). Celebratory drinking and intoxication: A contextual influence on alcohol consumption. *Environment and Behavior*, 39(3), 352–366.

18. Fournier, A. K., Ehrhart, I. J., Glindemann, K. E., & Geller, E. S. (2004). Intervening to decrease alcohol abuse at university parties: Differential reinforcement of intoxication level. *Behavior Modification*, 28, 167–181.

19. Glindeman, K. E., Ehrhart, I. J., Drake, E. A., & Geller, E. S. (2006). Reducing excessive alcohol consumption at university fraternity parties: A cost-effective incentive/reward intervention. *Addictive Behaviors*, 32(1), 39–48.

20. U.S. Department of Justice: Office of Justice Programs (2005). *Sexual assault on campus: What colleges and universities are doing about it.* Retrieved from https:// www.ncjrs.gov/pdffiles1/nij/205521.pdf.

21. Koss, M. C., Gidycz, C., & Wisniewski, N. (1987). The scope of rape: Incidence and prevalence of sexual aggression and victimization in a national sample of higher education students. *Journal of Consulting and Clinical Psychology*, 55(2), 162–170.

22. Abbey, A., McAuslan, P., & Ross, L. T. (1998). Sexual assault perpetration by college men: The role of alcohol, misperception of sexual intent, and sexual beliefs and experiences. *Journal of Social and Clinical Psychology*, 17, 167–195.

13

Actively Caring for Obesity

SALLIE BETH JOHNSON AND E. SCOTT GELLER

If we don't succeed in turning this epidemic around, we are going to face, for the first time in our history, a situation where our children are going to live shorter lives than we do.
– Francis S. Collins

I've always had struggles with my food and weight. But now, I know how to read these labels and only eat when I'm hungry. I'm eating less of that junk food and cooking more fresh food. That Healthy Living class got me going! My family is going to the Farmer's Market. We go to the park and get our steps. So far, I've lost 20 pounds and got my sugar under control. We're all just feelin' great.

These are the words of a participant in the Healthy Living in the Mid-Carolinas (HLMC) program.[1] As a health educator, Sallie Beth reflects with joy and curiosity on the beneficial behavior changes shared in success stories like this one. This participant reports making healthier choices, achieving her health goals, and involving her family. Yet we wonder if she will be able to keep the pounds off. We also wonder why more families aren't successful at adopting healthier lifestyles.

Designed to help people get active, eat healthy, and give up tobacco, HLMC is a lifestyle preventive health program. Offered by FirstHealth of Carolina's Community Health Services (FirstHealth),[2] this behavior-change program aims to reduce high rates of chronic diseases, such as heart disease, cancer, and diabetes. For nine years, Sallie Beth drove the FirstHealth "Green Machine" station wagon pictured in Figure 13.1. With more than 100,000 miles on its odometer, this station wagon helped spread strategies for adopting a healthy lifestyle in rural communities throughout North Carolina.

Sallie Beth's Green Machine – loaded with fresh fruits and vegetables, step counters, hula hoops, and stress balls – stopped at churches, schools,

FIGURE 13.1. The "Green Machine" station wagon.

and community centers. During these visits, she facilitated HLMC classes where participants performed "check our pace" walks to make sure they were reaching a health-benefiting level of physical activity, practiced cooking healthy meals, and devised quit-smoking plans to deal with the "nicotine crazies."

The tremendous fun and feel-good rewards associated with serving as a health educator on the frontlines were counterbalanced by all-too-common frustration and heartache. Sallie Beth quickly experienced the many challenges involved in motivating others to make lifestyle changes. It's especially difficult to help people lose weight and keep it off. Sallie Beth also witnessed firsthand the toll of unhealthy behaviors on the quality of life of children and adults, especially those living in lower socioeconomic sections of communities. Serving with a team of five other health educators was clearly insufficient for effecting positive large-scale lifestyle changes. Indeed, the change agents had difficulty maintaining an optimistic attitude about their health-promotion efforts. The need for a more effective macrobehavior-change system was obvious.

AN INTRODUCTION TO AC4P

Sallie Beth enrolled in the doctorate program at Virginia Tech in the Department of Human Nutrition, Foods and Exercise in 2012, interested in combining her frontline experiences with research and developing her communication skills in order to train the next generation of health educators. As a graduate student, she was introduced to the Actively Caring for People (AC4P) Movement and the value of applying humanistic behaviorism to the development and implementation of sustainable behavior-change interventions. "Here's the special ingredient that's missing. We need to try a new recipe for promoting healthy lifestyles," she thought.

A number of health-promotion programs effectively incorporate vision, goal setting, and program planning, but the power of consequences and the AC4P principles needed to influence behavior change are absent. Are people giving each other enough supportive and corrective feedback for individuals to initiate and maintain health-related behaviors? Does an individual's sense of independence trump the power of interdependence among people when it comes to health-related lifestyles? Obviously, we need more people going beyond the call of duty on behalf of the health and welfare of others. We need to cultivate a culture of compassion for wellness. We need the AC4P Movement to incorporate actively caring for a healthy lifestyle.

This chapter shares how the AC4P principles can be applied to one of the world's most significant health problems – the "obesity epidemic." First, we provide background on the complexities of obesity, including causes and consequences of this condition. Then we describe potential solutions, including our adaptation of an international health-counseling model to incorporate the AC4P principles. We refer to this model as the "Seven As Action Plan": (1) *assess*, (2) *advise*, (3) *ask*, (4) *agree*, (5) *assist*, (6) *arrange*, and (7) *AC4P Agent of Change*.

We specify how the seven As address obesity and improve healthy lifestyles by examining interactions between a healthcare team and clients with obesity. Finally, this chapter ends with suggestions about how each of us can "weigh in" with the seven As and thus have a large-scale AC4P impact on people's health and well-being.

WHAT IS OBESITY?

Type "obesity" into Google search and you'll receive approximately 73,000,000 hits.[3] Obesity is ubiquitous. From morning TV news to the halls of Congress and your physician's office, obesity is an omnipresent topic of conversation – the center of debates and a major issue for our healthcare system.

Definitions of obesity vary slightly. *Merriam-Webster* defines obesity as "a condition characterized by the excessive accumulation and storage of fat in the body."[4] The National Institutes of Health defines obesity as a label for a range of body weights that are greater than what is generally considered healthy for a given height.[5] In June 2013, the American Medical Association defined obesity as a disease.[6] This perspective is controversial, but some physicians believe declaring obesity a disease will generate more attention in the healthcare system and improve reimbursement for intensive behavioral therapy for obesity, including relevant medicines and surgery for extreme cases.

Overweight and obesity ranges are determined by using weight and height to calculate a number called the "body mass index" (BMI).[7] As a population measure for obesity, BMI is used because, for most people, it represents the amount of their body fat. Although it's not perfect, especially for large-framed individuals and athletes, BMI is the calculation used most often by physicians, researchers, and statisticians.[8] BMI is calculated by dividing weight in pounds by height in inches squared and multiplying by a conversion factor of 703.

Here's a calculation example:

Weight = 135 lb. Height = 5'5" (65 in.)
Calculation = $[135 \div (65)^2] \times 703$
BMI = **22.5**

BMI tables with calculations already computed are frequently used in healthcare settings to simplify the scoring process. Want to know your BMI? Look at Table 13.1 – find your closest weight in the horizontal row, then your height on the vertical column. The intersecting number is your approximate BMI score.

A BMI score is used as a screening tool to identify possible weight problems for adults, teens, and children. For adults age 20 years and older, BMI is interpreted through categories that do not take into account age or gender. The standard weight-status categories associated with BMI for adults are shown in Table 13.2.[9] An adult with a BMI between 25 and 29.9 kg/m^2 is considered overweight. An adult with a BMI of 30 kg/m^2 or higher is considered obese. Within the obesity range, there are three levels of severity. Class I is considered low-risk; Class II is considered moderate-risk; and Class III is considered high-risk.

TABLE 13.1. A table for estimating body mass index (BMI)

HEIGHT \ WEIGHT	95	100	105	110	115	120	125	130	135	140	145	150	155	160	165	170	175	180	185	190	195	200	205	210	215	220	225	230	235	240	245
5'0"	19	20	21	21	22	23	24	25	26	27	28	29	30	31	32	33	34	35	36	37	38	39	40	41	42	43	44	45	46	47	48
5'1"	18	19	20	21	22	23	24	25	26	26	27	28	29	30	31	32	33	34	35	36	37	38	39	40	41	42	43	43	44	45	46
5'2"	17	18	19	20	21	22	23	24	25	26	27	27	28	29	30	31	32	33	34	35	36	37	38	38	39	40	41	42	43	44	45
5'3"	17	18	19	19	20	21	22	23	24	25	26	27	27	28	29	30	31	32	33	34	35	35	36	37	38	39	40	41	42	43	43
5'4"	16	17	18	19	20	21	21	22	23	24	25	26	27	27	28	29	30	31	32	33	33	34	35	36	37	38	39	39	40	41	42
5'5"	16	17	17	18	19	20	21	22	22	23	24	25	26	27	27	28	29	30	31	32	32	33	34	35	36	37	37	38	39	40	41
5'6"	15	16	17	18	19	19	20	21	22	23	23	24	25	26	27	27	28	29	30	31	31	32	33	34	35	36	36	37	38	39	40
5'7"	15	16	16	17	18	19	20	20	21	22	23	23	24	25	26	27	27	28	29	30	31	31	32	33	34	34	35	36	37	38	38
5'8"	14	15	16	17	17	18	19	20	21	21	22	23	24	24	25	26	27	27	28	29	30	30	31	32	33	33	34	35	36	36	37
5'9"	14	15	16	16	17	18	18	19	20	21	21	22	23	24	24	25	26	27	27	28	29	30	30	31	32	32	33	34	35	35	36
5'10"	14	14	15	16	16	17	18	19	19	20	21	22	22	23	24	24	25	26	27	27	28	29	29	30	31	32	32	33	34	34	35
5'11"	13	14	15	15	16	17	17	18	19	20	20	21	22	22	23	24	24	25	26	27	27	28	29	29	30	31	31	32	33	33	34
6'0"	13	14	14	15	16	16	17	18	18	19	20	20	21	22	22	23	24	24	25	26	26	27	28	28	29	30	31	31	32	33	33
6'1"	13	13	14	15	15	16	16	17	18	18	19	20	20	21	22	22	23	24	24	25	26	26	27	28	28	29	30	30	31	32	32
6'2"	12	13	13	14	15	15	16	17	17	18	19	19	20	21	21	22	22	23	24	24	25	26	26	27	28	28	29	30	30	31	31
6'3"	12	12	13	14	14	15	16	16	17	17	18	19	19	20	21	21	22	22	23	24	24	25	26	26	27	27	28	29	29	30	31
6'4"	12	12	13	13	14	15	15	16	16	17	18	18	19	19	20	21	21	22	23	23	24	24	25	26	26	27	27	28	29	29	30

424

TABLE 13.2. *Classification of weight by BMI, waist circumference, and disease risks*

	Apple vs. pear		Disease risk relative to normal weight and waist circumference	
Classification	BMI (kg/m²)	Obesity class	Men ≤ 40 in. Women ≤ 35 in.	Men > 40 in. Women > 35 in.
Underweight	<18.5	–	–	–
Normal	18.5–24.9	–	–	Increased
Overweight/ pre-obese	25–29.9	–	Increased	High
Obesity	30–34.9	I	High	Very high
Severe obesity	35–39.9	II	Very high	Very high
Extreme obesity	≥40	III	Extremely high	Extremely high

For teens and children 2–19 years old, BMI is age- and gender-specific, and is often referred to as BMI-for-age. The BMI number is plotted on BMI-for-age growth charts (for either girls or boys) to obtain a percentile ranking. Copies of growth charts are available at cdc.gov/healthyweight.[10]

After calculating your BMI, measure your waistline. Physicians refer to waistline as the waist circumference. The goal for a healthy waist circumference is less than 40 in. (102 cm) for men and less than 35 in. (88 cm) for women.[11] To determine your waist circumference, measure your waist with a tape measure. A good way to identify your waist is to let your arms hang at your side and measure at the place where the point of your elbows falls. The tape should fit snugly, but not press into your skin.

Combining BMI and waist circumference provides a sharper picture of your health risk. Check out your relative standing from the measurements in Table 13.2. Men and women with a high BMI and a relatively large waist circumference are at increased risk for developing type 2 diabetes, hypertension, and cardiovascular disease. Individuals with a normal status BMI classification may still have increased disease risk if their waist circumference is in an unhealthy range.

Measuring waist circumference helps determine a person's amount of deep belly fat. Medical researchers claim large amounts of such fat, called "visceral" fat, are extremely dangerous.[12] People who are "apple-shaped" and store fat around their belly are more likely to develop weight-related diseases than people who are "pear-shaped" and store most of their fat around their hips.[13] However, more recent research from the University of California-Davis shows the pear is losing ground in the weight battle.[14]

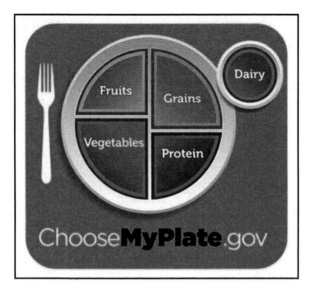

FIGURE 13.2. The MyPlate guide for healthy eating.

Unfortunately, fat stored in the thighs and buttocks is not risk-free. Actually, extra fat stored anywhere on the body poses health risks.

Fit versus Fat

A BMI or obesity classification is only one measure of health. A person who is not at a "normal" weight according to BMI charts may be healthy if s/he has healthy eating habits and exercises regularly.[15] And people who are thin but don't eat nutritious foods and don't exercise aren't necessarily healthy. This observation has led to the ongoing "fit versus fat" debate. Based on the most recent research, the winning argument is that people can be considered fat or obese by weight recommendation standards, but still be fit if they are meeting nutrition and physical activity recommendations.[16]

Current healthy lifestyle recommendations encourage a balance of healthy eating with regular exercise.[17] For Americans, nutrition recommendations are based on a plate icon. (This is different from the food pyramid many of us grew up learning.) As shown in Figure 13.2, the new MyPlate illustrates the five food groups considered the building blocks of a healthy diet: fruits, vegetables, grains, proteins, and dairy products. The recommendation is to fill half of our plate with fruits and vegetables, and the remainder with whole grains, lean protein, and low-fat dairy products.

We also want to watch out for added sugar, too much salt, and heart-clogging saturated and trans fats. Water instead of sugary drinks is the healthiest choice when it comes to beverages. Specific details on each of the food groups, sample daily food plans such as that shown in Figure 13.3, along with healthy recipes can be found at the choosemyplate.gov Website.[18]

Along with MyPlate recommendations, dietary guidelines emphasize that everyone has a personal calorie limit. Staying within your calorie limit based on gender, age, and level of physical activity helps achieve and maintain a healthy weight. For most individuals, this means enjoying your food but eating less, except for those fruits and vegetables. It's important to pay attention to serving size, the amount of food listed on a product's nutrition fact label and recommended in guidelines, along with portion size, the amount of food you actually choose to consume at a given time. People often indulge in more than one recommended serving.

To put food amounts into perspective, nutritionists recommend using your hand as a guide.[19] For instance, a cup equals your fist or cupped hand. To reach the recommended five or more servings of fruits and vegetables a day, you should aim to consume five "fists" throughout your breakfast, lunch, dinner, and snacks. Three ounces, the recommended portion of chicken or beef, is the size and width of your palm. One teaspoon, a serving of fat such as butter, is the size of your thumb tip.

For exercise, the U.S. physical activity recommendation for adults is to accumulate at least one hour and thirty minutes of moderate-intensity or 75 minutes of vigorous aerobic activity every week, combined with two or more days of fifteen minutes of muscle-strengthening activities (or resistance training).[20] Examples of moderate-intensity aerobic activity include brisk walking, riding a bike on level ground or with a few hills, dancing, or pushing a lawn mower. Examples of vigorous activity include running, swimming laps, or jumping rope. Blocks of at least ten minutes of activity are advised to reach the recommended duration. Thirty minutes of moderate-intensity activity a day for five days a week meets guidelines. For teens and children, the physical activity recommendation is higher than it is for adults: sixty minutes a day.

Resistance training should target each major muscle group, including legs, hips, back, abdomen, chest, shoulders, and arms. Examples of recommended strengthening activities include sit-ups, push-ups, free weights, resistance-band exercises, and yoga poses. For weight loss and weight-loss maintenance, the physical activity recommendation increases to 300 minutes of aerobic activity each week in order to achieve a negative energy balance, which occurs when more calories are burned than consumed from food.

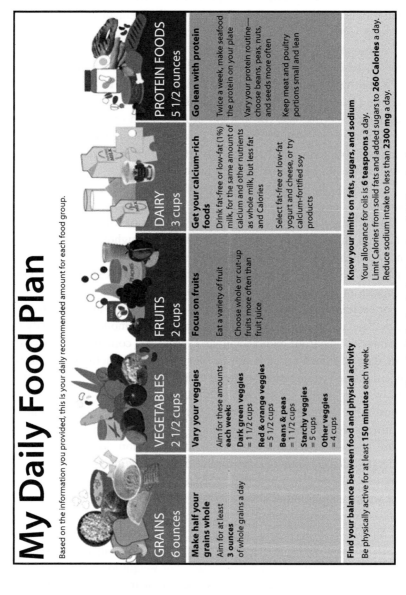

My Daily Food Plan

Based on the information you provided, this is your daily recommended amount for each food group.

GRAINS 6 ounces	VEGETABLES 2 1/2 cups	FRUITS 2 cups	DAIRY 3 cups	PROTEIN FOODS 5 1/2 ounces
Make half your grains whole Aim for at least **3 ounces** of whole grains a day	**Vary your veggies** Aim for these amounts **each week:** **Dark green veggies** = 1 1/2 cups **Red & orange veggies** = 5 1/2 cups **Beans & peas** = 1 1/2 cups **Starchy veggies** = 5 cups **Other veggies** = 4 cups	**Focus on fruits** Eat a variety of fruit Choose whole or cut-up fruits more often than fruit juice	**Get your calcium-rich foods** Drink fat-free or low-fat (1%) milk, for the same amount of calcium and other nutrients as whole milk, but less fat and Calories Select fat-free or low-fat yogurt and cheese, or try calcium-fortified soy products	**Go lean with protein** Twice a week, make seafood the protein on your plate Vary your protein routine—choose beans, peas, nuts, and seeds more often Keep meat and poultry portions small and lean

Find your balance between food and physical activity

Be physically active for at least 150 minutes each week.

Know your limits on fats, sugars, and sodium

Your allowance for oils is **6 teaspoons** a day.
Limit Calories from solid fats and added sugars to **260 Calories** a day.
Reduce sodium intake to less than **2300 mg** a day.

FIGURE 13.3. Sample daily food plan based on MyPlate food groups.

428

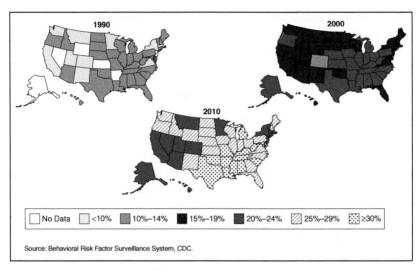

FIGURE 13.4. Map of obesity trends in the U.S. from 1990 to 2010.

THE WEIGHT OF THE WORLD

According to a 2014 report from the *Lancet*, of the 7 billion people on earth, more than 2 billion are overweight or obese.[21] Based on BMI, more than one-third (35.7 percent) of the U.S. adult population is obese and 17.5 percent of U.S. children are obese.[22] Surveys by the Centers for Disease Control and Prevention indicate that only 33 percent of adults consume the recommended servings of fruits and only 27 percent consume the recommended servings of vegetables.[23] Compounding matters, only 20 percent of adults meet physical activity recommendations.[24]

These discouraging reports of unhealthy behaviors, along with the number of individuals with obesity, have trended upward at an astonishing rate in the past twenty-five years.[25] For instance, as shown in Figure 13.4, twenty-five years ago, not one state had an obesity rate above 15 percent. Today, more than two-thirds of our nation's states have obesity rates above 25 percent. It's predicted that by 2030 every state in the country will have obesity rates ranging from 44 to more than 60 percent. These rates have increased in all segments of U.S. society. No matter their age, gender, race, ethnicity, income, education level, or geographic region, people are putting on the pounds.

Disparities do exist regarding who is gaining the most weight. The highest rates of obesity occur among African American women, low-income individuals, adults who did not graduate from high school, Baby Boomers

(45- to 64-year-olds), and those who live in the South.[26] Some say this is because southerners love their sweet tea, fried chicken, and biscuits and spend too much time sitting on their porch-swing rocking chairs.[27]

CAUSES OF OBESITY

Obesity is an enormously complex problem. It's much more than an issue of personal responsibility. We can't blame obesity solely on individuals eating too much and moving too little. Many additional factors influence a person's body weight, including genes (though the heredity effect is very small), prenatal and early-life influences, too much TV watching, too little sleep, and a toxic "obesogenic" environment.[28]

"Obesogenic" is a new term referring to an environment that promotes weight gain and at the same time prevents weight loss.[29] The obesogenic environments in which we live, learn, work, pray, and play often make it difficult to attain or maintain a healthy weight. Plus, decisions made by powerful food corporations, agriculture leaders, and government officials throughout the years have had negative effects on the health of our society.[30]

A Food Fight

Unhealthy foods are everywhere in America. We live in a fast-food culture, and we're exposed to a vast amount of junk food sold at schools, worksites, and grocery stores. In addition, we're constantly bombarded with food and beverage marketing.[31] Products with the highest amount of added fats and sugars have the largest advertising budgets. Relatively inexpensive, palatable, high-calorie foods and beverages, with no nutritional value, constantly attract our attention.

Consider a 20-ounce bottle of carbonated soft drink in a vending machine. Do you know it contains about seventeen teaspoons of added sugar? On average, Americans drink three carbonated soft-drink beverages every day, adding about fifty-one teaspoons of liquid sugar to their diet.[32] This sugar-sweetened consumption can be responsible for two to three extra pounds a month.[33]

Sure, many of us know we need to eat more fruits and vegetables and less fast-food. But healthy food choices are often inconvenient, relatively expensive, and sometimes seem impossible to prepare. The soon, certain, positive consequences of unhealthy food choices can overpower one's self-motivation to eat healthy food. Plus, the hectic pace of modern life adds to the inconvenience of eating healthy – and supports the consumption of fast food.

Consider this scenario: A divorced dad has custody of his three school-aged kids and it's time for dinner. They have spent a busy day at soccer games, gathering materials for science fair projects, and picking out a present for a friend's birthday party. The evening is quickly approaching and Dad finds himself once again at a fast-food drive-thru. He wants his kids to eat healthier, but a fast-food meal of burgers and fries is quick and easy; the kids like it and, most important for the moment, they will eat it.

There is no food fight. "Awesome, Dad. This is great!" are the words he hears. There's no whining or moaning about eating vegetables. He also has saved time since there is no kitchen to clean or dishes to wash. To change this scenario, this dad needs more supportive and corrective feedback (Chapter 3). He needs help making healthier choices for himself and his family.

Too Much Down Time

Whether we are working, playing, or traveling, we require less physical activity in our lives today.[34] We're dependent on our cars, mini-vans, and SUVs. Walking and biking to school, to work, and to the market have decreased markedly.[35] Many of our communities lack sidewalks or paths for safe walking, running, or biking. Technology – laptops, tablet devices, smartphones, wide-screen high-definition TVs, and so on – dominates our work and free time. We have a lot of downtime and not much "uptime." We spend most of our days sitting rather than moving. Schoolchildren face similar situations. Many U.S. schools no longer require daily physical education classes and have reduced their recess times.[36] Overall, downtime rather than uptime defines our lives.

Gaining weight is easy for people of all ages, given our obesogenic environment that continually promotes an abundance of unhealthy foods and sedentary behavioral options. Losing weight is not as easy. Keeping it off is even more difficult, and unfortunately there's no quick fix.

CONSEQUENCES OF OBESITY

The health, economic, and societal consequences of obesity are shocking and dismal.[37] Yet reviewing the alarming negative consequences of obesity has the potential to motivate behavior change or at least inspire individuals to consider the need to help others, as well as themselves, deal with the challenges of obesity.

Health Consequences

Each year, obesity contributes to at least 2.8 million adult deaths around the world.[38] In the United States, obesity is the second-leading cause of preventable death.[39] Smoking is the first. From high blood pressure to sleep apnea and depression, more than sixty diseases have been linked to obesity.[40]

During the next two decades, the increase in obesity-related diseases is anticipated to skyrocket.[41] Specifically, 6 million new cases of type 2 diabetes, the kind most closely associated with unhealthy weight, are expected in the United States. In addition, 5 million new cases of heart disease and stroke and more than 400,000 new cases of cancer will be associated with obesity. These new cases of disease caused by obesity will take a toll on the U.S. healthcare system. We have a dire need for healthcare practitioners to proactively and reactively address nutrition, physical activity, and weight loss with their patients.

Economic Consequences

Obesity exacts a tremendous toll in terms of national healthcare spending, workforce productivity, and corporate cost-containment efforts, as well as individuals' pocketbooks.[42] The estimated annual cost of obesity-related illness in the U.S. is $210 billion. Twenty-one percent of the total annual medical spending in the United States is attributed to obesity. Typically, obese individuals have annual healthcare costs averaging about 40 percent higher than those individuals of normal weight.

In the workplace, obese workers miss more days of work and cost employers more in medical disability and workers' compensation than do non-obese workers. As a result, an average U.S. firm with 1,000 employees faces $285,000 per year in extra costs associated with obesity.[43] Plus, the dubious U.S. diet industry is a profitable business. Each year, Americans spend more than $40 billion dollars on diets and "magic pills" in an attempt to lose weight.[44]

Of course, many of these costs would be prevented if people helped each other make comprehensive lifestyle changes. We don't need to wait for a new drug or a high-tech breakthrough. We simply need to implement effectively the evidence-based weight-management strategies currently available. We need to help each other eat healthy, get more active, and overcome the challenges of our obesogenic culture. We need to actively care for people with obesity and for those at risk for becoming obese.

Social Consequences

For those struggling with their weight, the social consequences can be extremely tough to endure. The adverse social consequences of obesity include (a) discrimination in employment; (b) barriers to education; (c) biased attitudes of healthcare professionals; (d) stereotypes in the media; and (e) stigma in interpersonal relationships.[45] All of these factors threaten to diminish quality of life for a vast number of people who are overweight or obese. These individuals suffer both immediate and long-term negative consequences related to their physical and emotional well-being.

Dealing with weight discrimination, bias, and stigma can undermine weight-loss efforts and diminish the person-states that affect one's propensity to perform AC4P behavior for oneself or others. As explained in Chapter 2, a lessening of self-esteem, self-efficacy, personal control, optimism, and belonging inhibits AC4P behavior for others as well as oneself. It's difficult to feel good about oneself when one is intermittently teased, ridiculed, or harassed about being overweight.

Even if an individual has made a number of changes to his/her eating and activity patterns, it's still possible to feel like a personal failure if desirable weight loss is not soon observed. We are a "quick-fix" society, and people readily get discouraged if the desired outcomes of our efforts are not readily evidenced. People need AC4P behavior from others to help maintain their self-motivation, involvement, and commitment to a healthy lifestyle.

Empathic AC4P communication (Chapter 5) is needed to help individuals with obesity understand that a number on the scale does not define one's worth (e.g., self-esteem). The media, teachers, employers, healthcare professionals, families, and friends need to learn and apply AC4P strategies to help individuals deal with weight issues.

SIZABLE SOLUTIONS

From our family dinner tables to our lunchrooms at school and break rooms at work, and to the fields and factories that produce our food, change is needed to both prevent and reduce the growth of our nation's expanding waistlines. In the 2012 Institute of Medicine (IOM) report, obesity is described as a complex problem with known solutions.[46] Presenting a multilevel cultural solution for change, the report suggests we can tackle the obesity problem by (a) integrating physical activity into our lives every day in every way; (b) making healthy foods available everywhere; (c) marketing strategies for a healthy lifestyle; (d) supporting health-promotion education and provisions in schools; and (e) motivating employers and healthcare professionals to discuss obesity and offer support for their employees and patients, respectively. The report emphasizes that any one of these five solutions will accelerate progress in preventing obesity; together, the beneficial impact will be optimal and synergistic.

Through weight-loss programs, health campaigns, and collaborations, individuals, organizations, schools, and communities are acting on the recommendations of the IOM report to reverse the obesity epidemic. At every level, the application of AC4P principles has great potential to enhance the positive impact of relevant interventions.

Weight-Loss Programs

Several substantial research trials of lifestyle interventions have shown that weight loss can be achieved and sustained.[47] One of the most well-known and referenced trials in lifestyle research is the National Diabetes Prevention Program randomized controlled trial.[48] The trial demonstrated that individuals could lose and maintain 5–10 percent of their initial body weight if they were taught diet, physical activity, and applied behavioral science (ABS) strategies, such as goal setting, self-monitoring, and pinpointing contextual determinants of behavior, and if they received AC4P support from family, friends, and colleagues. Studies of commercial programs, such as Weight Watchers and Jenny Craig, have demonstrated similar short-term benefits.[49]

Although these weight-loss percentages might seem small, they yield significant health benefits, such as improved blood pressure, cholesterol level, and glucose readings.[50] In fact, individuals in the National Diabetes Prevention trial showed that the lifestyle changes were 58 percent more effective than a drug called metformin in reversing risks for disease.[51] The key to weight-loss success in this lifestyle intervention approach is the attention paid to incorporating ABS strategies.[52]

In a community blog posted publicly on Weight Watchers' website, a participant named Mary wrote an entry entitled "Thanks B. F. Skinner!," demonstrating the effectiveness of ABS. As shown in Figure 13.5, the entry notes how ABS helped Mary improve her food choices and stay on track with her healthy eating goals.[53] In particular, Mary noted that Weight Watchers does not claim to "magically burn fat or make appetite disappear but aims to gradually establish healthful eating and moderate exercise as comfortable, rewarding routines of daily life rather than punishing battles of willpower and deprivation."

Thanks B.F. Skinner!

Written by newmary12 (Mary) on 5/25/2012 3:54pm

I learned from The Perfected Self in the June 2012 issue of The Atlantic that WW's "behavior modification plan" closely adheres to B.F. Skinner's theory of basic principles. In so doing, WW has "consistently garnered some of the best long-term weight loss results of any mass market program."

The article goes on to say that WW's key characteristic is the support and encouragement it provides to help participants stick with the plan.

Further - I like this part – WW does not claim to "magically burn fat or make appetite disappear but aims to gradually establish healthful eating and moderate exercise as comfortable, rewarding routines of daily life rather than punishing battles of willpower and deprivation."

Skinner's theory was denounced half century ago as a "manipulative vehicle for government control." But the article reports that his ideas have proven so successful, especially in today's world of smartphone apps, they are making a come-back.

Back in the 1950s, I would have been on the critics' side. Nobody, I believed, had the right to tell anyone else what to do and especially should not use tools to "modify" behavior.

I've changed. In my current fat-self life and daily battle with obesity, I realize that not only does my approach to eating and exercise need to be modified; I need help with the process.

I'm on track. For lunch today, I prepared a turkey burger, sliced tomato topped with fresh basil from my herb garden and a tiny bit of shredded mozzarella along with a side of fresh squash and a dessert of fresh strawberries.

Ten points. Total.

Lunch in my pre-WW days would have been *anything* fried: fried potatoes perhaps with a giant burger – fried – on rich buns topped with a thick slice of Jack cheese and for a dessert a slice of homemade pie or cake or a handful of homemade cookies, all loaded with sugar and saturated fat. Long story short, I will be the first to agree that my behavior is being modified. And that's a good thing. If I stay the course, in a few months I will wake to a slimmer, healthier me thanks to WW and in a round-about-way, B.F. Skinner.

FIGURE 13.5. A Weight Watchers community blog acknowledging the founder of ABS.

Of course, as pointed out in Chapter 1, without AC4P support for the desired behavior, an unhealthy lifestyle can return and the pounds can pile on again. In fact, most people experience significant weight regain in the first year following termination of a weight-loss program.[54] This is one of the critical gaps in the obesity research literature. Much attention has been given to lifestyle intervention for weight loss, but effective strategies for maintaining weight loss are still needed. Strategies that are practical, affordable, and effective for the long haul in healthcare and community settings are in great demand.[55]

MOBILIZING THE MEDICAL COMMUNITY

From the Office of the U.S. Surgeon General to the National Prevention Strategy, there has been a national effort to mobilize the medical community to address obesity as part of a comprehensive wellness strategy.[56] First Lady Michelle Obama's "Let's Move" childhood obesity campaign Website has a special section for healthcare providers to commit to measuring BMI and counseling patients about optimal nutrition and physical activity.[57] The American Hospital Association has a nationwide initiative for all hospitals and their employees to commit to creating a culture of health that promotes healthy eating, physical activity, and weight management.[58]

As beneficiaries of the authority principle (Chapter 6), healthcare providers are in a prime position to provide medical advice and treatment for obesity.[59] The outreach potential of the medical community to help solve the obesity problem is substantial. But obesity is not sufficiently addressed by the U.S. healthcare system.[60]

Physicians, nurses, and therapists do not adequately confront their patients' weight issues. Recent surveys indicate healthcare providers assess patients' BMIs and offer weight-loss counseling to only one-fifth of their obese patients.[61] In one study of patients who reported discussing their weight, only 5 percent received nutrition and exercise advice.[62] Why does the medical community so often choose to neglect this critical health issue?

Obesity Counseling

A variety of personal and professional factors contribute to frustration among physicians and other members of the healthcare team with regard to managing obesity.[63] The list of *personal* barriers includes (a) negative characterization of patients who are obese; and (b) a lack of training and low self-efficacy in obesity counseling and lifestyle management. *Professional* barriers include (a) a lack of reimbursement for obesity-related services; (b) failure to implement office systems to screen for obesity; (c) insufficient time during the office visit; and (d) a lack of precise guidelines and tools for effective counseling.

The STOP (Strategies to Overcome & Prevent) Obesity Alliance and the Rudd Center for Food Policy and Obesity have worked extensively to address personal barriers in the domain of weight bias and stigma among healthcare professionals.[64] They offer several recommendations, based on their research, for promoting empathetic communication that is productive and not stigmatizing. Here are a few tips that can be readily applied to provider–client conversations: (a) use AC4P language – instead of referring to or labeling a person as "obese;" (b) use desirable terms to refer to body weight (e.g., excess weight or a high BMI) rather than undesirable terms (e.g., fatness, heaviness, obesity, or large size) that may be hurtful or offensive because of negative connotations; and (c) emphasize that weight is about health, not appearance.[65]

To address professional barriers, the U.S. Preventive Services Task Force, the American College of Cardiology, the American Heart Association, and the Obesity Society published guidelines for obesity counseling.[66] It's now recommended that primary-care providers screen for obesity and offer or refer adult patients with a BMI of 30 kg/m^2 or higher to an intensive, multicomponent ABS weight-loss intervention. The Centers for Medicare Medicaid Services has started to reimburse primary-care physicians for conducting obesity counseling.[67]

It's suggested that providers use the international five As of behavior change as a tool to assist with counseling. The five As of obesity counseling involves a series of five sequential steps: (1) *assess* status, (2) *advise* to change, (3) *agree* on goals, (4) *assist* with support, and (5) *arrange* follow-up for change.[68]

More about the "Five As" Framework

Developed originally by the National Cancer Institute to assist physicians in getting patients to quit smoking, the five As framework is not a theory, but a how-to guide for health behavior-change counseling.[69] The five As have been found to promote competent health counseling and have been useful for initiating conversations on health behaviors and sensitive health issues.[70] This counseling tool has also increased the rate at which patients are referred for intensive behavioral counseling compared with what typically occurs during a healthcare clinic visit.[71]

The five As have been supported by research, but the five strategic steps are rarely practiced fully among healthcare professionals. Typically, if providers are able to counsel, only *assess* and *advise* are conducted. One of the most useful of the five As (*assist*) is least practiced.[72] This part of the framework includes essential ABS components, such as goal setting, self-monitoring, and behavioral feedback. As a result, evidence-based strategies shown to be effective in research studies have not been sustained in real-world clinical practice.[73]

THE AC4P "SEVEN AS" ACTION PLAN

The need and potential for a practical how-to guide for obesity counseling that will actually be used and integrated into the AC4P practice of a health-care team are clearly evident. In response, we've modified the five As of obesity.[74] By changing the formation, content, and number of A-words, we believe this new adapted framework has greater potential to make a beneficial and lasting difference.

Combining the humanism and behaviorism of the AC4P Movement (i.e., humanistic behaviorism), the new framework integrates principles of ABS to improve one's weight status, as well as overall health and well-being. Each word addresses AC4P principles to enhance the impact of providers' counseling behaviors on patients' nutrition, physical activity, and weight management. We refer to this framework as an "action plan" since it provides a detailed blueprint of actions needed by providers and clients to achieve healthy lifestyle and weight-loss goals.

First, as depicted in Figure 13.6, the formation of the A-steps are presented visually as a circular loop rather than in the linear or tabular fashion often used in most publications of the five As. The loop symbolizes how the A-components need to be continuous and ongoing. There is really no end to achieving and maintaining a healthier lifestyle.

Second, the content of the As has been enhanced with conversations about consequences, empowerment, behavior-based feedback, and AC4P behaviors from others. With choice, competence, and community embedded in the framework for both providers (benefactors) and clients (beneficiaries), self-motivation will increase for both parties (Chapter 3).

Third, the number of A-steps has been expanded from five to seven. As displayed in Figure 13.6, the seven As provide a new AC4P approach to healthy lifestyle counseling. The following is a brief description of each A-word and an example of how the seven As can address obesity and activate and support healthy lifestyles in real-world settings.

An important consideration: Who is the healthcare counselor? As healthcare delivery moves toward inter-professional team care, a physician, physician's assistant, nurse, dietician, exercise physiologist/physical therapist, social worker, health educator, or health coach could all serve as a counselor.[75] Ideally, a healthcare team would work together with a client to deliver the As.

1. *Assess* **weight status, behaviors, and contributing factors.** Assess BMI and waist circumference. Note whether the client is following

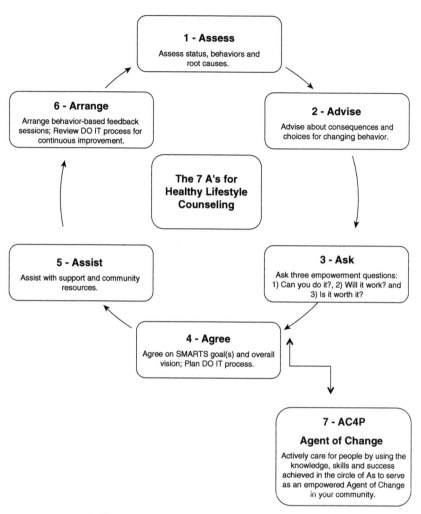

FIGURE 13.6. The "Seven As Action Plan" for healthy lifestyle counseling using an AC4P approach.

MyPlate guidelines and meeting physical activity recommendations for both aerobic and muscle-strengthening activities. Explore factors contributing to weight status, such as distress, overeating, consumption of sugar-sweetened beverages, excessive sit-down time during computer use, and lack of uptime (i.e., exercise). During the assessment, use the *overweight* or *BMI*, rather than a negatively perceived term such as *fat* or *obese*.

2. *Advise* **about consequences and choices for changing behaviors.** Discuss the health, economic, and social consequences of excessive weight. Provide an array of evidence-based choices for losing weight, such as reducing calorie consumption, watching portion sizes, limiting fast-food intake, and increasing physical activity.

3. *Ask* **the three empowerment questions.** In relation to the client's selected behavior-change choice(s), ask: (1) Can you do it? (2) Will it work? (3) Is it worth it? A yes answer to each of these questions reflects feeling empowered (Chapter 2). A no answer reflects a need for training (Question 1), education (Question 2), or motivation (Chapter 3). The counselor must prepare to address training, education, or motivation issues related to any particular weight-loss strategy selected by the client.

4. *Agree* **on SMARTS goal(s), an overall vision, and a DO IT process.** When feeling empowered, the patient is ready for goal setting (see Figure 2.2). The counselor and client set and agree upon SMARTS goals that are *specific, motivational, achievable, relevant, trackable,* and *shared* (Chapter 3). This aligns with the DO IT method for providing feedback to shape behavioral improvement, as described in Chapter 1.

   For instance, a client may set a goal of eating at least five servings ("fists") of fruits and vegetables a day to reduce his/her weight by 10 pounds for an upcoming high school reunion. S/he plans to track the number of daily fruits and vegetables and weight on a Smartphone to objectively observe and measure progress. S/he plans to consume more fruits and vegetables at breakfast and dinner and while snacking. S/he will add blueberries or a banana to her/his morning cereal, a salad to her/his dinner plate, and have carrot sticks and apples on hand for snacks. In addition, s/he will share weekly goal progress updates on Facebook, Twitter, Instagram, or some other preferred social media outlet.

5. *Assist* **with identifying support and community resources.** A counselor can link clients to people, places, and programs that help achieve health-related goals. For this example, a coach could share a fruits and vegetables recipe book, a calendar noting days the farmer's market is open, and a contact number to register for classes on nutrition. The counselor could also share a directory of exercise options available in the local community, along with a list of specific weight-loss and resistance-training exercises for use at home (e.g., walk for thirty minutes five days a week, take the spin class at the community exercise facility on Monday and Wednesday, etc.).

6. ***Arrange* behavior-based feedback sessions and review the DO IT process**. This additional A-word arranges supportive and corrective feedback for clients – an often overlooked area – to improve and maintain their health-related behaviors. Clients can download a Smartphone app to track their fruit and vegetable consumption and schedule a phone session with a health counselor to discuss successes and struggles. The counselor can ask for progress reports of beneficial behavior change and goal attainment. If relevant, the selected behavioral target(s) for weight loss and weight-loss maintenance can be adjusted as part of continuous improvement. These feedback seasons should be scheduled soon after relevant health-related behavior occurs. Excessive delays between behavior and feedback can be counterproductive, as reflected in the illustration.

7. ***AC4P change agent.*** The AC4P counselor becomes an empowered agent of change in the community by using the knowledge, skills, and success achieved in the circle of A-words. By participating in the obesity counseling process outlined here, both counselors and clients have worthwhile learning experiences to share. Their mutual success as benefactor and beneficiary of a successful weight-loss process fuels their self-motivation to help others sustain a health-enhancing program for family and friends.

With documented success, healthcare providers are more likely to counsel future clients and colleagues. Successful clients will likely help others with their weight-loss planning and goal setting for process activities leading toward a particular outcome goal (e.g., a certain amount of weight loss in one month).

GOING GLOBAL WITH THE SEVEN AS

The seven As approach provides a technique to start the AC4P conversation for health promotion, whether you are the one needing to lose a few pounds or the physician, coach, friend, or family member who is trying to help. Although the example given earlier involves a counselor and client, the seven As can certainly be used beyond the formal healthcare setting. It's a framework that guides action planning for macro applications in schools, worksites, community groups, and families, anywhere in the world.

As noted in the example, the use of high-tech communication has the potential to enhance applications of the seven As. From Smartphone apps to text messages and new wearable fitness wristbands with built-in accelerometers, such as the Fitbit®, Jawbone,® and Nike Fuel®, electronic technology can assist both parties in the circle of As with tracking, sharing, and providing behavior-based feedback. Organizations interested in adopting the seven As should consider ways to integrate technology for systematically documenting progress per each A-word and provide linkages to additional programs and services. This will be a dynamic area of rapid development in coming years.

By progressing through each A-component, both the counselor and client experience documented changes in behavior that increase competence, personal control, and courage, all fueling self-motivation to teach or perform AC4P behavior for personal health. With small changes in relevant person-states, more behavior change follows. In turn, successive small-win improvements lead to a personal commitment, total engagement in the process, and a desire to share the successful process with others.

Increased use of incentives for healthcare professionals to conduct obesity counseling and promote wellness is another strategy for accelerating implementation of the seven As. As discussed recently at the National Forum on Hospitals, Health Systems and Population Health, creating payment bundles with insurance companies that pay for performance rather than pay for service has promise.[76] Physicians would be paid on the basis of how healthy they keep their patient population, rather than the current system that compensates physicians for conducting tests and prescribing medications to treat illness.

In a system focused on health rather than sickness, evidence-based strategies for promoting healthy eating, physical activity, and weight management that are delivered effectively would be prioritized and bundled together as an AC4P care package. Advocating for improved environments to support healthy lifestyles would be part of the healthcare mission. Applying the AC4P approach of the seven As would be seen as a viable strategy for achieving the triple aims of healthcare: (1) to improve patients' experience of customized care; (2) to improve the health of populations; and (3) to reduce the per capita costs of healthcare.[77]

As described in Chapter 6, this *ripple effect* can lead to the seven As becoming not only a behavior-change counseling tool to tackle obesity, but a large-scale framework to create a culture of interpersonal compassion and wellness that is transferrable to any healthcare system, and beyond to any community, educational system, business enterprise, other organizations, groups, and families. Positive consequences of applying the seven As should improve the quality of AC4P coaching of others in need of healthier lifestyles. The result: more people actively caring effectively for the health, wellness, and well-being of themselves and others.

IN CONCLUSION

This chapter provided an overview of the obesity epidemic, its causes and consequences, and called for an AC4P approach to promoting healthy lifestyles. The recommended five As framework for behavioral-health counseling was reviewed and an adapted seven As action plan based on AC4P principles was introduced. As a result, a new tool is available to broaden the benefits of the AC4P Movement.

Most important, this chapter shared the special ingredients of evidence-based, AC4P principles for creating a recipe for promoting healthy lifestyles. As Julia Child once said, "You don't have to cook fancy or complicated masterpieces – just good food from fresh ingredients." Tackling our current obesity epidemic is like sitting down for a full-course meal. If each of us takes one bite, the meal can be devoured. With humanistic behaviorism as the seasoning, the meal will be consumed most efficiently and effectively, and with the least amount of displeasure.

DISCUSSION QUESTIONS

1. Why is it difficult to help people lose weight and keep it off?
2. What are the recommended behaviors for achieving and maintaining a healthy weight?

3. Define the term "obesogenic" using real-world illustrations.
4. Briefly describe the three negative consequences of obesity (a) health consequences, (b) economic consequences, and (c) social consequences.
5. Why did Mary thank B. F. Skinner in a community blog on the Weight Watchers' Web site?
6. Why does the medical community appear to neglect the obesity epidemic?
7. What changes to the popular five As framework for health behavior-change counseling do the authors propose?
8. Offer a rationale for the changes described in your answer to Question 7.
9. Explain how modes of high-tech communication (e.g., smartphone apps) can facilitate one or more of the aspects of the seven As action plan: (1) assess, (2) advise, (3) ask, (4) agree, (5) assist, (6) arrange, and (7) AC4P agent of change.
10. Provide an example of how the seven As could be applied beyond the healthcare setting.

REFERENCES

1. Healthy Living in the Mid-Carolinas (HLMC) is a $1.5 million community-based preventative health initiative funded by the Kate B. Reynolds Charitable Trust. From 2007 to 2014, FirstHealth of the Carolinas enrolled approximately 7,000 individuals living at or below 200% federal poverty level into HLMC behavior-change programs. More information about this initiative and healthy living programs offered by FirstHealth can be retrieved from https://www.firsthealth.org/lifestyle/community-health.
2. FirstHealth of the Carolinas is a nonprofit, private healthcare system based in Pinehurst, NC. Its mission is to "care for people." The Department of Community Health Services partners with churches, schools, and community groups to provide preventive care throughout a four-county rural service region, including Hoke, Montgomery, Moore, and Richmond counties. More information about the department can be retrieved from http://www.firsthealth.org/communityhealth.
3. Obesity. Retrieved March 1, 2015 from http://www.google.com.
4. Obesity. Retrieved March 1, 2015 from http://www.merriam-webster.com/dictionary/obesity.
5. National Institutes of Health (1998). Clinical guidelines on the identification, evaluation, and treatment of overweight and obesity in adults: The evidence report. *Obesity Research*, 6, Suppl. 2, 51–209.
6. Beal, E. (2013). The pros and cons of designating obesity a disease: The new AMA designation stirs debate. *American Journal of Nursing*, 113(11), 18–19; AMA Report of the Council on Science and Public Health. (2015, March 1). Retrieved March 1, 2015 from http://www.ama-assn.org/ama/pub/news/news/2013/2013-06-18-new-ama-policies-annual-meeting.page.

7. Stensland, S. H., & Margolis, S. (1990). Simplifying the calculation of body-mass index for quick reference. *Journal of the American Dietetic Association*, 90(6), 856.

8. Mazic, S., Djelic, M., Suzic, J., Suzic, S., Dekleva, M., Radovanovic, D., et al. (2009). Overweight in trained subjects: Are we looking at wrong numbers? *General Physiological Biophysics*, 28, Spec. No., 200–204.

9. U.S. Department of Health and Human Services (2005). Aim for a healthy weight. Retrieved March 1, 2015 from http://www.nhlbi.nih.gov/health/public/heart/obesity/aim_hwt.pdf.

10. Division of Nutrition, Physical Activity and Obesity. National Center for Chronic Disease Prevention and Health Promotion. (2015, March 1). In Healthy weight: It's not a diet, it's a lifestyle. Retrieved March 1, 2015 from http://www.cdc.gov/healthyweight.

11. Poirier, P., & Despres, J. P. (2003). Waist circumference, visceral obesity, and cardiovascular risk. *Journal of Cardiopulmonary Rehabilitation*, 23(3), 161–169.

12. Kaess, B. M., Pedley, A., Massaro, J. M., Murabito, J., Hoffmann, U., & Fox, C. S. (2012). The ratio of visceral to subcutaneous fat, a metric of body fat distribution, is a unique correlate of cardiometabolic risk. *Diabetologia*, 55(10), 2622–2630.

13. Thoma, M. E., Hediger, M. L., Sundaram, R., Stanford, J. B., Peterson, C. M., & Croughan, M. S. (2012). Comparing apples and pears: Women's perceptions of their body size and shape. *Journal of Women's Health*, 21(10), 1074–1081.

14. Jialal, I., Devaraj, S., Kaur, H., Adams-Huet, B., & Bremer, A. A. (2013). Increased chemerin and decreased omentin-1 in both adipose tissue and plasma in nascent metabolic syndrome. *Journal of Clinical Endocrinology Metabolism*, 98(3), 514–517.

15. Lee, C. D., Jackson, A. S., & Blair, S. N. (1998). U.S. weight guidelines: Is it also important to consider cardiorespiratory fitness? *International Journal of Obesity Relational Metabolic Disorder*, 22, Suppl. 2, 2–7.

16. Duncan, G. E. (2010). The "fit but fat" concept revisited: Population-based estimates using NHANES. *International Journal of Behavioral Nutrition and Physical Activity*, 7, 47; Fogelholm, M. (2010). Physical activity, fitness and fatness: Relations to mortality, morbidity and disease risk factors: A systematic review. *Obesity Reviews*, 11:202–221; Jakicic, J., Mishler, A., & Rogers, R. (2011). Fitness, fatness, and cardiovascular disease risk and outcomes. *Current Cardiovascular Risk Report*, 5:113–119.

17. U.S. Department of Health and Human Services. (2010). *The surgeon general's vision for a healthy and fit nation*. Rockville, MD: U.S. Department of Health and Human Services, Office of the Surgeon General; U.S. Department of Agriculture & U.S. Department of Health and Human Services (2010). *Dietary guidelines for Americans*(7th ed.), Washington, DC: U.S. Government Printing Office, 2010

18. Post, R., Haven, J., Maniscalco, S., & Brown, M. C. (2013). It takes a village to communicate the dietary guidelines for Americans and MyPlate. *Journal of the Academy of Nutrition and Dietetics*, 113(12): 1589–1590.

19. ExosNutrion. In Portion size strategy: A hand comes in handy. Retrieved March 1, 2015 from http://www.coreperformance.com/daily/nutrition/portion-size-strategy-a-hand-comes-in-handy.html.

20. U.S. Department of Health Human Services. (2008). *Physical activity guidelines for Americans.* Washington, DC: U.S. Government Printing Office.
21. Ng, M., Fleming, T., Robinson, M., Thomson, B., Graetz, N., Margono, C., et al. Global, regional, and national prevalence of overweight and obesity in children and adults during 1980–2013: A systematic analysis for the Global Burden of Disease Study, 2013. *Lancet*, 384(9945), 766–781.
22. Levi, J., Segal, L. M., Laurent, R. S., & Rayburn, J. (2014). The state of obesity: Better policies for a healthier America. Retrieved March 1, 2015 from http://healthyamericans.org/assets/files/TFAH-2014-ObesityReport%20FINAL.pdf.
23. Ollberding, N. J., Nigg, C. R., Geller, K. S., Horwath, C. C., Motl, R. W., & Dishman, R. K. (2012). Food outlet accessibility and fruit and vegetable consumption. *American Journal of Health Promotion*, 26(6), 366–370.
24. Centers for Disease Control and Prevention (2013). Adult participation in aerobic and muscle-strengthening physical activities – United States, 2011. *Morbidity and Mortality Weekly Report*, 62(17), 326–330.
25. Centers for Disease Control and Prevention, National Center for Health Statistics, The National Health and Nutrition Examination Survey. (2005–2008). Retrieved March 1, 2015 from National Indicator Warehouse, http://healthindicators.gov/Indicators/Obesity-in-adults-percent_1208/Profile/Data; Levi, J., Segal, L. M., Laurent, R. S., Lang, A., & Rayburn, J. (2012). F as if fat: How obesity threatens America's future. Retrieved March 1, 2015 from http://healthyamericans.org/assets/files/TFAH2012FasInFatFnlRv.pdf.
26. Suddath, C. (2009). Why are southerners so fat? *Time.* Retrieved March 1, 2015 from http://www.time.com/time/health/article/0,8599,1909406,00.html.
27. Akil, L., & Ahmad, H. A. (2011). Effects of socioeconomic factors on obesity rates in four southern states and Colorado. *Ethnicity & Disease Journal*, 21(1), 58–62.
28. Friedman, J. M. (2009). Obesity: Causes and control of excess body fat. *Nature*, 459(7245), 340–342.
29. Ard, J. D. (2007). Unique perspectives on the obesogenic environment. *Journal of General Internal Medicine*, 22(7), 1058–1060.
30. National Research Council. (2012). *Accelerating progress in obesity prevention: Solving the weight of the nation.* Washington, DC: National Academies Press.
31. Harris, J. L., Pomeranz, J. L., Lobstein, T., & Brownell, K. D. (2009). A crisis in the marketplace: How food marketing contributes to childhood obesity and what can be done. *Annual Reviews of Public Health*, 30, 211–225.
32. Risica, P. M., Kerr, S., Lawson, E., Belhumeur, R., & Ankoma, A. (2009). Self-report of sugar-sweetened beverage and fast food consumption by annual household income. *Medicine & Health*, 92(2), 63–64.
33. Blumenthal, S., &Shelby, J. (2012). Weighing in on sugary beverages and obesity. Retrieved March 1, 2015 from http://www.huffingtonpost.com/susan-blumenthal/soda-health_b_1627335.html.
34. Lee, I. M., Ewing, R., & Sesso, H. D. (2009). The built environment and physical activity levels: The Harvard Alumni Health Study. *American Journal of Preventive Medicine*, 37(4), 293–298.
35. Frank, L., & Kavage, S. (2009). A national plan for physical activity: The enabling role of the built environment. *Journal of Physical Activity & Health*, 6, Suppl. 2, 186–195.

36. National Association for Sport and Physical Education, American Heart Association (2012). *Shape of the Nation Report: Status of physical education in the USA*, Reston, VA: American Alliance for Health, Physical Education, Recreation and Dance.

37. National Research Council. (2012). *Accelerating progress in obesity prevention: Solving the weight of the nation*. Washington, DC: National Academies Press; Withrow, D., & Alter, D. A. (2011). The economic burden of obesity worldwide: A systematic review of the direct costs of obesity. *Obesity Review*, 12(2), 131–141; Friedman, R. R., & Puhl, R. M. (2012). Rudd Report: Weight bias as a social justice issue. Retrieved March 1, 2015 from http://www.yaleruddcenter .org/resources/upload/docs/what/reports/Rudd_Policy_Brief_Weight_Bias .pdf.

38. Flegal, K. M., Carroll, M. D., Kit, B. K., & Ogden, C. L. (2012). Prevalence and trends in obesity among U.S. adults, 1999–2010. *JAMA*, 307(5), 491–497.

39. Wang, Y. C., McPherson, K., Marsh, T., Gortmaker, S. L., & Brown, M. (2011). Health and economic burden of the projected obesity trends in the USA and the UK. *Lancet*, 378(9793), 815–825.

40. National Cancer Institute. (2012). Obesity and cancer risk. Retrieved March 1, 2015 from www.cancer.gov/cancertopics/factsheet/Risk/obesity.

41. Hoffman, J., & Saleno, J. A. (2012). *The weight of the nation: To win we have to lose*. New York: St. Martin's Press; Levi, J., Segal, L. M., Laurent, R. S., Lang, A., & Rayburn, J. (2012). F as if fat: How obesity threatens America's future. Retrieved March 1, 2015 from http://healthyamericans.org/assets/files/ TFAH2012FasInFatFnlRv.pdf

42. Bilger, M., Finkelstein, E. A., Kruger, E., Tate, D., & Linnan, L. (2013). The effect of weight loss on health, productivity and medical expenditures among overweight employees. *Medical Care*, 51(6): 471–477; Finkelstein, E. A., Khaviou, O. A., Thompson, H., Trogdon, J. G., Pan, L., Sherry, B., et al. Obesity and severe obesity forecasts through 2030. *American Journal of Preventive Medicine*, 42(6): 563–570.

43. Levi, J., Segal, L. M., Laurent, R. S., & Rayburn, J. (2014). The state of obesity: Better policies for ahealthier America. Retrieved March 1, 2015 from http:// healthyamericans.org/assets/files/TFAH-2014-ObesityReport%20FINAL.pdf.

44. Hoffman, J., & Saleno, J. A. (2012). *The weight of the nation: To win we have to lose*. New York: St. Martin's Press.

45. Friedman, R. R., & Puhl, R. M. (2012). Rudd Report: Weight bias as a social justice issue. Retrieved March 1, 2015 from http://www.yaleruddcenter.org/ resources/upload/docs/what/reports/Rudd_Policy_Brief_Weight_Bias.pdf; Puhl, R., & Huer, C. (2010). Obesity stigma: Important considerations for public health. *American Journal of Public Health*, 100(6), 1019–1028.

46. National Research Council. (2012). *Accelerating progress in obesity prevention: Solving the weight of the nation*. Washington, DC: National Academies Press.

47. Wadden, T. A., Butryn, M. L., & Byrne, K. J. (2004). Efficacy of lifestyle modification for long-term weight control. *Obesity Research*, 12, Suppl., 151S–162S; Wadden, T. A., Webb, V. L., Moran, C. H., & Bailer, B. A. (2012). Lifestyle modification for obesity: New developments in diet, physical activity, and behavior therapy. *Circulation*, 125(9), 1157–1170.

48. Knowler, W. C., & Diabetes Prevention Program Research Group. (2002). Reduction in the incidence of type 2 diabetes with lifestyle intervention or metformin. *New England Journal of Medicine*, 346(6), 393–403.

49. Jebb, S. A., Ahern, A. L., Olson, A. D., Aston, L. M., Holapfel, C., Stoll, J., et al. (2011). Primary care referral to a commercial provider for weight loss treatment versus standard care: a randomized controlled trial. *Lancet*, 378 (9801), 1485–1492.

50. Wing, R. R., Lang, W., Wadden, T. A., Safford, M., Knowler, W. C., Bertoni, A. G., et al. & Look AHEAD Research Group. (2011). Benefits of modest weight loss in improving cardiovascular risk factors in overweight and obese individuals with type 2 diabetes. *Diabetes Care*, 34(7), 1481–1486.

51. Knowler, W. C., & Diabetes Prevention Program Research Group. (2002). Reduction in the incidence of type 2 diabetes with lifestyle intervention or metformin. *New England Journal of Medicine*, 346(6), 393–403.

52. Burke, L. E., Wang, J., & Sevick, M. A. (2011). Self-monitoring in weight loss: A systematic review of the literature. *Journal of American Dietetic Association*, 111(1), 92–102.

53. Weight Watchers. Thanks B. F. Skinner. Retrieved March 1, 2015 from http://community.weightwatchers.com/Blogs/ViewPost.aspx?threadID=1646994.

54. Franz, M. J., VanWormer, J. J., & Crain, A. L. (2007). Weight-loss outcomes: A systematic review and meta-analysis of weight-loss clinical trials with a minimum one-year follow-up. *Journal of American Dietetic Association*, 107(10), 1755–1767.

55. Akers, J. D., Estabrooks, P. A., & Davy, B. M. (2010). Translational research: Bridging the gap between long-term weight-loss maintenance research and practice. *Journal of American Dietetic Association*, 110(10), 1511–1513.

56. U.S. Department of Health and Human Services. (2010). *The surgeon general's vision for a healthy and fit nation*. Rockville, MD: U.S. Department of Health and Human Services, Office of the Surgeon General; National Prevention Council (2011). *National prevention strategy*. Washington, DC: U.S. Department of Health and Human Services, Office of the Surgeon General.

57. Task Force on Childhood Obesity. Let's move: Five simple steps to success for healthcare providers. Retrieved March 1, 2015 from letsmove.gov/health-care-providers.

58. American Hospital Association. Hospital-based strategies for creating a culture of health. Retrieved March 1, 2015 from http://www.hpoe.org/resources/hpoehretaha-guides/1687.

59. Loureiro, M. L., & Nayga, R. M., Jr. (2006). Obesity, weight loss, and physician's advice. *Social Science Medicine*, 62(10), 2458–2468; Dietz, W. H., Baur, L. A., Hall, K., Puhl, R., Taveras, E. M., Uauy, R., et al. (2015). Management of obesity: Improvement of health-care training and systems for prevention and care. *Lancet*, 1–13.

60. Kraschnewski, J. L., Sciamanna, C. N., Stuckey, H. L., Chuang, C. H., Lehman, E. B., Hwang, K. O., et al. (2013). A silent response to the obesity epidemic: Decline in U.S. physician weight counseling. *Medical Care*, 51(2), 186–192.

61. Bleich, S. N., Pickett-Blakely, O., & Cooper, L. A. (2011). Physician practice patterns of obesity diagnosis and weight-related counseling. *Patient Education Counseling*, 82(1), 123–129.

62. Alexander, S., Ostbye, T., Pollak, K., Gradison, M., Bastian, L. A., & Brouwer, R. J. (2007). Physicians' beliefs about discussing obesity: Results from focus groups. *American Journal of Health Promotion*, 21, 498–500.

63. Kraschnewski, J. L., Sciamanna, C. N., Stuckey, H. L., Chuang, C. H., Lehman, E. B., Hwang, K. O., et al. (2013). A silent response to the obesity epidemic: Decline in U.S. physician weight counseling. *Medical Care*, 51(2), 186–192; Dietz, W. H., Baur, L. A., Hall, K., Puhl, R., Taveras, E. M., Uauy, R., et al. (2015). Management of obesity: Improvement of health-care training and systems for prevention and care. *Lancet*, 1–13.

64. Friedman, R. R., & Puhl, R. M. (2012). Rudd Report: Weight bias as a social justice issue. Retrieved March 1, 2015 from http://www.yaleruddcenter.org/resources/upload/docs/what/reports/Rudd_Policy_Brief_Weight_Bias.pdf; Gray, C. M., Hunt, K., Lorimer, K., Anderson, A. S., Benzeval, M., & Wyke, S. (2011). Words matter: A qualitative investigation of which weight status terms are acceptable and motivate weight loss when used by health professionals, *Biomedical Central Public Health*, 11 (513), 1–9.

65. STOP Obesity Alliance. (2014). Why weight? A guide to discussing obesity and health with your patients. Retrieved march 1, 2015 from http://www.stopobesityalliance.org/wp-content/themes/stopobesityalliance/pdfs/STOP-Provider-Discussion-Tool.pdf.

66. Moyer, V. A. (2012). Screening for and management of obesity in adults: US Preventive Services Task Force recommendation statement. *Annals of Internal Medicine*, 157(5), 373–378; Jensen, M. D., & Donna, H. R. (2014). New obesity guidelines: Promise and potential. *JAMA*, 311(1), 23–24.

67. Centers for Medicare and Medicaid Services (2011). Decision memo for intensive behavioral therapy for obesity. Retrieved March 1, 2015 from www.cms.gov/medicare-coverage-database.

68. Vallis, M., Piccinini-Vallis, H., Sharma, A. M., & Freedhoff, Y. (2013). Clinical review: Modified 5 A's minimal intervention for obesity counseling in primary care. *Canadian Family Physician*, 59(1), 27–31; Jensen, M. D., Ryan, D. H., Apovian, C. M., Ard, J., Comuzzie, A. G., Donato, K. A., et al. (2014). 2013 AHA/ACC/TOS Guideline for the management of overweight and obesity in adults: A report of the American College of Cardiology/American Heart Association task force on practice guidelines and the Obesity Society. *Journal of the American College of Cardiology*, 63(25_PA), 2985–3023.

69. Goldstein, M. G., Whitlock, E. P., & DePue, J. (2004). Multiple health risk behavior interventions in primary care: Summary of research evidence. *American Journal of Preventive Medicine*, 24, 61–79.

70. Estabrooks, P. A., & Glasgow, R. E. (2006). Translating effective clinic-based physical activity interventions into practice. *American Journal of Preventive Medicine*, 31(4), 45–56; Jay, M., Gillespie, C., Schlair, S., Sherman, S., & Kalet, A. (2010). Physicians' use of the 5 As in counseling obese patients: Is the quality of counseling associated with patients' motivation and intention to lose weight? *BMC Health Services Research*, 10(159), 1–10.

71. Alexander, S. C., Cox, M. E., Boling Turer, C. L., Lyna, P., Ostbye, T., Tulsky, J. A., et al. (2011). Do the five A's work when physicians counsel about weight loss? *Family Medicine*, 43(3), 179–184.

72. Schlair, S., Moore, S., Mcacken, M., & Jay, M. (2012). How to deliver high-quality obesity counseling in primary care using the 5As framework. *Journal of Communication*, 19(5), 221–230.

73. Estabrooks, P. A., & Glasgow, R. E. (2006). Translating effective clinic-based physical activity interventions into practice. *American Journal of Preventive Medicine*, 31(4S), S45–S56; Akers, J. D., Estabrooks, P. A., & Davy, B. M. (2010). Translational research: Bridging the gap between long-term weight-loss maintenance research and practice. *Journal of American Dietetic Association*, 110(10), 1511–1513.

74. Vallis, M., Piccinini-Vallis, H., Sharma, A. M., & Freedhoff, Y. (2013). Clinical review: Modified 5 As' minimal intervention for obesity counseling in primary care. *Canadian Family Physician*, 59(1), 27–31.

75. Interprofessional Education Collaborative Expert Panel. (2011). Core competencies for interprofessional collaborative practice: Report of an expert panel. Washington, DC: Interprofessional Education Collaborative.

76. Dentzer, S. (2014). Five takeaways from National Forum on Hospitals, Health Systems and Population Health. Retrieved March 1, 2015 from http://www.rwjf.org/en/blogs/culture-of-health/2014/11/five_takeaways_from.html.

77. Berwick, D. M., Nolan, T. W., & Whittington, J. (2008). The triple aim: Care, health, and cost. *Health Affairs*, 27(3), 759–769.

14

Actively Caring for Patient-Centered Healthcare

DAVE JOHNSON AND E. SCOTT GELLER

Only by changing how we think about kindness at the bedside, in the workplace and in our community can we deliver world-class care to our patients.

– Gary Greensweig

What could be more fertile ground for the AC4P Movement than healthcare? The aims of AC4P parallel what healthcare has been recently attempting to accomplish with patient-centered care – creating cultures of empathy, compassion, and interdependence.

The roots of patient-centered healthcare date back to 2000, when a landmark Institute of Medicine study estimated medical errors contributed to 44,000–98,000 preventable deaths and 1,000,000 excessive injuries each year in the United States.[1] The impact of these medical mistakes was widespread, extending beyond fatalities and permanent disabilities to include hospital-acquired infections, hospital readmissions, wrong-site surgeries, wrong medications and incorrect dosages given to patients, and emotional trauma for both patients and their families.

Subsequent to this awareness of healthcare errors, a paradigm shift has begun to slowly emerge: from physician-centered care to patient-centered care. From physician knows all to patients know best how well their healthcare providers are meeting their needs.[2] The traditional physician-centered approach to healthcare is humorously depicted in the illustration on the next page and is seemingly still the perception of many benefactors and beneficiaries of healthcare.

PHYSICIAN–PATIENT EMPATHY

One of the tenets of patient-centered care is a positive relationship between the recipient of healthcare and the caregiver, whether a surgeon, hospitalist,

resident, nurse, X-ray technician, MRI operator, primary-care physician, or the technician who draws blood and takes blood pressure readings in a patient's hospital room. Some healthcare facilities have taken this paradigm shift a step further by teaching the AC4P principles of patient-centered care to almost all new hires, from housekeepers and receptionists to maintenance workers and those who bring patients their meals.[3]

Patient-centered care has a long way to go before it becomes institutionalized in healthcare facilities and throughout the medical community. But the healthcare industry is now aware, if not always accepting, of the truism that patients want personal connections with their physicians, nurses, and other caregivers. This requires physician-to-patient communication that includes empathic listening and relationship-building conversations,[2] as discussed in Chapter 5.

Furthermore, some medical schools are teaching their students how to practice empathy.[4] Why? Empirical research has demonstrated substantial benefits of physician empathy. Specifically, patient perceptions of physician empathy have correlated directly with perceptions of physician expertise, interpersonal trust, and the value of information exchange. Plus, perceiving empathy in their physicians led to better recovery from patient discomforts and concerns, better emotional health two months after treatment, and fewer diagnostic tests and referrals to other specialists.[2]

Empathic Communication

The frequency of certain empathy-based communication strategies was systematically observed in hospital inpatient encounters and room visits at Johns Hopkins and the University of Maryland Medical Center.[5] The five communication strategies observed included (a) introducing oneself to the patient; (b) explaining one's role in the patient's care; (c) touching the patient; (d) asking open-ended questions such as, "How are you feeling today?"; and (e) sitting down in the patient's room for a face-to-face conversation, if only briefly.

These desirable communication tactics were disappointingly low among twenty-nine internal medicine interns – doctors in their first year out of medical school. Specifically, these interns touched their patients (either during a physical exam or by offering a handshake or extending a gentle, caring touch) during 65 percent of 732 total visits. They asked an open-ended question on 75 percent of these visits, but introduced themselves during only 40 percent of these. They explained their role during only 37 percent of their visits with a patient and sat down in the patient's room during only 9 percent of these visits. Indeed, all five of the recommended communication behaviors were observed during just 4 percent of the 732 doctor–patient encounters observed.

But when these doctors were questioned about their compliance with the five recommended communication behaviors, they estimated they introduced themselves to patients on 80 percent of the visits and sat down with their patients on 58 percent of the visits – far more often than they actually did. Obviously, these new physicians overestimated their communication skills in this context. "Our perception of ourselves is off a lot of the time," said one of the physicians. "It's no wonder patients don't feel connected to what we are telling them, because many times we are not doing as much as we could to make that connection." Researchers at Thomas Jefferson Medical College of Thomas Jefferson University in Philadelphia have developed a scale to measure a patient's perception of physician empathy.[6] The following five statements are answered by patients with a five-point Likert scale (from 1 = strongly disagree to 5 = strongly agree):

1. My physician understands my emotions, feelings, and concerns;
2. My physician seems concerned about me and my family;

3. My physician can view things from my perspective (i.e., can see things as I see them);
4. My physician asks about what is happening in my daily life;
5. My physician is an understanding doctor.

The scale was completed by 225 patients on 166 different resident physicians. The researchers concluded this five-item scale showed good psychometric qualities and could be used to assess the predictive validity of patient outcomes.[6] The authors of the study concluded that physician empathy, delivered *through* effective communication skills, can increase patients' satisfaction, improve patients' compliance, and enhance physicians' ability to effectively diagnose and treat their patients.[6]

In contrast, these authors concluded that a lack of empathy can have a negative effect on clinical outcomes. In fact, resident physicians' humanistic qualities, communication skills, and professionalism are considered important components of a trainee's evaluation by both the American Board of Internal Medicine, which certifies internists, and the Accreditation Counsel for Graduate Medical Education, which accredits programs in American medical schools.[6]

The faculty at Thomas Jefferson Medical College believes empathy can be taught and learned, as revealed in communication behavior. As a result, physicians in residence at Jefferson are expected to form effective therapeutic relationships with patients and their families; to build these relationships through empathic listening, relationship-building conversations, and appropriate nonverbal communication; and to develop skills for educating and counseling patients and their families with empathy and compassion.[7] Such cultivation of empathic engagement between physician and patient reflects the AC4P Movement and can be achieved if the AC4P principles in the first section of this book, especially Chapter 5 on AC4P communication, are followed.

Barriers to Physician Empathy

Awareness of the need to change physician–patient relationship paradigms is now acknowledged in the medical literature; and in some pockets of excellence, the relevant AC4P education/training of doctors-to-be has been initiated. But substantial barriers stand in the way of widespread practice of physician and caregiver empathy. First and foremost, current reimbursement and physician-practice models limit the availability of patient-centered healthcare. The income of primary-care physicians is not connected to the AC4P relationship between physicians and their patients. In other words, there is no financial incentive for doctors to change their long-standing communication patterns with their patients.[2]

Since primary-care physicians are paid relatively poorly per patient encounter, the emphasis is on increasing the volume of patients seen. This reduces the time doctors spend with individual patients and degrades the physician–patient experience. In other words, we get what we pay for (Chapter 1). Rewarding higher volume leads to shorter, less interactive patient–physician encounters, thereby reducing the quality of the patient's experience. Hurried and stressed physicians order tests or referrals and pre-scribe medicines, all with the intent of appearing competent and giving the illusion of high-quality healthcare.[2]

EXPERIENCING PATIENT-CENTERED CARE

On Friday, October 22, 2010, I (Dave Johnson) entered Thomas Jefferson Hospital in downtown Philadelphia for surgery – endoscopic transnasal/transphenoidal resection of a recurrent nonsecretory pituitary macroadenoma. In other words, with cutting-edge, minimally invasive technology, surgeons would delicately remove a tumor (almost all such tumors are benign) that had wrapped itself around my pituitary gland, at the base of my skull. This would be the second such surgery performed on me; the first took place in 1994 at Temple University Hospital.

The technological advancements since 1994 were, to a layperson, simply astounding. For my first surgery, I was eight days in the hospital. Second time around, I went in on Friday, my surgery was performed on Friday afternoon into the evening, and I returned to my home on Sunday evening. During my brief stay at Jefferson, I experienced both the power of physician empathy and the barriers to AC4P patient-centered healthcare.

My surgeon, Dr. James J. Evans, is both brilliant clinically and empathic personally, even charismatic. Before our first encounter, blood work by an endocrinologist showed I had elevated cortisol levels, suggesting a possible recurrence of a pituitary tumor. This was confirmed by a subsequent MRI. One of the surgeons who had operated on me in 1994, Dr. Robert H. Rosenwasser, was now director of Thomas Jefferson Hospital's Division of Neurovascular Surgery and Endovascular Neurosurgery. I put a call into his office, since the lead surgeon on my 1994 operation had retired. Dr. Rosenwasser's office referred me to Dr. Evans, and I set up a consultative visit with his office.

Meeting My Surgeon

My first meeting with Dr. Evans was positive and encouraging. Nurses biased me beforehand by saying, "Dr. Evans is one of the best and nicest surgeons in the Neurosurgery Department." He seemed to be everyone's favorite. Soon I discovered why. He greeted me with an engaging smile and strong handshake. He was disarmingly young, I'd guess in his late 30s, with a boyish look, trim and fit, crisply dressed in shirt and tie. He projected a warmth that immediately relaxed me, as well as a high energy level with obvious but understated confidence.

I've learned you can often predict the nature of a relationship before a word is spoken. You get a gut, instinctual feeling. Almost immediately the thought flashed through my mind, "I like this guy. I can work with this guy. He's obviously sharp, and from what I have read about him via the Internet, by all accounts he's a highly respected, innovative surgeon."

Dr. Evans outlined the different treatment options: "We could just wait and see if the tumor continues to grow, since it is causing no physical problems, no headaches, and no vision deterioration. We could radiate. Or we could go in there and remove it."

I liked how Dr. Evans repeatedly used the term "we," as though he was referring to a partnership. That's one of the key positive AC4P perceptions among patients: They want to feel they are in a partnership with their physician.[2]

Dr. Evans recommended surgery. I asked how many times he had removed pituitary tumors. "Hundreds and hundreds of times in my ten-year career," he said, "seemingly daily." I didn't want the wait-and-see approach. My tumor was indeed macro, measuring 1.5 centimeters by 2.0 centimeters by 1.1 centimeters. That's almost an inch long and a half-inch thick. Dr. Evans explained the pros and cons of radiation, which did not seem like a sure thing to eradicate the entire tumor. "Let's go in and get it," I said.

Again, the sense was, "Let *us* go in and get it." I trusted this man by the way he carried himself, articulated explanations, and looked me straight in the eye, and by the reputation that preceded him. Dr. Evans was one of *Philadelphia Magazine*'s "Top Docs" in 2010, and again after my surgery in 2012 and 2013.

The next time I saw Dr. Evans I was lying in a hospital bed, behind one of those flimsy curtains, in the pre-op "ready" room. He entered with the same calm air and confidence, the same crisp professionalism, and asked, "How are you feeling?" He then asked other questions: "Do you understand what I'm going to do in the OR?" He explained the risks of surgery, any type of surgery. "Do you understand the risks?" I signed the consent form. "Do you have any other questions?" he asked. "Is your family here? I'll talk with them afterwards. See you in a bit."

Soon I was wheeled into the operating theater, spoke briefly to the anesthesiologist, and saw Dr. Marc R. Rosen, who would assist Dr. Evans – they perform pituitary tumor removals as a team. I remember seeing a number of nurses moving about, and then I was knocked out.

I awoke several hours later in a dark, windowless room – the post-op recovery room. This is supposedly a pit stop for patients on their way to their rooms upstairs. I ended up spending almost twenty-four hours there, definitely not a patient-centered experience.

I was told in so many words there was no room at the inn. The hospital's patients had filled every available room, and I was marooned in the post-op room for the night. It was not pleasant. Due to the nature of my surgery, I could not lie down in a bed. So I spent the night seated in a chair, cushioned by a few pillows. I got no sleep.

Across the dark room I could hear a nurse trying to comfort a moaning woman patient, fearful and in pain. Later, an older gentleman patient, I could not see him behind his curtain, was making an ongoing loud fuss about this and that. He did not seem in full control of his faculties. He did not know where he was. He threatened to get up and walk out. Nurses alternately coddled him and scolded him. I was anything but relaxed.

Suddenly, an act of kindness came my way at about four in the morning. One of the nurses took mercy on me and my predicament and gave me a full-body sponge bath. She was young and did not say a word, but her caring actions spoke louder than any words.

Later, nurses told me the hospital had mistreated me by having me spend the night after surgery sitting up in the noisy post-op room. "You should file a complaint when you leave," I was told. "It's not right you're being treated like this."

Return of AC4P Care

At about seven or eight Saturday morning, Dr. Evans appeared, seemingly out of nowhere. He was dressed in a suit and tie, looking sharp at such an early hour, as though he was on his way to give a lecture. He asked how I was feeling, deplored the way I had just spent the night, and assured me I would be moved to a private room as soon as possible. I was simply impressed the man showed up at such an early hour, dressed so professionally for a Saturday morning. What time had he gotten up and left home that morning?

Looking back, I'm struck by how much the physician–patient relationship can be a matter of actions speaking louder than words. This was the case with Dr. Evans appearing at my bedside so early on a Saturday morning. It meant a lot to me. He obviously wanted to check in on his patient. He actively cared.

I would not see Dr. Evans again during my brief stay at Jefferson. Indeed, I was moved as promised to a private room Saturday afternoon. My attending nurse upstairs was a young man who bicycles to and from his apartment downtown and the hospital. He was attentive, engaging, talked about where he grew up and how he came to be a nurse. He made an initial personal connection with me that allowed me to relax and feel in good spirits.

When researchers conclude patients can't remember the names of the residents who visit them, I can understand why. The residents I saw that weekend in Jefferson Hospital seemed to be an ever-changing cast of characters. Most did introduce themselves, but I'm terrible with names and almost immediately forgot. And I was usually visited by three or four residents at a time, not just one, which made remembering names more difficult. They made it clear they were all under the direction of Dr. Evans, but since it was a weekend, the residents made the rounds and popped in on me. I was fine with that. I had no post-op complications. But the residents were less communicative and more hurried; there was scant give and take with them. No personal connections were made.

The Need to Leave

Any patient in a hospital has one thing on his/her mind: When do I get out? When can I go home? On this I received conflicting information. It was Sunday now and I was told by one resident I'd be leaving Monday morning. A nurse on another shift seemed to confirm this.

Suddenly a resident stood in my doorway, wearing a long leather jacket and a few days' growth of beard. He introduced himself quickly and I didn't catch his name. He spoke with a French accent, he was a muscular guy, and I later kidded with my wife that he seemed like a member of the French mafia, what with his black leather jacket, jeans, and grizzled face. He announced, "We're going to get you out of here today. Dr. Evans says you just need your follow-up MRI." And then he was gone.

I waited, and waited. Around four in the afternoon, a gurney rolled into my room and I was whisked away to have the MRI. I returned to my room an hour or so later and waited for someone to discharge me. I asked a nurse about it, but she knew nothing. I felt out of the loop. I was at the mercy of a very large, very busy city hospital on a late Sunday afternoon when key decision makers were at home. This was not a positive AC4P patient-centered experience.

Around dinnertime a different resident stopped by and said I could go home. Another nurse reviewed my discharge papers and made sure I understood my discharge instructions, including days and times of my follow-up appointments; the medications I should take; symptoms that should prompt me to call my doctor; and restricted activities such as no driving, no lifting, no exercise, "cardiac prudent" nutrition guidelines, and above all *no* blowing my nose. (The surgeons had used my nostrils and nasal cavity to gain access to my pituitary and removed the tumor.)

This was too much information presented too quickly, and it was not fully absorbed by a patient distracted by thoughts of going home, arranging a ride, scheduling a time to meet his ride. Fortunately all the instructions were printed on a form for me to take home.

The late-in-the-day decision to release me caught both my wife (who was my ride) and myself by surprise. We had both believed I would be discharged Monday morning.

My wife was taking our son back to college, so it would be several hours before she reached the hospital. Night came and as I waited alone in my dark room, I became the invisible patient. Since I had been officially discharged, my story was finished as far as the hospital was concerned. I would see no more nurses. I was no one's responsibility. No one entered my room. I was in limbo– again not a particularly patient-centered AC4P experience. All communication with me ceased. Finally my wife arrived and located a young nurse, who wheeled me to the parking garage.

TAKEAWAYS FROM DAVE'S EXPERIENCE

- Patient-centered care, compassion, and empathic communication are easier to come by in one-to-one encounters, such as the conversations I had with my physician, the nurse who gave me the unsolicited sponge bath, and the nurses who regularly visited me in my room.
- Nonverbal communication matters. Appearances, posture, facial expressions, how caregivers conduct themselves, whether they sit down with you or stand, whether they touch you, give you a handshake or a pat on the back, or keep their distance – all these things contribute to the perceived level of AC4P in the healthcare setting.
- Empathy can be taught, but some people seem to be naturally gifted "humanists," if you will, such as Dr. Evans. From his handshake and

personal demeanor to his empathic communication style and eye-to-eye contact, Dr. Evans put you at ease and earned your trust. Nurses had said he was especially friendly, outgoing, and personable. Indeed, I would consider him a "natural" AC4P physician.

- Large hospitals are complex, fast-moving environments with thousands of employees working in decentralized departments. The fragmentation of services – blood tests and other forms of testing, X-rays, MRIs, CAT scans, along with the fragmented of environments, such as laboratories, pharmacies, surgical theaters, food preparation areas, rehabilitation centers, and emergency rooms, to name but some – are barriers to consistent and reliable AC4P patient-centered care. So, too, is the constant churn of nurses changing shifts, physicians shuttling between the operating room, making patient rounds, and returning to their offices for outpatient appointments, and the volume of patients coming and going with shorter stays due to curtailed insurance reimbursements.

EXPERIENCING A LACK OF PATIENT-CENTERED CARE

In May 2002, I (Scott Geller) entered the Radford Hospital in the southwestern Virginia college town of Radford to receive a radical retropubic nerve-sparing prostatectomy. Simply put, I had been diagnosed with prostate cancer three weeks earlier and selected surgery over radiation.

Safety glasses? Check. Sterile gloves? Check. Now please be Actively Caring down there.

Elsewhere I explain the psychological dynamics of the initial diagnosis, the painful recovery, the subsequent return of the cancer, and the trials and tribulations of living with cancer.[8] Here I describe only my experience in the hospital, which I have not documented heretofore.

Reflecting on that three-day hospital stay, I realize the importance of recounting and sharing this unfortunate experience, especially in the context of this chapter. Unfortunately, this story will never reach those who need the feedback – the healthcare professionals who not only made my hospital stay miserable but who contributed to a medical error that could have been fatal. But I'm convinced such lack of corrective behavioral feedback for relevant healthcare workers is all too common. People share their negative hospital experience with friends and family days or weeks after recovery, but they avoid informing the perpetrators of undesirable and correctable healthcare behaviors. So without soon, sincere, behavior-based feedback, undesirable practices will continue with no chance for improvement (Chapter 3).

Indeed, this is a critical take away from my story (and so many others like it): Give specific written and verbal behavior-based feedback to each healthcare professional who affects your hospital experience, positively and/or negatively. It's too late for me, and I regret that to this day (twelve years later), but perhaps this personal story (and the obvious need for patient-centered healthcare) will inspire others to give supportive and corrective feedback to those doctors, nurses, and hospital staff who impact treatment and recovery in a healthcare facility.

Prior to Surgery

I felt a sense of personal control and optimism as I was driven to Radford Hospital at 6:30A.M. on Monday, May 23, 2002, to be prepped for an 8:30A.M. surgery. Although I'm not an early morning riser, I had asked to be the first patient of the surgery team that day, figuring everyone would be most alert at that time. Confident in the surgical skills of the two experienced urologists, I actually looked forward to the experience. Why? I had requested a local anesthetic so I could observe the surgery team in action and later relate the relatively complicated surgery process to others, especially my university students. My urologist, the chief surgeon on the team, had agreed to my unusual request. Moreover, I was guaranteed a private room for postoperative recovery.

I sat up from the operating room (OR) gurney in the pre-op "ready" room to sign the consent form. Then I lay down to receive a spinal anesthesia.

About thirty minutes later, I was wheeled into the operating theater and spoke briefly to the anesthesiologist, emphasizing, "I'm looking forward to watching the OR team in action." Those were the last words I remember. I awoke from a deep sleep in the post-op room at Radford Hospital.

As I gathered my senses in the post-op room, I realized the surgery was finished. I didn't remember anything about the process I had eagerly wanted to watch. I was confused, and I asked the post-op nurse who was monitoring my vital signs, "What happened?" "What do you mean?" she replied. "You've just come from the OR, and you're waking up from surgery, and I'm checking your heart rate and blood pressure. Everything looks good."

"But I didn't want to sleep through the surgery. I received a local anesthetic so I could watch," I reacted. The nurse replied, "I don't know anything about that. You'll have to ask the anesthesiologist."

Sometime later, the anesthesiologist came in to check on me. Before he said a word, I asked, "Why did I sleep throughout the operation? I wanted to watch." His response: "You did watch the beginning of the procedure, but you were asking too many questions, so I put you under." How's that for the opposite of patient-centered care?

Days later I asked my urologist about the anesthesiologist's decision to put me under. "He said I was asking you too many questions. Was that the case? Did my questions bother you?" "Not at all," said the surgeon. "In fact, I liked answering your questions. I didn't even realize the anesthesiologist had put you under." How's that for the opposite of interdependent teamwork in the OR?

Post-Op Recovery

I had a private room and was quite comfortable. I felt minimal pain, perhaps because I had had the spinal anesthesia. Visitors were allowed most of the day, and it was comforting to be with family, friends, and my graduate students. And I thoroughly enjoyed the three meals per day. All this sounds patient-centered, right? But here's a troublesome problem: I could not get the amount of sound sleep I needed.

Throughout each night I could hear periodic loud conversations outside my door, apparently from the night staff. And about every hour or so, a male nurse would bound loudly into my room to check my vitals. And I mean *bound* and *loudly*. So many times I would be suddenly aroused from a sound sleep by this nurse hurriedly busting into my room to record numbers from machines with wires and hoses attached to my body. This was particularly disconcerting because it was always a struggle to get to sleep amid the chattering voices outside my room.

After three noisy nights, enough was enough. I asked my urologist if I could please go home, so I could get some sleep. He looked me over, read the charts, and said, "This is a bit early, but everything looks fine. I will sign the release papers and you may go home."

Home Recovery

My wife drove me to our second home, in Newport, Virginia, with a magnificent mountain view. I was there alone, except for the times my wife and/ or one of my two daughters brought me food. It felt good to be in control of my day and to sleep soundly for eight to nine hours.

I experienced a special advantage of a urinary tract catheter: no need to wake up during the night to urinate. So the elimination of liquids went smoothly, but that was not the case for solid foods. I hadn't had a bowel movement since the surgery, and the concomitant discomfort steadily increased to become unbearable.

The first day of my home-alone recovery, I called my doctor's office to explain my difficulty to his nurse – Barb. She relayed the solution, "Give yourself a Fleets enema." "What is that?" I asked. "I've never given myself an enema." "It's easy," she explained, and proceeded to give me step-by-step instructions. I called my wife, who had frequently given herself a Fleets enema. She brought me the implement that evening and reiterated the instructions given me previously by Barb.

That evening, I locked myself in the bathroom, got down on all fours, and proceeded to ram the pointed plastic end of the Fleets container into my rectum. And to my surprise, it worked fabulously. Indeed, I had to flush the toilet more than five times, my lower abdomen flattened, and I felt so much better. I went to bed early and had the best night's sleep I'd experienced since the surgery.

Early the next morning the phone rang. I answered, and Barb said with an anxious tone, "Scott, are you okay?" "I'm great, Barb, I gave myself that enema and it worked fine. Thanks for your invaluable help." I sensed a sigh of relief on the other end of the phone, as Barb explained that she almost lost her job after telling the urologist about her enema solution. "He said no one but me should have given you that enema. The site of the tube insertion for the enema is millimeters from the surgical sutures. If your self-enema insertions had hit one of those sutures, you could have bled to death without immediate assistance and transportation to the hospital." Recall, I was alone that evening, inside a locked bathroom.

That potentially fatal healthcare error was never investigated and thus few lessons were learned from that mistake. This is a common problem in industry (see Chapter 9), but at least most industrial sites have a protocol for reporting close calls that could have resulted in a serious injury or fatality.

Where does a patient go to report a medical error? How do healthcare workers learn from medical errors perceived by their patients? In my case, who learned from my close call? Indeed, what was the error? The urologist blamed the nurse for giving me potentially deadly advice. But let's dig deeper. No one at the hospital had checked to see if I'd had a bowel movement. They checked many other vital signs ad nauseam, but nothing as basic as a bowel movement. My urologist should not have signed the release papers without making this simple observation, and after that check, he should have given me an enema.

Certainly, the urologist's behavior (or lack thereof) was a factor contributing to my close call. But what other factors were probably involved? Did the local anesthetic inhibit my propensity for a bowel movement? I was told later this was likely the case. If so, why didn't this factor direct attention to the possible need for an enema? Incidentally, I've also been told it's common protocol to ensure a patient's elimination system is working before release from a hospital. This was clearly not the case for me.

Did other factors contribute to my close call? How about my desire to leave the hospital early? If the noisy chatter and the startling interruptions had not made sound sleep impossible, I would not have requested the early release. I would have stayed in the hospital the recommended additional day, giving healthcare workers an opportunity to check my elimination system. Perhaps my discomfort would have reached a level to prompt me to say something – to ask for an enema.

TAKEAWAYS FROM SCOTT'S EXPERIENCE

- The last sentence of my story reflects a major issue. Most patients feel vulnerable and humble, and these person-states can be a barrier to reporting personal concerns, let alone giving feedback about a healthcare worker's behavior. I spent three restless nights at Radford Hospital and never told anyone about the excessive noise outside my room or the abrupt intermittent interruptions each night by the hurried nurse checking my vitals.
- Given the reluctance of patients to give unsolicited feedback to their doctors, nurses, and healthcare technicians, hospitals need to beseech

patients for behavioral feedback relevant to their healthcare, both during and after their hospital stay. Family members who visit a patient should also be given an opportunity to provide feedback on the patient-centered care they observed or did not observe.

- The lack of communication between the anesthesiologist and the urologist during my surgery was disconcerting, and I've been told this is common. The anesthesiologist rules from his/her silo and doesn't meddle with the other silos in the OR. Such independence made my OR experience less than patient-centered, preventing me from learning from my surgery and sharing it with my students.
- The close call I experienced alerted me to the large number of other unidentified medical errors that must occur every day in every healthcare facility, with no analysis of contributing factors, no behavioral feedback, no lessons learned, and no opportunity to improve or reduce the probability of similar errors. Behavior-based safety (BBS) and people-based safety (PBS) have been significantly successful at identifying and correcting human errors before they contribute to a workplace injury (see Chapter 9), and the authors have co-written a book that shows how BBS and PBS can be used to reduce medical error and cultivate an AC4P patient-centered culture in healthcare facilities.[9]

IN CONCLUSION

Regardless of the healthcare institution, we believe patient-centered healthcare requires long-term, early education of the AC4P principles in medical and nursing schools, mandatory training of all healthcare employees in empathic communication, ownership and interpersonal support for patient-centered healthcare, and further empirical research of the positive outcomes that result from an AC4P patient-centered approach to healthcare.

The authors are not alone in their thinking here. In his article "Recognizing the Value of Kindness in Healthcare," George Greensweig, DO, wrote, "In what has become an increasingly depersonalized world of electronic communication, advanced technology and self-service on the Internet, kindness may seem inconsequential. But kindness is, indeed, important to patients. Feeling comfort, experiencing a sense of community and being cared for as a whole person and not just as an illness, allow patients to focus on healing."[10]

What are the solutions to the hustle and bustle of busy healthcare facilities? Is disjointed, disconnected patient care less likely in a smaller facility? An answer to this second question requires empirical study, but it's worth noting that the hospital site for Scott's negative experience is much smaller than Jefferson Hospital and is nestled in the semirural town of Radford, Virginia.

Regardless of the size of the healthcare facility, a systematic patient-centered feedback system is needed – one that solicits meaningful observations from patients and their family members regarding the quality of healthcare services provided. Plus, there must be a protocol in place for reviewing the feedback forms and deriving action plans from the lessons learned. Analogous applications have been successful at preventing injuries in industry, and the evidence-based observation, feedback, and coaching techniques used in industries worldwide are readily adaptable to application in healthcare facilities.[11]

The journey to implementing AC4P values and behaviors that will result in better patient-centered care has begun. Competition between hospitals for patients will provide momentum. Education, training, coaching, and mentoring based on the AC4P principles covered in the first part of this book, combined with the adoption of AC4P values, can make this happen. Indeed, textbooks, DVDs, CDs, and workbooks are currently available to facilitate a paradigm shift toward patient-centered healthcare.[12] But what healthcare facility can afford the time and response cost required to teach, apply, and support these AC4P principles? Without a change in response-consequence contingencies, including financial incentives and/or salary adjustments for participants, we fear a large-scale improvement in healthcare is unlikely.

DISCUSSION QUESTIONS

1. Consider your most recent visit to your personal physician. In what ways could the exchange between you and the physician have been improved?
2. Explain the connection between healthcare and humanistic behaviorism.
3. Discuss barriers to physicians practicing empathy with their patients.
4. If possible, describe portions of a personal healthcare experience that was disappointing. Why was the experience disappointing?
5. If possible, describe particularly positive aspects of an experience with one or more healthcare workers. What human dynamics made the experience positive?
6. Explain how behavioral feedback could prevent the kind of negative healthcare events experienced by Scott Geller. Include suggestions

for providing relevant feedback to healthcare workers, including physicians.

7. What dispositional and/or situational factors could hinder your ability to speak up and give feedback to a busy, authority-figure physician who is not accustomed to receiving feedback from a patient?

8. What is meant by the term "patient-centered" healthcare?

9. Given present-day healthcare cultures, with overly scheduled physicians, limited time with patients, and long waiting times, how could healthcare professionals improve the culture of their organizations?

10. Discuss the role played by a patient advocate, perhaps the adult child of an elderly patient unable to ask all the right questions and absorb technical information. In what ways can a patient advocate actively care for both the patient and the healthcare providers?

REFERENCES

1. Institute of Medicine (2000). *To err is human: Building a safer health system.* Washington, DC: National Academies Press.

2. Richert, J. (2012, January 24). Patient-centered care: What it means and how to get there. *Health Affairs Blog.* Retrieved May 21, 2014 from http:healthaffairs .org/blog/2012/01/24/patient-centered-what-it-means-and-how-to-get-there/.

3. Rodak, S. (2012, October 18). Ten guiding principles for patient-centered care. *Becker's Hospital Review.* Retrieved May 21, 2014 from www.beckershospitalreview .com/quality/10-guiding-principles-for-patient-centered-care.htm.

4. WMCN, "Dawn," Interview with Mohammadreza Hojat, Ph.D., Thomas Jefferson Medical College research professor (February, 2014).

5. Block, L., Hutzler, L., Habicht, R., Wu, A. W., Desai, S. V., Silva, K. N., et al. (2013). Do internal medicine interns practice etiquette-based communication? A critical look at the inpatient encounter. *Journal of Hospital Medicine*, 8(11), 631–634.

6. Gregory, G. C., Gotto, J. L., Mangione, S., West, S., & Hojat, M. (2007) Jefferson scale of patients' perceptions of physician empathy: Preliminary psychometric data. *Croatian Medical Journal*, 48(1), 81–86.

7. Hojat, M., Axelrod, D., Spandorfer, J., & Mangione, S. (2013). Enhancing and sustaining empathy in medical students. *Medical Teacher*, 35(12) 996–1001.

8. Geller, E. S. (2014). Living with cancer: The survival power of AC4P. In E. S. Geller (Ed.). *Actively caring for people: Cultivating a culture of compassion* (4th ed.) (pp. 311–318). Newport, VA: Make-A-Difference, LLC.

9. Geller, E. S., & Johnson, D. (2007). *People-based patient safety: Enriching your culture to prevent medical error.* Virginia Beach, VA: Coastal Training Technologies.

10. Greensweig, G. (2011). *Recognizing the value of kindness in healthcare.* posted online March 13, 2014 at www.hhnmag.com, *Hospitals & Health Networks* magazine.

11. Cooper, M. D. (2003). Behavior-based safety: Still a viable strategy. *Safety & Health*, 4, 46–48; Daniels, A. C. (1989) *Performance management.* Tucker,

GA: Performance Management Publications; Fellner, D. J., & Sulzer-Azaroff, B. (1984). Increasing industrial safety practices and conditions through posted feedback. *Journal of Safety Research*, 15, 7–21; Geller, E. S., & Williams, J. H. (2001). *Keys to behavior-based safety from Safety Performance Solutions.* Rockville, MD: Government Institutes; Geller, E. S. (1998). *Understanding behavior-based safety: Step-by-step methods to improve your workplace* (2nd ed.). Neenah, WI: J. J. Keller & Associates; Geller, E. S. (1999).Behavior-based safety: Confusion, controversy, and clarification. *Occupational Health and Safety*, 68(1), 40–49; Krause, T. R., Hidley, J. H., & Hodson, S. J. (1996). *The behavior-based safety process: Managing involvement for an injury-free culture* (2nd ed.). New York: Van Nostrand Reinhold; McSween, T. E. (1995). *The value-based safety process: Improving your safety culture with a behavioral approach.* New York: Van Nostrand Reinhold; Sulzer-Azaroff, B., & de Santamaria, M. C. (1980). Industrial safety hazard reduction through performance feedback. *Journal of Applied Behavior Analysis*, 13, 287–297; Williams, J. H., & Geller, E. S. (2000) Behavior-based interventions for occupational safety: Critical impact of social comparison feedback. *Journal of Safety Research*, 31, 135–142; Zohar, D., Cohen, A., & Azar, N. (1980) Promoting increased use of ear protectors in noise through information feedback. *Human Factors*, 22(1), 69–79.

12. *People-based patient safety: A skills-building and life-changing process.* (2007). Virginia Beach, VA: Coastal Training Technologies. A videotape and DVD program with a workbook for each of five videotapes and DVDs designed to teach healthcare workers strategies for reducing errors in hospitals and medical centers in order to keep their patients out of harm's way.

15

Actively Caring for Our Children

ANGELA K. FOURNIER, KELLI ENGLAND WILL,
AND KATE LARSON

> It's not our job to toughen our children up to face a cruel and heartless
> world. It's our job to raise children who will make the world a little less
> cruel and heartless.
> – L. R. Knost

The applied behavioral science (ABS) principles of actively caring for people (AC4P) are critical for effective childcare. Appropriate applications of
these principles can dramatically improve behavior and the way caregivers
teach children healthy, prosocial behavior. Many parents and caregivers use
these principles already without knowing it. Others can benefit from learning the principles and their applications.

You may already be a parent or a teacher, or plan to care for children
someday. Perhaps you work as a nanny or help your family by caring for
younger siblings. Many careers involve working with children (e.g., teachers, healthcare professionals, and coaches). The ABS principles can be
applied to all of these situations to make the work of caring for children
more effective and enjoyable for both caregiver and child.

This chapter reviews the ways ABS can be used to benefit childcare. It
describes how the key principles explained in Chapter 1, which have been
effectively applied to the promotion of healthy behavior in the workplace,[1]
in healthcare facilities,[2] and in schools,[3] can be used every day in childcare situations. In addition, the most common childcare challenges are
addressed, as are specific solutions provided by ABS.

Relationships between the ABS approach and healthy development are
discussed throughout this chapter in order to make salient the connection
between ABS principles and AC4P behavior. We focus on *early childhood*,
addressing specific milestones and challenges in the care of children who

TABLE 15.1. *Baumrind's original parenting styles*[5]

Authoritative	Parents encourage independence with limits and controls, supportive feedback
	Children are cheerful, self-controlled, self-reliant, friendly, and cooperative
Authoritarian	Parents are restrictive and punitive, rigid, harsh
	Children are fearful, anxious, have poor initiation and communication skills
Neglectful	Parents are uninvolved
	Children are socially incompetent, have poor self-control and low self-esteem, at risk for deliquesce
Indulgent	Parents are very involved with few demands or controls
	Children are disrespectful, domineering, egocentric

are 3–8 years of age. Nonetheless, the ABS principles are critical to caring for children of all ages and in all stages of their development.

It's not until age 3 that children have the cognitive ability to learn from the ABS principles discussed here. Still, behavior management is certainly an important role for parents and caregivers of children under age 3. Discipline for children under age 3 consists essentially of ignoring unwanted behavior, distracting the child, and managing the environment to prevent unwanted behavior and ensure safety.[4] The use of ABS strategies effectively in early childhood, as soon as children are developmentally ready, can lay the foundation for continued success in the future, from middle childhood to adolescence.

RELEVANCE TO PARENTING LITERATURE

Diana Baumrind's four parenting styles, which have been shown to result in fairly predictable outcomes, are often described in the literature on parenting. Table 15.1 lists these four styles – authoritarian, authoritative, neglectful, and indulgent.[5] Authoritative parenting is recommended because it's associated with the most successful outcomes for children. Research consistently shows authoritarian, neglectful, and indulgent forms of parenting are associated with negative outcomes for children, including behavioral problems (e.g., poor initiation, low self-control, delinquency), poor psychosocial adjustment (e.g., low self-esteem, social incompetence, egocentrism) and negative emotional outcomes (e.g., fearfulness, anxiety).

Conversely, children raised by authoritative parents or caretakers are cheerful, self-controlled, friendly, and cooperative. As you read this chapter, you'll see that AC4P parenting is consistent with authoritative parenting. The AC4P process encourages parents to be involved, to have consistent limits and appropriate controls, and to be flexible and stay positive. *AC4P parenting* is the label we prefer, since the terms *authoritarian* and *authoritative* can be easily confused. (Recall the issue of language discussed in Chapter 5 with regard to nurturing a more compassionate culture.)

Given different parenting styles and predictable outcomes, researchers have developed interventions to improve childcare skills. ABS strategies are critical to the success of the most effective of these interventions, including Parent Management Training,[6] Incredible Years,[7] Triple P,[8] and Family Check-Up.[9] These training programs tend to target parents of children with significant behavioral or emotional problems, including psychological disorders such as conduct disorder. This chapter is aimed at applying ABS to everyday childcare practices, with the mission of increasing the frequency of healthy, adaptive behavior among all young children.

APPLYING ABS PRINCIPLES TO CHILDCARE

Identifying Target Behaviors

Many day-to-day goals and challenges of parents and other caregivers are connected to behavior – what adults want children to do – "Eat your vegetables," "Do your homework" – or *not* do – "Stop hitting your sister," "Don't run in the house." But often adults use language that addresses an internal state or characteristic – "Be nice," "Be good," "Don't be naughty." ABS tells us we will be much more effective when targeting *observable behaviors* – something we can see the child do (or not do). "Be good" is an ambiguous nonbehavioral label. It might imply certain desired behaviors (e.g., "Say please and thank you"; "Keep your hands to yourself"), but it can be interpreted differently by two parents, by parents versus teachers, and certainly by children versus their caregivers.

If an observable behavior is not specified, neither the caregiver nor the child knows whether an expectation has been met. For example, it may be difficult to determine whether a child has followed a parent's order to "be good," but it's easy to determine whether the child demonstrated good manners by saying "please" and "thank you" at dinner. With children more than any other age group, it's critical to be *specific* when referring to behavior. And since children don't develop the ability to think abstractly until around age 12,[10] caregivers should use concrete language when stating expectations and providing feedback to young children. In addition, it's critical to avoid the use of abstract internal characteristics and the use of negative labels.

The Impact of Labeling. Behavior can be changed much more easily than a personality trait. For example, telling a child you're disappointed s/he didn't clean her/his room is much less threatening to the child's sense of self than telling the child s/he is "sloppy" or "messy." *Sloppy* and *messy* are labels, suggesting the problem is global and permanent – a part of who they are. Using ability labels in this way can contribute to a negative self-concept,[11] with children identifying themselves as "bad," "naughty," or "sloppy."

People tend to live up to the labels they are given, whether the label is positive or negative, according to the work by Kraut[12] and Dweck[13] described in Chapter 6. This is true for both young children and adolescents. Children labeled "neat and tidy" are more likely to clean up after others and children labeled "delinquent" tend to engage in further delinquent behavior.[14]

We should move the focus from the actor to the act, as revealed in Chapter 6. Suppose a child is throwing a tantrum, for example. We could tell the child, "You're a naughty boy," or we could say, "Your behavior is naughty." The second statement addresses what the child is *doing*, while the first statement is more global, addressing *who he is* – always and everywhere. We can further improve the communication by identifying the specific "naughty" behavior – "Kicking and screaming is naughty behavior." This informs the child which behavior is unacceptable and transfers the negative label from the child to the behavior.

A seminal experiment by Rosenthal and Jacobson[15] showed that labeling children can have a powerful effect on their caregivers' behavior, changing the way children are treated by others. Teachers in an elementary school were told some of their students were top scorers on a test designed to identify students who would experience a period of intense intellectual development over the next year (i.e., "academic bloomers"). In reality, the students were randomly selected and were no different from the rest of the class.

A year later, the "bloomers" outperformed their peers by 10–15 IQ points. It was suggested the teachers had unknowingly treated these "bloomers" differently, fostering greater academic development. This phenomenon of treating a labeled person in a way consistent with the label is known as the self-fulfilling prophecy[16] – a powerful form of social influence.

State the Expectation Clearly. *Proactive* childcare is likely to be more effective and less frustrating than *reactive* childcare for both the caregiver and the child. In proactive childcare, the caregiver clearly states a behavioral expectation to the child before a problem begins. With reactive parenting, the parent or caregiver waits until a problem occurs and then reacts. Unfortunately, a reactive approach is much more common in our society.

Parents, teachers, coaches, and work supervisors often wait until a problem occurs and then react to it rather than address a potential problem by taking measures to prevent it. For example, we spend much more money on treating people already sick with *preventable* diseases than on efforts to *prevent* the disease (despite the fact that we could save billions by doing the latter).[17] Childcare is much the same. It seems easier or more convenient to wait until a problem occurs and then react than to think ahead and put contingencies in place for prevention.

Stating expectations and contingencies before a behavior problem occurs results in more successes and fewer corrections. This means less frustration for the caregiver and a more positive self-perception for the child. Parenting interventions designed to increase proactive and positive childcare result in improved skills among caregivers and decreased disruptive behavior among children.[18]

Instruct What to Do. Caregivers should tell children what to do by targeting *desired* behaviors, rather than what not to do by targeting *undesired* behaviors. Why? If we tell a child what not to do (e.g., "Don't bounce the ball in the house"), he might choose another undesired behavior instead (e.g., throw the ball in the house). On the other hand, if we tell a child what to do and address the undesired behavior(s) at the same time (e.g., "Keep the ball outside"), we can get the behavior we want and avoid a multitude of undesired behaviors. Think of it this way – in any given situation there is probably one behavior we want the child to do and many more behaviors we don't want the child to do.

" MOM, YOU SAID NOT TO BOUNCE THE BALL...BUT I THREW IT. "

Be clear about desired behavior. This is the best way to get desirable results and is least frustrating for the parent or caregiver. It's also the easiest way for children to succeed in meeting expectations. Thus, there is bound to be less negativity from parents. Giving clear expectations is AC4P behavior because it sets children up for success rather than failure. Imagine adapting this proactive approach to all aspects of childcare. Referring to Covington's[19] motivational typologies in Chapter 1, this approach promotes the desirable success-seeker state over the undesirable failure-avoider state.

Model the Desired Behavior. Tell children what to do and *show* them what to do, by modeling desired behavior. The old adage, "Do as I say, not as I do" doesn't work; kids do what they see their parents, caregivers, and peers doing. *Observational learning,* also referred to as *vicarious learning,* is the process of learning by observing other people's behavior and the conse-quences of their behavior.[20]

"WHY DON'T YOU HAVE TO WEAR A HELMET, MOM?"

A prime example of the power of observational learning with children is Albert Bandura's seminal Bobo doll research.[21] In this 1965 study, chil-dren watched a video of an adult model behaving aggressively with a toy Bobo Doll (i.e., punching and kicking the doll). The children were then put in a room with the Bobo Doll and given the freedom to play however they chose. The children played aggressively, using the same physical movements shown in the video. Plus, the children's responses were influenced by the *consequences* of the model's behavior. Children who saw that the model's aggressive behavior had negative consequences showed *less* imitative behavior than children who saw that the model's aggressive behavior had positive consequences or no consequences at all.

This was the first of many studies showing the powerful impact of observational learning through interpersonal interaction and the media. The strongest social influence on children's behavior, all the way through the college years, according to research, is the modeling behavior of parents and peers. A longitudinal study by Lau, Quadrel, and Hartman[22] explored factors influencing young adults' health beliefs and behavior regarding alcohol use, diet, exercise, and vehicle safety belt use. Parents have a significant influence on young people's health-related beliefs and behaviors, they concluded.

Parents were influential in all areas, with safety-belt use being almost completely influenced by parents rather than peers. These healthy lifestyle behaviors and beliefs develop over one's lifetime, beginning in early childhood, the authors emphasized. They also concluded that while explicit training efforts by parents did significantly influence children's health-related behavior, the direct association between parents' behavior and children's behavior had a substantially higher impact. What we *teach* our children is important, but what we *show* them is even more important.

Focusing on External Factors to Explain Behavior

A toddler's refusal to eat at mealtimes might be attributed to a "picky" palate or a "stubborn" personality. Frequent tantrums in a preschooler might be attributed to a "difficult" temperament. Note the pattern here – problem *behavior* (e.g., refusing food, throwing tantrums) is attributed to internal *characteristics* (e.g., stubborn, difficult). Referring to the fundamental attribution error[23] discussed in Chapter 9, we are likely to attribute the behavior of others, including our children, to internal or dispositional characteristics. The ABS principles advise us to look at external or situational factors instead – things in the environment – that can explain a behavioral problem.

Recall from Chapter 1 that Skinner acknowledged the impact of both internal and external variables on our behavior. ABS focuses on external variables because these can be directly observed and measured, making an objective ABS analysis feasible. External factors are also more controllable, allowing for potential intervention and behavior change.

A child's temperament is present from early infancy and is considered by developmental psychologists to be fairly stable.[24] Temperament has a significant influence on behavior, but trying to change this factor is impractical. Even dispositional factors that change more easily (e.g., mood, energy level, perception, and attitude) are inappropriate targets because they cannot be objectively observed and are not easily controlled. In addition, children, particularly younger ones, can have difficulty identifying and expressing their internal person-states. On the other hand, variables in the child's environment can be clearly observed and in many cases managed to shape healthy, adaptive behavior and influence the occurrence of positive internal person-states.

Let's return to the example of temper tantrums. Dispositional causal factors might include hunger, fatigue, or frustration. Observable behaviors may suggest these internal person-states (e.g., a child yawns and rubs her eyes moments before losing it – kicking and screaming in the middle of the grocery store), but we cannot directly observe or control these internal states. We can, however, note when and where tantrums are most likely to occur and what seems to happen just before and just after they are observed. Unfortunately, a major temper tantrum is difficult to ignore and often gets immediate attention from a caregiver.

Depending on the intensity (e.g., the child is screaming loud enough to wake the dead) and location (e.g., in the middle of a crowded store), parents can be quite motivated to stop a temper tantrum immediately. Regrettably, this often means giving children whatever they want, as illustrated on the following page. In this and many childcare situations, we actually sustain the problem behavior by inadvertently rewarding the undesired behavior. Becoming skilled at identifying and adjusting the antecedents and consequences of the problem behavior is key.

Directing with Activators and Motivating with Consequences

Activators. Remember from Chapter 1 that an activator, or behavioral antecedent, is a signal occurring before a certain behavior. It can be a condition in the environment that sets the stage for the behavior or an event that prompts the behavior. Parents and other caregivers can often control the environment. In general, caregivers control what, where, and when their children eat, sleep, play, and work. The younger the child, the more this is true. Thus, a parent can usually do something to set the stage (i.e., create

environmental conditions) for desired behavior. This entails factors like the physical space, the food, clothing, and activities available, as well as the rules of the home or classroom.

Caregivers need to be aware of the environment and how it affects a given child's behavior. If there's a behavior to change, caregivers should identify situational variables that make the behavior more or less likely to occur. For example, the presence of soda in the home likely increases the probability a child will consume sugar and caffeine, which can increase the probability of hyperactive and unruly behavior. Contingency management (e.g., manipulating response antecedents and consequences) can certainly be used to limit the quantity and frequency of soda consumption; an even easier and more effective approach is to merely eliminate soda from the home environment altogether.

As defined in Chapter 1, incentives are activators that announce the availability of a reward following a designated desirable behavior. A parent might announce that an A on the next report card will be rewarded with a trip to the zoo. Unfortunately, many parents are more apt to use disincentives to control their children's behavior. For example, children are told, "Practice your piano or no television the rest of the night" or "Eat your vegetables or no desert." A simple change in words can turn these disincentives into incentives: "Practice your piano for thirty minutes and you can watch television for one hour" or "Eat your vegetables and you can have the special desert."

Disincentives can be effective in the short term, but remember these effects are usually short-lived and accompanied by unintended side effects. Using disincentives or threats to control behavior can instill a sense of fear or anxiety and set up a child to avoid failure rather than seek success, with a long-term negative impact on self-motivation (Chapter 3).

Consequences. Alone or paired with activators, consequences motivate the occurrence and recurrence of behavior. Following a child's behavior with the right consequence is an excellent way to increase the frequency of the right behavior. Consequences can be verbal, as in verbal praise ("Atta boy! Good job!") or scolding ("Shame on you. I'm disappointed"). When using verbal consequences, whether rewarding or penalizing, it's important to designate the target behavior ("I like the way you cleaned your room") rather than make a vague statement ("Good job") or refer to a personal characteristic ("Bad boy"). Referring to the target behavior tells a child the behavior you want and avoids global statements or labels that are ineffective and potentially harmful.

Consequences can also be material – an object is given or taken away – or they can be behavioral – an activity the child wants to do or avoid. It's best if the consequence is closely related to the target behavior. For example, if a child breaks a window with a baseball, he can help repair the window or do chores to compensate for the cost of a replacement. The lesson becomes more influential the closer the consequence connects with the target behavior, in time and in kind.

People are motivated more by immediate consequences than delayed consequences. This is especially true for children, who live in the present and for whom attention span is limited.[10] Remember from Chapter 1 that a behavior is most likely to occur when it's followed by a *soon, certain,* and *significant* consequence. As illustrated on the next page, waiting until a later time to address a behavioral problem is not recommended. Reward charts are an effective way to increase desired behavior in children. They allow for a small, immediate consequence followed by a sizable consequence in the future.

Consequences should be consistent; children need to be certain their behavior will be followed by the announced consequence. The consequence should be *certain*. This is an important point for parents and other caregivers. Many consider consistency a cardinal rule of effective parenting,[25] whether the consequence is a reward or a penalty.[26] Giving consequences (good or bad) inconsistently is unfortunately one of the most common mistakes made by caregivers. Such inconsistency often occurs with the same caregiver or between different caregivers.

Focusing on Positive Consequences

The principle of focusing on positive rather than negative consequences is just as important when one is working with children as it is with adults in the workplace or in social settings. Positive rather than negative consequences should be used to shape children's behavior, if at all possible. The pitfalls of using negative consequences to control behavior were explained in Chapter 1, so we won't review them here. Still, certain issues specific to children arise when the ABS principles are applied to parenting or managing the behavior of children. The following issues – spanking and rewarding – are on either side of a continuum, from most undesirable and ineffective to most desirable and effective.

Spanking. Spanking, or corporal punishment as it's sometimes called, is an important topic to address. Each family has its own value system and cultural beliefs, which influence the treatment of children. Although the use of corporal punishment is quite common during early childhood,[27] it's not recommended by the American Academy of Pediatrics[28] – for good reason. As mentioned earlier with respect to the undesirable side effects of negative consequences, a spanking may result in compliance initially but noncompliance later. In addition, consistent use of negative consequences can have lasting negative effects on the recipient. The research on using corporal punishment on children is clear; it's often associated with extremely negative outcomes.

Children subjected to corporal punishment are more likely to show aggression and other conduct problems.[29] They are also at risk for depression, anxiety, and substance abuse.[30] Spanking is not very effective in getting the behavior you desire and comes with extra baggage you don't want. When a penalty is necessary to address an undesired behavior, the American Academy of Pediatrics recommends using the timeout technique. This technique is another way of applying the ABS principles to changing behavior and is discussed later in this chapter.

Too Many Rewards? On the other end of the consequence continuum, some complain that American society has gotten too soft and children are rewarded too often. Others suggest that rewarding or praising children for their behavior decreases intrinsic motivation, robbing them of the feeling of success or accomplishment. Alfie Kohn, author of the book *Punished by Rewards*, suggests rewarding behavior is a form of control that decreases intrinsic motivation and makes one dependent on extrinsic rewards.[31] Regarding parenting, he claims praise and other forms of reward are gentle forms of coercion that teach children to focus on what others think of their behavior rather than on what they think and feel about themselves.[32]

So are rewards good or bad? The answer depends on certain circumstances, research suggests, but Kohn is much more wrong than right. Let's refer again to Carol Dweck's research on children praised for either their ability or their effort. Praising *effort* results in better performance and more accurate self-evaluations than praising *ability*.[33] This line of research provides evidence for the ABS principle of focusing on behavior rather than internal characteristics. When a child's behavior (i.e., demonstrated effort) was praised, both performance and positive person-states improved.

Another concern about using praise: Children may become "praise junkies,"[31] requiring more and more recognition for even the most basic behavior. This brings up an important point: ABS strategies are implemented to facilitate *learning* – a relatively permanent change in behavior. The mission of parents or caretakers is to help children learn appropriate behavior in various situations. This often means using positive consequences to increase the frequency or improve the quality of a desired behavior.

An important caveat: Once a behavior has been learned and is performed consistently, we should reduce the delivery of extrinsic consequences over time.[33] However, the research literature consistently refutes concerns of over-rewarding children's behavior, and overwhelmingly supports the efficacy of using positive consequences to reward the behavior or effort of children.[34]

Due to its direct, objective nature, contingency management is often a critical component of educational and training plans for children, particularly children with limited cognitive abilities due to their young age or an intellectual disability. Understanding a child's abilities, as well as related internal feelings and attitudes, is key to effectively shaping healthy, adaptive behavior. In addition, as explained in Chapter 3, if the verbal behavior associated with the delivery of a reward facilitates a perception of competency, choice, and/or social support, self-motivation is activated, thus increasing the probability of behavioral sustainability.

Designing Interventions with Consideration of Internal Feelings and Attitudes

Contingency management should be successful across many people, places, and situations as a learning technique, but a comprehensive understanding of the learner is critical. We humans are complex, with unique thoughts, feelings, and attitudes. We have different preferences and aversions. We also have different abilities and challenges. Although we cannot necessarily observe or measure such dispositional factors as feelings, attitudes, and abilities, these person-states impact our behavior and we need to consider these when implementing a behavior-change plan. This is a fundamental principle of humanism, reflecting the term *humanistic behaviorism*, as introduced in the Preface of this book and explained further in Chapter 2.

Chapter 1 discussed the importance of accounting for internal feelings and attitudes when designing behavioral interventions. In addition to accounting for internal factors due to individual differences, working with children requires that we also account for their developmental stage.

Challenges	Responsbilities
• Testing Limits	• Homework
• Sleep/Wake Times	• Household Chores
• Eating	• Sharing
• Toilet Training	• Self-Care
• Tantrums	

FIGURE 15.1. Typical challenges and responsibilities for children in early childhood.

Developmental Stage. Children experience many physical, cognitive, and emotional changes throughout early childhood. These changes present particular challenges for parents and caregivers, and determine the kind of behavior-change intervention that should be used. Figure 15.1 lists certain developmentally appropriate responsibilities and behavioral challenges typical of early childhood. In addition to growing two to three inches per year, children in early childhood develop gross motor skills (e.g., running, catching, throwing) as well as fine motor skills (e.g., using eating utensils, dressing themselves).[24]

Cognitively, children in early childhood are in what Jean Piaget called the *preoperational* stage of development, which is characterized by two substages.[10] Between 2 and 4 years of age, children develop *symbolic function*: the ability to remember, understand, and replicate objects in their mind. This ability to understand that one thing can represent something else means children at this age can begin to understand if–then contingencies (Chapter 3) and benefit from incentive/reward programs. However, there is wide variability within this two-to four-year period, making it important to assess a child's symbolic function. Expecting children to understand and comply with a request that is beyond their cognitive ability will lead to disappointment and can spur shame and self-doubt.

The preoperational stage is also a time of *egocentrism*. Children see the world from their perspective and are generally unable to take the perspective of others. This likely contributes to some of the interpersonal challenges typical of early childhood (e.g., difficulty in sharing).

The second sub stage of the preoperational stage occurs between 4 and 7 years of age. Children develop *intuitive thought* at this time. Cognitive processes progress from holding magical beliefs to rational beliefs, and children can appreciate dual relationships, understanding that something can be an object itself *and* a symbol for something else. These developments improve children's understanding of if–then contingencies, allowing them to take a more collaborative role in developing and implementing basic incentive/reward programs, as well as understanding progressively more complex behavioral-improvement plans.

Language requires both physical and cognitive abilities, and these also change dramatically throughout early childhood. Language development influences behavior and should be considered in understanding early childhood behavior and applying interventions. For example, a toddler's inability to adequately express her wants and needs, can result in frustration, serving as an antecedent to undesired behavior. Similarly, interventions relying too much on verbal behavior may fall flat with a 5-year-old who has good verbal expression but still has limited comprehension.

Children with Special Needs. Some children have emotional or cognitive challenges, in addition to the developmental factors influencing all children, that have to be taken into consideration in the management of their behavior. The direct, present-focused nature of ABS intervention makes it ideal for children with learning disorders as well as those who have compromised cognitive abilities.

Attention deficit/hyperactivity disorder (ADHD) and autism spectrum disorder (ASD) are discussed here as examples of conditions that impact early childhood behavior and have been most successfully addressed with ABS. It's estimated that 5 percent of children in the United States meet the diagnostic criteria for attention deficit/hyperactivity disorder.[35] While an accurate diagnosis cannot be made before age 7, children often show signs in early childhood.

Both inattention and hyperactivity impact which behaviors should be targeted and the contingencies used to manage them. For example, a child who struggles with hyperactivity may not be able to follow the command, "Sit still and stay in your chair until dinner is over." It would be more realistic for the child to remain seated while eating but have a break during the dinner period to get out of his/her seat and "get some wiggles out." Again, we need to customize the process for the particular child (i.e., humanistic behaviorism).

The field of applied behavior analysis or ABS has addressed the special needs of children with developmental disabilities in general and autism spectrum disorder in particular for more than sixty years.[36] ASD is a neurotic developmental disorder present in early childhood, characterized by significant problems with social, emotional, and communication skills.[35] This disorder is diagnosed in early childhood, with diagnosis made as early as 2 years of age and remaining fairly stable throughout childhood.[37] Research consistently shows ABS intervention to be the most effective method for managing the behaviors of children with ASD.[38] Consequently, ABS has become the treatment of choice for ASD.[39]

Applying the Scientific Method

This ABS principle is critical for developing and implementing an effective AC4P process for optimum childcare. Once we have targeted a behavior we wish to change, identified external factors that influence it, and developed a plan to address the target behavior through activators and positive consequences appropriate for the child, we need to test our plan with the scientific method. We show we care when we apply the most effective technique to a particular target behavior.

We've discussed the importance of working within a child's abilities and customizing activators and consequences to direct and motivate desirable behavior, respectively. Applying the scientific method helps to determine if the selected activators and consequences *are* optimal. To test an ABS method for childcare, it's best to collect data before and after implementing an intervention. For example, you might record how many times during dinner the child breaks the mealtime rules by getting out of his/her seat, playing with the food, or belching across the table.

Take the same count after posting mealtime rules or initiating a reward chart for appropriate mealtime behavior. If the desired behavior change has not occurred, check the appropriateness of the target behavior, reexamine external factors that influence the behavior, and consider your activators and consequences. Adjust as needed and try again. Once an intervention is working, keep it going until the child performs the target behavior consistently.

Following are some examples of the AC4P principles put into action with specific childcare issues and challenges. First, we review two evidence-based tools for caregivers – reward charts and the timeout technique. Both adhere to the ABS intervention principles and are very effective in improving child behavior. They can be implemented by parents, grandparents, teachers, or daycare providers, and can be used throughout early childhood, with proper adaptation to a child's maturation.

Mia's Reward Chart

	Job	S	M	T	W	T	F	S
	Pick up Toys							
	Brush Teeth							
	Make Bed							
	Do Homework							
	Extra							

FIGURE 15.2. Reward chart for a 7-year-old girl.

THE REWARD CHART: USING ABS PRINCIPLES
TO IMPROVE BEHAVIOR

A reward chart like the one shown in Figure 15.2 can be quite effective for addressing most behavioral issues. Note that the focus on the chart is achievement: *doing* desired behaviors; *not* stopping undesired behavior. Reward charts put the ABS principles into action and are useful for children ages 3–10. By age 3 most children can make performance-related judgments and thus should be able to understand the concept of earning a sticker on a chart for performing a desired behavior.[40]

It's futile to use a reward chart before a child can understand if–then contingencies. The child needs to make the connection between the desired behavior and the rewarding consequence. When it's easily visible to the child, the chart serves as an activator, reminding the child of the desired behavior and the positive consequence(s) of performing the behavior.

The chart in Figure 15.2 was used with a 7-year-old girl. The goal was to increase several daily behaviors regarding schoolwork and self-care. Although her parents defined the desired behaviors, referred to as "jobs," the child was involved in negotiating the rewards, writing the rewards on the chart, and deciding where to keep the chart (see Figure 15.3). Involving the child gave her ownership in the process and increased her motivation to do the tasks and earn the rewards. Note the "Extra" row in the "Job" column. In the true spirit of self-motivation (Chapter 3), this allowed the child to be rewarded for going above and beyond required daily tasks (e.g., helping parents, caring for pets) and perceiving a sense of competence, choice, and connection to others.

The child earned a sticker to place on the chart after completing a chore. This served as an immediate positive consequence. After earning a

FIGURE 15.3. Establishing ownership in a reward chart: a reward chart printed from a home computer (upper left); child writes potential prizes to be earned (lower left); and child puts stickers on the chart for doing the desired behavior (right).

designated number of stickers, the child was rewarded with a larger prize, such as a chance to go on a special outing. This was a *significant* consequence.

Parents can make their own personalized reward charts or download charts available online. Several Websites (e.g., kiddycharts.com) provide reward charts that can be downloaded and printed at no cost. For the child who loves mobile games and applications, free mobile apps are available (e.g., Chore Monster) for maintaining engagement and helping both the caregiver and the child track behaviors and opportunities to provide a rewarding consequence.

Timeout: Applying ABS Principles to Eliminate Undesired Behavior

Consistent and frequent use of positive consequences is best for increasing the occurrence of desired behavior, but other techniques are sometimes necessary to decrease the frequency of undesired behavior. Ignoring minor infractions and providing redirection can work wonders with small children, but these are inappropriate for more serious misbehavior. Timeout, when used correctly, is a very effective technique for managing a child's misbehavior. It's a recommended alternative to spanking, which, as discussed earlier, has serious and potentially long-lasting negative effects on children's conduct, aggression, and mental health.[41] And with all that baggage, spanking only suppresses unwanted behavior temporarily.

It's surprising to many caregivers that an adult's emotional reaction to undesired behavior can actually reinforce such behavior. Indeed, attention of any kind can be reinforcing for some children, and thus while the parent is busy cooking dinner, a child misbehaves for parental attention. Timeout avoids this problem and also avoids a common pitfall for many parents – empty threats without a negative consequence (e.g., "Keep doing that and you will not go with us on the family vacation"). Timeout is easy to apply directly, consistently, and immediately, and without emotion.

"Timeout" is short for "timeout from positive consequences." Its purposeful removal of attention – good or bad – is the negative consequence for the child. Timeout occurs for a distinct span of time without stimulation, without parental or other attention, and without fun or any distracting activity. When done correctly, it's an unpleasant but passive experience. The general guidelines for implementing an effective timeout procedure are as follows:[42]

1. The caregiver makes some decisions in advance, including the length of time for timeout and the typical timeout location. A chair, stool, or spot on the floor that is removed from stimulation but can still be monitored by the caregiver is best (see Figure 15.4). In a pinch, any spot that is relatively devoid of stimulation can serve as a place for timeout. The recommended minimum length of timeout is one minute for every year of the child's age.

2. When misbehavior warrants a timeout, the caregiver first gives the child a warning. This involves making a command (not a request, but a command) in a businesslike but pleasant demeanor and tone of voice.

3. The caregiver waits for about five seconds. If the child does not comply (or if the unwanted behavior recurs in a short period of time), the child is immediately told to go sit in the timeout chair/spot. It may be necessary for the caregiver to lead him/her by the wrist to the timeout chair.

4. The caregiver tells the child to stay in the chair until s/he says it's okay to come out. It's helpful to set the stage for achieving success by

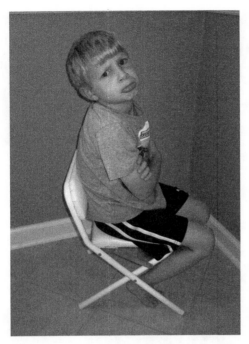

FIGURE 15.4. A child in timeout, appropriately removed from stimulation.

telling the child s/he must be quiet and stay in the chair before earning the right to leave timeout.

5. The caregiver goes about his/ her business while the timeout is served,
keeping an eye on the child's behavior. The caregiver does not interact, argue, or otherwise engage with the child. The key is to seemingly
ignore the child while unobtrusively monitoring his/her behavior
and watching a clock. Some caregivers use a timer, which is okay provided the caregiver determines when the child can leave timeout and
does not rely solely on the timer alarm for this determination.

6. The child can leave timeout when three conditions are met: (a) the
minimum one-minute-per-year-of-age sentence is served; b) the child
is no longer kicking/screaming/throwing a tantrum and is quiet for a
few moments; and (c) the child agrees to comply with the original command or correct the action that got him/ her in timeout (e.g., in cases of
hitting a sibling, the child apologizes and promises not to do it again).

7. To end timeout, the caregiver asks the child in a calm voice to explain
why s/he received a timeout. It's important for the child to understand
the behavior that led to the timeout and to immediately perform the

FIGURE 15.5. An inadequate timeout location.

necessary action to correct the inappropriate behavior. It's beneficial for the caregiver to reassure the child of his/ her love and comfort the child after a successfully served timeout.

It's amazing how often caregivers make mistakes when applying the timeout technique. The result: Timeout doesn't work because its hallmark purpose – removal of positive consequences – is spoiled when the technique is used incorrectly or inconsistently. Here are ten common ways caregivers use timeout incorrectly:

1. Multiple warnings are given, or no warning is given before timeout. (With the exception of particularly egregious behaviors such as hitting another child, *one* warning command should be given.)
2. Timeout is delayed to a later time.
3. The caregiver places the child in a timeout location that is interesting (e.g., in front of a window, in view of the TV, in the proximity of other children, with a book), or the child is allowed to have a comforting toy or blanket (Figure 15.5 shows a poor timeout location).

4. The child is sent to his/her room (or another room) unmonitored during timeout, or the timeout setting is a scary or unsafe place (e.g., closet, dark room, bathroom).

5. The caregiver or others interact with, talk to, argue with, or negotiate with the child during timeout.

6. The caregiver stares at the child rather than doing something else during the child's timeout.

7. The child is allowed to leave the location during the timeout period.

8. Timeout is too short or too long.

9. The child is permitted to leave timeout when the time is up regardless of his/her behavior during timeout, such as throwing a tantrum or yelling at a parent.

10. The caregiver fails to talk with the child in a calm and comforting manner immediately after the timeout to ensure the child understands what behavior led to the timeout; or the child is not required to correct or amend the inappropriate behavior after the timeout period (e.g., apologize for misbehavior, do the chore the child had refused to do).

Timeout applies key ABS principles, and when it is used correctly, the undesired behavior is quickly extinguished. Timeout also deescalates situations that could otherwise result in an emotionally charged parent–child interaction. For additional guidance in dealing with undesired behavior and *what-if* scenarios, Russell Barkley's *Your Defiant Child*[43] and *Defiant Children*[44] are useful evidence-based resources for parents and clinicians, respectively.

SPECIFIC CHILDCARE CHALLENGES: THE BASIC THREE

Caregivers struggle with many behaviors during early childhood; here we discuss three that deserve special attention. Roger McIntire[26] refers to these as "the basic three" – eating, sleeping, and toilet training. Why? Because they are so natural, necessary, and to some extent difficult to manage effectively and efficiently.

These behaviors relate to basic bodily functions, which are controlled by internal factors as much as external conditions. Perhaps because they seem difficult to control and also because they are necessary for survival, struggling with these behaviors can be especially distressful for caregivers. Unfortunately, caregiver distress can interfere with applying the ABS principles consistently and create a negative context for the child.

According to McIntire, the basic three are challenging because (a) they are somewhat out of the caregiver's control, (b) they are relatively difficult for the child to control, (c) the child's *need* for food, sleep, or elimination is not directly observable, (d) relevant behaviors are influenced by many other conditions (e.g., diet, exercise, mood), (e) cultural taboos are linked to these behaviors (e.g., "Your child still wears diapers?!"), and (f) they are somewhat private activities.

The basic three are still influenced by environmental factors, and parents can manage the environment so it connects with the child's body in ways that set the stage for success. The following sections describe the basic three in the context of ABS, illustrating how to apply key ABS principles.

Eating

Eating is the first of the basic three and can cause significant frustration among many parents.[45] Whether the problem is getting a child to try new foods, eat a balanced diet, or stop playing with food, eating behaviors can be extremely trying – for both caregivers and children. Remember that emotional reactions tend to be learned through classical conditioning. Continued pairings of mealtime with anger, fear, frustration, or anxiety can lead to negative associations with mealtime. This can result in food refusal in the short-term and clinical levels of anxiety or disordered eating in the long term.

One reason eating behavior is such a challenge: Parents and caregivers can take steps to improve a child's eating behavior, but the child has ultimate control over whether or not that broccoli makes it down the hatch. ABS can be used to greatly improve the odds of a child's eating *what* the caregiver wants *when* the caregiver wants. The key is for caregivers to manage the variables they *can* control (e.g., home or school environment) and work with or around variables beyond their control (e.g., individual food preferences, internal states of hunger or satiation).

The goal of changing *what* a child eats is complicated by the intrinsic or natural consequences of eating a particular food. Foods that taste good or make us feel good are *appetitive*; we seek these and eat them more often. On the other hand, the taste and texture of some foods are *aversive* and we avoid them. Combined with a state of hunger or satiation, these reactions to taste and texture have very powerful effects on eating behavior. Unlike young children, adults can rationally decide to put off the immediate rewards of eating what tastes good for the long-term expectation of a healthy body. Our country's obesity epidemic, though, illustrates it's not easy to do this.

Most children have difficulty making food choices beyond eating what tastes good now. In these cases, applying two strategies can greatly improve the eating behavior of the average child who fusses about eating broccoli, and even the picky eater who refuses to try any new food. In both cases, changing two environmental variables can have a dramatic impact.

Food Availability. In most homes, schools, or daycare settings the parent or caregiver has control over what food is available. McIntire suggests parents have the most control over a child's eating behavior when they are in the grocery store; they can control what foods are available. Simply put, a child can't eat junk food if it isn't in the house. So the first step in getting a child to eat well is to make sure the available food is healthy. For current health and nutrition information relevant for children see choosemyplate. gov/kids.

Scheduling. The eating schedule is a second environmental variable parents and caretakers can control. Caregivers cannot make a child hungry, but they can manage the child's schedule in order to stack the odds in their favor. A hungry child is more likely to eat the lunch or dinner s/he is served than a child who has filled up on snacks. Keeping a consistent eating schedule, with limited snacks in-between, can ensure a child is hungry at mealtime. This is similar to the concept of *establishing operations* – behavioral procedures that affect the appetitiveness or aversiveness of stimuli.[46] Food is more appetitive, even carrots and peas, when the child is hungry.

Prompting and Rewarding Desired Behavior. Finally, ABS intervention principles can be applied to eating in order to increase appropriate mealtime behavior. We can use activators to inform the child of the expected behaviors. Figure 15.6 illustrates a prompt to remind children of the rules at mealtime. Each rule clearly states the expected behavior.

This chart was used with a 4-year-old. Pictures were used instead of words, as the child was not yet literate. The parents determined the rules, but they gave the child ownership in the process by enabling her to create the chart. The pictures and numbers were printed, and the child cut them out, chose the order, and glued them onto the paper. She also chose where in the dining room the prompt would be posted. This allowed the child to be part of the process and was a fun activity for the parents and the child. Giving the child some control and spending quality time to make a prompt or behavioral chart can create a positive association with the rules, as well as a feeling of self-motivation (Chapter 3).

FIGURE 15.6. Prompt used to remind child of the rules at mealtime: (1) No TV; (2) Try it – take at least one bite of everything; (3) Stay in your seat; (4) Use your utensils; (5) If you try your fruits and vegetables, you may have dessert.

Sleeping

Many parents have spent sleepless nights battling with their toddler or pre-schooler over when and where to sleep. Research shows the quality of children's sleep is a strong predictor of parents' sleep, which in turn predicts negative mood, distress, and fatigue.[47] Sleep problems in early childhood are common, affecting 25–40 percent of pediatric patients.[48] As a specific example, one in three children regularly wakes in the night, requiring parental intervention.[49]

These sleep difficulties are behavioral in many cases and subject to ABS strategies rather than a physiological intervention. This section explains the application of ABS principles to common, nonclinical sleep difficulties in early childhood. For information on more serious sleep problems or sleep disorders, see the American Sleep Association's Website.[50]

The two most common nonclinical sleep problems parents face with their children are initiating sleep at bedtime and maintaining sleep throughout the night, each occurring among up to 30 percent of toddlers and preschoolers.[51] The research findings on ABS interventions to treat these problems among young children are clear; overwhelmingly, children show significant improvements in their sleep.[52] As with eating behavior, the proper application of ABS techniques can improve the odds of children sleeping where and when they want.

Extinction of Problem Bedtime Behavior. The combination of a tired child and a tired parent can be the perfect recipe for problem behavior from the child that is actually maintained by parental behavior. In general, we are not at our best when we're tired. We get upset more easily and have greater difficulty solving problems in a rational way. Children are more likely to meltdown when tired. So they are especially ripe for problem behavior when going to bed or waking in the middle of the night.

Typical problems at bedtime include the child's protests against going to bed at a certain time or the child insisting on sleeping with a parent or sibling instead of in his/her own bed. Protests can range from whining and crying to a full-blown tantrum. These protests can also occur at awakenings throughout the night.

These undesired behaviors may be inadvertently reinforced when the child's level of distress seems too severe or the parent is too tired to fight. Reinforcement might take the form of a parent delaying bedtime or agreeing to sleep with the child. Sleep protests tend to be intense and get parents' or caregivers' attention. If they happen in the middle of the night, they hit parents when they are most vulnerable. Whether reading one more story at bedtime, getting out of bed six times to gently tuck a child back in, or having a screaming match with a child who wants to crawl in with mom and dad in the middle of the night, a parent is giving the child attention that can serve to reinforce the maladaptive behavior. In this case, ignoring the undesired behavior is recommended.

In behavioral terms, this process is referred to as *extinction* – a response gradually disappears with repeated absence of an expected reward. This is referred to as the "cry-it-out" approach, since ignoring a child's requests or protests often results in crying, at least initially. Both *extinction* (i.e., totally ignoring the child after putting him or her to bed) and *graduated extinction* (i.e., ignoring a child's requests/protests for specified periods of time) are widely used. The latter has come to be known as the "Ferber method," popularized by Richard Ferber's book, *Solve Your Child's Sleep Problems.*[53] Research indicates both extinction and graduated extinction are highly effective in eliminating problem behaviors associated with sleep onset and night awakenings.[54]

Why don't all parents use these forms of extinction if they are so effective? Why do sleep problems persist? One reason is a lack of awareness of the method. A second is that ignoring a child's negative bedtime behavior can be difficult, particularly after a parent or guardian is awakened from a deep sleep in the middle of the night. Fortunately, environmental and behavior-management techniques can reduce the frequency and the intensity of such disruptive behaviors.

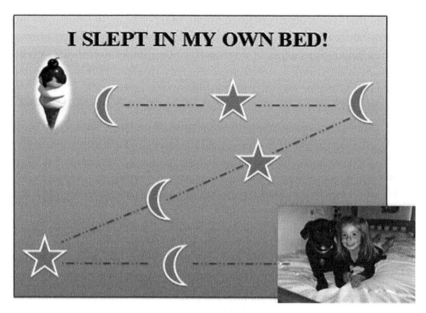

FIGURE 15.7. A sleep reward chart.

Environmental Management for Sleep Hygiene. Like hunger, sleep is an internal state that cannot be directly controlled but is influenced by external factors. Children are more likely to go to sleep and stay asleep when they're tired. We can increase the probability of a child being tired by scheduling bedtimes, wake times, and naps consistent with and appropriate to the child's age and need for sleep. Appropriate and consistent sleep schedules are part of a larger set of recommended practices referred to as *sleep hygiene*.

Sleep hygiene is a set of behaviors that support better quality and quantity of sleep.[55] Recommendations include eliminating caffeine and sugar intake before bedtime, developing a calming bedtime routine, maintaining a consistent bedtime and wake-time process, and avoiding television, exercise, and other stimulating activities before bedtime. Research indicates these behaviors reliably distinguish between healthy sleepers and problem sleepers, and are often a key component in the treatment of sleep disorders. For children, good sleep hygiene is associated with better sleep quantity and quality.[56] From an ABS perspective, consider the sleep hygiene guidelines as empirically supported recommendations for managing external factors that influence the target behavior – sleep.

Finally, a reward chart can be used to reward desired bedtime behavior (e.g., going to bed without fussing, staying in bed all night). Figure 15.7

illustrates a basic sleep reward chart, used with a 4-year-old girl who was having trouble staying in her own bed throughout the night. The chart is designed so each night the child successfully sleeps in her own bed, she earns a sticker, to be placed on a star/moon shape. Once she has earned seven stickers, she earns a trip to the ice-cream parlor.

In summary, ABS provides several tools to promote healthy sleep in early childhood. Extinction of undesired behavior, environmental management, and positive consequences can greatly reduce the bedtime brawls and midnight madness all too common among young children. Helping our children develop a healthy sleep routine in early childhood reflects AC4P; it prevents frustration and negative associations with sleep, promotes good health, and sets a foundation for sound sleep throughout the lifespan.

Toilet Training

Not needing to change diapers certainly appeals to many parents and is a significant accomplishment for children, but getting to this state can be challenging. Popular children's TV programs often feature commercials with children enjoying a celebration with a big parade, flashing lights, confetti, and music after they use the potty successfully. Although the celebration is a positive consequence, busy parents and caregivers with many competing demands cannot produce a parade each time the target behavior is completed. However, busy parents and caregivers can build excitement with clear expectations, verbal praise, and rewards. The AC4P approach provides a solid framework to customize an intervention for a particular child and setting.

Once the child has begun to show interest (even if just a little) in the process of toilet training, it's important to jump right in. The typical age range is between 22 and 24 months. However, research suggests looking for readiness behaviors of the child instead of relying on age.[57] Increasingly dry diapers after a nap, children saying they have to go potty, or wanting to imitate potty behaviors may reflect initial interest. At the start, spend time identifying what types of positive consequences might serve as a fitting reward for the child.[58] Understanding the individual child's currency is critical for success, as not all children are interested in mini M&Ms, coins, or stickers (though these can be very helpful).

For instance, if the target for toilet training is a little boy who finds all things about trains to be exciting, trains are the currency. Perhaps as the process continues, the little boy shows intense interest in fish. Recognizing this shift in interest can be central to continuing to motivate the child with a fitting consequence. The verbal commentary accompanying the reward is critical and can support self-motivation, as indicated earlier. More specifically, use words that support the child's perception of personal competency at toilet use.

Toilet training is a multistep process, and children need appropriate support, patience, and encouragement at each step. Showing interest in the potty or trying out the potty without actually going are behaviors that need a positive consequence just as much as actually completing the task. The *successive approximations* of behavioral shaping can be very effective with a toddler – the caregiver provides a positive consequence for each small step toward the target behavior until the desired behavior is completed.

"REMEMBER THE CONTINGENCY, TIMMY, IF YOU PERFORM THE TARGET BEHAVIOR, WE CAN ALL GO OUT FOR PIZZA!"

Positive recognition of the successive behavioral steps will increase the likelihood of the behaviors reoccurring, and in toilet training it's all about repetition in order to build personal competence and comfort with the child's body and relevant behavior. For instance, if a parent uses the verbal activator, "Potty

FIGURE 15.8. Potential ABC's for toilet training.

time, let's go try" and the child jumps up and runs to the potty, a high-five, "Way to go," or small sticker could serve to increase the chance of the behavior happening again.[59] Also, if a child tells you s/he needs to go or wants to try going potty, an immediate smile followed by "Great! Way to listen to your body" is a positive verbal consequence that rewards an important step in the process (i.e., knowing you need to go and moving toward the target location).

Invest time upfront to generate a list of the behaviors or steps associated with going potty. This helps set clear expectations. Figure 15.8 provides a list of potential activators (A), target behaviors (B), and consequences (C) for toilet training. Be sure to account for the type of potty being used – does it require a step stool, a child-size seat, or lifting the lid? Be aware of each step so it's easier to give instruction, anticipate need, and immediately reward the right behavior.

With all of the precursory work completed (i.e., the child is motivated, child-specific currency has been collected/purchased, and verbal praise for key behaviors has been identified), it's time to put the plan into action. Giving a verbal cue as an activator and then rewarding successive approximations toward the target behavior is the foundation, with consistency of action and immediacy of reward being critical. At the beginning, it's especially important to respond quickly to a signal to go potty and with excitement, even if it's at the worst possible moment (e.g., other kids are crying, you're in the middle of cooking, or you're trying to get out the door in the morning). The missed opportunity to go potty at the right time may result in the child being punished by the yucky feeling of having an "accident." Such consequences may decrease the desire to go on the big-kid potty, especially when they are accompanied by scolding or a look of disappointment.

"Accidents" will happen; the child is new to the process and working to figure out bodily signals while coordinating clothing manipulation with

the potty. Providing a patient and understanding reaction when "accidents" occur is important. We actively care for children when modeling the appropriate reaction when problems or messes occur. Most children know the "accident" is a behavior they are working to avoid and are punished by their own disappointment or soggy undies. A good-natured "Oops accidents happen, let's get cleaned up and try again" can go a long way.

One final practical note: An extremely negative consequence for the toilet newbie is the flushing of an auto-flushing toilet while the child is still seated. The experience is overwhelming and unexpected to say the least and could keep the little one from wanting to go potty again in public restrooms. One trick is to carry Post-it* notes with you to cover the sensor; then when the child is finished, remove the paper and allow the toilet to flush. Mastery over the public potty is often the final milestone in toilet training.

IN CONCLUSION

Parents and caregivers want their children to be healthy and happy. This chapter discussed ways ABS principles can make this happen. Each of the principles is critical for giving care to children in an effective, AC4P manner. Both the key principles and the two strategies – reward charts and timeouts – can be used to address most behavioral concerns in early childhood. Although the basic three – eating, sleeping, and toilet training – can present unique challenges for parents, ABS provides tools for working with those challenges and nourishing children as they grow.

The use of ABS in parenting is consistent with the AC4P Movement. Why? With these techniques, evidence-based methods (a) improve children's behavior, (b) result in the least negative side effects, (c) promote well-being, and (d) help maintain a healthy parent–child relationship.

DISCUSSION QUESTIONS

1. What is behavior-based parenting, and why is this approach desirable?
2. Why is it important to give behavior-focused rather than ability-focused labels to children?
3. Distinguish between proactive and reactive childcare with an example.
4. Describe problems that might arise from "what not to do" instructions as opposed to "what to do" instructions.
5. How does observational learning impact effective versus ineffective parenting?

6. Discuss the difference between dispositional and situational factors as they relate to effective parenting.

7. Describe an example of a parent's misuse of positive consequences that is maintained by negative reinforcement.

8. Why is corporal punishment a behavior-control technique frequently used by some parents?

9. Provide examples of using a "now-then" and an "if–then" reward to "motivate" a child.

10. Detail the components of an effective timeout procedure to correct a child's undesirable behavior.

REFERENCES

1. Geller, E. S. (2001). *The psychology of safety handbook.* Boca Raton, FL: CRC Press; Geller, E. S. (2002). *The participation factor: How to get more people involved in occupational safety.* Des Plaines, IL: American Society of Safety Engineers; Geller, E. S. (2005). *People-based safety: The source.* Virginia Beach, VA: Coastal Training and Technologies.

2. Geller, E. S., & Johnson, D. (2007). *People-based patient safety: Enriching your culture to prevent medical error.* Virginia Beach, VA: Coastal Training Technologies.

3. McCarty, S. M., & Geller, E. S. (2014). Actively caring to prevent bullying: Prompting and rewarding prosocial behavior in elementary schools. In E. S. Geller (Ed.). *Actively caring at your school: How to make it happen* (2nd ed.) (pp. 177–197). Newport, VA: Make-A-Difference, LLC.

4. Peters, R. A. (1998). *It's never too soon to discipline: A low-stress program that shows parents how to teach good behavior.* New York: Golden Books.

5. Baumrind, D. (1989). Rearing competent children. In W. Damon (Ed.). *Child development today and tomorrow* (pp. 349–378). San Francisco: Jossey-Bass; Baumrind, D., Larzelere, R. E., & Owens, E. B. (2010). Effects of preschool parents' power assertive patterns and practices on adolescent development. *Parenting, Science and Practice,* 10, 157–201.

6. Forgatch, M. S., & Patterson, G. R. (2010). Parent management training – Oregon model: An intervention for antisocial behavior in children and adolescents. *Evidence-Based Psychotherapies for Children and Adolescents,* 2, 159–178.

7. Webster-Stratton, C. (2001). *Leader's guide, the parent and children's series: A comprehensive course divided into four programs.* Seattle: University of Washington Press.

8. Sanders, M. R. (1999). Triple P-positive parenting program: Towards an empirically validated multilevel parenting and family support strategy for the prevention of behavior and emotional problems in children. *Clinical Child and Family Psychology Review,* 2(2), 71–90.

9. Dishion, T. J., & Kavanagh, K. (2005). *Intervening in adolescent problem behavior: A family-centered approach.* New York: Guilford Press.

10. Piaget, J. (1952). *The origins of intelligence in children.* New York: International Universities Press.

11. Griffin, C., & Al-Talib, N. I. (1994). Labeling effect on adolescents' self-concept. *International Journal of Offender Therapy and Comparative Criminology*, 38 (1), 47–57.

12. Kraut, R. E. (1973). Effects of social labeling on giving to charity. *Journal of Experimental Social Psychology*, 9, 551–562.

13. Dweck, C. S. (2006). *Mindset: The new psychology of success*. New York: Ballotine Books.

14. Tannenbaum, F. (1983). *Crime and community*. New York: Columbia University Press.

15. Rosenthal, R., & Jacobson, L. (1992). *Pygmalion in the classroom: Teacher expectation and pupils' intellectual development* (Expanded ed.). New York: Irvington Publishers.

16. Merton, R. K. (1948). The self-fulfilling prophecy. *Antioch Review*, 8(2), 195. doi: 10.2307/4609267.

17. Robert Wood Johnson Foundation. (2013, December). *Return on investments in public health: Saving lives and money*(Policy Highlight Brief). Princeton, NJ: Robert Wood Johnson Foundation. Retrieved August 2, 2014 from http://www.rwjf.org/content/dam/farm/reports/issue_briefs/2013/rwjf72446.

18. Gardner, F., Shaw, D. S., Dishion, T. J., & Burton, J. (2007). Randomized prevention trial for early conduct problems: Effects on proactive parenting and links to toddler disruptive behavior. *Journal of Family Psychology*, 21 (3), 398–406.

19. Covington, M. V. (1992). *Making the grade: A self-worth perspective on motivation and school reform*. Cambridge: Cambridge University Press; Martin, A. J., & Marsh, H. W. (2003). Fear of failure: Friend or foe? *Australian Psychologist*, 38, 31–38.

20. Bandura, A. (1977). *Social learning theory*. Englewood Cliffs, NJ: Prentice Hall.

21. Bandura, A. (1965). Influence of models' reinforcement contingencies on the acquisition of imitative response. *Journal of Personality and Social Psychology*, 1, 589–595.

22. Lau, R. R., Quadrel, M. J., & Hartman, K. A. (1990). Development and change of young adults' preventive health beliefs and behavior: Influence from parents and peers. *Journal of Health and Social Behavior*, 31, 240–259.

23. Ross, L. (1977). The intuitive psychologist and his shortcomings: Distortions in the attribution process. In Berkowitz, L. (Ed.). *Advances in experimental social psychology* (Vol. 10) (pp. 173–220). New York: Academic Press.

24. Damon, W., & Lerner, R. M. (Eds.) (2006). *Handbook of child psychology* (6th ed.) Hoboken, NJ: John Wiley.

25. Peters, R. (1998). *It's never too soon: A low-stress program that shows parents how to teach good behavior*. New York: Golden Books.

26. McIntire, R. (2012). *What every parent should know about raising children*. Columbia, MD: Summit Crossroads Press.

27. Knox, M. (2010). On hitting children: A review of corporal punishment in the United States. *Journal of Pediatric Health Care*, 24 (2), 103–107.

28. American Academy of Pediatrics. *Where we stand: Spanking*. Retrieved September 1, 2014, from http://www.healthychildren.org/English/family-life/family-dynamics/communication-discipline/Pages/Where-We-Stand-Spanking.aspx.

29. Knox, M. (2010). On hitting children: A review of corporal punishment in the United States. *Journal of Pediatric Health Care*, 24 (2), 103–107; Gershoff, E. T. (2002). Corporal punishment by parents and associate child behaviors and experiences: A meta-analytic and theoretical review. *Psychological Bulletin*, 128 (4), 539–579.

30. Afifi, T. O., Mota, N. P., Dasiewicz, P., MacMillan, H. L., & Sareen, J. (2012). Physical punishment and mental disorders: Results from a nationally representative U.S. sample. *Pediatrics*, 130 (2), 1–11.

31. Kohn, A. (1993). *Punished by rewards: The trouble with gold stars, incentive plans, A's, praise, and other bribes*. Boston: Houghton Mifflin.

32. Kohn, A. (2001). Five reasons to stop saying "Good Job!" *Young Children*, 56 (5), 24–30.

33. Timm, M. A., Strain, P. S., & Eller, P. H. (1979). Effects of systematic, response-dependent fading and thinning procedures on the maintenance of child–child interaction. *Journal of Applied Behavior Analysis*, 12, 308; Kratochwill, T. R., & Stoiber, K. C. (2000). Empirically supported interventions and school psychology. *School Psychology Quarterly*, 15, 233–253.

34. Strain, P. S., & Joseph, G. E. (2004). A not so good job with "Good job": A response to Kohn 2001. *Journal of Positive Behavior Interventions*, 6 (1), 55–59.

35. American Psychiatric Association. (2013). *Diagnostic and statistical manual of mental disorders* (5th ed.): *DSM-5*. Washington, DC: American Psychiatric Association.

36. Axelrod, S., McElrath, K. K., & Wine, B. (2012). Applied behavior analysis: Autism and beyond. *Behavioral Interventions*, 27, 1–15.

37. Lord, C., Risi, S., DiLavore, P. S., Shulman, C., Thurm, A., & Pickles, A. (2006). Autism from 2 to 9 years of age. *Archives of General Psychiatry*, 63(6), 694–701.

38. Bailey, J., & Burch, M. (2010). *25 essential skills and strategies for the professional behavior analyst: Expert tips for maximizing consulting effectiveness*. New York: Routledge; Friman, P. C. (2010). Come on in, the water is fine: Achieving mainstream relevance through integration with primary care. *Behavior Analyst*, 33, 19–36.

39. Satcher, D. (2000). Mental health: A report of the Surgeon General – Executive summary. *Professional Psychology: Research and Practice*, 31(1), 5.

40. Stipek, D. J., & Hoffman, J. M. (1980). Development of children's performance-related judgments. *Child Development*, 51, 912–914.

41. Geller, E. S. (Ed.) (2014). *Actively caring for people: Cultivating a culture of compassion* (4th ed.). Newport, VA: Make-A-Difference, LLC; Gershoff, E. T. (2002). Corporal punishment by parents and associated child behaviors and experiences: A meta-analytic and theoretical review. *Psychological Bulletin*, 128 (4), 539–579; Gershoff, E. T. (2013). Spanking and child development: We know enough now to stop hitting our children. *Child Development Perspectives*, 7 (3), 133–137.

42. MacKenzie, M. J., Nicklas, E., Brooks-Gunn, J., & Waldfogel, J. (2014). Spanking and children's externalizing behavior across the first decade of life: Evidence for a transactional process. *Journal of Youth and Adolescence*, 44, 658–659; Barkley, R. (2013). *Defiant children: A clinician's manual for assessment and parent training* (3rd ed.). New York: Guilford Press.

43. Barkley, R. A. (2013). *Your defiant child: Eight steps to better behavior* (2nd ed.). New York: Guilford Press.

44. Barkley, R. A. (1997). *Defiant children: A clinician's manual for assessment and parent training* (3rd ed.). New York: Guilford Press.

45. Leung, A. K. C., Marchland, V., & Suave, R. S. (2012). The 'picky eater': The toddler or preschooler who does not eat. *Pediatric Child Health*, 17(8), 455–457.

46. Michael, J. (1982). Distinguishing between discriminative and motivational functions of stimuli. *Journal of the Experimental Analysis of behavior*, 37, 149–155.

47. Meltzer, L. J., & Mindell, J. A. (2007). Relationship between child sleep disturbances and maternal sleep, mood, and parenting stress: A pilot study. *Journal of Family Psychology*, 21 (1), 67–73.

48. Owens, J. A. (2005). Epidemiology of sleep disorders during childhood. S. H. Sheldon, R. Ferber, & M. H. Kryger (Eds.). *Principles and practices of pediatric sleep medicine* (pp. 27–33). Philadelphia: Elsevier Saunders.

49. Moor, T., & Ucko, C. (1957). Night waking in early infancy: Part I. *Archives of Disease in Children*, 32, 333–342; Adair, R. H., & Bauchner, H. (1993). Sleep problems in childhood. *Current Problems in Pediatrics*, 23, 147–170.

50. American Sleep Association. *Children and sleep*. Retrieved September 15, 2014, from http://www.sleepassociation.org/patients-general-public/children-and-sleep/.

51. Thiedke, C. C. (2001). Sleep disorders and sleep problems in childhood. *American Family Physician*, 63 (2), 277–284.

52. Mindell, J. A., Meltzer, L. J., Carskadon, M. A., & Chervin, R. D. (2009). Developmental aspects of sleep hygiene: Findings from the 2004 national sleep foundation sleep in America poll. *Sleep Medicine*, 10(7), 771–779.

53. Ferber, R. (1985). *Solve your child's sleep problems*. New York: Simon &Schuster.

54. Mindell, J. A., Huhn, B., Lewin, D. S., Meltzer, L. J., & Sadeh, A. (2006). Behavioral treatment of bedtime problems and night wakings in infants and young children. *Pediatric Sleep*, 29(10), 1263.

55. Hauri, P. (1977). *Current concepts: The sleep disorders*. Kalamazoo, MI: Upjohn.

56. Lacks, P., & Rotert, M. (1986). Knowledge and practice of sleep hygiene techniques in insomniacs and good sleepers. *Behavior Research & Therapy*, 24, 365–368.

57. Azrin, N. H., & Foxx, R. M. (1989). *Toilet training in less than a day*. New York: Pocket Books.

58. Gorski, P. A. (1999). Toilet training guidelines: Parents – the role of parents in toilet training. *Pediatrics*, 103, 362–363.

59. Azrin, N. H., & Foxx, R. M. (1973). Dry pants: A rapid method of toilet training children. *Behaviour Research and Therapy*, 11(4), 435–442; Kaerts, N., Van Hal, G., Vermandel, A., & Wyndaele, J. J. (2012). Readiness signs used to define the proper moment to start toilet training: A review of the literature. *Neurourology and Urodynamics*, 31(4), 437–440.

16

Actively Caring for Preschoolers

JOCELYN H. NEWTON, KATIE C. GOULET,
AND KYRA L. HEIDELBERGER

> One looks back with appreciation to the brilliant teachers, but with grati-
> tude to those who touched our human feelings. The curriculum is so
> much necessary raw material, but warmth is the vital element for the
> growing plant and for the soul of the child.
> – Carl Jung

Actively caring for people (AC4P) of course includes children we commonly refer to as "preschoolers," ages 3–5 years. How do we best launch
these children for lifelong success? Kindergarten can be exciting, yet perhaps overwhelming or possibly scary – especially today, as many scholars
cite the academic rigor of kindergarten. The mission is no longer simply
learning to play and relate with others. Now kindergarten children must
master certain academic requirements.[1]

More children are engaged in preschool activities today, perhaps due to
increased kindergarten entry requirements. Currently, no federal or state
mandates for preschool exist, but approximately half of U.S. children aged
3–4 are enrolled in some sort of preschool/daycare experience.[2] Critical
questions arise: How important is the preschool experience, and what characteristics define an effective preschool program?

THE IMPORTANCE OF PRESCHOOL

This chapter explores the AC4P behaviors of teachers that can promote
early learning in preschool settings. We discuss how teachers can learn
to create an AC4P culture in their classrooms to effectively promote early
childhood development. Consistent with the theme of this book, information contained in this chapter clearly aligns with the basic principles of the
AC4P Movement introduced in Chapter 2.

Children of preschool age differ considerably in their readiness or ability to learn to read and do math.[3] These skills are highly predictive of later educational success.[4] With regard to reading, for example, early elementary years appear to be critical for learning basic reading skills. In later grades, elementary school teachers transition from teaching students *how* to read to expecting students to acquire knowledge and learn *through* reading.

Perhaps you recall how your fifth- and-sixth-grade teachers began asking you to read longer sections of textbooks as homework and to learn new and exciting information in domains such as science and history through the process of reading. Imagine that experience had you not yet learned how to read. If children have not learned to read rather fluently by fourth grade, their academic difficulties (which to that point were limited to reading) begin to generalize to other academic areas, putting those children further behind not only in reading but in all other subject areas as well.[5]

Early math skills (i.e., understanding numbers and their relationship to each other) are highly important for later success. Acquisition of early math or numeracy concepts and skills is another powerful predictor of later achievement in both math and reading.[6] We should be very invested in how children learn these early skills if we want to support their educational success – an investment that can be enriched by facilitating and supporting an AC4P classroom.

DIFFERENCES IN EARLY LEARNING SKILLS

Kindergarten and early school teachers are very much aware of how children differ from each other in their initial learning skills and abilities. Research has shown that demographic factors such as gender, race, and socioeconomic status account for at least some of this early cognitive variability.[7] These early differences matter because an achievement gap apparent in kindergarten persists and widens in later school years. The value of preschool: Children entering kindergarten with some basic early reading and math skills are ready to progress to learning more advanced skills.

In contrast, children who enter school without these basic skills will learn, but the focus for them (and their teachers) continues to be on the acquisition of basic skills fundamental to progress in reading and math. By the end of kindergarten, the skill gap present upon entry remains among various demographic groupings.[8] National education data indicate the academic skill gaps persist and broaden among these demographic groups throughout their educational careers.[9]

Current teaching/learning interventions nationally do not seem to address these gaps in knowledge and skills present before children arrive at elementary school. Those invested in education must define ways to enhance learning in preschool so more at-risk children can arrive in kindergarten well prepared to learn more advanced skills. It's difficult to address these factors in any meaningful way, although research on the demographic factors predicting ease of early learning is available (socioeconomic status being the primary factor). Intervening to enhance large-scale learning among young children is critical. The National Research Council has called for identifying both the "contexts that enhance development" and the dimensions in adult–child relationships that benefit children's skill development.[10]

HALLMARK STUDIES IN PRESCHOOL QUALITY

An AC4P culture can be created to enhance preschoolers' academic and psychosocial development. The advantage of preschool education is evident in two longitudinal projects with important implications for the design and social validity of a quality preschool experience: the HighScope Perry Preschool Project and the Carolina Abecedarian Project. Both offer compelling evidence for the significance of providing early educational experiences to children, especially those from disadvantaged backgrounds. The AC4P behaviors of teachers can be critical here, as we will see later in this chapter.

The HighScope Perry Preschool Project, conducted in Ypsilanti, Michigan, was initiated by an administrator of the local school system, David Weikart, who wanted to address the black/white and socioeconomic achievement gaps of the local school system in the 1950s.[11] Study participants included 123 African American children living in poverty with IQ scores between 70 and 85 and who were determined to be at high risk for school failure.[12] These 3- and- 4-year-old children were randomly assigned to either the Treatment or Control conditions, and data on individual outcomes were collected on a continual basis up through the most recent study, when participants were between 39 and 41 years of age.[13]

The preschool program (implemented for the children randomly assigned to the Treatment condition) consisted of two and a half hours of preschool programming each weekday with home visits of one and a half hours occurring weekly during the months of October through May.[13] The natural development of students was the basis for preschool programming, and cognitive development was stimulated by increasing student vocabulary, teaching letters and numbers, and using child-directed explor-atory learning (i.e., using a child's interests to teach basic concepts).[14]

When comparing the Treatment and Control groups of the Perry Preschool study, researchers noted significant differences. Initially, students who received the high-quality preschool programming demonstrated gains of 15 points on measures of intelligence, which resulted in fewer of those students being placed in special-education classes.[11] Although initial gains in intelligence scores were not maintained when the students entered for-mal schooling, other lasting and positive effects were found for the stu-dents in the preschool program.[15] Students in the preschool program were less likely to be held back a grade, displayed fewer behavior problems, per-formed better academically, showed more effort to complete homework assignments, were more likely to say school was important to them, and had higher graduation rates.[16]

These positive effects were sustained throughout the remainder of the child's educational career and even extended into adulthood. Adulthood benefits for those who attended preschool included (a) fewer arrests; (b) fewer drug-related offenses; (c) more positive financial indicators (e.g., higher earnings, greater likelihood of owning a home/second car, and less reliance on welfare or other governmental assistance); (d) a greater likelihood of being married; (e) a lower likelihood of being a single parent; and (f) a greater likelihood of pursuing higher education compared with their counterparts who did not receive preschool pro-gram services.[15]

Thus, the Perry Preschool study demonstrated lifelong benefits from high-quality preschool programming for children living in poverty, in terms of educational performance, economic development, and reduced crime. A significant return on taxpayer investment was calculated at $7.16 for every $1 invested.[12]

The Carolina Abecedarian Project confirmed many of the significant findings of the Perry Project. Between 1972 and 1977, the Abecedarian Project studied 112 primarily African American individuals from low-income fami-lies considered at risk for lower intellectual and social development.[17] These children were randomly assigned to Preschool and Non-preschool research groups. Those in the Preschool group participated in a high-quality pre-school education intervention at a childcare setting from infancy through age 5. Like the Perry Project, the Abecedarian Project was grounded in developmental systems theory and focused on increasing school readiness by creating a rich, AC4P-like, positive, and responsive learning culture that emphasized conversational language.[18]

Unlike the children in the Perry Project, those in the Abecedarian Project spent full days in preschool, without home visits. Instead of home visits, some students received supportive educational assistance from a teacher who directed homeschool teaching/learning collaboration with parents or caregivers from kindergarten through second grade. Individuals in the Carolina Abecedarian Project were followed up until age 21.[17]

Students who participated in this preschool program displayed higher cognitive test scores consistently from their toddler years up to age 21, according to results of the Carolina Abecedarian Project.[17] Children in the Preschool group also displayed (a) greater academic achievement in both reading and math throughout the primary grades; (b) enhanced language development; (c) fewer special-education placements; and (d) more years of education completed as compared with individuals who did not participate in the preschool program.[17]

As with the Perry Project, these benefits appeared to extend into adulthood. Through age 21, students in the Preschool group (a) were more likely to attend a four-year college; (b) demonstrated continued higher scores on reading and mathematics assessments; (c) evidenced higher employment percentages and a higher likelihood of obtaining a skilled job; and (d) were less likely to be a teen parent and to use marijuana than were the Non-preschool individuals.[17] Researchers of the Carolina Abecedarian Project identified a unique finding for the parents of the participants: Teen mothers of the preschool students in the Preschool condition were more likely to complete high school and obtain post-secondary training.[18]

These two landmark studies reveal convincingly the positive consequences of preschool for children, not only immediately, but later in life. A good preschool experience addresses achievement gaps that can put children at risk for lifetime difficulties. A compelling argument can be made for increasing AC4P support of high-quality early childhood education for all children.

So what are the qualities of an effective AC4P program for preschoolers? Let's examine a typical preschool program through the use of a case study. This case study program and three of its teachers illustrate how AC4P interventions can enhance preschool academic and psychosocial development.

CASE STUDY: TEACHERS AT THE GREEN MUSHROOM PRESCHOOL

Ms. Margaret, Ms. Ruby, and Mr. Sam teach at the Green Mushroom Preschool. Each teacher has his/her own classroom, with fifteen 3- and-4-year-old children. Each classroom has a lead teacher (Ms. Margaret, Ms. Ruby, or Mr. Sam) and an assistant teacher. The lead teachers are certified in their state as early childhood educators; all have a bachelor's degree in early childhood education and have passed a competency exam to meet these requirements. Their classrooms have a similar schedule each day, so children can eat lunch and play outside as a combined class.

Table 16.1 displays a sample daily schedule: As you can see, this is a busy day for children, and all activities are focused on learning and developing fundamental motor, communication, cognitive, social-emotional, and adaptive skills. Let's assume all three teachers are highly devoted to their students and motivated to create an AC4P culture in their classrooms. What does an AC4P culture look like in a preschool setting?

WHAT IS HIGH-QUALITY PRESCHOOL EDUCATION?

Two main sets of factors essential for preschool effectiveness have been identified in a number of research studies. First are structural/environmental factors, including teacher education qualifications and accreditation criteria. Depending upon the state in which the teacher works, requirements can range from a high school diploma to a bachelor's degree. All states require teacher certification.[19] Other regulatory guidance addresses the ratio of staff to children per classroom (about one adult to every eight or nine students at the 3- and 4-year-old ages).[20]

Research to date indicates structural/environmental factors are important for preschool effectiveness. The teacher's education and experience seem important for the emotional climate of the classroom, as well as for the use of activities optimal for child learning.[21] Also, teacher–student ratio and the use of a high-quality preschool curriculum appear to benefit child development outcomes.[22]

Applying important structural/environmental factors to the case study, we see that our Green Mushroom program meets the first characteristic of preschool effectiveness. All three teachers have bachelor's degrees, and each is certified within their state. And the teacher–student ratio (one head and one assistant teacher with fifteen children per classroom) meets the stated criterion.

The teachers themselves are an even more important part of an effective preschool experience than structural/environmental factors, according to research studies on preschool quality. Yes, the people matter most when creating an AC4P culture of interpersonal compassion in preschool. Structural/environmental characteristics are fundamental, but certain

TABLE 16.1. *Sample daily schedule of the Green Mushroom Preschool*

Time	Activity	Description
9–9:15 A.M.	Morning arrival	Students arrive at preschool on the school bus or via private vehicle.
9:15–10:00 A.M.	Free play	Students transition into the classroom and begin free play, where they can choose from a number of play-based learning opportunities, including reading books, coloring, playing with large construction blocks/other toys, playing in a kitchen area, listening to music on headphones, etc.
10:00–10:15 A.M.	Clean-up	Students clean up the classroom and transition to circle time.
10:15–10:30 A.M.	Circle time	Students take their seats in the front of the classroom. They engage in an interactive teacher-led activity, consisting of activities such as calendar review, weather report, followed by the main lesson for the day/week (a topic students are learning about). Typically, the teacher will read a book (pertaining to the day's topic) and engage in dialogue with students about the topic.
10:30–10:45 A.M.	Prep for outdoor play	Students transition from circle time to outdoor play
10:45–11:15 A.M.	Outdoor play	Students play outside (all three classes are combined) on the playground.
11:15–11:30 A.M.	Prep for lunch	Students transition back into to the classroom.
11:30 A.M.–12:30 P.M.	Lunch	Lunch in the cafeteria (all three classes are combined).
12:30–1:30 P.M.	Rest time	Students, each in their individual classrooms, rest on cots.
1:30–2:00 P.M.	Work time	Students are led through a teacher-directed activity that focuses on the topic for the day. They typically work on an arts-and-crafts project that enhances and supports their learning of the topic. For example, if the topic for the day is "frogs," students might color in a picture of a frog, then cut out pre-printed descriptive words (e.g., "hops" or "ribbet!") to glue onto their picture.
2:00–2:15 P.M.	Work cleanup	Transition to Gross Motor Circle Time

Time	Activity	Description
2:15–2:45 P.M.	Movement time	Students return to their assigned circle time spots and then are led through a gross motor activity. This typically involves songs and movement activities (e.g., "Heads-Shoulders-Knees-and-Toes" or the "Hokey Pokey" song)
2:45–3:15 P.M.	Snack	Teachers distribute a healthy afternoon snack in their individual classrooms and engage students in teacher–student or student–student dialogue.
3:15–3:30 P.M.	Prep to go home	Students clean up the classroom and prepare to travel home via bus or private vehicle.

teacher characteristics and behaviors have the largest impact on a child's learning outcomes in preschool.

Individual children may not flourish academically or psychosocially unless or until they are able to interact with teachers who provide them with warm, supportive, and nurturing care – even if a preschool program employs teachers who meet state requirements for education and certification and maintains the proper teacher–student ratio. Teacher qualities that align with the AC4P approach to creating a caring culture are essential. What are those qualities within the context of preschool?

Teacher Qualities in Preschool

Over the past few decades, many studies have examined the relationship between teacher qualities and child learning outcomes. Children unable to establish a warm and positive relationship with their teacher will not attain optimal educational and psychosocial outcomes, even when the ideal curricula are employed, this research suggests. Three key elements of teacher characteristics and behavior in the classroom seem to contribute to an effective preschool experience: organizational support, emotional support, and instructional support. Let's define (or operationalize) and explore each of these key teacher characteristics or behaviors and show how our three teachers from the Green Mushroom Preschool practice beneficial AC4P behaviors every day.

Organizational Support. Effective preschool teachers are effective classroom managers. They make the most of the time they have with their students. They have an organized, yet flexible schedule. They manage student behaviors effectively and maintain student interest in various learning activities.[23]

Ms. Margaret is particularly strong here. She plans activities to maximize the time her children spend learning. Correspondingly, she minimizes distractions and time spent on "housekeeping" chores (e.g., recording attendance). Additionally, Ms. Margaret uses every moment in her classroom as a teachable moment, even during transition times. For example, when her students are cleaning up from free play, she says to a student, "Let's clean up these blocks together, and while we do that, let's sort them by color and count them!"

In terms of behavior management, Ms. Margaret proactively identifies the behavioral expectations of the students in her classroom, and she communicates these clearly to her children each day. When her students are transitioning to outside play, she states, "Before we go outside, what are we are supposed to do when we are walking down the hallway past the other classrooms? What are some rules we follow when on the playground?"

Teachers such as Ms. Margaret who provide students with strong organizational support give feedback specific to behaviors they have identified as desirable for their students to perform. So in the hallway on the way to the playground, Ms. Margaret announces, "Wow, I love how you are *all* using your quiet walking feet and keeping your hands to yourselves!" Note the AC4P emphasis on supportive feedback.

A preschool teacher with ABS knowledge and skills finds ways to engage students and maintain their interest in learning activities. Ms. Margaret might begin a teacher-led work session by saying, "Class, today we are going to learn about frogs. Tell me what you know about frogs." Throughout these teacher–student interactions, Ms. Margaret uses multiple forms of instruction, starting with the use of pictures in a book (seeing), then listening to a song about frogs (hearing and expressing), and then finally getting out a stuffed frog to allow the children to pass around the group circle (feeling).

Instructional Support. Effective AC4P teachers provide their preschool students with high levels of instructional support. They use approaches that support child cognitive and language development – skills most closely associated with academic progress.[24] Teachers with knowledge of ABS who provide quality instructional support to students don't just relay factual information to students and request rote memorization. They facilitate critical thinking and concept-development skills. Students in classrooms with teachers who provide positive AC4P instructional support show the most academic gains – gains that are apparent later in kindergarten.[25] The instructional quality of preschool programs has correlated significantly with kindergarten performance in the areas of language, academic (reading), and social skills.[26]

The quality of feedback teachers provide to children in their classrooms is a second dimension of instructional support. When teachers promote concept development and provide one-to-one feedback in a clear, specific, and constructive manner, children demonstrate increased learning and are able to maintain that learning.[26] For example, during circle time, Ms. Ruby asks her class to describe the weather outside. When a student responds incorrectly, Ms. Ruby provides clear, corrective feedback in a positive way by saying, "Good try, Johanna, it was sunny outside yesterday, but not today. Can you look outside and tell me what the weather looks like today? Can you see the sun today?"

Effective teachers also provide behavioral feedback toward specific students. For instance, Ms. Ruby consistently demonstrates AC4P instructional support when students are tying their shoes following rest time. Rather than respond to her children's performance as a group (e.g., "You are all doing such a good job"), she gives each child specific and positive behavioral feedback (e.g., "Julio, I like how you started with making a knot" and "Mary, please look at your tie again. It looks like you forgot to double knot the laces").

High levels of instructional support also encourage exploration across concepts, as well as higher-level reasoning. When teaching the frog lesson to her students, Ms. Ruby asks her class, "Last week we learned about bumblebees. Can someone tell me how frogs are like bumblebees? How are they different from bumblebees?" Ms. Ruby gives specific feedback to her students when they respond to these questions to stimulate concept exploration. She challenges her students to persist in their learning (e.g., "Paco, yes, you are right – bumblebees and frogs move differently. Can you tell me how?").

Finally, AC4P-oriented instructional-supportive teachers prompt verbal reactions to questions and instigate more advanced language to encourage overall language development. For example, a child brings in a toy truck and tells Ms. Ruby, "Look at my truck!" Ms. Ruby responds, "Oh, wow, look at that blue truck; it looks like a dump truck. Tell me what you know about dump trucks."

Emotional Support. Preschool teachers need to provide their students with a high degree of emotional support, consistent with the AC4P mission of creating a kind and caring classroom culture. This means effective teachers develop and maintain a positive classroom culture of interpersonal compassion by showing sensitivity to their students' difficulties and exhibiting an empathic regard for their perspectives.[23] Students exposed to this emotionally supportive climate are much more likely to be engaged in learning and to perceive personal control over their learning. Regarding our case study, Mr. Sam is particularly strong in this area. What does he do to create such an AC4P classroom?

Experts in the field would describe Mr. Sam's style as *elaborative*. This interactional style communicates sensitivity and empathy to preschool students.[27] Mr. Sam gives frequent behavior-focused AC4P praise to his children, including statements such as, "Wow, Elizabeth, I like the yellow and green paint you are using to represent your garden! You are holding the brush with the correct grip we talked about earlier today – great work!"

Mr. Sam's elaborative style of teaching avoids redirecting or changing the focus of his student's ongoing behavior. For example, when reading a book with one of his students, Mr. Sam notices that Maria skips forward a number of pages to "get to the part with the monster." Mr. Sam follows her lead, letting Maria's interest in the material guide his interactions with her about the book. He doesn't redirect her focus by asking her to proceed through the pages in sequential order. This elaborative style reflects an AC4P humanistic approach to teaching.

An AC4P culture developed by an emotionally supportive preschool teacher minimizes the occurrence of disruptive behavior. For example, Mr. Sam looks for opportunities to provide specific behavioral compliments that promote classroom rules through positive rather than negative means (e.g., "Jacob, I really like how you sat in your chair the whole time you were working on that assignment!"). Mr. Sam also creates a more group-level AC4P classroom culture by recognizing and rewarding AC4P interactions among the children (e.g., "Sara, thank you for helping Deonte clean up the pencils. You're showing all of us how to be a good friend").

Mr. Sam builds close relationships with his students by using positive affective statements to communicate his warmth (e.g., "Jerry, I'm so glad you came to my class this morning; seeing your smile just made my day!"). When children experience negative emotions, Mr. Sam demonstrates empathy and uses the present moment to communicate empathy and facilitate a learning opportunity.

For example, during free play, a particular student in Mr. Sam's class becomes upset that he cannot play with the construction blocks because too many other children are using them. Harold begins throwing blocks across the room. Demonstrating emotional support and compassion, Mr. Sam says, "Harold, I see you are upset that you cannot play with the blocks right now. Instead of throwing those blocks across the room, is there a better way to express your feelings to me?"

In Summary

An AC4P culture can be created by teachers in their classrooms by providing high levels of emotional support, organizing their classrooms to customize the learning process per individual student, and stimulating critical thinking and language development. Exposed to such a culture, preschoolers demonstrate significant gains in learning, both socially and emotionally, and not only in preschool, but also later in kindergarten and beyond.[26]

Unfortunately, not all preschool programs employ teachers who possess and exhibit these AC4P emotional, instructional, and organizational skills. Children from lower socioeconomic status (SES) groups are less likely to have teachers with high levels of these qualities.[28] Classrooms with at least 60 percent of children living in poverty are rated significantly lower than middle and upper SES classrooms in terms of both teacher–child interactions and instructional support.[29] Hence, children from selected backgrounds (lower SES) most in need of an effective AC4P preschool program are least likely to get it.

We know children learn most effectively from emotionally sensitive and empathic AC4P teachers. Preschool teachers must be trained and encouraged to develop this skill set. Let's consider interventions that have been implemented to enhance the AC4P teacher skills that will most benefit the cognitive, emotional, and prosocial development of preschool children.

IMPROVING THE AC4P IMPACT OF PRESCHOOL TEACHERS

Using the principles of applied behavioral science (ABS) reviewed in Chapter 1, the authors of a number of studies identified a set of observable behaviors that reflect desirable teacher qualities. Next, interventions were designed to train samples of teachers to exhibit these qualities in their classrooms. The effectiveness of the interventions was evaluated on the basis of changes in teachers' classroom behavior and their one-to-one interactions with students, as well as in student-oriented outcomes. These research studies have focused primarily on developing beneficial teacher–child relationships.[26]

Our case study teachers (Ms. Margaret, Ms. Ruby, and Mr. Sam) are ded-icated and motivated to improve their teaching. They often wonder, "What specifically can we do to provide optimal support for our students?" Let's briefly review some relevant intervention studies. Following each part of the review, we revisit our three teachers to examine how they might use these intervention techniques to improve their teaching of preschool children.

Helping Teachers Define Relevant Behavior

Any intervention designed to improve preschool teaching should begin by identifying a set of desired teaching behaviors that can be observed and objectively assessed. This is consistent with ABS guidelines. The Classroom Assessment Scoring System (CLASS) developed by Pianta, La Paro, and Hamre is one such tool.[23] The CLASS is an observational assessment system that provides a list of desirable teacher–child interactions in classroom set-tings. External observers use it to measure and subsequently evaluate the effectiveness of individual teachers. When teachers are taught the desirable behaviors reflected in the CLASS, observe their own videotaped teaching behavior, and then evaluate themselves using the CLASS checklist, they can readily adjust their classroom instruction and interactions with their students.

The CLASS includes three domains of classroom quality, each consis-tent with the characteristics of quality teaching reviewed earlier. *Emotional Support* is the first domain. This includes teacher behaviors that focus on developing supportive AC4P teacher–student relationships by (a) increas-ing children's comfort levels; (b) helping them experience joy and excite-ment regarding learning; and (c) facilitating appropriate perceptions of choice and personal control. The Emotional Support items of the CLASS assess the classroom culture and the teacher's sensitivity and regard for stu-dent perspectives.

Classroom Organization is the second subscale of the CLASS. It's defined as effective pedagogical techniques that (a) regulate children's behavior; (b) support their productive learning; and (c) sustain student interest in classroom activities. Teachers' behavior-management skills are examined, as are their productive use of classroom learning time and application of appropriate instructional formats.

Instructional Support is the third subscale of the CLASS. It targets teach-ing behaviors that support children's growth in the cognitive and language domains. The focus is on literacy and reflects (a) concept development; (b) the quality of teachers' feedback; and (c) their language modeling.

To assess the behaviors exhibited by preschool teachers, a few large-scale, nationally based studies were conducted with the CLASS. These studies revealed that, on average, classroom teachers scored in the middle to high range on the Emotional Support domain, but scored much lower on the Instructional Support scale.[30] It appears preschool teachers differ in their use of effective teaching behaviors.

Most teachers did not have highly developed teaching skills across all three domains when these studies examined scores "within teachers" (i.e., looked at individual teacher's scores across all three scales). Given this variability in skill sets within individual teachers and across different teachers, can teachers be trained to acquire and then to demonstrate more effective teaching behaviors? Let's consider relevant intervention research.

Using the CLASS to Improve Teachers' Behaviors

Different intervention studies have been conducted with the CLASS to determine if teachers can be trained to demonstrate high-quality teaching across all three domains just discussed. The participants were either currently employed teachers or teachers in training. Many studies were delivered either via a Web-based program or through a professional development course. They were designed to determine if teaching outcomes (behaviors and knowledge) increased as a result of the intervention procedure. These studies are summarized in Table 16.2.

It's possible to have a beneficial impact on teacher behavior, as summarized in the intervention studies in Table 16.2. Every study resulted in significant improvement in participants' knowledge of effective teaching behaviors and/or in their classroom behaviors. A few key points regarding the design of effective teacher-training programs are apparent from these studies.

First, it's important for teachers to clearly understand all components of effective AC4P teaching behavior – in any teacher-training program. This can be accomplished by requiring teachers to learn about the dimensions of the CLASS and what behaviorally specific teaching skills are contained in the tool.

Second, in each of these studies, teachers were shown videos that presented concrete examples of quality teaching behaviors defined by the CLASS. Observation of master teachers will likely need to be incorporated in effective teacher-training modules.

Third, objective and systematic observation of teachers' behavior followed by individualized behavioral feedback is important. Expert trainers are best

TABLE 16.2. *A summary of intervention research using the CLASS*

Intervention study	Intervention procedure and outcomes
My Teaching Partner (MTP)[31]	In this intervention, early childhood teacher participants: 1. watched Web-based videos of "expert teaching" consistent with the CLASS, and 2. were then observed and rated on the CLASS by trained observers. 3. Some teachers also received individualized behavioral feedback from the trained observers to further develop their teaching skills on the CLASS. Intervention outcomes: • Teachers who watched videos and received individualized feedback on their teaching demonstrated positive growth in teacher–child interactions as measured by the CLASS.
Using the CLASS to train teachers in college settings[32]	In this intervention, early childhood teachers-in-training: 1. learned about the CLASS as a framework for promoting knowledge of effective teaching, viewed videos of expert teachers modeling teaching techniques, and 2. completed assignments that included readings, analyzing videos of expert teachers, and completing written reflections in response to content. Intervention outcomes: • Participants reported the videos helped them improve their intentional teaching style. • Participants demonstrated growth in their knowledge of early language and literacy, as well as in their knowledge of effective teacher–student interactions.
Using the CLASS to train teachers in college settings[33]	In this intervention, early childhood teachers-in-training: 1. videotaped themselves teaching, and 2. reviewed these videotapes with peer and instructor feedback to analyze their skills based on the CLASS observation system. 3. Tapes were also reviewed and scored by researchers using the CLASS observation system. Intervention outcomes: • Teachers generally made progress, as measured by improved skills on the CLASS. • Authors noted that even with intervention, teachers displayed variable skills across the three domains of the CLASS, indicating it's difficult to focus concurrently on all skills.

Intervention study	Intervention procedure and outcomes
A Semester-long professional development course for teachers[34]	Teachers in the intervention group: 1. received explicit instruction on quality teaching consistent with the CLASS, 2. were observed using the CLASS, 3. analyzed their teaching according to the CLASS, completing self-critiques/reflection, and 4. participated in role-plays. Intervention outcomes: • Teachers who took this course, as compared with a control group, displayed growth in their knowledge and skill with both the instructional and emotional support domains of the CLASS.

A yearlong professional development course for teachers[35]	Intervention procedure:
	 1. Self-reflection: Teachers videotaped their classrooms monthly and completed self-reflections on their own teaching skills.
	 2. Teachers received mentoring:
	   a. On-site supervisors used the CLASS to observe teaching.
	   b. On the basis of these observations, supervisors provided coaching for the teachers.
	 3. Teachers participated in bimonthly workshops regarding effective teaching behaviors.
	 Intervention outcomes:
	 • Participants demonstrated significant improvement in (a) behavior management skills; (b) productive use of classroom time; (c) effective use of language-modeling skills; and (d) quality of feedback given to children in their classes.

qualified to provide observations and feedback of teaching; still, some studies successfully incorporated peer observations or self-observations. This might make an intervention easier to accomplish within actual preschool settings.

Let's return to the three teachers from our Green Mushroom Preschool Program. We will use the information contained in previous sections of this chapter to design a CLASS-based intervention that could be used to enhance their AC4P classroom culture.

Revisiting the Case Study. Principles of ABS should guide professional development for preschool teachers. We propose a skill-development program that includes opportunities for practice (behavioral rehearsal), individualized feedback, multidimensional training/learning methods, expert coaching, and ongoing support (in order to transfer learning to a work setting).[36] Let's see how the three case study teachers, in conjunction with their supervisor, could use the CLASS to improve their teaching during the upcoming school year. Table 16.3 contains the plan these three teachers constructed. Note how this plan closely aligns with the scientific method explained in Chapter 1 specific to ABS – define, observe, intervene, test (DO IT).

The sample teacher-training program presented in Table 16.3 should increase teacher awareness of the importance of developing a classroom culture that provides high levels of support for children in all three domains: organizational, instructional, and emotional. The training program was based on ABS principles and could be conducted with relative ease within a preschool setting.

Much of the research on preschool teacher effectiveness and teacher training has been based on the CLASS, as evident from previous sections of this chapter and in the information contained in Tables 16.2 and 16.3. There are other ways to assess and improve teacher–child relationships in preschool settings. One approach examines and works toward improving teachers' level of sensitivity. This perspective is examined next.

Intervening to Improve Teacher–Child Relationships

Teacher sensitivity is one of the subdomains within the Emotional Support category of the CLASS. It's often considered to be a key interpersonal characteristic of effective preschool teaching. Teachers high in sensitivity exhibit high levels of awareness/responsiveness to each child, have the ability to address/resolve problems in a timely manner, and support and encourage students to set learning goals, seek support and guidance, and participate in classroom activities.[23]

Two techniques help teachers improve their sensitivity in the classroom. The first trains teachers to exhibit a more child-focused teaching style.[37] A child-focused style emphasizes following the child's lead and providing fewer directions during one-to-one interactions. Teachers also display positive affect during interactions with individual children and develop a sense of belongingness and interdependency. In contrast, teachers with a more adult-centered style attempt to structure their interactions with children using an individualistic top-down approach.

Imagine a teacher and child in a preschool classroom reading a book together. The child shows interest in a page and begins to tell the teacher a story about the picture. An adult-centered teacher responds with, "No,

TABLE 16.3. *Professional development plan for Green Mushroom Preschool Teachers*

Months	Scientific method stage	Description
August and September	Define behavior (what is quality teaching?)	Our teachers begin by learning the characteristics of quality teaching behavior. Although each teacher demonstrates particular skills within his/her classroom, all three are introduced to the components of the CLASS model (Instructional Support, Organizational Support, and Emotional Support). To accomplish this, the following steps are implemented: • Their supervisor leads them through lessons related to these components and introduces the CLASS observation tool. • Following each lesson, the teachers view a video of an expert teacher demonstrating "live" skills in each area. • While they are watching these videos, each teacher uses the CLASS observation tool to rate the expert teacher.
October	Define behavior (what is quality teaching?)	Once our three teachers are comfortable with the content of the CLASS and know how to behaviorally define each component, they • are assigned a video of a classroom and use the CLASS tool to rate the classroom teacher in each of the three areas. • Then they meet as a group with their supervisors to discuss their ratings and provide a personal example of what they viewed in the video. The supervisors provide feedback regarding the video ratings.
November	Observe (teaching behavior)	• Each teacher has someone videotape him/ her in the classroom. • They review their own video and rate themselves on the CLASS, reflecting on their own strengths and weaknesses. • In addition, the supervisors view their respective videotaped classroom segment and rate the teacher with the CLASS.

(continued)

TABLE 16.3 *(continued)*

Months	Scientific method stage	Description
December	Intervene (to improve quality of teaching behavior)	• The teachers meet individually with their supervisor to discuss ratings of the CLASS. • During this consultation and collaboration meeting, the supervisor offers specific, behavioral professional-development suggestions for each teacher (e.g., Ms. Ruby, who is strong in organizational support, might be guided to work on her emotional-support skills).
January	Intervene (to improve teaching behavior)	Following this feedback, all three teachers • complete any additional reading/activities suggested by the supervisor, and • compose and submit weekly reflections of their own progress in the three domains.
February	Test (effects of the intervention on teaching quality)	All three teachers re-videotape their classrooms and rate their own behavior again using the CLASS. • The supervisor also views these tapes and rates the teachers using the CLASS. • Another consultation meeting is scheduled to review their ratings, specifically focusing on how teachers have demonstrated progress in their skill development. • At the end of this consultation meeting, the teacher and supervisor discuss next steps of professional development.
March and April	Intervene (to continue to build quality teaching skills)	Following their second set of CLASS-specific feedback, teachers continue to compose weekly reflections and complete any additional readings/professional development activities suggested by the supervisor.
May	Test (perform a summative evaluation of progress toward goals)	Before adjourning for the summer, teachers • meet again with their supervisor, this time as a group, to reflect on both individual and group progress. • The group brainstorms ideas for professional development over the summer.

we don't have time for your story right now. Let's finish the book so we can move on to our next activity." In contrast, a child-centered teacher listens with great interest to the child's story, and perhaps even asks some learning-related follow-up questions (e.g., "So how did you feel when that happened?"). This child-focused (humanistic) style can be extremely beneficial, particularly with behaviorally challenged children.

The use of technology-assisted devices for reading with young children is a corresponding and more current issue regarding adult–child interactions during learning activities. In a recent study, researchers compared the interactions between parent and child interactions when they read a book together versus when they used an electronic device (i.e., a tablet).[38] The results of this study suggest that adults who use electronic devices when reading with children might focus on the correct use of the technology in lieu of a humanistic interaction with the child, although more research on this topic is needed. For example, an adult reading a book with a child on a technology device might interact with the child in more directive ways ("Don't touch the button to turn the page yet, Mary!"); the adult reading with a hard-copy book will likely interact with the child surrounding the content ("Mary, look at that car. We have a car that same color, don't we?"). A teacher (or parent) using technology to read with a child might risk exhibiting lower levels of sensitivity and undermine a more positive and warm adult–child interaction.

"Banking time" is the second technique used to enhance teacher sensitivity in the preschool classroom. Teachers "bank" or spend time with students in their classroom in a one-to-one focused interaction.[39] Teachers work with a consultant to identify target students within their classroom. They meet with these individual students on a regular basis (daily, if possible) for short sessions up to fifteen minutes. During these sessions, the teachers are encouraged to let the child direct the interaction and focus on observing the development of an AC4P adult–child relationship.

Emotional sensitivity may appear to be natural for some people and not for others. But preschool teachers can be trained to increase the frequency of their sensitivity-related behaviors in their classrooms, according to some studies. Two of these studies are briefly described in Table 16.4.

The first study focused on using self-reflection and self-evaluation to increase teachers' sensitivity and warmth; the second study examined the validity of the "banking time" approach. Preschool teachers (or teachers in training) can learn to be more sensitive to the needs of their students, as indicated in the outcomes section of this table. What might such an intervention look like? Let's see what happens when one of our teachers from the Green Mushroom Preschool takes on this challenge.

TABLE 16.4. *A summary of research on improving teacher sensitivity*

Intervention study	Intervention procedure and outcomes
Training graduate-student early childhood teachers to increase behaviors of sensitivity and warmth[37]	Intervention procedure: 1. Teachers complete a self-reflection statement; they are encouraged to think about how personal characteristics might impact their teaching and teacher–child relationships. 2. Teachers review videotapes of their own teaching and analyze their skills with peers and instructors. 3. Teachers are encouraged to build their sensitivity skills and behaviors through a series of guided problem-solving questions that encourage appropriate goal setting. 4. Teachers participate in group-based seminars to brainstorm on creative techniques and activities for demonstrating sensitivity in the classroom. Intervention outcomes: • Teacher participants enrolled in this course are better able to recognize specific quality-teaching behaviors. • The area of greatest gain is in the behaviors used to communicate emotional support to students.
Using "banking time" in the classroom[40]	Intervention procedure: • Teachers are trained to engage in "banking time" intervention in their classrooms. Intervention outcomes: Children of the teachers using "banking time" demonstrate: • Increases in frustration tolerance, task orientation, and competence • Decreases in conduct problems in the classroom • Increases in teacher-reported closeness.

Intervening to Increase Teacher Sensitivity

As part of their yearlong professional development project to improve teacher effectiveness, Ms. Margaret, Ms. Ruby, and Mr. Sam received feedback from a teacher consultant regarding their teaching skills. Ms. Margaret's behavior-focused feedback reveals she demonstrates teaching strengths in her organizational and instructional support of her students, but demonstrates a weakness in her emotionally supportive skills. After receiving this behavior-focused feedback, Ms. Margaret determines she

TABLE 16.5. *Sample banking time dialogue*

Ms. Margaret: "Hi, Jacob, I'm so excited for us to spend some time learning together today. What would you like to play with?"

Jacob: "Can we play with the cars?"

Ms. Margaret: "I would love to play with the cars. Let's go together and get them from the shelf." (Teacher leads Jacob to retrieve the cars and brings them back to the table. Jacob pours all of the cars out onto the table.)

Ms. Margaret: "I see you're getting out all of the cars for us to play with." (She's observing and narrating child's actions.)

Jacob: "Yeah, I'm trying to find the police car."

Ms. Margaret: "Oh, okay. I'll help you look for that. Perhaps we can find it quicker if we help each other. Can you tell me what color it is?" (Teacher is developing a relational theme of help and support.)

Jacob: "Black. Here it is!" (He holds car up for teacher to see.) "Here, you play with this police car, I'll find another one."

Ms. Margaret: "Oh, Jacob, thank you for sharing your police car with me. It's so much fun to play with you when you share your toys." (She's narrating the child's action and developing relational themes.)

Jacob: (after a bit longer searching) "Where is that stupid car?"

Ms. Margaret: "It sounds like you are frustrated that you can't find the other police car. What can I do to help?" (She is labeling the child's emotion and feelings, further developing relational themes.)

Jacob: "It's okay; I'll just play with these." (He picks up a red car and blue car and begins crashing them together.)

Ms. Margaret: "Wow, look at the blue car and the red car; you made them crash into each other" (She's narrating the child actions), and "I wonder if my police car can help your cars get along better?" (She's developing relational themes).

---

wants to improve her AC4P connection with her students, desiring to be more responsive, sensitive, and empathic when interacting with them. Ms. Margaret decides to implement the banking time intervention in her classroom after consulting with the teacher expert.

She schedules time in her school week to spend ten minutes of one-on-one time with certain children in her class to make this happen. She decides she will meet with two children each day during the free-play portion of the schedule. During this time, she counts on her teaching assistant to make sure all of the other children are supervised so she can focus her interactions on one child.

During her banking time sessions with each child, Ms. Margaret focuses on demonstrating the following behaviors: (a) observing the child's actions; (b) narrating (describing) the child's actions out loud; (c) labeling the child's emotions and feelings; and (d) developing relational themes. Table 16.5

depicts an example of this banking time with a child – Jacob. Where applicable, the desired teacher behavior is noted.

The dialogue depicted in Table 16.5 represents one example of how a humanistic-behaviorism intervention might be conducted for one teacher–student interaction. By encouraging the teacher to focus on observing the child, narrating his/her actions, applying feelings or emotion labels when possible, and developing relational themes, the teacher becomes more nondirective, empathic, and responsive to each child. This approach encourages teachers to focus their interactions with each child toward more child-directed interactions (i.e., directed by the child's interests and needs at that time) rather than adult-directed (i.e., directed by the teacher's perceptions).

Clearly, this intervention reflects the AC4P approach to developing an actively caring culture of compassion for preschool students. The overarching mission is to establish relational themes between the teacher and the student, specifically communicating to the student (through these short play-based sessions) that the teacher is a safe, reliable, responsive, helpful, accepting, and AC4P adult who believes in the child's potential.[39]

IN CONCLUSION

This chapter reviews research on the benefits of preschool and shows how preschool teachers can be trained to create an AC4P-centered culture that enhances children's academic and psychosocial well-being. Unfortunately, many children enter kindergarten without foundational pre-mathematics and pre-reading skills. As a result, these children continue to underperform as compared with their preschooler peers throughout the remainder of their educational careers. Children from lower socioeconomic status or racial minority groups comprise a disproportionately large part of the children who enter kindergarten without these skills. And quality preschool programs are apparently less available to those at-risk groups of children.

According to hallmark studies in preschool education, a quality preschool experience can buffer many of the negative effects of growing up in an at-risk demographic group, particularly those students from lower socioeconomic status groups. The positive effects of a quality preschool experience appear to be important upon entry to elementary school and beyond into adulthood. Children who have an exemplary preschool experience have better long-term outcomes, both educationally (e.g., higher reading and math scores in later grades, increased graduation rates) and socially (e.g., lower incidence of legal violations, improved financial circumstances).

A quality preschool experience that impacts children positively is defined by a quality curriculum and a solid organizational structure. What appears even more important to the quality of a preschool are its *teachers*. The degree to which teachers establish a warm climate within their classroom and display empathy toward their students is particularly meaningful. This is entirely consistent with the AC4P Movement. Clearly, instruction is important, but without the presence of an AC4P teacher–student relationship, child learning outcomes are not maximized.

Fortunately, research indicates that preschool teachers can be trained to act in accordance with AC4P principles. This chapter showed how ABS methods help teachers improve their instructional skills as well as their relational competencies with their students. Teachers who support their students emotionally, organizationally, and instructionally have a positive impact on their children that extends well beyond the preschool years.

Preschool is a particularly important context to examine because a positive, quality preschool experience gets young students off to a strong start. If we train the teachers who work with these preschool students to exhibit an AC4P demeanor of interpersonal compassion, their students will evidence not only academic gains, but also social-emotional growth. In doing so, we form the foundation of a peer-based academic culture that exemplifies the AC4P Movement. By intervening early with the important adults in these children's lives, we create an AC4P culture that students carry with them throughout the remainder of their educational experiences, and beyond.

DISCUSSION QUESTIONS

1. Imagine you know parents who are considering whether to incur the expense and inconvenience of sending their child to preschool. They ask, "Why not give our child another year of freedom and bonding with family, and we can teach basic life lessons at home?" How would you respond?
2. What beneficial consequences of effective preschool programming have been empirically demonstrated?
3. Discuss teacher behaviors linked to the three categories of teacher effectiveness in preschool: organizational support, instructional support, and emotional support.
4. How can preschool teachers facilitate critical thinking and concept-development skills among their young students?
5. How is the CLASS (Classroom Assessment Scoring System) used to enhance the effectiveness of preschool teachers?

6. Explain the connection between the ABS principles defined in Chapter 1 and effective training for preschool teachers.
7. Provide a behavioral (i.e., operational) definition of a student-centered teaching style.
8. How does "banking time" augment teacher sensitivity in the preschool classroom?
9. In what ways is "humanistic behaviorism" an appropriate label for training techniques designed to enhance the effectiveness of preschool teachers and cultivating an AC4P classroom culture?
10. Imagine you are deciding which of several preschools would be best for your child. What factors would you look for in making your decision, and how would you determine the availability of these factors?

REFERENCES

1. Russell, J. L. (2011). From child's garden to academic press: The role of shifting institutional logics in redefining kindergarten education. *Education and Educational Research*, 48(2), 236–267.
2. Kids Count Data Center (2012). In *The Annie E. Casey Foundation*. Retrieved October 6, 2014, from http://datacenter.kidscount.org/data/Tables/7188-children-ages-3-to-4-not-attending-preschool?loc=1&loc t=1#detailed/1/any/false/1049,995,932,757,470/any/14230,14231.
3. Chen, C., Lee, S., & Stevenson, H. W. (1996). Long-term prediction of academic achievement of American, Chinese, and Japanese adolescents. *Journal of Educational Psychology*, 88(4), 750–759; Shonkoff, J. P., & Phillips, D. A. (Eds.). (2000). *From neurons to neighborhoods: The science of early childhood development*. Washington, DC: National Academy Press.
4. Butler, S. R., Marsh, H. W., Sheppard, M. J., & Sheppard, J. L. (1985). Seven-year longitudinal study of the early prediction of reading achievement. *Journal of Educational Psychology*, 77, 349–361; Krajewski, K., & Schneider, W. (2009). Exploring the impact of phonological awareness, visual-spatial working memory, and preschool quantity-number competencies on mathematics achievement in elementary school: Findings from a three-year longitudinal study. *Journal of Experimental Child Psychology*, 103, 516–531; Stevenson, H. W., & Newman, R. S. (1986). Long-term prediction of achievement and attitudes in mathematics and reading. *Child Development*, 57(3), 646–659.
5. Annie E. Casey Foundation (2010). Early warning! Why reading by the end of third grade matters. Retrieved June 1, 2012, from http://aecf.org; Wilson, S. B., & Lonigan, C. J. (2009). An evaluation of emergent literacy screening tools for preschool children. *International Dyslexia Association*, 59, 115–131.
6. Duncan, G. J., Dowsett, C. J., Claessens, A., Magnuson, K., Huston, A. C., Klebanov P., et al. (2007). School readiness and later achievement. *Developmental Psychology*, 43(6), 1428–1446; Grissmer, D., Grimm, K. J., Aiyer, S. M., Murrah, W. M., & Steele, J. S. (2010). Fine motor skills and early comprehension of the

world: Two new school readiness indicators. *Developmental Psychology,* 46(5), 1008–1017.

7. Nisbett, R. E., Aronson, J., Blair, C., Dickens, W., Flynn, J., Halpern, D. F., et al. (2012). Intelligence: New findings and theoretical developments. *American Psychologist,* 67(2), 130–159.

8. Denton, K., & West, J. (2002). Children's reading and mathematics achievement in kindergarten and first grade. *Education Statistics Quarterly,* 4(1), 19–26; Lee, V. E., & Burkham, D. T. (2002). *Inequality at the starting gate: Social background differences in achievement as children begin school* Washington, DC: Economic Policy Institute; West, J., Denton, K., & Germino-Hausken, E. (2000). America's kindergartners: Findings from the early childhood longitudinal study, kindergarten class of 1998–99: Fall 1998. *Education Statistics Quarterly,* 2(1), 7–13; West, J., Denton, K., & Reaney, L. (2001). *The kindergarten year.* Washington, DC: U.S. Department of Education.

9. Aud, S., Hussar, W., Johnson, F., Kena, G., Roth, E., Manning, E., et al. (2012). *The condition of education 2012* (NCES 2012–045). Washington, DC: U.S. Department of Education, National Center for Education Statistics. Retrieved January 20, 2013 from http://nces.ed.gov/pubsearch.

10. Bowman, B. T., Donovan, M. S., & Burns, M. S. (2001). *Eager to learn: Educating our preschoolers.* Washington, DC: National Academies Press.

11. Hanford, E. (2014). Early lessons. *American Radio Works.* Retrieved September 6, 2014 from http://americanradioworks.publicradio.org/features/preschool/index.html.

12. Parks, G. (2000). The HighScope Perry Preschool Project. *Office of Juvenile Justice and Delinquency Prevention Bulletin.* Retrieved September 7, 2014 from https://www.ncjrs.gov/html/ojjdp/2000_10_1/contents.html.

13. Schweinhart, L. J. (2003). Benefits, costs, and explanation of the HighScope Perry Preschool Program. *Meeting of the Society for Research in Child Development.* Retrieved September 7, 2014 from http://www.highscope.org/file/Research/PerryProject/Perry-SRCD_2003.pdf.

14. Schweinhart, L. J. (2003). Benefits, costs, and explanation of the HighScope Perry Preschool Program. *Meeting of the Society for Research in Child Development.* Retrieved September 7, 2014 from http://www.highscope.org/file/Research/PerryProject/Perry-SRCD_2003.pdf; Hanford, E. (2014). Early lessons. *American Radio Works.* Retrieved September 6, 2014 from http://americanradioworks.publicradio.org/features/preschool/index.html.

15. Schweinhart, L. J. (2002). How the HighScope Perry Preschool study grew: A researcher's tale. Phi Delta Kappa Center for Evaluation, Development, and Research, 32. Retrieved September 7, 2014 from http://www.highscope.org/Content.asp?ContentId=232.

16. Schweinhart, L. J. (2002). How the HighScope Perry Preschool study grew: A researcher's tale. Phi Delta Kappa Center for Evaluation, Development, and Research, 32. Retrieved September 7, 2014 from http://www.highscope.org/Content.asp?ContentId=232; Hanford, E. (2014). Early lessons. *American Radio Works.* Retrieved from September 6, 2014 http://americanradioworks.publicradio.org/features/preschool/index.html.

17. Campbell, F. A., Ramey, C. T., Pungello, E., Sparling, J., & Miller-Johnson, S. (2002). Early childhood education: Young adult outcomes from the Abecedarian project. *Applied Developmental Science, 6*(1), 42–57.

18. Ramey, C. T., Campbell, F. A., Burchinal, M., Skinner, M. L., Gardner, D. M., & Ramey, S. L. (2000). Persistent effects of early intervention on high-risk children and their mothers. *Applied Developmental Science, 4*, 2–14.

19. Bureau of Labor Statistics, U.S. Department of Labor. (January, 2014). *Occupational outlook handbook, 2014–2015 ed., Preschool Teachers.* Retrieved October 2, 2014 from http://www.bls.gov/ooh/education-training-and-library/preschool-teachers-htm.

20. National Association for the Education of Young Children (2006). The 10 NAEYC Standards. Retrieved October 4, 2014 from http://families.naeyc.org/accredited-article/10-naeyc-program-standards#6.

21. McDonald-Connor, C. M., Son, S., Hindman, A., & Morrison, F. J. (2005). Teacher qualifications, classroom practices, family characteristics, and preschool experience: Complex effects on first graders' vocabulary and early reading outcomes. *Journal of School Psychology, 43*, 343–375; Pianta, R., Howes, C., Burchinal, M., Bryant, D., Clifford, R., Early, C., et al. (2005). Features of pre-kindergarten programs, classrooms, and teachers: Do they predict observed classroom quality and child-teacher interactions? *Applied Developmental Science, 9*(3), 144–159.

22. Mashburn, A. J., Pianta, R., Hamre, B. K., Downer, J. T., Barbarin, O., Bryant, D., et al. (2008). Measures of classroom quality in pre-kindergarten and children's development of academic, language and social skills. *Child Development, 79*, 732–749.

23. Pianta, R. C., La Paro, K. M., & Hamre, B. K. (2008). *Classroom assessment scoring system.* Baltimore: Brookes.

24. Downer, J. T., Sabol, T., & Hamre, B. K. (2010). Teacher–child interactions in the classroom: Toward a theory of within- and cross-domain links to children's developmental outcomes. *Early Education and Development, 21*, 699–723.

25. Curby, T., LoCasale-Crouch, J., Konold, T., Pianta, R., Howes, C., Burchinal, M., et al. (2009). The relations of observed pre-k classroom quality profiles to children's achievement and social competence. *Early Education & Development, 20*(2), 346–372.

26. Burchinal, M., Howes, C., Pianta, R., Bryant, D., Early, D., Clifford, R., et al. (2008). Predicting child outcomes at the end of kindergarten from the quality of pre-kindergarten teacher-child interactions and instruction. *Applied Developmental Science, 12*(3), 140–153

27. de Kruif, R. E. L., McWilliam, R. A., Ridley, S. M., & Wakely, M. B. (2000). Classification of teachers' interaction behaviors in early childhood classrooms. *Early Childhood Research Quarterly, 15*, 247–268.

28. McDonald-Connor, C. M., Son, S., Hindman, A., & Morrison, F. J. (2005). Teacher qualifications, classroom practices, family characteristics, and preschool experience: Complex effects on first graders' vocabulary and early reading outcomes. *Journal of School Psychology, 43*, 343–375.

29. Pianta, R., Howes, C., Burchinal, M., Bryant, D., Clifford, R., Early, C., et al. (2005). Features of pre-kindergarten programs, classrooms, and teachers: Do they predict observed classroom quality and child-teacher interactions? *Applied Developmental Science*, 9(3), 144–159.

30. Early, D., Barbarin, O., Bryant, D., Burchinal, M., Chang, F., Clifford, R., et al. (2005). Pre-kindergarten in eleven states: NCEDL's multi-state study of pre-kindergarten and study of state-wide early education programs (SWEEP). Preliminary descriptive report. Chapel Hill: University of North Carolina, Child Development Institute. Retrieved August 15, 2014, from http://fpg.unc.edu/sites/fpg.unc.edu/files/resources/reports-and-policy-briefs/NCEDL_PreK-in-Eleven-States_Working-Paper_2005.pdf; Pianta, R. C., Mashburn, A. J., Downer, J., Hamre, B. K., & Justice, L. (2008). Effects of web mediated professional development resources on teacher–child interactions in prekindergarten classrooms. *Early Childhood Research Quarterly*, 23, 431–451; La Paro, K. M., Maynard, C., Thomason, A., & Scott-Little, C. (2012). Developing teachers' classroom interactions: A description of a video review process for early childhood students. *Journal of Early Childhood Teacher Education*, 33, 224–238.

31. Pianta, R. C., Mashburn, A. J., Downer, J., Hamre, B. K., & Justice, L. (2008). Effects of web mediated professional development resources on teacher–child interactions in prekindergarten classrooms. *Early Childhood Research Quarterly*, 23, 431–451.

32. Scott-Little, C., La Paro, K. M., Thomason, A. C., Pianta, R. C., Hamre, B., Downer, J., et al. (2011). Implementation of a course focused on language and literacy within teacher-child interactions: Instructor and student perspectives across three institutes of higher education. *Journal of Early Childhood Teacher Education*, 32, 200–224.

33. La Paro, K. M., Maynard, C., Thomason, A., & Scott-Little, C. (2012). Developing teachers' classroom interactions: A description of a video review process for early childhood students. *Journal of Early Childhood Teacher Education*, 33, 224–238.

34. Hamre, B. K., Pianta, R. C., Burchinal, M., Field, S., LoCasale-Crouch, J., Downer, J. T., et al. (2012). A course on effective teacher–child interactions: Effects on teacher beliefs, knowledge, and observed practice. *American Educational Research Journal*, 49(1), 88–123.

35. Zan, B., & Donegan-Ritter, M. (2014). Reflecting, coaching, and mentoring to enhance teacher–child interactions in head start classrooms. *Early Childhood Education Journal*, 42, 93–104.

36. Sheridan, S. M., Edwards, C. P., Marvin, C. A., & Knoche, L. L. (2009). Professional development in early childhood programs: Process issues and research needs. *Early Education & Development*, 20, 377–401.

37. Rimm-Kaufman, S. E., Voorhees, M. D., Snell, M. E., & LaParo, K. M. (2003). Improving the sensitivity and responsivity of preservice teachers toward young children with disabilities. *Topics in Early Childhood Special Education*, 23, 151–163.

38. Parish-Morris, J., Mahajan, N., Hirsh-Pasek, K., Golinkoff, R. M., & Collins, M. F. (2013). Once upon a time: Parent–child dialogue and storybook reading in the electronic era. *Mind, Brain, and Education*, 7(3), 200–211.

39. Hamre, B. K., & Pianta, R. C. (2006). Student–teacher relationships. In G. G. Bear & K. M. Minke (Eds.). *Children's needs III: Development, prevention, and intervention* (pp. 59–71). Washington, DC: National Association of School Psychologists.

40. Driscoll, K. C. (2010). Banking time in Head Start: Early efficacy of an intervention designed to promote supportive teacher–child relationships. *Early Education and Development*, 21, 38–64.

17

Actively Caring Coaching for
Young Athletes

THELMA S. HORN

Somewhere behind the athlete you've become and the hours of practice
and the coaches who have pushed you is a little girl who fell in love with
the game and never looked back ... play for her.
– Mia Hamm

Participating in sports is a popular activity for children in the United
States.[1] Approximately 35–45 million children between the ages of 6 and
18 participate in some type of organized sport program each year, according to recent estimates. Youth participation in these programs (especially
in certain types of sports) varies significantly across gender, race/ethnicity,
geographic area, and family socioeconomic status.[2] In total, at least half or
up to three-quarters of all children in the United States participate in organized sports.

The number of children (especially girls) who participate in a competitive sport program has increased during the past several decades.[1] There
also appears to be a trend toward earlier entry into sports.[2] Today, it's not
unusual for children as young as 3 or 4 years of age to be participating in an
organized sports program and/or to begin training in what will ultimately
be a competitive sport. The intensity of physical training among young athletes may also be increasing, as parents hope to boost their children into
higher levels of play.[3]

There is also a trend in certain sports contexts toward earlier sport specialization. Children participate from an early age (e.g., 4 or 5 years) in
only one sport (e.g., tennis) to the exclusion of all other physical activities.[4]
In previous decades children participated more often in several different
sports or physical activities until they were into their adolescent years – at
which time they often focused on one sport. It's more common today for

children to be asked to, or perhaps pushed to, select one sport at an early age and train year round at that sport for the rest of their athletic career.

Participation in sports occurs during very important growth and development periods in the lives of children and adolescents. Significant developmentally-based changes occur between the ages of 6 and 18 in children's physical, socioemotional, psychological, and cognitive domains, and this development appears to be an interaction of nature and nurture.[5] And so engagement in competitive sports programs can significantly impact a child's development.[6]

In general, the research to date suggests that children who participate in youth sport programs are at an advantage with regard to (a) development of basic motor-skill competencies (e.g., coordination, balance, motor control); (b) levels of physical fitness (e.g., flexibility, strength, aerobic capacity); (c) physical health (e.g., decreased risk of obesity, type II diabetes, cardiovascular disease);[2] (d) academic and cognitive competences (e.g., attention/concentration, information-processing abilities, higher grades, decreased school dropout rates); (e) character and moral behavior (e.g., sportspersonship, self-discipline, persistence); (f) social skills and relationship-building; (g) positive self-perceptions (e.g., self-esteem, perceived competence, life satisfaction, body image); and (h) healthy lifestyle behaviors such as good nutrition, lower rates of drug use, and lower rates of juvenile delinquency.[7]

But other researchers and writers have identified potential negative outcomes of excessive participation in an organized youth sport program. Intensive training at a very young age can lead to injuries to the child's growing skeleton and brain, and these injuries can have lifelong consequences. Moreover, children and adolescents engaged in high levels of sport participation could be at risk for physical and emotional burnout and might even experience physical and sexual abuse by adults in their sport environment.[3] Youth sport participants also may develop negative health behaviors (e.g., disordered eating patterns, use of performance-enhancing drugs), negative self-perceptions (low self-esteem, low self-efficacy, and a negative body image), and possibly a decline in moral reasoning and behaviors.[8]

We have very different points of view here. Some researchers and writers cite positive effects of sport participation; others tout potential negative effects. How do we reconcile these divergent paradigms? What determines whether children will benefit or suffer by participating in a competitive sports program?

TABLE 17.1. *Quotes from current/former athletes*

Athlete	Quote
Former high school varsity basketball player	"He's the worst coach ever ... he didn't really influence me much ... aside from don't *ever* be anything like him!"
College softball player	"In all honesty ... well, I'm a senior ... and I guess I can say now that my coach made my four years of college sports a miserable experience! I loved playing softball in high school. But college – no way!"
Youth gymnast (10 years old)	"The worst thing is when she gets mad at me – I just want to cry, and then she gets even more mad 'cuz I do cry!"
College tennis player	"My coach? My college coach? Well ... he ... I would say that he had a big ... a huge ... influence on me. He was a really good coach and all that, but the big thing is that he really helped me through some kinda tough times. I still give him a call now and then – just to talk."
High school basketball player	"I want a college coach just like Coach T. She makes us work so hard in practices, but she's a true friend off the court."
Youth athlete	"He makes practices fun – even when we have to run (I *hate to* run!)"
Current youth sport coach/former athlete	"I just want my kids to love playing tennis as much as I did."
College football player	"Coach M ... he was more important than my high school football coach. He was ... I guess you could say a real good role model ... for real ... and maybe you'll think I'm stupid when I say this ... but ... um ... he just taught us how to be men."

The answer may well be the quality of the behavior among adults involved in the youth sport environment, from parents of young athletes to administrators or directors of youth sport programs and team coaches. In this chapter, I focus particularly on the role coaches play in determining whether young athletes will experience positive or negative outcomes. From two decades of evaluating relationships between coaches and young athletes, I've collected a number of quotes from current and former athletes. To illustrate the diversity of opinions, a few are presented in Table 17.1. As these comments make clear, coaches play important roles in their athletes' lives – most often in a positive way but sometimes in a strongly negative way.

THE AC4P APPROACH TO COACHING
YOUNG ATHLETES

In Chapter 1, Scott Geller advocates cultivating an organizational culture in which all participants actively care for the well-being of each other. He and his students have coined the phrase actively caring for people (AC4P) to capture the essence of this culture-improvement movement. This chapter illustrates applications of the AC4P approach to youth sports, first by reviewing the results of research that examined coaches' behaviors in youth sports. The conclusion: The action of coaches can reflect a desire to actively care for the children and adolescents with whom they work and help create a climate of humanistic AC4P concern for others. I begin with an examination of various behaviors characteristic of coaches.

BEHAVIORS OF YOUTH SPORT COACHES

More than forty years ago, Ron Smith, Frank Smoll, and their colleagues at the University of Washington began a series of studies that examined the behaviors of youth sport team coaches (i.e., of soccer, basketball, baseball, and football).[9] They developed an assessment tool to code and categorize coaches' behaviors during practices and games, and attempted to assess how the coaches' behaviors affected their young athletes' perceptions, attitudes, and beliefs. First, teams of observers (mostly undergraduate and graduate students) watched the practices and games of young athletes and used a time-sampling method to verbally record (in a "play-by-play" manner) the behaviors of their coaches.

The behavioral observations were tape-recorded and then content-analyzed using concepts from social learning theory to develop the instrument: the Coaching Behavior Assessment System (CBAS). This assessment tool provided a measure of the types of behaviors coaches of youth exhibit during practices and games. In particular, the CBAS captures twelve dimensions of coaching behavior, divided into two categories: (a) reactive behaviors displayed by coaches in response to athletes' behaviors (e.g., feedback to an athlete after a performance attempt, response to an athlete's misbehavior); and (b) spontaneous behaviors displayed by the coach and not in response to athlete behaviors (e.g., instructions, general encouragement, general communication).

Researchers and/or practitioners can observe coaches during an extended period of time with the CBAS and code their behaviors in both game and practice situations. After observation data are coded and compiled, a profile of each coach is developed. Typically, a coach's profile is based on the percentage of each type of behavior the coach exhibits over a large number of observed practice or game sessions. Table 17.2 presents example profiles of five youth volleyball coaches. Each of these coaches was observed for five total practice sessions (two hours per practice) by a team of observers using the CBAS. The number in the last row of the table shows the total number of behaviors coded per each coach. The numbers within each behavioral column (positive comment, no response, etc.) indicate the *percentage* of each coach's total behaviors per category.

Coach 1 (Shala) exhibited a total of 1,200 codable behaviors during five practices. Of this total, 22 percent (264 behaviors) were coded as a "positive comment;" 2 percent (24 behaviors) were coded as "no response," and so on. These data indicate substantial variation between the five coaches. Which behavioral profile is best? Which is worst? Answers are revealed at the end of the following section.

IMPACT OF COACHES' BEHAVIORS ON YOUNG ATHLETES

Smith and Smoll and their colleagues used the CBAS to determine what coaching behaviors were most effective for enhancing young athletes' psychosocial well-being.[9] This research team conducted several large-scale observation-based field studies in which they coded more than 80,000 coaching behaviors of 70 youth sport coaches. In addition, they interviewed and administered questionnaires to more than 1,000 of the young athletes in their homes following the end of their competitive season. Young athletes whose coaches engaged in higher frequencies of supportive and instructive behaviors liked their coaches and their teammates more, according to results, and they reportedly had more fun than did players whose coaches scored lower in supportive and instructive conversation and higher in the use of punitive consequences.

Teams' won-lost records, as compiled at the end of the season, related to players' evaluations of their coach's knowledge and teaching ability (i.e., players of teams that won more games perceived their coaches as more competent), noted Smith and Smoll and colleagues.[9] In contrast, players' perceptions of the fun and enjoyment they experienced and their attraction to their coach and teammates were determined primarily by the coach's behavioral style and much less by their won-lost record. The coaches' behavioral profiles had the greatest impact on the players who started the season with lower self-esteem. For athletes with lower self-esteem, the most

TABLE 17.2. *CBAS behavioral profiles for five youth volleyball coaches[1]*

		Coach 1: Shala	Coach 2: Damien	Coach 3: Jill	Coach 4: Darren	Coach 5: Nick
Coaches' reactive behaviors	**Responses to player successes**					
	Positive comment (e.g., "Good serve, Toni.")	**22**	9	**18**	5	5
	No response (e.g., coach ignores a good serve an athlete just made)	2	10	5	10	**15**
	Responses to player errors/mistakes					
	Ignoring mistakes (e.g., coach ignores a player's missed dig)	8	2	3	10	**15**
	Corrective feedback (e.g., "You missed that block because your hands were too far apart. Remember ... thumbs together ...")	4	4	**10**	3	2
	Encouragement (e.g., "It's OK. Even a college player serves into the net once in a while.")	6	2	6	6	2
Coaches' reactive behavior	**Negative comment** (e.g., "That was a terrible serve receive! You're gonna kill us in our next match!")	0	**10**	0	0	2

Coaches' impromptu behaviors							
Response to player(s) misbehaviors	**Punitive corrective feedback** (e.g., "How many times have I had to tell you to extend your elbow on the serve?")	2	0	2	10	0
	Keeping control (e.g., Jennifer, quit kicking the balls!")	10	1	2	5	3
Game-relevant	**Instruction** (e.g., "In this next drill, I want each of you to really concentrate on extending your elbow. You'll get more power on your serve.")	10	25	26	26	16
	General Encouragement (e.g., "OK, let's get fired up for this last drill.")	10	20	15	10	24
	Organization (e.g., "Janelle, you go into the scrimmage at setter. Jaleesa, you're our right-side hitter . . .")	10	12	8	10	5
Game-irrelevant	**General communication** (e.g., "Teresa, I hear you did really well on your science report!")	17	8	5	2	10
Total behaviors coded across 5 matches		500	1,100	1,000	800	1,200

¹ *Note:* Values in each column represent the percentage of total behaviors observed for each coach.

important coaching behavior seemed to be instruction-based (i.e., coaches who provided higher levels of behavioral instruction and responded to player errors with corrective behavior-based feedback).

At the end of the season, the researchers asked the coaches to rate their behavior with a questionnaire form of the CBAS.[9] Comparisons of coaches' perceptions of their own behavior with the observations from the CBAS indicated generally low and nonsignificant correlations, suggesting most coaches had limited awareness of the type of behaviors they exhibited in practices and games. In contrast, young athletes' ratings of their coaches' behavior (again using a questionnaire version of the CBAS) correlated significantly with the observation-based CBAS, indicating players were more aware of their coaches' actual coaching behavior than were the coaches themselves.

Verbal Feedback

Subsequently, additional studies were conducted using the CBAS (either the observational or the questionnaire form) with samples of young athletes in various sports.[10] These studies revealed similar findings: Athletes whose coaches exhibited higher frequencies of supportive and instruction-based behavioral feedback (e.g., praise for success and encouraging corrective feedback for performance errors) reported higher levels of perceived sport competence (i.e., higher confidence and self-efficacy), intrinsic motivation, and enjoyment/fun at the end of the season than did athletes whose coaches scored lower for supportive and instruction-based behaviors and/or who exhibited higher levels of punitive verbal behavior or ignoring behaviors (e.g., no positive comment following successes and ignoring mistakes).

In total, these results clearly support the notion that the behaviors coaches exhibit in practice and in game situations can dramatically affect a young athlete's perception of competence, thereby influencing self-motivation (as explained in Chapter 3), as well as their overall enjoyment and attraction to a certain sport activity.

This may be particularly true regarding the type of feedback coaches give their young athletes after a successful or unsuccessful performance. If a young basketball player makes a free throw in a game, her coach can respond with supportive feedback (e.g., "Good shot, Alicia!"), with supportive feedback plus technical instruction (e.g., "Great follow-through with the wrist, Alicia – that's why your shot went in"), or with no consequence (i.e., the coach says nothing after Alicia's good performance).

Similarly, if a young volleyball player misses a serve in a game, his coach can respond with encouragement (i.e., "That's OK, you'll get it next time"), with corrective feedback (e.g., "Jason, you didn't toss the ball high enough – that's why your serve went into the net. We'll work on that tomorrow in practice"), with negative consequences (e.g., "Jason, that was terrible"), or with no verbalization (i.e., the coach does or says nothing in response to the missed serve).

How a coach responds in each of these situations appears to be important in terms of the young athletes' perceptions of competence, motivation to continue playing, enjoyment and fun, and possibly overall self-esteem. Specifically, coaches' provision of high frequencies of supportive and corrective feedback leads to better performance and person-states than no feedback or negative reactions. Given this overview of results with the CBAS, let's examine more closely the behavioral profiles of each coach, as summarized in Table 17.2.

Coach Jill. It appears Coach 3 (Jill) has the best overall profile, based on results of the studies conducted to determine what coaching behaviors are most effective. Jill exhibited high frequencies of technical instruction (i.e., focusing primarily on skill instruction during practice), and she also provided her players with lots of AC4P corrective feedback in response to their performance errors (i.e., telling them in a positive way how to prevent an observed error), as indicated by the bold numbers in Table 17.2. This enhanced her young athletes' ability to learn the relevant skills. She also showed high levels of positive and encouraging behaviors (i.e., providing supportive feedback for successful player performance and corrective feedback and/or encouragement after player errors) combined with low levels of punitive-oriented commentary.

Coach Jill also exhibited a relatively small percentage of "keeping-control" behaviors. This suggests she had established at the beginning of the season a set of clear guidelines for acceptable/desirable player behaviors during practice, and she enforced those guidelines at the start of the season. As the season progressed, she spent minimal time disciplining her athletes.

Coach Damien. Coach 2 (Damien) scored high on technical instruction. So, like Coach Jill, Coach Damien focused primarily on skill development during practice. But he provided relatively high levels of punitive feedback in response to his athletes' performance errors. Correspondingly, his scores on positive and encouraging behaviors are low. Coach Damien seems to be a very good instructor in terms of helping his players develop their skills, but his high rate of negative comments (especially following player errors during practice) can lead to high levels of anxiety and fear of failure among his athletes.

Coach Shala. Coach 1 (Shala) scored very high on positive and supportive behavior (e.g., supportive feedback, general encouragement), but she was comparatively low in providing corrective feedback (i.e., she has relatively low scores in the "technical instruction" category). She tended to respond to her players' behavioral successes and errors with simple praise ("Good job") or encouragement (e.g., "Don't worry about it") without referencing relevant behavior. Such general support is positive, but it didn't provide her young athletes with corrective or technical information they could use to improve their skills. Coach Shala would be considered an effective coach in terms of being positive or supportive. But to develop her players' skill levels and enhance their perceptions of competence or ability, she should provide more quality behavior-based supportive and corrective feedback, as detailed in Chapter 3.

Coach Darren. Coach #4 (Darren) provided his athletes with large amounts of technical instruction during practice, but appeared to be quite low in any of the feedback categories. He did not respond to the actual play of his athletes (i.e., he has relatively high scores for the "no-response" and "ignoring mistakes" categories). Coach Darren is likely ineffective at enhancing his players' skills or their perceptions of competence in the sport of volleyball, since we know athletes learn best by getting specific feedback from their coaches in direct response to specific behavior (both successes and errors). We would recommend he increase his rate of responding to individual player behavior with appropriate supportive and corrective behavior-based feedback.

Coach Nick. Coach 5 (Nick) appears to be somewhat disengaged from teaching/coaching. He exhibited very low scores on most of the feedback categories (e.g., positive comment, technical or corrective instruction, encouragement, etc.), but received high scores on the no response and ignoring mistakes categories. His high scores on general communication suggest he spent quite a lot of time talking to his athletes about game-irrelevant topics during practice sessions. Young athletes might enjoy and even benefit from such non-sport-related interactions with their coach, but this does not enhance their skills and perceptions of competence at the sport. Game-irrelevant communication between coach and athletes should be conducted outside the actual practice session, if at all.

"Keeping control" is another high-frequency score for Coach Nick, indicating he responded to player misbehaviors unrelated to game-related competencies. All in all, this coach was quite uninvolved in the teaching aspects of his role. Perhaps he does not know much about the game of volleyball and cannot give his athletes the technical information and behavioral feedback they need to improve.

Codable Behaviors. Finally, the last row of Table 17.2 reveals considerable differences between the five coaches in the *number* of codable behaviors they exhibited. Coach Nick exhibited the lowest number (500 across five games), while Coaches Shala and Jill showed the highest number (1,200 and 1,100, respectively). This supports the notion that Coach Nick was less involved as a teacher/coach, and Coaches Shala and Jill were more actively engaged in the game and in the teaching of relevant skills.

Children want and need large amounts of verbal praise and support from their sport coaches, as indicated by the results of research conducted with the CBAS. There may be an important caveat to this notion, though. Carol Dweck, noted scholar in educational psychology, has argued convincingly that praise can actually undermine children's skill development if given the wrong way.[11] She recommends that praise for children and adolescents be given – but this praise should be linked directly to children's work effort and task mastery (process-oriented feedback) rather than to their abilities (see Chapter 6).

As an example, Susie is a 6-year-old child who has recently joined a gymnastics program. In one of the practice sessions, Susie and her team-mates are learning to do cartwheels. It's Susie's turn to perform, and she does a very good cartwheel. Rightfully so, her coach wants to reward her performance. She gives Susie ability-oriented feedback with the comment, "Susie, that was so good. You are a born gymnast!" This coach has given Susie an *ability* label, attributing her good performance to something innate or inborn. In contrast, an *effort* label is reflected by the comment, "Susie, that was so good. You have worked really hard the last few days to learn how to keep your elbows locked and your legs straight. And now look what you can do!"

The effort label is more effective, according to Dweck, because it helps Susie develop the mindset that her effortful behavior led to the successful outcome and she can control her performance outcomes and improve.[11] The ability-oriented feedback (although nice to hear) does not give Susie a perception of control of her outcomes. If Susie's coach continues to give high frequencies of ability-oriented feedback (e.g., "You are a natural athlete"), when Susie encounters a skill she initially cannot do (e.g., a more complicated gymnastics skill), her mindset may be that she does not possess the innate ability to develop that particular skillset. Plus, she might not attempt more difficult routines because she fears losing her positive ability label.

On the other hand, if Suzie's coach consistently gives her effort-based praise (e.g., "When you perform a skill really well, it's because you have worked hard to master it"), then when Suzie encounters a difficult routine she initially cannot do, she will have a growth mindset (i.e., "I can't do that routine now, but if I practice really hard, I will learn to do it").

A coach's reaction to a player's errors is also relevant to the distinction between *fixed-ability and growth-effort* mindsets. If a basketball defender fails to stop an offensive player's drive to the basket, the coach can give effort-oriented corrective feedback (e.g., "Deion, you just needed to take a longer step with your left foot to stop him; we'll work on that next week in practice"), or the coach might give more ability-oriented feedback (e.g., "Deion, you're too slow to stop that guy; we'll have to shift our defensive assignments"). Again, the effort/growth-oriented feedback tells Deion his performance error or mistake can be corrected. He can learn to be a better defensive player. The ability-oriented feedback suggests Deion does not have the innate talent to be a good defensive player, stifling his motivation to practice getting better.

The value of using effort rather than ability labels in behavioral feedback given to young athletes was demonstrated by Dweck's research.[11] Children provided with higher frequencies of effort-focused feedback had a growth mindset and higher levels of self-motivation than did their peers who developed a fixed mindset as the result of ability-focused feedback, according to Dweck and her colleagues. Thus, coaches should not just heap high frequencies of general praise and encouragement, but give behavior-based supportive and corrective feedback within the context of continuous growth and improvement.

Coaches (like teachers) also may differ from each other in the type of climate or environment they create for their teams or in their classrooms. This issue is explored next.

THE DIFFERENCES THE CULTURE MAKES

It's hypothesized from achievement-oriented goal theory that adults in achievement-oriented environments (e.g., academic classrooms, exercise settings, competitive sport settings) create one of two types of motivational cultures: independent or interdependent (Chapter 3).[12] A mastery-oriented, interdependent team culture in athletics is created by coaches who(a) place primary emphasis on skill improvement or task mastery as the measure of success (i.e., each child is successful if s/he is getting better at the skill and feedback is given for mastery of a task), (b) view mistakes as a natural part of the skill-learning process (e.g., "You will get better with practice"), (c) encourage players to work together to achieve common goals (e.g. "We are all in this together"), and (d) place value on the interdependent contributions of each athlete (e.g., "Each of you has an important and valued role on this team").

In contrast, some coaches create an ego-oriented (or performance-based) individualistic culture. They place primary emphasis on outcome rather than process or behavior (e.g., each child's success is based on the team's winning or losing). They use intra-team rivalry (e.g., drills that emphasize peer comparison or one-on-one conflict) to motivate their athletes and give the most one-on-one attention to the stars of the team.

To measure the type of motivational culture created by coaches, researchers have asked athletes to rate the culture their coach has cultivated by answering a series of questions. Since the advent of this method to classify coaches and teams, a number of studies have been conducted in youth sport settings.[13] Generally, the results indicate the following: Young athletes who play for mastery-oriented coaches with an interdependent mindset exhibit higher levels of perceived sport-related competence, sport-related enjoyment, self-motivation, persistence at difficult tasks, lower dropout and burnout rates, and more positive attitudes toward the sport and their coach than do athletes who play for ego-oriented coaches. In contrast, athletes who perceive that their coaches support a more ego-oriented, individualistic culture score higher on competitive anxiety, higher on sport-related burnout, and lower on measures of overall psychosocial well-being.

Whether or not coaches create an AC4P culture is another way to consider coaching effectiveness in youth sports. Noddings[14] and Hellison[15] suggest positive youth development is enhanced by contact with an AC4P adult. These roles can be filled by parents, older siblings, or adult relatives, but Noddings points to the value of more distant adults demonstrating

AC4P behavior, such as teachers or activity leaders (including youth sport coaches). These adults create an AC4P culture by (a) making sure individuals within the group exhibit concern for one another, (b) creating a non-judgmental or accepting climate, and (c) exhibiting and modeling value for all individuals within the group.

Newton and her colleagues developed the Caring Climate Scale to assess the type of culture in a youth sport or physical activity setting.[16] Subsequent research conducted with samples of youth attending summer sports camps or federally-funded summer activity programs revealed that young campers who perceived their adult staff as facilitating a more AC4P culture scored higher at the end of the program on self-motivation, endorsement of prosocial behavior, and psychological well-being (e.g., lower depression and sadness, higher feelings of hope and happiness) as compared to their peers who perceived their adult staff did not promote an AC4P culture.[17]

Coaches' Interpersonal Style

Researchers in sport psychology have examined the type of inter-personal styles used by youth sport coaches from the perspective of self-determination theory.[18] Some studies examined the relative effects of an autonomy-supportive leadership style versus a more controlling style on young athletes' psychosocial well-being.[19] An autonomy-supportive style refers to coaches who allow their athletes to perceive some personal choice and control.[20] These coaches provide choices for athletes, avoid top-down directives ("Do this because I told you"), provide a rationale for decisions ("In order to develop endurance, it will be important for you to run sprints in practice"), and acknowledge and take into account the athlete's feelings and perspectives. Coaches who are more controlling (or low in autonomy-supportive behavior) exhibit a leadership style high in top-down control ("My way or the highway") and low in providing opportunities for athletes to show personal initiative and independence (e.g., "I'm the leader, and you just need to do as you are told without opening your mouth").

The autonomy-supportive coaching style in youth sport settings has been recently examined in two studies.[19] In the first, Coatsworth and Conroy investigated the effects of the autonomy-supportive style on young (ages 10–17) swimmers' attitudes and perceptions. They found an autonomy-supportive coaching style predicted higher levels of perceived competence and feelings of connectedness or belongingness with their coaches and teammates.

In the second study, Adie and colleagues surveyed a sample of young soccer players (ages 11–18) and found that the athletes who perceived their coaches as using an autonomy-supportive coaching style had higher perceptions of sport competence, choice, community, and subjective well-being, as well as lower levels of perceived physical and emotional exhaustion than did peers who perceived their coaches to be low in autonomy support. Research in this domain provides clear support for the notion that an autonomy-supportive interpersonal coaching style will result in enhanced psychosocial well-being and self-motivation among young athletes. These findings are very consistent with the information on self-motivation presented in Chapter 3.

Desirable Coaching Behaviors

I created an evidence-based summary of *best practices* for coaches of youth sport athletes based on the prior discussion of coaches' behaviors in practice and game situations as well as the type of culture they create among their young athletes. This summary, presented in Table 17.3, reveals clear alignment with the AC4P principles illustrated in the first six chapters of this text. More specifically, if we consider a youth sport team to be a family, the attributes listed in Figure 2.8 are mirrored in the recommended coaching behaviors and practices listed in Table 17.3. Use of these best practices

TABLE 17.3. *Best AC4P practices for youth sport coaches*

Recommendations	"Do this …"	"Not this …"
1. Exhibit high frequencies of instructional behavior.	Place primary focus in practice sessions on athletes' development of the sport skills. Plan ahead! Select drills/activities that will be appropriate for the age and skill level of athletes. Run an organized and efficient practice. Set up drills and practice activities in such a way that all athletes are participating as much as possible (i.e., the more practice attempts or "touches" each player can get in an individual practice, the quicker they will learn). Make effective use of skill demonstrations and give clear and specific information on how to perform a skill.	Waste time in practices by not planning ahead. Design drills and activities in such a way that only a few of the athletes are engaged while the rest stand around and watch. Explain or describe how to perform a skill in an unclear, nonbehavioral and unorganized way (e.g., a long lecture on correct batting form for 10-year-olds would not be useful).
2. Decrease the need for exhibiting high frequencies of "keeping control" behaviors	Set up consistent behavioral guidelines for athletes' conduct and behavior (non-game-related) at the beginning of the season and consistently enforce them. This will reduce the need for "keeping control" behaviors as the season progresses.	Be unclear about the guidelines for player conduct and behavior. Deal with player misbehaviors in an inconsistent way (e.g., sometimes punishing them and sometimes ignoring them), or punishing some players but not others for the same undesirable behavior.

(*continued*)

551

TABLE 17.3 *(continued)*

Recommendations	"Do this ..."	"Not this ..."
3. Place greater emphasis on skill development and skill mastery than on performance outcomes for individual athletes and teams.	Look for opportunities to show individual athletes or groups of athletes how much they have improved (e.g., keep charts showing improvement scores or graphs; have athletes engage in the same drill on successive weeks and keep track of their improvement). Give feedback to athletes to recognize how far they have come in the acquisition of a skill rather than emphasize that they are not yet at the top of the skill continuum. Emphasize that complex sport skills are best developed or acquired in stages or steps. For young athletes, it's critical to give feedback contingent on the skill technique and not the outcome (e.g., if a young basketball player makes a nice offensive move but then misses the subsequent lay-up, the coach should reward the nice move).	If an athlete (or group of athletes) shows improvement in a skill but is still not perfect (e.g., a softball batter who used to strike out is now able to contact the ball even though she doesn't get a base hit), make a negative comment (e.g., "Sheila, you still haven't got it!"). Wait to recognize athletes for skill expertise until they have reached the final stage and are at a "perfect" level. Give feedback contingent on performance rather than behavior (e.g., if a young basketball player does not use correct form but makes the shot anyway, give a positive reaction because the outcome was successful even if the technique was not).
4. Convey the attitude that mistakes provide opportunities to learn (especially during practice).	When a defensive volleyball player misses a dig because she was in the wrong spot on the floor, give corrective feedback (e.g., "Watch the hitter's shoulders so you can get a better estimate of where the hit is going to land" followed by the comment, "Sometimes, you just have to get it wrong before you can figure out how to do it better, so every time you misread a hitter, take a minute to think back and figure out what you may have missed").	Whenever a mistake occurs in practice, yell at the offending athlete (or make her do push-ups or "suicide runs") in order to create enough fear in all teammates so they won't make the same mistake.

552

5. Apply peer learning and cooperative activities (especially during practice).

- Help athletes learn how to give each other feedback on relevant behavior. Do this by asking one athlete to watch a particular part of her/his teammate's behavior (e.g., "Watch where her hand contacts the ball") and give behavioral feedback to the performer. This can enhance both athletes' skills.
- Conduct team-building activities that require athletes to work together in order to reach a team goal.

- Pit individual athletes (or groups of athletes) against each other in practice with the intent of rewarding one and not the other.
- When an on-court player makes a mistake in a practice scrimmage, immediately blow the whistle and say to a sub, "Whitney, get in here and take Meredith's place. Apparently, she can't get the job done. If you can, then you're our new starting point guard."

6. Create a culture that emphasizes the important contributions each athlete makes to the team (i.e., an interdependency mindset).

- Make a concerted effort to identify the unique contributions each athlete makes for the team.
- Design team-building activities that ask individual athletes to tell the group what behaviors they really like and value about *each* of their teammates.
- After each game, point out the "little and often unnoticed contributions" from individual players.

- Devote most of your time and attention in practice on the starters or the "stars." Expect the subs to learn by watching their "star" teammates practice and play.
- Base positive recognition on game outcomes (e.g., post pictures after each game of the highest scorer, person with most rebounds, etc.).

7. Develop a culture where all individuals in the group are valued, accepted, and are cared for equally.

- Be very clear that you will not allow members of the team to make disparaging comments about any teammate.
- Be a role model by treating each athlete as a valued member of your team.

- Allow individual athletes (especially the leaders/"stars") to make negative comments about other players (either in public or behind their backs).
- Give the impression you appreciate certain athletes most (e.g., sit with the same team members on all bus trips, exhibit an interest in the non-sport activities of some athletes but not others).

(continued)

TABLE 17.3 (continued)

Recommendations	"Do this …"	"Not this …"
8. Allow athletes some choice in their sport-related behaviors.	Depending on athletes' age and skill level, allow them the opportunity to make some decisions (e.g., "What color uniforms shall we wear for tomorrow's game; what type of post-game food do we want; what pre-game chants will we use; shall we have our hardest practice on Tuesday or Wednesday of next week?").	Make it clear from the beginning of the season that all decisions (from big to little) will be made by you as the head coach.
9. Ask for athletes' opinions and feelings.	At the end of some (or even every) practice, spend a few minutes asking the athletes what they thought about the practice. Are there ways to help them learn more? At periodic points in the season, meet individually with each athlete to ask questions about progress as individuals and his/her reactions to the sport.	Act in ways that make it clear you think/know you have all the answers and there is no need for input from the athletes.
10. Provide a rationale for coach decisions.	"We looked a bit sluggish in the last five minutes of the game last night. For that reason, I've decided to incorporate more 'all-out' sprints into the end-of-the-practice drills in order to increase our level of endurance." Always be prepared to answer players' questions regarding decisions you have had to make (e.g., starting line-ups, substitutions, etc.).	"Run 20 laps, and go all out! If you don't, you will run another 20." When players ask questions about a coach's decision related to the team (e.g., "Why did I not play left field in the last game?), tell them you're the coach and you don't have to answer such questions.
11. Give high frequencies of supportive and encouraging corrective feedback and avoid negative commentary.	"That was a very smart play, Jalen." "I really like how you have been focusing hard in practice the last few days on taking a faster first step." "I know this skill is a really hard one to learn. But, if you keep working at it, I know you can get it."	"If you miss this free throw, the whole team will run sprints tomorrow!" "I've never seen such a lazy attitude in a player. You don't deserve to wear this uniform."

12. Provide high frequencies of process-oriented feedback and no ability-oriented feedback.

"Your shooting percentage has really improved over the past few weeks. I know you've been working on your shot and especially on your follow-through. It's really paid off for you."

"I know you are frustrated that you keep striking out. But you really are improving your swing. You used to be really late in getting the bat around, but now you are almost always making contact with the ball. Keep working on it. Maybe you can stay a little later after practice next week so you and I can work on it together."

"Derrick, you are never going to be tall enough to rebound with the big boys. Don't even try."

Coach to team: "Did you see the nice smooth move Tammy made in the third quarter? That was a 'money' move. Some athletes work their entire lives to learn that move. But not her! She can do it in her sleep! Lucky girl! She'll never have to work hard to be good at this sport!"

13. Give encouraging and corrective feedback in response to player errors/mistakes.

"That was a nice level swing, and you did make good contact with the ball. But now let's work on following through with your swing so you can get more power."

"Eric! You are and always will be way too slow to steal a base!"

14. Look for opportunities to offer behavior-based supportive and corrective feedback.

"Most of us (adults included) need feedback from skilled others when we are first learning a skill. If we get no feedback, then we will only be able to develop our skills through trial and error – an inefficient way to learn!"

"That was a great throw to first, and I'm glad you threw the runner out. But be sure to keep your glove low to the ground when you field the ball. You almost lost the ball because your glove was too high."

Coaches who generally give no feedback (either in response to player successes or errors) may as well not even come to practices or games!

15. Evaluate individual athletes as well as groups of athletes based on skill mastery and improvement rather than on performance outcomes.

"Although the other team out-scored us in the fourth quarter last night, I saw some really good things on the floor. For example, I saw Jared move over to help his teammate cover a drive, and I saw Tommy …"

"I realize that some of your parents may have told you that you played well last night, but the bottom line is that we lost. Now, we're out of the play-offs, and that's nothing to be happy about!"

by youth sport coaches should result in optimal development of not only young athletes' fundamental sport skills and abilities, but also their perceptions of competence, personal control, choice, and interdependence. Their perceived motivational orientation can become self-directed rather than other-directed or coerced.

It's clear sport coaches of youth differ considerably in their leadership style and feedback behavior at practice and at games, based on the information obtained from the studies described in the previous pages of this chapter. In the process, coaches create a culture that has a significant effect on the psychosocial well-being of young athletes. A key question: Can coaches be trained to be more effective leaders, capable of cultivating an interdependent culture that facilitates self-motivation and an AC4P growth mindset? An answer is explored in the following section.

TRAINING COACHES OF YOUNG ATHLETES

The first coach-training study was conducted by Smith, Smoll, and their colleagues at the University of Washington using Coach-Effectiveness Training (CET).[21] This coach-training program was founded on a cognitive behavioral framework and was intended to help coaches (a) become more aware of their coaching-related behaviors; (b) create expectations concerning the consequences of their behavior; (c) increase their desire to generate certain consequences; and (d) develop or enhance their ability to perform desired coaching behaviors.[22]

A sample of thirty-four Little League male coaches were recruited and randomly assigned to either a CET training program ($n = 18$) or a control group ($n = 16$). The CET coaches received two hours of pre-season training that included a verbal and written presentation of desirable behavior guidelines (based on the studies described earlier) and some examples of appropriate behaviors through modeling (i.e., observational learning).

In addition, during the first two weeks of the season, the behaviors of these CET coaches were observed and coded using the CBAS, and their behavioral profiles were mailed to them for feedback. After the first ten games of the season these coaches were asked to complete the questionnaire version of the CBAS as a self-monitoring technique. At the end of the season, the athletes who played for the CET coaches and the untrained coaches were interviewed in their homes.

CET was effective. Trained coaches exhibited more desirable changes in their behavioral profiles as a result of the pre-season and early-season training process.[21] At the end of the season, players of the CET coaches and untrained coaches differed in their perceptions of their coaches' behaviors (as assessed with the questionnaire version of the CBAS). Players of the CET coaches perceived a more desirable coaching profile. And players of the CET coaches scored higher than the players of the untrained coaches in their regard for their coach and teammates and in their desire to play for the same coach the following year.

No differences in overall self-esteem were found at the end of the season between players of the CET and untrained coaches. But for the players who began the season with the lowest self-esteem, those playing for the CET coaches exhibited significant increases in self-esteem from pre- to post-season. Those playing for the untrained coaches showed no change from pre- to post-season.

These results were replicated in a subsequent set of coach-training studies using the same CET program.[23] The 2.5-hour pre-season training program for coaches increased players' psychosocial well-being, as well as their perceptions of fun, enjoyment, and attraction to the coach. In addition, player attrition was examined as a function of CET by conducting phone and home interviews one year after CET. The result: 26 percent of the athletes from the untrained-coach teams stopped playing baseball after the previous season, whereas only 5 percent of the athletes from the CET-coach teams dropped out.

A third set of studies added training components from the motivational culture perspective reviewed earlier (i.e., achievement goal theory).[24] The name of the intervention program was changed from Coach Effective Training to the Mastery Approach to Coaching (MAC) to reflect the added material. For these studies, thirty-seven male and female youth league basketball coaches were divided into a Training ($n = 20$) or a Control group ($n = 17$). Coaches in the Training group were given a seventy-five-minute pre-season workshop that included the use of written and oral presentations, modeling, and role-playing with behavioral feedback.

In addition, the trained coaches completed behavioral self-monitoring activities immediately after the first ten games of the season. These coaches were asked to increase certain desirable behaviors (i.e., supportive and corrective behavioral feedback and overall encouragement) and decrease designated undesirable behaviors (i.e., punitive-oriented comments and all behaviors other than supportive or corrective feedback when such feedback was warranted). Consistent with the motivational-climate perspective, the MAC coaches were also instructed to emphasize effort, skill mastery, individualized attention, and goal setting rather than focus on performance outcomes, making peer-to-peer comparisons, and promoting intra-team rivalry.

The success of the training protocol was verified by the results of these studies.[24] At the end of the season, athletes of the coaches in the Training group rated their coaches as providing a more mastery-oriented team culture and a more supportive and encouraging behavioral style than athletes of the coaches in the Control group. In addition, athletes in the Control condition exhibited an increase from pre- to post-season in total competitive anxiety, somatic anxiety, and concentration/disruption. In contrast, athletes who played for coaches in the Training group showed a decrease over the season in total competitive anxiety, somatic anxiety, and worry.

Consistent with the motivational culture approach, the athletes of the trained coaches showed increases in their perceptions of a mastery goal orientation and corresponding decreases in ego-orientation scores; athletes of the coaches in the Control group exhibited no changes in these factors from pre- to post-season. And consistent with previous research on attrition, the athletes who played for the Training group coaches participated at a higher daily rate than did the athletes who played for the Control group coaches.

Using a somewhat different approach, Newton and colleagues conducted an intervention program with a large sample of 353 children and adolescents participating in a federally-funded summer program that targeted underserved populations and emphasized physical activity.[25] Staff members ($n = 32$) in one program participated in a two-day (twelve total hours) training module encouraging the development of an AC4P culture within a camp setting. Staff members engaged in a series of activities to increase staffers' perceptions of interpersonal unity and community, but also to encourage them to develop and subsequently apply student-centered learning strategies (e.g., activities to increase students' perceptions of choice and relatedness) and an AC4P approach to discipline.

In contrast, staff members in similar programs did not participate in this training module and constituted a Control group. At the end of the five-week camp program, children who participated in both sets of programs completed self-report questionnaires that assessed their perceptions of their camp experience.

Campers who participated in a program supervised by the trained staff perceived higher levels of an AC4P climate within their camp, exhibited more compassion for others, and were more apt to indicate a desire to return to camp for the following summer than did the campers in the non-trained group, according to systematic analysis of the results. These empirical findings, along with those described previously, indicate youth sport coaches (or sport camp staffers) can be trained to exhibit more desirable coaching behaviors and create a more AC4P sport culture.

IN CONCLUSION

Several conclusions are evident from the behavior-focused studies of coaches reviewed in this chapter. First, as illustrated in Table 17.2 and as found in related empirical studies, sport coaches of youth differ dramatically in the types of behaviors they exhibit in practice and during competitive contexts.

Second, research to date clearly indicates coaching behaviors differentially affect not only young athletes' ability to develop their sport-related skills, but also their self-perceptions, degree of self-motivation, enjoyment, and desire to continue their participation in the sport. The desirable (and less desirable) coaching behaviors are summarized in Table 17.3 and are clearly linked to the AC4P principles presented in the first six chapters of this text.

Third, coaches of youth sports can be trained to exhibit a more desirable behavioral profile, as evidenced by a review of the field intervention studies. In particular, effective coach-training programs can be accomplished within field settings by incorporating a brief (two-to-three hour) pre-season education/training session that includes role-playing with behavioral feedback, followed by self-monitoring assessment methods. Integrating these training procedures into the majority of youth sport programs would be cost-effective and enhance the AC4P benefits of those programs.

Fourth, creating and maintaining an AC4P culture in youth sport settings may ultimately impact the development of more humanistic and collectivistic generations. Childhood and adolescence are critical times for developing prosocial (rather than antisocial), moral, and humanistic attitudes, values, beliefs, and behaviors. Reaching out to children and adolescents within a real-world setting (e.g., a youth sport team) may be one of our most cost-effective ways to cultivate an AC4P culture.

DISCUSSION QUESTIONS

1. List some positive and negative outcomes for children who participate in youth sports programs.
2. How is the CBAS (Coaching Behavior Assessment System) used to improve the coaching of youth?
3. What coaching behaviors influence young players' perceptions of competence and hence self-motivation, as well as their enjoyment of particular sports?

4. How does the research of Carol Dweck and colleagues help to determine which coaching behaviors to perform and to avoid?

5. Contrast the interdependent (collectivistic) versus independent (individualistic) team culture with regard to athletes' behaviors and person-states, and to cultivating an AC4P culture.

6. What are some behavioral characteristics of coaches who adopt an autonomy-supportive coaching style, and what are some outcomes of this style?

7. List ten best AC4P practices among coaches of youth sports.

8. What empirical evidence (i.e., outcomes) indicates that the coaches of young athletes can become more effective with behavior-based training?

9. What AC4P qualities of youth have been observed as a result of a training program that uses student-centered learning strategies to promote an interdependent community perspective?

10. Imagine you had an opportunity to offer a daylong workshop on effective coaching for young athletes. What topics would you cover, and how would you get the coaches engaged in your workshop material?

REFERENCES

1. National Council of Youth Sports (NCYS) (2008). *Report on trends and participation in organized youth sports.* Stuart, FL: National Council of Youth Sports.

2. Sabo, D., & Veliz, P. (2008). *Go out and play: Youth sports in America.* East Meadow, NY: Women's Sports Foundation.

3. Malina, R. M. (2010). Early sport specialization: Roots, effectiveness, risks. *Current Sports Medicine Reports,* 9(6), 364–371.

4. Landers, R. Q., Carson, R. L., & Blankenship, B. T. (2010). Introduction. *Journal of Physical Education, Recreation, and Dance,* 81(8), 14–15; Russell, W. D. (2014). The relationship between youth sport success, reasons for participation and youth sport participation motivation: A retrospective study. *Journal of Sport Behavior,* 37(3), 286–305.

5. Sameroff, A. (2010). A unified theory of development: A dialectic integration of nature and nurture. *Child Development,* 81, 6–22.

6. Weiss, M. R. (2004). (Ed.). *Developmental sport and exercise psychology: A lifespan perspective.* Morgantown, WV: Fitness Information Technology.

7. Hedstrom, R., & Gould, D. (2004). *Research in youth sports: Critical issues status.* East Lansing, MI: Institute for the Study of Youth Sports; Weiss, M. R., Kipp, L. E., & Bolter, N. D. (2012). Training for life: Optimizing positive youth development through sport and physical activity. In S. M. Murphy (Ed.). *The Oxford handbook of sport and performance psychology* (pp. 448–475). New York: Oxford University Press.

8. Bar-Or, E. (1996) (Ed.). *The child and adolescent athlete.* London: Blackwell Science; Eklund, R., & Cresswell, S. (2007). Athlete burnout. In R. C. Eklund &

S. L. Cresswell (Eds.). *Handbook of sport psychology* (3rd ed.) (pp. 621–641). New York: John Wiley; Fraser-Thomas, J., & Cote, J. (2009). Understanding adolescents' positive and negative development experiences in sport. *Sport Psychologist*, 23, 3–23; Gearity, B. T., & Murray, M. A. (2011). Athletes' experiences of the psychologist effects of poor coaching. *Psychology of Sport and Exercise*, 12, 213–221; Murphy, S. (1999). *The cheers and the tears: A healthy alternative to the dark side of youth sports today*. San Francisco: Jossey-Bass.

9. Smoll, F. L., & Smith, R. E. (2015). Conducting evidence-based coach training programs: A social-cognitive approach. In J. M. Williams & V. Krane (Eds.). *Applied sport psychology: Personal growth to peak performance* (7th ed.) (pp. 359–383). New York: McGraw-Hill.

10. Black, S. J., & Weiss, M. R. (1992). The relationship among perceived coaching behaviors, perceptions of ability, and motivation in competitive age-group swimmers. *Journal of Sport and Exercise Psychology*, 14(3), 309–325; Horn, T. S. (1985). Coaches' feedback and changes in children's perceptions of their physical competence. *Journal of Educational Psychology*, 77(2), 174–186.

11. Dweck, C. S. (2007). The perils and promises of praise. *Educational Leadership*, 34–39; Dweck, C. S. (2008). Mindsets: How praise is harming youth and what can be done about it. *School Library Media Activities Monthly*, 34(5), 55–58.

12. Ames, C. (1992). Achievement goals, motivational climate, and motivational processes. In G. C. Roberts (Ed.). *Motivation in sport and exercise* (pp. 161–176). Champaign, IL: Human Kinetics; Dweck, C. S. (1999). *Self-theories: Their role in motivation, personality, and development*. Philadelphia: Taylor & Francis/ Psychology Press; Nicholls, J. (1989). *The competitive ethos and democratic education*. Cambridge, MA: Harvard University Press.

13. Erickson, K., & Gilbert, W. (2013). Coach–athlete interactions in children's sport. In J. Cote, & R. Lidor (Eds.). *Conditions of children's talent development in sport* (pp. 139–156). Morgantown, WV: Fitness Information Technology.

14. Noddings, N. (1992). *The challenge to care in schools: An alternative approach to education*. New York: Teachers College Press; Noddings, N. (1995). Teaching themes of care. *Phi Delta Kappan*, 76, 675–679.

15. Hellison, D. (2000). Physical activity programs for underserved youth. *Journal of Science and Medicine in Sport*, 3, 238–242; Hellison, D. (2003). *Teaching responsibility through physical activity* (2nd ed.). Champaign, IL: Human Kinetics.

16. Newton, M., Fry, M. D., Watson, D. L., Gano-Overway, L., Kim, M., Magyar, M., et al. (2007). Psychometric properties of the caring climate scale in a physical activity setting. *Revista de Psicologia del Deporte*, 16, 67–84.

17. Fry, M. D., Kim, M. S., Gano-Overway, L. A., Guivernau, M., Newton, M., & Magyar, T. M. (2012). Youth perceptions of a caring climate, emotional regulation, and psychological well-being. *Sport, Exercise, and Performance Psychology*, 1(1), 44–57; Gano-Overway, L. A., Newton, M., Magyar, T. M., Fry, M. D., Kim, M. S., & Guinernau, M. R. (2009). Influence of caring youth sport contexts on efficacy-related beliefs and social behaviors. *Developmental Psychology*, 45(2), 329–340.

18. Ryan, R. M., & Deci, E. L. (2000). Self-determination theory and the facilitation of intrinsic motivation, social development, and well-being. *American Psychologist*, 55(1), 68–78.

19. Adie, J., Duda, J. L., & Ntoumanis, N. (2012). Perceived coach-autonomy support, basic need satisfaction and the well- and ill-being of elite youth soccer players: A longitudinal investigation. *Psychology of Sport and Exercise*, 13(1), 51–59; Coatsworth, J. D., & Conroy, D. E. (2009). The effects of autonomy-supportive coaching, need satisfaction, and self-perceptions on initiative and identity in youth swimmers. *Developmental Psychology*, 45(2), 320–328.

20. Mageau, G. A., & Vallerand, R. J. (2003). The coach–athlete relationship: A motivational model. *Journal of Sports Sciences*, 21(11), 883–904.

21. Smith, R. E., Smoll, F. L., & Curtis, B. (1979). Coach effectiveness training: A cognitive-behavioral approach to enhancing relationship skills in youth sport coaches. *Journal of Sport Psychology*, 1(1), 59–75.

22. Bandura, A. (1977). *Social learning theory*. Englewood Cliffs, NJ: Prentice Hall.

23. Barnett, N. P., Smoll, F. L., & Smith, R. E. (1992). Effects of enhancing coach–athlete relationships on youth sport attrition. *The Sport Psychologist*, 6(2), 111–127; Smoll, F. L., Smith, R. E., Barnett, N. P., & Everett, J. J. (1993). Enhancement of children's self-esteem through social support training for youth sport coaches. *Journal of Applied Psychology*, 78(4), 602–610.

24. Smith, R. E., Smoll, F. L., & Cumming, S. P. (2007). Effects of a motivational climate intervention for coaches on young athletes' sport performance anxiety. *Journal of Sport and Exercise Psychology*, 29, 39–50; Smoll, F. L., Smith, R. E., & Cumming, S. P. (2007). Effects of a motivational climate intervention for coaches on changes in young athletes' achievement goal orientations. *Journal of Clinical Sport Psychology*, 1(1), 23–46.

25. Newton, M., Watson, D. L., Gano-Overway, L., Fry, M., Kim, M. S., & Magyar, M. (2007). The role of a caring-based intervention in a physical activity setting. *Urban Review*, 39(3), 281–299.

18

Actively Caring for Higher Education

DEREK D. REED, BRYAN T. YANAGITA, AMEL BECIREVIC,
JASON M. HIRST, BRENT A. KAPLAN, ELLIE EASTES,
AND TAYLOR HANNA

I never teach my pupils, I only attempt to provide the conditions in which they can learn.
– Albert Einstein

Action needs to be taken to improve education in the United States. The United States ranked seventeenth among thirty-four Organizations for Economic Co-operation and Development (OECD) countries in the 2012 results of the Programme for International Student Assessment (PISA).[1] The PISA is a standardized test of math, science, and reading comprehension skills, and is administered to more than five hundred thousand 15-year-olds internationally. At the forefront are students from China, Singapore, Korea, Japan, and Liechtenstein with mean PISA scores of 613, 573, 554, 536, and 535, respectively. With a mean score of 481, U.S. students scored significantly lower than the international average of 494, trailing Spain, the Russian Federation, and the Slovak Republic.[1]

According to the OECD, the assessment gauges knowledge and skills of students, which helps policymakers target and set reasonable goals in their education systems. The disconcerting PISA score of U.S. 15-year-olds raises several questions: What underlying factors contribute to relatively poor academic performance in the United States? What can be done to improve academic performance? Is it too late?

We do not believe it's too late; but a solution requires a greater understanding of the activators and consequences that affect academic-related behavior.

In *Declining by Degrees*, Hersh and Merrow[2] provide insight into possible reasons our American education system is failing. These include (a) the belief that college does nothing more than prepare students for a job; (b) the inability of educators to effectively communicate information to students; (c) the disconnection between supply and demand for available courses;

(d) an emphasis on teaching to assessment exams; and (e) insufficient preparation for college, among other factors.

Despite these barriers, we believe principles of applied behavioral science (ABS) can provide guidance for students, parents, educators, and the community as a whole toward a brighter future for education in the United States and beyond.

A MODEL FOR IMPROVING THE COLLEGE EXPERIENCE

The activator-behavior-consequence (ABC) model of ABS has a long and rich history of improving students' classroom performance.[3] Instructors and researchers have demonstrated methods to improve class attendance and punctuality,[4] ways to improve course structure so students can allocate more time for studying,[5] and approaches to enhancing students' ability to take notes during class lectures.[6]

Effective instructors who are passionate about educating students and fostering a love for learning seek empirically supported methods to structure their courses. Whether they are aware of it or not, these instructors are always changing the environment and the contingencies that promote student behavior for academic success. Put simply, academic behavior is a function of activators and consequences (as explained in Chapter 1). This behavior is no different than any other behavior discussed in this book as a target for actively caring for people (AC4P) intervention. If we know academic behavior is influenced by environmental arrangements imposed by course policies and instruction, why not purposefully and systematically program these arrangements to promote academic success?

This chapter explores the rich history of and strong potential for applying behavioral science to the improvement of higher education. We begin by summarizing Project Follow Through, the largest government-sponsored educational research in U.S. history. We then describe why traditional teaching methods are problematic. Finally, we take an in-depth look at various evidence-based ABS interventions in specific facets of education. As reflected in the Einstein quote at the beginning of this chapter, ABS focuses on changing the environmental conditions of instruction to cultivate learning.

THE AC4P MOVEMENT

AC4P is a reinforcement-based, culture enrichment movement developed by Scott Geller and his students at Virginia Tech.[7] The purpose of the AC4P

Movement is to create, nurture, and sustain a culture of positivity, aimed at increasing prosocial behaviors while decreasing problem behaviors on a societal level. Since many of the prosocial behaviors that individuals exhibit are learned in the classroom, it's important to understand various teaching interventions that support AC4P behaviors and outcomes.

Evidence-based interventions that apply AC4P principles (i.e., humanistic behaviorism) are described in the following sections. Diverse in their implementation, these interventions all adhere to humanistic behaviorism by (a) applying contingencies with positive consequences; (b) involving peer-to-peer interactions; and (c) modifying the environment to best support student success. As we investigate evidence-based instruction (EBI) techniques, we consider their relation to the AC4P Movement and their role in spreading positive change through ABS strategies.

PROJECT FOLLOW THROUGH

Imagine a scenario in which the U. S. government devotes tens of millions of dollars in a nine-year period to a comparison between an ABS approach (specifically, an approach called *direct instruction*) and other common methods of instruction. Consider this scientific study to be the largest and most expensive project ever conducted by the federal government to evaluate the relative impact of certain approaches to education. Now imagine that data from 200,000 students in this study are analyzed and clearly indicate the ABS approach to education is more effective than traditional approaches. In fact, imagine the data suggested certain other approaches actually *decreased* student performance. A reasonable taxpayer would demand that the ABS approach be implemented in schools nationwide, right? Instructors and policymakers across the country would champion the implementation of ABS in schools as a scientifically sound way to educate students most effectively.

Plot twist: This study actually took place in the context of a comprehensive evaluation titled "Project Follow Through," conducted from 1968 to 1977.[8] Unfortunately, when the data were summarized, no one celebrated. Few people championed the most successful ABS approach. Most students never received any trace of ABS-based EBI and the education system continued to decline.

What happened? What's going on in our education system? Welcome to Project Follow Through (PFT) – the multi-million-dollar, decade-long study that provided valuable scientific insight pertaining to effective and efficient education techniques.

PFT was designed to fix a problem, namely that "poor children tend to do poorly in school."[9] The first step in addressing this large-scale societal issue – the intersection between poverty and education – was to conduct a comprehensive assessment of twenty-two widely used educational models. In addition, PFT was designed to demonstrate that educational improvements documented in controlled studies extend to students from various socioeconomic backgrounds and across multiple grade levels.

To achieve these goals, more than 200,000 students participated in the most expensive longitudinal education-based study to date.[10] Participants were sampled from 178 different communities across the United States and represented a wide range of demographics, including ethnic composition and socioeconomic status. The PFT study used a comparison design in which each community selected a single approach it would apply for the duration of the study.

Of the twenty-two models considered, nine were selected to serve as independent variables in the PFT study.[11] The nine educational models assessed in PFT reflect three overarching teaching categories. The first category was the affective model. It's based on the assumption that the best way to improve learning in children is to foster their self-esteem. To accomplish this, the main focus of instruction is to provide educational experiences that improve children's self-esteem, thought to lead indirectly to the learning of basic skills and higher-order problem solving. Three specific educational techniques were systematically evaluated in the affective model category: (1) the Bank Street approach; (2) responsive education; and (3) open education.

The cognitive model was the second teaching category.[11] This model focuses on higher-order skills such as critical thinking and problem solving. It assumes students will learn affective and basic skills as a result of cognitive training. Three teaching techniques fall within the cognitive model category: (1) parent education; (2) the Tucson early education model (TEEM); and (3) cognitively-oriented curriculum.

The third category was the basic skills model.[11] This model presumes the best way to improve learning among children is to focus on lower-order skills. Those supporting the model suggest that the way to achieve higher-order thinking skills, as well as higher self-esteem, is to master basic skills. These teaching techniques are largely based on the ABS literature and use reinforcement-based procedures to teach basic skills. The three teaching techniques within the basic skills model are (1) direct instruction; (2) behavior analysis; and (3) the Southwest Labs approach. Each of these approaches is reviewed in the next several paragraphs.

Basic Skills Model

The basic skills model of instruction is based on the underlying assumption that all behaviors are learned.[12] This presumes that underprivileged children are behind in their learning because no one has effectively taught them the necessary skills needed to succeed in both social and academic settings. It follows that training methods must be behavioral and based on principles of positive consequences. The basic skills model represents an ABS approach to education with many shared AC4P features (see Chapters 1 and 2).

Direct Instruction. Direct instruction (DI) was developed by Siegfried Engelmann and Wes Becker at the University of Oregon.[13] This approach uses empirically validated teaching techniques from ABS. It places responsibility for student success on the shoulders of the teachers, rather than looking for differences between students to explain learning deficits. We address specifics of this approach later in this chapter.

Behavior Analysis. The behavior analysis approach was created at the University of Kansas by Donald Bushell.[14] This system uses simple reward-based procedures to teach basic reading comprehension, arithmetic, handwriting, and spelling. Participants are provided with rewards – contingent on correct responses – in the form of social praise and tokens exchangeable for desired activities. Shaping procedures are used, in which participants begin at their current level and build gradually to fluency. New skills are learned by applying positive consequences for observable success.

Southwest Approach (Language Development). The Southwest approach focuses primarily on language development. Material is often presented in multiple languages (e.g., English and Spanish), especially for bilingual students.[11]

Cognitive Skills Model

The cognitive skills model presumes disadvantaged children fall behind because they lack normal cognitive experiences. To address this deficiency, children learn to use verbal skills and solve problems through interactions with the teachers, who provide age-appropriate academic experiences.[11]

Cognitively-Oriented Curriculum. This curriculum is based on Piaget's educational theory, which suggests children must select their own educational activities to learn language, learn problem-solving skills, and enhance a positive self-concept to improve their own cognitive processes.[11]

Florida Parent Education Approach. The Florida parent education strategy, as with the cognitively-oriented curriculum, emphasizes the in-class Piaget approach. It also focuses on educating parents to effectively teach their children language, cognitive, affective, and motor skills.[11]

Tucson Early Education Approach. This approach assumes children have different learning styles, and it allows children a high level of choice in the classroom. The primary focus of this approach is to enhance language and educational experiences for each student.[11]

Affective Skills Model

The affective skills model bases teaching methods on the underlying assumption that the most effective learning occurs when the child exhibits sufficient socioemotional development.[11] The focus of these teaching methods is the use of humanistic approaches to improve self-esteem and peer-to-peer interaction. Classroom curricula consist of semi-structured learning environments focused on increasing self-esteem and the personal responsibility to learn. In practice, skills are not explicitly taught; children are expected to know what is best for their personal growth. While considered humanistic, this approach differs substantially from the form of humanistic behaviorism described throughout this book. The humanism in the affective skills model lacks a conceptual foundation regarding the role of the environment in fostering positive behavior change.

Bank Street Approach. The Bank Street approach adopted by Head Start, a national pre-kindergarten educational system, uses an open-learning environment.[11] The classroom is structured to provide multiple learning opportunities at a given time and allows children various options for engaging in these activities. The teacher is responsible for helping children take advantage of these learning opportunities.

Open Education Approach. The open education approach focuses on creating situations to enhance a child's desire to learn.[11] It's the child's responsibility to learn the material, as reading and writing skills are not directly taught. Instead, this approach aims to cultivate a desire to communicate personal preferences (wants and needs) so students take control of their own learning. By successfully controlling their learning experiences, students are expected to build their self-esteem.

Responsive Education Approach. This approach calls for several learning centers within the classroom environment that provide unique educational activities. Children can choose their preferred area of the classroom depending on personal interests at that time.[11] The purpose is to foster a sense of autonomy and control in the classroom. Proponents believe this builds self-esteem – presumably essential for learning academic skills.

Methods of Project Follow Through

Project Follow Through began in 1968 and was conducted for nine years.[15] Participants began in either kindergarten or first grade and were tested yearly through third grade. To compare the effects of the various instruction methods, each PFT school district was matched with a non-PFT district with similar demographics to serve as a control group. More than 200,000 students were exposed to PFT in total, with 9,255 PFT students and 6,485 non-PFT students included in the final analysis of data.[11]

The evaluation of PFT was completed in 1977.[9] All techniques were evaluated according to student progress in three categories: basic skills, affective skills, and cognitive skills. A relatively fair and holistic assessment was provided by an evaluation of all techniques using these three categories. Various empirically valid standardized assessments were used for each aspect of the evaluation, including the Metropolitan Achievement Test (MAT), the Wide Range Achievement Test (WRAT), the Raven's colored Progressive Matrices, the Intellectual Achievement Responsibility Scale (IARS), and the Coopersmith Self-Esteem Inventory (CSEI).[11]

These tools assessed a range of skills: sound–symbol relationships, vocabulary skills, word identification, math calculations, spelling, language and grammar, reading and oral math problems, and number recognition. Affective assessments with the IARS and CSEI asked participants how they perceived themselves, how they thought others perceived them, and whether they attributed success and failure to themselves and/or to external circumstances. All of the tests were administered each year for every education model site, for both the PFT and non-PFT schools.

Assessment scores were compared between PFT schools and the matched-control schools, as depicted in Figure 18.1. The x-axis displays the type of teaching technique used at the participating schools, and the y-axis shows student performance relative to control schools. The zero point on the y-axis represents the level of student performance at the control schools. The y-axis scale is a normalized range of points (maximum possible range: –100 to +100) awarded to each model for each statistically significant difference between the PFT and non-PFT schools.

Normalized scores below zero indicate that students at PFT schools demonstrate skill detriments compared with matched-control schools.

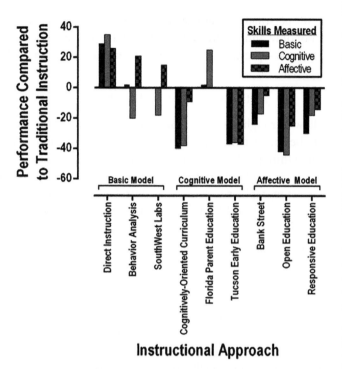

FIGURE 18.1. Average effects of nine PFT approaches compared with schools with traditional instruction (adapted from Engelmann & Carnine).[16]

Normalized scores above zero demonstrate that gains were made in the assessed skills of students in the PFT schools relative to the schools in the matched-control schools. Scores near or equal to zero indicate no differences between the skills gained from the teaching technique compared with the control schools.

The first takeaway from Figure 18.1 is that five of the assessed teaching approaches (i.e., Bank Street, responsive education, and open education from the affective skills model, and TEEM and cognitive curriculum from the cognitive skills model) resulted in *decreases* in all of the skills assessed (i.e., affective skills, cognitive skills, and basic skills) compared with matched control schools.[9] These data suggest that not only are these five teaching techniques ineffective, but student participants actually learned fewer skills than those exposed to traditional teaching methods used at the control schools.

Three education techniques resulted in small gains in at least one skills category.[9] Of the three, two were from the basic skills model (i.e., behavior analysis and Southwest model), while the other was from the cognitive skills model (i.e., parent education). Notably, in all three techniques, the largest gains were found in the self-esteem skills. Approaches from the basic skills model and cognitive skills model produced larger gains in the self-esteem assessments than did the technique specifically designed to enhance self-esteem.

The *only* teaching technique that yielded robust gains in all three assessment categories (i.e., basic skills, cognitive skills, and affective skills) was direct instruction (DI).[11] Compared with control schools, students who participated in the DI condition showed marked increases in all of the assessed skills. In addition, despite the focus on teaching only basic skills, substantial increases in the scores on the cognitive and affective skills assessments were found relative to control schools. These data suggest DI not only teaches basic skills, but can also improve higher-order thinking (i.e., cognitive skills) and boost self-reported self-esteem and peer-to-peer interaction (i.e., affective skills).

That DI increased basic and cognitive skills is not surprising given that these skills are directly instructed in the DI approach; however, it's noteworthy DI was the best intervention for increasing self-esteem, as well. As you learned in Chapter 3, self-motivation is a crucial component of sustainable behavior change. The heavy reliance on positive consequences in DI supports autonomous mastery of educational material. As you will learn later in this chapter, students receiving DI obtain frequent, immediate, and specific feedback on their performance. Autonomy is fostered, competency is ensured, and a sense of relatedness is achieved when a classroom experiences DI. It's not really surprising, then, that DI strengthens self-motivation for learning, which was likely captured in the affective-skills measures used in PFT.

PFT was a fruitful endeavor to demonstrate the relative effectiveness of various instructional methods. The extensive study supported the effectiveness of certain teaching approaches and highlighted the ineffectiveness of other teaching approaches. Still, there was no movement by education professionals or government agencies to implement DI in the U.S. school system. After nearly 1 billion dollars of taxpayers' money were poured into PFT (accounting for inflation to present-day value), few changes were made to the status quo.[10] Results related to the effectiveness of DI were ignored. Government organizations abandoned research on DI. Instead, investigations were funded to determine why the cognitive and affective techniques failed.[15]

DI is still missing from mainstream public education. Forty years have passed since the PFT findings. Is the neglect because DI is costly and complicated? No. DI is relatively inexpensive and requires minimal upfront costs. What is your reaction to these decisions – knowing the United States is falling behind the rest of the developed world in nearly all aspects of academics? If you were shown Figure 18.1 and asked which technique you would like to have a child, perhaps your own, experience, which would you choose?

You might ask yourself if policymakers actively care for education. You would hope evidence-based instruction (EBI) techniques would be commonplace in institutions of learning – if you are like us and believe objective data should be used for decision making. The remainder of this chapter reviews what behavioral scientists know about EBI, including ways in which DI and similar approaches can be used in higher education.

ISSUES WITH TRADITIONAL LECTURE-BASED COURSES

As Skinner[17] observed and as evidenced by the results of PFT, the traditional instructional paradigm has many flaws. Standard lecture-based courses often lack motivating contingencies and teach *at* students rather than create environments that best support learning (recall Einstein's quote). Students should be active participants in the learning process, not passive spectators. After all, learning does not happen to students; learning is something a student experiences. And experience involves behavior.

It's not surprising that the learning impact of lecture-based courses pales in comparison with that of other teaching methods based on ABS. We bet your favorite college courses involved some form of interaction and direct feedback – not an entirely lecture-based course. But how do we organize and create environments to best support learning? Consider the EBI methods described in the paragraphs that follow.

Boyce and Hineline[18] describe a few key problems with lecture-based courses that produce disadvantageous outcomes for students, and they propose an alternative instruction style. First, the contingencies in lecture-based courses are weak and delayed. As a result, students often put off studying throughout the semester and cram right before the tests. No soon and certain positive consequences are available to motivate ongoing engagement with the course material. In the classroom, students are passive sponges. Their job is to simply listen throughout the class period.

From an AC4P perspective, the student has no active role in his/her own learning in traditional lecture-based courses. Thus, the student has no sense of personal control, ownership, or belonging. Plus, the lack of positive consequences (e.g., soon, certain, and supportive feedback for learned behavior) hinders the optimal development of self-efficacy.

If only brief participation exercises are provided for homework, contingencies supporting social interaction and off-task behaviors outweigh contingencies supporting on-task academic interactions. Self-motivation is necessary, and factors that support or increase self-motivation are rare in a lecture class (see Chapter 3).

Another issue: Due to their size (e.g., hundreds of students in introductory courses), lecture-based courses assume all students begin at the same skill level and learn at the same pace. Of course, this is a flawed assumption. Some students learn at faster rates than others, and some students start with a better understanding of a course topic. The result: Some students are bored and want to move on to more difficult material; others lack required skill mastery and fall behind. Optimism and self-efficacy diminish, and self-esteem is jeopardized as students fall further behind.

It's no revelation that traditional lecture-based courses are relatively dull and ineffective, since the AC4P person-states (Chapter 2) are ignored, if not weakened. In addition, the contingencies applied in lecture-based settings are often aversive – students are motivated to avoid penalization or embarrassment from the instructor or peers. This is evident in attendance policies, exam formats, and quizzes. When the ABS and AC4P principles and techniques described throughout this book are absent, the result is an overall aversive and passive classroom environment.[18]

DIRECT INSTRUCTION

We have discussed the efficacy of DI but have not described its procedures. So what is DI? Direct instruction was pioneered by Siegfried Engelmann and Wesley C. Becker as a method to teach reading and math during primary education.[19] It applies the principles of ABS to effectively teach skills to students of all ages.[13] DI uses activators, often in the form of questions, hints, and prompts, to help students give correct responses with minimal errors. Delivery of positive consequences for correct responses is also heavily emphasized.

To demonstrate DI in practice, imagine a second-grade classroom with thirty students and a single teacher. In this example, let's assume the students are learning to read aloud, and let's consider the use of activators, consequences, and the pace of the trials:

TEACHER: First word?
STUDENTS (IN UNISON): Th-ere

TEACHER: *Exactly*! Second word?
STUDENTS (IN UNISON): were
TEACHER: Spell it?
STUDENTS (IN UNISON): W-E-R-E
TEACHER: *Yes*! Now read both words together, and faster!
STUDENTS (IN UNISON): There were!
TEACHER: *Excellent*! Last word?
STUDENTS (IN UNISON): Din-o-awleklh (mumbles from students)
TEACHER: Try again and sound it out, Dino-sa . . .
STUDENTS (IN UNISON): Di-no-saurs.
TEACHER: *Great*! Now read me all three words.
STUDENTS (IN UNISON): There were dinosaurs!

Note how the teacher uses positive consequences in response to correct answers to promote self-efficacy among the students. Note too that the students respond chorally, as a group, to foster belonging. Such use of DI positively affects the AC4P person-states associated with self-motivation explained in Chapter 3.

Following a series of such lessons, students meet briefly with the teacher, either one-on-one or in small groups, and read similar yet novel words. While the student is reading, the teacher records the number of incorrect responses, as well as the overall time it takes the student to finish reading the words. With these data, the teacher can decide whether the student needs more practice (if s/he did not achieve mastery) or if s/he is ready to move on to more difficult words. This component of the lesson tests the generality (the application of newly learned behavior to novel situations) of a student's reading skills to new words. In subsequent lessons, the teacher provides similar text while testing novel words and sounds to ensure students reliably use proper reading skills.

The DI approach is easily adapted for college instruction. Imagine a college-level course on neuropsychology: A professor stands in front of the room with a slide advancer and a projector depicting areas of the brain. As the professor advances the slide, a picture of the amygdala appears on the screen and the professor says, "What's this?" The class shouts, "Amygdala!" Students presumably learned this term when reading their textbook or completing homework.

The professor next advances to a slide that simply depicts the word "amygdala" on the screen and asks, "In what lobe would we find this?" The class shouts, "Temporal!" The professor gives the class some praise for their fluent responding and continues in this fashion. This form of DI at

the college level is an offshoot of an earlier ABS approach known as programmed instruction, which we will describe later.

Another aspect of DI consistent with the ABS approach is the continued measurement of student performance, or constant collection of
learning-relevant behavior. This enables teachers to understand what
should be taught next and whether further review is necessary for certain students. When teaching methods base the course of study on time
(i.e., after one week of addition the class moves onto subtraction), some
students are left behind. By taking data and measuring ongoing student
performance, the teacher ensures students have mastered a current skill
and are prepared for the next lesson. Such data help teachers understand
whether they are successfully teaching certain material. If the data indicate
a lack of learning, the teacher adjusts the curriculum so it's more effective.

Principles that guide the DI approach can be applied across a variety
of academic topics: (1) students are explicitly taught rules and strategies;
(2) multiple examples are used for each concept to establish correct answering in response to particular questions/cues; (3) each example is sequenced
so systematic steps occur between the examples provided; (4) systematic
withdrawal of prompts and activators ensures students can accurately and
independently respond to natural cues likely to be encountered in real life
outside of the classroom; (5) novel situations are presented; and (6) incorrect
responses are corrected.[20]

These six principles encompass the important aspects of ABS-style
instruction such as DI. To use common technical terms from ABS, students are prompted to respond correctly, and their behavior is followed
by a positive consequence such as supportive feedback or by earning high
marks/grades in the class. The activators are then systematically withdrawn until the students respond independently. As students demonstrate
independent mastery of the material, they gain an enhanced feeling of personal control and self-efficacy that motivates them to continue learning.

This ABS approach to learning teaches students to discriminate between
correct and incorrect examples of a concept or methodology by providing multiple examples that differ slightly. The application of newly learned
behavior to novel situations (generality) is programmed in DI curricula
by means of novel examples/situations where students are taught to properly adapt their newly learned behaviors. Finally, incorrect responses are
immediately corrected to ensure students make as few errors as possible
when engaging with course materials (DI lessons, homework, etc.). Bottom
line: DI ensures all students contact success.

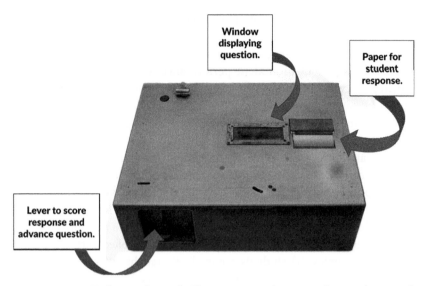

FIGURE 18.2. Early mechanical Skinnerian teaching machine. Photograph courtesy of Silly Rabbit on Wikimedia Commons under the Creative Commons Attribution 3.0 Unported license. Labels and arrows added by authors.

The pace of DI is quite fast, ensuring students have as many opportunities to respond and experience consequences as possible.[20] Learning opportunities are brief, discrete units of learning, such as one math problem or one vocabulary word. This emphasis on practice and feedback allows for students to efficiently master the topics. The DI methodology can be implemented at nearly every academic level. The topics depend on the age or academic level of the students, but the teaching methods described here remain the same. Note how this humanistic approach contradicts a common myth: "We learn more from our mistakes."

PROGRAMMED INSTRUCTION

Programmed instruction was developed by Skinner in the 1950s to assist independent student learning.[21] Based on ABS principles, this approach focuses on shaping techniques and positive-consequence contingencies to effectively teach a variety of academic topics. Course content for programmed instruction was administered through a teaching machine (see Figure 18.2), which was operated by individual students and enabled them to learn without the assistance of a classroom teacher.

1. **E. Scott Geller** is the **founder** of the **AC4P** Movement.
2. **E. Scott Geller** is the **founder** of the **AC4P** Movement.
3. **E. Scott Geller** is the **founder** of the _____ Movement.
4. **E. Scott Geller** is the _____ of the **AC4P** Movement.
5. _____ is the **founder** of the **AC4P** Movement.
6. E. Scott Geller is the _____ of the AC4P Movement.
7. _____ is the founder of the AC4P Movement.
8. E. Scott Geller is the founder of the _____ Movement.

FIGURE 18.3. An example of programmed instruction for students; initial activators gradually disappear over time.

Although there are several technological iterations of the teaching machine, the concepts are relatively simple.[22] The original teaching machines consisted of a display disk with roughly thirty frames, each frame representing a question for the student to answer. The machine displayed one of the thirty frames, and students responded to the displayed question prompt by writing an answer on another opening in the machine. Following the response, the student then lifted a lever to reveal the correct answer.

The original teaching machine included options to shape (as opposed to test) behaviors.[23] The frames that were displayed could either test the student or systematically and strategically withdraw particular activators (or prompts) so students eventually respond without an activator. For instance, while teaching spelling, the machine may provide a substantial activator to guarantee a correct response (i.e., "spell the word: dinosaur"). Following the correct responding in this frame, the next frame removes some letters (i.e., "spell the word: din_sau_"). The subsequent frames continue to fade these prompts until the frame simply consists of _____, in which a correct response is the entire word "dinosaur" (see Figure 18.3 for an additional example). With this teaching/learning format, students can self-direct their studying without teacher intervention. Learning is self-paced and builds self-efficacy and self-motivation through programmed instruction.

Technological breakthroughs and software development have rendered today's teaching machines more "virtual" than mechanical. These virtual machines are built into course content management systems (CMSs) such as Blackboard,˙ ANGEL˙, and Moodle˙. The CMSs enable instructors to program their own learning modules that operate identically to the original teaching machines. Such "e-teaching machines" have numerous benefits compared with old-school mechanical approaches: (a) instructors can pull questions from a very large bank of possible questions and aren't limited to what can fit onto a physical rotating disc; (b) student responses are typed and can be saved electronically by the instructor for office-hour discussions regarding performance; (c) the electronic nature of the student-response database provides instructors with an efficient means of diagnosing problematic questions (e.g., those missed by many students); and (d) the electronic display of the questions permits more creative activators and prompts, such as pictures or bold/colored fonts to evoke correct responding.

Programmed instruction provides three distinct advantages over traditional lecture-based teaching methods: First, the teaching machine reveals the correct answer immediately after the student responds, providing immediate feedback to foster learning and self-efficacy. This is a major advantage compared with traditional teaching methods, in which feedback is typically delayed by weeks and even months – say, until the final exam.

Second, the course of study is tailored to each individual student, enhancing personal control and self-efficacy. In a traditional class, students may be at different academic levels, resulting in boredom for some students and daunting challenges for others. Programmed instruction accounts for these individual differences by shaping students' responses at a self-directed pace that enables individual progress toward mastery. This shaping process was initially very time-intensive with the mechanical teaching machines, but it's now very efficient using CMSs and computer-aided instruction.

Third, stimulus-response teaching trials are presented at a high rate, leading to more learning opportunities within a teaching/learning session.

Initially, programmed-instruction presentations are challenging to create, requiring a great deal of time and effort. Once a program is created, though, it can be administered to large numbers of students, becoming quite efficient. Skinner[21] noted that many considerations go into creating a successful program, but some features are common to successfully program any topic. First, the program's success is largely based on the instructor's ability to tailor the lessons to each individual student. This level of oversight may seem overwhelming at first, but use of CMSs to automate the process makes this approach rather easy.

The major hurdle in modern programmed instruction is the initial programming of CMSs or computer software to deliver questions students can already answer correctly, and then programming in small steps a progression of more difficult subsequent questions to ensure students are likely to succeed with minimal errors. The assistance provided to students to facilitate success is gradually removed until a student can give the correct response independently. Once an instructor has programmed the system to achieve programmed-instruction goals, any student can be enrolled in the system without needing to re-create the process each time.

Teaching machines are commonly criticized for being limited to the instruction of only rote material. However, when programmed instruction is integrated into a personalized system of instruction described in the next section, these forms of instruction can be expanded to higher-order cognitive skills and critical thinking associated with topics such as calculus, English composition, physics, and biochemistry.[24]

PERSONALIZED SYSTEM OF INSTRUCTION

In the mid-1960s, Fred Keller developed an ABS teaching intervention called personalized system of instruction (PSI), expanding on the principles of programmed instruction proposed earlier by his friend B. F. Skinner.[25] Keller recognized problems with traditional lecture-based teaching methods and formalized five aspects of PSI to directly address these issues: (1) instruction is largely presented in written format; (2) lectures are used exclusively for motivational purposes; (3) the material covered is self-paced; (4) mastery is required before the student can move on to subsequent material; and (5) prior students tutor current students.

These five aspects of PSI mitigate specific deficiencies found in lecture-based courses. Lectures can be aversive for students, as previously discussed. Supporting contingencies involve aversive control (e.g., students working to avoid failure, embarrassment, penalties, etc.) and they make little use of positive consequences.[18] For PSI, instructors tailor lectures to be motivational. The material presented in lectures demonstrates the practicality and applicability of the course topics, augmenting the reinforcing value of learning the topics.

For instance, a PSI lecture on ABS principles might present multiple examples of ways students can use contingency-management principles in their everyday lives. The purpose of these lectures is to help students get excited about the topics and the prospect of learning. In fact, Keller's version of PSI requires students to reach a designated performance criterion before earning the *privilege* of attending the motivational lecture. As such, Keller's lectures were positive consequences for succeeding in the course.

We know of no peer-reviewed scientific article on the impact of such lectures, but we can anecdotally report that many of our ABS colleagues who champion PSI have made lectures *required* for *all* students to (a) ensure all students are exposed to all material; (b) circumvent issues regarding differential achievement of PSI criteria because students are progressing at different rates; and (c) compensate for changes in culture that result in lectures most likely being skipped if made optional. It's unknown whether these modern modifications of Keller's optional lecture contingency substantially lessen the benefits of PSI, but we actually expect a *gain* in performance by requiring lecture attendance.

The material presented in PSI is often presented in written format and can occur in the form of worksheets, study guides, and notes.[26] Students' engagement with written instruction means they can access as much practice as necessary to master certain lessons, adhering to the self-paced aspect of PSI. The distinction between self-pacing and teacher-led instruction is important, as instructor-paced courses often teach to the *average* student.

With the standard lecture course, some students are left behind while others are ready to move on, as previously noted. By pacing themselves, students can reach mastery for a given topic by a designated day. But PSI students might not pace themselves properly and be left in a worse position – further adrift – than those in an instructor-paced course. While this is possible, PSI instructors often provide incentive/reward contingencies to motivate mastery of the course material. Typically, this is achieved by basing students' final grades on the number of sections they completed with mastery. This approach to grading typically results in an all-or-none outcome where students either fail or earn an A.

Many universities frown on such outcomes. They are perceived as grade inflation and interfere with the grading system of most other courses. Instructors can mitigate this result by (a) changing the course to a pass/fail grading structure; (b) assigning other homework or quizzes so the course is not based solely on PSI mastery; or (c) assigning students an "incomplete" grade if they have not reached total mastery criteria by the end of the semester. Once the student later finishes the PSI mastery requirements, the incomplete is changed to a "pass" or a letter grade that reflects degree of mastery.

In lecture-based courses, content progresses according to the teacher's schedule – at the expense of ensuring mastery for all students. You've probably experienced this in your own education. For instance, Week 1 might cover the history of the field of study, Week 2 the basic principles across the entire field of study, and Week 3 might begin teaching details about specific principles. But what happens if some students still have a poor understanding of the material covered in Week 2? Unfortunately, those students are out of luck and have to struggle with the instructor's pace. From an AC4P perspective, self-motivation is weakened because students' personal control over their pace of achieving mastery is restricted.

The PSI approach addresses this problem by requiring students to master each topic before moving on to the next. Some students might master the material in two days; others might require an extra week or two. Bottom line: Students have mastered the necessary topics by the end of the course, as opposed to being simply *introduced* to those topics.

The use of undergraduate proctors in the course structure is another unique aspect of PSI. Proctors hold office hours so students have a forum to ask for clarification of the PSI work and to discuss why certain answers are correct or incorrect. The proctors are authorized to discuss the correct answers with the students. If students wish to appeal an incorrect answer, the proctor asks them to defend their answer, and the proctor relays this information to the instructor during weekly team meetings.

Becoming a proctor typically entails a highly competitive application process. Only students with high grades in the course can be considered to serve as proctors. Instructors compile teams of proctors with the understanding these proctors will work closely with the faculty and graduate teaching assistants within an AC4P community of interdependent teaching and learning. Proctors ultimately receive highly personalized letters of recommendation for jobs or graduate school applications. This incentive/reward contingency motivates students to succeed in the course and earn the opportunity to serve as a proctor, and then to perform diligently as a proctor.

Numerous considerations and assumptions must be made to implement PSI effectively.[27] Students must actively participate rather than passively listen and attempt to soak up lecture material. Both corrective and supportive feedback is necessary to motivate students in PSI curricula. Students also must understand the learning objectives associated with the course assignments to better track their mastery.

The material should be sequentially organized in the same format as a shaping procedure. Course content should begin at a place where the student will respond correctly, and successively get more difficult as the student learns. The rate of correct responding should remain high as the response requirements systematically increase.

Consider how children learn mathematics. It would certainly be disadvantageous for a student in math to start the learning sequence with complex division. Preferably, students master all aspects of arithmetic, beginning with the mastery of single-digit numbers and moving on to larger numbers. After students have demonstrated mastery of larger numbers, they are introduced to simple and more complex division.

The key is to maintain a high rate of correct responses followed by positive consequences (or supportive feedback) to strengthen the learning process of vocabulary terms or basic information. Higher-order processing can be assessed using short essays or assignments that demonstrate learned behavior, such as differential equations in a calculus course. Students should be frequently evaluated on their current skills, and this information should inform subsequent lessons. This process illustrates the personalized (humanistic) nature of PSI, caring for the needs of individual students as opposed to the average student in a large class.

Students succeed and feel empowered in their own education when PSI is implemented correctly. As discussed, students often succeed so well that PSI instructors are suspected of grade inflation. It's noteworthy the PSI structure results in students spending substantially more time in active learning than do students passively attending traditional lecture courses. Instructors need only show administrators the sheer number of learning responses given by PSI students to deflect grade-inflation critiques.

From our personal experience of adapting online testing to formal PSI, we found that students in online testing that was void of PSI components encountered approximately one-tenth the number of questions experienced by PSI students. These data suggest students in our PSI course received ten times more feedback than students in a standard lecture-based course. By requiring students to master material before proceeding with the course content, instructors are essentially guaranteeing *all* students who remain enrolled in the course will succeed.

In conclusion, PSI is an efficient and effective teaching technique, aimed at providing individualized instruction in a classroom setting. The research-based components of PSI described here correct certain disadvantages of a traditional lecture-based course and provide a framework for instructors who may wish to adapt this EBI in their classroom setting.

MAKING IT HAPPEN: EXAMPLES FROM THE UNIVERSITY OF KANSAS

Actively caring for higher education can be achieved via a myriad of approaches.[28] This chapter presented these approaches in isolation, but they need not be implemented this way. Now we describe our approach to actively caring for higher education at the University of Kansas, which has historically served as the hotbed for ABS approaches to instruction.

The authors of this chapter are a team of instructors who regularly teach "Introduction to Applied Behavioral Science" (ABSC 100).[29] The ABSC 100 course is the gateway course to the applied behavioral science undergraduate major at the University of Kansas. Concepts covered in ABSC 100 range from the philosophy of behaviorism to the principles of positive behavior change. ABSC 100 is a large lecture course that combines aspects of DI and PSI with more than two hundred students enrolled in each section every semester.

Each class meeting in ABSC 100 features highly engaging lectures with contemporary and real-world examples that are meaningful to our undergraduate population. All students are required to attend lectures to learn the material for later application to PSI modules. We recognize that pop culture constantly evolves, and our teaching team must strive to stay hip. The use of undergraduate teaching proctors is one way to stay culturally relevant to the undergraduate population.

Students who previously excelled in ABSC 100 are invited to fill one of twelve slots in a teaching apprenticeship course for PSI proctors. This teaching apprenticeship course entails a weekly discussion of articles on evidence-based instruction with the ABSC 100 instructor and the graduate teaching assistants. The proctors have a second meeting with the ABSC 100 teaching team each week to discuss whether current teaching practices are promoting student success (assessed by students' performance on PSI tasks) and ways to update course material to stay contemporary with pop culture. Proctors assist with the PSI component of ABSC 100 by holding office hours.

The PSI component of ABSC 100 involves an online course content-management system (CMS). The CMS houses relevant content such as syllabi, links to campus resources, and an online gradebook students can access in order to monitor their performance. We have also programmed our CMS to offer PSI learning modules that expand upon content from lectures and the required textbook.

Nearly 50 percent of the entire course grade is based upon PSI module performance. The modules contain ten fill-in-the-blank questions (written by prior proctors and edited each semester to update the materials). The fill-in-the-blank questions fulfill the PSI mission to rely on the written word for learning. Students are allowed to complete the PSI module from any computer, any time of the day, and at their selected pace.

The proctors for the course write new questions for the module banks each semester; currently, each module contains a bank of more than two hundred questions. When students access a module, they are presented with ten random questions from the bank, presented in random order, making it nearly statistically impossible for multiple students to simultaneously access an identical sequence of quiz questions. This design eliminates the potential for cheating. Students work through the modules and receive immediate feedback on their written responses. This fulfills the core ABS concept of consequence-based learning. Students are assigned a PSI module for each unit from the course textbook. The highest grade they earn on a PSI module for each unit is the grade entered into the gradebook.

The PSI modules also rely on unit-perfection mastery to advance – another core component of this teaching approach.[24] Mastery is achieved by requiring students to earn 80 percent of the points on a module before the next module is made available. Students cannot progress through the material until they have demonstrated adequate mastery. Why 80 percent rather than 100 percent accuracy? To align our course with best practices in PSI, we allow students to learn at their own pace with unlimited attempts on each PSI module.[25] Students are in complete control of their PSI module scores because we allow unlimited attempts and provide feedback for every question. Students have the choice to retake a module or settle with a score between 80 and 100 percent before progressing to the next module.

Two additional incentive/reward contingencies increase motivation for better-than-adequate responding: (a) if students earn 100 percent on all PSI modules, they are exempt from the 100-item final examination for the course; (b) students earn a voucher to drop an assignment score if they complete all twenty PSI modules with 100 percent accuracy by mid-semester.

The reliance on fill-in-the-blank questions opens the possibility for multiple correct answers. Students can petition to have an answer counted as correct by attending undergraduate proctoring hours where proctors review the answer and hear a student's appeal for why his/her answer should be considered correct.[25] Students are not permitted an appeal unless they can also provide a reasonable rationale for their answer.

Beyond the PSI modules, students engage in active learning via DI drills at the start of each lecture, as well as in-class quizzes associated with the lecture. The DI drills consist of "virtual" flashcards (or "e-flashcards") projected from a software program onto the screen, where a brief phrase is presented in black text with the associated vocabulary term presented on the reverse side. Various forms of software can be used to create virtual flashcards, including PowerPoint. There are far too many flashcard computer/smartphone applications to list here (we use the StudyBlue® program).

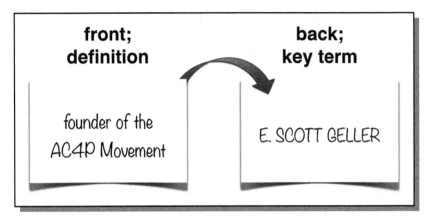

FIGURE 18.4. A SAFMEDS card.

In DI, such flashcards are presented using a strategic ABS format known as SAFMEDS: *Say All Fast, One Minute Each Day, Shuffled.*[30] The goal of SAFMEDS is to develop fluent (i.e., rapid and accurate) responding. We offer our students a brief training on SAFMEDS during the first class lecture and grant online access to SAFMEDS cards developed by our teaching team and our proctors to complement the lectures and course readings. Students can adapt any flashcard program to use within the SAFMEDS approach. No grade points are provided for using SAFMEDS, but many students access the online resources to practice on their own between lectures and before completing relevant PSI modules.

The DI drills using SAFMEDS at the start of lecture are led by a graduate teaching assistant who controls the pace of the SAFMEDS trials. The teaching assistant reads the definition/phrase (depicted in black font) and provides a cue to "Go!" that prompts students to chorally shout the associated vocabulary term on the reverse side of the virtual flashcard. The teaching assistant then flips the card to provide immediate feedback to students. Figure 18.4 provides an example of a SAFMEDS card.

Our online resource for students allows students to click a "yes" or "no" to indicate whether they know the answer. This allows for the tracking of correct responding. Online data tracking permits visual monitoring of students' personal mastery of the content. Students tell us the online SAFMEDS effectively prepares them for in-class quizzes given during each lecture class.

Our in-class quizzes make use of a personal response system ("clickers") during lecture. The in-class quizzes are multiple-choice questions. Two review questions are asked at the start of class to ensure retention of the previous lecture's material; and three questions are asked at the end of class to ensure students mastered the three main points of the lecture before they are dismissed. For both sets of questions, the instructor reviews the answers following each question and provides a brief mini-lecture on the content if less than 90 percent of the students answered correctly.

With so many resources (proctors, PSI, SAFMEDS) in the course, it's reasonable to ask whether a personal response system is necessary. The literature on personal response systems indicates that students – especially those in large lecture courses – are reluctant to raise their hand in class for fear of speaking incorrectly or providing inadequate verbal responses.[31] While a personal response system does not significantly improve grades, it does foster self-efficacy and optimism when students respond correctly. This promotes a humanistic element to the course within the AC4P framework.[32]

The use of a personal response system in class has an additional benefit. It offers another form of learning in the classroom, beyond the content mastery of PSI or fluency-building SAFMEDS exercises. The multiple-choice nature of the personal-response-system quizzes requires students to critically compare content and arrive at one correct answer.

The personal response system allows us to monitor student mastery within class. We also provide activators to students during the lecture to promote attention to important details. All students are provided guided notes at the start of class that contain fill-in-the-blank phrases associated with lecture content. These guided notes have been evaluated by other behavioral scientists who demonstrated guided notes result in fewer errors on quizzes than sharing completed notes (i.e., the lecture slides in their entirety).[6]

Beyond the ABS research on guided notes, we were inspired to adopt guided notes when recent research in psychology demonstrated that students who take notes on their computer during lecture actually perform *worse* than those using pen and paper.[33] Plus, students' use of laptops during lectures for note taking or off-task behavior can negatively impact the learning of other students in close proximity.[34] These findings prompted us to ban the use of laptops in class in order to promote a more engaging culture and limit students' disruption from other students' laptop use.

A real-life demonstration of actively caring is an AC4P capstone assignment. As an introductory course in applied behavioral science, ABSC 100 focuses on the scientific foundations and practical applications of ABS. Before teaching procedures such as positive reinforcement, we teach skills such as observational recording and behavioral definitions.

To integrate AC4P into the course, we break the assignment into two activities: students select and define an instance of AC4P behavior they will target and observe throughout the semester; and they follow the four steps of the AC4P process (see, act, pass, share). To facilitate the experience, we use a major portion of our operating budget to purchase AC4P wristbands for every student in the class. This ensures all students have the opportunity to fully experience the AC4P process.

After lecturing on behavioral definitions and identifying target behaviors, we release an online discussion blog so students can post an act of caring they plan to look for throughout the semester. Students are instructed to select something of personal relevance, not just a generic good deed (not that there's anything wrong with that, though). Responses are publicly posted to a course blog on our Blackboard' CMS page.

We personally review each entry and provide specific feedback on whether the student has selected an appropriate target AC4P behavior (something meaningful, and both observable and countable). Students who post targets such as "someone being nice to someone else" are prompted to reevaluate their response and behaviorally define "nice" such that two independent observers would agree. Less generic and more specific targets would be along the lines of "someone holding the door open for a stranger" or "someone telling a stranger that s/he dropped something."

Students provide a personal rationale for their target behavior to ensure they are looking for actions they genuinely value and would like to reward. If they do not provide a personal rationale, we prompt them to do so before assigning them a grade. Examples are shown in Figure 18.5.

Active participation in the AC4P four-step process is the second component of our AC4P assignment. Students are instructed on each step. In Step 1 (see), students are told to actively monitor their environment for instances of their target behavior. This obviously works toward the end goal of the assignment. It also serves a secondary and more meaningful purpose: Become actively engaged in seeing the goodness in humanity. Our goal is to open students' eyes to the surprising amount of charity, hospitality, and compassion far too often overlooked. Acts of caring rarely make the evening news, reinforcing the impression that our communities are full of apathy, selfishness, tragedy and malevolence.

In Step 2 (act), students approach the individuals they observed demonstrating the target behavior and thank them for actively caring. Step 3 (pass) entails passing the wristband to the individual and telling the individual about the class assignment and the AC4P Movement. This step uses the principle of reinforcement that students learn about in our class. Specifically, students learn about behavior-specific contingent praise, and they are expected to apply the principle through this stage of the assignment.

My target act of caring is "communication." It may sound simple, but far too often Americans forget how to verbally communicate with each other. Maybe it's due to a reliance on technology or the general hustle and bustle of modern life? It is not difficult to greet another with, "hello, how are you?" Likewise, it shouldn't be hard to tell another person that we admire some quality they possess; e.g., "you're a great role model to your sister." From my experience, simple comments such as these could potentially lead to more happiness, success, and value to a person's daily life. If everyone took the time to simply communicate in a personal manner, everyone would feel a lot more respected!

The actively caring behavior that I would like to see happen more often around campus is picking up trash and recycling. I am disheartened when I see students throw paper scraps on the floor or toss empty water bottles on the ground... it's disrespectful to our campus and the janitors that have to pick up after them (let alone the Earth!). Imagine if every student took a few moments to identify litter or empty bottles/cans around their desk at the end of class and properly disposed of them as they left the room...campus would looks so much better! The next time I see someone picking up someone else's trash, I will be sure to give them my bracelet!

FIGURE 18.5. Two examples of student entries from the AC4P assignment.

Sharing the story via the ac4p.org Website and on the course's Blackboard® discussion blog is the final step (share).

Our students are instructed to describe the scenario of passing the AC4P wristband and to personally reflect on their emotions and the observed reaction of the individual receiving the wristband. Student grades are privately assigned, but their stories are publicly displayed to all other students in the class. This serves two functions. First, it forces students to actively reflect on their experience and to be mindful of the emotions associated with the relevant social exchange. Second, public posting demonstrates the collective compassion experienced and propagated within the class and during a single semester.

We hope this public posting of collective compassion will portray our campus and community as cultures of kindness and camaraderie rather than a collection of nameless and faceless persons blindly sharing space in the name of education. Our vision: Students' AC4P experiences will reach far beyond the classroom.

IN CONCLUSION

This chapter reviewed evidenced-based instruction approaches firmly grounded in humanistic behaviorism and actively supporting the AC4P Movement. These approaches emanate from both human and nonhuman research in ABS and have decades of science to support their efficacy. Despite these successes, do you ever recall being taught with any of these procedures? Sure, there may have been traces of some of these components, but if you're like most students we've surveyed, it's unlikely you've experienced any of these approaches as they were designed to be used. Why aren't these EBI approaches mandated, or even recommended, by the U.S. Department of Education and supported by teachers' unions everywhere?

Programmed instruction, DI, PSI, and various other ABS teaching technologies enhance learning beyond traditional approaches – on this there is no debate. But the number of students receiving these EBI approaches is embarrassingly small. Inexcusably small, even. Researchers, instructors, and policymakers are failing to actively care for higher education. So what should we do?

You can help to cultivate a campus culture of respect for learning and an appreciation for EBI. Start by learning about SAFMEDS and creating your own empirically supported study materials. Take notes by hand and not on a computer. Create peer study groups to create your own sense of personal control and belongingness in the course while emulating the proctor aspect of PSI. In your study groups, practice choral responding and provide feedback – both supportive and corrective – for peer responding.

Share your successes with your instructors. Hold on to an optimistic expectation that they will share these tips with other students. We hope these simple modifications to your personal study routine will foster enough self-efficacy, self-esteem, personal control, optimism, and belongingness that you will volunteer your time to help an instructor integrate some of these components into his or her course structure. You'll be actively caring for your peers' education, as well as your own. Yes, you can do it!

DISCUSSION QUESTIONS

1. How critical is the level of education in the United States compared with that in other industrialized countries? Why do you think this is the case?
2. How did Project Follow Through (PFT) attempt to improve public education?

3. Distinguish between the three fundamental approaches to education that were evaluated by PFT: the affective model, the cognitive model, and the basic skills model.

4. Which PFT approach resulted in the greatest substantial gains in all three assessment categories? Why was this approach most effective at increasing self-esteem?

5. Why are traditional lecture-based courses relatively ineffective?

6. Why do traditional lecture-based courses continue to be the most common approach to college and university instruction?

7. Compare the PSI (Personalized System of Instruction) approach to education with that of traditional lecture-based courses.

8. Why are PSI courses relatively rare at colleges and universities?

9. How do the authors of this chapter apply ABS and DI principles to their applied behavioral science course at the University of Kansas?

10. How do the authors address AC4P specifically in their capstone course on applied behavioral science?

REFERENCES

1. OECD. (2012). *Programme for International Student Assessment (PISA)*. Retrieved July 23, 2015 from http://www.oecd.org/pisa/keyfindings/pisa-2012-results.htm.

2. Hersh, R. H., & Merrow, J. (Eds.). (2005). *Declining by degrees: Higher education at risk*. New York: Macmillan.

3. Gardner III, R., Sainato, D. M., Cooper, J. O., Heron, T. E., Heward, W. L., Eshleman, J. W., et al. (1994). *Behavior analysis in education: Focus on measurably superior instruction*. Belmont, CA: Thomson Brooks/Cole; Geller, E. S. (Ed.). (2014). *Actively Caring for People: Cultivating a culture of compassion* (4th ed.). Newport, VA: Make-A-Difference, LLC. Geller, E. S. (2014). (Ed.). *Actively caring at your school: How to make it happen* (2nd ed.). Newport, VA: Make-A-Difference, LLC.

4. Bicard, D. F., Lott, V., Mills, J., Bicard, & Baylot-Casey, L. (2012). Effects of text messaged self-monitoring on class attendance and punctuality of at-risk college student athletes. *Journal of Applied Behavior Analysis, 45*, 205–210.

5. Neef, N. A., Perrin, C. J., Haberlin, A. T., & Rodrigues, L. C. (2011). Studying as fun and games: Effects on college students' quiz performance. *Journal of Applied Behavior Analysis, 44*, 897–901.

6. Neef, N. A., McCord, B. E., & Ferreri, S. J. (2006). Effects of guided notes versus completed notes during lectures on college students' quiz performance. *Journal of Applied Behavior Analysis, 39*, 123–130.

7. Geller, E. S. (Ed.). (2014). (*Actively Caring for People: Cultivating a culture of compassion* (4th ed.). Newport, VA: Make-A-Difference, LLC.

8. Becker, W. C., & Carnin, D. (1981). Direct instruction: A behavior theory model for comprehensive educational intervention with the disadvantaged. In S. W. Bijou & R. Ruiz (Eds.). *Behavior modification: Contributions to education*

(pp. 145–210). Hillsdale, NJ: Lawrence Erlbaum; Engelmann, S. (2007). *Teaching needy kids in our backward system*. Atlanta: ADI.

9. Stebbins, L. B., St. Pierre, R. G., & Proper, E. C. (1977). *Education as experimentation: A planned variation model*, Vols. IVA &IVB. Cambridge, MA: Abt Associates, p. xxxiii.

10. Grossen, B. (1996). Overview: The story behind Project Follow Through. *Effective School Practices*, vol. 15, n. 1. Retrieved July 23, 2015 from http://darkwing.uoregon.edu/~adiep/ft/grossen.htm.

11. Adams, G. (1996). Project Follow Through: In-depth and beyond. *Effective School Practices*, vol. 15, n. 1. Retrieved July 23, 2015 from http://pages.uoregon.edu/adiep/ft/adams.htm.

12. Becker, W. C. (1978). National evaluation of follow through: Behavior-theory-based programs come out on top. *Education and Urban Society*, 10, 431–458.

13. Becker, W., & Carnine, D. (1981). Direct Instruction: A behavior theory model for comprehensive educational intervention with the disadvantaged. In S. Bijou & R. Ruiz (Eds.). *Contributions of behavior modification in education* (pp. 1–106). Hillsdale, NJ: Laurence Erlbaum.

14. Bushell, D. (1978). An engineering approach to the elementary classroom: The behavior analysis follow-through project. In A. C. Catania & T. A. Brigham (Eds.). *Handbook of applied behavior analysis* (pp. 525–563). New York: Irvington.

15. Watkins, C. L. (1996). Follow through: Why didn't we? *Effective School Practices*, Vol. 15, No. 1. Retrieved July 23, 2015 from http://pages.uoregon.edu/adiep/ft/watkins.htm.

16. Engelmann, S., & Carnine, D. (1982). *Theory of instruction: Principles and applications*. New York: Irvington Press.

17. Skinner, B. F. (1961). Why we need teaching machines. *Harvard Educational Review*, 31, 377–398.

18. Boyce, T. E., & Hineline, P. N. (2002). Interteaching: A strategy for enhancing the user-friendliness of behavioral arrangements in the college classroom. *Behavior Analyst*, 25, 215–226.

19. Engelmann, S., Becker, W. C., Carnine, D., & Gersten, R. (1988). The direct instruction follow through model: Design and outcomes. *Education and Treatment of Children*, 11, 303–317.

20. Gersten, R., Carnine, D., & White, W. (1984). The pursuit of clarity: Direct instruction and applied behavior analysis. In W. L. Heward, T. E. Heron, D. S. Hill, & J. Trapp-Porter (Eds.). *Focus on behavior analysis in education* (pp. 38–57). Columbus, OH: Merrill.

21. Skinner, B. F. (1958). Teaching machines. *Science*, 128, 969–977.

22. Benjamin, Jr., L. T. (1988). A history of teaching machines. *American Psychologist*, 43, 703–712.

23. Skinner, B. F. (1986). Programmed instruction revisited. *Phi Delta Kappan*, 68, 103–110.

24. Reboy, L. M., & Semb, G. B. (1991). PSI and critical thinking: Compatibility or irreconcilable differences? *Teaching of Psychology*, 18, 212–215.

25. Keller, F. S. (1968). "Goodbye, Teacher ..." *Journal of Applied Behavior Analysis*, 1, 79–89.

26. McGaw, D. (1975). *Personalized system of instruction.* Paper presented at the annual meeting of the American Political Science Association. San Francisco: McGaw.

27. Kemp, J. (1971). *Instructional design.* Belmont, CA: Fearon.

28. Geller, E. S. (Ed.). (2014). *Actively Caring for People: Cultivating a culture of compassion* (4th ed.). Newport, VA: Make-A-Difference, LLC; Geller, E. S. (Ed.). (2014). *Actively caring at your school: How to make it happen* (2nd ed.). Newport, VA: Make-A-Difference, LLC.

29. Reed, D. D., Hirst, J. M., Kaplan, B. A. & Becirevic, A. (2014). The AC4P Movement at the University of Kansas. In E. S. Geller (Ed.). *Actively caring at your school: How to make it happen* (2nd ed.). Newport, VA: Make-A-Difference, LLC.

30. Graf, S., & Lindsley, O. R. (2002). *Standard celeration charting.* Poland, OH: Graf Implements.

31. Shaffer, D. M., & Collura, M. J. (2009). Evaluating the effectiveness of a personal response system in the classroom. *Teaching of Psychology, 36,* 273–277.

32. Mayer, R. E., Stull, A., DeLeeuw, K., Almeroth, K., Bimber, B., Chun, D., et al. (2009). Clickers in college classrooms: Fostering learning with questioning methods in large lecture classes. *Contemporary Educational Psychology, 34,* 51–57.

33. Mueller, P. A., & Oppenheimer, D. M. (2014). The pen is mightier than the keyboard: Advantages of longhand over laptop note taking. *Psychological Science, 25,* 1159–1168.

34. Sana, F., Weston, T., & Cepeda, N. J. (2013). Laptop multitasking hinders classroom learning for both users and nearby peers. *Computers & Education, 62,* 24–31.

19

Actively Caring for Mother Earth

E. SCOTT GELLER

Thank God men cannot fly, and lay waste the sky as well as the earth.
– Henry David Thoreau

This chapter addresses the human dynamics of environmental protection and ecological sustainability. An ecologically sustainable future depends on a large-scale increase in environmentally responsible behavior (ERB) and a global decrease in environmentally harmful behavior (EHB). Some behaviors degrade the environment, while others protect our Mother Earth. Indeed, the sustainability of our planet is inextricably linked to human behavior. Consider the issues that confront and challenge environmental resources: overpopulation; climate change; loss of biodiversity; inadequate access to water; ocean acidification; pollution; ozone layer depletion; the extinction of many fish species; and deforestation.

Applied behavioral science (ABS) can play a crucial role in addressing our environmental crises. Almost three decades ago, B. F. Skinner[1] defined this crisis elegantly and succinctly:

> Most thoughtful people agree that the world is in serious trouble ... fossil fuels will not last forever, and many other critical resources are nearing exhaustion; the earth grows steadily less habitable; and all this is exacerbated by a burgeoning population that resists control. The timetable may not be clear, but the threat is real. That many people have begun to find a recital of these dangers tiresome is perhaps an even greater threat.

Some claim our environmental crisis has reached proportions beyond salvation; others maintain a relentless optimism regarding planetary concerns. A "business as usual" stance has been adopted in some quarters (as if environmental problems will correct themselves naturally); others believe high-technology engineering, physics, biology, and chemistry will rescue us.

Today, organizations and individuals routinely incorporate "green" or pro-environment ideas into their language, but the rhetoric has not resulted in large-scale actively caring behaviors on behalf of Mother Earth. Or noticeably positive results. We have a problem of environmental sustainability and a problem of human denial, helplessness, and apathy.[2]

Current theories and intervention approaches need to be considered (which are reviewed in this chapter) if the three main sources of the earth's environmental threats are to be effectively addressed – human overpopulation, *over*consumption, and *under*conservation.

In his *Psychology: An Introduction* textbook, Lahey lists these psychological barriers to sustaining a healthy ecology: (a) denial; (b) bad habits; (c) diffusion of responsibility (as in bystander apathy introduced in Chapter 2); (d) lack of self-efficacy (i.e., not believing one's actions can make a difference); and (e) short-term self-interest (or the reality that human behavior is guided by immediate and certain consequences, whereas ecological sustainability usually requires some inconvenience, discomfort, and financial costs to reap distant and uncertain benefits).[3] Each barrier relates directly or indirectly to the theories, interventions, and recommendations we review here.

Interventions to actively care for Mother Earth are grounded in behaviorism and humanism. As explained in Chapter 1, behaviorists study overt behavior and its observable environmental, social, and physiological manifestations. As behavior is determined by its consequences, behaviors can be changed by altering those consequences. Humanists argue that behavior is determined by internal attitudes, beliefs, and values, and behavior change can be achieved by targeting these internal states by reasoning with people or appealing to their guilt or "social conscience."

In general, behaviorism offers the technology (practical tools and observable practices or "hardware") for changing behaviors and attitudes in pro-environment directions, and humanism addresses the attitudes, expectancies, or person-states people need (the internal "software") to increase their propensity to use behavioral technology for environmental protection. Combine these approaches and you have *humanistic behaviorism* – the academic theme of this book. Each of the theories relating to behaviorism and humanism that follow is relevant to the development of large-scale and long-term community and organizational programs to increase ERB and decrease EHB.

THEORETICAL AND EMPIRICAL FOUNDATIONS

The AC4P Model

More than two decades ago, I proposed integrating behavioral and humanistic perspectives by reviewing behavior-change techniques applicable to ecological sustainability and by suggesting that certain dispositions or person-states increase the probability of people performing ERB.[4] The occurrence of ERB partly depends on people having certain person-states. As discussed in Chapter 2, I use the term *person-state* rather than *personality trait* to reflect the malleability of these human characteristics; personality *traits* are generally assumed to remain stable over time. Person-*states* can benefit from particular interpersonal and contextual factors (including education and training), and they can increase an individual's propensity to perform AC4P behavior on behalf of ecological sustainability or environmental conservation.

These five person-states were defined in Chapter 2 (see Figure 2.9) and are human dynamics discussed frequently by humanists but rarely by behaviorists. The potential to integrate behaviorism and humanism can be realized by this truism: Operations and contingencies developed and evaluated by behavioral scientists can influence the person-states defined and appreciated by humanists. In Chapter 2, I proposed these states (or personality dispositions) influence one's propensity to emit AC4P behavior, which includes performing ERBs and serving as an intervention agent who motivates others to actively care for Mother Earth.

These AC4P principles have been combined with ABS and are the foundation of various topical interventions, including an effective bully-prevention process implemented throughout an elementary school,[5] a large-scale effort to promote peace and reduce interpersonal conflict,[6] and an injury-prevention program at several industrial sites[7] (see Chapter 9). The AC4P model is also reflected in each of the chapters in this application portion of the book.

Empirical research supports certain components of the AC4P model. Specifically, Roberts and Geller[8] found that employees who scored higher on measures of self-esteem and group cohesion (i.e., belongingness) were more likely to give and/or receive an actively caring thank you card (Figure 2.6) that recognized workers for performing discretionary safety-related behaviors. Geller and colleagues also showed that measures of workers' personal control and group cohesion correlated directly with employees' reported willingness to perform AC4P behavior.[9] Plus, Allen and Ferrand found one's perception of personal control to be a strong predictor of ERB.[10]

Self-Determination Theory

The second theory reviewed here is self-determination theory (SDT). This theory rests on the notion that people have needs for competency (self-efficacy), autonomy (personal control or choice), and relatedness (belongingness or community). These human needs are presumed to direct and motivate our behavior.[11] Note that SDT is the same as the self-motivation person-states discussed and illustrated in Chapter 3.

A distinction between various modes of motivation representing differences along the spectrum of autonomy versus control was proposed by Deci and colleagues.[12] *External regulation* is lowest on the scale of autonomy. This refers to a person's behavior being driven exclusively by external if–then rewards or penalties. *Interjected motivation* occurs when one performs a certain behavior due to socially driven, internal consequences (e.g., in order to feel proud of oneself or to avoid the shame and guilt of *not* performing the behavior).

Identified motivation is the most autonomous of the levels of *extrinsic motivation*. Here an individual performs a behavior because it's consistent with one's personal values. *Intrinsic motivation*, on the other hand, is present when a behavior is satisfying and enjoyable because of its natural or inherent consequences.[12] These motivations and needs can predict the occurrence of ERB.

The relationship between ERB and internal motives was reported by De Young in a series of studies.[13] Competence, frugality, and participation were three types of internal motives investigated. No single motive was found to be optimal for promoting ERB, but De Young did note the importance of harnessing the human urge toward competence.[14] Each type of personal satisfaction investigated can be reframed as issues of personal competence (relating to self-efficacy and personal control in the AC4P model). Give individuals a context in which they can feel competent and the result will likely benefit the promotion and maintenance of ERB.

Osbaldiston's meta-analysis of the ERB literature examined results from experiments that tested SDT empirically.[15] Of the four types of motivation included in this theory (external, interjected, identified, and internal), Osbaldiston found only *identified* motivation to significantly relate to occurrences of ERB. Since identified motivation implies individuals perform a behavior because they value or identify with its importance, increasing individuals' perceptions of the personal importance or relevance of a targeted ERB should benefit AC4P interventions to benefit Mother Earth.

Theory of Planned Behavior

The third theory reviewed here, Ajzen's theory of planned behavior (TPB), has also been applied to ERB.[16] We need to consider three components – attitude toward the behavior (Is the target ERB evaluated favorably?), subjective norm (What do important others think about the ERB?), and perceived control (Do I have control over performing this ERB?) – when predicting an individual's behavior, according to this theory. Perceived control is also referred to as self-efficacy in Bandura's social cognitive theory,[17] and it dovetails nicely with self-efficacy and personal control in the AC4P model.

The weak relationship between environmental concern and ERB could be explained by TPB, Bamberg concluded.[18] How we interpret specific situations and our resulting perceptions affect our level of concern for the environment and predict the likelihood of ERB. The intentions of those highly concerned about the environment align closely to situation-specific issues; the intentions of those with low levels of concern related closely to perceptions about social norms. This suggests interventions for highly concerned individuals should target perceived empowerment, and interventions for minimally concerned individuals should target social norms or feelings of belongingness. A notable limitation of Bamberg's study: It relied on self-reporting for most of the measures, and the ERB in question was merely a request for additional pro-environment information (i.e., asking for a brochure on green energy).

A goal-directed extension of Ajzen's TPB[19] was applied by Carrus, Passafaro, and Bonnes to promote ERB.[20] Attitudes, perceived behavioral control, frequency of past behavior, subjective norms, anticipated emotions, desire, and other factors were evaluated to predict ERB intention. The use of public transportation was addressed in one study, and the other focused on household recycling. The results of both suggest designers of future eco-friendly interventions should consider the impact of anticipated emotional experiences, which can be affected by marketing campaigns that link desired behaviors with people's positive emotional experiences or expectations.

Competence Theory

The fourth theory to consider is competence theory. Focusing on altruism as a key motive for performing an ERB is problematic, Kaplan proposed, because such behavior is seen as sacrificial and not in one's self-interest.[21] According to De Young, presuming "humans are egocentric gain-maximizers" with no concern for ecological sustainability saps the potential internal motivation derived from ERB.[22] Both perspectives subscribe to the theory that our human concern for competence is a primary source of motivation.

This desire for competence is self-initiating and self-rewarding, White argues; and behaviors relating to a sense of competence are highly focused activities that are inherently reinforcing.[14] This notion is quite similar to self-efficacy theory.[17] It also bears resemblance to the AC4P model, which in addition to self-efficacy includes two other concepts directly linked to perceived competency – personal control[23] and optimism.[24]

Kaplan refers to the issue of competence as the "reasonable person model."[21] He assumes "reasonable" people are motivated to know, to understand what is going on, to learn, to discover, and to participate. They work to avoid feeling incompetent or helpless. Given this, ERB interventions should focus on increasing competence, maintaining personal control, and avoiding perceptions of helplessness.

If you presume people are naturally motivated to make a positive difference, as Kaplan does, it's not necessary to call on guilt or sacrifice to get people to actively care for our Mother Earth. Participating in pro-ecology activities can satisfy a basic human need – the need for competence.[14]

(Recall the discussion of competence in Chapter 3 as a key determinant of self-motivation.)

Social Labeling

The fifth theory reviewed here is social labeling, as introduced in Chapter 6 with the social influence principle of consistency. Can ERB be promoted by social labeling? This hypothesis was tested by Cornelissen and colleagues.[25] By giving people's spontaneous behaviors high environmental relevance, the probability of future ERBs recurring from these individuals can be increased. For example, telling someone s/he is "very concerned with the environment and is ecologically conscious" because s/he has chosen an energy-efficient and nonpolluting product can cause that person, who might have been motivated by nonenvironmental reasons, to attribute the ERB to being "environmentally conscious." This social labeling has a beneficial impact on ERB: people whose actions are labeled "ecologically conscious" are more likely to display ERB in a subsequent situation.

The level of social attention paid to a particular ERB can influence the occurrence of another ERB, as a series of experiments documented.[26] People normally do not consider their behavior to be environmentally conscious when an ERB is relatively commonplace (e.g., recycling). Emphasizing the pro-environmental relevance of a routine ERB can lead people to view their ERB as reflecting a pro-environmental self-image. This is consistent with self-perception theory.[27] The result: People see themselves as environmentally responsible and perform additional ERBs in order to be consistent with the social label.

Community-Based Social Marketing

The sixth theory we consider is the marketing theory of perceived consumer effectiveness, which suggests that prosocial or AC4P behavior is determined by the perceived beneficial impact of the behavior. Ellen and colleagues attempted to empirically separate perceived consumer *effectiveness* from other constructs of *social consciousness*.[28] They argued that social consciousness makes a unique contribution to the promotion of ERB. They found individuals who believe their actions will have a pro-environmental impact are more willing to accept the cost of ERB, according to a survey of 387 residents, age 21 or older, of a major metropolitan area in southeastern United States. This suggests that interventions to promote ERB should persuade individuals of the *potential* beneficial impact of their ERB, as well as provide supportive feedback regarding the *actual* benefits of their ERB.

Merely providing information is insufficient to motivate people to perform ERB (see Chapter 1). Artz and Cooke[29] used social-marketing techniques (i.e., an application of social-influence principles, Chapter 6) to develop an email campaign among employees at the Department of Environmental Protection for the state of Maine. An ERB advocate within the department sent a series of emails requesting commitment, follow-up, and feedback about four different ERBs. Increases in the frequency of all four target ERBs were found, with greater changes in those ERBs easier to perform and having no financial cost to the consumer.

This email intervention removed two barriers to performing ERB: (a) lack of information and instructional knowledge, which were addressed by the email newsletter; and (b) failure of the ERB to achieve social-norm status, which the newsletter addressed by emphasizing the "green power" of other individuals.

Recognizing that information-intensive campaigns alone fail to foster ERB, McKenzie-Mohr proposed a community-based social-marketing model for the large-scale promotion of environmental sustainability.[30] This approach merged principles from ABS and social marketing[31] to maximize the community-wide dissemination and impact of behavior-change techniques.

The following procedural steps were included in his approach: (1) select potential ERBs to target; (2) identify the barriers associated with each of the potential actions, and decide whether resources and strategies are available to remove these barriers; (3) on the basis of an analysis of these barriers, decide which ERB to target with an intervention; (4) design an intervention process to overcome the identified barriers to the target ERB; (5) pilot the behavior-change program on a small scale to identify the most cost-effective approach and refine specific strategies; (6) implement the refined intervention throughout the community; and (7) evaluate changes in the target ERB, as well as actual environmental impact (e.g., decreases in electricity or water consumption) and participants' opinions of the intervention program.

Summary

From this review of six eco-relevant theories, the following points emerge as elements of a successful intervention to promote ERB: (a) associate the target ERB with positive emotional experiences;[20] (b) use social norms for individuals with low concern and apply situational issues for individuals with high concern;[18] (c) apply social-labeling techniques to help people identify themselves as environmentally conscious;[25] and (d) highlight the beneficial impact (or consequences) of specific ERBs.[28]

No single approach reviewed here has demonstrated significant durable impact on environmental sustainability. Greater attention must be given to developing ABS technology that can support both ERB and relevant AC4P person-states over the long term. Let's review prior ABS research in this area in order to realize what it might take to advance applications of ABS principles on behalf of Mother Earth.

INTERVENING TO INCREASE ECOLOGICAL SUSTAINABILITY

Let's go back to the first Earth Day in the spring of 1970, when behavioral scientists began implementing ABS interventions to protect the environment. They followed the basic activator-behavior-consequence scheme (the ABC model) introduced in Chapter 1. The basic premise: Activators direct behavior and consequences motivate behavior. Given that behaviors are motivated by the consequences they deliver, understanding the expected consequences of an individual's ERB will enable AC4P intervention designers to predict whether that individual will perform the ERB.

Activators

Activators for environmental protection have taken the form of (a) written or spoken messages (e.g., films, television commercials, promotional fliers, verbal reminders, and road signs); (b) awareness or education sessions; (c) behavioral modeling or demonstrations (e.g., on videotape or by live exemplars); (d) goal setting (to reach certain individual or group process outcomes relevant to environmental conservation); (e) commitment techniques (e.g., signing a promise card to perform a particular ERB); and (f) engineering and design techniques to make a desired ERB more salient or convenient (e.g., adding decorated trash receptacles or recycling bins to a setting).

A wealth of field research has evaluated the impact of activator techniques on various ERBs. Generally, activators alone (without consequences) were effective at increasing the frequency of an ERB when the instructions were behavior-specific and given in close physical and temporal proximity with opportunities to exhibit the target ERB, and when performing the

ERB was relatively easy and convenient (e.g., like turning off lights in unoccupied rooms, using a particular trash receptacle or recycling container, or purchasing drinks in returnable bottles).[32]

When the target ERB is perceived as relatively time-consuming, costly or otherwise inconvenient to perform, a behavior-change intervention usually requires extrinsic or extra consequences in order to have a substantial impact. A notable exception has been the application of *promise-card commitment* activators introduced in Chapter 4. Field researchers have markedly increased participation in community recycling programs by asking residents to sign cards promising their participation.[33]

Activator by Design

This section covers engineering design techniques to activate ERB. Here I present more specifics about the experimental design, data collection, and results than for any of the other intervention studies. My rationale: (a) These were among the earliest field studies of ERB; (b) The results were straightforward, socially valid, and robust; (c) Remarkable behavioral impact of simple environmental changes was demonstrated; (d) The ERB impact of these simple design changes could be sustained as long as the design changes remained in place; (e) The data from one field study activated a large-scale positive environmental change throughout a shopping mall; and (f) This type of field research was extremely rare among behavioral scientist in the 1970s and laid the foundation for *behavioral community psychology* – the systematic evaluation of public behavior to develop and refine community-based interventions for increasing the frequency of behaviors that benefit public health, safety, and/or well-being.[34]

Figure 19.1 depicts a special trash receptacle designed in 1976 to commemorate the U.S. bicentennial.[35] In one field study, my students placed litter in front of this receptacle and in front of the standard 50-gallon trash can on our university campus. As expected, significantly more people passing by these receptacles stopped to pick up the litter in front of the eagle receptacle. But the number of passers-by who stopped to pick up the litter was disappointingly small in both conditions (i.e., 15 of 407 passing the eagle vs. 1 of 329 passing the standard trash can).

In another field study at an indoor shopping mall, my students weighed the trash deposited in six trash receptacles three times a week for forty-one consecutive weeks.[36] For a seven-week intervention phase, we replaced two of the standard 50-gallon trash cans with attractive bird receptacles; one was an eagle (as depicted in Figure 19.1) and the other was shaped and painted to represent

FIGURE 19.1. The eagle-shaped trash receptacle.

a cardinal – the state bird of Virginia. These bird receptacles were 4.5 feet tall and had the same 50-gallon capacity as the standard trash cans in the mall. Boldly printed on the side of each bird receptacle was the message, "Please be a litter bit thoughtful," and on the front of these two receptacles was placed a "Keep America Clean" emblem in bright red, white, and blue colors.

In this study, the clear behavioral influence of the bird receptacles was shown by the substantially smaller quantity of litter in the vicinity of the two bird receptacles and the significantly greater amount of litter in the bird receptacles than in the 50-gallon unobtrusive trash cans. The overall weekly contents of the six trash receptacles weighed 15.5lb. per bird receptacle versus 9.34lb. per standard trash can.

In a third field study at the same indoor shopping mall, we installed a speaker and amplifier system inside the eagle receptacle and connected it to a microphone 20 feet away. When I talked into the microphone, the sound came from the eagle. I attempted to activate trash-can use by remarking, "Help, please feed me with litter." Then, when a passer-by put trash in the opening, I announced, "Thank you for caring for the environment."

Obviously, this verbal activator from the eagle turned lots of heads in the mall. When litter was placed in the vicinity of this special trash receptacle,

FIGURE 19.2. Ash tray (left) and trash can (right) with results of improper disposal behavior.

passers-by (especially children) were quick to respond to my "Feed me" prompt. It was also reinforcing to see people's positive reactions to the "Thank you" consequence. Besides turning their heads and smiling, many said something nice to another person, even a stranger, like "Isn't that cool?", "What a great way to keep our environment clean," or "There should be more trash cans like that."

Next we placed a tape recorder inside the eagle receptacle that gave a "Thank you for pitching in" verbal consequence whenever the lid to the can was pushed. Unfortunately, the tape recorder was stolen after three days. Today's technology can put this ABC contingency in place with minimal expense to automate an intermittent "Feed me" activator and a response-contingent "Thank you" consequence. A problem with our low-tech design – the verbal message occurred whenever the lid was pushed, whether or not trash was deposited – could be overcome readily with contemporary technology.

While conducting these field studies, we noticed consistent misuse of the standard trash cans and the receptacles designed for ash-tray litter (i.e., cigarette and cigar butts and matches). Figure 19.2 shows photographs of these two types of trash receptacles, and indicates that people placed paper trash on ash trays and smokers used the lids of the trash cans to put out their cigarettes or cigars. Remember, these field observations occurred in 1976 when cigarette smoking was the norm, and proper disposal of cigarette and cigar butts was a noticeable environmental issue. Improper disposal could also cause a fire.

I contacted some students and faculty in Virginia Tech's College of Architecture with an idea for a trash receptacle that enabled convenient disposal of both cigarette/cigar trash and other litter (e.g., paper, packaging material, and beverage containers) in the same receptacle. This ash-tray/

FIGURE 19.3. The ash-tray\trash-can combo designed for this research.

trash-can combo is depicted in Figure 19.3. The design is quite common these days. However, in 1976, I had never seen it before, and no such receptacle was available in our university community in Blacksburg.

On forty-eight consecutive evenings my students systematically collected, counted, and categorized as appropriate or inappropriate all daily disposals in the three trash-can receptacles: (1) the regular ash tray, which looked identical to the regular trash cans, except the flip-top trash-can cover was replaced by a sand-filled pan; (2) the regular ash tray positioned next to the standard trash can, and (3) the specially designed ash-tray/trash-can combo pictured in Figure 19.3.

The results: A significant direct relationship was found between frequency of appropriate ash-tray disposals and the proximity of the ash tray to a trash can.[36] Table 19.1 shows the daily averages of appropriate versus inappropriate ash-tray disposals for the three ash-tray settings. These data convinced the mall manager to adopt the combo receptacle for exclusive use throughout the shopping mall.

Consequences

Let's continue our review of ABS principles applicable to actively caring for Mother Earth. As defined in Chapter 1, incentives and disincentives

TABLE 19.1. *Average frequency of ash-tray contents per day*

Ash-tray/trash-can Proximity	Appropriate disposals[a]	Inappropriate disposals[b]
Ash-tray/trash-can combo	22.19	2.64
Ash tray next to trash can	7.67	7.56
Ash tray alone	3.17	16.33

[a] Cigarette and cigar butts, matches.

[b] Paper, candy, peanut shells, toothpicks, gum, cans, bottles, straws, pull tops, cups and covers, other inorganic matter, other organic matter.

are activators that announce the availability of a rewarding or a penalizing consequence, respectively, in order to motivate a designated behavior. Traditionally, local, state, and federal governments have used disincentives and penalties to motivate ERB. These attempts to protect the environment usually take the form of ordinances or laws (e.g., fines for littering, illegal dumping, using excessive water, or polluting of land, water, or air).

To be effective, disincentive/penalty interventions usually require extensive promotion (activators) and enforcement (consequences). As discussed in Chapter 1, behavioral scientists have deemphasized this approach because negative affect, feelings, or attitudes typically accompany attempts to mandate behavior change through disincentive/penalty tactics. Plus, the enforcement approach can stifle self-motivation, as detailed in Chapter 3.[37]

Rewarding Consequences. The reward contingencies implemented for environmental protection have been diverse. Some rewards have been given after the performance of a desired ERB; others have been contingent upon a particular outcome (e.g., for reaching a designated level of environmental cleanliness, energy conservation, or water savings). The rewards themselves have varied widely; they include monetary rebates, verbal commendations, merchandise discount coupons, raffle tickets, self-photographs, soft drinks, and recognition on an "energy efficient" honor roll.

The U.S. Environmental Protection Agency (EPA) uses both negative enforcement contingencies (monetary penalties for, e.g., violations of the Clean Air Act and the Clean Water Act) and positive rewards, such as its voluntary "Energy Star" program (started in 1992 and cofounded by the Department of Energy), which recognizes energy efficiency products, new homes, commercial buildings, and industrial plants.[38]

Several documents have shown that most reward contingencies produce dramatic increases in the targeted ERB; but unfortunately, the ERB usually returned to pre-intervention baseline levels when the reward contingency was withdrawn.[32] Most of the intervention phases in this research were relatively short term, though, and likely did not allow sufficient time for natural consequences such as social approval, media recognition, or visible environmental improvement to gain control. Still, many of the rewarding consequences (e.g., raffle coupons for prizes donated by community merchants) were inexpensive enough to keep in place for long period of time.

In some cases it's cost-effective to maintain a consequence strategy indefinitely. Consider, for example, the if–then incentive programs that offer financial refunds for the return of certain beverage containers when individuals turn in returnable bottles or cans at a designated location instead of throwing them in the trash. Plus, many feedback strategies are inexpensive and effective, and do not have to be withdrawn.

Feedback Techniques. Most of the feedback research on ecological sustainability has addressed residential energy consumption, and the feedback has usually gone to residents.[39] The more labor-intensive procedures included the delivery of feedback cards showing the amount of kilowatt-hours or cubic feet of gas used (and the cost) for a particular time period. Today, technology is available to deliver this sort of feedback directly and automatically to homes equipped with appropriate displays.

Analogous devices have been tested and have shown much promise for dramatic energy savings. Among these are a hygrothermograph that gives continuous readings of room temperatures and humidity, an electronic feedback meter with a digital display of electricity cost per hour, a special device with a light that illuminates whenever electricity use exceeds 90 percent of a household's peak level, and a fuel-flow meter that displays continuous miles-per-gallon or gallons-per-hour consumption of gasoline during vehicle travel.

Building on the social-influence research reviewed in Chapter 6, intervention studies have used social feedback to encourage energy conservation.[40] In one field study, researchers found that providing residents feedback about the average household energy used in their neighborhood attracted attention like a magnet. Households that used more than average electricity started reducing their energy consumption, while households that used less energy than average increased their consumption.[41]

Similarly, hotel guests were more likely to reuse their towels when they received a message indicating the majority of former guests reused them.[42] These studies support the belongingness person-state of the AC4P model; people will change their behavior in ways that maintain or increase a sense of peer support or community.

LARGE-SCALE INTERVENTION IMPACT

To achieve a sustainable ecology, large-scale changes in behavior are needed in various settings. As we've seen, substantial research has demonstrated the beneficial impact of applying the basic ABC contingency of ABS (i.e., activator-behavior-consequence). However, there have been few large-scale applications of any of these behavior-change strategies for ecological sustainability. The direct behavioral approach is clearly the most cost-effective strategy for increasing occurrences of ERB and decreasing the frequency of EHB,[43] but this approach has only recently started to produce large-scale benefits. Let's consider reasons for this lack of impact and ways to overcome these barriers.

Who Is the Audience?

Most of the research relating to eco-sustainability is published in professional journals and books read almost exclusively by other psychologists. The authors present convincing demonstrations of the efficacy of their behavior-change techniques almost exclusively to an audience of people who have little interest or influence in large-scale dissemination and application of the interventions. The critical social-marketing aspects of behavior-change technology have not been adequately addressed.[31]

Bailey comments on this dissemination problem: "We have a great science (the experimental analysis of behavior) and a pretty good technology (applied behavior analysis) but no product development or marketing."[44] He explains further that "we do not value marketing" and have "neglected to develop socially acceptable terminology for presenting our concepts to consumers ... we have, in our zest for science and technology, taken the human concerns out of behavior analysis."[44] This commentary, presented more than twenty-five years ago, sets the stage for the academic theme of this book – *humanistic behaviorism.*

Even when the right audience is reached, the question remains whether the general public will provide sufficient support and participation to justify implementation of eco-friendly interventions. Individuals may not share scientists' sense of urgency when it comes to combating environmental problems.[45] For instance, despite growing evidence of the need to address climate change through the collaborative efforts of countries around the world, skepticism still exists regarding the severity and urgency of this issue.

Interestingly, skepticism about climate change seems most prevalent among prosperous white males who stand to lose most through efforts to reduce lavish consumer consumption of energy resources, suggesting that many climate-change beliefs are self-serving.[46]

On a related note, Li, Johnson, and Zaval found people are less likely to believe in global warming on unusually cold days, but they are more likely to believe in global warming on relatively hot days (despite the fact that local temperature is unrelated to global temperature).[47] People's level of environmental concern is often lower than warranted by scientific consensus. This may prevent the public from seeing the benefits of ERB, making it difficult to garner support for relevant AC4P "green" interventions.

What Behaviors Are Targeted?

Another barrier to eco-caring could be the selection of a target ERB to change. Oskamp, for example, identified overpopulation and overconsumption as the key threats to ecological sustainability – not litter control or recycling, which have been prime ERB targets for applied behavioral scientists.[48] Stern and Gardner distinguish between *curtailment* ERB (such as reducing consumption) and *efficiency* ERB (reducing the resource consumption of equipment and machinery).[49] They emphasize people can do more to save environmental resources by purchasing energy-efficient vehicles and water heaters than by carpooling or reducing showering time.

Efficiency ERBs require a onetime purchase of an environmentally responsible product (e.g., from vehicles and major appliances to home heating and cooling systems), while curtailment ERB typically involves repeated inconvenient or sacrificial action (e.g., from carpooling and collecting recyclables to reducing water use and adjusting thermostats). The early applications of behavioral science to ecological sustainability did not target one-shot efficiency ERB. And this trend has continued to the present,[50] despite the recommendation of Gardner and Stern more than two decades ago to focus interventions on efficiency ERB.[51]

Osbaldiston's meta-analysis of sixty-two studies on the promotion of ERB examined the types of interventions employed, the ERB targeted, the potential moderators of successful interventions, and the applicability of various theoretical interpretations.[15] The greatest behavioral benefits were found for interventions that included a commitment or goal-setting strategy. Similar to Lehman and Geller,[50] Osbaldiston found the ERB targeted was often the easiest to manipulate and measure (such as litter control and recycling), rather than ERB with the greatest potential impact (such as pollution control and climate change).

The ERB targeted with ABS largely related to recycling and energy conservation. Osbaldiston suggests future intervention studies related to ecological sustainability should address ERB not previously targeted and apply commitment and goal-setting interventions that have been used relatively infrequently to increase the occurrence of ERB.[15]

Who Should Change?

Efficiency ERB requires efficiency options, and such availability is greatly determined by the policies of organizations and local, state, and federal governments. Stern and Gardner emphasize, "Corporations make a greater direct contribution to environmental problems than individuals, and it is worth examining whether more can be done to alleviate these problems by modifying corporate rather than individual behavior."[52] Thirteen years later, Stern made the same point, reminding us: "Organizations usually do more to degrade the environment than individuals and households,"[53] and "If manufacturers adopt 'greener' production technologies and product designs, this will further increase the potential to help solve environmental problems without sacrificing well-being."[54]

THE MAINTENANCE CHALLENGE

All of the applications of ABS designed to increase the frequency of ERB have been short-term demonstration projects, conducted to show that a particular intervention procedure had a desired effect. Methods to sustain the environmental impact of a behavior-change technique have not been systematically addressed. This is not critical for onetime efficiency ERB, but is obviously necessary for the regular repetition of curtailment ERB.

Boyce and Geller addressed this challenge of response maintenance by reviewing the research literature related to applying ABS to occupational safety.[55] They found no systematic study of factors related to the successful institutionalization of an effective behavior-change process. However, they did identify factors conducive to sustaining a successful behavior-change process, and these have been verified by practitioners.[56] The following factors have contributed to the long-term impact of ABS interventions in industrial settings:

- Workers at each level of an organization (from management to line workers) need education and training to understand the rationale behind a behavior-focused intervention and to realize their specific roles in making the process work.

- Indigenous staff need to implement the intervention procedures and have substantial input into the design of an ABS intervention.
- A formal accountability system is required, which is best handled by an employee-manned steering committee that monitors intervention results and develops action plans for enhancing intervention benefits.
- A formal procedure for collecting, reviewing, and using behavioral results is needed to support the accountability system and enable continuous improvement.
- Group and individual rewards are needed to support ongoing participation in the process, as well as to recognize exemplary accomplishments.

These conclusions (see Chapter 9 for applications for occupational safety) are certainly relevant to sustaining environmental-protection interventions, especially in organizational settings, which should be a prime target.[57] Direct behavior-change approaches are most cost-effective over the short term, but they may not be the best strategy for long-term environmental sustainability.

It's important to persuade the right audience to adopt and maintain an ERB, but there are inherent problems with direct persuasion. Aronson suggested indirect or self-persuasion is necessary for durable behavior change, and substantial empirical research supports this viewpoint.[58] As indicated in Chapter 1, advertisers use direct persuasion, but they do not request behavior that is inconvenient or difficult to perform. Usually, the purpose of an advertisement is only to persuade a consumer to select a certain brand of merchandise.

Ecology-sustaining behavior is usually more inconvenient and requires more effort than choosing one brand over another. It often requires significant adjustment in a highly practiced and regular routine at work, at home, or on the road. Adopting a pro-environment way of doing something might first require eliminating an efficient and convenient habit that wastes environmental resources. Plus, participation in an ecology-sustaining effort usually requires the regular performance of several inconvenient ERBs.

Consequently, direct persuasion might not be the most effective approach to increasing the frequency of ERB. Since other people are not usually around to hold us accountable for selecting the most pro-environment behavior available, we need to hold ourselves accountable. We need to view ERB as consistent with our perception of ourselves to sustain behavior change. We need to perceive ourselves as pro-environment and ecology-sustaining. I'm talking about *indirect persuasion*, which was introduced in Chapter 1.

Indirect Persuasion

Empirical research supports the notion that self-persuasion is more likely to occur within an individual when the extrinsic control of an ABC contingency is less obvious or perhaps indirect. When there are sufficient external consequences to justify the amount of effort required for an ERB, the performer does not develop an internal justification for the behavior. There is no self-persuasion,[58] and performing the behavior does not alter self-perception.[27] In these circumstances, maintenance of ERB is unlikely, unless it's possible to keep a sufficient accountability system in place over the long term (e.g., incentives or disincentives, or a feedback contingency).

The Hypocrisy Effect

Which of the following intervention conditions will produce the most desirable change in behavior and attitude? (a) *Awareness* – participants receive a clear and persuasive rationale about the need to conserve water in their community; (b) *Awareness + Commitment* – participants receive the convincing rationale and then publicly sign a pledge card, promising to use less water for one month, particularly when bathing or taking showers; or (c) *Commitment + Hypocrisy* – participants publicly sign the pledge card to use less water for one month and then list the recent occasions on which they used more water than necessary, from bathing and showering to watering their gardens and washing their cars.

The first condition represents the typical education approach to persuading people to perform a particular ERB. I bet basic intuition tells you the second condition will be more influential than the first. Recall the reference to promise-card commitment as an effective activator of an ERB. The principle of consistency is in effect here, as explained in Chapter 6.

You should expect more water conservation under the Awareness + Commitment intervention condition than with Awareness only. When people make a public statement to do something, they encounter both personal and social pressures to follow through. But behavioral research has shown the third condition – Commitment + Hypocrisy – to be the most influential in motivating ERB.

Aronson and colleagues timed the showers taken by female college students after they experienced one of the three intervention conditions listed above. The results: The girls who made a commitment to conserving water and then listed circumstances in which they wasted water (i.e., Commitment + Hypocrisy condition) took significantly shorter showers than the girls who experienced the other two intervention conditions.[58]

These researchers replicated this hypocrisy effect in two additional studies – one targeting resource recycling and the other addressing the use of condoms among sexually active college males. As with the water conservation study, hypocrisy was induced by having participants publicly commit to taking a certain course of action and then complete an exercise that reminded the participants of their failures to perform in accordance with their commitment. In both studies, the Hypocrisy condition influenced more of the desired behavior – recycling and the purchase and use of condoms – than the Awareness or Commitment condition.[58]

Why does this kind of intervention influence more behavior change than standard awareness and commitment procedures? Consider the consistency principle and the notion of indirect or self-persuasion explained above. Given people's desire to keep their words in line with their actions and vice versa, having people remind themselves of an inconsistency between what they say they will do and what they actually did leads to internal conflict or tension. Social psychologists call this *cognitive dissonance*, as introduced in Chapter 6.[59]

This internal tension or cognitive dissonance is not a pleasant state. It challenges one's personal integrity. How can such tension be reduced and a sense of integrity restored? Easy – simply change your behavior to make it consistent with the commitment. The important point here is that evoking this tension by prompting people to perceive an inconsistency between personal commitment and action led to more desired behavior change than a standard awareness or commitment intervention. Does this inspire any ideas for increasing the impact of your next attempt to persuade others to perform a certain ERB?

Applying the Hypocrisy Effect to ERB. Suppose you ask people to commit publicly to performing a particular ERB, and then ask people to think of times when their behavior has been inconsistent with their commitment. Your objective is to stir up feelings of being hypocritical or inconsistent. Of course, you need to obtain the initial commitment, and that could be a challenge in some situations. However, it should not be difficult to get people to state openly that they care about environmental conservation or sustainability. You might even persuade some that actively caring for our planet should be a *core* value.

Such value statements about Mother Earth voiced publicly might be a sufficient commitment to establish a context for the hypocrisy effect. Now ask the participants who claim environmental sustainability as a value to list things they do daily that are inconsistent with holding ERB as a value. Should this list be private or public? That's an empirical question in need of research.

Suppose it's possible to create *group* tension by obtaining group consensus that ERB is a value and then listing specific behaviors observed by group members that are inconsistent with ERB as a value. Would such a group exercise lead to a group hypocrisy effect – with team members motivated to reduce the group tension by adjusting their personal and interpersonal behaviors? Would this group application of the hypocrisy manipulation be more efficient and effective at increasing the occurrence of ERB than the individual approach used in the research literature? And how long will the beneficial behavioral impact of the hypocrisy effect last?

According to theory and some research comparing direct and indirect persuasion, the hypocrisy effect should facilitate self-persuasion and more long-term behavior change than more direct ABC attempts to influence ERB. Such direct comparisons of these divergent approaches are rare in the behavioral-intervention literature, and the need for intervention research in this domain is obvious.

Should Dispositions Be Considered?

A substantial amount of environmentally focused research has attempted to measure individual propensity to perform ERB. The construct reflecting a person's natural internal motivation to protect the environment has been termed *environmental concern,*[60] *ecological consciousness,*[61] *pro-environmental orientation,*[62] *ecological worldview,*[63] and *biospheric value orientation.*[64] It might be theoretically useful to search for person-states and traits that relate to the performance of ERB; this would allow matching specific intervention strategies to characteristics of the target audience.[65]

This is clearly a promising direction for developing more effective ways to promote and sustain ERB, and thereby actively care for our Mother Earth. Indeed, this is the basic rationale for combining humanism with behaviorism – *humanistic behaviorism.*

If a consistent pro-environment profile were identified (which has not happened yet), it might be possible to use this information to select AC4P agents for community-wide promotion of ERB. Or if individual difference variables were transient person-states (rather than permanent traits), it might be possible to move such states in a pro-environmental direction, as proposed by the AC4P model. These possibilities are far removed from current reality, however, and given our need for immediate large-scale promotion of ERB, the dispositional profile approach should be abandoned in favor of systematic searches for practical applications of ABS and AC4P principles to directly and indirectly increase and institutionalize ERB.

IN CONCLUSION

Each of the six theories reviewed at the beginning of this chapter is relevant for the development of large-scale and long-term community programs designed to increase the frequency of ERB and decrease the occurrence of EHB. Plus, the AC4P model and the self-determinism and competence theories were detailed in the opening chapters of this text (i.e., Chapters 2 and 3, respectfully) as fundamental to cultivating an AC4P culture. In addition, the various challenges to disseminating and implementing a behavior-change process and maintaining its effects need to be considered in the design of a far-reaching environmental-protection program. This chapter also presented several critical questions about intervention design (e.g., direct vs. indirect approaches) in dire need of behavior-based research.

External contingencies are not typically available for motivating ERB. It's often necessary to implement an ABS intervention process to motivate ERB on a large scale. However, to promote self-persuasion and self-accountability for long-term behavior change, it's critical for the ABC contingency of ABS to be strong enough to get an ERB started but not overly powerful to provide complete justification for the effort. This relates only to curtailment ERB – or pro-environment behavior that needs to be repeated regularly in order to substantially benefit ecological sustainability. In the case of one-shot ERB, a single extrinsic application of an ABC contingency can motivate the purchase of certain equipment or machinery, which saves environmental resources whenever it's used.

In sum, achieving an ecologically sustainable future involves the following ten steps:

1. Define specific curtailment and efficiency ERBs;
2. Order this list from most to least critical with regard to environmental impact;
3. Identify barriers related to each ERB and define ways to remove these barriers;

4. Decide on ERBs to target, considering resources available to remove certain barriers;

5. Develop and implement a process to instruct, support, and motivate the occurrence of each selected ERB;

6. If motivational contingencies must eventually be withdrawn, make them only strong enough to get the ERB started, but not powerful enough to provide complete justification for the effort and thereby hinder self-persuasion and perceptions of self-motivation for ecological sustainability;

7. Derive a marketing plan to disseminate and implement the behavior-change intervention on a large scale;

8. Involve community leaders and relevant stakeholders as much as possible in the various steps of the process, from selecting a target ERB and identifying relevant barriers to designing, supporting, and evaluating the behavior-change process;

9. Use the competence motive to initiate and maintain participation – refer to the target ERB as reflecting competence and personal control rather than self-sacrifice, and solicit social support to provide positive behavior-based recognition for those leading ERB efforts and performing ERB; and

10. Make allowances for the potential impact of the AC4P person-states to create the kind of personal dispositions that can increase an individual's propensity to perform a target ERB, and perhaps champion a community-based or organizational intervention process to promote and support a designated curtailment or efficiency ERB.

DISCUSSION QUESTIONS

1. Explain how social labeling (as introduced in Chapter 6) can influence ERB (environmentally responsible behavior).

2. Explain how the ABC model of ABS was applied to the design of an eagle-shaped trash receptacle.

3. How did the author and his students demonstrate the influence of convenience in people's disposal of trash-can versus ash-tray litter?

4. How have feedback techniques been used to increase the frequency of ERB?

5. Distinguish between curtailment ERB and efficiency ERB with real-world examples.

6. Discuss strategies for initiating and maintaining an ERB-promotion program in an organization.

7. Explain how hypocrisy was used as an activator by Eliot Aronson to influence ERB among college students.
8. How can the hypocrisy effect be explained by the Consistency Principle (introduced in Chapter 6)?
9. Explain the dispositional profile approach to increasing the frequency of ERB. Do you believe this approach is viable? Why or why not?
10. How should the overjustification effect be considered in the design of an intervention to increase the frequency of ERB?

REFERENCES

1. Skinner, B. F. (1987). *Upon further reflection.* Englewood Cliffs, NJ: Prentice Hall, p. 1.
2. Frantz, C. M., & Mayer, F. S. (2009). The emergency of climate change: Why are we failing to take action? *Analyses of Social Issues & Public Policy,* 9, 205–222.
3. Lahey, B. B. (2011). *Psychology: An introduction* (11th ed.). New York: McGraw-Hill.
4. Geller, E. S. (1995). Integrating behaviorism and humanism for environmental protection. *Journal of Social Issues,* 51, 179–195.
5. McCarty, S. M., & Geller, E. S. (2013). Actively caring to prevent bullying: Activating and rewarding prosocial behavior in elementary school. In E. S. Geller (Ed.). *Actively caring at your school: How to make it happen* (2nd ed.) (pp. 177–199). Newport, VA: Make-A-Difference, LLC; McCarty, S. M., & Geller, E. S. (2011). Want to get rid of bullying? Then reward behavior that is incompatible with it. *Behavior Analysis Digest International,* 23(2), 5–7.
6. McCarty, S. M., Teie, S., & Geller, E. S. (2011). *Redefining peace through an actively-caring perspective.* Technical report submitted to the Center for Peace Studies and Violence Prevention, Virginia Tech, Blacksburg, VA.
7. Geller, E. S., Bolduc, J. E., Foy, M. J., & Dean, J. (2012). In pursuit of an actively-caring safety culture: Practical methods, empirical results, and provocative implications. *Professional Safety,* 57(1), 44–50.
8. Roberts, D. S., & Geller, E. S. (1995). An "actively caring" model for occupational safety: A field test. *Applied and Preventive Psychology,* 4, 53–59.
9. Geller, E. S., Roberts, D. S., & Gilmore, M. R. (1996). Predicting propensity to actively care for occupational safety. *Journal of Safety Research,* 27, 1–8.
10. Allen, J. B., & Ferrand, J. L. (1999). Environmental locus of control, sympathy, and proenvironmental behavior: A test of Geller's actively caring hypothesis. *Environment and Behavior,* 31(3), 338–353.
11. Deci, E. L., & Ryan, R. M. (2002). *Handbook of self-determination research.* Rochester, NY: University of Rochester Press.
12. Moller, A. C., Deci, E. L., & Ryan, R. M. (2006). Choice and ego-depletion: The moderating role of autonomy. *Personality and Social Psychology Bulletin,* 32(8), 1024–1036.
13. De Young, R. (2000). Expanding and evaluating motives for environmentally responsible behavior. *Journal of Social Issues,* 56(3), 509–526.
14. White, R. W. (1959). Motivation reconsidered: The concept of competence. *Psychological Review,* 66, 297–333.

15. Osbaldiston, R. (2004). *Meta-analysis of the responsible environmental behavior literature*. Unpublished doctoral dissertation. University of Missouri–Columbia.
16. Ajzen, I. (1991). The theory of planned behavior. *Organizational Behavior and Human Decision Processes*, 50, 179–211.
17. Bandura, A. (1997). *Self-efficacy: The exercise of control*. New York: W.H. Freeman.
18. Bamberg, S. (2003). How does environmental concern influence specific environmentally related behaviors? A new answer to an old question. *Journal of Environmental Psychology*, 23(1), 21.
19. Perugini, M., & Bagozzi, R. P. (2001). The role of desires and anticipated emotions in goal-directed behaviours: Broadening and deepening the theory of planned behaviour. *British Journal of Social Psychology*, 40(1), 79–98.
20. Carrus, G., Passafaro, P., & Bonnes, M. (2008). Emotions, habits, and rational choices in ecological behaviours: The case of recycling and use of public transportation. *Journal of Environmental Psychology*, 28(1), 51–62.
21. Kaplan, S. (2000). Human nature and environmentally responsible behavior. *Journal of Social Issues*, 56, 491–508.
22. De Young, R. (2000). Expanding and evaluating motives for environmentally responsible behavior. *Journal of Social Issues*, 56(3), 514.
23. Rotter, J. B. (1966). Generalized expectancies for internal versus external control of reinforcement. *Psychological Monographs*, 80(1).
24. Seligman, M. E. (1991). *Learned optimism*. New York: Alfred A. Knopf.
25. Cornelissen, G., Dewitte, S., Warlop, L., & Yzerbyt, V. (2007). Whatever people say I am, that's what I am: Social labeling as a social marketing tool. *International Journal of Research in Marketing*, 24(4), 278–288.
26. Cornelissen, G., Pandelaere, M., Warlop, L., & Dewitte, S. (2008). Positive cueing: Promoting sustainable consumer behavior by cueing common environmental behaviors as environmental. *International Journal of Research in Marketing*, 25(1), 46–55.
27. Bem, D. J. (1972). Self-perception theory. In L. Berkowitz (Ed.). *Advances in experimental social psychology*, Vol. 6 (pp. 1–60). New York: Academic Press.
28. Ellen, P. S., Wiener, J. L., & Cobb-Walgren, C. (1991). The role of perceived consumer effectiveness in motivating environmentally conscious behaviors. *Journal of Public Policy & Marketing*, 10(2), 102–117.
29. Artz, N., & Cooke, P. (2007). Using e-mail listservs to promote environmentally sustainable behaviors. *Journal of Marketing Communications*, 13(4), 257–276.
30. McKenzie-Mohr, D. (2000). Fostering sustainable behavior through community-based social marketing. *American Psychologist*, 55, 531–537; McKenzie-Mohr, D. (2000). Promoting sustainable behavior: An introduction to community-based social marketing. *Journal of Social Issues*, 56(3), 543–554.
31. Geller, E. S. (1989). Applied behavior analysis and social marketing: An integration for environmental preservation. *Journal of Social Issues*, 45, 17–36.
32. Abrahamse, W., Steg, L., Vlek, C., & Rothengatter, T. (2005). A review of intervention studies aimed at household energy conservation. *Journal of Environmental Psychology*, 25, 273–291; Cone, J. D., & Hayes, S. C. (1980). *Environmental problems/behavioral solutions*. Monterey, CA: Brooks/Cole; Dwyer, W. O., Leeming, F. C., Cobern, M. K., Porter, B. E., & Jackson, J. M. (1993). Critical review of

behavioral interventions to preserve the environment: Research since 1980. *Environment and Behavior*, 25, 275–321; Geller, E. S., Winett, R. A., & Everett, P. B. (1982). *Preserving the environment: New strategies for behavior change.* New York: Pergamon Press; Lehman, P. A., & Geller, E. S. (2004). Behavior analysis and environmental protection: Accomplishments and potential for more. *Behavior and Social Issues*, 13(1), 13–32.

33. Burn, S. M., & Oskamp, S. (1986). Increasing community recycling with persuasive communication and public commitment. *Journal of Applied Social Psychology*, 16, 29–41; Wang, T. H., & Katzev, R. (1990). Group commitment and resource conservation: Two field experiments on promoting recycling. *Journal of Applied Social Psychology*, 20, 265–275.

34. Glenwick, D., & Jason, L. (Eds.) (1980). *Behavioral community psychology.* New York: Praeger.

35. The bird trash receptacles were designed, manufactured, and donated to our field research by the Jackson Company, Pomona, CA.

36. Geller, E. S., Brasted, W. S., & Mann, M. (1979). Waste receptacle designs as interventions for litter control. *Journal of Environmental Systems*, 9(2), 146–160.

37. Deci, E. L., & Ryan, R. M. (2002). *Handbook of self-determination research.* Rochester, NY: University of Rochester Press; Geller, E. S., & Veazie, B. (2011). *When no one's watching: Living and leading self-motivation.* Newport, VA: Make-A-Difference.

38. Energy Star (n.d.). About Energy Star. Retrieved January 19, 2015, from http://www.energystar.gov/about.

39. Fischer, C., & Newell, R. G. (2008).Environmental and technology policies for climate mitigation. *Journal of Environmental Economics and Management*, 55(2), 142–162; Winett, R. A. (1980). An emerging approach to energy conservation. In D. Glenwick & L. Jason (Eds.). *Behavioral community psychology.* (pp. 320–350). New York: Praeger.

40. Cialdini, R. B., Reno, R. R., & Kallgren, C. A. (1990). A focus theory of normative conduct: Recycling the concept of norms to reduce littering in public places. *Journal of Personality and Social Psychology*, 58(6), 1015–1026; Kallgren, C. A., Reno, R. R., & Cialdini, R. B. (2000). A focus theory of normative conduct: When norms do and do not affect behavior. *Personality and Social Psychology Bulletin*, 26(8), 1002–1012.

41. Schultz, P. W., Nolan, J. M., Cialdini, R. B., Goldstein, N. J., & Griskevicius, V. (2007). The constructive, destructive, and reconstructive power of social norms. *Psychological Science*, 18, 429–434.

42. Goldstein, N., Cialdini, R., & Griskevicius, R. (2008). A room with a viewpoint: Using social norms to motivate environmental conservation in hotels. *Journal of Consumer Research*, 35, 472–482.

43. Allcott, H., & Mullainathan, S. (2010). Behavior and energy policy. *Science*, 327, 1204–1205.

44. Bailey, J. S. (1991). Marketing behavior analysis required different talk. *Journal of Applied Behavior Analysis*, 24(3), 39.

45. Frantz, C. M., & Mayer, F. S. (2009). The emergency of climate change: Why are we failing to take action? *Analyses of Social Issues & Public Policy*, 9, 205–222; Lahey, B. B. (2011). *Psychology: An introduction* (11th ed.). New York: McGraw-Hill.

46. McCright, A. M., & Dunlap, R. E. (2011). The politicization of climate change: Political polarization in the American public's views of global warming. *Sociological Quarterly*, 52(2), 155–194.

47. Li, Y., Johnson, E. J., & Zaval, L. (2011). Local warming. *Psychological Science*, 22, 454–459.

48. Oskamp, S. (2000). A sustainable future for humanity? How can psychology help? *American Psychologist*, 55, 496–508.

49. Stern, P. C., & Gardner, G. T. (1987). Managing scarce environmental resources. In D. Stokols & I. Altman (Eds.). *Handbook of environmental psychology*, Vol. 2 (pp. 1043–1088). New York: Wiley.

50. Lehman, P. A., & Geller, E. S. (2004). Behavior analysis and environmental protection: Accomplishments and potential for more. *Behavior and Social Issues*, 13(1), 13–32.

51. Gardner, G. T., & Stern, P. C. (1996). *Environmental problems and human behavior*. Needham Heights, MA: Allyn & Bacon.

52. Stern, P. C., & Gardner, G. T. (1987). Managing scarce environmental resources. In D. Stokols & I. Altman (Eds.). *Handbook of environmental psychology*, Vol. 2 (p. 1050). New York: Wiley.

53. Stern, P. C. (2000). Psychology and the science of human-environment interactions. *American Psychologist*, 55, 523.

54. Stern, P. C. (2000). Psychology and the science of human-environment interactions. *American Psychologist*, 55, 525.

55. Boyce, T. E., & Geller, E. S. (2001). Applied behavior analysis and occupational safety: The challenge of response maintenance. *Journal of Organizational Behavior Management*, 21(1), 31–60.

56. McSween, T. E., & Mathews, G. A. (2001). Maintenance in organizational behavior management. *Journal of Organizational Behavior Management*, 21, 75–83.

57. Stern, P. C. (2000). Psychology and the science of human–environment interactions. *American Psychologist*, 55, 523–530; Stern, P. C., & Gardner, G. T. (1987). Managing scarce environmental resources. In D. Stokols & I. Altman (Eds.). *Handbook of environmental psychology*, Vol. 2 (pp. 1043–1088). New York: Wiley.

58. Aronson, E. (1999). The power of self-persuasion. *American Psychologist*, 54(11), 875–884.

59. Festinger, L. (1957). *A theory of cognitive dissonance*. Stanford, CA: Stanford University Press.

60. Weigel, R. H., & Weigel, J. (1978). Environmental concern: The development of a measure. *Environment and Behavior*, 10, 3–15.

61. Ellis, R. J., & Thompson, F. (1997). Culture and the environment in the Pacific Northwest. *American Political Science Review*, 91, 885–897.

62. Dunlap, R. E., Van Liere, K. D., Mertig, A. G., & Jones, R. E. (2000). Measuring endorsement of the new ecological paradigm: A revised NEP scale. *Journal of Social Issues*, 56, 425–442.

63. Dunlap, R. E., & Van Liere, K. D. (1978). The "new environmental paradigm": A proposed measuring instrument and preliminary results. *Journal of Environmental Education*, 9, 10–19.

64. de Groot, J. I. M., & Steg, L. (2008). Value orientations to explain beliefs related to environmental significant behavior: How to measure egoistic,

altruistic, and biospheric value orientations. *Environment and Behavior*, 40, 330–354.

65. Abrahamse, W., Steg, L., Vlek, C., & Rothengatter, T. (2007). The effect of tailored information, goal setting, and tailored feedback on household energy use, energy-related behaviors, and behavioral antecedents. *Journal of Environmental Psychology*, 27, 265–276.

20

The AC4P Power of Pets

KRISTA S. GELLER

Some of our greatest historical and artistic treasures we place in museums; others, we take for walks.

– Roger Caras

Are you wondering how a chapter about pets is connected to a book about using principles of humanistic behaviorism to nurture a culture of AC4P behavior? For me it's obvious, and I bet this is also the case for readers who have a pet they care for on a regular basis, especially a pet they consider part of their family.

How has your pet enriched your life? Compassionate pet owners surely actively care for their pets. And I contend the reciprocal benefits from our pets surpass any costs. How do these benefits both reflect and influence AC4P behavior? This chapter illustrates how pets, and caring for pets, can improve one's quality of life, family culture, and the human condition, as derived from both empirical research and personal experience.

MY AC4P AGENTS

Animals have always been a significant part of my life.[1] Ever since I was able to walk, I was on the back of a pony; and ever since I was able to beg, I was asking for a kitten or a puppy to hold. Pets have been a huge inspiration for me, opening the social world, offering lasting friendships, and teaching me to cherish life itself. The positive and loyal affect pets have had on me is clear when I reflect on two of my most influential childhood pets – Goldie and Lady Champayne. I've come to understand the profound AC4P influence an animal can have on a child and the importance of a pet's AC4P-like unconditional affection. My relationship with these two special pets affected my other relationships within my family and beyond, especially facilitating my verbal interactions with others.[2]

From a Beginning

This enriching connection with pets began when I (at age 5) put my hands around a stray cat and refused to let go, obligating my mother to bring him home. This was my pet cat – Goldie. We did more than just play together; we grew up together. We shared a unique friendship so incredible to me as a little girl that it seemed to contain the very meaning of life. At least it made my life meaningful. Goldie wasn't just my cat; he was my most cherished companion whose presence seemed to fill every corner of my world with love and devotion. Goldie made a little five-year-old girl smile when the rest of the world got her down.

It's not unusual for pets like Goldie to play a distinct AC4P-like role in the family.[3] Goldie was there when I needed support; he was there to help me escape from a troubled day; and he was there when I felt all alone. He was my beloved companion with the comforting quality of being my best childhood friend.

Goldie opened up my social world and interpersonal relationships throughout my early life. He gave me the opportunity to express my feelings to my family and others. I conveyed my emotions to Goldie. He seemed to listen when I tried to express my innermost feelings, something I found difficult to do with people. I was shy and conflicted when needing to communicate with others, from family members to peers. But talking to my cat enabled me to (a) understand my own emotions; (b) open up a discussion about how I really felt; (c) practice verbalizing thoughts and ideas to express later to family members; and (d) develop self-efficacy and courage to disclose my emotions to others.

Goldie brought me out of my shell. Did his unconditional affection for me and his patient nonjudgmental listening to my endless verbalizing make him a humanistic AC4P companion? I believe so. Figure 20.1 shows Goldie and me napping together one Sunday afternoon. The photo on the right shows Goldie darned with jewelry; he often played the role of my doll with extraordinary patience and tolerance for a cat.

My beloved Goldie was taken from me one very miserable morning. I remember it as if it happened yesterday. It began as an unexplained ache in my heart that just seemed to sit there when I awoke, as if it had some hidden meaning waiting to be exposed. That night I had gone to bed early without saying goodnight to anyone, not even Goldie, as I had done routinely every

FIGURE 20.1. Krista and Goldie napping (left); Goldie dressed in jewels (right).

night. In the morning I expected to feel relieved and rested, but instead I was even more depleted and incredibly upset. It was as if I knew my entire adolescent life was about to change in some profound way.

When my mom drove her car out of the driveway that morning, I saw the source of my strange heartache. I spotted a drab and wet, orange-colored image on the lawn. I knew deep down what was lying there, but I found it impossible to look closer. My mother got out of her car to investigate and confirmed the orange lifeless body was indeed Goldie. All I could do at that point was go to school. Perhaps then I would wake up from the hideous nightmare I was experiencing. But school didn't help; things only got worse.

At school I just sat expressionless in my first class, attracting unwanted attention. When class started I didn't move. I had my backpack on my desk with the side of my face pressed into it. I had only one thought: "When will I wake up?" When one of my friends asked me if I was okay, I was hit with the reality that this nightmare was not a dream. My lifelong best friend whom I cherished with all my heart was gone from my life. Who would listen to me now? Who would make me feel better after a bad day at school, especially a day like this awful one? I had an urge to fall to the floor in hopes I would hit hard enough to make the pain disappear. I didn't and the pain continued. Instead, the reality of my loss only became more profound.

When the school day finally ended, I had to deal with the certainty that the little furry creature who was always there to greet me at the door and fuel the rest of my day with a cheerful spirit would not be there this time – or any time thereafter. Goldie, once filled with awesome vigor and love, was now a lifeless body tucked in a box. All I could do was hold him closely and curse the world for taking my one-and-only (it seemed) true friend.

He was my buffer against life's negative realities. He was the best communication tool I had within my family. He enabled me to reveal my deepest feelings, express my thoughts, and adjust my outlook on life. To a young girl, this pet – a mere cat – made every problem in the world seem understandable and solvable.

The day Goldie died I learned more about myself than I could ever have imagined. Looking back, I learned I had developed the ability to communicate effectively; I saw that talking about my emotions is allowed and others will listen; I also realized I had a deep ability and desire to love, and to feel loved, even by a simple cat.

What a rude awakening I experienced when Goldie left us. It felt as though I had lost critical *peer support* I assumed would always be there – a comfort zone I had always nestled into. Goldie was a substitute for missing interpersonal relationships in my early years. With him I had talked out my problems, my emotions, and my daily challenges.

The AC4P Power of Lady Champayne

I need to mention a second influential pet in my life. She allowed me to believe everything was okay when my teenage adolescent fears got me down. I would run to her when things didn't make sense, and I would lay across her back in the middle of the field when I looked for an escape. She was my oasis from real-world distress and discomfort. She helped me stand tall through all my college and graduate-school studies. Are you wondering? This miraculous pet was a stocky, spirited, buckskin pony, as shown in Figure 20.2.

Lady Champayne stepped in when Goldie was taken from me. She was the next AC4P agent in my life, guiding me through the anxieties and complexities of my teenage years, and still acting as a comforting escape when I became a young adult. She was there for me when I needed a nudge from her nose or a neck to hug. Much like Goldie, she listened to my ranting and raving, she heard all about my stressors, she participated willingly in all the riding exercises I invented, and she always came running whenever she heard my voice. Our relationship started when I was 14 and she was 4.

Lady was not the first pony I rode in horse shows. She was my third and last. I remember well the first night I was compelled to ride Lady. In fact, I had previously dismissed her and decided she was not the pony for me. Just after midnight, a group of my equestrian friends decided to play cops and robbers in our horse-riding ring. Everyone jumped eagerly on

FIGURE 20.2. Krista and Lady sharing a smooch.

the backs of their ponies and headed to the ring. Only one pony remained riderless and bare – Lady Champayne.

I was not fond of this 4-year-old mare. She was stubborn, rude, and extremely ornery. In fact, she was nicknamed "the bucking bronco with an attitude." But if I wanted to join in the game, I had to pony up. Reluctantly, I jumped on her bareback and entered the ring with the rest of my friends. Once in the ring, I felt Lady gracefully gain a spunky speed. She readily picked up her feet and began trotting to the opposite side of the ring. Her gait was effortless and flowing, a little choppy, but ever so vibrant and full of life. A mere five minutes on Lady's back and I knew we had a unique connection.

Our relationship flourished. Lady took me to show-jumping competitions, fox hunts, stadium jumping, cross country, dressage, and she enabled us to achieve a high ridership ranking in Pony Club. You name it, we did it, and we did it together. We forged one of the strongest and most heartfelt relationships I've ever experienced. From the moment we trotted across that ring, Lady and I were a team.

The most remarkable aspect of her kindness was the way she actively cared for me. She was always there – she was my AC4P agent. She helped me get through high school, comforted me throughout my college years, and inspired me during my graduate school studies, from M.S. to Ph.D. in human development. She was my best friend for twenty-three years.

I was so captivated by her AC4P heart I decided to breed her – twice with the same stallion. First, I set it up so the foal would be born near my graduation date with an M.S. degree. The second breeding was timed so the foal would be born close to my Ph.D. hooding.

Breeding Lady enabled me to focus on something other than my graduate school studies, obligating me to make time in my busy schedule for her. It was my turn to reciprocate – to actively care for Lady. She had run round and round various horse rings for me, doing her very best in competitions. Now it was payback time. She deserved the joy of motherhood, something very different from her daily routine.

Thanks to our extraordinary bond, Lady allowed me to help her deliver each foal, letting me pick them up immediately. She allowed me to play with them, and participate 100 percent in introducing each filly to the life of a pony, from bathing to feeding and training. No one else enjoyed such caretaking privileges. Indeed, she warned everyone, horses and humans, to back off her foals by kicking both back legs into the air and snorting loudly. Figure 20.3 shows me tending to Lady and her first filly (Koko Puff) two hours after her birth.

FIGURE 20.3. Lady Champayne, Koko Puff, and I.

Even though our competitive adventures were over, Lady still waited eagerly for my visits to the barn. We had a rhythm to our time together; we fit like an old shoe. She was my best link to my childhood. Some people visit a childhood home, neighborhood, or a vacation spot to recall special moments that contributed to their development. For me, I just looked toward Lady to reminisce and truly appreciate my life, and to find myself centered again. Figure 20.4 shows Lady and me on July 31, 2010. I had to tread through muddy water to give her a well-deserved AC4P hug.

Sadly, as most of us pet owners learn, we eventually say good-bye to our pets, and we're rarely ready for such grief. I lost Lady on April 20, 2012. Although the experience was painful, my vet and I did what was best for my companion and longest AC4P agent. After much persuasion, I convinced Lady to lie down in the center of the barn with her head resting on my lap. I held her face tightly to my sopping-wet cheeks and whispered softly in her ear as the vet administered the drug that would take away my treasured friend. As I held her head tightly to my chest, I realized how lucky I was to have had this wonderful creature in my life.

FIGURE 20.4. Taking a bath with my best friend.

Lady took care of me after Goldie; she listened to me when others didn't, loved me unconditionally when I needed it most, and gave me peace when life got tough. Both Lady and Goldie were my AC4P agents, teaching me the value of friendship and the significance and reciprocity of actively caring.

From Personal Experience to Research

My story illustrates the AC4P power a pet can possess. A pet can be positively intertwined within a family culture and drastically influence a child's outlook. My two long-term wonderful pet experiences demonstrate how an individual's social interactions within family and among peers can be improved by an AC4P friendship with a pet.

Let's consider more specifically and empirically the AC4P benefits of pets. A variety of animals, including birds, chinchillas, guinea pigs, hamsters, horses, ferrets, bunnies, snakes, cats, and dogs, serve as pets. Most of the research literature on this topic does not specify the kind of animal referred to as a "pet." The term used throughout the research reviewed is simply "pet," leaving the role of "pet" open to any possible animal.

Dogs and cats are the most common animals playing the pet role in American culture. Regardless of species, pets have been shown to promote self-assurance and personal adequacy, conveying positive regard for the owner and providing a special comfort that does not impose standards on a person's performance.[4]

SOME CONCLUSIONS FROM RESEARCH

Pets are often viewed as a best friend, an important other, or even a family member. Plus, talking to a pet can be a therapeutic exercise.[5] Katcher[6] reported that nearly all pet owners talk to their pets and almost half confide in them. Beck and Katcher[7] found that more than 70 percent of adolescents share confidences with their pets. They tell their pets secrets. Young children reported they have intimate talks with their pets on a routine basis.[4]

Some people experience a decrease in blood pressure when talking to their pets, suggesting a more relaxed state with pets than with people.[8] Spicer[9] concluded, "Who else listens so well to irrational ranting and raving without once interrupting?"

More than 50 percent of households in the world have a pet.[10] There are more than 60 million pet dogs and nearly 70 million pet cats in the United

States.[11] The positive impact of pets on humans is self-evident to all who care for one or more. Pets can decrease the loneliness and depression of owners by providing a source of companionship and affection.[12]

In several questionnaire surveys of pet owners, researchers observed a common theme: More than 50 percent of pet owners reported they talked to their pets frequently, as if they were people, and considered their pets to be sensitive to their moods.[13] This kind of attachment shows that when close and affectionate contact with others is needed, the family pet can be extremely beneficial.[14] Close relationships with pets help individuals cope with physical and psychological stressors in their everyday lives.[15] Pets serve as AC4P agents for stress reduction and happiness.

A pet can actually open communication lines between family members, especially when some family members rarely speak to each other except through their pets.[9] Some people relate better to pets than humans. But the relationship between a human and a pet is not as simple as might be expected. Human–pet relationships can be quite complex and help individuals deal with family crises and emotional distress.[16] Moreover, pets can facilitate pleasure, fun, humor, and exercise. Some pets also provide security and protection, as well as a way to teach children responsibility and a respect for life. The AC4P service of pets is diverse and invaluable.

Pet and human interaction can be a positive, healthy, and significant dynamic in life. A pet can boost self-esteem, interpersonal competence, life satisfaction, happiness, and marital health. Pets can add a substantial dose of genuine affection to the family.[17] They can serve as a social lubricant, increasing the quantity and improving the quality of interpersonal conversation. Pet–human interactions can supplement human-to-human interactions or even substitute for certain human relationships.[18]

A pet can benefit an individual's physical and psychological health. In another context, researchers found that simply viewing aquarium fish lowered blood pressure. Thus, even without physical contact, a pet can provide a soothing and relaxing atmosphere.[19] Some pets help people socialize with others and often increase duration of survival after a heart attack.[20] In addition, pets are often a replacement or a surrogate for a human relationship[21] and prevent episodes of depression.[22]

In summary, it's likely that owning and developing a profound attachment to a pet may help (a) protect people from the debilitating effects of distress; (b) relieve loneliness and depression; (c) provide interdependent comfort and friendship; and (d) serve as an activator and supporter of healthy recreation and exercise.

Communication

Communication is key to any healthy relationship, and in some cases a pet facilitates open dialogue. Pets can open the lines of conversation for a family. They can provide an active or passive medium for interpersonal verbalization, giving people something to talk about.[23] It's not necessary to hide your identity when communicating with a pet. In contrast, when exchanging feelings with a human it's often necessary to take on the role of the other person in order to communicate effectively.[24] This can cause distress. Connecting with a pet has been considered simpler and less stressful.[25]

Due to misunderstandings or controversy resulting from communicating – or miscommunicating – with a family member, talking with the family pet could be preferred. Misinterpretations and conflicts in human relationships are frequent and diverse because perceptions are so personal and so readily biased. We all see life through our own filters.

Communicating with another human being can be more of a burden than a benefit. We will often avoid talking to someone due to anticipated conflict or distress. But communication is central to family life, and expressing one's feelings with family members is critical for healthy relationships.[26] Davis and Juhasz[4] showed in their survey research that some children find it easier to communicate and express their emotions with a pet rather than a person, because the young person feels safe and trusts the animal.

Emotional Support

Pets can show a unique concern for a human that only its owner truly understands. Most people who are empathic and caring in their views of animals are likely to have the same sentiments toward people. Past and present ownership of a pet can lead to greater concern about the treatment and welfare of animals.[27] Paul[27] showed that those respondents who had owned pets during their childhood had significantly higher animal-oriented empathy scores than those who did not have a childhood pet.

Brickel[28] examined how individuals acquire and maintain an emotional bond with animals throughout their lifetime. He found that some people perceive animals as emotional wards in the family. Both Brickel and Larsen and colleagues[29] suggest compassion for pets may be greater than for humans. It seems intuitive that bonding with a pet is often easier and less complicated than with another person.

Eckstein[25] developed the Pet Relationship Impact Inventory and found two different types of people: those who love and treat pets as regular members of the family, and those who don't. The researchers concluded the relationship between child and pet is often simpler and less conflicted than human relationships. Pets were characterized as providing a "living security blanket for children."[30] For many children, their pet provides an emotional attachment created through deep bonds of mutual affection. Pets are not only a medium for a child's verbal and nonverbal communication exchanges; they are also agents of security, emotional support, and most important, unconditional love.[25]

A Powerful Role

Each stage of a person's life can be characterized by varying and changing roles. A role is any set of behaviors with a commonly accepted definition.[31] Pets can take on distinct roles. For instance, pets can provide companionship and affection for an individual.[12] Pets can assume the role of best friend, the surrogate mate, the caretaker, the listener. Indeed, a pet can play many different roles, each accompanied by profound feelings.[32]

Children have fewer and very differing roles than adults. Some authors claim every child should own a pet and assume the various roles required to care for an animal.[31] Young children can develop a sense of responsibility when actively caring for a pet, and a preadolescent caretaker of a pet might identify his/her pet as "something that makes me feel good about myself."[33] In some situations a pet can be a replacement for another significant relationship. Some children have a limited number of playmates when growing up, and their pet serves as the ideal playmate.[31]

Cain[3] studied the valuable role a pet plays in the family system with a 32-item questionnaire completed by 896 families with at least one pet at home. The results: 93 percent of the respondents had pets while growing up; 99 percent reported they thought children should have pets; 98 percent considered their pet a family member or a close friend; and 72 percent said their pet usually had "people status" in the family.

Of all the pet owners, 70 percent reported an increase in family happiness and fun after getting a pet; 60 percent indicated an increased expression of affection around the pet; and 52 percent said family time spent together increased with a pet. Asked what special characteristics their pet displayed, 77 percent of the respondents believed their pet understood when they talked or confided in them; 73 percent reported their pet communicated back to them; and 59 percent believed their pet understood them and was sensitive to their moods.[3]

The author provided examples of how a pet can break tension in a household. He described situations when the pet acted as a peacemaker, and in one case a dog was described as a diversion from a crisis. There were also times when the pet would do something cute and people would forget they were angry, or occasions when the pet requested attention during periods of tension. There were even situations in which the pet seemed to sense anger and did something silly to make people laugh. This "pet therapy" helped family members develop a sense of balance again. Paying attention to the pet allowed them to reflect on their perceptions and get control of their feelings.

Conclusion: Pets serve several positive and significant AC4P roles in the family culture, providing a means for happiness, enjoyment, and recreation, as well as a source of physical security and protection. They also teach children responsibility and a respect for life.[3]

Humanizing Pets

Pets today have become humanized. Most grooming services for humans are available for dogs, cats, and other animals. Poodles regularly get their hair done at beauty parlors, which includes a shampoo, a cut, a blow-dry, and a manicure. Sometimes poodles arrive at these parlors by limousine, wearing a custom-made sweater. Expensive and attractive pets are often viewed as a personal accessory, similar to an expensive car or diamond ring.[18]

As mentioned, a pet can be a replacement or a surrogate for a human relationship. Some childless couples consider their pets to be their children – loving their pets as they would their own offspring. A pet can serve as a surrogate parent, enabling a child to practice a variety of interactions later to be incorporated into other social relationships.

EXPLORING THE AC4P VALUE OF PETS

My master's thesis research in the Human Development Department at Virginia Tech (VT) used a survey with twelve open-ended questions to explore the impact and importance of a pet on family members, especially the influence of a pet on relationships between its caretaker and other family members.[34] A total of 102 surveys were distributed to university students; 96 students completed the survey. Of these, 82 respondents (85.4 percent) indicated a pet had influenced their life in important ways.

An underlying assumption of this study was that pets provide an important dynamic for families. As previously discussed, they can decrease stress and anxiety, and provide personal comfort and protection. The results of my study supported this premise and were consistent with the findings of the research reviewed in the preceding sections. Answers to the survey questions were diverse, but nearly all supported the AC4P power of pets in benefiting family relationships.

Many participants reported their pets reduced stress by facilitating laughter and distractions when human interaction became too demanding or negative. Pets were commonly considered another playmate who stimulated family bonding, improving relationships among family members. Many respondents appreciated the consistency of their pets' behavior, especially the unique love each expressed. It was common for pets to be viewed as a respondent's best friend – a loyal, stable companion at times when love and attention were most needed.

Pets were perceived as being "consistent" in their actions and in their relationships within the family. Respondents described their pets as "keeping the peace," "providing an escape," "nuzzling for attention," "lovable," "consistent," "dependent," "non-authoritative," "building self-esteem," "listening," and "providing brighter days." They can hear all the problems and worries that might be causing distress. They are "happy to have you around," and they maintain a friendly countenance that benefits individuals' moods and their interactions with other family members.

The unconditional love a pet can bestow on the entire family exemplifies the kind of AC4P behavior family members need to show toward each other. Respondents recognized their pets as being present to "keep company," "make you happy," and "help you to forget your problems." This form of AC4P interaction is sometimes preferred over interpersonal communication.[35]

Many participants used my survey to project personal and strong positive feelings about their pets. Such self-disclosure revealed solid evidence of the valuable role pets play in developing and maintaining healthy family relationships. One of my research questions asked, "In what ways can a pet replace or act as a beneficial substitute for other interpersonal, significant relationships?" Through personal anecdotes, respondents depicted their pets as a "best friend" – providing special companionship consistently whenever needed.

Many pets were described as great listeners who never pass critical judgment, never interrupt, never force opinions upon the individual, and never hold a grudge. This implies that connecting with a pet is usually simpler and less stressful than building relationships with humans, as indicated in the research cited earlier. Pets are often depicted as protectors, whether they protect the entire family or just a particular individual in that family. They can also be an affectionate playmate and a resilient sounding-board for verbal expressions of emotional and/or physical pain.

Participants in my thesis research indicated the family pet is often perceived as a tremendous source of joy. The pet is the one they look forward to seeing when they come home; the one to whom they confide their problems and worries; and the one they know has unconditional positive regard for them. Self-esteem can be boosted by a pet who shows genuine appreciation for simple acts of affection, kindness, and caring. The family pet welcomes and reciprocates unconditional love. It can be a source of stability within a family culture.

Beck[36] and Brickel[28] conclude that a pet can be present for attention and affection when no one else is available; a pet can appear to listen when the rest of the world seems disinterested; a pet can offer unconditional love when love from people seems to be conditional.

Beck[36] discusses the special advantages of communicating with a pet: A pet does not argue, interrupt, or disagree, but rather seems to take it all in. As such, pets become a person's special friend – an escape from a seemingly negative, uncaring, or misunderstanding world. As most participants in my thesis research confirmed: Pets bring love to the family, listen with apparent interest when no one else seems interested, and are loyal unconditionally, unlike many relationships with humans that vary according to conditions and contingencies.[37]

QUANTIFYING HUMAN–PET ATTACHMENT

For my dissertation research I developed and evaluated a scale to measure the amount of attachment pet owners feel toward their pets.[38] A total of 398 pet owners, ranging in age from 18 to 87, completed a 34-item Pet Attachment Scale (PATS) that asked respondents about their emotional connection to their pets and how their pets influence their lives.

A factor analysis of the PATS results yielded the reliable 19 items listed in Table 20.1. Two independent factors relating to attachment were found: emotional fulfillment (Items 1–10) and companionship (Items 11–19). In other words, my dissertation research indicated that companionship and emotional fulfillment are two distinct AC4P functions of pets. The survey results suggested these are two separate benefits of pets, but further research is needed to define the operational or behavioral differences between emotional fulfillment and companionship.

TABLE 20.1. *The pet attachment scale*[39]

Circle the scale value after each item that best describes your feelings at this time:
*1-Strongly Disagree; 2-Disagree; 3-Somewhat Disagree; 4-Neutral; 5-Somewhat Agree;
6-Agree; 7-Strongly Disagree*

1.	I love my pet.	1	2	3	4	5	6	7
2.	My pet loves me.	1	2	3	4	5	6	7
3.	I feel emotionally attached to my pet.	1	2	3	4	5	6	7
4.	My pet is emotionally attached to me.	1	2	3	4	5	6	7
5.	My pet brings me happiness.	1	2	3	4	5	6	7
6.	I bring happiness to my pet.	1	2	3	4	5	6	7
7.	I would be lost without my pet.	1	2	3	4	5	6	7
8.	I count on my pet being there when I need comfort.	1	2	3	4	5	6	7
9.	My pet is often my best friend.	1	2	3	4	5	6	7
10.	I am emotionally dependent on my pet.	1	2	3	4	5	6	7
11.	I prefer to be with my pet more than others.	1	2	3	4	5	6	7
12.	I talk to my pet as a friend.	1	2	3	4	5	6	7
13.	I confide in my pet.	1	2	3	4	5	6	7
14.	I spend time each day training my pet.	1	2	3	4	5	6	7
15.	I show photos of my pet to my friends.	1	2	3	4	5	6	7
16.	When I feel bad, I seek my pet for comfort.	1	2	3	4	5	6	7
17.	I feel sad when I am separated from my pet.	1	2	3	4	5	6	7
18.	My pet means more to me than most of my friends.	1	2	3	4	5	6	7
19.	My pet adds happiness to my life.	1	2	3	4	5	6	7

Can a pet be a companion and not fulfill emotional needs? Can emotional fulfillment occur without substantial caretaking? Is pet companionship necessary for emotional fulfillment, or can emotional fulfillment come without companionship? Do certain kinds of pets provide more companionship then emotional fulfillment, and vice versa? Are certain independent variables predictive of companionship but not emotional fulfillment, and vice versa? How do these two factors of human–pet relationships mirror aspects of human-to-human relationships? Clearly, my dissertation research activated more questions than it answered.

Benefits of Human–Animal Relationships

The amount of responsibility people felt toward their pet was the strongest predictor of the degree-of-attachment scores on the PATS, as common sense suggests. The other predictors of pet attachment were gender and the favorite pet chosen. Women showed greater attachment to their pets and more caretaking for pets.

Participants who did not choose a favorite pet scored highest on the PATS, followed by dog lovers and next by cat lovers. Those who had a pet other than a cat or a dog showed the least amount of attachment and caretaking. Greater attachment among those who selected all pets as their favorite suggests those with more than one pet experience greater human–pet attachment.

The AC4P theme of this chapter was demonstrated by participants receiving both emotional fulfillment and companionship from their pets. This underscores the AC4P power of pets and supports earlier findings by Sable[40] that showed dogs and cats have the potential to provide an emotional bond of attachment that promotes a sense of well-being and security.

Pets uniquely fill a combination of emotional needs, sometimes substituting for an absence of human attachment.[40] Similarly, Gunter[19] claims pets meet many fundamental human needs of their owners, providing companionship and feelings of security and affection. This reflects the emotional fulfillment factor revealed in the factor analysis of the PATS.

My dissertation research indicated that dogs provide more AC4P benefits than cats. Is this because dogs require more care and are less independent? Or perhaps the behavior of a dog is more conducive to the development of an animal–human bond. More follow-up research is needed. Sable[40] also found dogs to be favored over cats. He explains that dogs show more affection toward their owners and enable more opportunities for human–animal interaction. Obviously, dogs engage in a wider range of activities conducive to AC4P human involvement. For example, dog owners take their pets on more errands than owners of other pets.[19] Dog owners also feel the most secure with their pet.

Interestingly, pet owners who did not choose a particular pet as their favorite showed the most attachment. These individuals might have had more than one pet and could not choose a favorite among them. Perhaps the more animals in one's household, the greater the level of animal–human attachment experienced. I found a significant positive correlation between number of pets and attachment scores on the PATS.

Is there a direct relationship between pet attachment and number of pets? Perhaps the relationship between number of pets and pet attachment is an inverted U-shaped function. More than one or two pets could increase attachment; but after three or more pets, attachment might decrease. This likely depends, of course, on the amount of AC4P care provided the pets.

Emotional Fulfillment

The emotional fulfillment factor reflects a heartfelt AC4P connection to one's pet, as assessed by Items 1–10 in Table 20.1. Emotional fulfillment is not typically viewed as independent from companionship in human–animal relationships. But according to my dissertation results, it's possible to find *both* companionship and emotional fulfillment in a companion animal, and it's possible to experience just one or the other.

Companionship

Companionship is reflected by Items 11–19 on the PATS. Consider two of these items: "I talk to my pet as a friend," and "My pet is often my best friend." These questions represent camaraderie between individuals and their pets. Companionship and friendship go hand-in-hand. Harker and collegues[41] reported that the general term *companionship* usually translates into shared activities with one's pet. For example, riding a horse, walking a dog, playing with a cat, singing with a bird, and similar behaviors are shared activities. And these can be mutual AC4P behaviors.

In summary, individuals who scored high on this PATS factor have a strong sense of AC4P companionship with their pets. They like to do things with their pets, they enjoy the company of their pets, and they have a genuine friendship with, and compassion for, their pets.

IN CONCLUSION

When I decided to study the impact of pets in people's lives, I realized how pets have always had a positive AC4P influence in my life. They have been inspiring, encouraging, calming, and comforting. I've always been intrigued by the relationship between pets and individuals, and entire families. In my thesis surveys, respondents reported a dramatic influence of pets in their lives that parallels AC4P benefits throughout society. Pets were consoling when respondents wanted to cry, self-disclose, express anger about a family member, practice their confrontation, or cuddle before bedtime. In this sense, our pets exemplify *humanistic behaviorism*.

My thesis research began with this assumption: Pets are powerful AC4P agents in family relationships. This hypothesis was strongly supported by the results of my surveys. Most respondents commented that their pets are "influential," "consistent," "happy to have you around," "an escape," "listeners," "dependent," "lovable," and "always there." These are only a sample of the many positive AC4P qualities my research participants attributed to their pets.

When reading the surveys, I was astonished by the number of personal stories respondents provided to illustrate AC4P attachment to their pets. Pets were portrayed as "the biggest joy in my life," "almost another child," "better than people," "one of the family," "younger brother or sister," "significant relationship," "another playmate," "more comforting," and "a facilitator of family bonding." Indeed, pets are powerful, influential, important, and beloved.

Pets actively care unconditionally, and in turn likely increase the recipient's propensity to perform AC4P behavior for others. The facilitating mechanism could be the reciprocity principle (Chapter 6) or a boost in one or more of the person-states that enhance one's propensity to perform AC4P behavior (Chapter 2).

The theme of this chapter – the AC4P power of pets – was also illustrated by the finding that two distinct functions of pets determine the degree of human–pet attachment: emotional fulfillment and companionship. Pets give owners something to actively care about, provide a special comradeship, and offer opportunities to experience human-to-animal bonding. These contributions of pets certainly reflect the AC4P emotional fulfillment factor revealed in the factor analysis of the participants' scores on the Pet Attachment Scale (PATS) I developed and evaluated for my Ph.D. research.

While completing the first draft of this chapter, I glanced to my right and then to my left, and I saw my three current AC4P agents: two Pomeranians, "Teddy" and "Chewy," and a Pomeranian/Shepherd mix, "Paddington." Figure 20.5 depicts my current team – my three AC4P agents who keep my

FIGURE 20.5. My AC4P agents: Teddy (front), Chewy (left), and Paddington (back).

life aligned, who actively care for my heart, and who offer constant companionship, emotional fulfillment, and life enrichment.

DISCUSSION QUESTIONS

1. Explain why a chapter on pets is relevant for a book on cultivating an AC4P culture.
2. How have special pets influenced the author's life? In what ways can you relate to her experiences with pets?
3. How can a pet build a child's self-responsibility and self-motivation?
4. How can a pet facilitate interpersonal conversation and togetherness among family members?
5. In what specific ways do pets serve as AC4P agents to benefit human welfare?
6. How does pet ownership connect with positive psychology (Chapter 7)?
7. In what ways, if any, can a pet be considered humanistic?
8. The author's dissertation research that developed and evaluated a Pet Attachment Scale (PATS) revealed that pets fulfill two independent human needs. What are these and how do pets fulfill them?
9. In what ways can a pet have a positive impact in a person's life?
10. Why or why not do you currently have a pet in your life? If you do not, do you intend to have a pet later? Why or why not?

REFERENCES

1. I owe my pet attachments to my mom, Carol Hillis Geller. She always allowed me to bring home and actively care for the stray cats and dogs I found. She encouraged and inspired my love for pets. Her adoration and devotion to all pets and animals of any kind generalized to me. Thanks, Mom!
2. Gergen, K. J. (1999). *An invitation to social construction*. London: Sage.
3. Cain, A. O. (1985). A study of pets in the family system. In A. H. Katcher & A. M. Beck (Eds.). *New perspectives on our lives with companion animals*. Philadelphia: University of Pennsylvania Press, 1983; Cain, A. O. (1985). Pets as family members. *Marriage and Family Review*, 8(3–4), 5–10.
4. Davis, J. H., & Juhasz, A. M. (1985). The preadolescent/pet bond and psychosocial development. *Marriage and Family Review*, 8(3–4), 79–94.
5. Brickel, C. M. (1985). Initiation and maintenance of the human–animal bond: Familial roles from a learning perspective. *Marriage and Family Review*, 8(3–4), 31–48; Davis, J. H., & Juhasz, A. M. (1985).The preadolescent/pet bond and psychosocial development. *Marriage and Family Review*, 8(3–4), 79–94; Eckstein, D. (2000).The pet relationship impact inventory. *Family Journal: Counseling and Therapy for Couples and Families*, 8, 192–198.

6. Katcher, A. H. (1981). Interactions between people and their pets: Form and function. In B. Fogle (Ed.). *Interactions between people and pets* (pp. 41–67). Springfield, IL: Charles C. Thomas.

7. Beck, A. M., & Katcher, A. H. (1996). *Between pets and people: The importance of animal companionship*. West Lafayette, IN: Purdue University Press.

8. Barone, M. (1998). The truth about cats and dogs. *Fairfield County Woman*, 30, 36–39; Beck, A. B. (1999). Companion animals and their companions: Sharing a strategy for survival. *Technology and Society*, 19, 201–203; Eckstein, D. (2000). The pet relationship impact inventory. *Family Journal: Counseling and Therapy for Couples and Families*, 8, 192–198; Friedman, E., & Thomas, S. A. (1985). Health benefits of pets for families. In M. B. Sussman (Ed.). *Pets and the family* (pp. 191–202). New York: Haworth Press; Serpell, J. (1996). *In the company of animals: A study for human-animal relationships*. New York: Cambridge University Press.

9. Spicer, L. (1990). Our furry relations. *Optimist*, 16, 9.

10. Beck, A. B. (1999). Companion animals and their companions: Sharing a strategy for survival. *Technology and Society*, 19, 201–203; Bonas, S., McNicholas, J., & Collis, G. (2000). *Pets in the network of family relationships: An empirical study*. In A. Podberscek, E. Paul, & J. Serpell (Eds.). *Companion animals & us: Exploring the relationships between people and pets* (pp. 209–236). New York: Cambridge University Press; Fogle, B. (1983). *Pets and their people*. London: Collins Harvill.

11. American Veterinary Association (1983). *The veterinary services market*, Vols. I & II. Overland Park, KS: Charles, Charles & Associates.

12. Entin, A. D. (1986). The pet focused family: A systems theory perspective. *Psychotherapy in Private Practice*, 4, 13–17; Friedman, E., & Thomas, S. A. (1985). Health benefits of pets for families. In M. B. Sussman (Ed.). *Pets and the family* (pp. 191–202). New York: Haworth Press.

13. Friedman, E., & Thomas, S. A. (1985). Health benefits of pets for families. In M. B. Sussman (Ed.). *Pets and the family* (pp. 191–202). New York: Haworth Press.

14. Serpell, J. (1996). *In the company of animals: A study for human–animal relationships*. New York: Cambridge University Press.

15. Brickel, C. M. (1985). Initiation and maintenance of the human–animal bond: Familial roles from a learning perspective. *Marriage and Family Review*, 8(3–4), 31–48; Davis, J. H., & Juhasz, A. M. (1985). The preadolescent/pet bond and psychosocial development. *Marriage and Family Review*, 8(3–4), 79–94; Serpell, J. (1996). *In the company of animals: A study for human–animal relationships*. New York: Cambridge University Press.

16. Entin, A. D. (1986). The pet focused family: A systems theory perspective. *Psychotherapy in Private Practice*, 4, 13–17.

17. Spicer, L. (1990). Our furry relations. *Optimist*, 16, 13–14; Sussman, M. B. (1985). Pet/human bonding: Applications, conceptual and research issues. *Marriage and Family Review*, 8, 1–3.

18. Veevers, J. E. (1985). The social meanings of pets: Alternative roles for companion animals. In M. B. Sussman (Ed.). *Pets and the family* (pp. 11–31). New York: Haworth Press.

19. Gunter, B. (1999). *Pets and people: The psychology of pet ownership*. London: Whurr.

20. Brasic, J. (1998). Pets and health. *Psychological Reports*, 83(3), 1211–1024; Gunter, B. (1999). *Pets and people: The psychology of pet ownership*. London: Whurr.

21. LaRossa, R., & Reitzes, D. C. (1993). Symbolic interactionism and family studies. In P. G. Boss, W. J. Doherty, R. Larossa, W. R. Schumm, & S. K. Steinmetz (Eds.). *Sourcebook of family theories and methods: A contextual approach* (pp. 135–163). New York: Plenum.

22. Kehoe, M. (1990). Loneliness and the aging homosexual: Is pet therapy an answer? *Journal of Homosexuality*, 20, 137–142.

23. Davis, J. H., & Juhasz, A. M. (1985). The preadolescent/pet bond and psychosocial development. *Marriage and Family Review*, 8(3–4), 79–94; Friedman, E., & Thomas, S. A. (1985). Health benefits of pets for families. In M. B. Sussman (Ed.). *Pets and the family* (pp. 191–202). New York: Haworth Press; Spicer, L. (1990). Our furry relations. *Optimist*, 16, 13–14.

24. Gergen, K. J. (1999). *An invitation to social construction*. London: Sage, p. 124.

25. Eckstein, D. (2000). The pet relationship impact inventory. *Family Journal: Counseling and Therapy for Couples and Families*, 8, 192–198.

26. Fitzpatrick, M. A., & Ritchie, L. D. (1993). Communication theory and the family. In P. G. Boss, W. J. Doherty, R. Larossa, W. R. Schumm & S. K. Steinmetz (Eds.). *Sourcebook of family theories and methods: A contextual approach* (pp. 565–585). New York: Plenum.

27. Paul, E. S. (2000). Empathy with animals and with humans: Are they linked? *Anthrozoos*, 13, 194–202.

28. Brickel, C. M. (1985). Initiation and maintenance of the human–animal bond: Familial roles from a learning perspective. *Marriage and Family Review*, 8(3–4), 31–48.

29. Brickel, C. M. (1985). Initiation and maintenance of the human–animal bond: Familial roles from a learning perspective. *Marriage and Family Review*, 8(3–4), 31–48; Larsen, K. S., Ashlock, J., Caroll, C., Foote, S., Feeler, J., Keller, E., et al. (1974). *Laboratory aggression where the victim is a small dog. Social Behavior and Personality*, 2, 174–176.

30. Eckstein, D. (2000). The pet relationship impact inventory. *Family Journal: Counseling and Therapy for Couples and Families*, 8, 196.

31. Netting, F. E., Wilson, C. C., & New, J. C. (1987). The human–animal bond: Implications for practice. *Social Work*, 32, 60–64.

32. Sussman, M. B. (1985). Pet/human bonding: Applications, conceptual and research issues. *Marriage and Family Review*, 8, 1–3.

33. Davis, J. H., & Juhasz, A. M. (1985). The preadolescent/pet bond and psychosocial development. *Marriage and Family Review*, 8(3–4), 79–94.

34. Geller, K. S. (2002). *The power of pets: How animals affect family relationships*. Unpublished master's thesis, Virginia Tech, Blacksburg.

35. Klein, D. M., & White, J. M. (1996). *Family theories: An introduction*. Thousand Oaks, CA: Sage; LaRossa, R., & Reitzes, D. C. (1993). Symbolic interactionism and family studies. In P. G. Boss, W. J. Doherty, R. Larossa, W. R. Schumm, & S. K. Steinmetz (Eds.). *Sourcebook of family theories and methods: A contextual approach* (pp. 135–163). New York: Plenum.

36. Beck, A. B. (1999). Companion animals and their companions: Sharing a strategy for survival. *Technology and Society*, 19, 201–203.

37. Beck, A. B. (1999). Companion animals and their companions: Sharing a strategy for survival. *Technology and Society*, 19, 201–203; Brickel, C. M. (1985). Initiation and maintenance of the human–animal bond: Familial roles from a learning perspective. *Marriage and Family Review*, 8(3–4), 31–48.

38. Geller, K. S. (2005). *Quantifying the power of pets: An instrument to assess attachment between humans and companion animals.* Unpublished Ph.D. dissertation, Virginia Tech, Blacksburg, VA.

39. Geller, K. S. (2005). Adapted from the Pet Attachment Scale developed and evaluated in my dissertation.

40. Sable, P. (1995). Pets, attachment, and well-being across the life cycle. *Social Work*, 40, 334–341.

41. Harker, R., Collis, G., & McNicholas, J. (2000). The influence of current relationships upon pet animal acquisition. In A. Podberscek, E. Paul, & J. Serpell (Eds.). *Companion animals & us: Exploring the relationships between people and pets* (pp. 109–121). New York: Cambridge University Press.

Epilogue

Where Do We Go from Here?

E. SCOTT GELLER

I believe most people want to do the right thing, and care profoundly about the hardships of others. Unfortunately, the majority of us remain silent until after misfortune falls on someone else. Consider this discerning statement by Martin Luther King, Jr.: "History will have to record that the greatest tragedy of this period of social transition was not the strident clamor of the bad people, but the appalling silence of the good people."[1]

Our challenge is to shatter the "appalling silence" sooner rather than later. This call for proactive AC4P behavior is easier for me to proclaim than for all of us to do. We don't instinctively know how to offer advice, feedback, or support to promote well-being or prevent possible misfortune, even a tragedy. And it's certainly easier to avoid proactive AC4P behavior and reflexively continue working for soon, certain, positive and self-serving consequences than to intervene – to actively care.

This book introduced and explained effective techniques for intervening on behalf of the welfare of others. Lack of knowledge is no excuse. This book shared evidence-based advantages of using AC4P principles – humanistic behaviorism – to improve the quality of life in various situations. Indeed, it *is* better (i.e., more reinforcing) to give (i.e., to actively care) than to receive. So a lack of motivation is no excuse.

To the silent majority: Let's no longer stay passive, quiet, and inconspicuous. Reflect on these issues and resolve to join the AC4P Movement to make our world safer, healthier, and more positive. To read and understand the contents of this book is not sufficient. Teach others the AC4P principles and applications shared here. Yet education alone will not suffice.

PRACTICE AC4P PRINCIPLES

If we are to make the vision of an AC4P culture of compassion real, we need you to put AC4P principles into practice. And it's important to note the worthwhile outcomes of your AC4P endeavors. When you document the methods and results of your AC4P behavior on behalf of one or more persons' well-being, your competence to teach AC4P to others and convince them to get on board will be enhanced considerably.

The best teachers relate the information they're teaching to personal experiences – they are intimate storytellers. The authors of each chapter of this text have observed direct and/or indirect benefits of one or more AC4P interventions. In some cases, these authors experienced a multiplicative effect of their positive interventions extending to other circumstances and settings.

Documenting your practice of AC4P principles will do more than increase your proficiency in teaching others the techniques for creating an AC4P culture. When you report AC4P experiences in words, you contribute to making a culture of compassion happen. Post your AC4P stories on the ac4p.org Website; email your friends and business colleagues about your positive exposures to the AC4P Movement; tweet, text-message, blog, use Facebook and LinkedIn to spread the word through social media; write a brief newspaper report or magazine article about one or more AC4P stories; and contact your local TV news stations about your notable AC4P interventions and findings.

Here's an example with awesome potential that was reported in June 2015 on Fox News (see the link http://video.foxnews.com/v/4349936151001/beyond-the-dream-actively-caring-for-people/?playlist_id=926093635001#sp=show-clips). Recently, Bobby Kipper, a retired police officer who had served for twenty-five years and then founded the National Center for the Prevention of Community Violence (www.NCPCV.com), collaborated with me in the development and initiation of an AC4P policing process that inspires police officers to reward AC4P behavior among the citizens they serve.[2] Police departments can order sequentially numbered AC4P wristbands from this Website: www.AC4PPolicing.org.

First, the police officers define potential AC4P behaviors from citizens in their communities. Then they look for those behaviors during their shifts. When they observe them, they reward the performer with an AC4P wristband. The officers report their daily AC4P exchanges at www.AC4PPolicing.org. This designated Website enables police departments to track each officer's participation in the AC4P policing process.

At the time of this writing (August 2015), AC4P policing is practiced among police officers in Arizona, Florida, Illinois, Texas, and Virginia. The process is supported by the International Association of the Chiefs of Police. Thus, I hope some readers of this text are already aware of this method for encouraging positive connections between police officers and the citizens they serve. Students and faculty at Virginia Tech and the University of North Texas are planning to systematically evaluate the behavioral and attitudinal impact of this AC4P policing process.

I hope in time many additional examples of people bringing to life the AC4P principles explicated in this book will occur and be shared broadly. Why? Because I'm certain an AC4P culture of compassion will become a reality only if the AC4P principles and applications are disseminated and practiced by large numbers of people. We're talking about cultures, families, communities, schools, organizations – a prosocial movement. To meet this monumental challenge, we need your help to get the word out. And in doing so there is evidence such AC4P behavior will bolster your personal happiness (see Chapter 7).

Our challenge is to convince ourselves and others that effective AC4P behavior is followed by soon, certain, and positive consequences. How do we do this? Through ongoing, mindful practice and feedback, of course. We need the humility to accept behavior-based feedback from others about ways to improve; and we need the courage to offer behavior-based feedback whenever it can support or improve AC4P-related behavior.

HUMANISTIC BEHAVIORISM

We also need to consider the humanistic principles of empathy, empowerment, and compassion when giving and receiving behavior-based supportive and corrective feedback. Yes, actively caring integrates the best of humanism and behaviorism – *humanistic behaviorism*. As indicated earlier, *actively* means action (behavior) and *caring* is feeling (humanistic).

Some Background

To be sure, this book is not the first to entertain the concept of humanistic behaviorism. More than forty years ago, F. William Dinwiddie proposed humanistic behaviorism as "a working model for modern, dynamic, and successful treatment centers for children [because] ... behaviorism modulated by traditional humanistic approaches helps in the molding of an efficient helping environment for children."[3] Similarly, Carl E. Thoresen claimed that "humanistic psychology offers directions for the kind of behavior that individuals should be able to engage in; contemporary behaviorism offers principles and procedures to help individuals increase their humanistic actions."[4]

In fact, a number of behavioral scientists in the 1970s considered themselves humanists[5] because they (a) focused on individual behavior under present circumstances; (b) emphasized the role of learning in explaining and resolving human problems; (c) examined how environments can be changed to prevent or alleviate human problems; and (d) used the scientific method to develop and improve intervention techniques.[6] Given these criteria, B. F. Skinner would be considered a humanist, and as indicated in the Preface, he was honored as "Humanist of the Year" in 1972.[7]

Yes, integrating humanistic and behavioristic concepts was proposed by several scholars in the 1970s, but since then there has been very little discussion of this notion, especially with respect to behavior change beyond the clinic – which is the focus of all interventions in this textbook. Few, if any, students who have taken a psychology course have heard of humanistic behaviorism. I've been reviewing introductory psychology textbooks annually for forty-five years, and I've never seen the term *humanistic behaviorism* in a textbook for a psychology course. Instead, the focus is on explicating distinct differences between the humanistic and behavioristic approaches to clinical therapy.

It's not difficult to find critics of integrating humanism and behaviorism. Bobby Newman, a board-certified behavior analyst and licensed psychologist in New York, censures an alliance between humanism and behaviorism, claiming, "The unfortunate truth is that many problems in living will not be alleviated by empathy, a supportive environment or even unconditional positive regard."[8] And a reviewer of Newman's case against humanistic behaviorism concludes, "Based on the evidence we have thus far, there is little reason to believe that integrating humanistic psychotherapy and education with behavior analysis will do anything but attenuate the efforts of behavior analysis."[9]

Please note that these critiques of a humanistic behaviorism alliance were written more than two decades ago in the context of clinical therapy, not large-scale improvement of quality of life. Plus, the integration of humanism and behaviorism proposed in this text selected certain (not all) concepts from humanism to augment the impact of behavior-focused intervention. A variety of humanistic concepts were chosen on the basis of empirical evidence (e.g., the person-states that increase self-motivation and propensity to perform AC4P behavior); others were rejected for lack of research support (e.g., unconditional positive regard).

Bottom line: The notion of humanistic behaviorism is certainly not new, and integrating these seemingly disparate domains to develop sustainable behavior-change interventions for the large-scale benefit of individual, public, and environmental safety, health, and well-being is not particularly innovative. However, a textbook that teaches effective and practical ways to enhance the impact of behavior-improvement techniques with humanistic principles *is* unique and significant. Relatively few individuals have learned the AC4P principles revealed in this book; and without such an education, the frequency of *quality* AC4P behavior needed to solve so many societal problems is unlikely to increase.

Selection by Consequences

Let me address another criticism of what we aspire to achieve through the widespread dissemination of this textbook. Psychologist and scholar Paul Chance purports that we must prove B. F. Skinner wrong in order to solve the major problems facing humanity.[10] Sure, it's a challenge to move people beyond their self-serving desires to achieve soon, certain, and positive *consequences*. And I do not disagree entirely with his point that these primary principles of behaviorism give us "impulses that undermine our health; impel us toward violence; turn us into cheats, liars, and brigands, and threaten to make our world uninhabitable."[11]

Strong language, is it not? I do disagree with the implication that self-serving contingencies compel all of "us" to perform undesirable behaviors, from cheating and lying to engaging in interpersonal conflict and violence. That's a disturbing negative generalization – an indictment. We hear about destructive and harmful individuals – too often – in the news and in stories that go viral via social media and the Internet perhaps these outliers convince some of us that these undesirable acts reflect normative behavior. Not so. Cheating, lying, conflict, and violence are not the norm.

I must also disagree with Dr. Chance's premise that the ultimate challenge is to prove B. F. Skinner wrong.[10] Skinner was not wrong. We *are* motivated most frequently by soon, certain, and positive consequences – and effective AC4P behavior *is* usually followed by soon, certain, and positive consequences. We need to help people experience the positive consequences of AC4P behavior.

INTEGRATING RESEARCH WITH
PRACTICAL APPLICATIONS

This book offers leading-edge strategies you can readily use to improve the health, safety, and well-being of people in various situations – from the workplace to schools, homes, and everywhere along the spectrum of life.

Throughout my lengthy career as teacher, researcher, and author, I've had the good fortune to play the role of both an academic professor and organizational consultant. While the academic researcher in applied psychology develops and evaluates interventions to improve the behavior of individuals and groups, the consultant selects and implements interventions to address problems defined by a particular client.

Consider the advantage of learning from professionals in both the academic and consulting worlds. This can ensure the most effective intervention technologies are applied to current problems in ways that are acceptable, cost-effective, and employable by the affected personnel. Such is the mission of this volume. All of the intervention tactics in the application chapters were developed from the results of both empirical research and practical implementations.

Only the Beginning

We've only started to address large-scale, people-related social ills that can be mitigated with AC4P intervention. To be sure, many of the AC4P methods in this book are incomplete, inconclusive, or inefficient. The potential is obvious, but more research and development are needed to demonstrate the durable beneficial impact of the proactive interventions illustrated in this book. Please contact us with ideas and application possibilities for researching the implementation of AC4P principles. The Actively Caring for People Foundation, Inc., was established to explore and evaluate applications of AC4P principles that improve the health, safety, and well-being of people worldwide.

Continuous Learning

Tim, a participant at a recent leadership retreat at my home – Make-A-Diff-Ranch in the rolling hills of Newport, Virginia – made my day with the following comment. He shook my hand and said:

> What a pleasure it was to hear your latest thoughts about person-to-person actively caring to benefit individuals, organizations, and communities.

I first became aware of your research and scholarship when attending your day-long workshop at the ASSE (American Society of Safety Engineers) Convention in 2002. Since then I've read four of your books, and taught many of your principles to my colleagues at Cummins. [Cummins, Inc., is a Fortune 500 corporation that designs and manufactures engines, filtration, and power generation equipment.]

I'm not sharing this comment to shine a light on me, but rather to provide context for the rest of Tim's commentary, which was most reinforcing to me. Obviously, I was genuinely pleased to hear his positive remarks, but I had to interject, "It's so nice to learn that my teachings are reaching others through other teachers. But since you've already read several of my recent books, much of my workshop material today was redundant, right?" He replied:

For sure, I understood where you were coming from and I predicted where you were going throughout that session, and it was reassuring to hear it again. But what I really liked best was learning how your perspectives, principles, and application suggestions have evolved over the ten years I've been following your work.

Tim's last comment was the big reinforcer for me. My teaching of practical ways to apply psychology for solving real-world problems has progressed significantly over the years, as I continuously learn from ongoing research and from my own and others' consulting experiences. Contrary to the illustration on the next page, we're never too old to learn. For me, it's very meaningful to have an organizational leader recognize, understand, and appreciate the *evolution* of recommendations for managing the human dynamics of organizational and societal problems.

You see, this kind of feedback justifies continuous collaboration and mutual learning from researchers and consultants. Tim's commentary also validates the mission of this book – to connect research and practice for optimal intervention design and application relevant to cultivating cultures of compassion.

We've merely scratched the surface of societal afflictions that can be solved in part by applications of AC4P principles. The particular issues addressed in this book are diverse, yet the AC4P interventions within each of these problem domains are far from being comprehensive and optimal. Plus, the AC4P principles are applicable to so many additional domains. Indeed, the practical applied psychology presented in this textbook is relevant for any situation influenced by human dynamics. And isn't it true that most circumstances are influenced by human behavior?

We have so much more to learn from the synergistic integration of behavioral and humanistic psychology – *humanistic behaviorism*. Share your AC4P ideas and document your AC4P stories. They could incite relevant research, suggest real-world practice, or inspire participation by others. The outcome could very well end up in a subsequent edition of this book. More important, your personal AC4P leadership – your ownership of AC4P principles – is necessary to encourage others to live an AC4P lifestyle and help champion the AC4P Movement.

REFERENCES

1. King Jr., M. L. *Martin Luther King Quotes*. Retrieved September 18, 2013 from http://www.inspirationpeak.com/cgi-bin/search.cgi?search=Dr.%20Martin%20Luther%20King&method=all
2. Geller, E. S., & Kipper, B. (2015). AC4P Policing: A research-based process for cultivating positive police-community relations. *Police Chief*, September.

3. Dinwiddie, F. W. (1975). Humanistic behaviorism: A model for rapprochement in residential treatment milieus. *Child Psychiatry and Human Development,* 5(4), 259.

4. Thoresen, C. E. (1972, April). *Behavioral humanism.* Research and Development Memorandum No. 88. Stanford, CA: Stanford University, School of Education, p. 4.

5. Day, W. F. (1971). Humanistic psychology and contemporary humanism. *Humanist,* 31, 13–16; Hosford, R. E., & Zimmer, J. (1972). Humanism through behaviorism. *Counseling and Values,* 16, 1–7; Kanfer, F. H., & Phillips, J. S. (1970). *Learning foundations of behavior therapy.* New York: Wiley; Lazarus, A. (1971). *Behavior therapy and beyond.* New York: McGraw-Hill; MacCorquodale, K. (1971). Behaviorism is a humanism. *Humanist,* 31, 12–13; Staats, A. W. (1971). *Child learning, intelligence and personality.* New York: Harper & Row; Thoresen, C. E., & Mahoney, M. J. (1974). *Behavioral self-control.* New York: Holt, Rinehart & Winston; Ullmann, L. P., & Krasner, L. (1969). *A psychological approach to abnormal behavior.* Englewood Cliffs, NJ: Prentice Hall.

6. Thoresen, C. E. (1972, April). *Behavioral humanism.* Research and Development Memorandum No. 88.Stanford, CA: Stanford University, School of Education, pp. 1–35.

7. American Humanist Association. (2008). Retrieved September 9, 2012 from http://www.americanhumanist.org/.

8. Newman, B. (1992). *The reluctant alliance: Behaviorism and humanism.* Buffalo, NY: Prometheus Books, p. 47.

9. Houts, A. C. (1993). Review of "The reluctant alliance: Behaviorism and humanism." *Child & Family Behavior Therapy,* 15(4), 70.

10. Chance, P. (2007). The ultimate challenge: Prove B. F. Skinner wrong. *Behavior Analyst,* 30(2), 153–160.

11. Chance, P. (2007). The ultimate challenge: Prove B. F. Skinner wrong. *Behavior Analyst,* 30(2), 158.

SUBJECT AND NAME INDEX